P9-CTA-497

How PRODUCTS Are MADE

How PRODUCTS Are MADE

An Illustrated Guide to

Product Manufacturing

Volume 1

NEIL SCHLAGER, Editor

 **Gale Research Inc.** • DETROIT • WASHINGTON, D.C. • LONDON

STAFF

Neil Schlager, *Editor*

Elisabeth Morrison, *Associate Editor*

Christine Jeryan, Kyung-Sun Lim, Kimberley A. McGrath, Bridget Travers, Robyn V. Young,
Contributing Editors

Meggin M. Condino, Jeffrey Muhr, Janet Witalec, *Contributing Associate Editors*

Victoria B. Cariappa, *Research Manager*
Maureen Richards, *Research Supervisor*
Donna Melnychenko, *Research Associate*
Jaema Paradowski, *Research Assistant*

Mary Beth Trimper, *Production Director*
Shanna Heilveil, *Production Assistant*

Cynthia Baldwin, *Art Director*
Bernadette M. Gornie, *Page Designer*
Mark C. Howell, *Cover Designer*

Electronic illustrations provided by Hans & Cassady, Inc. of Westerville, Ohio.

ISBN 0-8103-8907-X
ISSN 1072-5091

Printed in the United States of America
Published simultaneously in the United Kingdom
by Gale Research International Limited
(An affiliated company of Gale Research Inc.)
10 9 8 7 6 5 4 3 2 1

I(T)P

The trademark **ITP** is used under license.

Contents

Introduction

About the Series

Welcome to *How Products Are Made: An Illustrated Guide to Product Manufacturing*. This series provides detailed yet accessible information on the manufacture of a variety of items, from everyday household products to heavy machinery to sophisticated electronic equipment. With step-by-step descriptions of processes, simple explanations of technical terms and concepts, and clear, easy-to-follow illustrations, the series will be useful to a wide audience.

In each volume of *How Products Are Made*, you will find products from a broad range of manufacturing areas: food, clothing, electronics, transportation, machinery, instruments, sporting goods, and more. Some are intermediate goods sold to manufacturers of other products, while others are retail goods sold directly to consumers. You will find products made from a variety of materials, and you will even find products such as precious metals and minerals that are not "made" so much as they are extracted and refined.

Organization

Every volume in the series is comprised of many individual entries, each covering a single product; Volume 1 includes more than 100 entries, arranged alphabetically. Although each entry focuses on the product's manufacturing process, it also provides a wealth of other information: who invented the product or how it has developed, how it works, what materials it is made of, how it is designed, quality control procedures used, byproducts generated during its manufacture, future applications, and books and periodical articles containing more information.

To make it easier for users to find what they are looking for, the entries are broken up into standard sections. Among the sections you will find are:

• Background

• History

• Raw Materials

• Design

- The Manufacturing Process
- Quality Control
- Byproducts
- The Future
- Where To Learn More

The illustrations accompanying each entry provide you with a better sense of how the manufacturing process actually works. Uncomplicated and easy to understand, these illustrations generally follow the step-by-step description of the manufacturing process found in the text.

Bold-faced items in the text refer the reader to other entries in this volume.

Volume 1 also contains an added bonus: approximately ten percent of the entries include special boxed sections. Written by William S. Pretzer, a manufacturing historian and curator at the Henry Ford Museum, these sections describe interesting historical developments related to a product.

Finally, Volume 1 contains a general subject index with important terms, processes, materials, and people. Here as in the text, bold-faced items refer the reader to main entries on the subject.

Contributors/Advisors

The entries in Volume 1 were written by a skilled team of technical writers and engineers, often in cooperation with manufacturers and industry associations.

In addition, a group of advisors assisted in the formulation of the series and of Volume 1 in particular. They are:

Marshall Galpern
Staff Engineer
General Motors Corporation

Dr. Michael J. Kelly
Director
Manufacturing Research Center
Georgia Institute of Technology

Jeanette Mueller-Alexander
Reference Librarian/Business Subject Specialist
Hayden Library
Arizona State University

Dr. William S. Pretzer
Curator
Henry Ford Museum & Greenfield Village

Diane A. Richmond
Head
Science and Technology Information Center
Chicago Public Library

Suggestions

Your questions, comments, and suggestions are welcome. Please send all such correspondence to:

The Editor
How Products Are Made
Gale Research Inc.
835 Penobscot Building
Detroit, MI 48226

Contributors

Jim Acton

William L. Ansel

Lawrence H. Berlow

Douglas E. Betts

Rick Bockmiller

Robert A. Cortese

Blaine Danley

Matthew Fogel

Suzy Fucini

Theodore L. Giese

Alicia Haley

David Harris

Catherine Kolecki

Greg Ling

Peter S. Lucking

Barry M. Marton

Steve Mathias

Leslie G. Melcer

L. S. Millberg

Robert C. Miller

Dan Pepper

Rashid Riaz

Rose Secrest

Eva Sideman

Frank Sokolo

Edward J. Stone

Peter Toeg

Phillip S. Waldrop

Jim Wawrzyniak

Glenn G. Whiteside

Craig F. Whitlow

Acknowledgments

The editor would like to thank the following individuals, companies, and associations for providing assistance with Volume 1 of *How Products Are Made:*

Air Bag: Morton International Incorporated—Automotive Products Division; TRW Vehicle Safety Systems Incorporated. **Artificial Limb:** Bob Burleson, Southeastern Orthotics & Prosthetics; Jim Colvin, Ohio Willow Wood Company; Douglas Turner, Becker Orthopedic; Al Pike, Otto Bock. **Baking Soda:** Church & Dwight Company Incorporated; FMC Corporation. **Ball Bearing:** Thomson Precision Ball Company. **Baseball:** Scott Smith, Rawlings Sporting Goods Company. **Baseball Glove:** Bob Clevenhagen, Rawlings Sporting Goods Company; Robby Storey, Nocona Athletic Goods Company. **Battery:** John Daggett, Rayovac Corporation; Steve Wicelinski, Duracell Incorporated. **Bicycle Shorts:** Cannondale Manufacturers. **Blue Jeans:** Bill Dunnahoo, Thomaston Mills Incorporated; Allen Slagle, Bristol Jeans Incorporated. **Bulletproof Vest:** Al Baker, American Body Armor; Bob Coppage, Progressive Technologies of America; Lester Gray, Keramont Corporation. **Carbon Paper:** Jim Sellers, NER Data Products Incorporated. **Cellophane Tape:** Jerry Miron, Skeist Incorporated. **Chalk:** Roger Taylor, Dixon Ticonderoga Company. **Chocolate:** Bob Zedik, Chocolate Manufacturers Association. **Combination Lock:** Master Lock Company. **Combine:** Dick Corken, John Deere Harvester Division. **Compact Disc Player:** Sanyo Fisher Company. **Corrugated Cardboard:** Rod Johnson, Packaging Corporation of America—Containerboard Products Division. **Cutlery:** Sandra E. Finley, Oneida, Limited. **Expanded Polystyrene Foam (EPF):** E. S. Clark, University of Tennessee—Materials Engineering Department; Ralph Taylor, Constar International Incorporated. **File Cabinet:** Phil Bradley, Kwik File Incorporated; Debbie Kniegge, Accuride; K. C. Thomsen, Electro Painters Incorporated. **Golf Cart:** Textron Incorporated—E-Z Go Division. **Laundry Detergent:** Larry Byrne, Sr., Byrne Laboratories. **Lawn Mower:** Dan Ariens, Ariens Company. **Optical Fiber:** James Bratton, Corning Incorporated—Telecommunications Products Division. **Pantyhose:** National Association of Hosiery Manufacturers. **Peanut Butter:** Russell E. Barker, Peanut Butter and Nut Processors Association. **Pesticide:** Reed Bacon, Bacon Products Corporation. **Postage Stamp:** Kelly Keough, American Banknote Company. **Rubber Band:** Michael Halperson, Plymouth Office Supply Company. **Running Shoe:** Craig Cartley, Athletic Footwear Association. **Saddle:** John DePietra, Equitation Synergist. **Salsa:** Caroline Fee, Del Monte Corporation; Lou Rasplicka, Pace Foods Incorporated. **Satellite Dish:** Jonathan

Peschko, Sky Link. **Screwdriver:** Glenn Allen, Stanley Works. **Seismograph:** Gene Tafra, Spreng-Nethers; Teledyne Incorporated—Geotech Division. **Shaving Cream:** Leonard Giglio, Contract Packaging Company. **Soda Bottle:** E. S. Clark, University of Tennessee—Materials Engineering Department; Ralph Taylor, Constar International Incorporated. **Solar Cell:** Mark Stimson, Siemens Solar Industries Incorporated. **Stethoscope:** Marc Blitstein, American Diagnostic Corporation; Tom Edmundson, Tycos; Cynthia Runyon, Minnesota Mining and Manufacturing Company (3M). **Sugar:** Suzanne Arnold, Sugar Association Incorporated. **Super Glue:** Lou Baccei, Loctite Corporation. **Tire:** Bill Brown II, Pirelli Armstrong Tire Corporation. **Tortilla Chip:** Tortilla Industry Association. **Trumpet:** Cliff Blackburn, Blackburn. **Umbrella:** Ann Cain, Totes Incorporated; Bob Storey and Manny Dubinsky, Zip Jack Industries, Limited. **Washing Machine:** Speed Queen Company. **Watch:** Scott Chou, SEIKO Corporation of America. **Wind Turbine:** Kerri E. Miller and Robert Sims, U.S. Windpower Incorporated.

The historical photographs on pages 25, 51, 81, 175, 225, 257, 321, 454, and 495 are from the collections of **Henry Ford Museum & Greenfield Village,** Dearborn, Michigan. The cover photograph of a tire is courtesy of **AP/Wide World Photos.**

Finally, the editor would like to thank **Hans & Cassady Incorporated** of Westerville, Ohio, for providing the electronic illustrations for Volume 1.

How
PRODUCTS
Are MADE

Air Bag

Background

An air bag is an inflatable cushion designed to protect **automobile** occupants from serious injury in the case of a collision. The air bag is part of an inflatable restraint system, also known as an air cushion restraint system (ACRS) or an air bag supplemental restraint system (SRS), because the air bag is designed to supplement the protection offered by seat belts. Seat belts are still needed to hold the occupant securely in place, especially in side impacts, rear impacts, and rollovers. Upon detecting a collision, air bags inflate instantly to cushion the exposed occupant with a big gas-filled pillow.

A typical air bag system consists of an air bag module (containing an inflator or gas generator and an air bag), crash sensors, a diagnostic monitoring unit, a steering wheel connecting coil, and an indicator lamp. These components are all interconnected by a wiring harness and powered by the vehicle's **battery**. Air bag systems hold a reserve charge after the ignition has been turned off or after the battery has been disconnected. Depending on the model, the backup power supply lasts between one second and ten minutes. Since components vital to the system's operation might sit dormant for years, the air bag circuitry performs an internal "self-test" during each startup, usually indicated by a light on the instrument panel that glows briefly at each startup.

The crash sensors are designed to prevent the air bag from inflating when the car goes over a bump or a pothole, or in the case of a minor collision. The inflator fits into a module consisting of a woven nylon bag and a break-away plastic horn pad cover. The module, in turn, fits into the steering wheel for driver's-side applications and above the glove compartment for front passenger applications.

In a frontal collision equivalent to hitting a solid barrier at nine miles per hour (14.48 kilometers per hour), the crash sensors located in the front of the car detect the sudden deceleration and send an electrical signal activating an initiator (sometimes called an igniter or squib). Like a **light bulb**, an initiator contains a thin wire that heats up and penetrates the propellant chamber. This causes the solid chemical propellant, principally sodium azide, sealed inside the inflator to undergo a rapid chemical reaction (commonly referred to as a pyrotechnic chain). This controlled reaction produces harmless nitrogen gas that fills the air bag. During deployment the expanding nitrogen gas undergoes a process that reduces the temperature and removes most of the combustion residue or ash.

The expanding nitrogen gas inflates the nylon bag in less than one-twentieth (1/20) of a second, splitting open its plastic module cover and inflating in front of the occupant. As the occupant contacts the bag, the nitrogen gas is vented through openings in the back of the bag. The bag is fully inflated for only one-tenth (1/10) of a second and is nearly deflated by three-tenths (3/10) of a second after impact. Talcum powder or corn starch is used to line the inside of the air bag and is released from the air bag as it is opened.

History

The air bag traces its origin to air-filled bladders outlined as early as 1941 and first patented in the 1950s. Early air bag systems

The expanding gas inflates the bag in less than one-twentieth of a second, splitting open its plastic cover and inflating in front of the occupant. The bag is fully inflated for only one-tenth of a second and is nearly deflated by three-tenths of a second after impact.

A typical driver's-side air bag fits neatly on the steering wheel column. In case of a collision, the crash sensor sends an electric spark to the inflator canister, setting off a chemical reaction that produces nitrogen gas. The gas expands, inflating the air bag and protecting the driver.

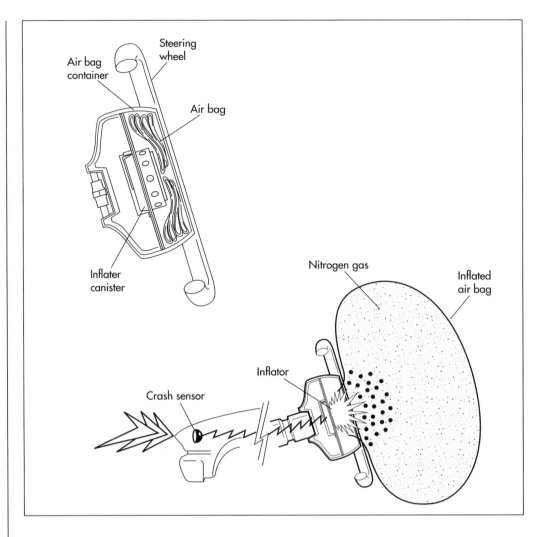

were large and bulky, primarily using tanks of compressed or heated air, compressed nitrogen gas (N_2), freon, or carbon dioxide (CO_2). Some of the early systems created hazardous byproducts. One particular system used gunpowder to heat up freon gas, producing phosgene gas ($COCl_2$)—an extremely poisonous gas.

One of the first patents for automobile air bags was awarded to industrial engineer John Hetrick on August 18, 1953. Conceived by Hetrick after a near accident in 1952, the design called for a tank of compressed air under the hood and inflatable bags on the steering wheel, in the middle of the dashboard, and in the glove compartment to protect front seat occupants, and on the back of the front seat to protect rear seat passengers. The force of a collision would propel a sliding weight forward to send air into the bags. Many other inventors and researchers followed suit, all exploring slightly different designs, so that the exact technical trail from

the early designs to the present system is impossible to note with certainty.

In 1968, John Pietz, a chemist for Talley Defense Systems, pioneered a solid propellant using sodium azide (NaN_3) and a metallic oxide. This was the first nitrogen-generating solid propellant, and it soon replaced the older, bulkier systems. Sodium azide in its solid state is toxic if ingested in large doses, but in automotive applications is carefully sealed inside a steel or aluminum container within the air bag system.

Since the 1960s, air bag-equipped cars in controlled tests and everyday use have demonstrated the effectiveness and reliability. The Insurance Institute For Highway Safety conducted a study of the federal government's Fatal Accident Reporting System using data from 1985 to 1991, and concluded that driver fatalities in frontal collisions were lowered by 28 percent in automobiles equipped with air bags. According to

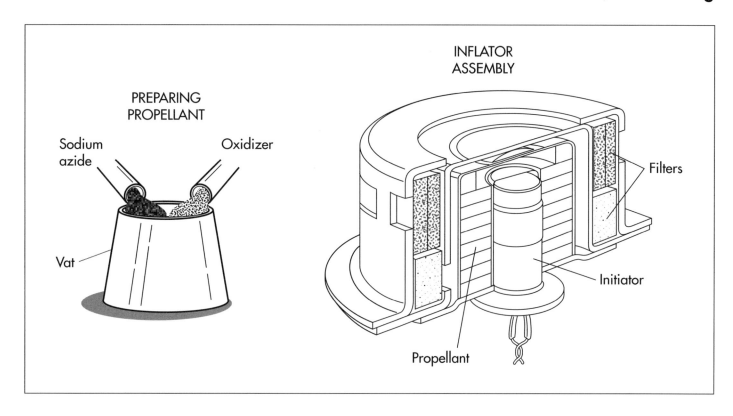

PREPARING
PROPELLANT

Sodium azide

Oxidizer

Vat

INFLATOR
ASSEMBLY

Filters

Initiator

Propellant

another study conducted in 1989 by General Motors, the combination of lap/shoulder safety belts and air bags in frontal collisions reduced driver fatalities by 46 percent and front passenger fatalities by 43 percent.

In response to consumers' increased safety concerns and insurance industry pressure, the federal government has forced automobile manufacturers to upgrade their safety features. First, Department of Transportation (DOT) regulations require all cars, beginning with model year 1990, sold in the United States to be equipped with a passive restraint system. (Passive restraint systems—requiring no activation by the occupant—involve the use of automatic seat belts and/or the use of air bags.) If car manufacturers choose an air bag, then regulations require only a driver's-side system until model year 1994, when air bag-equipped cars must include passive protection on the passenger's side as well. A 1991 law requires driver and passenger air bags in all cars by the 1998 model year and in light trucks and vans by 1999.

Raw Materials

As stated above, an air bag system consists of an air bag module, crash sensors, a diagnostic monitoring unit, a steering wheel connect-ing coil, and an indicator lamp. Both this section and the next ("The Manufacturing Process") will focus on the air bag module itself.

An air bag module has three main parts: the air bag, the inflator, and the propellant. The air bag is sewn from a woven nylon fabric and can come in different shapes and sizes depending on specific vehicle requirements. The driver's-side air bag material is manufactured with a heat shield coating to protect the fabric from scorching, especially near the inflator assembly, during deployment. Talcum powder or corn starch is also used to coat the air bag; either substance prevents the fabric from sticking together and makes it easier to assemble. Newer silicone and urethane coated air bag materials require little or no heat shield coating, although talcum powder or corn starch will probably still be used as a processing aid.

The inflator canister or body is made from either stamped **stainless steel** or cast aluminum. Inside the inflator canister is a filter assembly consisting of a stainless steel wire mesh with ceramic material sandwiched in between. When the inflator is assembled, the filter assembly is surrounded by metal foil to maintain a seal that prevents propellant contamination.

Preparation of the propellant, the first step in air bag manufacture, involves combining sodium azide and an oxidizer. The propellant is then combined with the metal initiator canister and various filters to form the inflator assembly.

The propellant, in the form of black pellets, is primarily sodium azide combined with an oxidizer and is typically located inside the inflator canister between the filter assembly and the initiator.

The Manufacturing Process

Air bag production involves three different separate assemblies that combine to form the finished end product, the air bag module. The propellant must be manufactured, the inflator components must be assembled, and the air bag must be cut and sewn. Some manufacturers buy already-made components, such as air bags or initiators, and then just assemble the complete air bag module. The following description of the manufacturing process is for driver-side air bag module assembly. Passenger-side air bag module assemblies are produced slightly differently.

Propellant

1 The propellant consists of sodium azide mixed together with an oxidizer, a substance that helps the sodium azide to burn when ignited. The sodium azide is received from outside vendors and inspected to make sure it conforms to requirements. After inspection it is placed in a safe storage place until needed. At the same time, the oxidizer is received from outside vendors, inspected, and stored. Different manufacturers use different oxidizers.

2 From storage, the sodium azide and the oxidizer are then carefully blended under sophisticated computerized process control. Because of the possibility of explosions, the powder processing takes place in isolated bunkers. In the event safety sensors detect a spark, high speed deluge systems will douse whole rooms with water. Production occurs in several redundant smaller facilities so that if an accident does occur, production will not be shut down, only decreased.

3 After blending, the propellant mixture is sent to storage. Presses are then used to compress the propellant mixture into disk or pellet form.

Inflator assembly

4 The inflator components, such as the metal canister, the filter assembly—

stainless steel wire mesh with ceramic material inside—and initiator (or igniter) are received from outside vendors and inspected. The components are then assembled on a highly automated production line.

5 The inflator sub-assembly is combined with the propellant and an initiator to form the inflator assembly. Laser welding (using CO_2 gas) is used to join stainless steel inflator sub-assemblies, while friction inertial welding is used to join aluminum inflator sub-assemblies. Laser welding entails using laser beams to weld the assemblies together, while friction inertial welding involves rubbing two metals together until the surfaces become hot enough to join together.

6 The inflator assembly is then tested and sent to storage until needed.

Air bag

7 The woven nylon air bag fabric is received from outside vendors and inspected for any material defects. The air bag fabric is then die cut to the proper shapes and sewn, internally and externally, to properly join the two sides. After the air bag is sewn, it is inflated and checked for any seam imperfections.

Final assembly of air bag module

8 The air bag assembly is then mounted to the tested inflator assembly. Next, the air bag is folded, and the breakaway plastic horn pad cover is installed. Finally, the completed module assembly is inspected and tested.

9 The module assemblies are packaged in boxes for shipment and then sent to customers.

Other components

10 The remaining components of the air bag system—the crash sensors, the diagnostic monitoring unit, the steering wheel connecting coil, and the indicator lamp—are combined with the air bag module during vehicle assembly. All the components are connected and communicate through a wiring harness.

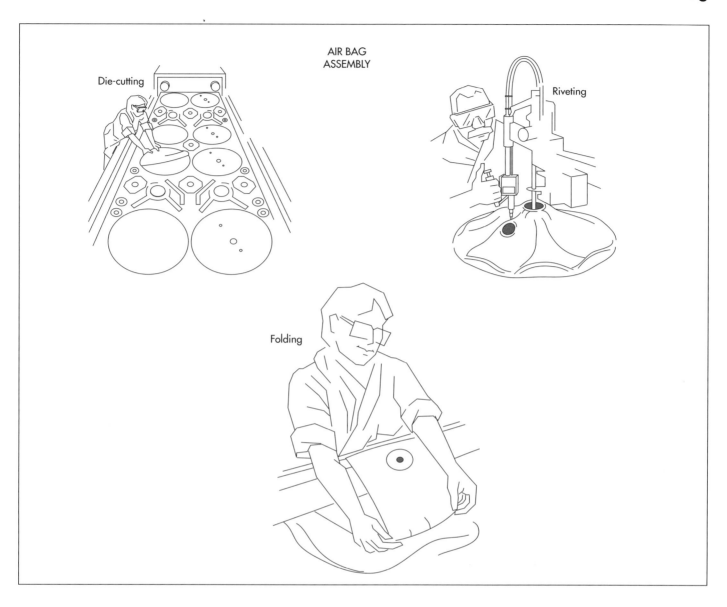

Die-cutting

AIR BAG
ASSEMBLY

Riveting

Folding

Quality Control

The quality control aspect of air bag production is, obviously, very important because many lives depend on the safety feature. Two major areas where quality control is critical are the pyrotechnic or propellant tests and the air bag and inflator static and dynamic tests.

Propellants, before being inserted into inflators, are first subjected to ballistic tests to predict their behavior. A representative sample of inflators are pulled from the production line and tested for proper operation by a full-scale inflator test, which measures pressure—created by the generated gas inside a large tank 15.84 or 79.20 gallons (60 or 300 liters)—versus time in milliseconds. This gives an indication of the inflator system's

ability to produce an amount of gas at a given rate, ensuring proper air bag inflation. The air bags themselves are inspected for fabric and seam imperfections and then tested for leaks.

Automated inspections are made at every stage of the production process line to identify mistakes. One air bag manufacturer uses radiography (x-rays) to compare the completed inflator against a master configuration stored in the computer. Any inflator without the proper configuration is rejected.

The Future

The future for air bags looks extremely promising because there are many different applications possible, ranging from aircraft seating to motorcycle helmets. The air bags of the future will be more economical to pro-

The air bag parts are die-cut out of woven nylon, sewn together, and riveted. The bag is then carefully folded so that it will fit inside the plastic module cover.

Crash sensors can be located in several spots on the front of the automobile. These sensors are connected to the air bag module with a wiring harness. Two other key components of an air bag system are the diagnostic module and the indicator lamp. The diagnostic module performs a system test each time the car is started, briefly lighting up the indicator lamp mounted on the dashboard.

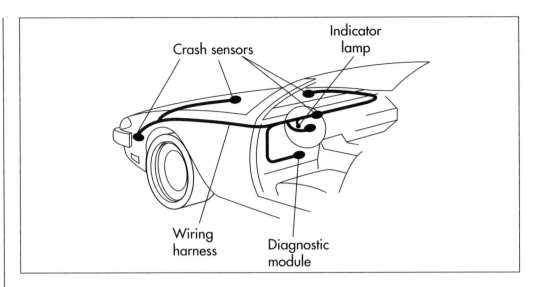

duce and lighter in weight; will involve smaller, more integrated systems; and will use improved sensors.

Side-impact air bags are another possibility that would work similar to driver- and passenger-side air bags. Side-impact air bags will most likely be mounted in the car door panels and deployed towards the window during impact to protect the head. Foam padding around the door structure would also be used to cushion the upper body in a side impact. Head and/or knee bolsters (energy absorbing pads) to complement the air bag system are also being investigated. Rear-seat air bags are also being tested but consumer demand is not expected to be high.

Aftermarket air bag systems—generic systems that can be installed on any vehicle already built—are not currently available. Since the effectiveness of an air bag depends on its sensors recognizing if a crash is severe enough to trigger deployment, a system must be precisely tuned to the way a specific car model behaves in a crash. Still, companies are exploring the future possibility of producing a modified air bag system for retrofit.

A hybrid inflator is currently being tested that uses a combination of pressurized inert gas (argon) and heat from a propellant to significantly expand the gas's volume. These systems would have a cost advantage, since less propellant could be used. Air bag manufacturers are also developing systems that would eliminate the sodium azide propellant, which is toxic in its undeployed form. Work

is also underway to improve the coatings that preserve the air bag and facilitate its opening. Eventually the bags may not need coatings at all.

In the future, more sophisticated sensors called "smart" sensors will be used to tailor the deployment of the air bag to certain conditions. These sensors could be used to sense the size and weight of the occupant, whether the occupant is present (especially in the case of passenger-side air bags where deployment may be unnecessary if there are no passengers), and the proximity of the driver to the steering wheel (a driver slumped over the steering wheel could be seriously injured by an air bag deployment).

Where To Learn More

Periodicals

Chaikin, Don. "How It Works—Airbags," *Popular Mechanics.* June, 1991, p. 81.

Frantom, Richard L. "Buckling Down on Passenger Safety," *Design News.* October 2, 1989, pp. 116-118.

Gottschalk, Mark A. "Micromachined Airbag Sensor Tests Itself," *Design News.* October 5, 1992, p. 26.

Grable, Ron. "Airbags: In Your Face, By Design," *Motor Trend.* January, 1992, pp. 90-91.

Haayen, Richard J. "The Airtight Case for Air Bags," *Saturday Evening Post.* November, 1986.

Reed, Donald. "Father of the Air Bag," *Automotive Engineering.* February, 1991, p. 67.

Sherman, Don. "It's in the Bag," *Popular Science.* October, 1992, pp. 58-63.

Spencer, Peter L. "The Trouble with Air Bags," *Consumers' Research.* January, 1991, pp. 10-13.

— *Glenn G. Whiteside*

Aluminum Foil

The preference for aluminum in flexible packaging has become a global phenomenon. In Japan, aluminum foil is used as the barrier component in flexible cans. In Europe, aluminum flexible packaging dominates the market for pharmaceutical blister packages and candy wrappers.

Background

Aluminum foil is made from an aluminum alloy which contains between 92 and 99 percent aluminum. Usually between 0.00017 and 0.0059 inches thick, foil is produced in many widths and strengths for literally hundreds of applications. It is used to manufacture thermal insulation for the construction industry, fin stock for air conditioners, electrical coils for transformers, capacitors for radios and televisions, insulation for storage tanks, decorative products, and containers and packaging. The popularity of aluminum foil for so many applications is due to several major advantages, one of the foremost being that the raw materials necessary for its manufacture are plentiful. Aluminum foil is inexpensive, durable, non-toxic, and grease-proof. In addition, it resists chemical attack and provides excellent electrical and non-magnetic shielding.

Shipments (in 1991) of aluminum foil totaled 913 million pounds, with packaging representing seventy-five percent of the aluminum foil market. Aluminum foil's popularity as a packaging material is due to its excellent impermeability to water vapor and gases. It also extends shelf life, uses less storage space, and generates less waste than many other packaging materials. The preference for aluminum in flexible packaging has consequently become a global phenomenon. In Japan, aluminum foil is used as the barrier component in flexible cans. In Europe, aluminum flexible packaging dominates the market for pharmaceutical blister packages and candy wrappers. The aseptic drink box, which uses a thin layer of aluminum foil as a barrier against oxygen, light, and odor, is also quite popular around the world.

Aluminum is the most recently discovered of the metals that modern industry utilizes in large amounts. Known as "alumina," aluminum compounds were used to prepare medicines in ancient Egypt and to set cloth dyes during the Middle Ages. By the early eighteenth century, scientists suspected that these compounds contained a metal, and, in 1807, the English chemist Sir Humphry Davy attempted to isolate it. Although his efforts failed, Davy confirmed that alumina had a metallic base, which he initially called "alumium." Davy later changed this to "aluminum," and, while scientists in many countries spell the term "aluminium," most Americans use Davy's revised spelling. In 1825, a Danish chemist named Hans Christian Ørsted successfully isolated aluminum, and, twenty years later, a German physicist named Friedrich Wöhler was able to create larger particles of the metal; however, Wöhler's particles were still only the size of pinheads. In 1854 Henri Sainte-Claire Deville, a French scientist, refined Wöhler's method enough to create aluminum lumps as large as marbles. Deville's process provided a foundation for the modern aluminum industry, and the first aluminum bars made were displayed in 1855 at the Paris Exposition.

At this point the high cost of isolating the newly discovered metal limited its industrial uses. However, in 1866 two scientists working separately in the United States and France concurrently developed what became known as the Hall-Héroult method of separating alumina from oxygen by applying an electrical current. While both Charles Hall and Paul-Louis-Toussaint Héroult patented their discoveries, in America and France respectively, Hall was the first to recognize the financial potential of his purification process. In 1888

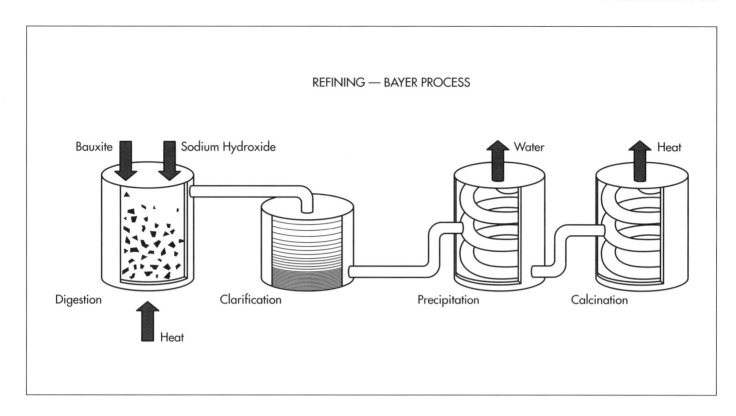

REFINING — BAYER PROCESS

Bauxite   Sodium Hydroxide   Water   Heat

Digestion   Clarification   Precipitation   Calcination

Heat

he and several partners founded the Pittsburgh Reduction Company, which produced the first aluminum ingots that year. Using hydroelectricity to power a large new conversion plant near Niagara Falls and supplying the burgeoning industrial demand for aluminum, Hall's company—renamed the Aluminum Company of America (Alcoa) in 1907—thrived. Héroult later established the Aluminium-Industrie-Aktien-Gesellschaft in Switzerland. Encouraged by the increasing demand for aluminum during World Wars I and II, most other industrialized nations began to produce their own aluminum. In 1903, France became the first country to produce foil from purified aluminum. The United States followed suit a decade later, its first use of the new product being leg bands to identify racing pigeons. Aluminum foil was soon used for containers and packaging, and World War II accelerated this trend, establishing aluminum foil as a major packaging material. Until World War II, Alcoa remained the sole American manufacturer of purified aluminum, but today there are seven major producers of aluminum foil located in the United States.

Raw Materials

Aluminum numbers among the most abundant elements: after oxygen and silicon, it is the most plentiful element found in the earth's surface, making up over eight percent of the crust to a depth of ten miles and appearing in almost every common rock. However, aluminum does not occur in its pure, metallic form but rather as hydrated aluminum oxide (a mixture of water and alumina) combined with silica, iron oxide, and titania. The most significant aluminum ore is bauxite, named after the French town of Les Baux where it was discovered in 1821. Bauxite contains iron and hydrated aluminum oxide, with the latter representing its largest constituent material. At present, bauxite is plentiful enough so that only deposits with an aluminum oxide content of forty-five percent or more are mined to make aluminum. Concentrated deposits are found in both the northern and southern hemispheres, with most of the ore used in the United States coming from the West Indies, North America, and Australia. Since bauxite occurs so close to the earth's surface, mining procedures are relatively simple. Explosives are used to open up large pits in bauxite beds, after which the top layers of dirt and rock are cleared away. The exposed ore is then removed with front end loaders, piled in trucks or railroad cars, and transported to processing plants. Bauxite is heavy (generally, one ton of aluminum can be produced from four to six tons of the ore), so, to reduce

The Bayer process of refining bauxite consists of four steps: digestion, clarification, precipitation, and calcination. The result is a fine white powder of aluminum oxide.

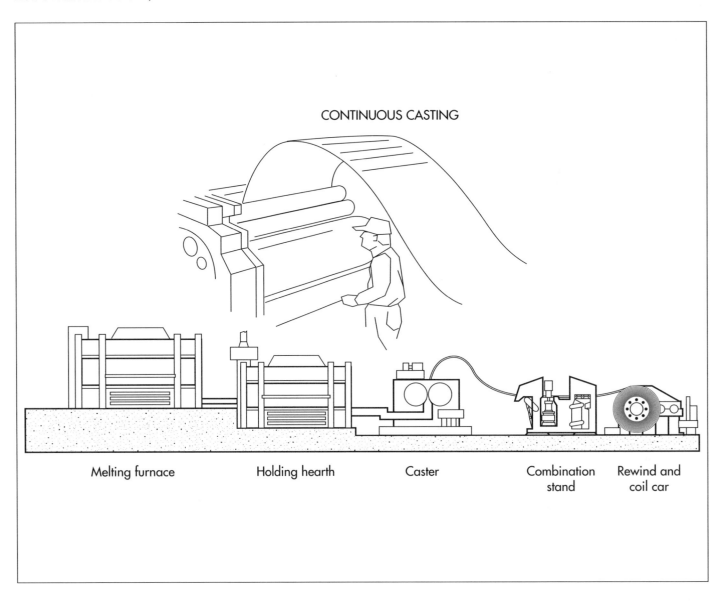

CONTINUOUS CASTING

Melting furnace · Holding hearth · Caster · Combination stand · Rewind and coil car

Continuous casting is an alternative to melting and casting aluminum. An advantage of continuous casting is that it does not require an annealing (heat treatment) step prior to foil rolling, as does the melting and casting process.

the cost of transporting it, these plants are often situated as close as possible to the bauxite mines.

The Manufacturing Process

Extracting pure aluminum from bauxite entails two processes. First, the ore is refined to eliminate impurities such as iron oxide, silica, titania, and water. Then, the resultant aluminum oxide is smelted to produce pure aluminum. After that, the aluminum is rolled to produce foil.

Refining—Bayer process

1 The Bayer process used to refine bauxite comprises four steps: digestion, clarification, precipitation, and calcination. During

the digestion stage, the bauxite is ground and mixed with sodium hydroxide before being pumped into large, pressurized tanks. In these tanks, called digesters, the combination of sodium hydroxide, heat, and pressure breaks the ore down into a saturated solution of sodium aluminate and insoluble contaminants, which settle to the bottom.

2 The next phase of the process, clarification, entails sending the solution and the contaminants through a set of tanks and presses. During this stage, cloth filters trap the contaminants, which are then disposed of. After being filtered once again, the remaining solution is transported to a cooling tower.

3 In the next stage, precipitation, the aluminum oxide solution moves into a large silo, where, in an adaptation of the Deville

method, the fluid is seeded with crystals of hydrated aluminum to promote the formation of aluminum particles. As the seed crystals attract other crystals in the solution, large clumps of aluminum hydrate begin to form. These are first filtered out and then rinsed.

4 Calcination, the final step in the Bayer refinement process, entails exposing the aluminum hydrate to high temperatures. This extreme heat dehydrates the material, leaving a residue of fine white powder: aluminum oxide.

Smelting

5 Smelting, which separates the aluminum-oxygen compound (alumina) produced by the Bayer process, is the next step in extracting pure, metallic aluminum from bauxite. Although the procedure currently used derives from the electrolytic method invented contemporaneously by Charles Hall and Paul-Louis-Toussaint Héroult in the late nineteenth century, it has been modernized. First, the alumina is dissolved in a smelting cell, a deep steel mold lined with carbon and filled with a heated liquid conductor that consists mainly of the aluminum compound cryolite.

6 Next, an electric current is run through the cryolite, causing a crust to form over the top of the alumina melt. When additional alumina is periodically stirred into the mixture, this crust is broken and stirred in as well. As the alumina dissolves, it electrolytically decomposes to produce a layer of pure, molten aluminum on the bottom of the smelting cell. The oxygen merges with the carbon used to line the cell and escapes in the form of carbon dioxide.

7 Still in molten form, the purified aluminum is drawn from the smelting cells, transferred into crucibles, and emptied into furnaces. At this stage, other elements can be added to produce aluminum alloys with characteristics appropriate to the end product, though foil is generally made from 99.8 or 99.9 percent pure aluminum. The liquid is then poured into direct chill casting devices, where it cools into large slabs called "ingots" or "reroll stock." After being annealed—heat treated to improve workability—the ingots are suitable for rolling into foil.

An alternative method to melting and casting the aluminum is called "continuous casting."

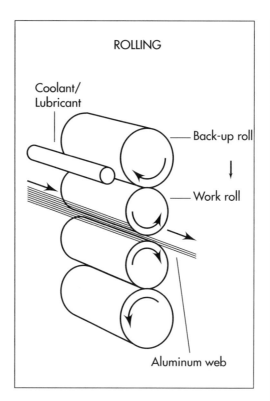

ROLLING

Coolant/ Lubricant

Back-up roll

Work roll

Aluminum web

This process involves a production line consisting of a melting furnace, a holding hearth to contain the molten metal, a transfer system, a casting unit, a combination unit consisting of pinch rolls, shear and bridle, and a rewind and coil car. Both methods produce stock of thicknesses ranging from 0.125 to 0.250 inch (0.317 to 0.635 centimeter) and of various widths. The advantage of the continuous casting method is that it does not require an annealing step prior to foil rolling, as does the melting and casting process, because annealing is automatically achieved during the casting process.

Rolling foil

8 After the foil stock is made, it must be reduced in thickness to make the foil. This is accomplished in a rolling mill, where the material is passed several times through metal rolls called work rolls. As the sheets (or webs) of aluminum pass through the rolls, they are squeezed thinner and extruded through the gap between the rolls. The work rolls are paired with heavier rolls called backup rolls, which apply pressure to help maintain the stability of the work rolls. This helps to hold the product dimensions within tolerances. The work and backup rolls rotate in opposite directions. Lubricants are added to facilitate the rolling process. During this

Foil is produced from aluminum stock by rolling it between heavy rollers. Rolling produces two natural finishes on the foil, bright and matte. As the foil emerges from the rollers, circular knives cut it into rectangular pieces.

rolling process, the aluminum occasionally must be annealed (heat-treated) to maintain its workability.

The reduction of the foil is controlled by adjusting the rpm of the rolls and the viscosity (the resistance to flow), quantity, and temperature of the rolling lubricants. The roll gap determines both the thickness and length of the foil leaving the mill. This gap can be adjusted by raising or lowering the upper work roll. Rolling produces two natural finishes on the foil, bright and matte. The bright finish is produced when the foil comes in contact with the work roll surfaces. To produce the matte finish, two sheets must be packed together and rolled simultaneously; when this is done, the sides that are touching each other end up with a matte finish. Other mechanical finishing methods, usually produced during converting operations, can be used to produce certain patterns.

9 As the foil sheets come through the rollers, they are trimmed and slitted with circular or razor-like knives installed on the roll mill. Trimming refers to the edges of the foil, while slitting involves cutting the foil into several sheets. These steps are used to produce narrow coiled widths, to trim the edges of coated or laminated stock, and to produce rectangular pieces. For certain fabricating and converting operations, webs that have been broken during rolling must be joined back together, or spliced. Common types of splices for joining webs of plain foil and/or backed foil include ultrasonic, heat-sealing tape, pressure-sealing tape, and electric welded. The ultrasonic splice uses a solid-state weld—made with an ultrasonic transducer—in the overlapped metal.

Finishing processes

10 For many applications, foil is used in combination with other materials. It can be coated with a wide range of materials, such as polymers and resins, for decorative, protective, or heat-sealing purposes. It can be laminated to papers, paperboards, and plastic films. It can also be cut, formed into any shape, printed, embossed, slit into strips, sheeted, etched, and anodized. Once the foil is in its final state, it is packaged accordingly and shipped to the customer.

Quality Control

In addition to in-process control of such parameters as temperature and time, the finished foil product must meet certain requirements. For instance, different converting processes and end uses have been found to require varying degrees of dryness on the foil surface for satisfactory performance. A wettability test is used to determine the dryness. In this test, different solutions of ethyl alcohol in distilled water, in increments of ten percent by volume, are poured in a uniform stream onto the foil surface. If no drops form, the wettability is zero. The process is continued until it is determined what minimum percent of alcohol solution will completely wet the foil surface.

Other important properties are thickness and tensile strength. Standard test methods have been developed by the American Society For Testing and Materials (ASTM). Thickness is determined by weighing a sample and measuring its area, and then dividing the weight by the product of the area times the alloy density. Tension testing of foil must be carefully controlled because test results can be affected by rough edges and the presence of small defects, as well as other variables. The sample is placed in a grip and a tensile or pulling force is applied until fracture of the sample occurs. The force or strength required to break the sample is measured.

The Future

The popularity of aluminum foil, especially for flexible packaging, will continue to grow. Four-sided, fin-sealed pouches have gained wide popularity for military, medical, and retail food applications and, in larger sizes, for institutional food service packs. Pouches have also been introduced for packaging 1.06 to 4.75 gallons (4-18 liters) of **wine** for both retail and restaurant markets, and for other food service markets. In addition, other products continue to be developed for other applications. The increase in popularity of **microwave oven**s has resulted in the development of several forms of aluminum-based semi-rigid containers designed specifically for these ovens. More recently, special cooking foils for barbecuing have been developed.

However, even aluminum foil is being scrutinized in regard to its environmental "friendliness." Hence, manufacturers are increasing their efforts in the recycling area; in fact, all U.S. foil producers have begun recycling programs even though aluminum foil's total tonnage and capture rate is much lower than that of the easy-to-recycle aluminum cans. Aluminum foil already has the advantage of being light and small, which helps reduce its contribution to the solid waste stream. In fact, laminated aluminum foil packaging represents just 17/100ths of one percent of the U.S. solid waste.

For packaging waste, the most promising solution may be source reduction. For instance, packaging 65 pounds (29.51 kilograms) of **coffee** in steel cans requires 20 pounds (9.08 kilograms) of steel but only three pounds (4.08 kilograms) of laminated packaging including aluminum foil. Such packaging also takes up less space in the landfill. The Aluminum Association's Foil Division is even developing an educational program on aluminum foil for universities and professional packaging designers in order to help inform such designers of the benefits of switching to flexible packaging.

Aluminum foil also uses less energy during both manufacturing and distribution, with in-plant scrap being recycled. In fact, recycled aluminum, including cans and foil, accounts for over 30 percent of the industry's yearly supply of metal. This number has been increasing for several years and is expected to continue. In addition, processes used during foil manufacturing are being improved to reduce air pollution and hazardous waste.

Where To Learn More

Books

Aluminum Foil. The Aluminum Association. 1981.

Periodicals

"Barrier Qualities Stimulate Aluminum Foil Packaging Growth," *FoilPak News.* The Aluminum Association. Fall, 1992.

"The Best Ways to Keep Food Fresh: A Roundup of the Most Effective and Most Economical Wraps, Bags, and Containers," *Consumer Reports.* February, 1989, p. 120+.

Gracey, Kathryn K. "Aluminum in Micro-waves," *Consumers' Research Magazine.* January, 1989, p. 2.

"Promote Even Cookery with Foil," *Southern Living.* December, 1987, pp. 130-131.

— *L. S. Millberg*

Artificial Limb

The most exciting development of the twentieth century has been the development of myoelectric prosthetic limbs. Myoelectricity involves using electrical signals from the patient's arm muscles to move the limb.

Background

Artificial arms and legs, or *prostheses*, are intended to restore a degree of normal function to amputees. Mechanical devices that allow amputees to walk again or continue to use two hands have probably been in use since ancient times, the most notable one being the simple peg leg. Surgical procedure for amputation, however, was not largely successful until around 600 B.C. Armorers of the Middle Ages created the first sophisticated prostheses, using strong, heavy, inflexible iron to make limbs that the amputee could scarcely control. Even with the articulated joints invented by Ambroise Paré in the 1500s, the amputee could not flex at will. Artificial hands of the time were quite beautiful and intricate imitations of real hands, but were not exceptionally functional. Upper limbs, developed by Peter Baliff of Berlin in 1812 for below-elbow amputees and Van Peetersen in 1844 for above-elbow amputees, were functional, but still far less than ideal.

The nineteenth century saw a lot of changes, most initiated by amputees themselves. J. E. Hanger, an engineering student, lost his leg in the Civil War. He subsequently designed an artificial leg for himself and in 1861 founded a company to manufacture prosthetic legs. The J. E. Hanger Company is still in existence today. Another amputee named A. A. Winkley developed a slip-socket below-knee device for himself, and with the help of Lowell Jepson, founded the Winkley Company in 1888. They marketed the legs during the National Civil War Veterans Reunion, thereby establishing their company.

Another amputee named D. W. Dorrance invented a terminal device to be used in the place of a hand in 1909. Dorrance, who had lost his right arm in an accident, was unhappy with the prosthetic arms then available. Until his invention, they had consisted of a leather socket and a heavy steel frame, and either had a heavy cosmetic hand in a glove, a rudimentary mechanical hand, or a passive hook incapable of prehension. Dorrance invented a split hook that was anchored to the opposite shoulder and could be opened with a strap across the back and closed by rubber bands. His terminal device (the hook) is still considered to be a major advancement for amputees because it restored their prehension abilities to some extent. Modified hooks are still used today, though they might be hidden by realistic-looking skin.

The twentieth century has seen the greatest advances in prosthetic limbs. Materials such as modern plastics have yielded prosthetic devices that are strong and more lightweight than earlier limbs made of iron and wood. New plastics, better pigments, and more sophisticated procedures are responsible for creating fairly realistic-looking skin.

The most exciting development of the twentieth century has been the development of myoelectric prosthetic limbs. Myoelectricity involves using electrical signals from the patient's arm muscles to move the limb. Research began in the late 1940s in West Germany, and by the late sixties myoelectric devices were available for adults. In the last decade children have also been fitted with myoelectric limbs.

In recent years computers have been used to help fit amputees with prosthetic limbs. Eighty-five percent of private prosthetic facilities use a CAD/CAM to design a model

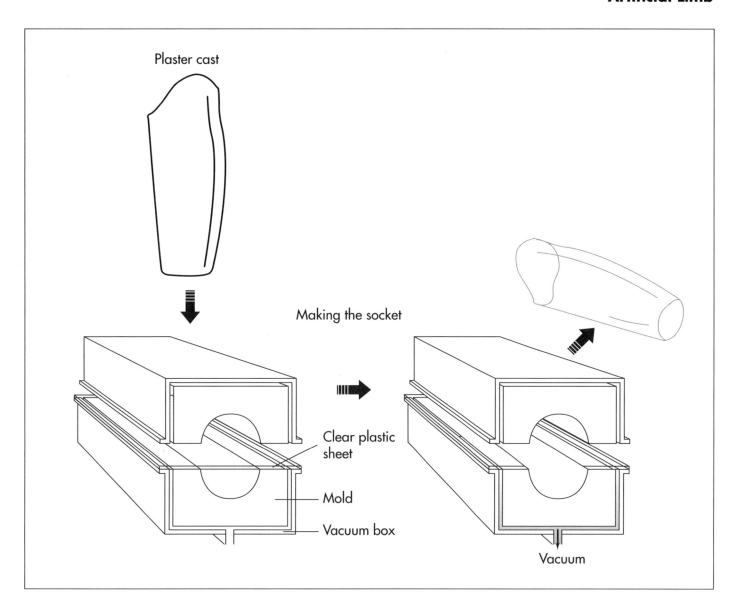

Plaster cast

Making the socket

Clear plastic sheet

Mold

Vacuum box

Vacuum

of the patient's arm or leg, which can be used to prepare a mold from which the new limb can be shaped. Laser-guided measuring and fitting is also available.

Raw Materials

The typical prosthetic device consists of a custom fitted socket, an internal structure (also called a pylon), knee cuffs and belts that attach it to the body, prosthetic socks that cushion the area of contact, and, in some cases, realistic-looking skin. Prosthetic limb manufacture is currently undergoing changes on many levels, some of which concern the choice of materials.

A prosthetic device should most of all be lightweight; hence, much of it is made from plastic. The socket is usually made from polypropylene. Lightweight metals such as titanium and aluminum have replaced much of the steel in the pylon. Alloys of these materials are most frequently used. The newest development in prosthesis manufacture has been the use of carbon fiber to form a lightweight pylon.

Certain parts of the limb (for example, the feet) have traditionally been made of wood (such as maple, hickory basswood, willow, poplar, and linden) and rubber. Even today the feet are made from urethane foam with a wooden inner keel construction. Other materials commonly used are plastics such as polyethylene, polypropylene, acrylics, and polyurethane. Prosthetic socks are made from a number of soft yet strong fabrics. Earlier socks were made of **wool**, as are some

After a plaster cast of the amputee's stump is made, a thermoplastic sheet is vacuum-formed around this cast to form a test socket. In vacuum-forming, the plastic sheet is heated and then placed in a vacuum chamber with the cast (or mold). As the air is sucked out of the chamber, the plastic adheres to the cast and assumes its shape. After testing, the permanent socket is formed in the same way.

modern ones, which can also be made of cotton or various synthetic materials.

Physical appearance of the prosthetic limb is important to the amputee. The majority of endoskeletal prostheses (pylons) are covered with a soft polyurethane foam cover that has been designed to match the shape of the patient's sound limb. This foam cover is then covered with a sock or artificial skin that is painted to match the patient's skin color.

The Manufacturing Process

Prosthetic limbs are not mass-produced to be sold in stores. Similar to the way dentures or eyeglasses are procured, prosthetic limbs are first prescribed by a medical doctor, usually after consultation with the amputee, a prosthetist, and a physical therapist. The patient then visits the prosthetist to be fitted with a limb. Although some parts—the socket, for instance—are custom-made, many parts (feet, pylons) are manufactured in a factory, sent to the prosthetist, and assembled at the prosthetist's facility in accordance with the patient's needs. At a few facilities, the limbs are custom made from start to finish.

Measuring and casting

1 Accuracy and attention to detail are important in the manufacture of prosthetic limbs, because the goal is to have a limb that comes as close as possible to being as comfortable and useful as a natural one. Before work on the fabrication of the limb is begun, the prosthetist evaluates the amputee and takes an impression or digital reading of the residual limb.

2 The prosthetist then measures the lengths of relevant body segments and determines the location of bones and tendons in the remaining part of the limb. Using the impression and the measurements, the prosthetist then makes a plaster cast of the stump. This is most commonly made of plaster of paris, because it dries fast and yields a detailed impression. From the plaster cast, a positive model—an exact duplicate—of the stump is created.

Making the socket

3 Next, a sheet of clear thermoplastic is heated in a large oven and then vacuum-formed around the positive mold. In this process, the heated sheet is simply laid over the top of the mold in a vacuum chamber. If necessary, the sheet is heated again. Then, the air between the sheet and the mold is sucked out of the chamber, collapsing the sheet around the mold and forcing it into the exact shape of the mold. This thermoplastic sheet is now the test socket; it is transparent so that the prosthetist can check the fit.

4 Before the permanent socket is made, the prosthetist works with the patient to ensure that the test socket fits properly. In the case of a missing leg, the patient walks while wearing the test socket, and the prosthetist studies the gait. The patient is also asked to explain how the fit feels; comfort comes first. The test socket is then adjusted according to patient input and retried. Because the material from which the test socket is made is thermoplastic, it can be reheated to make minor adjustments in shape. The patient can also be fitted with thicker socks for a more comfortable fit.

5 The permanent socket is then formed. Since it is usually made of polypropylene, it can be vacuum-formed over a mold in the same way as the test socket. It is common for the stump to shrink after surgery, stabilizing approximately a year later. Thus, the socket is usually replaced at that time, and thereafter when anatomical changes necessitate a change.

Fabrication of the prosthesis

6 There are many ways to manufacture the parts of a prosthetic limb. Plastic pieces—including soft-foam pieces used as liners or padding—are made in the usual plastic forming methods. These include vacuum-forming (see no. 3 above), injecting molding—forcing molten plastic into a mold and letting it cool—and extruding, in which the plastic is pulled through a shaped die. Pylons that are made of titanium or aluminum can be die-cast; in this process, liquid metal is forced into a steel die of the proper shape. The wooden pieces can be planed, sawed, and drilled. The various components are put together in a variety of ways, using bolts, adhesives, and laminating, to name a few.

7 The entire limb is assembled by the prosthetist's technician using such tools as a torque wrench and screwdriver to bolt the

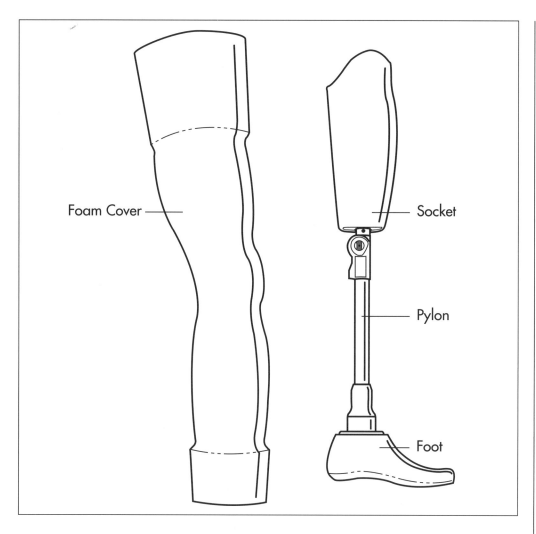

Foam Cover

Socket

Pylon

Foot

prosthetic device together. After this, the prosthetist again fits the permanent socket to the patient, this time with the completed custom-made limb attached. Final adjustments are then made.

Physical Therapy

Once the prosthetic limb has been fitted, it is necessary for the patient to become comfortable with the device and learn to use it in order to meet the challenges of everyday life. At the same time, they must learn special exercises that strengthen the muscles used to move the prosthetic device. When the patient has been fitted with a myoelectric device, it is sometimes true that the muscles are too weak to effectively signal the device, so again the muscles are exercised to strengthen them. Some new amputees are trained to wash the devices—including the socks— daily, and to practice getting them on and off.

A patient fitted with an artificial arm must learn to use the arm and its locking device as well as the hand. If the amputee lost an arm due to an accident and is subsequently fitted with a myoelectric device, this is relatively easy. If the loss of the limb is congenital, this is difficult. An instruction system has been developed to teach amputees how to accomplish many small tasks using only one hand.

Some patients fitted with an artificial leg also undergo physical therapy. It typically takes a new amputee 18-20 weeks to learn how to walk again. Patients also learn how to get in and out of bed and how to get in and out of a car. They learn how to walk up and down hill, and how to fall down and get up safely.

Quality Control

No standards exist for prosthetic limbs in the United States. Some manufacturers advocate instituting those of the International Standards Organization of Europe, particularly because U.S. exporters of prosthetic limbs to Europe must conform to them anyway.

Others believe these regulations to be confusing and unrealistic; they would rather see the United States produce their own, more reasonable standards.

Lack of standards does not mean that prosthetic limb manufacturers have not come up with ways to test their products. Some tests evaluate the strength and lifetime of the device. For instance, static loads test strength. A load is applied over a period of 30 seconds, held for 20 seconds, then removed over a period of 30 seconds. The limb should suffer no deformation from the test. To test for failure, a load is applied to the limb until it breaks, thus determining strength limits. Cyclic loads determine the lifetime of the device. A load is applied two million times at one load per second, thus simulating five years of use. Experimental prosthetic limbs are usually considered feasible if they survive 250,000 cycles.

The Future

Many experts are optimistic about the future of prosthetic limbs; at least, most agree that there is vast room for improvement. A prosthetic limb is a sophisticated device, yet it is preferably simple in design. The ideal prosthetic device should be easy for the patient to learn how to use, require little repair or replacement, be comfortable and easy to put on and take off, be strong yet lightweight, be easily adjustable, look natural, and be easy to clean. Research aims for this admittedly utopian prosthetic device, and strides have been made in recent years.

Carbon fiber is a strong, lightweight material that is now being used as the basis of endoskeletal parts (the pylons). In the past it was used primarily for reinforcement of exoskeletal protheses, but some experts claim that carbon fiber is a superior material that will eventually replace metals in pylons.

One researcher has developed software that superimposes a grid on a CAT scan of the stump to indicate the amount of pressure the soft tissue can handle with a minimum amount of pain. By viewing the computer model, the prosthetist can design a socket

that minimizes the amount of soft tissue that is displaced.

An experimental pressure-sensitive foot is also in the works. Pressure transducers located in the feet send signals to electrodes set in the stump. The nerves can then receive and interpret the signals accordingly. Amputees can walk more normally on the new device because they can feel the ground and adjust their gait appropriately.

Another revolutionary development in the area of prosthetic legs is the introduction of an above-knee prosthesis that has a built-in computer that can be programmed to match the patient's gait, thereby making walking more automatic and natural.

Where To Learn More

Books

Forester, C. S. *Flying Colours*. Little, Brown, 1938.

Sabolich, John. *You're Not Alone*. Sabolich Prosthetic and Research Center, 1991.

Shurr, Donald G. and Thomas M. Cook. *Prosthetics and Orthotics*. Appleton and Lange, 1990.

Periodicals

Abrahams, Andrew. "An Amazing 'Foot' Puts Legless Vet Bill Demby Back in the Ballgame," *People Weekly*. April 4, 1988, p. 119.

Hart, Lianne. "Lives that Are Whole," *Life*. December, 1988, pp. 112-116.

Heilman, Joan Rattner. "Medical Miracles," *Redbook*. May, 1991, p. 124+.

"A Helping Hand for Christa," *National Geographic World*. November, 1986, p. 10.

"Off to a Running Start," *National Geographic World*. August, 1991, pp. 29-31.

—*Rose Secrest*

Aspirin

Background

Aspirin is one of the safest and least expensive pain relievers on the marketplace. While other pain relievers were discovered and manufactured before aspirin, they only gained acceptance as over-the-counter drugs in Europe and the United States after aspirin's success at the turn of the twentieth century.

Today, Americans alone consume 16,000 tons of aspirin tablets a year, equaling 80 million pills, and we spend about $2 billion a year for non-prescription pain relievers, many of which contain aspirin or similar drugs.

Currently, the drug is available in several dosage forms in various concentrations from .0021 to .00227 ounces (60 to 650 milligrams), but the drug is most widely used in tablet form. Other dosage forms include capsules, caplets, suppositories and liquid elixir.

Aspirin can be used to fight a host of health problems: cerebral thromboses (with less than one tablet a day); general pain or fever (two to six tablets a day; and diseases such as rheumatic fever, gout, and rheumatoid arthritis. The drug is also beneficial in helping to ward off heart attacks. In addition, biologists use aspirin to interfere with white blood cell action, and molecular biologists use the drug to activate genes.

The wide range of effects that aspirin can produce made it difficult to pinpoint how it actually works, and it wasn't until the 1970s that biologists hypothesized that aspirin and related drugs (such as ibuprofen) work by inhibiting the synthesis of certain hormones that cause pain and inflammation. Since then, scientists have made further progress in understanding how aspirin works. They now know, for instance, that aspirin and its relatives actually prevent the growth of cells that cause inflammation.

History

The compound from which the active ingredient in aspirin was first derived, salicylic acid, was found in the bark of a willow tree in 1763 by Reverend Edmund Stone of Chipping-Norton, England. (The bark from the willow tree—Salix Alba—contains high levels of salicin, the glycoside of salicylic acid.) Earlier accounts indicate that Hippocrates of ancient Greece used willow leaves for the same purpose—to reduce fever and relieve the aches of a variety of illnesses.

During the 1800s, various scientists extracted salicylic acid from willow bark and produced the compound synthetically. Then, in 1853, French chemist Charles F. Gerhardt synthesized a primitive form of aspirin, a derivative of salicylic acid. In 1897 Felix Hoffmann, a German chemist working at the Bayer division of I.G. Farber, discovered a better method for synthesizing the drug. Though sometimes Hoffmann is improperly given credit for the discovery of aspirin, he did understand that aspirin was an effective pain reliever that did not have the side effects of salicylic acid (it burned throats and upset stomachs).

Bayer marketed aspirin beginning in 1899 and dominated the production of pain relievers until after World War I, when Sterling Drug bought German-owned Bayer's New

Today, Americans alone consume 16,000 tons of aspirin tablets a year, equaling 80 million pills, and we spend about $2 billion a year for non-prescription pain relievers, many of which contain aspirin or similar drugs.

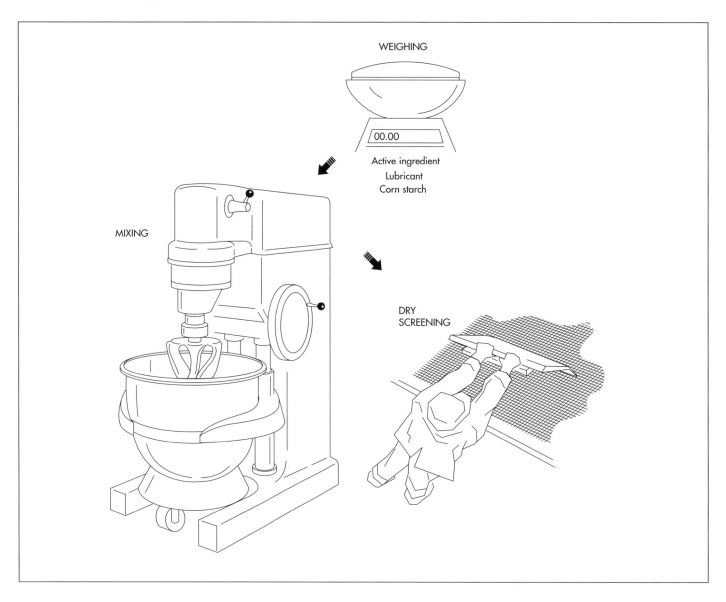

WEIGHING

00.00

Active ingredient
Lubricant
Corn starch

MIXING

DRY
SCREENING

The first three steps in aspirin manufacture: weighing, mixing, and dry screening. Mixing can be done in a Glen Mixer, which both blends the ingredients and expels the air from them. In dry screening, small batches are forced through a wire mesh screen by hand, while larger batches can be screened in a Fitzpatrick mill.

York operations. Today, "Aspirin" is a registered trademark of Bayer in many countries around the world, but in the United States and the United Kingdom aspirin is simply the common name for acetylsalicylic acid.

The manufacture of aspirin has paralleled advancements in pharmaceutical manufacturing as a whole, with significant mechanization occurring during the early twentieth century. Now, the manufacture of aspirin is highly automated and, in certain pharmaceutical companies, completely computerized.

While the aspirin production process varies between pharmaceutical companies, dosage forms and amounts, the process is not as complex as the process for many other drugs. In particular, the production of hard aspirin tablets requires only four ingredients: the

active ingredient (acetylsalicylic acid), corn starch, water, and a lubricant.

Raw Materials

To produce hard aspirin tablets, corn starch and water are added to the active ingredient (acetylsalicylic acid) to serve as both a binding agent and filler, along with a lubricant. Binding agents assist in holding the tablets together; fillers (diluents) give the tablets increased bulk to produce tablets of adequate size. A portion of the lubricant is added during mixing and the rest is added after the tablets are compressed. Lubricant keeps the mixture from sticking to the machinery. Possible lubricants include: hydrogenated vegetable oil, stearic acid, talc, or aluminum stearate. Scientists have performed considerable investigation and research to isolate the most effective lubricant for hard aspirin tablets.

Chewable aspirin tablets contain different diluents, such as mannitol, lactose, sorbitol, sucrose, and inositol, which allow the tablet to dissolve at a faster rate and give the drug a pleasant taste. In addition, flavor agents, such as saccharin, and coloring agents are added to chewable tablets. The colorants currently approved in the United States include: FD&C Yellow No. 5, FD&C Yellow No. 6, FD&C Red No.3, FD&C Red No. 40, FD&C Blue No. 1, FD&C Blue No. 2, FD&C Green No. 3, a limited number of D&C colorants, and iron oxides.

The Manufacturing Process

Aspirin tablets are manufactured in different shapes. Their weight, size, thickness, and hardness may vary depending on the amount of the dosage. The upper and lower surfaces of the tablets may be flat, round, concave, or convex to various degrees. The tablets may also have a line scored down the middle of the outer surface, so the tablets can be broken in half, if desired. The tablets may be engraved with a symbol or letters to identify the manufacturer.

Aspirin tablets of the same dosage amount are manufactured in batches. After careful weighing, the necessary ingredients are mixed and compressed into units of granular mixture called slugs. The slugs are then filtered to remove air and lumps, and are compressed again (or punched) into numerous individual tablets. (The number of tablets will depend on the size of the batch, the dosage amount, and the type of tablet machine used.) Documentation on each batch is kept throughout the manufacturing process, and finished tablets undergo several tests before they are bottled and packaged for distribution.

The procedure for manufacturing hard aspirin tablets, known as *dry-granulation* or *slugging*, is as follows:

Weighing

1 The corn starch, the active ingredient, and the lubricant are weighed separately in sterile canisters to determine if the ingredients meet pre-determined specifications for the batch size and dosage amount.

Mixing

2 The corn starch is dispensed into cold purified water, then heated and stirred until a translucent paste forms. The corn starch, the active ingredient, and part of the lubricant are next poured into one sterile canister, and the canister is wheeled to a mixing machine called a Glen Mixer. Mixing blends the ingredients as well as expels air from the mixture.

3 The mixture is then mechanically separated into units, which are generally from 7/8 to 1 inches (2.22 to 2.54 centimeters) in size. These units are called *slugs*.

Dry screening

4 Next, small batches of slugs are forced through a mesh screen by a hand-held **stainless steel** spatula. Large batches in sizable manufacturing outlets are filtered through a machine called a Fitzpatrick mill. The remaining lubricant is added to the mixture, which is blended gently in a rotary granulator and sifter. The lubricant keeps the mixture from sticking to the tablet machine during the compression process.

Compression

5 The mixture is compressed into tablets either by a single-punch machine (for small batches) or a rotary tablet machine (for large scale production). The majority of single-punch machines are power-driven, but hand-operated models are still available. On single-punch machines, the mixture is fed into one tablet mold (called a dye cavity) by a feed shoe, as follows:

• The feed shoe passes over the dye cavity and releases the mixture. The feed shoe then retracts and scrapes all excess mixture away from the dye cavity.

• A punch—a short steel rod—the size of the dye cavity descends into the dye, compressing the mixture into a tablet. The punch then retracts, while a punch below

This drawing illustrates the principle of compression in a single-punch machine. First, the aspirin mixture is fed into a dye cavity. Then, a steel punch descends into the cavity and compresses the mixture into a tablet. As the punch retracts, another punch below the cavity rises to eject the tablet.

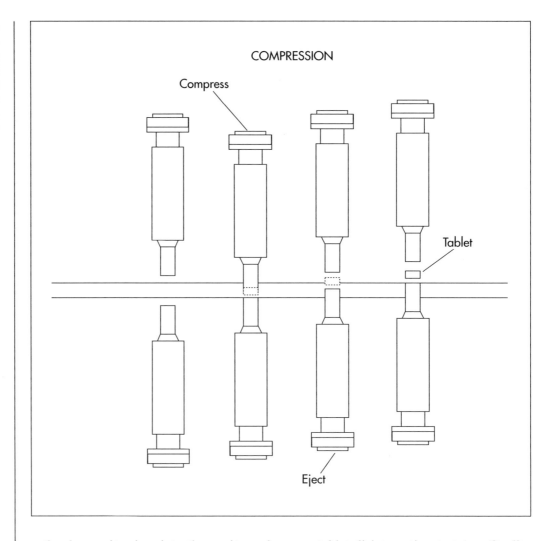

COMPRESSION

Compress

Tablet

Eject

the dye cavity rises into the cavity and ejects the tablet.

- As the feed shoe returns to fill the dye cavity again, it pushes the compressed tablet from the dye platform.

On rotary tablet machines, the mixture runs through a feed line into a number of dye cavities which are situated on a large steel plate. The plate revolves as the mixture is dispensed through the feed line, rapidly filling each dye cavity. Punches, both above and below the dye cavities, rotate in sequence with the rotation of the dye cavities. Rollers on top of the upper punches press the punches down onto the dye cavities, compressing the mixture into tablets, while roller-activated punches beneath the dye cavities lift up and eject the tablets from the dye platform.

Testing

6 The compressed tablets are subjected to a tablet hardness and friability test, as well as a tablet disintegration test (see Quality Control section below).

Bottling and packaging

7 The tablets are transferred to an automated bottling assembly line where they are dispensed into clear or color-coated polyethylene or polypropylene plastic bottles or glass bottles. The bottles are topped with cotton packing, sealed with a sheer aluminum top, and then sealed with a plastic and rubber child-proof lid. A sheer, round plastic band is then affixed to the circular edge of the lid. It serves as an additional seal to discourage and detect product tampering.

8 The bottles are then labeled with product information and an expiration date is affixed. Depending on the manufacturer, the bottles are then packaged in individual cardboard boxes. The packages or bottles are then boxed in larger cardboard boxes in preparation for distribution to distributors.

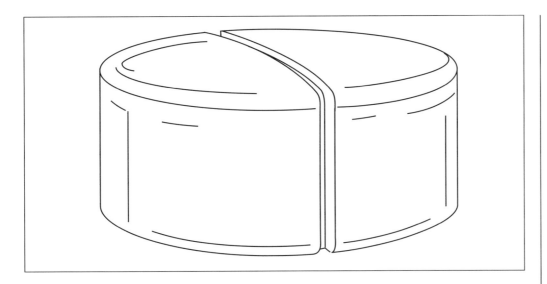

Quality Control

Maintaining a high degree of quality control is extremely important in the pharmaceutical manufacturing industry, as well as required by the Food and Drug Administration (FDA). All machinery is sterilized before beginning the production process to ensure that the product is not contaminated or diluted in any way. In addition, operators assist in maintaining an accurate and even dosage amount throughout the production process by performing periodic checks, keeping meticulous batch records, and administering necessary tests. Tablet thickness and weight are also controlled.

Once the tablets have been produced, they undergo several quality tests, such as tablet hardness and friability tests. To ensure that the tablets won't chip or break under normal conditions, they are tested for hardness in a machine such as the Schleuniger (or Heberlein) Tablet Hardness Tester. They are also tested for friability, which is the ability of the tablet to withstand the rigors of packaging and shipping. A machine called a Roche Friabilator is used to perform this test. During the test, tablets are tumbled and exposed to repeated shocks.

Another test is the tablet disintegration test. To ensure that the tablets will dissolve at the desirable rate, a sample from the batch is placed in a tablet disintegration tester such as the Vanderkamp Tester. This apparatus consists of six plastic tubes open at the top and bottom. The bottoms of the tubes are covered with a mesh screen. The tubes are filled with tablets and immersed in water at 37 degrees Fahrenheit (2.77 degrees Celsius) and retracted for a specified length of time and speed to determine if the tablets dissolve as designed.

Where To Learn More

Books

HIJSA'S Pharmaceutical Dispensing, 6th edition, Mack Publishing Company, 1966.

History of Pharmacy, 4th edition, The American Institute of History of Pharmacy, 1986.

An Introduction to Pharmaceutical Formulation, Pergamon Press, 1965.

Mann, Charles C. *The Aspirin Wars: Money, Medicine & One Hundred Years of Rampant Competition.* Alfred A. Knopf, Inc. 1991.

Remington's Pharmaceutical Sciences, 17th edition, Mack Publishing, 1985.

Periodicals

Draper, Roger. "A Pharmaceutical Cinderella (History of Aspirin)," *The New Leader.* January 13, 1992, p. 16.

Weissmann, Gerald. "Aspirin," *Scientific American.* January, 1991, pp. 84-90.

Wickens, Barbara. "Aspirin: What's in a Name?," *Maclean's.* July 16, 1990, p. 40.

— *Greg Ling*

Automobile

The development of the electric automobile will owe more to innovative solar and aeronautical engineering and advanced satellite and radar technology than to traditional automotive design and construction. The electric car will have no engine, exhaust system, transmission, muffler, radiator, or spark plugs. It will require neither tune-ups nor gasoline.

Background

In 1908 Henry Ford began production of the Model T automobile. Based on his original Model A design first manufactured in 1903, the Model T took five years to develop. Its creation inaugurated what we know today as the mass production assembly line. This revolutionary idea was based on the concept of simply assembling interchangeable component parts. Prior to this time, coaches and buggies had been hand-built in small numbers by specialized craftspeople who rarely duplicated any particular unit. Ford's innovative design reduced the number of parts needed as well as the number of skilled fitters who had always formed the bulk of the assembly operation, giving Ford a tremendous advantage over his competition.

Ford's first venture into automobile assembly with the Model A involved setting up assembly stands on which the whole vehicle was built, usually by a single assembler who fit an entire section of the car together in one place. This person performed the same activity over and over at his stationary assembly stand. To provide for more efficiency, Ford had parts delivered as needed to each work station. In this way each assembly fitter took about 8.5 hours to complete his assembly task. By the time the Model T was being developed Ford had decided to use multiple assembly stands with assemblers moving from stand to stand, each performing a specific function. This process reduced the assembly time for each fitter from 8.5 hours to a mere 2.5 minutes by rendering each worker completely familiar with a specific task.

Ford soon recognized that walking from stand to stand wasted time and created jam-ups in the production process as faster workers overtook slower ones. In Detroit in 1913, he solved this problem by introducing the first moving assembly line, a conveyor that moved the vehicle past a stationary assembler. By eliminating the need for workers to move between stations, Ford cut the assembly task for each worker from 2.5 minutes to just under 2 minutes; the moving assembly conveyor could now pace the stationary worker. The first conveyor line consisted of metal strips to which the vehicle's wheels were attached. The metal strips were attached to a belt that rolled the length of the factory and then, beneath the floor, returned to the beginning area. This reduction in the amount of human effort required to assemble an automobile caught the attention of automobile assemblers throughout the world. Ford's mass production drove the automobile industry for nearly five decades and was eventually adopted by almost every other industrial manufacturer. Although technological advancements have enabled many improvements to modern day automobile assembly operations, the basic concept of stationary workers installing parts on a vehicle as it passes their work stations has not changed drastically over the years.

Raw Materials

Although the bulk of an automobile is virgin steel, petroleum-based products (plastics and vinyls) have come to represent an increasingly large percentage of automotive components. The light-weight materials derived from petroleum have helped to lighten some models by as much as thirty percent. As the price of fossil fuels continues to rise, the preference for lighter, more fuel efficient vehicles will become more pronounced.

Design

Introducing a new model of automobile generally takes three to five years from inception to assembly. Ideas for new models are developed to respond to unmet pubic needs and preferences. Trying to predict what the public will want to drive in five years is no small feat, yet automobile companies have successfully designed automobiles that fit public tastes. With the help of computer-aided design equipment, designers develop basic concept drawings that help them visualize the proposed vehicle's appearance. Based on this simulation, they then construct clay models that can be studied by styling experts familiar with what the public is likely to accept. Aerodynamic engineers also review the models, studying air-flow parameters and doing feasibility studies on crash tests. Only after all models have been reviewed and accepted are tool designers permitted to begin building the tools that will manufacture the component parts of the new model.

The Manufacturing Process

Components

1 The automobile assembly plant represents only the final phase in the process of manufacturing an automobile, for it is here that the components supplied by more than 4,000 outside suppliers, including company-owned parts suppliers, are brought together for assembly, usually by truck or railroad. Those parts that will be used in the chassis are delivered to one area, while those that will comprise the body are unloaded at another.

Chassis

2 The typical car or truck is constructed from the ground up (and out). The frame forms the base on which the body rests and from which all subsequent assembly components follow. The frame is placed on the assembly line and clamped to the conveyer to prevent shifting as it moves down the line. From here the automobile frame moves to component assembly areas where complete front and rear suspensions, gas tanks, rear axles and drive shafts, gear boxes, steering box components, wheel drums, and braking systems are sequentially installed.

Workers install engines on Model Ts at a Ford Motor Company plant. The photo is from about 1917.

The automobile, for decades the quintessential American industrial product, did not have its origins in the United States. In 1860, Étienne Lenoir, a Belgian mechanic, introduced an internal combustion engine that proved useful as a source of stationary power. In 1878, Nicholas Otto, a German manufacturer, developed his four-stroke "explosion" engine. By 1885, one of his engineers, Gottlieb Daimler, was building the first of four experimental vehicles powered by a modified Otto internal combustion engine. Also in 1885, another German manufacturer, Carl Benz, introduced a three-wheeled, self-propelled vehicle. In 1887, the Benz became the first automobile offered for sale to the public. By 1895, automotive technology was dominated by the French, led by Emile Lavassor. Lavassor developed the basic mechanical arrangement of the car, placing the engine in the front of the chassis, with the crankshaft perpendicular to the axles.

In 1896, the Duryea Motor Wagon became the first production motor vehicle in the United States. In that same year, Henry Ford demonstrated his first experimental vehicle, the Quadricycle. By 1908, when the Ford Motor Company introduced the Model T, the United States had dozens of automobile manufacturers. The Model T quickly became the standard by which other cars were measured; ten years later, half of all cars on the road were Model Ts. It had a simple four-cylinder, twenty-horsepower engine and a planetary transmission giving two gears forward and one backward. It was sturdy, had high road clearance to negotiate the rutted roads of the day, and was easy to operate and maintain.

William S. Pretzer

3 An off-line operation at this stage of production mates the vehicle's engine with its transmission. Workers use robotic arms to install these heavy components inside the engine compartment of the frame. After the engine and transmission are installed, a

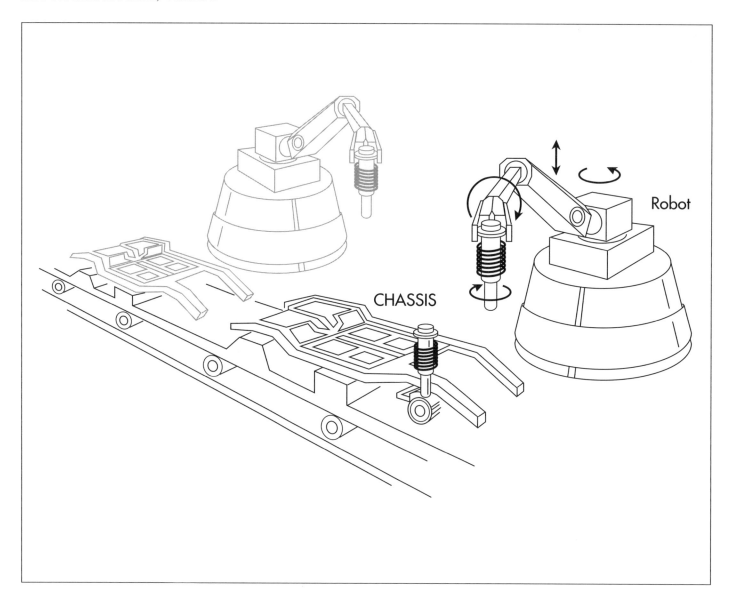

CHASSIS

Robot

On automobile assembly lines, much of the work is now done by robots rather than humans. In the first stages of automobile manufacture, robots weld the floor pan pieces together and assist workers in placing components such as the suspension onto the chassis.

worker attaches the radiator, and another bolts it into place. Because of the nature of these heavy component parts, articulating robots perform all of the lift and carry operations while assemblers using pneumatic wrenches bolt component pieces in place. Careful ergonomic studies of every assembly task have provided assembly workers with the safest and most efficient tools available.

Body

4 Generally, the floor pan is the largest body component to which a multitude of panels and braces will subsequently be either welded or bolted. As it moves down the assembly line, held in place by clamping fixtures, the shell of the vehicle is built. First, the left and right quarter panels are robotically disengaged from pre-staged shipping

containers and placed onto the floor pan, where they are stabilized with positioning fixtures and welded.

5 The front and rear door pillars, roof, and body side panels are assembled in the same fashion. The shell of the automobile assembled in this section of the process lends itself to the use of robots because articulating arms can easily introduce various component braces and panels to the floor pan and perform a high number of weld operations in a time frame and with a degree of accuracy no human workers could ever approach. Robots can pick and load 200-pound (90.8 kilograms) roof panels and place them precisely in the proper weld position with tolerance variations held to within .001 of an inch. Moreover, robots can also tolerate the

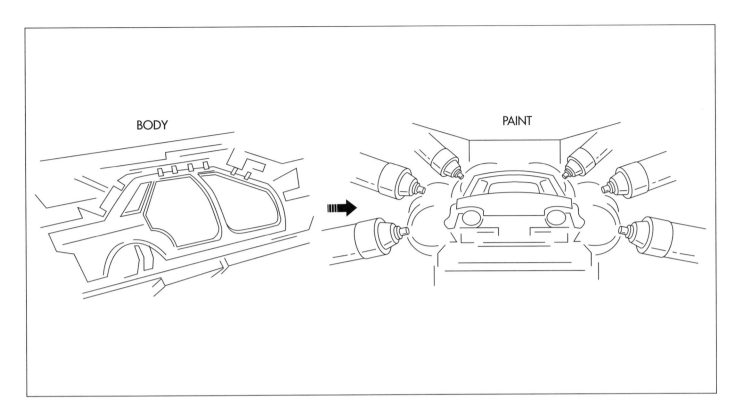

BODY

PAINT

smoke, weld flashes, and gases created during this phase of production.

6 As the body moves from the isolated weld area of the assembly line, subsequent body components including fully assembled doors, deck lids, hood panel, fenders, trunk lid, and bumper reinforcements are installed. Although robots help workers place these components onto the body shell, the workers provide the proper fit for most of the bolt-on functional parts using pneumatically assisted tools.

Paint

7 Prior to painting, the body must pass through a rigorous inspection process, the *body in white* operation. The shell of the vehicle passes through a brightly lit white room where it is fully wiped down by visual inspectors using cloths soaked in hi-light oil. Under the lights, this oil allows inspectors to see any defects in the sheet metal body panels. Dings, dents, and any other defects are repaired right on the line by skilled body repairmen. After the shell has been fully inspected and repaired, the assembly conveyor carries it through a cleaning station where it is immersed and cleaned of all residual oil, dirt, and contaminants.

8 As the shell exits the cleaning station it goes through a drying booth and then through an undercoat dip—an electrostatically charged bath of undercoat **paint** (called the *E-coat*) that covers every nook and cranny of the body shell, both inside and out, with primer. This coat acts as a substrate surface to which the top coat of colored paint adheres.

9 After the E-coat bath, the shell is again dried in a booth as it proceeds on to the final paint operation. In most automobile assembly plants today, vehicle bodies are spray-painted by robots that have been programmed to apply the exact amounts of paint to just the right areas for just the right length of time. Considerable research and programming has gone into the dynamics of robotic painting in order to ensure the fine "wet" finishes we have come to expect. Our robotic painters have come a long way since Ford's first Model Ts, which were painted by hand with a brush.

10 Once the shell has been fully covered with a base coat of color paint and a clear top coat, the conveyor transfers the bodies through baking ovens where the paint is cured at temperatures exceeding 275 degrees Fahrenheit (135 degrees Celsius).

The body is built up on a separate assembly line from the chassis. Robots once again perform most of the welding on the various panels, but human workers are necessary to bolt the parts together. During welding, component pieces are held securely in a jig while welding operations are performed. Once the body shell is complete, it is attached to an overhead conveyor for the painting process. The multi-step painting process entails inspection, cleaning, undercoat (electrostatically applied) dipping, drying, topcoat spraying, and baking.

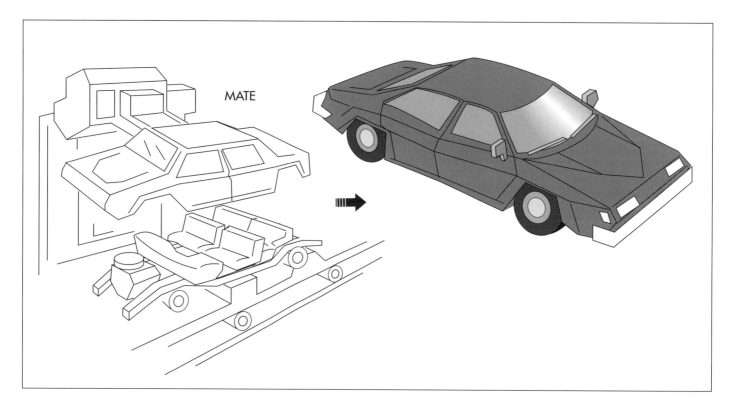

MATE

The body and chassis assemblies are mated near the end of the production process. Robotic arms lift the body shell onto the chassis frame, where human workers then bolt the two together. After final components are installed, the vehicle is driven off the assembly line to a quality checkpoint.

After the shell leaves the paint area it is ready for interior assembly.

Interior assembly

11 The painted shell proceeds through the interior assembly area where workers assemble all of the instrumentation and wiring systems, dash panels, interior lights, seats, door and trim panels, headliners, radios, speakers, all glass except the **automobile windshield**, steering column and wheel, body weatherstrips, vinyl tops, brake and gas pedals, carpeting, and front and rear bumper fascias.

12 Next, robots equipped with suction cups remove the windshield from a shipping container, apply a bead of urethane sealer to the perimeter of the glass, and then place it into the body windshield frame. Robots also pick seats and trim panels and transport them to the vehicle for the ease and efficiency of the assembly operator. After passing through this section the shell is given a water test to ensure the proper fit of door panels, glass, and weatherstripping. It is now ready to mate with the chassis.

Mate

13 The chassis assembly conveyor and the body shell conveyor meet at this stage of production. As the chassis passes the body conveyor the shell is robotically lifted from its conveyor fixtures and placed onto the car frame. Assembly workers, some at ground level and some in work pits beneath the conveyor, bolt the car body to the frame. Once the mating takes place the automobile proceeds down the line to receive final trim components, **battery**, **tires**, antifreeze, and gasoline.

14 The vehicle can now be started. From here it is driven to a checkpoint off the line, where its engine is audited, its lights and horn checked, its tires balanced, and its charging system examined. Any defects discovered at this stage require that the car be taken to a central repair area, usually located near the end of the line. A crew of skilled trouble-shooters at this stage analyze and repair all problems. When the vehicle passes final audit it is given a price label and driven to a staging lot where it will await shipment to its destination.

Quality Control

All of the components that go into the automobile are produced at other sites. This means the thousands of component pieces that comprise the car must be manufactured, tested, packaged, and shipped to the assembly plants, often on the same day they will be used. This requires no small amount of planning. To accomplish it, most automobile manufacturers require outside parts vendors to subject their component parts to rigorous testing and inspection audits similar to those used by the assembly plants. In this way the assembly plants can anticipate that the products arriving at their receiving docks are *Statistical Process Control* (*SPC*) approved and free from defects.

Once the component parts of the automobile begin to be assembled at the automotive factory, production control specialists can follow the progress of each embryonic automobile by means of its *Vehicle Identification Number* (*VIN*), assigned at the start of the production line. In many of the more advanced assembly plants a small radio frequency transponder is attached to the chassis and floor pan. This sending unit carries the VIN information and monitors its progress along the assembly process. Knowing what operations the vehicle has been through, where it is going, and when it should arrive at the next assembly station gives production management personnel the ability to electronically control the manufacturing sequence. Throughout the assembly process quality audit stations keep track of vital information concerning the integrity of various functional components of the vehicle.

This idea comes from a change in quality control ideology over the years. Formerly, quality control was seen as a final inspection process that sought to discover defects only after the vehicle was built. In contrast, today quality is seen as a process built right into the design of the vehicle as well as the assembly process. In this way assembly operators can stop the conveyor if workers find a defect. Corrections can then be made, or supplies checked to determine whether an entire batch of components is bad. Vehicle recalls are costly and manufacturers do everything possible to ensure the integrity of their product before it is shipped to the customer. After the vehicle is assembled a validation process is conducted at the end of the assembly line to verify quality audits from the various inspection points throughout the assembly process. This final audit tests for properly fitting panels; dynamics; squeaks and rattles;

functioning electrical components; and engine, chassis, and wheel alignment. In many assembly plants vehicles are periodically pulled from the audit line and given full functional tests. All efforts today are put forth to ensure that quality and reliability are built into the assembled product.

The Future

The development of the electric automobile will owe more to innovative solar and aeronautical engineering and advanced satellite and radar technology than to traditional automotive design and construction. The electric car has no engine, exhaust system, transmission, muffler, radiator, or spark plugs. It will require neither tune-ups nor—truly revolutionary—gasoline. Instead, its power will come from alternating current (AC) electric motors with a brushless design capable of spinning up to 20,000 revolutions/minute. Batteries to power these motors will come from high performance cells capable of generating more than 100 kilowatts of power. And, unlike the lead-acid batteries of the past and present, future batteries will be environmentally safe and recyclable. Integral to the braking system of the vehicle will be a power inverter that converts direct current electricity back into the battery pack system once the accelerator is let off, thus acting as a generator to the battery system even as the car is driven long into the future.

The growth of automobile use and the increasing resistance to road building have made our highway systems both congested and obsolete. But new electronic vehicle technologies that permit cars to navigate around the congestion and even drive themselves may soon become possible. Turning over the operation of our automobiles to computers would mean they would gather information from the roadway about congestion and find the fastest route to their instructed destination, thus making better use of limited highway space. The advent of the electric car will come because of a rare convergence of circumstance and ability. Growing intolerance for pollution combined with extraordinary technological advancements will change the global transportation paradigm that will carry us into the twenty-first century.

Where To Learn More

Books

Abernathy, William. *The Productivity Dilemma: Roadblock to Innovation in the Automobile Industry.* Johns Hopkins University Press, 1978.

Gear Design, Manufacturing & Inspection Manual. Society of Manufacturing Engineers, Inc., 1990.

Hounshell, David. *From the American System to Mass Production.* Johns Hopkins University Press, 1984.

Lamming, Richard. *Beyond Partnership: Strategies for Innovation & Lean Supply.* Prentice Hall, 1993.

Making the Car. Motor Vehicle Manufacturers Association of the United States, 1987.

Mortimer, J., ed. *Advanced Manufacturing in the Automotive Industry.* Springer-Verlag New York, Inc., 1987.

Mortimer, John. *Advanced Manufacturing in the Automotive Industry.* Air Science Co., 1986.

Nevins, Allen and Frank E. Hill. *Ford: The Times, The Man, The Company.* Scribners, 1954.

Seiffert, Ulrich. *Automobile Technology of the Future.* Society of Automotive Engineers, Inc., 1991.

Sloan, Alfred P. *My Years with General Motors.* Doubleday, 1963.

Periodicals

"The Secrets of the Production Line," *The Economist.* October 17, 1992, p. S5.

— *Rick Bockmiller*

Automobile Windshield

Background

Glass is a versatile material with hundreds of applications, including windshields. Glass has a long history and was first made more than 7,000 years ago in Egypt, as early as 3,000 B.C. Glass is found in a natural state as a by-product of volcanic activity. Today, glass is manufactured from a variety of ceramic materials (main components are oxides). The main product categories are flat or float glass, container glass, cut glass, fiberglass, optical glass, and specialty glass. Automotive windshields fall into the flat glass category.

There are more than 80 companies worldwide that produce automotive glass, including windshields. Major producers in the United States include PPG, Guardian Industries Corp., and Libby-Owens Ford. According to the Department of Commerce, 25 percent of flat glass production is consumed by the automotive industry (including windows) at a total value of approximately $483 million. In Japan, 30 percent of flat glass goes to the automotive industry, valued at around $190 billion in 1989. Major Japanese flat glass manufacturers include Asahi Glass Co., Central Glass Co., and Nippon Sheet Glass Co. Little growth is expected for the flat glass industry overall in both countries. Germany has a more positive outlook, with high growth rates expected from the automotive industry.

Glass windshields first appeared around 1905 with the invention of safety glass—glass tempered (tempering is a heat treatment) to make it especially hard and resistant to shattering. This type of windshield was popular well into the middle of the century, but it was eventually replaced by windshields made of laminated glass—a multilayer unit consisting of a plastic layer surrounded by two sheets of glass. In many countries, including the U.S., auto windshields are required by law to be made of laminated glass. Laminated glass can bend slightly under impact and is less likely to shatter than normal safety glass. This quality reduces the risk of injury to the **automobile**'s passengers.

Raw Materials

Glass is composed of numerous oxides that fuse and react together upon heating to form a glass. These include silica (SiO_2), sodium oxide (Na_2O), and calcium oxide (CaO). Raw materials from which these materials are derived are sand, soda ash (Na_2CO_3), and limestone ($CaCO_3$). Soda ash acts as a flux; in other words, it lowers the melting point of the batch composition. Lime is added to the batch in order to improve the hardness and chemical durability of the glass. Glass used for windshields also usually contains several other oxides: potassium oxide (K_2O derived from potash), magnesium oxide (MgO), and aluminum oxide (Al_2O_3 derived from feldspar).

The Manufacturing Process

1 The raw materials are carefully weighed in the appropriate amounts and mixed together with a small amount of water to prevent segregation of the ingredients. Cullet (broken waste glass) is also used as a raw material.

2 Once the batch is made, it is fed to a large tank for melting using the float

A bi-layer windshield has been developed that consists of one sheet of glass joined to a single sheet of polyurethane. Unique features of this windshield include ultraviolet resistance, self-healing of scratches, weight savings, more complex shapes, increased safety due to retention of glass splinters, and anti-fog capability.

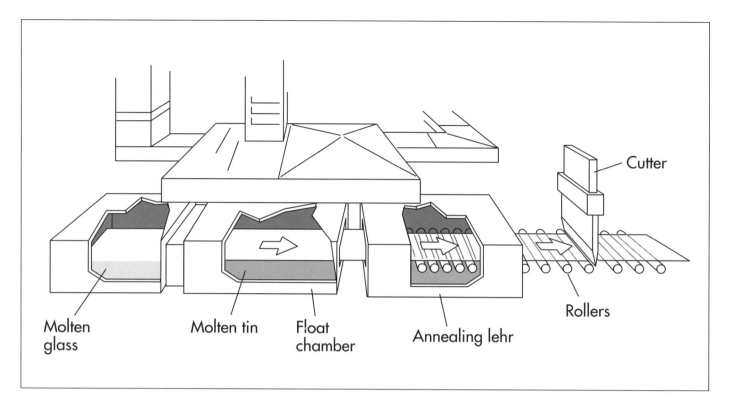

Molten glass

Molten tin

Float chamber

Annealing lehr

Rollers

Cutter

The glass for automibile windshields is made using the float glass process. In this method, the raw material is heated to a molten state and fed onto a bath of molten tin. The glass literally floats on top of the tin; because the tin is perfectly flat, the glass also becomes flat. From the float chamber, the glass passes on rollers through an oven (the "annealing lehr"). After exiting the lehr and cooling to room temperature, the glass is cut to the proper shape and tempered.

glass process. First, the batch is heated to a molten state, and then it is fed into a tank called the float chamber, which holds a bath of molten tin. The float chamber is very large—from about 13 feet to 26.25 feet (4 to 8 meters wide and up to almost 197 feet (60 meters) long; at its entrance, the temperature of the tin is about 1,835 degrees Fahrenheit (1,000 degrees Celsius), while at the exit the tin's temperature is slightly cooler—1,115 degrees Fahrenheit (600 degrees Celsius). In the float chamber, the glass doesn't submerge into the tin but floats on top of it, moving through the tank as though on a conveyor belt. The perfectly flat surface of the tin causes the molten glass also to become flat, while the high temperatures clean the glass of impurities. The decreased temperature at the exit of the chamber allows the glass to harden enough to move into the next chamber, a furnace.

3 After the glass exits from the float chamber, rollers pick it up and feed it into a special furnace called a lehr. (If any solar coatings are desired, they are applied before the glass enters the lehr.) In this furnace, the glass is cooled gradually to about 395 degrees Fahrenheit (200 degrees Celsius); after the glass exits the lehr, it cools to room temperature. It is now very hard and strong and ready to be cut.

Cutting and tempering

4 The glass is cut into the desired dimensions using a diamond scribe—a tool with sharp metal points containing diamond dust. Diamond is used because it is harder than glass. The scribe marks a cut line into the glass, which is then broken or snapped at this line. This step is usually automated and is monitored by cameras and optoelectronic measuring systems. Next, the cut piece must be bent into shape. The sheet of glass is placed into a form or mold of metal or refractory material. The glass-filled mold is then heated in a furnace to the point where the glass sags to the shape of the mold.

5 After this shaping step, the glass must be hardened in a heating step called tempering. First, the glass is quickly heated to about 1,565 degrees Fahrenheit (850 degrees Celsius), and then it is blasted with jets of cold air. Called quenching, this process toughens the glass by putting the outer surface into compression and the inside into tension. This allows the windshield, when damaged, to break into many small pieces of glass without sharp edges. The size of the pieces can also be changed by modifying the tempering procedure so that the windshield breaks into larger pieces, allowing good vision until the windshield can be replaced.

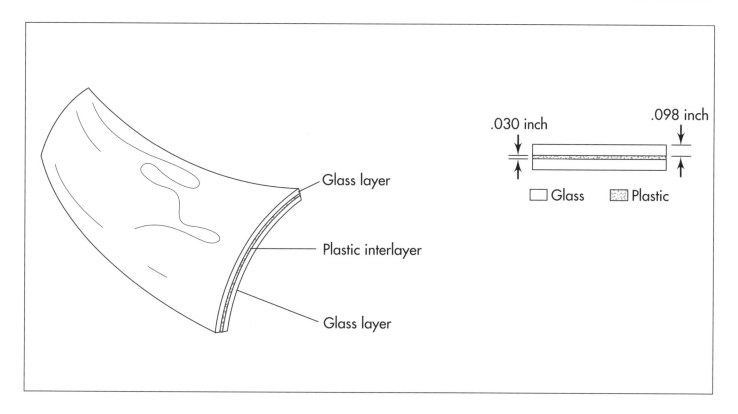

.030 inch .098 inch

☐ Glass ▨ Plastic

Glass layer

Plastic interlayer

Glass layer

Laminating

6 After the glass is tempered and cleaned, it goes through a laminating process. In this process, two sheets of glass are bonded together with a layer of plastic (the plastic layer goes inside the two glass sheets). The lamination takes place in an autoclave, a special oven that uses both heat and pressure to form a single, strong unit that is resistant to tearing. The plastic interlayer is often tinted to act as an ultraviolet filter. When laminated glass is broken, the broken pieces of glass remain bound to the internal tear-resistant plastic layer, and the broken sheet remains transparent. Thus, visibility remains good. Unlike traditional safety glass, laminated glass can be further processed—cut, drilled, and edge-worked, as necessary. A typical laminated windshield is very thin: each glass layer is approximately .03 inch (.76 millimeter) thick, while the plastic interlayer is approximately .098 inch (2.5 millimeters) thick.

Assembly

7 After laminating, the windshield is ready to be assembled with plastic moldings so it can be installed on the car. Known as glass encapsulation, this assembly process is usually done at the glass manufacturer. First, the peripheral section of the windshield is set in a predetermined position in a mold cavity.

Next, molten plastic is injected into the mold; when it cools, it forms a plastic frame around the glass. The windshield assembly is then shipped to the car manufacturer, where it is installed in an automobile. The installation is done by direct glazing, a process that uses a polyurethane adhesive to bond the windshield and automobile body.

Quality Control

Process control includes testing of raw materials and monitoring such process variables as melting temperature, furnace atmosphere, and glass level. As the glass is formed, photoelectric devices are used to inspect for defects automatically. Other automatic devices have been developed to measure dimensions and radius of curvature after the windshield has been formed.

Safety glass used in windshields must meet certain specifications regarding properties such as chemical durability, impact resistance, and strength. Standards have been developed by the American Society for Testing of Materials (ASTM) for measuring these properties. Specifications have also been developed for windshield performance by SAE International, an organization of automotive engineers.

A finished windshield consists of two glass layers sandwiched around a plastic interlayer. Although very thin—about .25 inch thick—such laminated glass is very strong and is less likely to shatter than normal safety glass. In the United States, windshields are required by law to be made of laminated glass.

The Future

Despite the recent downturn in the automotive industry, long-term prospects are more optimistic. Motor vehicle production markets will be stronger than in recent years, raising demand for flat glass products such as windshields. Windshields are also increasing in size in order to accommodate newer aerodynamic designs, and thus the use of glass is increasing relative to the total surface area of vehicles. (In fact, some models are incorporating glass roofs as well.)

Such increase in glass area, in turn, has a negative impact on comfort systems, namely air conditioners, which must be able to adjust the higher interior temperatures to a comfortable level. To avoid having to use larger air conditioning systems, new glass compositions, coated glasses, and aftermarket films are being evaluated. These include angle-selective glazings that reject high-angle sun, and optical switching films that actively or passively change transmittance properties.

One recently developed film, a polymer multilayer solar control film, can also act as a deicing device. The coated plastic substrate simply replaces the laminated plastic film in conventional windshields. The film can be made in any color and can transmit up to 90 percent of the visible light. Another coating is a glaze that consists of silver coating used in combination with other metal oxide layers. This glaze can reject up to 60 percent of the total solar energy, reducing the infrared energy by 56 percent.

In addition, new types of laminated-glass windshields are being researched. A bi-layer windshield has been developed that only requires one outer sheet of glass, .08 to .16 of an inch (2-4 millimeters) thick, joined to a .254 of an inch (1 millimeter) sheet of polyurethane. The polyurethane sheet consists of two layers, one having high absorption properties and the other high surface resistance. Unique features of this bi-layer windshield include ultraviolet resistance, self-healing of scratches, weight savings, more complex shapes, increased safety due to retention of glass splinters, and anti-fog capability.

Recycling of windshield components may also become a standard practice. Though traditionally recycling has been difficult because of the plastic laminated films, one manufacturer has recently developed a cost-effective process to remove these layers. The recycled glass can be used in several applications, including glassphalt for road repair. Legislation may also speed up recycling practices, with the introduction of the Municipal Solid Waste and Hazardous Waste Research Act of 1992. This bill seeks to determine the obstacles to increased automotive components recycling and find ways to overcome these obstacles. This may eventually require using fewer resins during manufacturing or making sure these resins are compatible for recycling.

Where To Learn More

Books

McLellan, George W. and E. B. Shand, eds. *Glass Engineering Handbook*. 3rd ed., McGraw-Hill, 1984.

Pfaender, Heinz G. and Hubert Schroeder. *Schott Guide To Glass*. Van Nostrand Reinhold, 1983.

Scholes, Samuel R. *Modern Glass Practice*. CBI Publishing Company, 1975.

Periodicals

"Bill To Overcome Recycling Obstacles," *Autoglass*. July/August, 1992.

"Guardian Produces Largest Production Car Windshield," *Autoglass,* March/April, 1992.

Leventon, William. "Press and Vacuum Form Complex Windshields," *Design News*. November 9, 1992, p. 159.

Olosky, M. L. and M. J. Watson. "Silicon Film Adhesives: Bonding Automotive Fixtures to Glass," *SAE Paper No. 931013.* SAE International, 1993.

Peters, G. M. and T. W. Karwan, et al. "A Cost Effective Quality Improvement for Automotive Glass Encapsulation," *SAE Paper No. 931012.* SAE International, 1993.

Sheppard, L. M. "Automotive Performance Accelerate with Ceramics," *Ceramic Bulletin.* 1990, pp. 1012-1021.

—*L. S. Millberg*

Baking Soda

Background

Baking soda is a white crystalline powder ($NaHCO_3$) better known to chemists as sodium bicarbonate, bicarbonate of soda, sodium hydrogen carbonate, or sodium acid carbonate. It is classified as an acid salt, formed by combining an acid (carbonic) and a base (sodium hydroxide), and it reacts with other chemicals as a mild alkali. At temperatures above 300 degrees Fahrenheit (149 degrees Celsius), baking soda decomposes into sodium carbonate (a more stable substance), water, and carbon dioxide.

The native chemical and physical properties of baking soda account for its wide range of applications, including cleaning, deodorizing, buffering, and fire extinguishing. Baking soda neutralizes odors chemically, rather than masking or absorbing them. Consequently, it is used in bath salts and deodorant body powders. Baking soda tends to maintain a pH of 8.1 (7 is neutral) even when acids, which lower pH, or bases, which raise pH, are added to the solution. Its ability to tabletize makes it a good effervescent ingredient in antacids and denture cleaning products. Sodium bicarbonate is also found in some anti-plaque mouthwash products and toothpaste. When baking soda is used as a cleaner in paste form or dry on a damp sponge, its crystalline structure provides a gentle abrasion that helps to remove dirt without scratching sensitive surfaces. Its mild alkalinity works to turn up fatty acids contained in dirt and grease into a form of soap that can be dissolved in water and rinsed easily. Baking soda is also used as a leavening agent in making baked goods such as bread or pancakes. When combined with an acidic agent (such as lemon juice), carbon dioxide gas is released and is absorbed by the product's cells. As the gas expands during baking, the cell walls expand as well, creating a leavened product.

In addition to its many home uses, baking soda also has many industrial applications. For instance, baking soda releases carbon dioxide when heated. Since carbon dioxide is heavier than air, it can smother flames by keeping oxygen out, making sodium bicarbonate a useful agent in **fire extinguisher**s. Other applications include air pollution control (because it absorbs sulfur dioxide and other acid gas emissions), abrasive blastings for removal of surface coatings, chemical manufacturing, leather tanning, oil well drilling fluids (because it precipitates calcium and acts as a lubricant), rubber and plastic manufacturing, paper manufacturing, textile processing, and water treatment (because it reduces the level of lead and other heavy metals).

Imported from England, baking soda was first used in America during colonial times, but it was not produced in the United States until 1839. In 1846, Austin Church, a Connecticut physician, and John Dwight, a farmer from Massachusetts, established a factory in New York to manufacture baking soda. Dr. Church's son, John, owned a mill called the Vulcan Spice Mills. Vulcan, the Roman god of forge and fire, was represented by an arm and hammer, and the new baking soda company adopted the arm and hammer logo as its own. Today, the Arm & Hammer brand of baking soda is among the most widely recognized brand names.

Named after Nicolas Leblanc, the French chemist who invented it, the Leblanc process was the earliest means of manufacturing soda

In addition to its many home uses, baking soda also has many industrial applications: in fire extinguishers (because it smothers flames); in air pollution control (because it absorbs sulfur dioxide and other acid gas emissions); and in water treatment (because it reduces the level of lead and other heavy metals).

ash (Na_2CO_3), from which sodium bicarbonate is made. Sodium chloride (table salt) was heated with sulfuric acid, producing sodium sulfate and hydrochloric acid. The sodium sulfate was then heated with coal and limestone to form sodium carbonate, or soda ash.

In the late 1800s, another method of producing soda ash was devised by Ernest Solvay, a Belgian chemical engineer. The Solvay method was soon adapted in the United States, where it replaced the Leblanc process. In the Solvay process, carbon dioxide and ammonia are passed into a concentrated solution of sodium chloride. Crude sodium bicarbonate precipitates out and is heated to form soda ash, which is then further treated and refined to form sodium bicarbonate of *United States Pharmacopoeia* (U.S.P.) purity.

Although this method of producing baking soda ash is widely used, it is also problematic because the chemicals used in the process are pollutants and cause disposal problems. An alternative is to refine soda ash from trona ore, a natural deposit.

Raw Materials

Baking soda, or sodium bicarbonate, comes from soda ash obtained either through the Solvay process or from trona ore, a hard, crystalline material. Trona dates back 50 million years, to when the land surrounding Green River, Wyoming, was covered by a 600-square-mile (1,554-square-kilometer) lake. As it evaporated over time, this lake left a 200-billion-ton deposit of pure trona between layers of sandstone and shale. The deposit at the Green River Basin is large enough to meet the entire world's needs for soda ash and sodium bicarbonate for thousands of years.

Because the synthetic process used in the Solvay method presented some pollution problems, Church & Dwight Co. Inc. is basing more and more of its manufacturing on trona mining. Another large producer of soda ash, the FMC Corporation, also relies on trona to manufacture soda ash and sodium bicarbonate. Trona is mined at 1,500 feet (457.2 meters) below the surface. FMC's mine shafts contain nearly 2,500 (4,022.5 kilometers) miles of tunnels and cover 24 square miles (62 square kilometers). Fifteen

feet (4.57 meters) wide and nine feet (2.74 meters) tall, these tunnels allow the necessary equipment and vehicles to travel through them.

The Manufacturing Process

Making soda ash

1 Soda ash can be manufactured chemically using the Solvay process, or it can be made from trona ore. If trona ore is used, it must first be mined. After it has been brought to the surface, the trona ore is transported to a variety of processing plants. There, the ore is refined into a slurry of sodium sesquicarbonate, an intermediate soda ash product that actually contains both soda ash (sodium carbonate) and baking soda (sodium bicarbonate).

Making baking soda

2 Next, the intermediate soda ash solution is put into a centrifuge, which separates the liquid from the crystals. The crystals are then dissolved in a bicarbonate solution (a soda ash solution made by the manufacturer) in a rotary dissolver, thereby becoming a saturated solution. This solution is filtered to remove any non-soluble materials and is then pumped through a feed tank to the top of a carbonating tower.

3 Purified carbon dioxide is introduced into the bottom of the tower and held under pressure. As the saturated sodium solution moves through the tower, it cools and reacts with the carbon dioxide to form sodium bicarbonate crystals. These crystals are collected at the bottom of the tower and transferred to another centrifuge, where excess solution (filtrate) is filtered out. The crystals are then washed in a bicarbonate solution, forming a cake-like substance ready for drying. The filtrate that is removed from the centrifuge is recycled to the rotary dissolver, where it is used to saturate more intermediate soda ash crystals.

4 The washed filter cake is then dried on either a continuous belt conveyor or in a vertical tube drier called a *flash dryer*. The theoretical yield from the process, according to the Church & Dwight Company, is between 90 and 95 percent, and the baking soda manufactured is more than 99 percent pure.

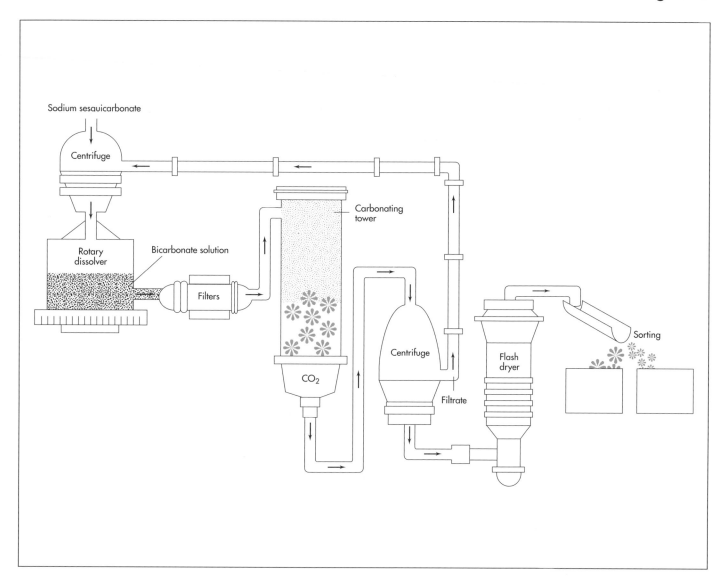

An illustration of the baking soda manufacturing process. A key step in the process occurs in the carbonating tower. Here, the saturated soda ash solution moves from the top of the tower downward. As it falls, the solution cools and reacts with carbon dioxide to form sodium bicarbonate crystals—baking soda. After filtering, washing, and drying, the crystals are sorted by particle size and packaged appropriately.

Sorting and storing the different grades

5 Next, the dried crystals of sodium bicarbonate are separated into various grades by particle size. Standard grades of sodium bicarbonate and special grades are manufactured to meet customers' specific requirements, and particle size is the major determinant of grades. Powdered #1 and fine granular #2 have a wide range of uses in foods, chemicals, and pharmaceuticals. Granular grades #4 and #5 are found in foods and doughnuts, cleaning compounds, pharmaceuticals, and many other products. Industrial grade sodium bicarbonate is used in diverse applications, including oil well drilling fluids, fire extinguishing materials, and water treatment.

6 Each grade goes to a holding bin wherein atmosphere, carbon dioxide, and moisture content are controlled to "cure" the product. Once cured, the grades are ready to be packaged and shipped.

Quality Control

The quality of sodium bicarbonate is controlled at every stage of the manufacturing process. Materials, equipment, and the process itself are selected to yield sodium bicarbonate of the highest possible quality. According to FMC sources, when the company constructed plants, it chose materials and equipment that would be compatible with the stringent quality requirements for making pharmaceutical grade sodium bicarbonate. FMC also uses *Statistical Process Control* (SPC) to maintain unvarying daily quality, and key operating parameters are charted to maintain process control. Product quality parameters are recorded by lot number, and samples are kept for two to three years.

All U.S.P. grades meet the *United States Pharmacopoeia and Food Chemicals Codex* specifications for use in pharmaceutical and food applications. In addition, food grade sodium bicarbonate meets the requirements specified by the U.S. Food and Drug Administration as a substance that is *Generally Recognized as Safe* (GRAS).

The Future

At the turn of the twentieth century, 53,000 tons (48,071 metric tons) of baking soda were sold annually. While the population increased dramatically, sales by 1990 were down to about 32,000 tons (29,024 metric tons) per year. Self-rising flour and cake and biscuit mixes have decreased the demand for baking soda as an important baking ingredient. Nevertheless, demand for the product is still significant. Commercial bakers (particularly cookie manufacturers) are one of the major users of this product. One of the most important attributes of sodium bicarbonate is that, when exposed to heat, it releases carbon dioxide gas (CO_2) which makes the baking goods rise. Sodium bicarbonate is also used in the pharmaceutical and health industries, and it has other industrial applications as well. It therefore continues to be an important product for today and for the future.

Where To Learn More

Books

Coyle, L. Patrick, Jr. *The World Encyclopedia of Food.* Facts on File, 1982.

Root, Waverley and Richard de Rochemont. *Eating in America: A History.* William Morrow & Co., Inc., 1976.

Periodicals and Pamphlets

Grosswirth, Marvin. "The Wonders of $NaHCO_3$," *Science Digest.* March, 1976.

History of the Arm & Hammer Trademark. Church & Dwight Co., Inc.

Sodium Bicarbonate. FMC Corporation.

Sodium Bicarbonate—Chemical Properties, Manufacturing. Church & Dwight Co., Inc.

—*Eva Sideman*

Ball Bearing

Background

Ever since man began to need to move things, he has used round rollers to make the job easier. Probably the first rollers were sticks or logs, which were a big improvement over dragging things across the ground, but still pretty hard work. Egyptians used logs to roll their huge blocks of stone for the pyramids. Eventually, someone came up with the idea of securing the roller to whatever was being moved, and built the first "vehicle" with "wheels." However, these still had bearings made from materials rubbing on each other instead of rolling on each other. It wasn't until the late eighteenth century that the basic design for bearings was developed. In 1794, Welsh ironmaster Philip Vaughan patented a design for ball bearings to support the axle of a carriage. Development continued in the nineteenth and early twentieth centuries, spurred by the advancement of the bicycle and the **automobile**.

There are thousands of sizes, shapes, and kinds of rolling bearings; ball bearings, roller bearings, needle bearings, and tapered roller bearings are the major kinds. Sizes run from small enough to run miniature motors to huge bearings used to support rotating parts in hydroelectric power plants; these large bearings can be ten feet (3.04 meters) in diameter and require a crane to install. The most common sizes can easily be held in one hand and are used in things like electric motors.

This article will describe only ball bearings. In these bearings, the rolling part is a ball, which rolls between inner and outer rings called races. The balls are held by a cage, which keeps them evenly spaced around the races. In addition to these parts, there are a lot of optional parts for special bearings, like seals to keep oil or grease in and dirt out, or screws to hold a bearing in place. We won't worry here about these fancy extras.

Raw Materials

Almost all parts of all ball bearings are made of steel. Since the bearing has to stand up to a lot of stress, it needs to be made of very strong steel. The standard industry classification for the steel in these bearings is 52100, which means that it has one percent chromium and one percent carbon (called alloys when added to the basic steel). This steel can be made very hard and tough by heat treating. Where rusting might be a problem, bearings are made from 440C **stainless steel**.

The cage for the balls is traditionally made of thin steel, but some bearings now use molded plastic cages, because they cost less to make and cause less friction.

The Manufacturing Process

There are four major parts to a standard ball bearing: the outer race, the rolling balls, the inner race, and the cage.

Races

1 Both races are made in almost the same way. Since they are both rings of steel, the process starts with steel tubing of an appropriate size. Automatic machines similar to lathes use cutting tools to cut the basic shape of the race, leaving all of the dimensions slightly too large. The reason for leaving them too large is that the races must be heat treated before being finished, and the steel

There are thousands of sizes, shapes, and kinds of rolling bearings. Sizes run from small enough to run miniature motors to huge bearings used to support rotating parts in hydroelectric power plants; these large bearings can be ten feet in diameter and require a crane to install.

Surprisingly, the rolling balls start out as thick steel wire. Then, in a cold heading process, the wire is cut into small pieces smashed between two steel dies. The result is a ball that looks like the planet Saturn, with a ring around its middle called "flash."

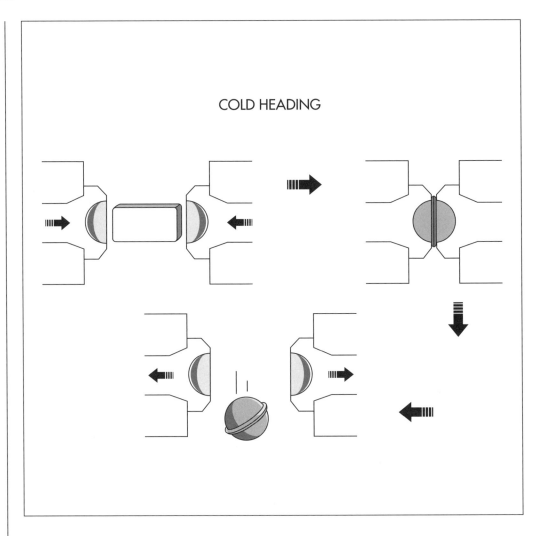

COLD HEADING

usually warps during this process. They can be machined back to their finished size after heat treating.

2 The rough cut races are put into a heat treating furnace at about 1,550 degrees Fahrenheit (843 degrees Celsius) for up to several hours (depending on the size of the parts), then dipped into an oil bath to cool them and make them very hard. This hardening also makes them brittle, so the next step is to temper them. This is done by heating them in a second oven to about 300 degrees Fahrenheit (148.8 degrees Celsius), and then letting them cool in air. This whole heat treatment process makes parts which are both hard and tough.

3 After the heat treatment process, the races are ready for finishing. However, the races are now too hard to cut with cutting tools, so the rest of the work must be done with **grinding wheel**s. These are a lot like what you would find in any shop for sharpen-

ing drill bits and tools, except that several different kinds and shapes are needed to finish the races. Almost every place on the race is finished by grinding, which leaves a very smooth, accurate surface. The surfaces where the bearing fits into the machine must be very round, and the sides must be flat. The surface that the balls roll on is ground first, and then lapped. This means that a very fine abrasive slurry is used to polish the races for several hours to get almost a mirror finish. At this point, the races are finished, and ready to be put together with the balls.

Balls

4 The balls are a little more difficult to make, even though their shape is very simple. Surprisingly, the balls start out as thick wire. This wire is fed from a roll into a machine that cuts off a short piece, and then smashes both ends in toward the middle. This process is called cold heading. Its name comes from the fact that the wire is not

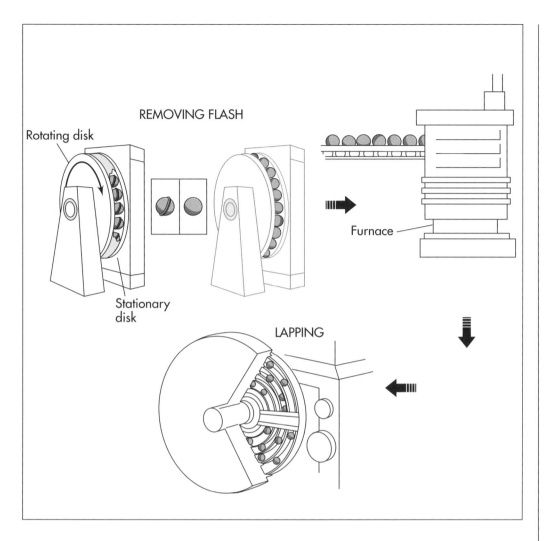

REMOVING FLASH

Rotating disk

Stationary disk

Furnace

LAPPING

The bulge around the middle of the rolling balls is removed in a machining proess. The balls are placed in rough grooves between two cast iron discs. One disc rotates while the other one is stationary; the friction removes the flash. From here, the balls are heat treated, ground, and lapped, which leaves the balls with a very smooth finish.

heated before being smashed, and that the original use for the process was to put the heads on nails (which is still how that is done). At any rate, the balls now look like the planet Saturn, with a ring around the middle called "flash."

5 The first machining process removes this flash. The ball bearings are put between the faces of two cast iron disks, where they ride in grooves. The inside of the grooves are rough, which tears the flash off of the balls. One wheel rotates, while the other one stays still. The stationary wheel has holes through it so that the balls can be fed into and taken out of the grooves. A special conveyor feeds balls into one hole, the balls rattle around the groove, and then come out the other hole. They are then fed back into the conveyor for many trips through the wheel grooves, until they have been cut down to being fairly round, almost to the proper size, and the flash is completely gone. Once again, the balls are left oversize so that they can be ground to

their finished size after heat treatment. The amount of steel left for finishing is not much; only about 8/1000 of an inch (.02 centimeter), which is about as thick as two sheets of paper.

6 The heat treatment process for the balls is similar to that used for the races, since the kind of steel is the same, and it is best to have all the parts wear at about the same rate. Like the races, the balls become hard and tough after heat treating and tempering. After heat treatment, the balls are put back into a machine that works the same way as the flash remover, except that the wheels are grinding wheels instead of cutting wheels. These wheels grind the balls down so that they are round and within a few ten thousandths of an inch of their finished size.

7 After this, the balls are moved to a lapping machine, which has cast iron wheels and uses the same abrasive lapping compound as is used on the races. Here, they will be lapped for 8–10 hours, depending on

The four parts of a finished ball bearing: inner race, outer race, cage, and ball.

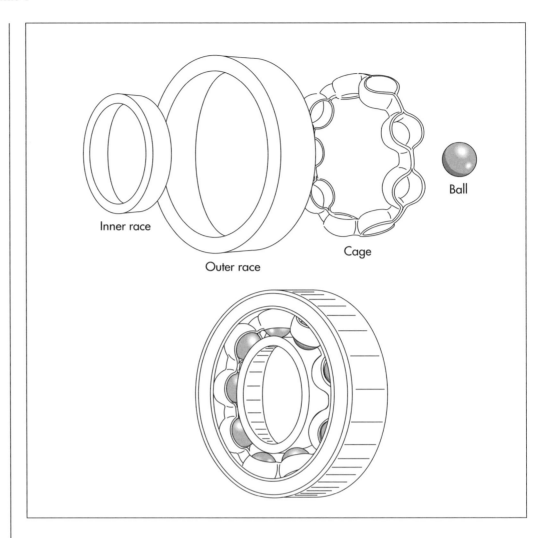

Inner race

Outer race

Cage

Ball

how precise a bearing they are being made for. Once again, the result is steel that is extremely smooth.

Cage

8 Steel cages are stamped out of fairly thin sheet metal, much like a cookie cutter, and then bent to their final shape in a die. A die is made up of two pieces of steel that fit together, with a hole the shape of the finished part carved inside. When the cage is put in between and the die is closed, the cage is bent to the shape of the hole inside. The die is then opened, and the finished part is taken out, ready to be assembled.

9 Plastic cages are usually made by a process called injection molding. In this process, a hollow metal mold is filled by squirting melted plastic into it, and letting it harden. The mold is opened up, and the finished cage is taken out, ready for assembly.

Assembly

10 Now that all of the parts are made, the bearing needs to be put together. First, the inner race is put inside the outer race, only off to one side as far as possible. This makes a space between them on the opposite side large enough to insert balls between them. The required number of balls is put in, then the races are moved so that they are both centered, and the balls distributed evenly around the bearing. At this point, the cage is installed to hold the balls apart from each other. Plastic cages are usually just snapped in, while steel cages usually have to be put in and riveted together. Now that the bearing is assembled, it is coated with a rust preventative and packaged for shipping.

Quality Control

Bearing making is a very precise business. Tests are run on samples of the steel coming to the factory to make sure that it has the right amounts of the alloy metals in it. Hardness and toughness tests are also done at several stages of the heat treating process. There are also many inspections along the way to make sure that sizes and shapes are correct. The surface of the balls and where they roll on the races must be exceptionally smooth. The balls can't be out of round more than 25 millionths of an inch, even for an inexpensive bearing. High-speed or precision bearings are allowed only five-millionths of an inch.

The Future

Ball bearings will be used for many years to come, because they are very simple and have become very inexpensive to manufacture. Some companies experimented with making balls in space on the space shuttle. In space, molten blobs of steel can be spit out into the air, and the zero gravity lets them float in the air. The blobs automatically make perfect spheres while they cool and harden. However, space travel is still expensive, so a lot of polishing can be done on the ground for the cost of one "space ball".

Other kinds of bearings are on the horizon, though. Bearings where the two objects never touch each other at all are efficient to run but difficult to make. One kind uses magnets that push away from each other and can be used to hold things apart. This is how the "mag-lev" (for magnetic levitation) trains are built. Another kind forces air into a space between two close-fitting surfaces, making them float apart from each other on a cushion of compressed air. However, both of these bearings are much more expensive to build and operate than the humble, trusted ball bearing.

Where To Learn More

Books

Deere & Company Staff, eds. *Bearings & Seals*, 5th ed. R. R. Bowker, 1992.

Eschmann, Paul. *Ball & Roller Bearings: Theory, Design & Application*, 2nd ed.

Harris, Tedric A. *Rolling Bearing Analysis*, 3rd ed. John Wiley & Sons, Inc., 1991.

Houghton, P. S. *Ball & Roller Bearings*. Elsevier Science Publishing Company, Inc., 1976.

Nisbet, T. S. *Rolling Bearings*. Oxford University Press, 1974.

Shigley, J. E. *Bearings & Lubrication: A Mechanical Designer's Workbook*. McGraw-Hill, Inc., 1990.

Periodicals

Gardner, Dana. "Ceramics Adds Life to Drives," *Design News*. March 23, 1992, p. 63.

Hannoosh, J. G. "Ceramic Bearings Enter the Mainstream," *Design News*. November 21, 1988, p. 224.

McCarty, Lyle H. "New Alloy Produces Quieter Ball Bearings," *Design News*. May 20, 1991, p. 99.

—*Steve Mathias*

Bar Code Scanner

The supermarket scanners commonplace today are known as point-of-sale scanners, since the scanning is done when merchandise is purchased. Supermarket scanners represent the most advanced bar code scanners because of the particular difficulties associated with reading bar codes on oddly shaped items or items that may be dirty, wet, or fragile.

Background

Many different types of bar code scanning machines exist, but they all work on the same fundamental principles. They all use the intensity of light reflected from a series of black and white stripes to tell a computer what code it is seeing. White stripes reflect light very well, while black stripes reflect hardly any light at all. The bar code scanner shines light sequentially across a bar code, simultaneously detecting and recording the pattern of reflected and non-reflected light. The scanner then translates this pattern into an electrical signal that the computer can understand. All scanners must include computer software to interpret the bar code once it's been entered. This simple principle has transformed the way we are able to manipulate data and the way in which many businesses handle recordkeeping.

Bar code scanning emerged in the early 1970s as a way to improve the speed and accuracy of data entry into computers. Businesses were just beginning to exploit computer tracking of stock and billing. The challenge was to find a quick, efficient, and relatively fool-proof method of record entry for companies (for example warehouses or mail order companies) that maintain a small stock of high volume items. The use of bar codes enabled clerks to keep track of every item they sold, shipped or packed without a tedious and error-prone keyboard data entry process. Bar coding caught on quickly in clothing stores, manufacturing plants (such as car makers), airline baggage checks, libraries, and, of course, supermarkets. The supermarket scanners which are commonplace today are known as point-of-sale scanners, since the scanning is done when merchandise is purchased; point-of-sale scanning is perhaps the most challenging bar code scanning application in use today. Supermarket scanners represent the most advanced design of the various types of bar code scanners, because of the particular difficulties associated with reading bar codes on oddly shaped items or items that may be dirty, wet, or fragile.

The first scanners required human action to do the scanning and used very simple light sources. The most common was the wand, which is still popular because it is inexpensive and reliable. Wand scanners require placing the end of the scanner against the code, because the light source they use is only narrow (focused) enough to distinguish between bars and stripes right at the wand tip. If the labeled products are oddly shaped or dirty, this method is impractical if not impossible.

To make a scanner that works without touching the code requires a light source that will remain in a narrow, bright beam over longer distances—the best source is a laser. Using a laser beam, the code can be held several inches or more from the scanner, and the actual scanning action can then take place inside the scanner. Rotating, motor-driven mirror assemblies, developed in the mid-1970s, allowed laser light to be swept over a surface so the user didn't need to move the scanner or the code; this technology improved scanner reliability and code reading speed.

Later, holograms were chosen to replace mirrors, since they can act just like a mirror but are lightweight and can be motorized more easily. A hologram is a photographic image that behaves like a three-dimensional object when struck by light of the correct wavelength. A hologram is created by shining a laser beam split into two parts onto a glass or plastic plate coated with a photographic emulsion. Whereas the previous generation of scanners worked by rotating a mirror assembly, holographic scanners operate by spinning a disk with one or more holograms recorded on it.

Researchers at IBM and NEC simultaneously developed holographic point-of-sale scanners in 1980. Holographic scanning was chosen not only because the hologram disks could be spun more easily than mirror assemblies, but also because a single disk could reflect light in many different directions, by incorporating different hologram areas on the same disk. This helped to solve the problem of bar code positioning; that is, codes no longer needed to directly face the scan window. Modern bar code scanners will scan in many different directions and angles hundreds of times each second. If you look at the surface of a scanner in the checkout lane, you will see lots of criss-crossed lines of light; this pattern was chosen as the most reliable and least demanding on particular package orientation.

Raw Materials

A holographic bar code scanner consists of an assembly of preformed parts. The laser—a small glass tube filled with gas and a small power supply to generate a laser beam—is usually a helium neon (HeNe) laser. In other words, the gas tube is filled with helium and neon gases, which produce a red light. Red light is easiest to detect, and HeNe's are less expensive than other kinds of lasers. They are much smaller versions of the types of lasers used in light shows or discotheques.

Lenses and mirrors in the optical assembly are made of highly polished glass or plastic, which is sometimes coated to make it more or less reflective at the red wavelength of light being used. The light detection system is a photodiode—a semiconductor part that conducts electrical current when light shines on it, and no current when no light is present; silicon or germanium photodiodes are the two types of photodiodes most commonly used.

The housing consists of a sturdy case, usually made of **stainless steel**, and an optical window that can be glass or a very resilient plastic. The window material must have good optical and mechanical properties; that is, it must remain transparent but must also seal the scanner from the air, so no dirt or dust gets inside and blocks the light or the light detector. Defects in the window can cause light to be transmitted at an unpredictable angle or not at all; both scenarios affect the accuracy of the scanner.

The holographic disks are made of a substance called *dichromated gelatin* (DCG) sealed between two plastic disks. DCG is a light-sensitive chemical used to record laser images, much like photographic film records light. It was developed by Dow Chemical and Polaroid for their own holographic work, and it is sold in liquid form so that it can be coated onto a variety of surfaces. DCG holograms are common in holographic jewelry (pendents, watch faces, etc.) and in the holographic spinner disks sold in toy stores. DCG will lose a recorded image if it is left in the open air, which is why it must be sealed between two layers of plastic.

The spinning motor drive that turns the disk is a small electric cylinder with a central spinning shaft, similar to the kind available in an erector set. The shaft is attached to the center of the hologram disk, so that when the motor is turned on, the disk spins.

Design

Bar code scanners require a team of designers to produce the completed assembly. First, a laser recording engineer designs the hologram disk. There are a number of important features to be considered in this design. For instance, the disk must reflect the majority of light that hits it (high efficiency), it must not distort the light so that the reflected beam remains narrow, and it must reflect light in the chosen scan pattern while it is spinning. Also, the scan pattern must maximize the number of readable orientations at which a bar code can be passed over the scan window and still be read.

The finished disk consists of many different holograms recorded in wedges on the same disk. Each wedge reflects light at a different angle. As the disk spins, the light is scanned in a line. The orientation of the lines changes from wedge to wedge. The hologram designer also specifies the exact power of laser to be used, a choice based on longevity, efficiency and safety to the user.

After the hologram disk is designed, an optical engineer designs the placement of the laser and hologram disk, specifies any lenses or mirrors required to steer the light in the right direction, and designs the detection system so that light reflected from a bar code can be read efficiently and reliably. The designer must optimize the scanner's *optical throw*, defined as the furthest distance an object can be held away from the scanner window and still be read correctly. It is the job of the optical designer to consider how best to fit the components into the smallest space, with the smallest weight and expense, while still placing the window at a convenient angle for normal use. For example, a supermarket scanner must have the window facing up on the checkout stand, even though it may be more convenient to put the spinning disk sideways inside the box. Additional mirrors can allow both of these constraints to be met.

An electrical engineer determines the best method of interpreting the electrical signals coming from the photodetector. Electrically, the signals must be received and interpreted as a sequence of ON signals, (light reflected from a white bar), and OFF signals, (no light reflected from a black bar). The resulting pattern is then converted by a computer into the product information the pattern represents. A computer programmer may be employed to design the computer software that will translate the code into product information, but the job of correctly interpreting the ON/OFF pattern is left to the electrical engineer.

The Manufacturing Process

After all of the components have been designed, they are ready to be made and assembled. The hologram disk is generally manufactured in-house, while the other components—lenses, mirrors, and laser—are usually purchased from other manufacturers. The various parts are then assembled and tested.

Hologram disk

1 The first step in the manufacturing process is to mass produce the hologram disk. This disk is replicated from a master hologram. All the disks, master and reproductions, are sandwiches made of plastic "bread" with DCG filling. Master disks are made in sections, one wedge for each different reflection angle required in the final disk. A typical point-of-sale scanner will have between 7 and 16 wedges on a single disk. Holographic recording is done with two laser beams that intersect at the surface of the DCG sandwich, creating the holographic pattern. Adjusting the angle at which the two beams meet will change the reflective properties of each hologram. Each wedge created in this way will act like a mirror that is turned in a different direction.

2 Once all the required wedges have been recorded, they are assembled and glued down on a single transparent plate, which can then be replicated. The glue used has optical properties that will not distort the hologram image, such as glycerin-based adhesives will. There are many ways to replicate a hologram, but the most common for DCG holograms is optical replication. The master disk is placed close to, but not touching, a blank DCG sandwich disk, and a single laser beam is used to illuminate the master from behind. This transfers the pattern onto the blank.

Lenses, mirrors, laser

3 Other components—lenses, mirrors, laser, etc.—are usually purchased from an outside manufacturer. Lens, mirror and scan window properties are specified during the design process. The manufacturer tests all of these components as they arrive to confirm that they meet specification. Motors and lasers are tested for proper operation, and some are lifetime tested to make sure that the bar code scanner will not fail within a reasonable period of time.

Housing

4 Housing can be purchased from a metal job shop, or it can be fabricated by the manufacturer. The size and exact shape of the box is specified in design, and manufacturing converts those specifications into realizable sketches. The parts are machined, assembled and tested for strength and durability.

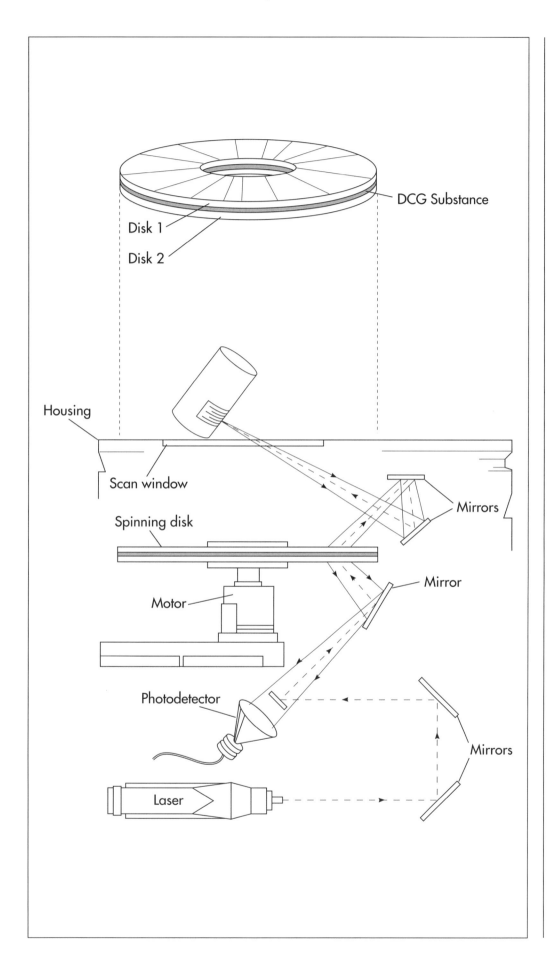

DCG Substance

Disk 1

Disk 2

Housing

Scan window

Spinning disk

Motor

Mirrors

Mirror

Photodetector

Mirrors

Laser

In a bar code scanner, a laser beam is directed toward an item with a black and white bar code symbol. The light is reflected back and recorded on a spinning holographic disk. A photodetector then converts this light into an electrical signal that can be read by a computer.

The spinning disk consists of a chemical substance, DCG, sandwiched between two plastic disks. A typical holographic disk contains between 7 and 12 wedges, each of which reflects light at a different angle. To make these disks, a disk master—comprising the various wedges glued onto a single transparent plate—is first prepared. Next, a single laser beam illuminates the master from behind, transfering the pattern onto a blank DCG disk placed next to (but not touching) the master.

Final assembly

5 Finally, the hologram disk is assembled with the spinning motor drive and tested. Scanning pattern, direction, and speed are all examined. The spinning disk is then assembled with the optical system (the laser and mirrors). Placement of the laser often depends on space considerations: the laser can be aimed directly at the spinning disk, or at a mirror that guides the beam to the disk, if this makes the package smaller.

6 The disk and optical system are tested as a unit. When the assembly passes inspection, it is mounted permanently inside the housing and sealed with the scanning window.

Quality Control

There are several stages to quality control in bar code scanner manufacturing. To begin with, there are several test criteria that are defined within the bar code industry and that must be specified by all manufacturers. These include:

• First Pass Read Rate (FPRR)—the percentage of time that a code can be read the first time it passes the scan window

• Rejection Rate—the number of scans per million which simply won't be read

• Read Velocity—the range of speeds with which a code may be passed over the surface of a scanner

These properties will relate to the optical, electrical and mechanical properties of the scanner. Mechanically, scanners are run for several days (and some select units will be pulled from production for longer lifetime tests—up to several years) to insure that the motor will continue to turn the disk consistently at the expected speed. Since the ability to differentiate between wide and narrow bars in a code is related to the speed at which the disk turns, it is critical that the motorized disk continue to operate in a predictable way. Spinning speed will also relate to Read Velocity, and may need to be adjusted to match the average speed that a clerk will use to drag items through a supermarket checkout. Mechanical failures may indicate a mismounted or imbalanced disk or other mechanical problems that need to be corrected.

Optically, scanners are tested for code reading consistency. For a good bar code scanner, this number should be greater than 85 percent. Commonly, 75 percent to 85 percent is achieved. If the scanner cannot meet this criteria, it is sent back for an inspection of the optical system—cleanliness of components and proper functioning of the laser and detection system.

Electrically, scanners are tested for the Rejection Rate. Holographic scanners scan the light over a bar code 100-200 times per second. This allows the computer to compare many different readings of the code for accuracy. But if there is some problem with the electronics, the computer will begin to "reject" scans, or simply refuse to read them. Part of this test uses bar codes that are imperfect in some way—codes containing ink spots, bars of non-uniform width, etc. The manufacturer has to produce a scanner that can tolerate some glitches in the code printing process. This is another reason to use a multiple scan and cross-check technique.

The Future

The future of bar code scanning technology will take a number of diverging pathways. More general use of bar code scanning requires cheaper and smaller light sources that will improve simple instruments like the wand scanner. Semiconductor lasers, for instance, may make the wand a more attractive instrument to users. In addition, some children's learning tools and toys are starting to appear with interactive bar codes rather than push buttons. In this way, new modules can be added to the same bar code scanning toy. There are some home-shopping systems that are beginning to exploit this technology, allowing people to do grocery or clothes shopping at home by scanning selections from a catalog using their telephone and a modem.

Laser scanners, on the other hand, are beginning to find more and more complex applications as the technology becomes more reliable and easier to use. More industries are using bar coding to track complicated lots of custom-manufactured items, record steps in a manufacturing process, and monitor activities in their plants. Other optical assemblies may be developed that will allow this technology to become even more flexible in size and utility.

Where To Learn More

Books

Adams, Russ. *Reading Between the Lines: An Introduction to Bar Code Technology*, 4th ed. Helmers Publishing, Inc., 1989.

Brophy, Peter. *Computers Can Read.* Gower Publishing Co, 1986.

Burke, Harry E. *Handbook of Bar Coding Systems.* Van Nostrand Reinhold Co., 1984.

Marshall, Gerald F., *Laser Beam Scanning*, Marcel Dekker, 1985.

Sobczak, Thomas. *Applying Industrial Bar Coding.* Society of Manufacturing Engineers, 1985.

Periodicals

Kramer, Charles. "Holographic Laser Scanners for Non-Impact Printing," *Laser Focus.* June, 1981, p. 70.

"Bar Code Scanner Replaces Data Entry Without a Decoder," *Purchasing.* September 27, 1990, p. 101.

Schwartz, Evan I. "They Just May Have Built a Better Bar Code," *Business Week.* September 28, 1992, p. 122K.

Stamper, Bonney. "What Happens When a Scanner Reads a Bar Code?," *Industrial Engineering.* October, 1992, p. 34.

—Leslie G. Melcer

Baseball

The baseball has undergone only one significant change since 1930: a shortage in the supply of horses in 1974 prompted a switch from horsehide to cowhide covers.

Background

The baseball traces its origin to the game of the same name. Modern baseball evolved from the English game of "rounders" in the first half of the 19th century. Alexander Cartwright of New York formulated the basic rules of baseball in 1845, calling for the replacement of the soft ball used in rounders with a smaller hard ball.

Despite its uncomplicated appearance, the baseball is in fact a precision-made object, and one that has often been the subject of heated controversy throughout its history. Although baseballs have changed very little in this century, either in terms of their physical dimensions or raw materials, some observers have suggested that the balls have secretly been "juiced up" to increase the output of crowd-pleasing homeruns during periods of lagging attendance at major league baseball games. The manufacturers of baseballs and Major League Baseball have steadfastly denied such allegations, however, and no proof of any covert alterations in the ball's design or composition has ever been produced.

An official Major League baseball consists of a round cushioned cork center called a "pill," wrapped tightly in windings of **wool** and polyester/cotton yarn, and covered by stitched cowhide. Approximately 600,000 baseballs are used by all Major League teams combined during the course of a season. The average baseball remains in play for only five to seven pitches in a Major League game. Each ball must weigh between 5 and 5.25 ounces (141.75-148.83 grams) and measure between 9 and 9.25 inches (22.86-23.49 centimeters) in circumference to conform to Major League standards.

Such uniformity was nonexistent in the early years of baseball's history, when balls were either homemade or produced on a custom-order basis as a sideline by cobblers, tanners and other small business owners. In 1872, the modern standard for the baseball's weight and size was established. The production of balls became more consistent during the remainder of the decade, thanks largely to the demands made on manufacturers by the newly formed National League, the first professional baseball league.

At the turn of the century, the baseball had a round rubber core. This gave way in 1910 to the livelier cork-centered ball, which was itself replaced two decades later by the even more resilient cushioned cork model. The baseball has undergone only one significant change since that time, when a shortage in the supply of horses in 1974 prompted a switch from horsehide to cowhide covers.

Raw Materials

A baseball has three basic parts: the round cushioned cork pill at its core, the wool and poly/cotton windings in its midsection, and the cowhide covering that makes up its exterior.

The pill consists of a sphere, measuring $13/16$ of an inch (2.06 centimeters) in diameter, made of a cork and rubber composition material. This sphere is encased in two layers of rubber, a black inner layer and a red outer layer. The inner layer is made up of two hemispheric shells of black rubber that are joined by red rubber washers. The entire pill measures 4-$1/8$ inches (10.47 centimeters) in circumference.

There are four distinct layers of wool and poly/cotton windings that surround the cushioned cork pill in concentric circles of varying thickness. The first winding is made of four-ply gray woolen yarn, the second of three-ply white woolen yarn, the third of three-ply gray woolen yarn, and the fourth of white poly/cotton finishing yarn. The first layer of wool is by far the thickest. When wrapped tightly around the pill, it brings the circumference of the unfinished ball to 7-¾ inches (19.68 centimeters). The circumference increases to 8-³⁄₁₆ inches (20.77 centimeters) after the second winding has been applied, 8-¾ inches (22.22 centimeters) after the third, and 8-⅞ (22.52 centimeters) after the fourth.

Wool was selected as the primary material for the baseball's windings because its natural resiliency and "memory" allow it to compress when pressure is applied, then rapidly return to its original shape. This property makes it possible for the baseball to retain its perfect roundness despite being hit repeatedly during a game. A poly/cotton blend was selected for the outer winding to provide added strength and reduce the risk of tears when the ball's cowhide cover is applied.

The baseball's outer cover is made of Number One Grade, alum-tanned full-grained cowhide, primarily from Midwest Holstein cattle. Midwest Holsteins are preferred because their hides have a better grain and are cleaner and smoother than those of cattle in other areas of the United States. The cover of an official baseball must be white, and it must be stitched together with 88 inches (223.52 centimeters) of waxed red thread. Cowhides are tested for 17 potential deficiencies in thickness, grain strength, tensile strength and other areas before they are approved for use on official Major League baseballs.

The Manufacturing Process

The production of a baseball can be viewed as a process of placing successive layers of material (rubber, fabric and cowhide) around a rubbery sphere not much bigger than a cherry. These materials are placed around the small sphere in three distinct ways: the rubber is molded, the fabric is wound, and the cowhide is sewn. The placement of materi-

BASE BALLS.

	Price.	
League Ball		$1.00
Professional Dead	"	.75
Amateur Dead	"	.50
Half Dollar Dead	"	.25
Boys' League	"	.25
Rocket	"	.15
Bounding Rock	"	.10
Daisy	"	.05

An advertisement for baseballs from the trade catalog of Horace, Partridge & Co., from about 1891.

Baseball," wrote Mark Twain (Samuel L. Clemens), "is the very symbol, the outward and visible expression of the drive and push and rush and struggle of the raging, tearing, booming nineteenth century." Baseball initially evolved into a favorite American sport because it was faster paced and more physical than its English predecessors, cricket, town-ball, and rounders. Though cricket was played wherever English immigrants congregated in the United States, Americans seemed to prefer the more aggressive character of baseball. Initially played by gentlemen in fashionable clothing, the game and its equipment—and its popularity—began to change once rules were written down in the 1840s. In particular, the game gained tremendous popularity after the Civil War. The ball itself was changed at least twice in that century: the first ball was too lively (scores sometimes exceeded 100 runs); the second was too dead (a scoreless 24-inning game convinced many that hitters were disadvantaged).

A. G. Spalding made headline news in 1888-89 when he led a widely popular tour of American baseball players that played demonstration games in countries around the world. By the turn of the century, Spalding was marketing four baseballs in boy's size and eight in regulation size, each costing from four cents to one dollar.

William S. Pretzer

als around the sphere is done under carefully controlled conditions to ensure that consistent size, shape and quality are maintained.

Molding rubber

1 Two hemispheric shells of black rubber, each approximately ⁵⁄₃₂ of an inch (.39 centimeter) thick, are molded to a sphere of rubberized cork measuring ¹³⁄₁₆ of an inch (2.06 centimeters) in diameter. The two small openings that separate these shells are sealed with red rubber gaskets.

The first step in manufacturing a baseball involves molding two shells of black rubber to a rubberized cork. After a thin layer of red rubber is molded to the ball and a layer of cement is applied, wool yarn is wound around the ball. The yarn is wound in three layers: four-ply gray yarn, followed by three-ply white yarn, and finally three-ply gray yarn.

A final layer of poly/cotton finishing yarn is next wrapped around the ball. The final layer is the cowhide cover, consisting of two figure-eight pieces that are stapled to the ball and then stitched together.

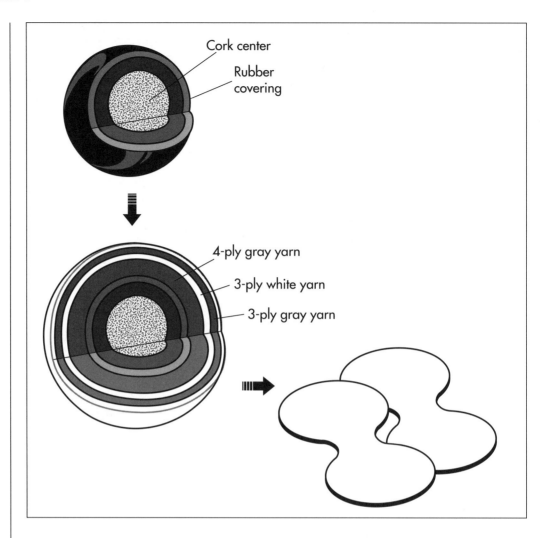

Cork center

Rubber covering

4-ply gray yarn

3-ply white yarn

3-ply gray yarn

2 Next, a layer of red rubber roughly ³⁄₃₂ of an inch (.24 centimeter) thick is molded to the black rubber encasement. The entire "pill" is then molded into a perfect circle weighing approximately ⅞ of an ounce (24.80 grams) with a circumference of roughly 4-⅛ inches (10.48 centimeters). Once the pill has been molded, a thin layer of cement is applied to its surface. This layer keeps the wool yarn in place on the pill at the start of the first winding operation.

Winding fabric

3 Wool yarn, stored under controlled fabric temperature and humidity conditions, is wound around the pill. This is done by computerized winding machines that maintain a constant level of very high tension to eliminate "soft spots," and create a uniform surface. After each step in the winding process, the ball is weighed and measured by computer to assure that official size requirements have been met. The wool yarn is wound so tightly that it has the appearance of thread when a baseball is dissected. Three layers of wool are wound around the baseball: the first, 121 yards (110.6 meters) of four-ply gray yarn; the second, 45 yards (41.13 meters) of three-ply white; and the third, 53 yards (48.44 meters) of three-ply gray.

4 A layer of 150 yards (137.1 meters) of fine poly/cotton finishing yarn is wrapped around the ball to protect the wool yarn and hold it in place. The wound ball is then trimmed of any excess fabric and prepared for the application of the external cowhide covering by being dipped in an adhesive solution.

Sewing hide

5 The cowhide covering is cut into two figure-8 patterns. Each pattern covers half the wound ball. Before they are stitched to the wound ball, the cowhide coverings are dampened to increase their pliability. The insides of the coverings also receive a coating of the same adhesive that was applied to the wound ball.

6 The two figure-8 coverings are stapled to the wound ball, then they are hand-sewn together using 88 inches (223.52 centimeters) of waxed red thread. There are 108 stitches in the sewing process, with the first and last completely hidden. An average of 13 to 14 minutes is required to hand-sew a baseball.

7 After the covers have been stitched together, the staples are removed and the ball is inspected. The ball is then placed in a rolling machine for 15 seconds to level any raised stitches. The baseballs are then measured, weighed and graded for appearance. Acceptable baseballs are stamped with the manufacturer's trademark and league designation.

Quality Control

A statistically representative sample of each shipment of baseballs is tested to measure *Co-Efficient Of Restitution* (COR), using Major League Baseball's officially sanctioned testing procedures. Essentially, the COR is an indication of the resiliency of a baseball.

The COR test involves shooting a baseball from an air cannon at a velocity of 85-feet-a-second (25.90-meters-a-second) at a wooden wall from a distance of eight feet (2.43 meters), and measuring the speed with which the ball rebounds off the wall. Major League COR specifications stipulate that a baseball must rebound at 54.6 percent of the initial velocity, plus or minus 3.2 percent.

A baseball must also retain its round shape after being hit 200 times by a 65-pound (29.51 kilograms) force. As proof of its strength, a baseball must distort less than 0.08 of an inch (.20 centimeter) after being compressed between two anvils.

The Future

The size of baseballs and the raw materials used to make them are likely to remain unchanged in the foreseeable future. Also,

few, if any, changes are expected in the process by which baseballs are manufactured.

Attempts have been made to automate the process of sewing cowhide covers on baseballs, but none has been successful. Automated machines that have been experimented with have exhibited two serious problems: first, they have been unable to start or stop the stitching process without manual assistance; and second, they have been unable to vary the tension of their stitches, something that is essential if the two figure-8 coverings are to fit securely on the wound ball without tearing.

It is also probable that the controversy about juiced-up balls will continue as long as the game of baseball is played and fans seek an explanation for fluctuations in the homerun output of favorite teams and players.

Where To Learn More

Books

Cleary, David Powers. *Great American Brands.* Fairchild Applications, 1981.

Danzig, Allison and Joe Reichler. *The History of Baseball.* Prentice Hall, 1959.

A finished baseball, with 88 inches of waxed red thread holding the two cowhide covering pieces together, weighs between 5 and 5.25 ounces and measures between 9 and 9.25 inches in circumference.

James, Bill. *The Bill James Historical Baseball Abstract*. Villard Books, 1986.

Seymour, Harold. *Baseball: The People's Game*. Oxford University Press, 1990.

Thorn, John and Bob Carroll, eds. *The Whole Baseball Catalog*. Fireside Books, 1990.

Periodicals

"Batter Up for a Baseball Factory Tour," *Southern Living*. November, 1989, p. 34.

—*Suzy Fucini*

Baseball Glove

Background

Wearing a glove to protect one's catching hand was not considered a manly thing to do in the years following the Civil War, when the game of baseball spread through the country with the speed of a cavalry charge. It's uncertain who was the first to wear a baseball glove; nominees include Charles G. Waite (or Waitt), who played first base for a professional Boston team in 1875, and Doug Allison, a catcher for the Cincinnati Red Stockings in 1869. Waite was undoubtedly concerned about his reputation; the gloves were flesh colored to make them less obvious.

By 1880, a padded catcher's mitt had appeared, and by the turn of the twentieth century, most players were wearing gloves of one sort or another. By today's standards of workmanship, and by current expectations of what a glove can do for a fielder, the gloves of that time were primitive.

Although the early gloves were not impressive by today's standards, they still required a high level of craftsmanship to produce. Gloves were and are a labor-intensive product calling for a large amount of individual attention. Most of them were heavily padded affairs that covered and protected the catching hand by virtue of the glove's thickness, but did little else. It wasn't until the late 1930s that the design of the glove as an aid to both catching and playing became a matter of importance. Even baseball gloves of twenty years ago seem antique compared to present-day relatives in their ability to protect the hand and help a player catch a ball.

A modern player can now, with his modern glove, make one handed catches; behind the plate, a catcher uses his flexible, fitted mitt with the surgical sureness of a doctor, plucking a ball from the air as if he were using a pair of tweezers to remove a splinter. The two-handed catch, a fielding skill required up to only a few years ago and necessary when gloves were just large pads, now is considered a useful but hardly necessary talent.

Differences among today's gloves vary from the thickness of the heel to the design of the web to the deepness of the palm. Outfielders tend to prefer large gloves with deep palms, to make catching fly balls easier. Infielders generally like smaller gloves into which they can reach easily to grip and throw the ball to another player. Most outfielders will break a glove in vertically; infielders tend to prefer gloves broken in horizontally.

Improvements in the design of the glove and the efficiency and protection it offers a ball player are ongoing. It looks like quite a simple thing, yet a baseball glove is the fruit of more than one hundred years of history and more than thirty patents. A baseball glove is reflective of a very special creative design process that is still very much alive.

Raw Materials

Except for small plastic reinforcements at the base of the small finger and the thumb, and some nylon thread, a glove is made totally of leather, usually from cattle. The Texas-based Nocona Glove Company, however, uses a large quantity of kangaroo hide from Australia in addition to leather from cattle. Kangaroo hide is somewhat softer than leather, and the glove can be used after a shorter breaking-in period than usual.

Outfielders tend to prefer large gloves with deep palms, to make catching fly balls easier. Infielders generally like smaller gloves into which they can reach easily to grip and throw the ball to another player.

55

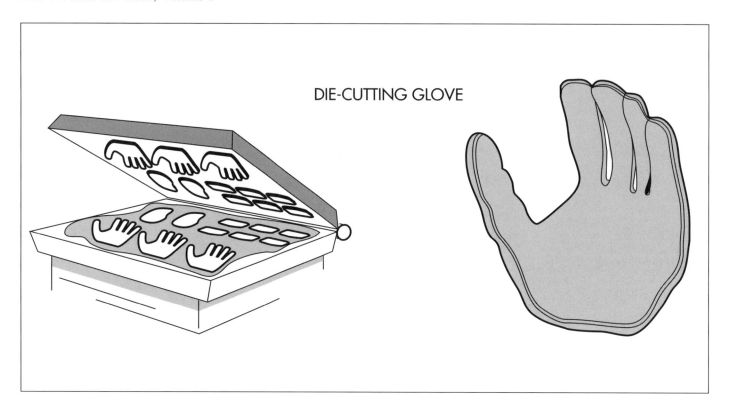

DIE-CUTTING GLOVE

The first step in baseball glove manufacture involves die-cutting the cowhide into four pieces: shell, lining, pad, and web. In die-cutting, the pieces are cut out of the hide with a machine that simulates a cookie cutter.

Generally, cowhides are the predominant material in use today, as in the past. Beef cattle hides (two to a steer) are processed by a tannery, and the finest hides, those without brands, nicks, or other blemishes are sent to the glove factories. Tanning is a chemical treatment of the hides to give them required characteristics, such as flexibility and durability. If leather were not tanned, it would dry and flake in extremely short order. Some glove companies compete for quality hides with makers of other fine leather products. The Rawlings Company depends on one tannery and buys all of the tannery's product.

Each cowhide provides the leather for three or four gloves. Rawlings, however, cuts and tans its own leather for lacing, which has different requirements for durability and flexibility than the rest of the glove. Various synthetic materials have been tested for baseball gloves, but so far none have demonstrated the resilience, the stretchability, and the feel that leather has, and no replacement for leather is on the immediate horizon.

The Manufacturing Process

By the time cowhides arrive at the factory, they have already been cured (salting or drying to kill bacteria) and tanned (chemically

treated to prevent putrefaction), all of which prepares them to be turned into gloves. Once at the factory, the cowhides are graded for such things as color and tested in a laboratory for strength.

The manufacturing process for baseball gloves is fairly simple: the various parts of the glove are cut and then sewn together with a long string of rawhide leather. Below is a more detailed explanation:

Die-cutting the glove parts

1 The parts of the hide that will be used for gloves are die-cut (i.e. cut automatically with a machine that simulates a cookie cutter) into four parts—the shell, lining, pad, and web.

2 Early in the process, sometimes even before the leather is cut, the lettering—usually foil tape—identifying the manufacturer is burned into the leather with a brass stamping die.

Shell and lining

3 The shell of the glove is sewn together while inside-out. It is then turned right-side-out, and its lining is inserted. Before being reversed, the shell is mulled (wetted or

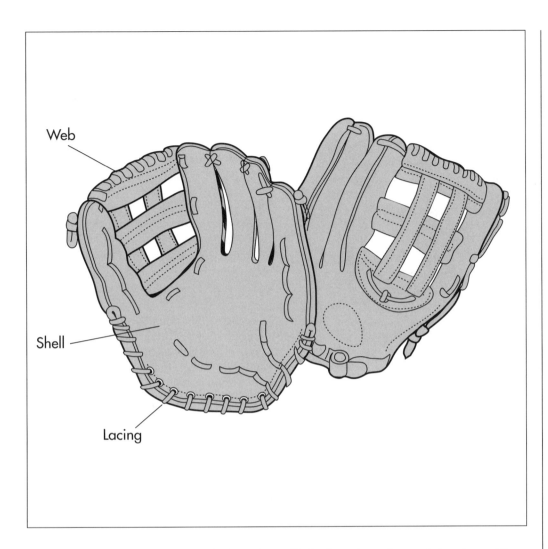

Web

Shell

Lacing

The lacing around the edges of a glove is usually one piece of rawhide that might be as much as 80 to 90 inches in length. The lacing begins at the thumb or little finger and holds the entire glove together. Like nearly every other step in baseball glove manufacture, the lacing must be done manually.

steamed for flexibility) so that it doesn't crack or rip when it is turned.

4 The turned shell is put on a device known as a hot hand, which is a hand-shaped metallic form; its heat helps the shell form to its correct size. At this point, the hot hand also assures that all the openings for the fingers (finger stalls) are open correctly.

Inserting the pad and plastic reinforcements

5 A pad is inserted into the heel of a glove. Better gloves have two-part pads that make it easier for the glove to flex in the correct direction when squeezed. The padding in a glove is made of two layers of leather, hand stitched together. Catchers' mitts, which need a thicker palm than other gloves, are made with five layers of leather padding.

6 At this same point, plastic reinforcements are inserted at the thumb and toe

(little finger) sections of the glove. These devices provide added support for the glove and protect the player's fingers from being bent backwards accidentally.

Web

7 Before all the parts of the glove are laced together, the web is fabricated out of several pieces of leather. The web can consist of anywhere from two to six pieces of leather, depending on the type of web desired.

Lacing and stitching

8 The lacing around the edges of a glove is usually one piece of rawhide that might be as much as 80-90 inches (203-228 centimeters) long. The lacing begins at the thumb or little finger and holds the entire glove together. The final lacing operation is at the web section. Some non-leather stitching is needed for the individual parts—the

web, for instance, is usually stitched together with nylon thread.

9 The strap across the back of the hand of a glove used to be lined with shearling (sheepskin); a synthetic material is now used.

10 Catchers' mitts and first base gloves are hand assembled and sewn from four parts—palm, pad, back, and web. The palm and back are sewn together first, and then joined together with the other pieces with rawhide lacing.

11 The final step is called a lay off operation; the glove is again placed on a hot hand to adjust any shaping problems and to make sure that the openings for the fingers (finger stalls) have remained open throughout the manufacturing process.

Quality Control

Quality control starts when the hides arrive at the factory, where they are graded for such things as color and tested in a laboratory for strength. Even after a hide is accepted by a manufacturer, only a part of it will be usable; Rawlings uses about 30 percent of a hide, from which it is able to make three or four gloves.

Because making a glove requires so much personal attention at each step, there is little need for a manufacturer to maintain a full-blown, quality control department. Each craftsman involved in the process functions as his or her own quality control person, and if a defect in a glove becomes apparent, the person who is working on the glove is expected to see that the glove is removed from production.

As happens in many areas where a product has undergone almost continuous design changes for years and years, there are those who believe that the older methods and products are better than the new ones. The Gloveman (Fremont, California), operated by Lee Chilton, specializes in restoring old gloves for current use (although it has its own line of catcher's mitts), and Chilton is quite serious in his assertion that one of the best ways to get a good glove is to buy an old one at a flea market, tag sale or second hand store, and let his company restore it.

Professional Gloves

Although professional gloves might be examined with a more critical eye before use, and might be the choicest specimens, they are the same gloves, sans autographs, that anyone can buy in a store. In exchange for autograph endorsements, professionals receive free gloves (and a fee) from manufacturers.

It is unusual for a professional ball player to experiment with different models of gloves, or to request an unusual design. According to Bob Clevenhagen, Master Glove Designer at Rawlings, ball players tend to be "conservatives who stick with what works." By the time a ballplayer is a professional, he has found the right glove for himself, and keeps using it. Most professionals are using the same or similar model glove that they used in college, high school, or even little league.

The Future

As is true of many older products where refinement is the primary goal of the manufacturers, baseball glove design is not changing as rapidly as it did in the past. Previous developments included such things as holding the fingers of the glove together with lacing, changes in the design of the pocket and the heel of the glove, and redesigning the catcher's glove so that a catcher can handle a ball with one hand, like other fielders. In the 1950s, Rawlings even devised a six-fingered glove at the request of Stan Musial, who wanted a single glove that could be used both at first base and at other infield positions.

Large glove manufacturers have seen different designs go in and out of style, and some of their most famous models have been retired from production (such as the Rawlings Playmaker, a popular glove of the 1950s).

Current changes have focused on how the glove is used in relation to other players. Catchers' mitts, for example, now have a bright, fluorescent edging to make a better target for a pitcher. In August, 1992, The Neumann Tackified Glove Company (Hoboken, New Jersey) announced that it would begin making black gloves with a white palm so that the glove will be a better target for one player throwing a ball to another.

Where To Learn More

Books

Thorn, John and Bob Carroll, eds. *The Whole Baseball Catalogue*. Fireside, 1990.

Periodicals

Feldman, Jay. "Working Hand In Glove," *Sports Illustrated*. April 6, 1987, pp. 146-150.

Javor, Ted. "His Innovation Really Caught On," *Sporting News*. June 25, 1990, p. 6.

Lindburgh, Richard. "It's a Brand New Ballgame: Sports Equipment for the 1990s," *USA Today*. May 2, 1990, p. 90-92.

Lloyd, Barbara. "A Baseball Glove Made To Help With Throwing," *New York Times*. August 22, 1992, p. 46a.

Wulf, Steve and Jim Kaplan. "Glove Story," *Sports Illustrated*. May 7, 1990, pp. 66-82.

—*Lawrence H. Berlow*

Battery

Volta's invention consisted of alternating discs of silver and zinc separated by leather or pasteboard that had been soaked in salt water, lye, or some alkaline solution. Strips of metal at each end of the pile were connected to small cups filled with mercury. When Volta touched both cups of mercury, he received an electric shock.

Background

Benjamin Franklin's famous experiment to attract electricity by flying a kite in a lightning storm was only one of many late eighteenth- and early nineteenth-century experiments conducted to learn about electricity. The first battery was constructed in 1800 by Italian Alessandro Volta. The so-called *voltaic pile* consisted of alternating discs of silver and zinc separated by leather or pasteboard that had been soaked in salt water, lye, or some alkaline solution. Strips of metal at each end of the pile were connected to small cups filled with mercury. When Volta touched both cups of mercury with his fingers, he received an electric shock; the more discs he assembled, the greater the jolt he received.

Volta's discovery led to further experimentation. In 1813, Sir Humphrey Davy constructed a pile with 2,000 pairs of discs in the basement of the Royal Institution of London. Among other applications, Davy used the electricity he produced for electrolysis—catalyzing chemical reactions by passing a current through substances (Davy separated sodium and potassium from compounds). Only a few years later, Michael Faraday discovered the principle of electromagnetic induction, using a magnet to induce electricity in a coiled wire. This technique is at the heart of the dynamos used to produce electricity in power plants today. (While a dynamo produces alternating current (AC) in which the flow of electricity shifts direction regularly, batteries produce direct current (DC) that flows in one direction only.) A lead-acid cell capable of producing a very large amount of current, the forerunner of today's **automobile** battery, was devised in 1859 by Frenchman Gaston Planté.

In the United States, Thomas Edison was experimenting with electricity from both batteries and dynamos to power the light bulb, which began to spread in the United States in the early 1880s. During the 1860s, Georges Leclanché invented the wet cell, which, though heavy because of its liquid components, could be sold and used commercially. By the 1870s and 1880s, the Leclanché cell was being produced using dry materials and was used for a number of tasks, including providing power for Alexander Graham Bell's telephone and for the newly-invented flashlight. Batteries were subsequently called upon to provide power for many other inventions, such as the radio, which became hugely popular in the years following World War I. Today, more than twenty billion power cells are sold throughout the world each year, and each American uses approximately 27 batteries annually.

Design

All batteries utilize similar procedures to create electricity; however, variations in materials and construction have produced different types of batteries. Strictly speaking, what is commonly termed a battery is actually a group of linked cells. The following is a simplified description of how a battery works.

Two important parts of any cell are the anode and the cathode. The cathode is a metal that is combined, naturally or in the laboratory, with oxygen—the combination is called an *oxide*. Iron oxide (rust), although too fragile to use in a battery, is perhaps the most familiar oxide. Some other oxides are actually strong enough to be worked (cut, bent, shaped, molded, and so on) and used in a cell. The anode is a metal that would oxidize if it were allowed to and, other things being equal, is more likely to oxidize than the metal that forms part of the cathode.

A cell produces electricity when one end of a cathode and one end of an anode are placed into a third substance that can conduct electricity, while their other ends are connected. The anode draws oxygen atoms toward it, thereby creating an electric flow. If there is a switch in the circuit (similar to any wall or lamp switch), the circuit is not complete and electricity cannot flow unless the switch is in the closed position. If, in addition to the switch, there is something else in the circuit, such as a light bulb, the bulb will light from the friction of the electrons moving through it.

The third substance into which the anode and the cathode are placed is called an *electrolyte*. In many cases this material is a chemical combination that has the property of being alkaline. Thus, an alkaline battery is one that makes use of an alkaline electrolyte. A cell will not produce electricity by itself unless it is placed in a circuit that has been rendered complete by a simple switch, or by some other switching connection in the appliance using the battery.

Designing a cell can lead to many variations in type and structure. Not all electrolytes, for example, are alkaline. Additionally, the container for the electrolyte can act as both a container and either the cathode or the anode. Some cells draw their oxygen not from a cathode but right out of the air. Changes in the compositions of the anode and the cathode will provide more or less electricity. Precise adjustment of all of the materials used in a cell can affect the amount of electricity that can be produced, the rate of production, the voltage at which electricity is delivered through the lifetime of the cell, and the cell's ability to function at different temperatures.

All of these possibilities do, in fact, exist, and their various applications have produced the many different types of batteries available today (lithium, mercury, and so on). For years, however, the most common cell has been the 1.5 volt alkaline battery.

Different batteries function better in different circumstances. The alkaline 1.5 volt cell is ideal for photographic equipment, handheld computers and calculators, toys, tape recorders, and other "high drain" uses; it is also good in low temperatures. This cell has a sloping discharge characteristic—it loses power gradually, rather than ceasing to produce electricity suddenly—and will lose perhaps four percent of its power per year if left unused on a shelf.

Other types of batteries include a lithium/manganese dioxide battery, which has a flat discharge characteristic—it provides approximately the same amount of power at the beginning of its life as at the end—and can be used where there is a need for small, high-power batteries (smoke alarms, cameras, memory backups on computers, and so on). Hearing aids, pagers, and some other types of medical equipment frequently use zinc air button type batteries, which provide a high energy density on continuous discharge. A mercury battery is frequently used in many of the same applications as the zinc air battery, because it, too, provides a steady output voltage.

Raw Materials

This section, as well as the following section, will focus on alkaline batteries. In an alkaline battery, the cylinder that contains the cells is made of nickel-plated steel. It is lined with a separator that divides the cathode from the anode and is made of either layered paper or a porous synthetic material. The canister is sealed at one end with an asphalt or epoxy sealant that underlies a steel plate, and at the other with a brass nail driven through the cylinder. This nail is welded to a metal end cap and passed through an exterior plastic seal. Inside the cylinder, the cathode consists of a mixture of manganese dioxide, graphite, and a potassium hydroxide solution; the anode comprises zinc powder and a potassium hydroxide electrolyte.

The Manufacturing Process

The cathode

1 In an alkaline battery, the cathode actually doubles as part of the container. Huge loads of the constituent ingredients—manganese dioxide, carbon black (graphite), and an electrolyte (potassium hydroxide in solu-

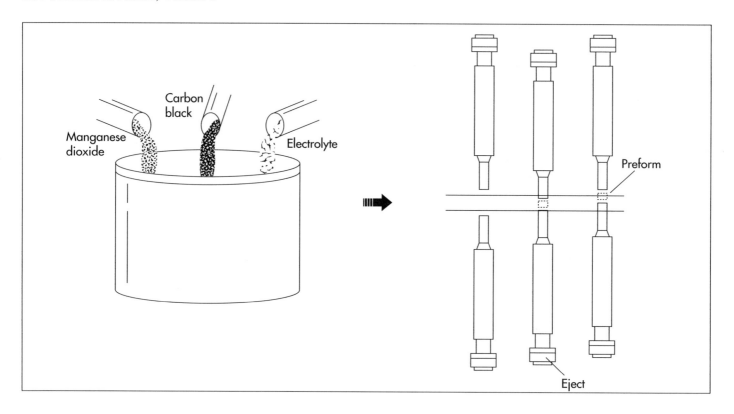

Manganese dioxide

Carbon black

Electrolyte

Preform

Eject

Mixing the constituent ingredients is the first step in battery manufacture. After granulation, the mixture is then pressed or compacted into preforms—hollow cylinders. The principle involved in compaction is simple: a steel punch descends into a cavity and compacts the mixture. As it retracts, a punch from below rises to eject the compacted preform.

tion)—are delivered by train and mixed in very large batches at the production site. The mixture is then granulated and pressed or compacted into hollow cylinders called *preforms.* Depending on the size of the battery being made, several preforms may be stacked one on top of another in a battery. Alternatively, the series of preforms can be replaced by an extruded ring of the same material.

2 The preforms are next inserted into a nickel-plated steel can; the combination of the preforms and the steel can make up the cathode of the battery. In a large operation, the cans are made at the battery factory using standard cutting and forming techniques. An indentation is made near the top of the can, and an asphalt or epoxy sealant is placed above the indentation to protect against leakage.

The separator

3 A paper separator soaked in the electrolyte solution is then inserted inside the can against the preforms; the separator is made from several pieces of paper laid at crossgrains to each other (like plywood). Looking down at an open can, one would see what looks like a paper cup inserted into the can. The separator keeps the cathode mater-

ial from coming into contact with the anode material. As an alternative, a manufacturer might use a porous synthetic fiber for the same purpose.

The anode

4 The anode goes into the battery can next. It is a gel composed primarily of zinc powder, along with other materials including a potassium hydroxide electrolyte. This gel has the consistency of a very thick paste. Rather than a solution, it is chemically a suspension, in which particles do not settle (though an appropriate filter could separate them). The gel does not fill the can to the top so as to allow space for the chemical reactions that will occur once the battery is put into use.

The seals

5 Though the battery is able to produce electricity at this point, an open cell is not practical and would exhaust its potential rapidly. The battery needs to be sealed with three connected components. The first, a brass "nail" or long spike, is inserted into the middle of the can, through the gel material and serves as a "current collector." The second is a plastic seal and the third a metal end cap. The nail, which extends about two-

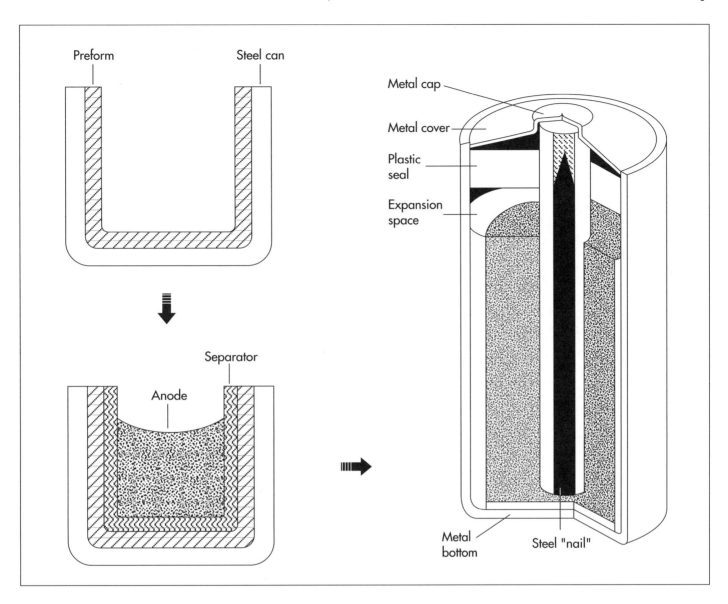

Preform   Steel can

Separator

Anode

Metal cap

Metal cover

Plastic seal

Expansion space

Metal bottom

Steel "nail"

thirds of the way into the can, is welded to the metal end cap and then passed through the plastic seal.

6 This seal is significantly thinner in some places than in others, so that if too much gas builds up in the can, the seal will rupture rather than the entire battery. Some battery designs make use of a wax-filled hole in the plastic; excess gas pushes through the wax rather than rupturing the battery. The seal assembly meets the indentation made in the can at the beginning of the process and is crimped in place.

7 The opposite end of the can (the positive end of the battery) is then closed with a steel plate that is either welded in place or glued with an epoxy-type cement.

The label

8 Before the battery leaves the factory, a label is added identifying the type of battery, its size, and other information. The label is often paper that is simply glued to the battery. One large manufacturer has its label design printed on plastic shrink wrap: a loose fitting piece of heat-sensitive plastic is wrapped around the battery can and then exposed to a blast of heat that makes the plastic shrink down to fit tightly around the can.

Quality Control

Because battery technology is not especially new or exotic, quality control and its results are especially important as the basis for brand competition. The ability of a battery to resist corrosion, to operate well under a vari-

The container of a typical alkaline battery, consisting of preform inserted into a steel can, also doubles as the cathode. The anode in the middle is a gel composed primarily of zinc powder. The separator between the anode and cathode is either paper or synthetic fiber that has been soaked in an electrolyte solution.

In the finished battery, a plastic seal, a steel nail, and a metal top and bottom have been added. The nail is welded to the metal bottom and extends about two-thirds of the way into the can, through the anode.

ety of conditions, to maintain a good shelf and usage life, and other factors, are the direct results of quality control. Batteries and ingredients are inspected and tested at almost all stages of the production process, and the completed batches are subjected to stringent tests.

Environmental Issues

Although making batteries does present some environmental obstacles, none are insurmountable. Zinc and manganese, the major chemicals in alkaline batteries, do not pose environmental difficulties, and both are considered safe by the Food and Drug Administration (FDA). The major potential pollutant in batteries is mercury, which commonly accompanies zinc and which was for many years added to alkaline batteries to aid conductivity and to prevent corrosion. In the mid-1980s, alkaline batteries commonly contained between five and seven percent mercury.

When it became apparent several years ago that mercury was an environmental hazard, manufacturers began seeking ways to produce efficient batteries without it. The primary method of doing this focuses on better purity control of ingredients. Today's alkaline batteries may contain approximately .025 percent mercury. Batteries with no added mercury at all (it is a naturally occurring element, so it would be difficult to guarantee a product free of even trace qualities) are available from some manufacturers and will be the industry-wide rule rather than the exception by the end of 1993.

The Future

Batteries are currently the focus of intense investigation by scientists and engineers around the world. The reason is simple: several key innovations depend on the creation of better batteries. Viable electric automobiles and portable electronic devices that can operate for long periods of time without needing to be recharged must wait until more lightweight and more powerful batteries are developed. Typical lead-acid batteries currently used in automobiles, for instance, are too bulky and cannot store enough electricity to be used in electric automobiles. Lithium batteries, while lightweight and powerful, are prone to leaking and catching fire.

In early 1993, scientists at Arizona State University announced that they had designed a new class of electrolytes by dissolving polypropylene oxide and polyethylene oxide into a lithium salt solution. The new electrolytes appear to be highly conductive and more stable than typical lithium electrolytes, and researchers are now trying to build prototype batteries that use the promising substances.

In the meantime, several manufacturers are developing larger, more powerful nickel-metal hydride batteries for use in portable computers. These new batteries are expected to appear in late 1994.

Where To Learn More

Books

Packaged Power. Duracell International Inc., 1981.

Periodicals

"Plastic May Recharge Battery's Future," *Design News.* November 17, 1986, p. 24.

Greenberg, Jeff. "Packing Power: Subnotebook Batteries, Power Management," *PC Magazine.* October 27, 1992, p. 113.

Leventon, William. "The Charge Toward a Better Battery: Designing a Long-Life Battery," *Design News.* November 23, 1992, p. 91.

Methvin, Dave. "Battery Contenders Face-Off in Struggle To Dominate Market," *PC Week.* November 12, 1990, p. S21.

Schmidt, K. F. "Rubbery Conductors Aim at Better Batteries," *Science News.* March 13, 1993, p. 166.

Zimmerman, Michael R. "Better Batteries on the Way: Nickel-Metal Hydride Is Short-Term Winner," *PC Week.* April 26, 1993, p. 25.

—Lawrence H. Berlow

Bicycle Shorts

Background

Bicycle shorts are form-fitting shorts designed specifically for the cyclist. A close inspection reveals that they differ significantly from typical jogging or beach shorts. Bicycle short material is usually a lightweight micro denier or close-knit woven fabric that protects against excessive moisture build-up during cycling. Upon removing a pair from its package and shaking it, you'll notice that it retains its contoured form, the legs slightly bent to accommodate the cyclist's position on a bicycle. Each leg extends to just above the knee and ends in an elasticized band that prevents the shorts from crawling up as the cyclist peddles. To better accommodate the contours of the lower body, the shorts are usually constructed of four, six, or eight separate panels that have been seamed together, and their streamlined design produces a slimming effect on waist, hips, and legs. The shorts also feature a padded lining stitched inside the crotch area to protect against saddle abrasion and other forms of irritating friction and to cushion against road bumps.

Photos of cyclists at the turn of the century show them wearing shorts, knickers, or simply pants with the legs rolled up (although women sometimes rode bicycles, only men rode competitively at that time). Early bicycle shorts were generally made of cotton or **wool** fabric. As the sport became more popular and more competitive, cyclists continually sought ways to improve their speed. All aspects of cycling were examined and improved, including not only the bicycle, protective headgear, and footwear, but the clothing as well. Cyclists discovered that hunching forward over the handlebars reduced wind resistance to their upper bodies and helped to shave seconds off their time. However, baggy trousers that caught the wind negated the benefits of this streamlined position. Another problem related to loose-fitting shorts was that they formed irritating folds that chafed, causing saddle sores that could easily become infected from bacteria accumulating between sweat and clothing. Cyclists responded to these problems by utilizing new fabrics and designs. Wind tunnel tests have shown that smooth, shiny, satiny material affords the least resistance, while stretchy, tight-fitting fabric offers an additional advantage: it won't bunch up in the groin area. Today, cyclists use synthetic fabrics designed with these characteristics, some of the most popular being Dupont's *Lycra, Coolmax,* and *Supplex.* To reduce the problem of moisture buildup, cyclists today favor black bicycle shorts. Whereas sweat between the legs caused discoloration in early bicycle shorts, today even multicolored shorts typically feature black inner panels to combat discoloration.

To lessen chafing, cyclists experimented with a number of liner fabrics before settling on chamois. This soft cloth not only protected best against abrasion, it also provided *wicking,* meaning that it absorbed moisture from the skin, carrying it to the surface where air currents could dry it. Today's liners are contoured to fit the groin area, and they extend from front to back, cut in a Y- or an hourglass shape. The chamois, usually synthetic, will have several layers: the layer that comes in direct contact with the skin will be a soft "ultrasuede" fabric; the next layer, a cotton terry cloth with wicking properties; the third layer, a foam or gel cushion, and the outermost layer, a close-knit fabric such as nylon or combination nylon/Lycra for extra protection

The shorts also feature a padded lining stitched inside the crotch area to protect against saddle abrasion and other forms of irritating friction and to cushion against road bumps.

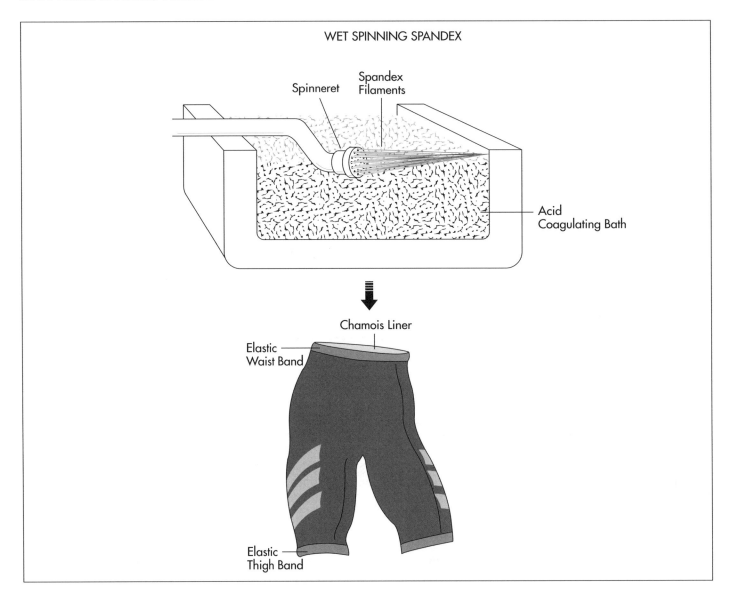

WET SPINNING SPANDEX

Spinneret

Spandex
Filaments

Acid
Coagulating Bath

Chamois Liner

Elastic
Waist Band

Elastic
Thigh Band

The fabric used in bicycle shorts usually consists of a blend of polyester, cotton, spandex, and nylon. Regardless of the materials used, they are usually spun and then combined into a single fabric. In spinning, filaments are drawn out of a spinneret, a device that works much like a shower head. Some filaments (such as spandex) are spun into an acid bath, while others are spun into open air.

After combining the threads into a single fabric and then washing and dyeing, the fabric is cut into various panels. After attaching the chamois liner, the panels are sewn together to form the finished piece.

against outside elements. Current versions of the chamois are also treated with an antibacterial agent to prevent fungal infections (similar to athlete's foot) in the groin area.

Today, there are two types of shorts: the more common bicycle short with an elastic waistband and a one-piece, bib type short without a waistband that is held up with suspender-type straps attached to a high Y- or U-shaped back panel. This short is mainly used by those who feel that the elastic waist on standard bicycle shorts hampers their breathing. Over the past decade, the tight-fitting or "skin" short has grown in popularity, and it can now be found in most major department and sports apparel specialty stores. Although these shorts are designed for cycling, many people wear them for comfort and exercise other than cycling.

Raw Materials

Choosing fabrics for bicycle shorts entails considering several requirements, including the degree of waterproofing or water-resistance for wick-dry capabilities, drying time, breathability, and windproofing.

Manufacturers tend to use synthetic fabrics such as spandex, a polyurethane fiber that returns to its original shape after stretching, although they are now blending these fabrics with natural fibers like cotton. Spandex is a stable fabric that retains its elasticity through dyeing, finishing, and frequent laundering.

The inner liner is called a chamois because it was originally made from the chamois, a goatlike antelope found in Europe and the Caucasus Mountains. Today, the liner is usually made from synthetic chamois mechanically molded to match anatomical contours. The liner also contains a petroleum-based fiber such as polypropylene, which enhances its wicking capabilities. Most manufacturers have their own fabric labels with similar fabric properties and wicking capabilities. One manufacturer, Cannondale, has a patented Biosuede ó chamois liner. Other trade names such as Ultrasuede and Supersuede have similar properties.

Design

Cyclists choose their apparel carefully, particularly if they compete: a raised seam can prove very irritating after several hours of strenuous cycling. Designers thus strive to develop the optimal cyclewear. Designs range from the less expensive four-panel cut to the more expensive eight-panel cut. The more panels used, the better the contours of the final product will match the shape of legs, waist, and groin. To accommodate the bent-over rider, the panels are cut higher in back and lower in front. Designers also consider sizing needs, and today this means designing bicycle shorts for both men and women. For example, the female cyclist needs a bicycle short with a small, high waistline that has more fullness in the hips than a male cyclist's bicycle short. The liner is also different for men and women, offering support and protection for the former, and a cotton/polyester blend for women. Designers first develop prototypes that are subjected to rigorous testing and revising before a bicycle short is approved for mass production.

The Manufacturing Process

Although more clothing manufacturers are making and distributing bicycle shorts for general sport and even nonathletic use, this section will describe how the short designed for the professional cyclist is manufactured.

Shorts

1 First, the fabric (usually a blend of polyester, cotton, spandex, and nylon) must be manufactured. This involves spinning and combining the various threads into a single fabric, washing and drying the fabric, and then dyeing it. Next, it is saturated or sprayed with a water resistant finish before being cut into panels according to pattern specifications set by the designer. The various panels are then carefully sewn together. To avoid raised "ridges," seams may be offset for a smoother finish. Finally, elastic is inserted in the waistband of the sewn short. Gripper elastic bands are also sewn into the cuffs at the short's hem.

Chamois liner

2 The chamois liner's layers are cut out according to pattern specifications before being bonded or laminated together. After assembly, they are stitched along the outer edges to prevent fraying. Sometimes, a special thread similar to a "soft floss" is used to prevent chafing. The finished product will have a molded look. It is usually inserted inside the bicycle short with a strip of tape to hold it in place. Several manufacturers have developed a one-piece chamois that does not require any seams and avoids any overlapping of material.

Inspection and shipping

3 The completed bicycle short is tested for defects. After passing inspection, it is ready to be packaged and shipped to a retailer.

Quality Control

Perhaps the most important quality control steps occur during the fabric manufacture. Chemical make-up, timing and temperature are essential factors that must be monitored and controlled in order to produce the fabric blend with the desired qualities.

The percentages of the various fibers used in a blended fabric must be controlled to stay within in the legal bounds of the Textile Fiber Identification Act. This act legally defines seventeen groups of man-made fibers. Six of these seventeen groups are made from natural material. They include **rayon**, acetate, glass fiber, metallics, rubber, and azion. The remaining eleven fabrics are synthesized solely from chemical compounds. They are nylon, polyester, acrylic, modacrylic, olefin, spandex, anidex, saran, vinal, vinyon, and nytril.

The Future

Apparel companies will continue to improve both the function and the fashion of bicycle shorts. A number of manufacturers have begun to use sponsored athletes to design, test, and market their products. Designers will continue to experiment with various fiber blends.

Where To Learn More

Books

Ballantine, Richard and Richard Grant. *Richards' Ultimate Bicycle Book.* Dorling Kindersley, Inc., 1992.

Chauner, David and Michael Halstead. *The Tour De France Complete Book of Cycling.* Villard Books, Inc., 1990.

Periodicals

Bradford, C. "Action Softwear," *Health.* September, 1988, pp. 45-51.

Herman, Hank. "Cool Threads," *Men's Health.* August, 1990, p. 24.

Smutko, Liz. "The Seat of Your Pants: When It Comes to Cycling Comfort, the Butt Stops Here," *Bicycling.* February, 1991, pp. 70-73.

—*Catherine Kolecki*

Blood Pressure Monitor

Background

Blood pressure is the pressure that the blood exerts against the walls of the arteries as it passes through them. Pulse refers to the periodic ejection of blood from the heart's left ventricle into the aorta. The left ventricle, or chamber, receives blood from the left atrium, another of the heart's chambers. By contracting, the left ventricle drives the blood into the aorta, a central artery through which blood is relayed into the arteries of all limbs and organs except the lungs. Pulse, transmitted though the arteries as a repeated pressure wave, is the mechanism that moves blood through the body.

The high and low points of this pressure wave are measured with the *sphygmomanometer*, or blood pressure monitor, and are expressed numerically in millimeters of mercury. The higher number, *systolic pressure,* measures the maximum pressure exerted on arteries and the heart muscle; the lower figure, *diastolic pressure*, measures the minimum pressure exerted. The reading of the two measurements indicates how hard the human system is working. All physicians consider a patient's blood pressure when determining general health or diagnosing disease.

The blood pressure monitor is used in conjunction with a stethoscope. After fastening the constricting band, or cuff, around one of the patient's arms above the elbow, the clinician inflates the cuff by pumping air into it with a rubber squeeze bulb until the mercury column or the needle of the gauge (also known as an *aneroid dial*) stops moving, usually at a point between 150 and 200 millimeters of mercury. The stethoscope is then placed over the brachial artery, on the inside of the arm at the elbow, while air is slowly released from the system via a small valve attached to the bulb. The technician watches carefully as the air escapes and the pressure indicator correspondingly declines. The point on the gauge at which the pulse can first be heard through the stethoscope indicates systolic pressure, and the gauge's reading when the sound disappears indicates diastolic pressure. Normal pressures vary with the individual, but systolic pressure typically ranges between 110 and 140, while diastolic runs from 65 to 80. Pressure above normal levels predisposes the patient to such health problems as heart disease, stroke, and kidney failure.

Many early attempts at measuring blood pressure involved attaching an instrument directly to one of the patient's arteries, a painful and dangerous practice. The first sphygmomanometer to use an inflated armband was developed in 1876 by Samuel Siegfried von Basch. Twenty years later, the Italian physician Scipione Riva-Rocci developed a more accurate device that soon replaced von Basch's instrument. Riva-Rocci's design was much like today's monitor, but its operating procedure allowed for measuring blood pressure only while the heart was contracted. In 1905, the measurement procedure was further refined by Nikolai Korotkoff, who added the use of a stethoscope to detect pulse rate, thereby enabling doctors to measure blood pressure while the heart was relaxed as well. Korotkoff suspected that both pressure readings were important, and today we realize that certain indications, such as a rise in the systolic with a stable or falling diastolic pressure, may suggest brain damage.

Many early attempts at measuring blood pressure involved attaching an instrument directly to one of the patient's arteries, a painful and dangerous practice. The first sphygmomanometer to use an inflated armband was developed in 1876 by Samuel Siegfried von Basch

The neoprene bulb is commonly made using vacuum-assisted injection molding. In this process, molten neoprene is injected into a mold of the proper shape. The mold is equipped with tiny holes, through which the air in the chamber is drawn out just before the neoprene enters. The resulting vacuum causes the neoprene to flow into the cavity evenly. Within a few seconds after injection, the neoprene cools and hardens and can be removed.

The pressure gauge contains two phosphor-bronze disks soldered together. Some blood pressure monitors utilize either a mercury manometer or an electronic display.

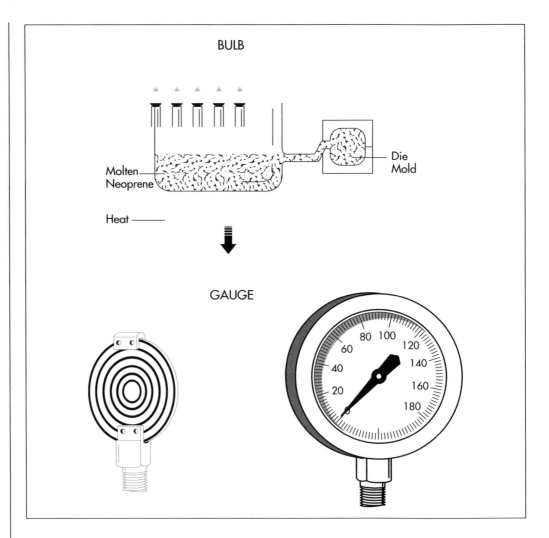

Design

All blood pressure monitors feature an air pump device equipped with a control valve, a means of indicating pressure, a constricting band to be attached to the patient, and the various connecting hoses that operate the system. Although three distinct types of blood pressure monitors exist, they differ basically in their means of registering pressure: one type uses a pressure gauge or dial; another type uses a mercury manometer (a manometer is an instrument that measures the pressure of liquids and gases); and the third uses an electronic or digital display. Despite the availability of electronic display sphygmomanometers, instruments that use a manometer or a dial are still more popular because they are easier to service as well as accurate, durable, and inexpensive. This article will focus on the dial or pressure gauge type.

A typical blood pressure monitor features a neoprene or rubber pump bulb that a medical technician squeezes to build air pressure in the system. Increasing air pressure inflates the constricting band and provides a pressure signal to the manometer or indicating gauge. The process is controlled by a valve, which has a hose fitting to attach the tube leading to the constricting band and gauge. Integral to the valve is a one-way flow device that operates only when the valve is closed. It usually consists of a small rubber disk or ball that is placed over the air passage from the squeeze bulb opening and secured by a screw or clip. The compressed air raises the ball slightly when the bulb is squeezed, sealing the opening to the atmosphere and forcing air to enter the cuff. Upon release of the bulb, the ball seals the opening between the bulb and the hose, opening the former to the atmosphere and allowing it to refill with air. This cycle is repeated until the correct starting pressure is reached. The manual valve opens a bypass route to release the air while readings are being taken.

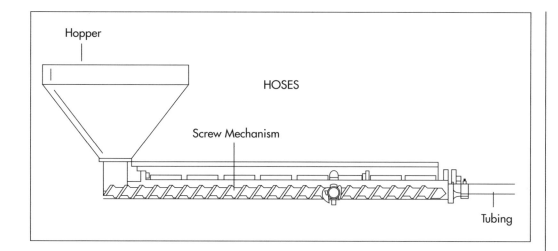

Hopper

HOSES

Screw Mechanism

Tubing

The rubber hoses are made by continuous extrusion, in which molten rubber is forced through a die block by a rotating screw device. Within the block is a rod the same size as the inside of the tubing; as the rubber flows around this rod and out of the die, it cools and assumes the shape of the tubing. It is then cut to the proper length.

Raw Materials

The dial, or aneroid type, instrument is a mechanical pressure gauge that has a pointer and dial calibrated in millimeters of mercury. The pressure gauge consists of three basic groups of parts: a pressure element and socket assembly; a movement and dial assembly; and a protective case and lens assembly enclosing them. The pressure element comprises two phosphor-bronze disks of approximately .010 inch (.025 centimeter) with a formed lip on the outer edge. The movement is usually made of polycarbonate and brass materials and contains a small gear train that amplifies the short travel distance of the disks. The movement assembly also supports the dial, which may be brass, aluminum, or plastic. The output shaft of the movement is mounted with the aluminum pointer.

The squeeze bulb is usually rubber or neoprene, as are the connecting hoses. The band, or cuff, is basically a fabric-covered neoprene bladder with a hook and loop (Velcro) fastener. The bladder is enclosed in a nylon or synthetic fiber fabric, which protects it from cuts during use by on-scene rescue technicians and reduces patient discomfort. The band must be very flexible and durable to accommodate the infinite differences in patients and situations. The control valve can be made of polycarbonate, brass, **stainless steel**, or combinations of these materials.

The Manufacturing Process

Many manufacturers purchase the components of the blood pressure monitor sepa-

rately, then assemble and package the unit for sale. Each part has its own manufacturing and assembly process.

The bulb

1 The bulb can be made using various processes, but it is most commonly produced using vacuum-assisted injection molding. Compressed air is used to blow the melted rubber or neoprene material into the cavity of a two-piece metal die set featuring the negative image of the bulb (the operation resembles blowing a gum bubble inside a bottle). The die also contains small holes through which air is drawn out just before the material is injected, helping it flow into the die cavity at a uniform thickness. While these holes are large enough to allow air to escape, they are too small to permit significant amounts of the rubber to seep out. The remnant of the rubber material that is drawn into the holes produces small protuberances that resemble the small "whiskers" visible on a new tire. Within a few seconds of its injection, the material has cooled so that the die may be opened, revealing the finished bulb. After a minimal amount of hand work to remove the whiskers, the bulb is ready to be attached to the other components.

The valves

2 The valves are made by die casting, plastic injection molding, and machining from bar material. They incorporate connection features that allow the bulb and hose to be attached. Machined valves can be made on a lathe controlled by a computer program that instructs it to turn the shape, threads, and other features.

A finished blood pressure monitor. While monitors that use pressure gauges for pressure display will continue to be popular because of their portability, electronic displays will increase in use as new power sources are developed and the design is made more rugged. Mercury monitors will likely drop from favor because of the hazardous effects of mercury.

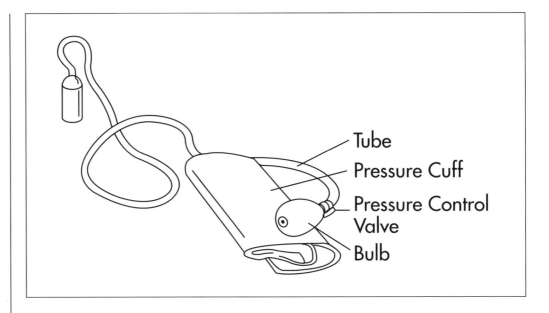

Tube

Pressure Cuff

Pressure Control Valve

Bulb

The gauge

3 The gauge consists of further sub-assemblies, each of which contains machined, molded, and stamped parts. The most important component of the gauge is the pressure element. It is constructed by soldering two disks together at the formed lip to construct a hollow wafer. The pressure from the system is introduced into the wafer though a hole in the socket connection, which in turn is connected to the squeeze bulb and cuff. As the internal pressure increases, the wafer swells. It is this swelling that is detected by the movement assembly, causing the pointer to rotate about the dial. After assembly, the gauge must be calibrated. This is accomplished by connecting it to a pressure source with a master gauge of known accuracy. Slight adjustments are made in the movement linkage until the pointer of the gauge reflects the correct pressure readings.

The cuff

4 The constricting cuff, or bladder, is made by heat sealing two rubber sheets together to form a flexible band. A tubing fitting is incorporated into this sealing process, providing a connection for the air supply. A fabric covering is then sewn to the bladder by conventional methods.

The hoses

5 The hoses are made by continuous extrusion, a process in which pellets of rubber or similar material are heated to the melting point, at which they become clay-like and viscous. Within the same machine, a rotating screw device forces this molten material through a die block, which is simply a hole in an aluminum block the same size as the outside of the tubing. Secured within the block is a rod that is the same size as the inside of the tubing and positioned in the center of the hole. As the material flows around the rod and out the hole, it cools and assumes the shape of the tubing. At this point, it is cut to length and coiled onto spools for shipment to the assembly facility.

Assembling the components

6 At final assembly, hoses are used to connect the components discussed above. The hoses are then checked for leaks and the calibration is verified. This is a good example of JIT (*just-in-time*) material requirements planning and TQC (*total-quality-concept*) management. Missing any one of the components, the entire assembly is useless. The plant must receive the parts and supplies in a timely manner to assure delivery of the finished product to the customer. The items must be of satisfactory quality, so they can be assembled correctly and without compromising the design. Many companies today have established quality management procedures. These procedures are simply intensive studies of all aspects of manufacture to eliminate or reduce the possibility of producing a defective part. It is not just making the part, but also designing it, selecting the materials, choosing packaging selection, and all other

aspects that determine the quality of the finished product.

The Future

Medical product manufacturers and their suppliers are prone to liability suit due to failure (or perceived failure) of their products. A portion of the cost of the instruments stems from the costs of insuring and defending the company against these lawsuits. Many companies have discontinued products because the liability risk is too much of a financial burden for them. For example, the mercury type instrument will probably be discontinued due to hazardous materials issues as discussed above. The electronic versions will most likely increase as new power source designs and improved ruggedness are achieved. Medical technicians and therapists rely on measurements of blood pressure as a benchmark for health, and consequently, some type of sphygmomanometer will always be used.

Where To Learn More

Books

Emergency Care and Transportation of the Sick and Injured. The American Academy of Orthopedic Surgeons.

Sphygmomanometers: Electronic or Automated. Association for the Advancement of Medical Instrumentation, 1987.

Travers, Bridget, ed. *World of Invention.* Gale Research, 1994.

Periodicals

Calem, Robert E. "Monitoring Blood Pressure Without Skipping a Heartbeat," *New York Times.* March 28, 1993, p. F16 (N).

—*Douglas E. Betts*

Blue Jeans

In 1937 the rivets on the back pockets were moved inside in response to complaints from school boards that the jeans students wore were damaging chairs and from cowboys that their jeans were damaging their saddles.

Background

Blue jeans are casual pants made from denim, noted for their strength and comfort. They have been worn by sailors and California **gold** miners as sturdy work pants, by the young as a statement of their generation, and by the fashionable, who are conscious of the prestige conveyed by designer names.

Denim cloth itself has an unusual history. The name comes from *serge de Nimes*, or the serge of Nimes, France. Originally, it was strong material made from **wool**. By the 1700s, it was made from wool and cotton. Only later was it made solely from cotton. Originally, it was used to make sails, but eventually, some innovative Genovese sailors thought it fit that such fine, strong material would make great pants, or "genes."

The name for blue jeans was derived from the color of the fabric used to make them. Denim was treated with a blue dye obtained from the indigo plant. Indigo had been used as a dye since 2500 B.C. in such diverse places as Asia, Egypt, Greece, Rome, Britain, and Peru. Blue jean manufacturers imported indigo from India until the twentieth century, when synthetic indigo was developed to replace the natural dye.

Blue jeans in the form we know them today didn't come about until the middle of the nineteenth century. Levi Strauss, an enterprising immigrant who happened to have a few bolts of blue denim cloth on hand, recognized a need for strong work pants in the mining communities of California. He first designed and marketed "Levi's" in 1850, and they have stayed essentially the same ever since; there have been only minor alterations to the original design.

Original Levi's did not contain rivets. A tailor by the name of Jacob Davis invented riveted pants at the request of a miner who complained that regular pants were not rugged enough to hold his mining tools. Davis subsequently granted Strauss the use of his rivet idea, which was patented on May 20, 1873. Few other changes were made over the next century. **Zipper**s replaced button flies in 1920 (although later button flies had a resurgence of popularity) and in 1937 the rivets on the back pockets were moved inside in response to complaints from school boards that the jeans students wore were damaging chairs and from cowboys that their jeans were damaging their **saddle**s. In the 1960s, they were removed entirely from the back pockets.

Blue jeans started becoming popular among young people in the 1950s. In the year 1957, 150 million pairs were sold worldwide. This growing trend continued until 1981 and jeans manufacturers were virtually guaranteed annual sales increases. In the United States, 200 million pairs of jeans were sold in 1967, 500 million in 1977, with a peak of 520 million in 1981. When jeans first caught on, apologists reasoned that their low price determined their huge success. During the 1970s, however, the price of blue jeans doubled, yet demand always exceeded supply. Sometimes manufacturers met the demand by providing stores with irregulars; that is, slightly defective merchandise that would not normally be sold.

Although the demand for jeans actually decreased in the 1980s, a brief surge occurred with the introduction of designer jeans to the market. Despite the apparent success of designer jeans, however, they did not capture the majority of the market; jeans have not

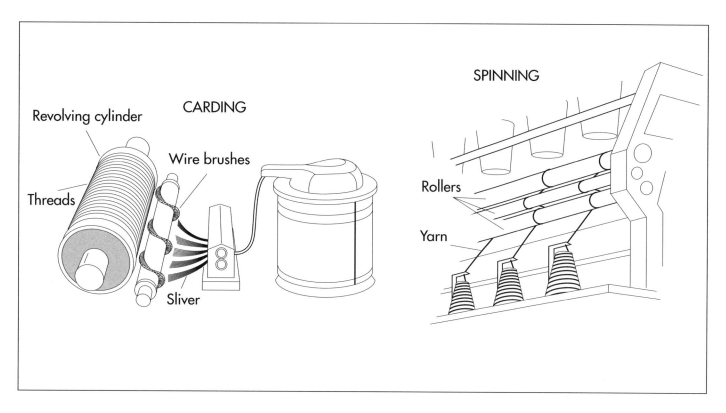

CARDING

Revolving cylinder

Wire brushes

Threads

Sliver

SPINNING

Rollers

Yarn

returned to the height of popularity they achieved in the seventies. Manufacturers must therefore constantly seek ways to keep the demand for blue jeans high. Believing that the decrease in demand reflects the changing needs of an aging population, jeans manufacturers have begun to cater to the mature customer by providing roomier, more comfortable jeans. Sally Fox, an entomologist, has developed cottons that naturally come in beige, brown, and green. The Levi Strauss Company now markets multicolored jeans as well. The company hopes to ride the popular wave of environmentalism, even advertising their new product on recycled denim.

Although blue jeans have remained basically the same since they were first designed, they have always been versatile enough to meet market demands. Since futuristic, yet familiar, "Levi's" appeared in the movie *Star Trek V*, it can be surmised that manufacturers as well as the public, expect blue jeans to be around indefinitely.

Raw Materials

True blue jeans are made out of 100 percent cotton, including the threads. Polyester blends are available, however, the overwhelming majority of jeans sold are 100 per-

cent cotton. The most common dye used is synthetic indigo. The belt loops, waistband, back panel, pockets, and leggings of a pair of blue jeans are all made of indigo-dyed denim. Other features of blue jeans include the zipper, buttons, rivets, and label. Rivets have been traditionally made of copper, but the zippers, snaps and buttons are usually steel. Designers' labels are often tags made out of cloth, leather, or plastic, while others are embroidered on with cotton thread.

The Manufacturing Process

Denim, unlike many types of cloth (which are woven in one place and sent to another for dying), is woven and dyed at one location.

Preparing the cotton yarn

1 There are several steps between ginned cotton (cotton after it has been picked from fields and processed) and cotton yarn. The incoming cotton is removed from tightly packed bales and inspected before undergoing a process known as *carding*. In this process, the cotton is put through machines that contain brushes with bent wire teeth. These brushes—called *cards*—clean, disentangle, straighten, and gather together the

The first two steps in blue jeans manufacture are carding and spinning. In carding, the cotton is put through a machine with bent wire brushes. The brushes clean, disentangle, straighten, and gather the cotton threads into sliver. After several slivers are joined together, they are put on spinning machines that twist and stretch the cotton to form yarn.

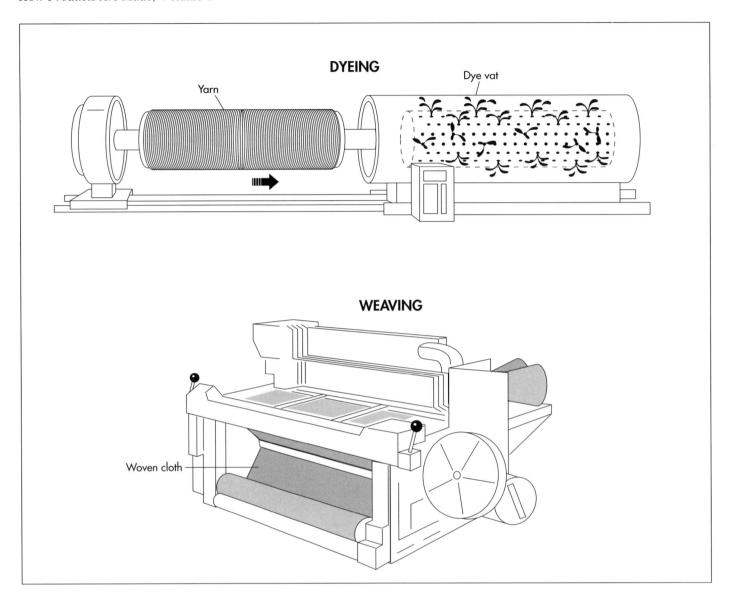

DYEING

Yarn

Dye vat

WEAVING

Woven cloth

Unlike many other cloths, denim is dyed before it is woven. The dye used is generally a chemically synthesized indigo. The denim is dipped in the dye vat several times so that the dye forms many layers. This explains why blue jeans fade after washing.

The yarn is then woven on large shuttle-less looms. The blue threads are woven with white threads, but because the blue threads are packed closer together than the white ones, the blue color dominates the cloth.

cotton fibers. At this point, the fibers are called *slivers.*

2 Other machines join several slivers together, and these slivers are then pulled and twisted, which serves to make the threads stronger. Next, these ropes are put on spinning machines that further twist and stretch the fibers to form yarn.

Dyeing the yarn

3 Some cloths are woven (see step 5 below) and then dyed, but denim is usually dyed with chemically synthesized indigo before being woven. Large balls of yarn, called ball warps, are dipped in the indigo mixture several times so that the dye covers the yarn in layers. (These many layers of indigo dye explain why blue jeans fade

slightly with each washing.) Although the exact chemicals used in such dyeing procedures remain trade secrets, it is known that a small amount of sulfur is often used to stabilize the top or bottom layers of indigo dye.

4 The dyed yarn is then *slashed*; that is, it is coated with sizing (any one of a variety of starchy substances) to make the threads stronger and stiffer. Once this operation is complete, the yarn threads are ready to woven with undyed filling yarn threads.

Weaving the yarn

5 The yarn is then woven on large mechanical looms. Denim is not 100 percent blue, as the blue dyed threads forming the *warp* (long, vertical threads) are combined with white threads forming the *weft* (shorter, hori-

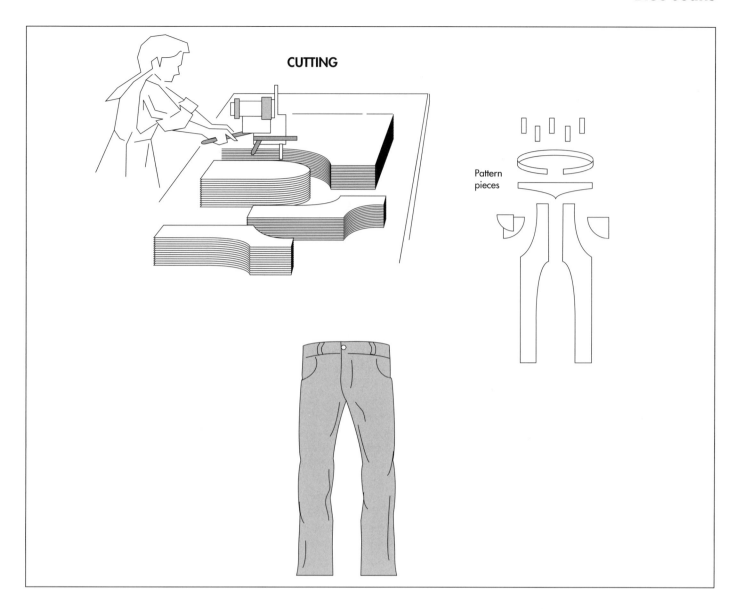

CUTTING

Pattern
pieces

zontal threads). Because denim is woven with the blue threads packed closer together than the white threads and with the blue threads covering three out of four white threads, the blue threads dominate. (By examining a piece of denim closely one can detect the steep diagonal pattern that results from this process, which is known as a three-by-one right-hand twill weave.) Although mechanized looms make use of the same basic weaving procedure as a simple hand loom, they are much larger and faster. A modern "shuttle-less" loom (which uses a very small carrier instead of the traditional shuttle to weave the weft threads between the warp threads) may produce as much as 3,279 yards (3,000 meters) of cloth 3.28 or 4.37 yards (three or four meters) wide in a single week. As much as 1,093 yards (1,000 meters) of cloth may be rolled into a single huge bolt.

6 At this point the denim is ready for finishing, a term referring to a variety of treatments applied to cloth after it is woven. With denim, finishing is usually fairly simple. The cloth is brushed to remove loose threads and lint, and the denim is usually skewed in a way that will prevent it from twisting when it is made into clothing. The denim may then be *sanforized*, or preshrunk. Preshrunk denim should shrink no more than three percent after three washings.

Making the blue jeans

7 Once the desired design is selected, patterns from the design are cut from heavy paper or cardboard. Up to 80 different sizes are possible from one pattern. The pieces of denim are then cut with high speed cutting machines from stacks 100 layers thick.

The denim cloth is cut into pattern pieces from stacks 100 layers thick. High-speed cutting machines are used for this process. Once the pieces are cut, they are sewn into completed pairs of blue jeans. Sewing is done in assembly-line fashion using human-operated sewing machines.

Excluding rivets, buttons, and zippers, a pair of blue jeans contains about ten different pieces, from the pockets to the leg panels to the waistband and belt loops.

8 The pieces of denim are ready to be sewn at this point. Sewing is done in an assembly line fashion, with rows of industrial human-operated sewing machines. Each sewer is assigned a specific function, such as making only back pockets. First, the various pockets and belt loops are assembled. Next, one sewer attaches the pockets to the leg seams, another then sews the leg seams together, and still another attaches the waistband. Once the waist band is secure, the belt loops may be stitched on and the buttons attached. If the jeans include a zipper, it is then sewn into place, and the pants are hemmed. Finally, the rivets are placed in the appropriate places and the maker's label is sewn on last.

9 Some jeans are prewashed and/or stone-washed to alter the appearance or texture of the finished jeans. Prewashing involves washing the jeans in industrial detergent for a short time to soften the denim. Stone-washing also means washing the jeans, but pumice is added to the load, resulting in a faded appearance. Small stones (less than one inch [one centimeter] in diameter) produce an even abrasion, while large stones (about four inches [10 centimeters] in diameter) highlight the seams and pockets and produce a more uneven appearance.

10 The completed pair of blue jeans is then pressed. They are placed into a large pressing machine that steam irons the entire garment at once in about a minute. A size tag is punched into the material and the jeans are folded, stacked, and placed in boxes according to style, color, and size before being sent to the warehouse for storage. When the jeans are selected to be sent to a store, they are put in large shipping cartons and sent on freight trains or trucks.

Byproducts/Waste

The process of cloth making involves treating the fabric with a number of chemicals in order to produce clothing with such desirable characteristics such as durability, colorfastness, and comfort. Each step of finishing the cotton fabric (dyeing, sanforizing, etc.) produces byproducts, most of which are biodegradable.

Byproducts of denim manufacture include organic pollutants, such as starch and dye, which can be treated through biological methods. These organic wastes may not be dumped into streams or lakes because of their high biochemical oxygen demand. To decompose, such waste materials utilize so much oxygen that the lifeforms in the body of water would be denied the oxygen necessary for survival.

Denim manufacturers process their own wastes in compliance with all relevant government regulations.

Quality Control

Cotton is a desirable natural fiber for several reasons. Cloth made from cotton is wear resistant, strong, flexible, and impermeable. Blue jeans are only as good as the cotton that goes into them, however, and several tests exist for cotton fiber. All bales of cotton are inspected by the denim manufacturer for the desired color, fiber length, and strength. Strength is the most important factor in blue jeans. It is measured by using a weight to pull it. When the fiber breaks, the force used to break it is measured. The cotton's strength index (weight of weight divided by weight of sample) is then calculated.

The finished denim cloth is carefully inspected for defects. Each defect is rated on a government-defined scale ranging from one point for very small flaws to four points for major defects. Although government regulations allow cloth with a high defect rating to be sold, in reality customers will not accept denim with more than seven to ten defect points per square meter. Poor cloth is sold as damaged. Denim is also tested for durability and its tendency to shrink. Samples of cloth are washed and dried several times to see how they wear.

Blue jeans are also inspected after they are completed. If a problem can be corrected, the jeans are sent back for re-sewing. The pair is then inspected again and passed. The buttons are inspected to ensure that they and the buttonholes are of the proper size; the snaps, metal buttons, and rivets are checked for durability and their ability to withstand rust. The zippers must be strong enough to withstand the greater pressures of heavy cloth, and their teeth durability must be checked as well. This is done by subjecting a sample zipper to a lifetime of openings and closings.

Where To Learn More

Books

Cray, Ed. *Levi's*. Houghton Mifflin, 1978.

Fehr, Barbara. *Yankee Denim Dandies*. Piper Publishing, 1974.

Finlayson, Iain. *Denim*. Simon and Schuster, 1990.

Henry, Sondra and Emily Taitz. *Everyone Wears His Name: A Biography of Levi Strauss*. Dillon Press, 1990.

Periodicals

Adkins, Jan. "The Evolution of Jeans: American History 501," *Mother Earth News*. July/August, 1990, pp. 60-63.

Brooks, John. "Annals of Business: A Friendly Product," *The New Yorker*. November 12, 1979, pp. 58-94.

— Rose Secrest

Book

Background

A book can be broadly defined as a written document of at least 49 text pages that communicates thoughts, ideas, or information. Throughout the ages, books have changed dramatically, assuming a number of different forms. To a great extent, the evolution of the book has followed the expansion of communication forms and methods and the ever-increasing demand for information.

The first known forms of written documentation were the clay tablet of Mesopotamia and the papyrus roll of Egypt. Examples of both date back as early as 3000 B.C. Independent of these developments were Chinese books, made of wood or bamboo strips bound together with cords. These books dated back to 1300 B.C.

Modern book production came about as a result of the invention of printing press. Although the invention of printing most likely occurred earlier in China as well, the introduction of movable type and the printing press to Europe is credited to Johann Gutenberg of Germany. Gutenberg, in collaboration with his partners Johann Fust and Peter Schoffer, printed a Latin Bible using a hand printing press with movable lead type by about 1456. Each individual letter of early hand-set type was designed in a style closely resembling script or handlettering. Thus, the first books printed in Europe appeared much like books produced by scribes. Books printed in the fifteenth century are now called *incunabula*, a word derived from the Latin word for cradle. In 1640, Stephen Day printed the first book in North America, in Cambridge, Massachusetts.

Because the printing press and moveable type mechanized the book production process, books became available in greater numbers. By the nineteenth century, however, the demand for books could not be met quickly enough by the process of hand printing. Printers developed larger presses to accommodate larger sheets of paper and/or the newly invented continuous rolls of paper. These improvements allowed printers to produce books at a much faster rate. During the decades of the mid-1800s, further progress was made, including the invention of the papermaking machine (1820s), binding machinery (1860), and the cylinder press (1840s); later, the linotype (invented in 1884), cast type by line rather than by individual letter.

Book production in America and throughout the industrialized world has flourished and expanded during the twentieth century. Important advances in printing, such as the introduction of the offset printing press and computerized typesetting, have made mass production more economical. The development of the paperback book, which was introduced in the 1940s to provide a less expensive alternative to the traditional hardback book, has also made books more accessible to the public. While the invention of other forms of media, such as radio and television, has had an adverse impact on reading in general, books remain the primary source of knowledge throughout most of the world.

Raw Materials

Books are made from a variety of different coated and uncoated paper stocks that differ in weight and size. In addition, different color inks may be used. Also, while front and back covers are generally made from a heavier stock of paper, they will vary in terms of weight. For example, hardback books have a durable cardboard stock cover while paperback books are made from a thinner paper stock. Usually, cover stocks are coated with different colors or designs.

Since the nineteenth century, book production has entailed the use of sophisticated machinery, including typesetting machines, a web or sheet-fed printing press, and book binding machines.

Design

The process of designing a book is ongoing throughout the stages of production. Initially, the author, in conjunction with an editor and book agent, will consider elements of design that pertain to the scope and purpose of the book, the desired approach to the subject matter, whether illustrations should be used, and other issues such as chapter headings and their placement. In determining those elements, the intended audience for the manuscript will be considered, along with accepted editorial standards. Other design considerations include whether a book should have a preface, a foreword, a glossary to define specific terms, an index to reference key words and concepts, and an appendix of supplementary material.

Once the book manuscript is written, editors and authors must refine the manuscript to attain a final edited version prior to production. In most cases, this involves a process of reviewing, editing, proofreading, revising and final approval. After such manuscript design factors are completed, editors and art directors will determine the following features:

- page size and style

- typeface size and style

- the type and weight of paper for the text and cover

- use of color

- presentation of visuals/illustrations in the text, if needed

- cover art/illustrations

A typesetter, or compositor, works at his type stand in this mid-nineteenth century engraving.

Since the days of Johannes Gutenberg and well into the twentieth century, printers have considered themselves a special lot. They needed to be literate to set type by hand, and they needed physical strength and endurance to operate a hand press. Because their work put them into contact with intellectuals, politicians, and community leaders, they often had social contacts beyond those commonly available to workers. Because they had constant access to ideas and information, they were generally considered to be learned individuals. Sometimes called the intellectuals of the working class, printers were distinguished by the fact that their work was a unique combination of mental and manual labor.

Like most skilled tradesmen, nineteenth-century printers developed a special language for their work. There were, of course, technical terms naming processes or tools. But much of the language, drawing on Anglo-European traditions, dealt with social relationships. Knowledge of this language was part of the training of an apprentice and separated the "fraternity" from the uninitiated. The youngest apprentice was called a "devil," reflecting his low status, responsibility for menial work, and propensity for getting dirty. Workers "jeffed," or used type as dice, to see who got certain work, who paid for drinks, or who laid off a night so that a "sub" (substitute) could get some work. The workers in an office would unofficially organize themselves into a "chapel" and elect a "chairman" or "father." These traditions eventually evolved into the union shop and union steward.

William S. Pretzer

The Manufacturing Process

After the book is written and appropriate design elements are agreed upon, book production can begin. The first stage is *type-*

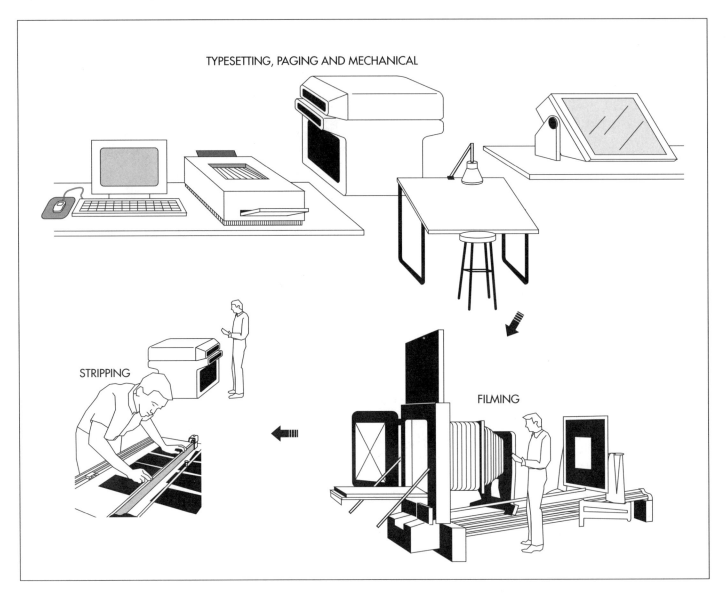

TYPESETTING, PAGING AND MECHANICAL

STRIPPING

FILMING

The first step in book production is typesetting, which increasingly is being done with desktop computer programs. With a computer, the proper software, and a laser printer, manuscript can be typeset that has the same quality as that produced by traditional typesetting methods.

Once typeset, the mechanical or "camera-ready copy" of the manuscript is sent to a printer. This vendor then photographs the pages to produce page negatives. Next, these negatives are stripped by hand onto large flat sheets known as "goldenrods," and the goldenrods are exposed with ultraviolet light. This results in "blueprints," a positive reproduction of the book that is then checked for accuracy.

setting, in which the actual text is converted into the appropriate typeface style (known as *font*) and size (known as *point size*). After the typeset version of the book has been reviewed and any necessary changes made, it is ready for printing and binding, in which the actual pages are printed and bound together with the cover, resulting in a finished book. The typesetting and printing—"printing" consists of filming and all subsequent steps—are typically done not by the publisher but by specialized vendors.

Typesetting

1 First, the manuscript is converted into the desired font and point size. If the manuscript has not been completed on a computer, it must be typed into a computer by the typesetter. If it is already in electronic form, how-

ever, the typesetter simply has to make programming changes to convert the manuscript into the proper style. The result is generally (but not always; see step #3 below) a *galley* of the text. A galley form of manuscript consists of long pages of text in a single column. The galley includes the proper typeface, but the proper pagination still must be worked out.

2 Galleys are then proofread and edited for errors by the publisher. This stage is particularly important if the manuscript has been typeset (typed) from a hard copy of the text. If the manuscript was typeset from a computer disk, most of the errors should have already been corrected during a review of the manuscript. The single-column format of galleys facilitates the proofreading.

Pages and mechanical

3 After galleys are thoroughly proofed and edited, pages (or lasers) are produced. An exact layout of typeset pages but usually printed on standard typing paper, pages are also reviewed for accuracy by the publisher. Some books skip the galley stage and proceed directly to pages. Once any necessary changes have been made, the typesetter then produces a mechanical of the typeset pages. Also called camera copy, the mechanical is printed on high-quality paper that is suitable for filming, the first stage in the printing process. The work of the typesetting vendor—if different from the publisher—is now done.

Filming

4 The typeset mechanical now goes to the printing and binding vendor. First, each text page, including line drawings, is photographed (or shot) using a large camera to produce page negatives. These negatives are the opposite of what will actually print. In other words, the text and photos will appear backward in negative form. Negatives are then checked to make sure there are no blemishes present. While printed words and line drawings are all one shade of black, photographs have many shades from palest gray to deepest black and must be filmed using a special process to maintain these shades. The process converts the shades into black and white dots—very light areas have many dots, while darker areas have fewer dots. The converted photographs are known as *halftones*. If the book will have more than one color of ink, a separate negative for each color is made. For color photos, for instance, four negatives are generally used: cyan, magenta, yellow, and black. For this reason, books with color will have negative overlays (one negative overlay for each color). Because of the added overlays, a book printed in more than one color involves additional preparation and cost.

Stripping

5 The negatives are then taped or "stripped" into their proper place onto a large sheet called a *goldenrod* or a *flat*. Each flat holds 32 or 64 pages, and enough flats are used to equal the number of pages in the book. Strippers examine each finished flat on a lineup table to ensure that text and illustrations are properly lined up and in sequence. (The book pages are not lined up in consecutive order on the flat, and in fact some of the pages are placed upside down. Such placing is necessary because the finished paper version of each flat will be folded several times; once the flat is folded, the 32 or 64 pages will be in the proper order. This placement method is known as *imposition*.) To make this examination process easier, the lineup tables are equipped with a fluorescent light that shines up through the negatives, so it is easier for the stripper to read and align the text.

Blueprints

6 To make sure the book is progressing properly, a proof of each flat is made by shining ultraviolet light through the negatives to expose their images onto a special light-sensitive paper. The resulting pages are called *blueprints* (or silverprints, bluelines, or dyluxes) because the paper and ink are blue or silver in appearance. The blueprints are then checked carefully by the publisher. If an editor or art director finds an error on a blueprint or decides to make a change, the page in question has to be rephotographed. The new negative will then be stripped onto the flat.

Plate making

7 After final approval, each flat is photographed, with the negatives being exposed onto (or "burned" onto) a thin sheet of aluminum called a *plate*. The sections of the plates that contain text and illustrations are then treated with a chemical that attracts ink, thereby ensuring that the text and illustrations will print when on press.

Printing

8 The plates are then sent to press. If printing in only one color, each plate will require only one pass through the press. If printing more than one color, an additional pass will be required for each color. For example, if two colors are used, the paper is fed through the press twice.

There are three main printing processes used in book production: *offset lithography, letterpress*, and *gravure*. The process used depends less on quality differences than on economic factors such as availability of

Printing is often done on an offset lithography printing press, in which the paper is fed through rolls that are exposed to the proper ink. If colored ink is necessary, either for text or for photographs, each of the four major colors is offset onto its own set of rollers.

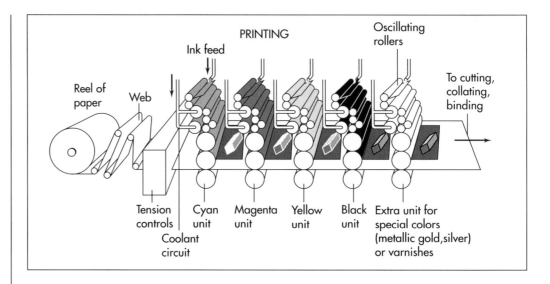

machines, number of books being printed (the print run), and the speed of delivery. Presses are either *sheet-fed* (single sheets of paper are fed through) or *web-fed* (huge rolls of paper are unwound and run through).

Binding

9 After the sheets are printed and dry, they are delivered to the bindery. While many large printing companies have their own binderies, other smaller printers must send the printed sheets to a outside bindery. At the bindery, the flats are folded and collated into book *signatures*—properly folded 32- or 64-page sections—that are then bound in proper sequence. All of these functions are automated.

10 Book binding also involves sewing the signatures together, gluing the spine, and inserting lining and trimming the edges. The amount and type of binding depends on the type of book (paperback or hardback) and its size. In the final step, the book is "cased in," or enclosed in a cover.

Quality Control

To help ensure that a quality product is produced, print shops conduct a number of periodic checks. In addition to checking blueprints for accuracy, printers will pull a press proof, or sample, before the print run is begun. If certain areas of the proof are too light or too dark, adjustments to the press may be required.

After the book signatures are sewn together, the print shop will spot-check them to make sure they have been folded and sewn correctly. They will also check to see if the book covers are properly bound to prevent the books from deteriorating with use.

Some of the instruments used to control quality include *densitometers* and *colorimeters*, both of which are used to evaluate color printing processes; *paper hygroscopes*, which measure the moisture balance of paper against the relative humidity of printing rooms; and *inkometers*, which measure the quality of the ink to be used in printing.

The Future

Book production has remained much the same since the early twentieth century, except for changes in typesetting. While dedicated typesetting machines (linotype or monotype) have been standard equipment in print shops and typesetting businesses since 1900, desktop publishing on microcomputers has become a cost-effective alternative. With the proper typesetting software and a laser printer, users can generate text, insert graphics, and create layouts and page designs that are as sophisticated and detailed as those produced by traditional typesetting machines. As a result, authors, publishers, print shops, and virtually any other business have been able to set type and perform page layout and design on microcomputers. Furthermore, depending on the resolution and quality of the laser printer, users can create type that a printer can use to shoot a negative. Such type is referred to as camera-ready.

In addition, desktop publishing accessories such as scanners and graphics software allow

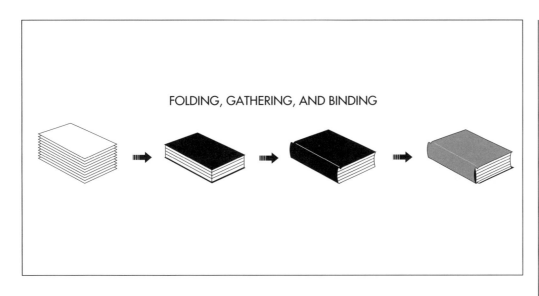

FOLDING, GATHERING, AND BINDING

After printing, the sections of the book—in 32- or 64-page pieces—are folded properly, sewn together, and bound with the book jacket or cover. All of these steps are automated.

users to insert still more computer graphics and scan in photographs, hard-copy graphics, and text into their desktop system.

For book production, many authors, publishers, and design shops now have their own desktop publishing equipment, allowing them to give printers camera-ready copy. If they do not have laser printers with sufficient print-quality resolution, they can simply give the printer the book in disk form and have the printer run the type out on a laser printer with high resolution. Either way, desktop publishing gives the user more design control and cuts down on production costs.

Because desktop publishing is relatively new, changes and enhancements continue to make the systems more user-friendly. As more people gain access to such systems, book publication and publishing in general will see more widespread use of desktop publishing in the future.

Where To Learn More

Books

Foot, Miriam. *Studies in the History of Bookbinding*. Ashgate Publishing Co., 1992.

Harrison, Thomas. *The Bookbinding Craft & Industry*. Garland Publishing, Inc., 1990.

Hollick, Richard. *Book Manufacturing*. Cambridge University Press, 1986.

Lyman, Ralph. *Binding & Finishing*. Graphic Arts Technical Foundation, 1993.

Matthews, Brander. *Bookbinding Old & New*. Garland Publishing, Inc., 1990.

McMurtrie, Douglas C. *The Book: Story of Printing & Bookmaking*. Dorset Press, 1990.

Pocket Pal: A Graphic Arts Production Handbook. International Paper, 14th ed., 1989.

Poynter, Dan. *Book Production: Composition, Layout, Editing & Design—Getting It Ready for Printing*, 3rd ed. Para Publishing, 1992.

Periodicals

Angstadt, Richard. "Why Typesetting Isn't as Good as It Should Be: An Experienced Typesetter Laments the Communications Problems in a Changing Industry," *Publishers Weekly*. September 7, 1990, p. 60.

Monkerud, Don. "Plate Full of Promises: Direct-to-Plate Technology Offers Faster and Cheaper Short-Run Color Printing," *Publish*. January, 1993, p. 48.

—Greg Ling

Brick

Modern bricks are seldom solid. Some are pressed into shape, which leaves a frog, or depression, on their top surface. Others are extruded with holes that will later expedite the firing process by exposing a larger amount of surface area to heat. Both techniques lessen weight without reducing strength.

Background

The term brick refers to small units of building material, often made from fired clay and secured with mortar, a bonding agent comprising of cement, sand, and water. Long a popular material, brick retains heat, withstands corrosion, and resists fire. Because each unit is small—usually four inches wide and twice as long, brick is an ideal material for structures in confined spaces, as well as for curved designs. Moreover, with minimal upkeep, brick buildings generally last a long time.

For the above-cited practical reasons and because it is also an aesthetically pleasing medium, brick has been used as a building material for at least 5,000 years. The first brick was probably made in the Middle East, between the Tigris and Euphrates rivers in what is now Iraq. Lacking the stone their contemporaries in other regions used for permanent structures, early builders here relied on the abundant natural materials to make their sun-baked bricks. These, however, were of limited use because they lacked durability and could not be used outdoors; exposure to the elements caused them to disintegrate. The Babylonians, who later dominated Mesopotamia, were the first to fire bricks, from which many of their tower-temples were constructed.

From the Middle East the art of brickmaking spread west to what is now Egypt and east to Persia and India. Although the Greeks, having a plentiful supply of stone, did not use much brick, evidence of brick kilns and structures remains throughout the Roman Empire. However, with the decline and fall of Rome, brickmaking in Europe soon diminished. It did not resume until the 1200s, when the Dutch made bricks that they seem to have exported to England. In the Americas, people began to use brick during the sixteenth century. It was the Dutch, however, who were considered expert craftsmen.

Prior to the mid-1800s, people made bricks in small batches, relying on relatively inefficient firing methods. One of the most widely used was an open clamp, in which bricks were placed on a fire beneath a layer of dirt and used bricks. As the fire died down over the course of several weeks, the bricks fired. Such methods gradually became obsolete after 1865, when the Hoffmann kiln was invented in Germany. Better suited to the manufacture of large numbers of bricks, this kiln contained a series of compartments through which stacked bricks were transferred for pre-heating, burning, and cooling.

Brickmaking improvements have continued into the twentieth century. Improvements include rendering brick shape absolutely uniform, lessening weight, and speeding up the firing process. For example, modern bricks are seldom solid. Some are pressed into shape, which leaves a *frog*, or depression, on their top surface. Others are extruded with holes that will later expedite the firing process by exposing a larger amount of surface area to heat. Both techniques lessen weight without reducing strength.

However, while the production process has definitely improved, the market for brick has not. Brick does have the largest share of the opaque materials market for commercial building, and it continues to be used as a siding material in the housing industry. However, other siding materials such as

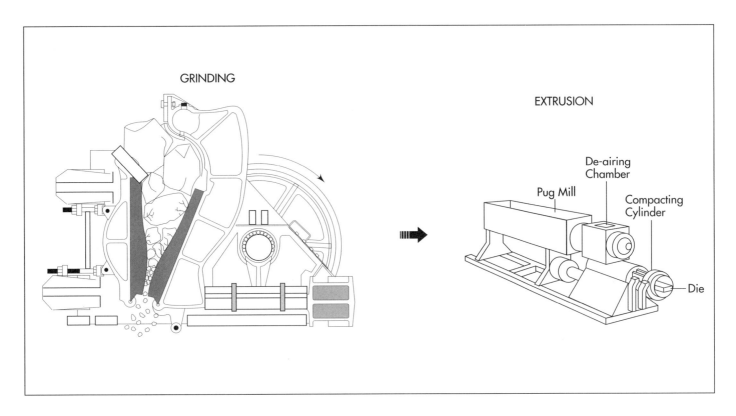

GRINDING

EXTRUSION

De-airing Chamber

Pug Mill

Compacting Cylinder

Die

wood, stucco, aluminum, plaster, and vinyl are strong competitors because they cost up to 50 percent less, and some (notably stucco and plaster) offer built-in insulation. Yet these systems can cost up to 1.75 times that of brick, which also requires less maintenance. Other materials that compete with brick despite their usually higher cost include precast **concrete** panels, glass, stone, artificial stone, concrete masonry, and combinations of these materials, because advances in manufacturing and design have made such materials more attractive to the builder. According to the U.S. Industrial Outlook, the use of brick as a siding material for single-family homes dropped from 26 percent in 1984 to 17 percent in 1989.

Raw Materials

Natural clay minerals, including kaolin and shale, make up the main body of brick. Small amounts of manganese, barium, and other additives are blended with the clay to produce different shades, and barium carbonate is used to improve brick's chemical resistance to the elements. Many other additives have been used in brick, including byproducts from papermaking, ammonium compounds, wetting agents, *flocculents* (which cause particles to form loose clusters) and *deflocculents* (which disperse such clusters).

Some clays require the addition of sand or *grog* (pre-ground, pre-fired material such as scrap brick).

A wide variety of coating materials and methods are used to produce brick of a certain color or surface texture. To create a typical coating, sand (the main component) is mechanically mixed with some type of colorant. Sometimes a *flux* or *frit* (a glass containing colorants) is added to produce surface textures. The flux lowers the melting temperature of the sand so it can bond to the brick surface. Other materials including graded fired and unfired brick, nepheline syenite, and graded aggregate can be used as well.

The Manufacturing Process

The initial step in producing brick is crushing and grinding the raw materials in a separator and a jaw crusher. Next, the blend of ingredients desired for each particular batch is selected and filtered before being sent on to one of three brick shaping processes—extrusion, molding, or pressing, the first of which is the most adaptable and thus the most common. Once the bricks are formed and any subsequent procedures performed, they are dried to remove excess moisture that might

To produce brick, the raw materials are first crushed and ground in a jaw crusher. Next, the ingredients are formed using one of several methods. In extrusion, the pulverized ingredients are mixed togther with water, passed into a de-airing chamber (which removes the air to prevent cracking), compacted, and extruded out of a die of the desired shape.

otherwise cause cracking during the ensuing firing process. Next, they are fired in ovens and then cooled. Finally, they are dehacked—automatically stacked, wrapped with steel bands, and padded with plastic corner protectors.

Grinding, sizing, and combining raw materials

1 First, each of the ingredients is conveyed to a separator that removes oversize material. A jaw crusher with horizontal steel plates then squeezes the particles, rendering them still smaller. After the raw materials for each batch of bricks have been selected, a scalping screen is often used to separate the different sizes of material. Material of the correct size is sent to storage silos, and oversized material goes to a hammermill, which pulverizes it with rapidly moving steel hammers. The hammermill uses another screen to control the maximum size of particle leaving the mill, and discharge goes to a number of vibrating screens that separate out material of improper size before it is sent on to the next phase of production.

Extrusion

2 With extrusion, the most common method of brick forming, pulverized material and water are fed into one end of a *pug mill*, which uses knives on a rotating shaft to cut through and fold together material in a shallow chamber. The blend is then fed into an extruder at the far end of the mill. The extruder usually consists of two chambers. The first removes air from the ground clay with a vacuum, thereby preventing cracking and other defects. The second chamber, a high-pressure cylinder, compacts the material so the auger can extrude it through the die. After it is compressed, the plastic material is forced out of the chamber though a specially shaped die orifice. The cross-section of the extruded column, called the "pug," is formed into the shape of the die. Sections of desired length are cut to size with rotating knives or stiff wires.

In molding, soft, wet clay is shaped in a mold, usually a wooden box. The interior of the box is often coated with sand, which provides the desired texture and facilitates removing the formed brick from the mold. Water can also be used to assist release.

Pressing, the third type of brick forming, requires a material with low water content. The material is placed in a die and then compacted with a steel plunger set at a desired pressure. More regular in shape and sharper in outline than brick made with the other two methods, pressed bricks also feature frogs.

Chamfering the brick

3 Chamfering machines were developed to produce a furrow in brick for such applications as paving. These machines use rollers to indent the brick as it is being extruded. They are sometimes equipped with wire cutters to do the chamfering and cutting in one step. Such machines can produce as many as 20,000 units per hour.

Coating

4 The choice of sand coating, also applied as the brick is extruded, depends on how soft or hard the extruded material is. A continuous, vibrating feeder is used to coat soft material, whereas for textured material the coating may have to be brushed or rolled on. For harder materials a pressure roller or compressed air is used, and, for extremely hard materials, sand blasting is required.

Drying

5 Before the brick is fired, it must be dried to remove excess moisture. If this moisture is not removed, the water will burn off too quickly during firing, causing cracking. Two types of dryers are used. Tunnel dryers use cars to move the brick through humidity-controlled zones that prevent cracking. They consist of a long chamber through which the ware is slowly pushed. External sources of fan-circulated hot air are forced into the dryer to speed the process.

6 Automatic chamber dryers are also used, especially in Europe. The extruded bricks are automatically placed in rows on two parallel bars. The bricks are then fed onto special racks with finger-like devices that hold several pairs of bars in multiple layers. These racks are then transferred by rail-mounted transfer cars or by lift trucks into the dryers.

Firing

7 After drying, the brick is loaded onto cars (usually automatically) and fired to

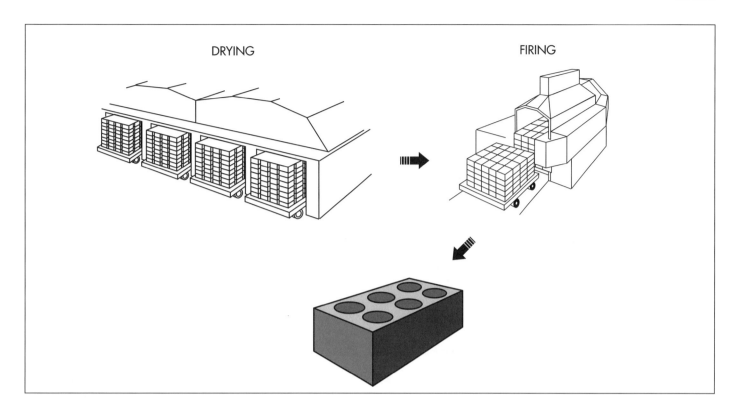

DRYING

FIRING

high temperatures in furnaces called kilns. In general, the cars that moved the bricks through the drying process are also used to convey them through the tunnel kiln. These cars are pushed through the kiln's continuously maintained temperature zones at a specific rate that depends on the material. The majority of kilns in the United States use gas as a fuel source, though a third of the brick currently produced is fired using solid fuels such as sawdust and coal. Tunnel kilns have changed in design from high-load, narrow-width kilns to shorter, lower-set wider kilns that can fire more brick. This type of design has also led to high-velocity, long-flame, and low-temperature flame burners, which have improved temperature uniformity and lowered fuel consumption.

Setting and packaging

8 After the brick is fired and cooled, it is unloaded from the kiln car via the dehacking process, which has been automated to the point where almost all manual brickhandling is eliminated. Automated setting machines have been developed that can set brick at rates of over 18,000 per hour and can rotate the brick 180 degrees. Usually set in rows eleven bricks wide, a stack is wrapped with steel bands and fitted with plastic strips that serve as corner protectors.

The packaged brick is then shipped to the job site, where it is typically unloaded using boom trucks.

Quality Control

Though the brick industry is often considered unsophisticated, many manufacturers are participating in total quality management and statistical control programs. The latter involves establishing control limits for a certain process (such as temperature during drying or firing) and tracking the parameter to make sure the relevant processes are kept within the limits. Therefore, the process can be controlled as it happens, preventing defects and improving yields.

A variety of physical and mechanical properties must be measured and must comply with standards set by the American Society of Testing and Materials (ASTM). These properties include physical dimensions, density, and mechanical strength. Another important property is freeze-thaw durability, where the brick is tested under conditions that are supposed to simulate what is encountered in the outdoors. However, current tests are inadequate and do not really correlate to actual conditions. What passes in the laboratory may not pass in the field. Therefore, the

After forming and coating, the bricks are dried using either tunnel dryers or automatic chamber dryers. Next, bricks are loaded onto cars automatically and moved into large furnaces called tunnel kilns. Firing hardens and strengthens the brick. After cooling, the bricks are set and packaged.

brick industry is trying to develop a more accurate test.

A similar problem exists with a condition known as *efflorescence*, which occurs when water dissolves certain elements (salt is among the most common) in exterior sources, mortar, or the brick itself. The residual deposits of soluble material produce surface discoloration that can be worsened by improper cleaning. When salt deposits become insoluble, the efflorescence worsens, requiring extensive cleaning. Though a brick may pass the laboratory test, it could fail in the field due to improper design or building practices. Therefore, brick companies are developing their own in-house testing procedures, and research is continuing to develop a more reliable standard test.

The Future

Currently, the use of brick has remained steady, at around seven to nine billion a year, down from the 15 billion used annually during the early 1900s. In an effort to increase demand, the brick industry continues to explore alternative markets and to improve quality and productivity. Fuel efficiency has also improved, and by the year 2025 brick manufacturers may even be firing their brick with solar energy. However, such changes in technology will occur only if there is still a demand for brick.

Even if this demand continues, the brick industry both here and abroad faces another challenge: it will soon be forced to comply with environmental regulations, especially in the area of fluorine emissions. Fluorine, a by-product of the brickmaking process, is a highly reactive element that is dangerous to humans. Long-term exposure can cause kidney and liver damage, digestive problems, and changes in teeth and bones, and the Environmental Protection Agency (EPA) has consequently established maximum exposure limits. To lessen the dangers posed by fluorine emissions, brickworks can install scrubbers, but they are expensive. While some plants have already installed such systems, the U.S. brick industry is trying to play a more important role in developing less expensive emissions testing methods and establishing emission limits. If the brick industry cannot persuade federal regulators to lower their requirements, it is quite possible that the industry could shrink in size, as some companies cannot afford to comply and will go out of business.

Where To Learn More

Books

Bender, Willi and Frank Handle. *Brick and Tile Making.* Bauverlag GmbH, 1985.

Jones, J. T. and M. F. Berard. *Ceramics: Industrial Processing and Testing.* Iowa State University Press, 1972.

Robinson, Gilbert C. *Ceramics and Glasses.* ASM International, 1992, pp. 943-950.

Periodicals

"Trends in Brick Plant Operations," *The American Ceramic Society Bulletin.* 1992, pp. 69-74.

Hall, Alvin. "Using Computer-Aided Manufacturing to Build Better Brick," *The American Ceramic Society Bulletin.* 1990, pp. 80-82.

Richards, Robert W. "Brick Manufacturing from Past to Present," *The American Ceramic Society Bulletin.* May, 1990, pp. 807-813.

Sheppard, Laurel M. "Making Brick and Meeting Regulations," *The American Ceramic Society Bulletin.* 1993.

"Lodge Lane Brickworks: A Breakthrough in the Reduction Firing of Bricks," *Ziegelindustrie.* September, 1992, pp. 344-341.

— *L. S. Millberg*

Bulletproof Vest

Background

Bulletproof vests are modern light armor specifically designed to protect the wearer's vital organs from injury caused by firearm projectiles. To many protective armor manufacturers and wearers, the term "bulletproof vest" is a misnomer. Because the wearer is not totally safe from the impact of a bullet, the preferred term for the article is "bullet resistant vest."

Over the centuries, different cultures developed body armor for use during combat. Mycenaeans of the sixteenth century B.C. and Persians and Greeks around the fifth century B.C. used up to fourteen layers of linen, while Micronesian inhabitants of the Gilbert and Ellice Islands used woven coconut palm fiber until the nineteenth century. Elsewhere, armor was made from the hides of animals: the Chinese—as early as the eleventh century B.C.—wore rhinoceros skin in five to seven layers, and the Shoshone Indians of North America also developed jackets of several layers of hide that were glued or sewn together. Quilted armor was available in Central America before Cortes, in England in the seventeenth century, and in India until the nineteenth century.

Mail armor comprised linked rings or wires of iron, steel, or brass and was developed as early as 400 B.C. near the Ukrainian city of Kiev. The Roman Empire utilized mail shirts, which remained the main piece of armor in Europe until the fourteenth century. Japan, India, Persia, Sudan, and Nigeria also developed mail armor. *Scale armor*, overlapping scales of metal, horn, bone, leather, or scales from an appropriately scaled animal (such as the scaly anteater), was used throughout the Eastern Hemisphere from about 1600 B.C. until modern times. Sometimes, as in China, the scales were sewn into cloth pockets.

Brigandine armor—sleeveless, quilted jackets—consisted of small rectangular iron or steel plates riveted onto leather strips that overlapped like roof tiles. The result was a relatively light, flexible jacket. (Earlier coats of plates in the twelfth-century Europe were heavier and more complete. These led to the familiar full-plate suit of armor of the 1500s and 1600s.) Many consider brigandine armor the forerunner of today's bulletproof vests. The Chinese and Koreans had similar armor around A.D. 700, and during the fourteenth century in Europe, it was the common form of body armor. One piece of breastplate within a cover became the norm after 1360, and short brigandine coats with plates that were tied into place prevailed in Europe until 1600.

With the introduction of firearms, armor crafts workers at first tried to compensate by reinforcing the *cuirass*, or torso cover, with thicker steel plates and a second heavy plate over the breastplate, providing some protection from guns. Usually, though, cumbersome armor was abandoned wherever firearms came into military use.

Experimental inquiry into effective armor against gunfire continued, most notably during the American Civil War, World War I, and World War II, but it was not until the plastics revolution of the 1940s that effective bulletproof vests became available to law enforcers, military personnel, and others. The vests of the time were made of ballistic nylon and supplemented by plates of fiberglass, steel, ceramic, titanium, Doron, and composites of ceramic and fiberglass, the last being the most effective.

Ballistic nylon was the standard cloth used for bulletproof vests until the 1970s. In 1965, Stephanie Kwolek, a chemist at Du Pont, invented *Kevlar*, trademark for poly-para-phenylene terephthalamide, a liquid polymer that can be spun into aramid fiber and woven into cloth. Originally, Kevlar was developed for use in **tire**s, and later for such diverse products as ropes, gaskets, and various parts for planes and boats. In 1971, Lester Shubin of the National Institute of Law Enforcement and Criminal Justice advocated its use to replace bulky ballistic nylon in bulletproof vests. Kevlar has been the standard material since. In 1989, the Allied Signal Company developed a competitor for Kevlar and called it *Spectra*. Originally used for sail cloth, the polyethylene fiber is now used to make lighter, yet stronger, nonwoven material for use in bulletproof vests alongside the traditional Kevlar.

Raw Materials

A bulletproof vest consists of a panel, a vest-shaped sheet of advanced plastics polymers that is composed of many layers of either Kevlar, Spectra Shield, or, in other countries, *Twaron* (similar to Kevlar) or *Bynema* (similar to Spectra). The layers of woven Kevlar are sewn together using Kevlar thread, while the nonwoven Spectra Shield is coated and bonded with resins such as Kraton and then sealed between two sheets of polyethylene film.

The panel provides protection but not much comfort. It is placed inside of a fabric shell that is usually made from a polyester/cotton blend or nylon. The side of the shell facing the body is usually made more comfortable by sewing a sheet of some absorbent material such as *Kumax* onto it. A bulletproof vest may also have nylon padding for extra protection. For bulletproof vests intended to be worn in especially dangerous situations, built-in pouches are provided to hold plates made from either metal or ceramic bonded to fiberglass. Such vests can also provide protection in car accidents or from stabbing.

Various devices are used to strap the vests on. Sometimes the sides are connected with elastic webbing. Usually, though, they are secured with straps of either cloth or elastic, with metallic buckles or velcro closures.

The Manufacturing Process

Some bulletproof vests are custom-made to meet the customer's protection needs or size. Most, however, meet standard protection regulations, have standard clothing industry sizes (such as 38 long, 32 short), and are sold in quantity.

Making the panel cloth

1 To make Kevlar, the polymer poly-para-phenylene terephthalamide must first be produced in the laboratory. This is done through a process known as *polymerization*, which involves combining molecules into long chains. The resultant crystalline liquid with polymers in the shape of rods is then extruded through a spinneret (a small metal plate full of tiny holes that looks like a shower head) to form Kevlar yarn. The Kevlar fiber then passes through a cooling bath to help it harden. After being sprayed with water, the synthetic fiber is wound onto rolls. The Kevlar manufacturer then typically sends the fiber to throwsters, who twist the yarn to make it suitable for weaving. To make Kevlar cloth, the yarns are woven in the simplest pattern, plain or tabby weave, which is merely the over and under pattern of threads that interlace alternatively.

2 Unlike Kevlar, the Spectra used in bulletproof vests is usually not woven. Instead, the strong polyethylene polymer filaments are spun into fibers that are then laid parallel to each other. Resin is used to coat the fibers, sealing them together to form a sheet of Spectra cloth. Two sheets of this cloth are then placed at right angles to one another and again bonded, forming a nonwoven fabric that is next sandwiched between two sheets of polyethylene film. The vest shape can then be cut from the material.

Cutting the panels

3 Kevlar cloth is sent in large rolls to the bulletproof vest manufacturer. The fabric is first unrolled onto a cutting table that must be long enough to allow several panels to be cut out at a time; sometimes it can be as

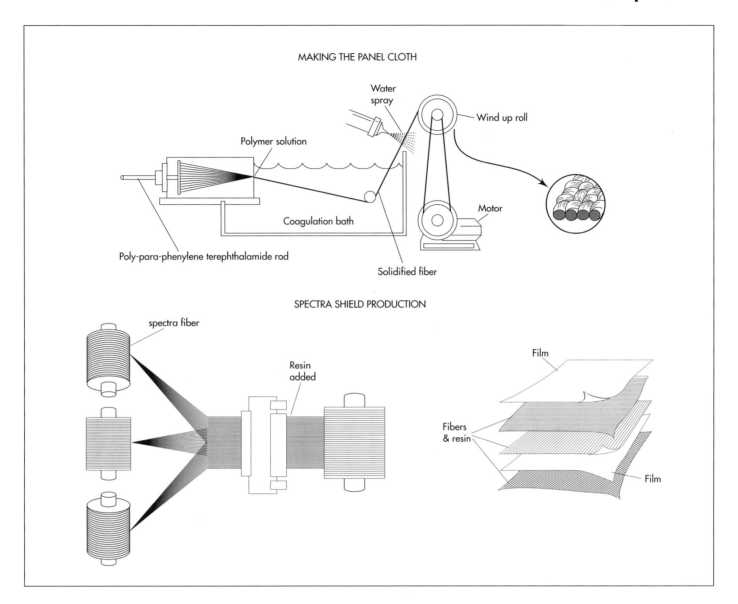

MAKING THE PANEL CLOTH

Water spray
Wind up roll
Polymer solution
Motor
Coagulation bath
Poly-para-phenylene terephthalamide rod
Solidified fiber

SPECTRA SHIELD PRODUCTION

spectra fiber
Resin added
Film
Fibers & resin
Film

long as 32.79 yards (30 meters). As many layers of the material as needed (as few as eight layers, or as many as 25, depending on the level of protection desired) are laid out on the cutting table.

4 A cut sheet, similar to pattern pieces used for home sewing, is then placed on the layers of cloth. For maximum use of the material, some manufacturers use computer graphics systems to determine the optimal placement of the cut sheets.

5 Using a hand-held machine that performs like a jigsaw except that instead of a cutting wire it has a 5.91-inch (15-centimeter) cutting wheel similar to that on the end of a pizza cutter, a worker cuts around the cut sheets to form panels, which are then placed in precise stacks.

Sewing the panels

6 While Spectra Shield generally does not require sewing, as its panels are usually just cut and stacked in layers that go into tight fitting pouches in the vest, a bulletproof vest made from Kevlar can be either quilt-stitched or box-stitched. Quilt-stitching forms small diamonds of cloth separated by stitching, whereas box stitching forms a large single box in the middle of the vest. Quilt-stitching is more labor intensive and difficult, and it provides a stiff panel that is hard to shift away from vulnerable areas. Box-stitching, on the other hand, is fast and easy and allows the free movement of the vest.

7 To sew the layers together, workers place a stencil on top of the layers and rub chalk on the exposed areas of the panel,

Kevlar has long been the most widely used material in bulletproof vests. To make Kevlar, the polymer solution is first produced. The resulting liquid is then extruded from a spinneret, cooled with water, stretched on rollers, and wound into cloth.

A recent competitor to Kevlar is Spectra Shield. Unlike Kevlar, Spectra Shield is not woven but rather spun into fibers that are then laid parallel to each other. The fibers are coated with resin and layered to form the cloth.

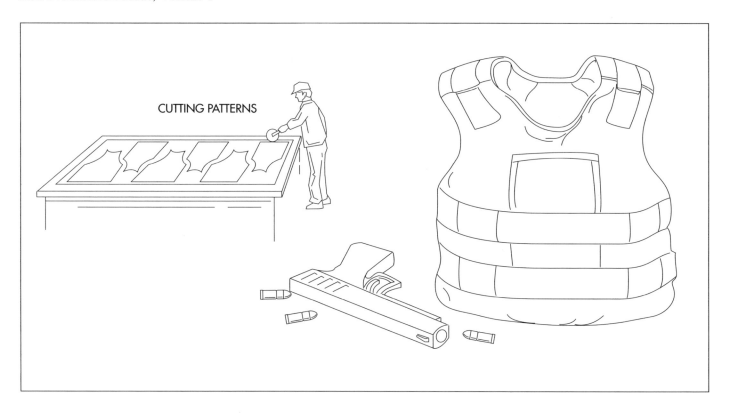

CUTTING PATTERNS

After the cloth is made, it must be cut into the proper pattern pieces. These pieces are then sewn together with accessories (such as straps) to form the finished vest.

making a dotted line on the cloth. A sewer then stitches the layers together, following the pattern made by the chalk. Next, a size label is sewn onto the panel.

Finishing the vest

8 The shells for the panels are sewn together in the same factory using standard industrial sewing machines and standard sewing practices. The panels are then slipped inside the shells, and the accessories—such as the straps—are sewn on. The finished bulletproof vest is boxed and shipped to the customer.

Quality Control

Bulletproof vests undergo many of the same tests a regular piece of clothing does. The fiber manufacturer tests the fiber and yarn tensile strength, and the fabric weavers test the tensile strength of the resultant cloth. Nonwoven Spectra is also tested for tensile strength by the manufacturer. Vest manufacturers test the panel material (whether Kevlar or Spectra) for strength, and production quality control requires that trained observers inspect the vests after the panels are sewn and the vests completed.

Bulletproof vests, unlike regular clothing, must undergo stringent protection testing as required by the National Institute of Justice (NIJ). Not all bulletproof vests are alike. Some protect against lead bullets at low velocity, and some protect against full metal jacketed bullets at high velocity. Vests are classified numerically from lowest to highest protection: I, II-A, II, III-A, III, IV, and special cases (those for which the customer specifies the protection needed). Each classification specifies which type of bullet at what velocity will not penetrate the vest. While it seems logical to choose the highest-rated vests (such as III or IV), such vests are heavy, and the needs of a person wearing one might deem a lighter vest more appropriate. For police use, a general rule suggested by experts is to purchase a vest that protects against the type of firearm the officer normally carries.

The size label on a vest is very important. Not only does it include size, model, style, manufacturer's logo, and care instructions as regular clothing does, it must also include the protection rating, lot number, date of issue, an indication of which side should face out, a serial number, a note indicating it meets NIJ approval standards, and—for type I through type III-A vests—a large warning that the vest will not protect the wearer from sharp instruments or rifle fire.

Bulletproof vests are tested both wet and dry. This is done because the fibers used to make a vest perform differently when wet.

Testing (wet or dry) a vest entails wrapping it around a modeling clay dummy. A firearm of the correct type with a bullet of the correct type is then shot at a velocity suitable for the classification of the vest. Each shot should be three inches (7.6 centimeters) away from the edge of the vest and almost two inches from (five centimeters) away from previous shots. Six shots are fired, two at a 30-degree angle of incidence, and four at a 0-degree angle of incidence. One shot should fall on a seam. This method of shooting forms a wide triangle of bullet holes. The vest is then turned upside down and shot the same way, this time making a narrow triangle of bullet holes. To pass the test, the vest should show no sign of penetration. That is, the clay dummy should have no holes or pieces of vest or bullet in it. Though the bullet will leave a dent, it should be no deeper than 1.7 inches (4.4 centimeters).

When a vest passes inspections, the model number is certified and the manufacturer can then make exact duplicates of the vest. After the vest has been tested, it is placed in an archive so that in the future vests with the same model number can be easily checked against the prototype.

Rigged field testing is not feasible for bulletproof vests, but in a sense, wearers (such as police officers) test them everyday. Studies of wounded police officers have shown that bulletproof vests save hundreds of lives each year.

Where To Learn More

Books

Tarassuk, Leonid and Claude Blair, eds. *The Complete Encyclopedia of Arms and Weapons*. Simon and Schuster, 1979.

Periodicals

Anderson, Jack and Dale Van Atta. "Standoff Over Bullet-Proof Vest Standard," *Washington Post*. April 9, 1990, p. B-9.

Chapnick, Howard. "The Need for Body Armor," *Popular Photography*. November 1982, pp. 62+.

Faison, Seth, Jr. "Police Insist on Complete Vests," *New York Times*. September 15, 1991, p. 34.

Flanagan, William G., ed. "Arms and the Man," *Forbes*. July 6, 1981, p. 135.

Lappen, Alyssa A. "Step Aside, Superman," *Forbes*. February 6, 1989, pp. 124-126.

—*Rose Secrest*

Candle

In the United States, standard commercial candles usually contain 60 percent paraffin, 35 percent stearic acid, and 5 percent beeswax. Some candles contain small amounts of candelilla or carnauba waxes (from the carnauba palm) to regulate the softening or melting point of the finished wax.

Background

One of the earliest forms of portable illumination, candles have served vital functions for humankind throughout history, a fact chronicled through the discovery of candles or candle-like objects in virtually every society. Historians believe the original candle may have been invented by primitive men who dipped dried branches in animal fat, thus producing a slow-burning and reliable source of light. Reliefs belonging to the ancient Egyptians depict the use of candles by writers and philosophers who worked well after sundown. These early candles were most likely developed from tapers that were made of fibrous materials mixed with wax or tallow (the white, nearly tasteless fat of cattle or sheep that was also used to make soap, margarine, and lubricants). As far back as 3000 B.C., dish-shaped candles were used on the island of Crete.

Candles have also been used for religious purposes. The Bible, for instance, makes numerous references to the use of candles, including the story of King Solomon who, after building the Temple, used ten candlesticks to light the north and south ends of the structure. In the Middle Ages, candlemaking became a popular occupation, as evidenced by the creation of many candlemakers' guilds throughout Europe. Later, candles were used as a means of keeping time. At auctions, the bidding time was limited by inserting a pin into a candle and letting the wax melt until the pin dropped, thus concluding that period of time.

Although the materials that comprise a candle have changed through the years, the art of candlemaking has remained surprisingly similar to the original production processes.

Candle wicks were, at first, made of reeds or rushes; eventually, various natural fibers were used. In 1824, Frenchman Jean-Jacques Cambaracérès introduced an important refinement in wick technology with the plaited wick, which burned more evenly than unplaited wicks. Twisted or plaited cotton still makes up most wicks today.

Animal or vegetable fats were used for the first candles. As candlemaking technology progressed, beeswax became widely used, mainly because of its pleasing odor and the absence of the mess that melting fats produced.

After the Revolutionary War, the whaling industry in America skyrocketed. However, not every type of whale was cherished solely for its blubber. The sperm whale was also used for its spermaceti—the wax taken from the oil of this huge mammal. This wax was used extensively as the fishing industry began to expand. The spermaceti candle was popular because it had no acrid odor, did not soften in summer temperatures, and burned evenly. Ozokerite, a colorless mineral hydrocarbon wax with a high melting point, was also popular in the seventeenth and eighteenth centuries. As candle technology advanced, animal fats were separated, leaving behind more desirable solid fatty acids such as stearine that had no odor and gave a brighter light. Paraffin, a wax crystallized from petroleum, became popular during the 1860s and was eventually blended with spermaceti and ceresin—a byproduct of refined petroleum oil—to create a more durable wax.

The original candles were produced through the dipping method. Dating back to the Middle Ages, this method used wicks made

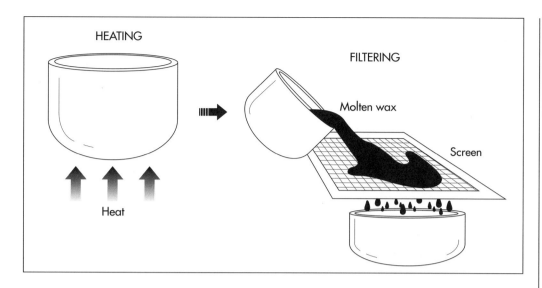

HEATING

FILTERING

Molten wax

Screen

Heat

After the wax base is heated into a clear, near-liquid state, it is filtered to remove any impurities that might interfere with the finished candle's burning process. Any dyes or perfumes are added at this time.

from dried rushes, which were peeled on all but one side, revealing the pith. The wicks were repeatedly dipped into the molten fat until the fat had stuck to the wick at a desired thickness. Beeswax candles were constructed using both the dipping method and pouring method. In the pouring method, the melted beeswax is poured over a suspended cotton wick while the wick is simultaneously and manually twirled. After a sufficient amount of wax has gathered at the bottom of the wick, the candled is reversed and poured from the other end.

Large-scale manufacture of candles became a reality only after 1834, when Joseph Morgan introduced the first mass-production candlemaking machine. Today's modern machines are strikingly similar to that original machine, with speed, accuracy and finished quality the only major differences.

Raw Materials

As mentioned earlier, the types of wax used in the construction of candles have changed greatly during the past few centuries. Today, substances are often mixed together to create stronger candles with higher melting points. In the United States, standard commercial candles usually contain 60 percent paraffin, 35 percent stearic acid, and 5 percent beeswax. Some candles contain small amounts of candelilla or carnauba waxes (from the carnauba palm) to regulate the softening or melting point of the finished wax. Beeswax candles are made of only pure insect wax and paraffin plus a small amount of stiffening wax. The wick is made of a high

grade of cotton or linen. The material is woven (or braided) so that it will burn in one direction and will curl so that its end remains in the candle flame's oxidizing zone for even and intense burning. Often, wire-core wicks are used. These wicks have a wire center that allows them to burn slightly hotter than cotton and remain erect in the melted wax.

Decorative candles often use waxes other than beeswax and paraffin. Bayberry wax (or wax myrtle, as it is sometimes referred to) is derived from the fruit of the bayberry bush and has a distinctive aroma making it especially popular for use at Christmas. Non-burning wax is used in those parts of a candle—mostly the shells or ornaments of decorative candles—that are not intended to burn.

The Manufacturing Process

The manufacturing of candles consists of three steps: preparation of the wicking, preparation of the wax base, and continuous molding or extrusion of the finished candles.

Making the wick

1 The cotton or linen wicks are braided and then treated with chemicals or inorganic salt solutions so that they bend at a 90 degree angle when burning. This angle allows the end to remain in the outer mantle of the flame and causes it to be shortened naturally. If the wick is not treated, it will burn too quickly and the flame will be extinguished by the melted wax. However, if the wick burns too

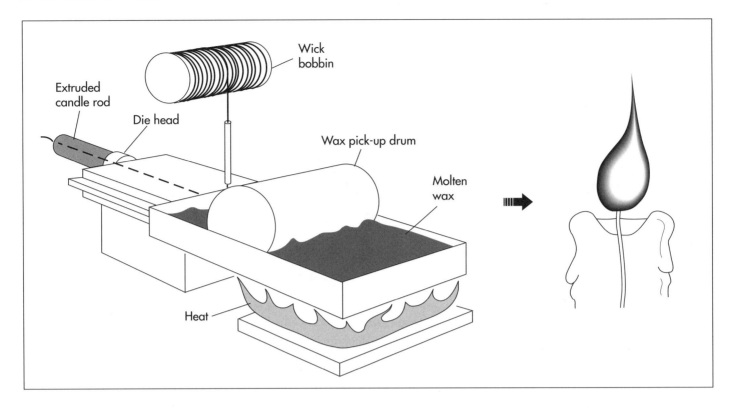

Extruded candle rod

Die head

Wick bobbin

Wax pick-up drum

Molten wax

Heat

One method of forming candles is to extrude the wax through a die of the desired shape. A wick bobbin feeds wick into the center of the mold so that the wax forms around the wick. Unlike molding, extrusion forms one continuous length of candle that must be cut into the proper sizes.

slowly, then the amount of exposed wick increases and the candle becomes dangerous.

Preparing the wax base

2 First, the wax is heated and melted into a clear, near-liquid state in huge metal kettles. Wax melted by direct flame can become dark-colored or can contain small pieces of carbon char. Next, the molten wax must be carefully filtered to remove impurities that may interfere with the burning process. Any desired perfumes and dyes are added at this time. Although most wax arriving at the manufacturer conforms to strict purity standards, many companies still filter their wax to be sure of a high-quality finished product.

Molding the candle

3 Since the invention of Morgan's first candlemaking machine, the construction of candles has been performed mainly by continuous molding machines, although manual machines are still used by some companies. Continuous molding machines are designed to make candles in groups ranging anywhere from 50 to 500 per load. The entire process takes almost 30 minutes per load.

4 Prior to the pouring of the wax, the wick is pulled through the tip of the mold.

This tip has a hole in it through which the wick passes from a spool located beneath the entire molding machine. The molds, which are made of tin, have polished interior surfaces and are slightly tapered for easier ejection of the finished candle.

5 The wax is cooled to slightly above its melting point and poured into a molding table located above the molds. The wax then works its way into each mold; the molds are pre-heated so the wax will flow evenly into them. After the wax is poured, a jacket around each mold is filled with cold water to speed up the solidification process. Once the wax has solidified, the finished candles are pulled upwards out of the molds, allowing the wicks to again thread through the molds in preparation for the next load of candles. The wicks are snipped, and the process begins again. Excess wax is trimmed, collected and re-used. The continuous molding process is used to make cylindrical, tapered or fluted candles as long as they can be easily ejected from the mold.

Extrusion

6 An alternate method uses extrusion, a process in which crushed paraffin wax is forced through a heated steel die under extreme pressure. At the same time, the wax is consolidated around the wick. Unlike molding machines, extrusion machines produce a continuous length of candle, which is then cut into specific sizes. Next, the tips of the candles are formed by rotation cutters, and the candles are sent to an automated packing machine.

Where To Learn More

Books

Constable, David. *Candlemaking*. Schwartz, Arthur & Co., Inc., 1993.

Millington, Deborah. *Tradition Candlemaking: Simple Methods of Manufacture*. Intermediate Technology Development Group of North America, 1992.

Shaw, Ray. *Candle Art*. William Morrow, 1973.

Taylor, Richard. *Beeswax Molding & Candle Making*. Linden Books, 1985.

Webster, William and Claire McMullen. *Contemporary Candlemaking*. Doubleday, 1972.

Webster, William and Claire McMullen. *The Complete Book of Candlemaking*. Doubleday, 1973.

Periodicals

Rupp, Becky. "The Art of Candle Making," *Blair & Ketchum's Country Journal*. January, 1986, p. 57.

—*Jim Acton*

Carbon Paper

A typical piece of carbon paper consists of a sheet of paper that has been impregnated with carbon and sandwiched between two sheets of regular paper.

Background

Carbon paper is an inexpensive reprographic device used to make a single copy concurrently with the original, as in credit card transaction receipts, legal documents, manuscripts, letters, and other simple forms.

Even up to the twentieth century, copying documents for business purposes was a difficult, labor-intensive process. Copy clerks, like the scribes of churches and government offices before them, were common in the business offices of the nineteenth century.

The first attempt at copying important business correspondence is attributed to the Scottish engineer James Watt, who improved the steam engine. Watt disliked trusting scribes to copy business letters, so he invented a method of pressing a tissue paper that had been moistened with special liquids onto an original, which had been written using special ink. By 1779, he was ready to market the process, but it didn't catch on.

In 1806 Ralph Wedgwood invented the Stylographic Manifold Writer. A paper saturated with printer's ink was placed between a piece of tissue paper and a piece of regular paper. A metal stylus then scratched an impression onto the tissue paper, creating a copy that read correctly and another that was a **mirror** image, though easily read through the thin tissue paper. It was necessary to prepare copies in this manner because the pens of the time (quills) couldn't press hard enough, and pencils could be erased. Around 1820 it became possible to use paper that had been inked on one side only and an indelible **pencil** to produce the original. This early carbon paper was not a huge success, appar-

ently because business owners, fearing forgery, preferred items written in ink.

In 1823 Cyrus P. Dakin began making carbons, papers coated with oil and carbon black. In the 1860s Lebbeus H. Rogers attempted to sell these carbons to businesses, but it wasn't until the invention of the typewriter in 1867 that carbon paper came to be accepted (typewriters produced a cleaner copy as well as a quality original). Rogers originally made carbon paper by placing paper on a stone table and slathering it with a mixture containing carbon black (soot), oil, and naphtha (a liquid hydrocarbon). Later he developed a machine that applied hot wax to the carbon paper, doing away with the manual brushing.

The production of carbon paper has stayed basically the same since Rogers's technological advances. In a quaint manufacturing tradebook put out around the turn of this century, carbon paper is described as consisting of various pigments, including carbon black, and wax or oils brushed onto thin, strong paper. While modern carbon paper is made using essentially the same formula, manufacturers have concentrated on increasing the cleanliness of the process and improving the quality of the reproduction by using more refined materials.

Raw Materials

A typical piece of carbon paper consists of a sheet of paper that has been impregnated with carbon and sandwiched between two sheets of regular paper. All components are standard, except for the coated sheet that performs the reprography. Its coating is made up of several materials, the most important of which is carbon black. Carbon black is a very

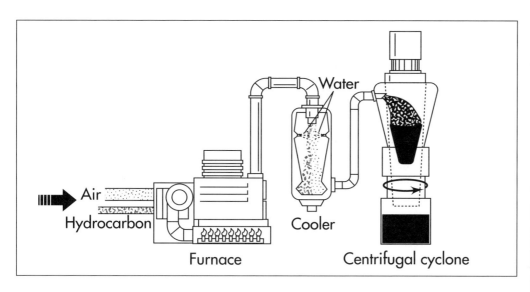

Air
Hydrocarbon
Furnace
Water
Cooler
Centrifugal cyclone

The key ingredient in carbon paper is carbon black. To make it, air and a hydrocarbon (such as petroleum oil) are fed into a furnace. In the furnace, part of the petroleum oil undergoes combustion, helping to raise the temperature up to 3,000 degrees Fahrenheit and causing the unburned hydrocarbon to decompose to carbon black. The carbon black is then cooled with water and recovered by putting in a centrifugal cyclone or bag filter.

fine, spherical, amorphous form of carbon that is not as crystalline as graphite. Mostly carbon, it also contains small amounts of oxygen, hydrogen, and sulfur. The carbon black adheres to the paper with the help of various waxes. Familiar one-time black carbon paper (the kind used for credit card receipts, for example) is coated with a mixture commonly composed of paraffin wax (33%), mineral oil (25%), carbon black (15%), china clay or kaolin (12%), montan wax (8%), carnauba wax (6%), and methyl violet or gentian violet (1%). Less common one-time blue carbon paper is commonly coated with a mixture composed of iron blue (21%), paraffin wax (20%), petrolatum (20%), mineral oil (15%), carnauba wax (10%), china clay (10%), and montan wax (4%).

Some carbon paper can be reused. This comes in handy for use in sales **book**s, for example, because only one sheet of carbon paper is needed to write out receipts for several sales. Reusable oil-soluble pencil carbon produces indelible copy. It is commonly coated with a mixture of talc (39%), carnauba wax (23%), lard oil (16%), oleic acid (15%), and victoria blue base (7%). Reusable pigment pencil carbon paper produces erasable copy. It is coated with a mixture that commonly consists of milori blue (25%), carnauba wax (20%), mineral oil (16%), amber petrolatum (11%), petrolatum (11%), toning iron blue (10%), and paraffin wax (7%). Typewriter carbon is also reusable, and because of the heavy striking force of the typewriter key, it uses higher quality carbon black and finer ingredients than one-time or pencil carbon paper. It is

commonly coated with an ink that consists of carnauba wax (32%), mineral oil (26%), carbon black (12%), amber petrolatum (6%), beeswax (5%), ouricury wax (5%), ozokerite wax (5%), oleic acid (3%), pigmented purple toner (3%), crystal violet dye (2%), and victoria blue base (1%). For further protection, it also has a backing wax composed of carnauba wax (40%), ouricury wax (40%), and microcrystalline wax (20%).

The Manufacturing Process

Carbon paper's most important ingredient, carbon black, has changed in recent years. Before 1940, 90 percent of the carbon black produced in the United States was made from channel or impingement carbon, where tiny jets of gas flame impinged (struck) onto a cool metallic surface, such as an iron channel (or groove). The resultant soot from the partial combustion was then scraped off, producing carbon particles of approximately 10^{-8} meters in diameter. This superb method of creating fine carbon black was abandoned in 1976, however, because of a large increase in the price of natural gas. The current method of producing carbon black uses the furnace process, described below. The finished carbon black is then coated onto paper using a series of offset rollers.

Making carbon black

1 A hydrocarbon (such as petroleum oil) and air are fed into a chamber. Part of the hydrocarbon undergoes incomplete combustion, raising the temperature inside the cham-

Two methods used to produce one-time carbon paper are the Mayer Method and the Flexographic Method. The two methods are similar in that both feature paper moving around a series of rolls, one of which contacts a carbon ink pan.

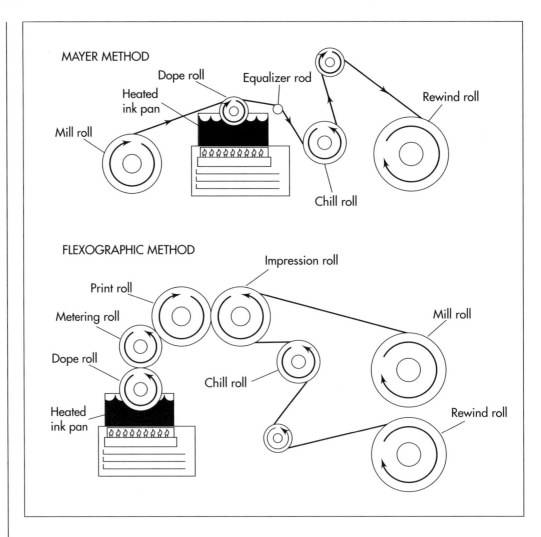

MAYER METHOD

Dope roll   Equalizer rod

Heated ink pan

Rewind roll

Mill roll

Chill roll

FLEXOGRAPHIC METHOD

Impression roll

Print roll

Metering roll

Mill roll

Dope roll

Chill roll

Heated ink pan

Rewind roll

ber to 2,012-3,092 degrees Fahrenheit (1100-1,700 degrees Celsius). At this temperature, the unburned hydrocarbon decomposes to carbon black.

2 The newly created carbon black is routed to a cooler, where it is sprayed with water. The fine black substance is then recovered using a centrifugal cyclone or a bag filter.

Making one-time carbon paper (Mayer method)

3 A large roll of coating paper (called the mill roll) unwinds and passes over another roll (the dope roll) sitting in a pan of carbon ink. The ink pan has been heated to between 168.8 and 179.6 degrees Fahrenheit (76 and 82 degrees Celsius). As the paper passes over this roll, the heated ink is transferred onto one side of the paper.

4 Next, the paper passes over an equalizer rod, which scrapes the coated paper to

smooth it out and remove excess ink. The equalizer rod may be either smooth or ridged. The paper then passes over another roll, the chill roll, which cools and solidifies the ink onto the paper. Finally, the completed paper is rewound onto another roll.

5 In the case of manifold business forms, the carbon paper is glued to another form, so the paper must have an uncoated strip without carbon where the adhesive can be applied. To accomplish this in the Mayer method, a strip of metal is simply placed in the proper place on the dope roll. This part of the roll thus picks up no ink from the ink pan to pass onto the paper.

Flexographic method

6 Another method, called the Flexographic method, can also be used to produce one-time carbon paper. First, a dope roll is coated with carbon ink from a heated pan below it. A metering roll contacts the dope roll and

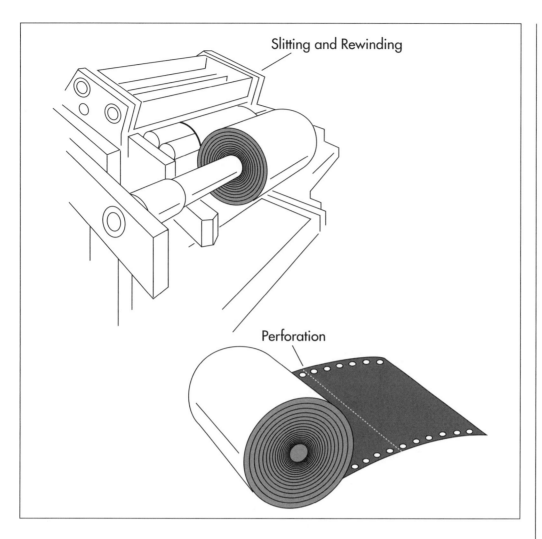

Slitting and Rewinding

Perforation

The final step in carbon paper man-ufacture is perforation. This is per-formed automatically by a spot carbonizer-processing machine and includes both the perforations between sheets of carbon paper and the tiny holes (produced by slit-ting) along the edges of the paper.

squeezes the ink to a uniform thickness. The ink is then transferred to a third roll, the print roll.

7 Meanwhile, the paper is fed from a mill roll onto an impression roll that contacts the print roll, the third roll mentioned in step #5 above. When these two rolls come into contact, ink from the print roll is passed onto the paper on the impression roll. The paper then passes over a chill roll that solidifies the ink, before being rolled onto the rewind roll. For manifold business forms being produced with the Flexographic method, a shallow groove is formed on the print roll. Where this groove contacts the paper on the impression roll, no ink gets transferred.

Perforation

8 The final stage in the manufacture of one-time carbon paper is perforation. First, the carbon and the printed forms are slitted while they are being collated. Next,

the huge rolls of carbon paper are cut into forms or sheets of the proper size. If neces-sary, line holes can also be punched into the paper. All of these operations are carried out automatically by a spot carbonizer-process-ing machine. Finally, the paper is stacked, boxed, and shipped to the customer.

Typewriter Carbon Paper

Typewriter carbon paper differs from one-time carbon paper in that it usually has an ink coating and backing wax, as well as printed material on the back. In this production method, a Flexographic set-up comprising a dope roll, metering roll, print roll, and impres-sion roll provides the means to print on the back of paper that has been supplied from a mill roll. After printing, the paper passes over a dope roll to receive a carbon ink coating that is smoothed with an equalizer rod as in the Mayer method. Next, the paper travels to a wax dope roll, which coats it with backing wax. As in the other methods, a chill roll then solidifies the wax. A felt buffing roll is sometimes used to improve the product's appearance before it is rolled onto a rewind roll.

Quality Control

The principle behind carbon paper is simple, yet producing it is difficult. A modern manufacturer of carbon paper tests all incoming raw materials for quality. A large number of tests can be applied to carbon black, including those for pigments and sulfur content. The carbon black selected should also be of fine particle size, which is determined by measuring the average diameter of a carbon black particle with an electron microscope. In addition, it should have low oil absorption, and the absorbency and pH of the carbon black are tested prior to use. The inks are tested for fineness of grain, which affects the final smoothness of the coating. The wax binder should penetrate only slightly into the paper and have the proper viscosity. To ensure proper lettering, the amount of wax released under pressure is tested. The paper itself should be smooth, nonporous, and free of surface defects. Although it must be a thin tissue, it should also be strong and dense. The finished carbon paper must be free of defects: no offset, flaking, wrinkles, or curl. It must work properly; the resultant copy must be clean and legible. The coating should be hard enough to meet its intended use; for example, one-time carbon doesn't require as hard a coating as typewriter carbon, which must also have a compounded coating of good color so it can be reused.

Other tests exist for finished carbon paper. To determine the amount of ink that was deposited, a specimen of carbon paper is selected and weighed. Its deposit of ink is then chemically removed before it is reweighed. The difference in weight indicates the amount of ink deposited. Curl is a frequent complaint about carbon paper, even though carbon paper is frequently coated on both sides (one side with the carbon, the other with backing wax) to combat the problem. To test for curl under different conditions, a piece of carbon paper is placed on a flat surface and, under controlled temperature, subjected to different humidities. The durability of reusable typewriter carbon paper is checked by repeatedly typing on one space until the carbon wears out. The cleanliness of both the copy and the carbon paper itself is important. To test the first, a document is typed and the copy is examined to see if it is clean. To test the second, the carbon side is rubbed with a clean, crumpled sheet of paper, which is then examined to see how much carbon has rubbed off. The color and thickness of the carbon must be inspected visually to see if they meet quality standards.

The Future

In 1991, over 62,000 metric tons of carbon paper were produced in the United States. However, during the same period, over 600,000 metric tons of carbonless transfer paper were manufactured. Ideal for handwritten records, carbonless paper utilizes chemically coated sheets that react under pressure, producing a colored image. Although carbonless paper weighs significantly more than carbon paper and is less suitable for typewritten and computerized records, its demand is increasing at the expense of carbon paper. (This demand for "regular" paper can also be attributed to the increasing availability of photocopiers.) It is likely that, as electronic communication becomes more prevalent, carbon paper will become obsolete. Presently, though, there is enough demand from businesses that utilize carbon paper for credit card receipts and computerized records to insure the survival of this simple, inexpensive product for some time to come.

Where To Learn More

Books

Casey, James P. *Chemistry and Chemical Technology*, Vol. IV, *Pulp and Paper*. John Wiley and Sons, 1983.

Mantell, Charles L. *Carbon and Graphite Handbook*. John Wiley and Sons, 1968.

The Manufacture of Pulp & Paper: Science & Engineering Concepts. Technical Association of the Pulp & Paper Industry, 1988.

Mosher, Robert H. and Dale S. Davis. *Industrial and Specialty Papers*, Vol. III: *Applications*. Chemical Publishing, 1969.

Proudfoot, W. B. *The Origin of Stencil Duplicating*. Hutchinson and Company, 1972.

—*Rose Secrest*

Cellophane Tape

Background

Cellophane tape consists of a backing to which an adhesive substance is affixed for the purpose of joining materials with a surface bond. Usually, a film of cellulose (a man-made textile fiber produced from plant matter) provides the backing for adherends made from chemically treated petroleum byproducts that create the tape's stickiness. Cellophane tape belongs to a family of adhesives known as pressure sensitive tapes: while other types of adhesives are activated by heat or water, pressure sensitive tapes adhere when only slight pressure is applied. These tapes are marketed primarily in the labeling industry, and includes such products as generic cellophane tape, masking tape, packing labels, and, perhaps the best known, transparent tape.

Early adhesives—the term denotes any substance used to join discrete materials by forming a surface attachment—were made from natural substances including tree pitch, beeswax, flour paste, and vegetable resins. These primitive glues were used extensively from ancient times through the Middle Ages, when more effective glues made from animal tissues were developed. During the nineteenth century, the introduction of rubber-based adhesives provided a still more effective alternative.

Pressure sensitive tapes were discovered during the mid-1800s, as scientists sought new applications for rubber. In 1845, Dr. Horace Day invented a rubber-based pressure sensitive tape for use in surgery. Because rubber possesses limited stickiness, the early adhesive tapes based on Day's invention required supplemental tackifying agents—oils and resins added to enhance adhesion.

The first adhesive tape was developed in the early twentieth century, due to a problem in the fledgling **automobile** industry. During the 1920s, when two-toned cars were popular, manufacturers had problems achieving a clean, crisp line between the two **paint** finishes. They tried using surgical tape but had problems because it did not form a proper seal and tended to lift off paint when it was removed. At that time, the Minnesota Mining and Manufacturing company (now better known as 3M) manufactured **sandpaper**. The firm entered the adhesive tape business when Richard Drew, a 3M lab worker who often visited the auto shops to test sandpaper, took on the challenge of finding a tape that would form a seal without damaging the car's paint when it was removed. The product Drew eventually devised, a rubber-based adhesive coated on a paper backing, resembled today's masking tape.

According to corporate legend, the brand name "Scotch tape" was coined when a prototype batch of Drew's tape received an adhesive coating only along its edges. This proved insufficient, prompting one irked painter to complain to his 3M sales rep about the company's "stingy Scotch bosses." Company executives seized upon the word "Scotch" because they hoped it would suggest that 3M tape was an economical product. After realizing that it would be necessary to coat the entire strip with adhesive, 3M began mass producing masking tape for auto painting and soon went on to make a transparent, or cellophane, tape for general consumer use. Transparent tape eventually became a household material used primarily to mend torn pages and wrap packages.

The development of synthetic resins and compounds after World War II made possible

While other types of adhesives are activated by heat or water, pressure sensitive tapes adhere when only slight pressure is applied. These tapes are marketed primarily in the labeling industry, and include such products as generic cellophane tape, masking tape, packing labels, and, perhaps the best known, transparent tape.

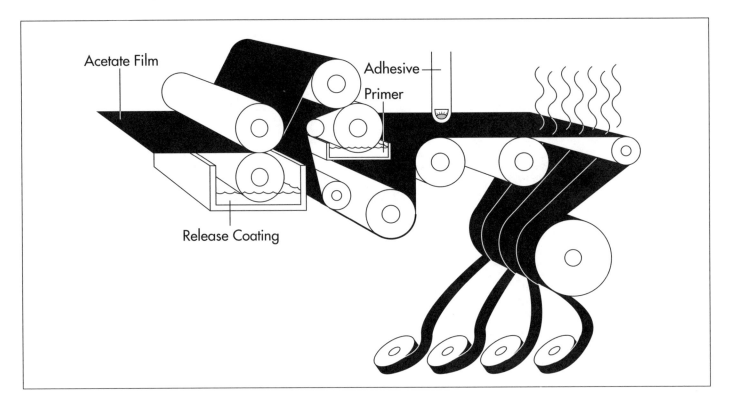

Acetate Film

Adhesive

Primer

Release Coating

Once the acetate film is produced, it is wound on large spools and loaded into a machine that applies the adhesive. The machine uses a series of rollers, much like a printing press. After the adhesive is applied, the film is heated and dried and then cut into individual strips that are packaged inside plastic dispensers.

great refinements of adhesive technology. Unlike Drew's invention, contemporary tape does not yellow or ooze adhesive as it ages. It can be written on, resists water, unwinds and rewinds easily, and is transparent. Today, more than 400 varieties of pressure sensitive tapes are manufactured. Some examples include electrical tape, masking tape, packaging tape, band aids, transparent tape and labels—all available in different sizes, widths, and, in some cases, shapes.

Raw Materials

While some pressure sensitive tapes are still prepared with natural rubber, the majority are now made using mostly synthetic materials. The backing for cellophane tape usually consists of cellulose acetate, a synthetic derivative of cellulose, which comes from wood pulp or cotton seeds. The cellulose is chemically treated with acetic acid and anhydride, and the side that won't receive an adhesive coating is treated with a release agent that enables the tape to be wound and unwound without sticking together. Although this compound varies among manufacturers, some commonly used substances include stearato chromic chloride and polystearic carbonate. Prior to the application of the adhesive, the adherend side of the backing may be primed with a solvent or aqueous dispersions such as nitrile rubber or

chlorinated rubber. To produce the final adhesive substance, some manufacturers use as many as 29 raw materials that go through various stages of production. However, the generic adherend is made up of acrylic resins, petroleum byproducts that are broken down into alcohols and acids before being fused into a polymer compound. This compound is then mixed with mineral spirits or a hydrocarbon solvent, creating an aqueous emulsion (a solution in which the microscopic resin particles are held suspended) that is applied to the backing.

The Manufacturing Process

Three separate manufacturing operations are necessary to produce a single roll of household pressure sensitive tape. First, the cellulose acetate backing is prepared, and then the adhesive is made. After the two materials are combined, the final product is cut into small batches for individual consumer use, inspected, packaged, and shipped.

Preparing the backing

1 First, wood pulp or cotton seeds are broken down into cellulose fibers through both physical crushing and chemical decomposition. Next, the raw cellulose fibers are treated

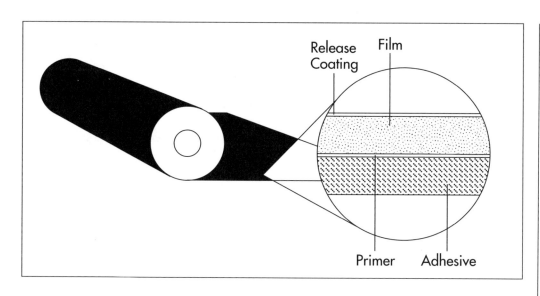

Release Coating   Film

Primer   Adhesive

This drawing shows the makeup of a layer of cellophane tape. The release coating makes the tape easier to unwind, while the primer helps secure the adhesive to the film.

with acetic acid and acetic anhydride to create a new compound, triacetate. This material is then treated with a mixture of chemicals and water to produce the basic form of cellulose acetate. After being heated to remove all moisture, the cellulose acetate is mixed with a plasticizing material similar to oil, and the resulting cellulose acetate plastic is made into pellets, or *pelletized*. The pellets are melted into a liquid and spread over a wide, flat conveyer belt to form extremely thin plastic sheets—it would take about five such sheets to equal the thickness of common paper. The completed backing, or film, is then wound on large rolls several thousand yards long to await the application of the adhesive.

Making the adhesive

2 Modern adhesives differ from their nineteenth century precursors in that *adhesomers*, the synthetic polymers they're based on, are inherently sticky and so require no additional tackifying agents. Such polymers are made from crude oil distillate that is chemically reacted to form alcohols and acids. These materials are then mixed with a hydrocarbon solvent that catalyzes their polymerization, the process by which they combine to form a complex molecular chain made up of repeating structural sequences. The resulting adhesomer may be used in this form or redissolved with more coating solvents, depending on its intended application. It is then stored until needed.

Combining film and adhesive

3 First, the non-adhesive side of the backing is treated with a release agent that makes the tape easy to unwind. Before the adhesive is applied to the sticky side, the side may be treated with a primer to anchor the adhesive. This coating is applied by routing the film over a large roller that rotates in an open vat of primer. As the tape moves over the roller, it applies the primer. Once these surface coats have been applied, the tape travels over heated drums (known as hot cans) that dry it. A very thin layer of pressure sensitive adhesive is metered onto the primed side of the tape, which is then rolled into long ovens for high-temperature drying.

Rolling, cutting, and packaging the tape

4 Once dried, the tape is wound onto large jumbo rolls and routed over slicers that divide it into varying widths. The individual bands of tape are then wound around a small plastic core, which is next fitted inside a plastic dispenser whose serrated edge can be used to cut lengths of tape. Both tape rolls and dispensers come in a variety of sizes to fit varying customer needs.

Quality Control

Pressure sensitive tape performance depends on three factors known in the adhesive industry as quick stick, cohesion, and adhesion. These properties must be properly balanced to achieve maximum performance. Quick stick is the tack of the adhesive where it forms an instantaneous bond on contacting another surface. The adhesive must "wet" any surface to which it is applied with only light finger pressure. The second criterion, cohesion, refers to the ability of the adhesive to remain bonded to an object without splitting when lifted away from that object. Pressure sensitive tape performs best with a high cohesive property. The tape's stickiness, or adhesion, is commonly measured by a "peel" test that examines the tape before and after it is applied to a surface and determines how it reacts to pressure and temperature changes.

Additional specifications and test methods are described in documents released by the federal government, the military, and organizations such as the American Society for Testing and Materials (ASTM) and the Pressure Sensitive Tape Council. Specifications essentially describe the characteristics of the adhesive while the methods protocols address testing procedures, forms, types, grades, and sizes.

Environmental Concerns

As the regulation of manufacturing processes under the Clean Air Act becomes stricter, the adhesive tape industry continues its efforts to shift from petroleum-based to water-based adhesives. Manufacturers must also comply with varying state and local regulations concerning groundwater contamination and wastewater treatment. As regulatory issues become more defined with specific mandates, the adhesive industry manufacturing process will continue to adapt its technologies. Currently, adhesive tape manufacturers are concentrating on increasing *repulpability*, the recyclability of paper adhesives, and *compostability*, the adhesive's ability to biodegrade. While several repulpable mills are already in operation, there are few compost-treatment sites.

The Future

In 1990, the adhesive industry reported overall sales of $6.5 billion. Of those sales, $2 bil-lion were in packaging adhesives. Experts list environmental consciousness as a big selling point, and manufacturers will seek to obtain the "environmental tag" on their products as they develop tape products that perform well while meeting environmental regulations.

Where To Learn More

Books

Dunning, Henry R. *Pressure Sensitive Adhesives: Formulations and Technology.* Noyes Data Corporation, 1977.

Katz, Irving. *Adhesive Materials.* Foster Publishing, 1964.

Skeist, Irving. *Handbook of Adhesives.* Van Nostrand Reinhold, 1977.

Periodicals

Axinn, David. "High-Tech Advance," *Chemical Marketing Reporter.* August 26, 1991, p. 21.

Jensen, Timothy B. "PSA Tapes Offer Environmental Advantages in Packaging," *Adhesives Age.* September, 1992, p. 10.

Loesel, Andrew. "Sticky Solutions," *Chemical Marketing Reporter.* August 26, 1991, pp. 15-16.

Mattes, Eileen. "Pressure Sensitive, Growth-Prone," *Chemical Marketing Reporter.* August 26, 1991, pp. 17 and 20.

Pamphlets

3M Tape and Specialties Division. *The "Big Idea."*

— Catherine Kolecki

Ceramic Tile

Background

Wall and floor tile used for interior and exterior decoration belongs to a class of ceramics known as whitewares. The production of tile dates back to ancient times and peoples, including the Egyptians, the Babylonians, and the Assyrians. For instance, the Step Pyramid for the Pharoah Djoser, built in ancient Egypt around 2600 B.C., contained colorful glazed tile. Later, ceramic tile was manufactured in virtually every major European country and in the United States. By the beginning of the twentieth century, tile was manufactured on an industrial scale. The invention of the tunnel kiln around 1910 increased the automation of tile manufacture. Today, tile manufacture is highly automated.

The American National Standards Institute separates tiles into several classifications. Ceramic mosaic tile may be either **porcelain** or of natural clay composition of size less than 39 cm^2 (6 in.^{2}). Decorative wall tile is glazed tile with a thin body used for interior decoration of residential walls. Paver tile is glazed or unglazed porcelain or natural clay tile of size 39 cm^2 (6 in.^{2}) or more. Porcelain tile is ceramic mosaic tile or paver tile that is made by a certain method called dry pressing. Quarry tile is glazed or unglazed tile of the same size as paver tile, but made by a different forming method.

Europe, Latin America, and the Far East are the largest producers of tile, with Italy the leader at 16.6 million ft.^{2}/day as of 1989. Following Italy (at 24.6 percent of the world market) are Spain (12.6 percent), Brazil and Germany (both at 11.2 percent), and the United States (4.5 percent). The total market for floor and wall tile in 1990 according to one estimate was $2.4 billion.

The United States has approximately 100 plants that manufacture ceramic tile, which shipped about 507 million ft.^{2} in 1990 according to the U.S. Department of Commerce. U.S. imports, by volume, accounted for approximately 60 percent of consumption in 1990, valued at around $500 million. Italy accounts for almost half of all imports, with Mexico and Spain following. U.S. exports have seen some growth, from $12 million in 1988 to about $20 million in 1990.

Because the tile industry is a relatively mature market and dependent on the building industry, growth will be slow. The United States Department of Commerce estimates a three to four percent increase in tile consumption over the next five years. Another economic analysis predicts that 494 million ft.^{2} will be shipped in 1992, a growth of about 4 percent from the previous year. Some tile manufacturers are a bit more optimistic; an American Ceramic Society survey showed an average growth of around 36 percent per manufacturer over the next five years.

Raw Materials

The raw materials used to form tile consist of clay minerals mined from the earth's crust, natural minerals such as feldspar that are used to lower the firing temperature, and chemical additives required for the shaping process. The minerals are often refined or beneficiated near the mine before shipment to the ceramic plant.

The raw materials must be pulverized and classified according to particle size. Primary crushers are used to reduce large lumps of material. Either a jaw crusher or gyratory crusher is used, which operate using a hori-

Among the pollutants produced in tile manufacture are fluorine and lead compounds, which are produced during firing and glazing. Lead compounds have been significantly reduced with the recent development of no-lead or low-lead glazes. Fluorine emissions can be controlled with scrubbers, devices that spray the gases with water to remove harmful pollutants.

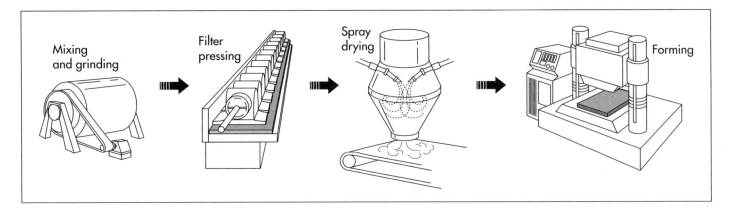

Mixing and grinding

Filter pressing

Spray drying

Forming

The initial step in ceramic tile manufacture involves mixing the ingredients. Sometimes, water is then added and the ingredients are wet milled or ground in a ball mill. If wet milling is used, the excess water is removed using filter pressing followed by spray drying. The resulting powder is then pressed into the desired tile body shape.

zontal squeezing motion between steel plates or rotating motion between steel cones, respectively.

Secondary crushing reduces smaller lumps to particles. Hammer or muller mills are often used. A muller mill uses steel wheels in a shallow rotating pan, while a hammer mill uses rapidly moving steel hammers to crush the material. Roller or cone type crushers can also be used.

A third particle size reduction step may be necessary. Tumbling types of mills are used in combination with grinding media. One of the most common types of such mills is the ball mill, which consists of large rotating cylinders partially filled with spherical grinding media.

Screens are used to separate out particles in a specific size range. They operate in a sloped position and are vibrated mechanically or electromechanically to improve material flow. Screens are classified according to mesh number, which is the number of openings per lineal inch of screen surface. The higher the mesh number, the smaller the opening size.

A glaze is a glass material designed to melt onto the surface of the tile during firing, and which then adheres to the tile surface during cooling. Glazes are used to provide moisture resistance and decoration, as they can be colored or can produce special textures.

The Manufacturing Process

Once the raw materials are processed, a number of steps take place to obtain the finished product. These steps include batching, mix-

ing and grinding, spray-drying, forming, drying, glazing, and firing. Many of these steps are now accomplished using automated equipment.

Batching

1 For many ceramic products, including tile, the body composition is determined by the amount and type of raw materials. The raw materials also determine the color of the tile body, which can be red or white in color, depending on the amount of iron-containing raw materials used. Therefore, it is important to mix the right amounts together to achieve the desired properties. Batch calculations are thus required, which must take into consideration both physical properties and chemical compositions of the raw materials. Once the appropriate weight of each raw material is determined, the raw materials must be mixed together.

Mixing and grinding

2 Once the ingredients are weighed, they are added together into a shell mixer, ribbon mixer, or intensive mixer. A shell mixer consists of two cylinders joined into a V, which rotates to tumble and mix the material. A ribbon mixer uses helical vanes, and an intensive mixer uses rapidly revolving plows. This step further grinds the ingredients, resulting in a finer particle size that improves the subsequent forming process (see step #4 below).

Sometimes it is necessary to add water to improve the mixing of a multiple-ingredient batch as well as to achieve fine grinding. This process is called wet milling and is often performed using a ball mill. The resulting water-filled mixture is called a slurry or slip. The water is then removed from the slurry by filter pressing (which removes 40-50 percent of the moisture), followed by dry milling.

Spray drying

3 If wet milling is first used, the excess water is usually removed via spray drying. This involves pumping the slurry to an atomizer consisting of a rapidly rotating disk or nozzle. Droplets of the slip are dried as they are heated by a rising hot air column, forming small, free flowing granules that result in a powder suitable for forming.

Tile bodies can also be prepared by dry grinding followed by granulation. Granulation uses a machine in which the mixture of previously dry-ground material is mixed with water in order to form the particles into granules, which again form a powder ready for forming.

Forming

4 Most tile is formed by dry pressing. In this method, the free flowing powder—containing organic binder or a low percentage of moisture—flows from a hopper into the forming die. The material is compressed in a steel cavity by steel plungers and is then ejected by the bottom plunger. Automated presses are used with operating pressures as high as 2,500 tons.

Several other methods are also used where the tile body is in a wetter, more moldable form. Extrusion plus punching is used to produce irregularly shaped tile and thinner tile faster and more economically. This involves compacting a plastic mass in a high-pressure cylinder and forcing the material to flow out of the cylinder into short slugs. These slugs are then punched into one or more tiles using hydraulic or pneumatic punching presses.

Ram pressing is often used for heavily profiled tiles. With this method, extruded slugs of the tile body are pressed between two halves of a hard or porous mold mounted in a hydraulic press. The formed part is removed by first applying vacuum to the top half of the mold to free the part from the bottom half, followed by forcing air through the top half to free the top part. Excess material must be removed from the part and additional finishing may be needed.

Another process, called pressure glazing, has recently been developed. This process combines glazing and shaping simultaneously by pressing the glaze (in spray-dried powder form) directly in the die filled with the tile body powder. Advantages include the elimination of glazing lines, as well as the glazing waste material (called sludge) that is produced with the conventional method.

Drying

5 Ceramic tile usually must be dried (at high relative humidity) after forming, especially if a wet method is used. Drying, which can take several days, removes the water at a slow enough rate to prevent shrinkage cracks. Continuous or tunnel driers are used that are heated using gas or oil, infrared lamps, or microwave energy. Infrared drying is better suited for thin tile, whereas microwave drying works better for thicker tile. Another method, impulse drying, uses pulses of hot air flowing in the transverse direction instead of continuously in the material flow direction.

Glazing

6 To prepare the glaze, similar methods are used as for the tile body. After a batch formulation is calculated, the raw materials are weighed, mixed and dry or wet milled. The milled glazes are then applied using one of the many methods available. In centrifugal glazing or discing, the glaze is fed through a rotating disc that flings or throws the glaze onto the tile. In the bell/waterfall method, a stream of glaze falls onto the tile as it passes on a conveyor underneath. Sometimes, the glaze is simply sprayed on. For multiple glaze applications, screen printing on, under, or between tile that have been wet glazed is used. In this process, glaze is forced through a screen by a rubber squeegee or other device.

Dry glazing is also being used. This involves the application of powders, crushed *frits* (glass materials), and granulated glazes onto a wet-glazed tile surface. After firing, the glaze particles melt into each other to produce a surface like granite.

Firing

7 After glazing, the tile must be heated intensely to strengthen it and give it the desired porosity. Two types of ovens, or

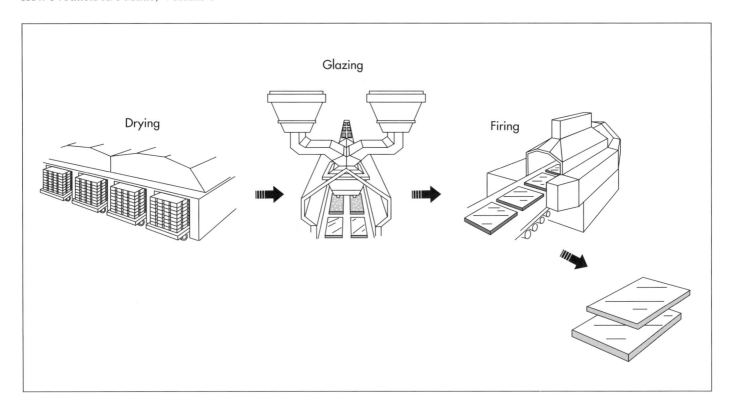

Drying   Glazing   Firing

After forming, the tile is dried slowly (for several days) and at high humidity, to prevent cracking and shrinkage. Next, the glaze is applied, and then the tile is fired in a furnace or kiln. Although some types of tile require a two-step firing process, wet-milled tile is fired only once, at temperatures of 2,000 degrees Fahrenheit or more. After firing, the tile is packaged and shipped.

kilns, are used for firing tile. Wall tile, or tile that is prepared by dry grinding instead of wet milling (see #2 and #3 above), usually requires a two-step process. In this process, the tile goes through a low-temperature firing called bisque firing before glazing. This step removes the volatiles from the material and most or all of the shrinkage. The body and glaze are then fired together in a process called glost firing. Both firing processes take place in a tunnel or continuous kiln, which consists of a chamber through which the ware is slowly moved on a conveyor on refractory batts—shelves built of materials that are resistant to high temperatures—or in containers called saggers. Firing in a tunnel kiln can take two to three days, with firing temperatures around 2,372 degrees Fahrenheit (1,300 degrees Celsius).

For tile that only requires a single firing— usually tile that is prepared by wet milling— roller kilns are generally used. These kilns move the wares on a roller conveyor and do not require kiln furnitures such as batts or saggers. Firing times in roller kilns can be as low as 60 minutes, with firing temperatures around 2,102 degrees Fahrenheit (1,150 degrees Celsius) or more.

8 After firing and testing, the tile is ready to be packaged and shipped.

Byproducts

A variety of pollutants are generated during the various manufacturing steps; these emissions must be controlled to meet air control standards. Among the pollutants produced in tile manufacture are fluorine and lead compounds, which are produced during firing and glazing. Lead compounds have been significantly reduced with the recent development of no-lead or low-lead glazes. Fluorine emissions can be controlled with scrubbers, devices that basically spray the gases with water to remove harmful pollutants. They can also be controlled with dry processes, such as fabric filters coated with lime. This lime can then be recycled as a raw material for future tile.

The tile industry is also developing processes to recycle wastewater and sludge produced during milling, glazing, and spray-drying. Already some plants recycle the excess powder generated during dry-pressing as well as the overspray produced during glazing. Waste glaze and rejected tile are also returned to the body preparation process for reuse.

Quality Control

Most tile manufacturers now use statistical process control (SPC) for each step of the manufacturing process. Many also work closely with their raw material suppliers to ensure that specifications are met before the material is used. Statistical process control consists of charts that are used to monitor various processing parameters, such as particle size, milling time, drying temperature and time, compaction pressure, dimensions after pressing, density, firing temperature and time, and the like. These charts identify problems with equipment, out of spec conditions, and help to improve yields before the final product is finished.

The final product must meet certain specifications regarding physical and chemical properties. These properties are determined by standard tests established by the American Society of Testing and Materials (ASTM). Properties measured include mechanical strength, abrasion resistance, chemical resistance, water absorption, dimensional stability, frost resistance, and linear coefficient of thermal expansion. More recently, the slip resistance, which can be determined by measuring the coefficient of friction, has become a concern. However, no standard has yet been established because other factors (such as proper floor design and care) can make results meaningless.

The Future

In order to maintain market growth, tile manufacturers will concentrate on developing and promoting new tile products, including modular or cladding tile, larger-sized tile, slip- and abrasion-resistant tile, and tile with a polished, granite or marble finish. This is being accomplished through the development of different body formulations, new glazes, and glaze applications, and by new and improved processing equipment and techniques. Automation will continue to play an important role in an effort to increase production, lower costs, and improve quality. In addition, changes in production technology due to environmental and energy resource issues will continue.

Where To Learn More

Books

Bender, W. and F. Handle, eds. *Brick and Tile Making: Procedures and Operating Practices in the Heavy Clay Industries.* Bauverlag GmbH, 1982.

Jones, J. T. and M. F. Berard. *Ceramics: Industrial Processing and Testing.* Iowa State University Press, 1972.

Pellacani, G. and T. Manfredini. *Engineered Materials Handbook.* ASM International, 1991, pp. 925-929.

Periodicals

Burzacchini, B. "Technical Developments in Ceramic Tile Glazes and Related Applications," *American Ceramic Society Bulletin.* March, 1991, pp. 394-403.

Fugmann, K. "Rapid Changes in Tile Technology," *Tile & Brick International.* March, 1991, pp. 165-166.

Gehringer, George. "Tile Glossary: A Guide to Techniques and Surface Designs," *American Ceramic Society Bulletin.* December, 1990, pp. 1950-1952.

Geiger, Greg. "Developments in the Tile Industry," *American Ceramic Society Bulletin.* December, 1991, pp. 1879-1885.

—*L. S. Millberg*

Chalk

Almost all chalk produced today is dustless. Earlier, softer chalk tended to produce a cloud of dust that some feared might contribute to respiratory problems. Dustless chalk still produces dust; it's just that the dust settles faster. Manufacturers accomplish this by baking their chalk longer to harden it more.

Background

Chalk used in school classrooms comes in slender sticks approximately .35 of an inch (nine millimeters) in diameter and 3.15 inches (80 millimeters) long. Lessons are often presented to entire classes on chalkboards (or blackboards, as they were originally called) using sticks of chalk because this method has proven cheap and easy.

As found in nature, chalk has been used for drawing since prehistoric times, when, according to archaeologists, it helped to create some of the earliest cave drawings. Later, artists of different countries and styles used chalk mainly for sketches, and some such drawings, protected with shellac or a similar substance, have survived. Chalk was first formed into sticks for the convenience of artists. The method was to grind natural chalk to a fine powder, then add water, clay as a binder, and various dry colors. The resultant putty was then rolled into cylinders and dried. Although impurities produce natural chalk in many colors, when artists made their own chalk they usually added pigments to render these colors more vivid. Carbon, for example, was used to enhance black, and ferric oxide (Fe_2O_3) created a more vivid red.

Chalk did not become standard in schoolrooms until the nineteenth century, when class sizes began to increase and teachers needed a convenient way of conveying information to many students at one time. Not only did instructors use large blackboards, but students also worked with individual chalkboards, complete with chalk sticks and a sponge or cloth to use as an eraser. These small chalkboards were used for practice, especially among the younger students. Pens dipped in ink wells were the preferred tool for writing final copy, but these were reserved for older students who could be trusted not to make a mess: paper—made solely from rags at this time—was expensive.

An important change in the nature of classroom chalk paralleled a change in chalkboards. Blackboards used to be black, because they were made from true slate. While some experts advocated a change to yellow chalkboards and dark blue or purple chalk to simulate writing on paper, when manufacturers began to fashion chalkboards from synthetic materials during the twentieth century, they chose the color green, arguing that it was easier on the eyes. Yellow became the preferred color for chalk.

Almost all chalk produced today is dustless. Earlier, softer chalk tended to produce a cloud of dust that some feared might contribute to respiratory problems. Dustless chalk still produces dust; it's just that the dust settles faster. Manufacturers accomplish this by baking their chalk longer to harden it more. Another method, used by a French company, is to dip eighty percent of each dustless chalk stick in shellac to prevent the chalk from rubbing off onto the hands.

Raw Materials

The main component of chalk is calcium carbonate ($CaCO_3$), a form of limestone. Limestone deposits develop as *coccoliths* (minute calcareous plates created by the decomposition of plankton skeletons) accumulate, forming sedimentary layers. Plankton, a tiny marine organism, concentrates the calcium found naturally in seawater from .04 percent to 40 percent, which is then precipitated when the plankton dies.

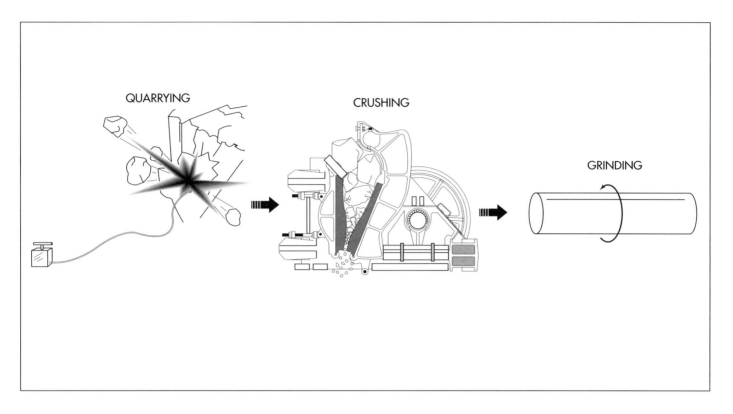

QUARRYING   CRUSHING   GRINDING

The base of pastel chalks is calcium sulfate ($CaSO_4$), which is derived from gypsum ($CaSO_4 \cdot 2H_2O$), an evaporite mineral formed by the deposition of ocean brine; it also occurs disseminated in limestone. Chalk and dehydrated gypsum thus have similar origins and properties. Pastels also contain clays and oils for binding, and strong pigments. This mixture produces sticks that write smoothly without smearing and draw better on paper than on chalkboards. Although great care is taken to eliminate contaminants when chalk is manufactured, some impurities inherent to the mineral remain. Chief among these are silica, alumina, iron, phosphorus, and sulfur. In less significant, amounts, manganese, copper, titanium, sodium oxide, potassium oxide, fluorine, arsenic, and strontium may also occur.

The Manufacturing Process

Quarrying limestone

1 Approximately 95 percent of the limestone produced in the United States is quarried. After a sufficient reserve (twenty-five years' worth is recommended) has been prospected, the land that covers the deposit is removed with bulldozers and scrapers. If the chalk is close to the surface, an open shelf quarry method can be used; however, this is very rare. Usually an open pit quarry method is used instead. In this method, holes are drilled into the rock, explosives are placed inside, and the rock is blown apart. Depending on the nature of the deposit, a pit can be enlarged laterally or vertically.

Pulverizing the chalk

2 Once comparatively large chunks of limestone have been quarried, they need to be transported to crushing machines, where they are pulverized to meet the demands of the chalk industry. The first step is primary crushing. Various crushers exist, but the principle is the same: all compress the stone with jaws or a cone, or shatter it through impact. Secondary crushing is accomplished by smaller crushers that work at higher speeds, producing pebbles which are then ground and pulverized.

3 The next phase, wet grinding, washes away impurities. It is used to make the fine grade of limestone necessary to make chalk suitable for writing purposes. Wet grinding is carried out in ball mills—rotating steel drums with steel balls inside that pulverize the chalk until it is very fine.

To make chalk, limestone is first quarried, generally by an open pit quarry method. Next, the limestone must be crushed. Primary crushing, such as in a jaw crusher, breaks down large boulders; secondary crushing pulverizes smaller chunks into pebbles. The limestone is then wet-milled with water in a ball mill—a rotating steel drum with steel balls inside to further pulverize the chalk. This step washes away impurities and leaves a fine powder.

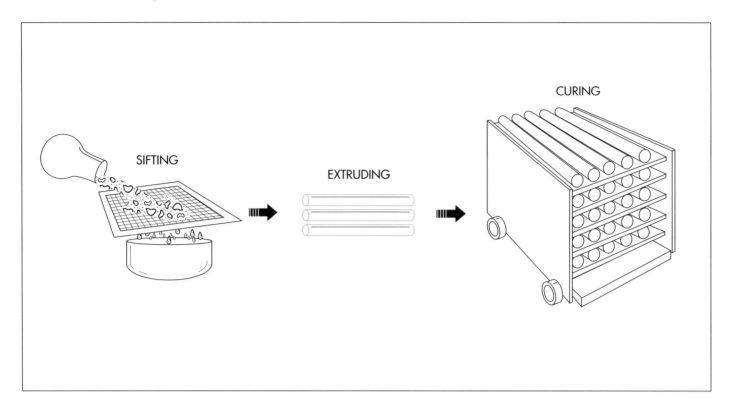

SIFTING

EXTRUDING

CURING

After grinding, the chalk particles are sifted over vibrating screens to separate the finer particles. The particles are then mixed with water, extruded through a die of the proper size, and cut to the proper length. Finally, the chalk is cured in an oven for four days.

Dehydrating gypsum

4 Gypsum, like limestone, is also quarried and pulverized. The major difference in processing gypsum is that it must be dehydrated to form calcium sulfate, the major component of colored chalk. This is done in a kettle, a large combustion chamber in which the gypsum is heated to between 244 and 253 degrees Fahrenheit (116-121 degrees Celsius). It is allowed to boil until it has been reduced by twelve to fifteen percent, at which point its water content will have been reduced from 20.9 percent to between 5 and 6 percent. To further reduce the water, the gypsum is reheated to about 402 degrees Fahrenheit (204 degrees Celsius), at which point it is removed from the kettle. By now, almost all of the water has evaporated, leaving calcium sulfate.

Sifting, cleaning, and shipping the chalk

5 The particles of chalk or calcium sulfate are now conveyed to vibrating screens that sift out the finer material. The ensuing fine chalk is then washed, dried, packed in bags, and shipped to the manufacturer. Upon receiving chalk or calcium sulfate, the chalk factory usually grinds the materials again to render them smooth and uniformly fine.

Making white classroom chalk

6 To make white classroom chalk, the manufacturer adds water to form a thick slurry with the consistency of clay. The slurry is then placed into and extruded from a die—an orifice of the desired long, thin shape. Cut into lengths of approximately 24.43 inches (62 centimeters), the sticks are next placed on a sheet that contains places for five such sticks. The sheet is then placed in an oven, where the chalk cures for four days at 188 degrees Fahrenheit (85 degrees Celsius). After it has cured, the sticks are cut into 80 millimeters lengths.

Making colored classroom chalk

7 Pigments (dry, natural, colored materials) are mixed in with the calcium carbonate while both are dry (the procedure is similar to sifting flour and baking powder together before adding liquid, as in a cake recipe). Water is then added to the mixture, which is then baked in the same manner as white classroom chalk.

Making pastels

8 Another manufacturing method is used for pastels, the chalks used for art drawing. The procedure resembles that used for colored classroom chalk, but calcium sulfate

is used instead of calcium carbonate. In addition, the dry material is mixed with clay and oils, and more pigments are added to produce a slurry that has the consistency of toothpaste. Because the final products must be relatively moist, pastels are usually air-dried rather than baked.

Boxing the chalk

9 Placed in small boxes, the completed chalk sticks are stacked in large boxes to be shipped to supply stores.

Quality Control

Chalk that is intended for the classroom must undergo stringent tests in order to perform well and be labeled nontoxic. All incoming materials are tested for purity before being used. After the chalk has been made into sticks, one stick from each batch is selected for tests. The density and break strength of the sample stick are determined. The sample is then used to write with, and the quality of the mark is studied. Erasability is also studied. First, the chalk mark is erased using a dry eraser, and the quality of erasure is examined. Then, the chalkboard is washed, and again the amount of chalk left on the board is examined. Furthermore, a sample from each batch is kept for five years so that it can be inspected if in the future its quality is questioned.

Chalk for classroom use adheres to the American National Standards Institute performance standards. Written specifications state the proper length of the chalk stick, as well as how many sticks should go in a box. On November 18, 1990, a Federal Act (*Public Law 100-695*) went into effect, mandating that all art materials sold in the United States must be evaluated by a qualified toxicologist who must then issue a label explaining their toxicity. Toxicologists are concerned not with cost but with safety, and they must consider many factors before granting approval. Each ingredient, the quantity in which it is used, and its possible adverse reactions with other ingredients are studied. The product's size and packaging, its potential harm to humans, and its tendency to produce allergic reactions are also considered. Toxicologists also take into account the products use and potential misuse, as well as all federal and state regula-

tions. Formulas for every color and every formula change must meet approval.

Classroom chalk is labeled "CP [certified product] nontoxic" if it meets the standards of the Art and Craft Materials Institute, a nonprofit manufacturers' association. This label certifies that art materials for children are nontoxic and meet voluntary standards of quality and performance, and that the toxicity of art materials for adults has been correctly labeled. The CP seal also indicates that the product meets standards of material, workmanship, working qualities, and color developed by the Art and Craft Materials Institute and others such as the American National Standards Institute and the American Society for Testing and Materials (ASTM). To ensure honesty, most chalk manufacturers are tested at random by an independent toxicologist, who checks to see that they are meeting nontoxic standards. Most manufacturers conform to such exacting standards because knowledgeable schools will not purchase chalk that is not properly labeled.

The Future

Many people consider using chalk and chalkboards to present material outdated. Some experts claim that teachers have stubbornly resisted new technologies that could improve teaching—and eliminate the chalkboard entirely. A study which recently investigated whether teaching with overhead projectors was more effective than using chalkboards concluded that chalkboards were more interactive, progressive, and fruitful.

A development much in the educational news lately is the electronic chalkboard. In place of a regular chalkboard, a teacher uses a large TV screen, inputting materials from a computer terminal. In a more advanced scenario, each student uses a terminal, to which the teacher sends information from a master computer. Experts claim that such set-ups are more visually exciting to students, more versatile than the old-fashioned chalkboards, cleaner than dusty chalk, easier for the teacher to use, and better able to present more complex material through the use of graphics and animation. Many studies on the feasibility of electronic chalkboards have been made, however, and most seem to favor keeping the traditional chalkboard, at least for now. Electronic chalkboards that are sophisticated and easily readable lie beyond the budget constraints and technological capabilities of most schools. Further, studies of the electronic system's effectiveness report that teachers who use it spent more time preparing their lessons, teachers and students were less interactive, students were dissatisfied with the electronic chalkboards, and the new devices divided the students' attention between the screen and the teacher conveying the information. Although the enthusiasm for electronic blackboards in some areas remains high, chalk use in the classroom is guaranteed for some time to come.

Where To Learn More

Books

Boynton, Robert. *Chemistry and Technology of Lime and Limestone.* John Wiley & Sons, 1980.

Cobb, Vicki. *The Secret Life of School Supplies.* J. B. Lippincott, 1981.

Institution of Civil Engineers Staff, eds. *Chalk.* American Society of Civil Engineers, 1990.

Periodicals

Toth, Beth. "Jeanne Otis: A Color Dialogue," *Ceramics Monthly.* January, 1988, p. 40.

—*Rose Secrest*

Cheese

Background

Cheese is a fermented food derived from the milk of various mammals. Since humans began to domesticate milk-producing animals around 10,000 B.C., they have known about the propensity of milk to separate into curds and whey. As milk sours, it breaks down into curds, lumps of phosphoprotein, and whey, a watery, grey fluid that contains lactose, minerals, vitamins, and traces of fat. It is the curds that are used to make cheese, and practically every culture on Earth has developed its own methods, the only major exceptions being China and the ancient Americas.

The first cheeses were "fresh," that is, not fermented. They consisted solely of salted white curds drained of whey, similar to today's cottage cheese. The next step was to develop ways of accelerating the natural separation process. This was achieved by adding rennet to the milk. Rennet is an enzyme from the stomachs of young ruminants—a ruminant is an animal that chews its food very thoroughly and possesses a complex digestive system with three or four stomach chambers; in the United States, cows are the best known creatures of this kind. Rennet remains the most popular way of "starting" cheese, though other starting agents such as lactic acid and various plant extracts are also used.

By A.D. 100 cheese makers in various countries knew how to press, ripen, and cure fresh cheeses, thereby creating a product that could be stored for long periods. Each country or region developed different types of cheese that reflected local ingredients and conditions. The number of cheeses thus developed is staggering. France, famous for the quality and variety of its cheeses, is home to about 400 commercially available cheeses.

The next significant step to affect the manufacture of cheese occurred in the 1860s, when Louis Pasteur introduced the process that bears his name. *Pasteurization* entails heating milk to partially sterilize it without altering its basic chemical structure. Because the process destroys dangerous micro-organisms, pasteurized milk is considered more healthful, and most cheese is made from pasteurized milk today.

The first and simplest way of extending the length cheese would keep without spoiling was simply ageing it. Aged cheese was popular from the start because it kept well for domestic use. In the 1300s, the Dutch began to seal cheese intended for export in hard rinds to maintain its freshness, and, in the early 1800s, the Swiss became the first to process cheese. Frustrated by the speed with which their cheese went bad in the days before refrigeration, they developed a method of grinding old cheese, adding filler ingredients, and heating the mixture to produce a sterile, uniform, long-lasting product. Another advantage of processing cheese was that it permitted the makers to recycle edible, second-grade cheeses in a palatable form.

Prior to the twentieth century, most people considered cheese a specialty food, produced in individual households and eaten rarely. However, with the advent of mass production, both the supply of and the demand for cheese have increased. In 1955, 13 percent of milk was made into cheese. By 1984, this percentage had grown to 31 percent, and it continues to increase. Interestingly, though

Based on its moisture and fat content, a cheese is labeled soft, semi-soft, hard, or very hard. It must then fall within the range of characteristics considered acceptable for cheeses in its category. For example, cheddar, a hard cheese, can contain no more than 39 percent water and no less than 50 percent fat.

processed cheese is now widely available, it represents only one-third of the cheese being made today. Despite the fact that most cheeses are produced in large factories, a majority are still made using natural methods. In fact, small, "farmhouse" cheese making has made a comeback in recent years. Many Americans now own their own small cheese-making businesses, and their products have become quite popular, particularly among connoisseurs.

Raw Materials

Cheese is made from milk, and that milk comes from animals as diverse as cows, sheep, goats, horses, camels, water buffalo, and reindeer. Most cheese makers expedite the curdling process with rennet, lactic acid, or plant extracts, such as the vegetable rennet produced from wild artichokes, fig leaves, safflower, or melon.

In addition to milk and curdling agents, cheeses may contain various ingredients added to enhance flavor and color. The great cheeses of the world may acquire their flavor from the specific bacterial molds with which they have been inoculated, an example being the famous *Penicillium roqueforti* used to make France's Roquefort and England's Stilton. Cheeses may also be salted or dyed, usually with *annatto,* an orange coloring made from the pulp of a tropical tree, or carrot juice. They may be washed in brine or covered with ashes. Cheese makers who wish to avoid rennet may encourage the bacterial growth necessary to curdling by a number of odd methods. Some cheeses possess this bacteria because they are made from unpasteurized milk. Other cheeses, however, are reportedly made from milk in which dung or old leather have been dunked; still others acquire their bacteria from being buried in mud.

The unusual texture and flavor of processed cheese are obtained by combining several types of natural cheese and adding salt, milk-fat, cream, whey, water, vegetable oil, and other fillers. Processed cheese will also have preservatives, emulsifiers, gums, gelatin, thickeners, and sweeteners as ingredients. Most processed cheese and some natural cheeses are flavored with such ingredients as paprika, pepper, chives, onions, cumin, caraway seeds, jalapeño peppers, hazelnuts, raisins, mushrooms, sage, and bacon. Cheese can also be smoked to preserve it and give it a distinctive flavor.

The Manufacturing Process

Although cheese making is a linear process, it involves many factors. Numerous varieties of cheese exist because ending the simple preparation process at different points can produce different cheeses, as can varying additives or procedures. Cheese making has long been considered a delicate process. Attempts to duplicate the success of an old cheese factory have been known to fail because conditions at a new factory do not favor the growth of the proper bacteria.

Preparing the milk

1 Small cheese factories accept either morning milk (which is richer), evening milk, or both. Because it is generally purchased from small dairies which don't pasteurize, this milk contains the bacteria necessary to produce lactic acid, one of the agents that triggers curdling. The cheese makers let the milk sit until enough lactic acid has formed to begin producing the particular type of cheese they're making. Depending on the type of cheese being produced, the cheese makers may then heat the ripening milk. This process differs slightly at large cheese factories, which purchase pasteurized milk and must consequently add a culture of bacteria to produce lactic acid.

Separating the curds from the whey

2 The next step is to add animal or vegetable rennet to the milk, furthering its separation into curds and whey. Once formed, the curds are cut both vertically and horizontally with knives. In large factories, huge vats of curdled milk are cut vertically using sharp, multi-bladed, wire knives reminiscent of oven racks. The same machine then agitates the curds and slices them horizontally. If the cutting is done manually, the curds are cut both ways using a large, two-handled knife. Soft cheeses are cut into big chunks, while hard cheeses are cut into tiny chunks. (For cheddar, for instance, the space between the knives is about one-twentieth of an inch [half a centimeter].) After cutting, the curds may be heated to hasten the separa-

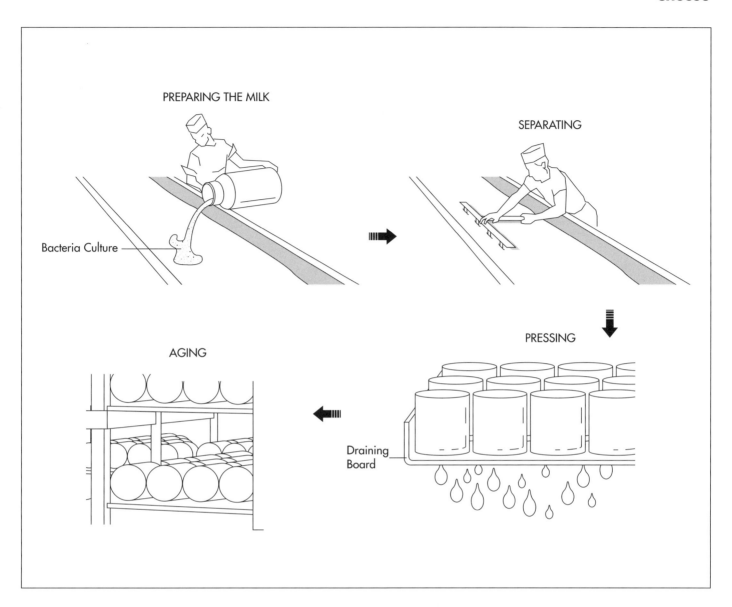

PREPARING THE MILK

Bacteria Culture

SEPARATING

PRESSING

Draining Board

AGING

tion from the whey, but they are more typically left alone. When separation is complete, the whey is drained.

Pressing the curds

3 Moisture must then be removed from the curds, although the amount removed depends on the type of cheese. For some types with high moisture contents, the whey-draining process removes sufficient moisture. Other types require the curds to be cut, heated, and/or filtered to get rid of excess moisture. To make cheddar cheese, for example, cheese makers *cheddar,* or finely chop, the curd. To make hard, dry cheeses such as parmesan, cheese makers first cheddar and then cook the curd. Regardless, if the curds are to be aged, they are then put into molds. Here, they are pressed to give the

proper shape and size. Soft cheeses such as cottage cheese are not aged.

Ageing the cheese

4 At this stage the cheese may be inoculated with a flavoring mold, bathed in brine, or wrapped in cloth or hay before being deposited in a place of the proper temperature and humidity to age. Some cheeses are aged for a month, some for up to several years. Ageing sharpens the flavor of the cheese; for example, cheddar aged more than two years is appropriately labeled extra sharp.

Wrapping natural cheese

5 Some cheeses may develop a rind naturally, as their surfaces dry. Other rinds

In a typical cheese-making operation, the first step is preparing the milk. Although smaller factories purchase unpasteurized milk that already has the bacteria present to produce lactic acid (necessary for curdling), larger factories purchase pasteurized milk and must add bacteria culture to produce the lactic acid.

Next, the curds must be separated from the whey. Animal or vegetable rennet is added, and then the curds are agitated and cut using large knives. As the whey separates, it is drained. The curds are then pressed into molds, if necessary, to facilitate further moisture drainage, and aged for the proper amount of time. Some cheeses are aged for a month, others for several years.

may form from the growth of bacteria that has been sprayed on the surface of the cheese. Still other cheeses are washed, and this process encourages bacterial growth. In place of or in addition to rinds, cheeses can be sealed in cloth or wax. For local eating, this may be all the packaging that is necessary. However, large quantities of cheese are packaged for sale in distant countries. Such cheeses may be heavily salted for export (such as Roquefort) or sealed in impermeable plastic or foil.

Making and wrapping processed cheese

6 Edible yet inferior cheeses can be saved and made into processed cheese. Cheeses such as Emmental (commonly called Swiss), Gruyere (similar to Swiss),Colby, or cheddar are cut up and very finely ground. After this powder has been mixed with water to form a paste, other ingredients such as salt, fillers, emulsifiers, preservatives, and flavorings are added. The mixture is then heated under controlled conditions. While still warm and soft, the cheese paste is extruded into long ribbons that are sliced. The small sheets of cheese are then put onto a plastic or foil sheet and wrapped by a machine.

Quality Control

Cheese making has never been an easily regulated, scientific process. Quality cheese has always been the sign of an experienced, perhaps even lucky cheese maker insistent upon producing flavorful cheese. Subscribing to analytical tests of cheese characteristics may yield a good cheese, but cheese making has traditionally been a chancy endeavor. Developing a single set of standards for cheese is difficult because each variety of cheese has its own range of characteristics. A cheese that strays from this range will be bad-tasting and inferior. For example, good soft blue cheese will have high moisture and a high pH; cheddar will have neither.

One controversy in the cheese field centers on whether it is necessary to pasteurize the milk that goes into cheese. Pasteurization was promoted because of the persistence of *Mycobacterium tuberculosis,* a pathogen or disease-causing bacteria that occurs in milk products. The United States allows cheeses that will be aged for over sixty days to be made from unpasteurized milk; however, it requires that many cheeses be made from pasteurized milk. Despite these regulations, it is possible to eat cheeses made from unpasteurized milk to no ill effect. In fact, cheese connoisseurs insist that pasteurizing destroys the natural bacteria necessary for quality cheese manufacture. They claim that modern cheese factories are so clean and sanitary that pasteurization is unnecessary. So far, the result of this controversy has merely been that connoisseurs avoid pasteurized milk cheeses.

Regulations exist so that the consumer can purchase authentic cheeses with ease. France, the preeminent maker of a variety of natural cheeses, began granting certain regions monopolies on the manufacture of certain cheeses. For example, a cheese labeled "Roquefort" is guaranteed to have been ripened in the Combalou caves, and such a guarantee has existed since 1411. Because cheese is made for human consumption, great care is taken to insure that the raw materials are of the highest quality, and cheese intended for export must meet particularly stringent quality control standards.

Because they possess such disparate characteristics, different types of cheese are required to meet different compositional standards. Based on its moisture and fat content, a cheese is labeled soft, semi-soft, hard, or very hard. Having been assigned a category, it must then fall within the range of characteristics considered acceptable for cheeses in that category. For example, cheddar, a hard cheese, can contain no more than 39 percent water and no less than 50 percent fat. In addition to meeting compositional standards, cheese must also meet standards for flavor, aroma, body, texture, color, appearance, and finish. To test a batch of cheese, inspectors core a representative wheel vertically in several places, catching the center, the sides, and in between. The inspector then examines the cheese to detect any inconsistencies in texture, rubs it to determine body (or consistency), smells it, and tastes it. Cheese is usually assigned points for each of these characteristics, with flavor and texture weighing more than color and appearance.

Processed cheese is also subject to legal restrictions and standards. Processed American cheese must contain at least 90 percent real cheese. Products labeled "cheese food" must be 51 percent cheese, and most are 65 percent. Products labeled "cheese spread" must also be 51 percent cheese, the difference being that such foods have more water and gums to make them spreadable. "Cheese product" usually refers to a diet cheese that has more water and less cheese than American cheese, cheese food, or cheese spread, but the specific amount of cheese is not regulated. Similarly, "imitation cheese" is not required to contain a minimum amount of cheese, and cheese is usually not its main ingredient. In general, quality processed cheese should resemble cheese and possess some cheesy flavor, preferably with a "bite" such as sharp cheddar cheese has. The cheese should be smooth and evenly colored; it should also avoid rubberiness and melt in the mouth.

Where To Learn More

Books

Brown, Bob. *The Complete Book of Cheese.* Gramercy Publishing, 1955.

Carr, Sandy. *The Simon and Schuster Pocket Guide to Cheese.* Simon and Schuster, 1981.

Kosikowski, Frank. *Cheese and Fermented Milk Foods.* Cornell University, 1966.

Mills, Sonya. *The World Guide to Cheese.* Gallery Books, 1988.

Timperley, Carol and Cecilia Norman. *A Gourmet's Guide to Cheese.* HP Books, 1989.

Periodicals

"American Cheese and 'Cheeses'," *Consumer Reports.* November, 1990, pp. 728-732.

Birmingham, David. "Gruyere's Cheesemakers," *History Today.* February, 1991, pp. 21-26.

Raichlen, Steven. "Farmhouse Cheeses," *Yankee.* February, 1991, pp. 84-92.

—*Rose Secrest*

Chewing Gum

In 1906, the first attempt to make bubble gum failed when consumers found "Blibber Blubber" too wet and grainy. It wasn't until 1928 that the Fleer company developed an acceptable bubble gum, marketed as "Dubble Bubble." The gum's familiar pink color was practically an accident: it was the color Fleer had most on hand.

Background

Chewing gum is a sweetened, flavored confection composed primarily of latex, both natural and artificial. Organic latex, a milky white fluid produced by a variety of seed plants, is best known as the principle component of rubber. Used as a snack, gum has no nutritive value, and, when people have finished chewing, they generally throw it away rather than swallow it.

Throughout history, people in many regions have selected naturally chewy and aromatic substances as breath fresheners or thirst quenchers. The Greeks used mastic tree resin; the Italians, frankincense; the West Indians, aromatic twigs; the Arabs, beeswax. Tree resins appear to have been the most popular, and spruce sap had been a favored chewing substance for centuries in North America before New England colonists adopted it for their own enjoyment. Although spruce gum was available to anyone willing to go out into the woods and extract it from a tree, John Curtis and his son, John Bacon Curtis, thought they could package and market it. In the mid-1800s, they experimented with the first manufacture of chewing gum sticks. First they boiled the spruce gum and skimmed off impurities such as bark before adding **sugar** and other fillers. Then they rolled it, let it cool, and cut it into sticks which they dipped in cornstarch, wrapped in paper, and placed in small wooden boxes. The Curtis company thrived, and business grew still further when the younger Curtis developed a machine to mass produce gum and founded the first chewing gum factory. The Curtis's manufacturing process is roughly the same one used to produce chewing gum today.

Despite the Curtis's success, very few other spruce gum factories were established during the nineteenth century. However, in 1869 William F. Semple took out the first patent on chewing gum. His formula was the earliest attempt to create latex-based gum, yet he never manufactured or marketed it. However, chewing gum as we know it today was first manufactured that year by Thomas Adams. Adams began mass-producing latex-based gum after meeting with the famous Mexican general Antonio López de Santa Anna, who wanted Adams to help him introduce chicle, a rubbery tree sap from the Sapodilla trees of Mexico and Central America, as a cheap replacement for rubber. Adams could find no way of treating the chicle to render it useable, but he thought it would make an excellent chewing gum that could easily replace paraffin, the tasteless wax that dominated the chewing gum market at the time. To give his gum the proper size and consistency, Adams put the chicle in hot water until it was the consistency of putty. He then flavored it with sassafras and licorice, kneaded it, and shaped it into little balls. In 1871 Adams was the first to patent a gum-making machine. The machine kneaded the gum and ran it out in long, thin strips that could be cut off by druggists, who were the most common direct seller of chewing gum in the early days. Adams' venture proved successful, and his American Chicle Company and its gum are still around today.

The most successful chewing gum company ever is that established by William Wrigley, Jr., in 1892. Although the company, run by the founder's son and grandson after his death in 1932, developed a wide array of flavored gums, it dropped many of these to concentrate on its biggest sellers: "Juicy Fruit,"

"Doublemint," and "Wrigley's Spearmint." Recently, the company introduced gum for denture wearers, sugar-free gum, cinnamon-flavored gum, and non-stick bubble gum. Like earlier Wrigley products, all have proven popular. The secrets behind the success of Wrigley gums—the company has never made anything else—are strong flavor and prominent advertising. As William Wrigley, Jr., said early in the century, "Tell 'em quick and tell 'em often."

Today bubble gum is probably more popular than chewing gum, at least among young people. In 1906, however, the first attempt to make bubble gum failed when consumers found "Blibber Blubber" too wet and grainy. It wasn't until 1928 that Walter Diemer, a young employee of the Fleer company, developed an acceptable bubble gum, marketed as "Dubble Bubble." (The gum's familiar pink color was practically an accident: it was the color Fleer had most on hand.) During the 1930s and 1940s, the invention of synthetic rubbers assisted chewing gum manufacturers greatly, because they no longer had to rely on irregular supplies of imported natural rubber.

Although basic chewing gum has stayed about the same for over a century, several different types have recently become available. For instance, sugarless gum debuted in the 1970s, along with nicotine gum, liquid center gum, athlete's gum, chewing gum that doesn't stick to dental work, and bubble gum that doesn't stick to the face. More recently, some manufacturers have tried adding abrasives to chewing gum, marketing it as good for the teeth.

Raw Materials

The manufacture of chewing gum in the United States has come a long way from loggers chopping off wads of spruce gum for chewing pleasure, yet the base of the gum remains the sap of various rubber trees, or, in most cases, a synthetic substitute for such sap. Natural gum bases include latexes like chicle, jelutong, gutta-percha, and pine rosin. Increasingly, natural resins other than chicle have been used because chicle is in extremely short supply: a chicle tree yields only 35 ounces (one kilogram) of chicle every three to four years, and no chicle plantations were ever established. However, natural latex in general is being replaced by synthetic substi-

tutes. Most modern chewing gum bases use either no natural rubber at all, or a minimal amount ranging from ten to twenty percent, with synthetic rubbers such as butadiene-styrene rubber, polyethylene, and polyvinyl acetate making up the rest.

After the latex used to form bases, the most common ingredient in chewing gum is some type of sweetener. A typical stick contains 79 percent sugar or artificial sweetener. Natural sugars include cane sugar, corn syrup, or dextrose, and artificial sweeteners can be saccharine or aspartame. Popular mint flavors such as spearmint and peppermint are usually provided by oils extracted from only the best, most aromatic plants. Thus, while the aroma of a stick of spearmint gum is quite strong, flavoring comprises only one percent of the gum's total weight. Fruit flavors generally derive from artificial flavorings, because the amount of fruit grown cannot meet the demand. For example, apple flavor comes from ethyl acetate, and cherry from benzaldehyde. In addition to sweeteners and flavorings, preservatives such as butylated hydroxytoluene and softeners like refined vegetable oil are added to keep the gum fresh, soft, and moist. Fillers such as calcium carbonate and corn starch are also common.

Federal regulations allow a typical list of ingredients on a pack of chewing gum to read like this: gum base, sugar, corn syrup, natural and/or artificial flavor, softeners, and BHT (added to preserve freshness). This vagueness is mainly due to the chewing gum manufacturers' insistence that all materials used are part of a trade secret formula.

The Manufacturing Process

While the specific ingredients in gum might be a secret, the process for making gum is not. The first chewing gum making machine wasn't even patented, and today the procedure is considered standard throughout the industry.

Preparing the chicle

1 If natural latex is to be used, it must first be harvested and processed. The tall 32.79 yard (30-meter) chicle tree is scored with a series of shallow Xs, enabling the chicle to flow down into a bucket. After a significant

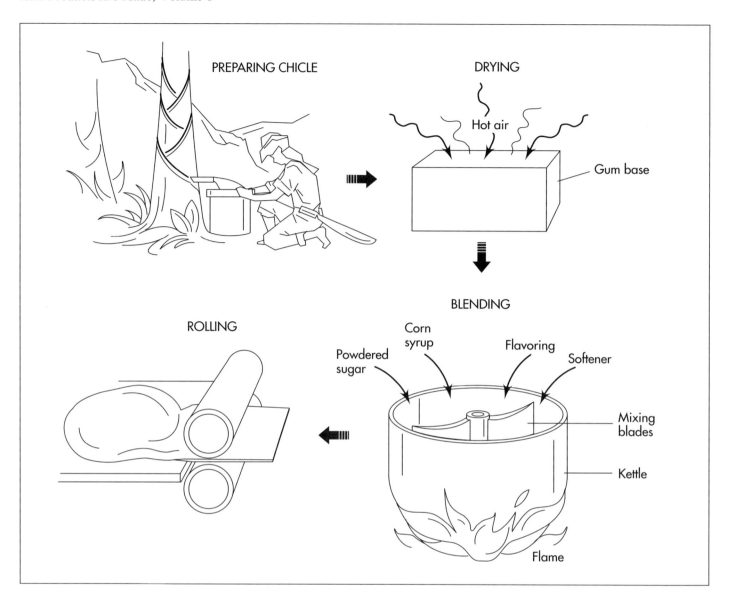

PREPARING CHICLE

DRYING

Hot air

Gum base

ROLLING

BLENDING

Corn syrup

Powdered sugar

Flavoring

Softener

Mixing blades

Kettle

Flame

Chewing gum base consists either of natural latex or a synthetic substitute. Natural latex such as chicle is harvested by making large X-marks on rubber trees and then collecting the substance as it runs down the tree. After grinding the base to form a coarse meal, the mixture is dried for a day or two.

Next, the mixture is heated in large kettles while the other ingredients are added. Large machines then pummel, or "knead," the mass until it is properly smooth and rubbery, and it is put on a rolling slab and reduced to the proper thickness.

amount of chicle has accumulated, it is strained and placed in large kettles. Stirred constantly, it is boiled until it reduces to two-thirds of its original volume. It is then poured into greased wooden molds and shipped.

Grinding, mixing, and drying the latex

2 The natural and/or artificial gum bases are first ground into a coarse meal and mixed to ensure uniform consistency. The blend is then placed in a warm room to dry for a day or two. During drying, hot air continually passes over the mixture.

Cooking and purifying the base

3 Next, the gum base is cooked in kettles at 243 degrees Fahrenheit (116 degrees

Celsius) until it has melted into a thick syrup. To purify it, workers pass it through screens and place it in a high speed centrifuge before refiltering it, this time through finer screens.

Blending additional ingredients

4 The gum base is now ready for additives. It is placed in kettles to be cooked, and additional ingredients are stirred in by large steel blades. First, extremely fine powdered sugar and corn syrup are added. Flavorings are added next, followed by softeners. When the mixture is smooth enough, it is rolled out onto belts and cooled by being exposed to cold air.

Kneading and rolling the gum

5 The next step is kneading. For several hours machines gently pummel the mass

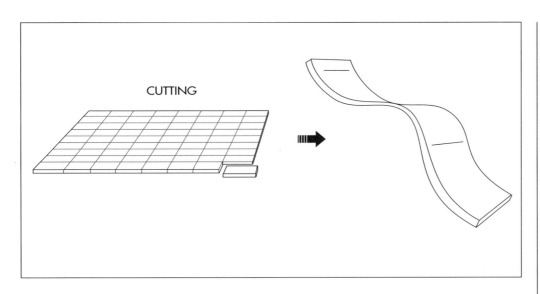

CUTTING

of chewing gum until it is properly rubbery and smooth. Large chunks are then chopped off the mass, to be flattened by rollers until they reach the proper thickness of nearly .17 inches (about .43 cm). During this process, the sheet of chewing gum is dusted with powdered sugar to prepare it for cutting.

Cutting and seasoning the gum

6 A cutting machine first scores the sheet in a pattern of rectangles, each 1.3 inches (3.3 centimeters) long and .449 of an inch (1.14 centimeters) wide. The sheet is then put aside at the proper temperature and humidity to "season."

Packaging the gum

7 Once seasoned, the gum sheets are broken into sticks, wrapped in **aluminum foil** or wax paper, wrapped in paper, and put into plastic packs that are then sealed. Put into boxes or plastic bags, the gum is ready to be shipped to retail outlets.

Other types of gum

8 Amazingly, gum balls make up only three percent of chewing gum sales, yet their unique merchandising makes them intriguing. Gumballs are made by scoring a cylinder of gum twice to form balls, which are then stored several hours at 55-60 degrees Fahrenheit (13-16 degrees Celsius) to harden. The balls are put into huge kettles to be coated with a flavored and colored sucrose solution. After seven hours, the coated balls are dried with hot air, then rolled in beeswax or other wax to make them shiny.

The nature of gumball machines determined the next step. An enclosed plastic globe is subject to interior condensation. The water collected ruins untreated gumballs, so they are usually coated with a plastic, water-repellent glaze to protect them. Candy-coated gums are made in essentially the same way, their final destination being boxes, not gumball machines.

A recent development has been the introduction of gums with a liquid center. To make this gum, the gum base is extruded to form a hollow rope. The liquid is then fed into the hollow area, and a cutting machine chops the ropes into bite-size pieces and wraps them.

Quality Control

Perhaps because chewing gum has always had a bad reputation as an unsanitary and crass junk food, but more likely because it is intended for human consumption, chewing gum factories have for decades been known for immaculate conditions.

Standards for raw materials are equally high. If natural rubber such as chicle is used, it must pass several tests for cleanliness and texture. Before shipment, chicle is inspected for rocks, dirt, and other obvious impurities. If it is too milky, dry, or dirty, it is rejected. Chewing gum is manufactured completely untouched by human hands, its entire production process taking place in clean, air-conditioned facilities. Each ingredient is tested for purity before being used, and only the highest quality ingredients are accepted. Every large company has a research laboratory on its premises, thereby simplifying the standard procedure of inspecting and testing ingredients at every stage of the manufacturing process. The research and development department is also responsible for investigating new ways to produce and package gum, and for developing new products.

A successful piece of gum must be chewy and fresh, and bubble gum in particular must be both resilient and soft. With all types of gum, freshness and texture depend upon moistness. Gum must also contain the right amount of flavor oil. While too much solvent will make a gum sticky and hard to cut, it must contain enough flavor to mask the taste of the gum base and to last for a reasonably long time. For these reasons, the flavor oils used in gum are highly concentrated. A long shelf-life is also desirable, and every pack of gum is dated. After that date, the manufacturer asks that the gum be disposed of. To ensure that merchants do this, one manufacturer will replace unsold, out-of-date gum for free.

The Future

Much current research is directed towards producing longer-lasting gum. At present, the flavor of a typical chewing gum lasts five minutes. The most promising idea for long-lasting gum entails coating each stick with a polymer film that releases flavor molecules slowly; studies suggest that the flavor of such gum can last more than ten hours. Another recent innovation is a chewing gum imbued with a patented compound that helps to repair tooth enamel. The compound, amorphous calcium phosphate, crystallizes when chewed, triggering the natural remineralization process by which the body rebuilds damaged teeth. Under ideal circumstances, the body generates enough amorphous calcium phosphate to repair teeth organically, but many people eat more sugar than their bodies can fight. This experimental gum would help to protect these people against tooth decay. Researchers hope to have the enhanced gum in stores by 1996.

Where To Learn More

Books

Hendrickson, Robert. *The Great American Chewing Gum Book.* Chilton Book Company, 1976.

Lasky, Michael S. *The Complete Junk Food Book.* McGraw-Hill, 1977.

Periodicals

Hendrickson, Robert. "Since 1928 It's Been Boom and Bust with Bubble Gum," *Smithsonian,* July, 1990, pp. 74-83.

Plaut, Josh. "Pop Secret," *Science World,* September, 1992, pp. 16-21.

Raulston, J. C. "Sweet Gum," *The Magazine of American Gardening.* February, 1989, p. 80.

—Rose Secrest

Chocolate

Background

Chocolate, in all of its varied forms (candy bars, cocoa, cakes, cookies, coating for other candies and fruits) is probably America's favorite confection. With an annual per capita consumption of around 14 pounds (6 kilograms) per person, chocolate is as ubiquitous as a non-essential food can be.

Cocoa trees originated in South America's river valleys, and, by the seventh century A.D., the Mayan Indians had brought them north into Mexico. In addition to the Mayans, many other Central American Indians, including the Aztecs and the Toltecs, seem to have cultivated cocoa trees, and the words "chocolate" and "cocoa" both derive from the Aztec language. When Cortez, Pizarro, and other Spanish explorers arrived in Central America in the fifteenth century, they noted that cocoa beans were used as currency and that the upper class of the native populations drank *cacahuatl*, a frothy beverage consisting of roasted cocoa beans blended with red pepper, vanilla, and water.

While the Spanish initially found the bitter flavor of unsweetened cacahuatl unpalatable, they gradually introduced modifications that rendered the drink more appealing to the European palate. Grinding **sugar**, cinnamon, cloves, anise, almonds, hazelnuts, vanilla, orange-flower water, and musk with dried cocoa beans, they heated the mixture to create a paste (as with many popular recipes today, variations were common). They then smoothed this paste on the broad, flat leaves of the plantain tree, let it harden, and removed the resulting slabs of chocolate. To make *chocalatl*, the direct ancestor of our hot chocolate, they dissolved these tablets in hot water and a thin corn broth. They then stirred the liquid until it frothed, perhaps to distribute the fats from the chocolate paste evenly (cocoa beans comprise more than fifty percent cocoa butter by weight). By the mid-seventeenth century, an English missionary reported that only members of Mexico's lower classes still drank cacahuatl in its original form.

When missionaries and explorers returned to Spain with the drink, they encountered resistance from the powerful Catholic Church, which argued that the beverage, contaminated by its heathen origins, was bound to corrupt Christians who drank it. But the praise of returning conquistadors—Cortez himself designated chocalatl as "the divine drink that builds up resistance and fights fatigue"—overshadowed the church's dour prophecies, and hot chocolate became an immediate success in Spain. Near the end of the sixteenth century, the country built the first chocolate factories, in which cocoa beans were ground into a paste that could later be mixed with water. Within seventy years the drink was prized throughout Europe, its spread furthered by a radical drop in the price of sugar between 1640 and 1680 (the increased availability of the sweetener enhanced the popularity of **coffee** as well).

Chocolate consumption soon extended to England, where the drink was served in "chocolate houses," upscale versions of the coffee houses that had sprung up in London during the 1600s. In the mid-seventeenth century, milk chocolate was invented by an Englishman, Sir Hans Sloane, who had lived on the island of Jamaica for many years, observing the Jamaicans' extensive use of chocolate. A naturalist and personal physician to Queen Anne, Sloane had previously

When missionaries and explorers returned to Spain from Latin America with chocalatl—the direct ancestor of our hot chocolate—they encountered resistance from the powerful Catholic Church, which argued that the beverage, contaminated by its heathen origins, was bound to corrupt Christians who drank it.

considered the cocoa bean's high fat content a problem, but, after observing how young Jamaicans seemed to thrive on both cocoa products and milk, he began to advocate dissolving chocolate tablets in milk rather than water.

The first Europeans to drink chocolate, the Spaniards were also the first to consume it in solid form. Although several naturalists and physicians who had traveled extensively in the Americas had noted that some Indians ate solid chocolate lozenges, many Europeans believed that consuming chocolate in this form would create internal obstructions. As this conviction gradually diminished, cookbooks began to include recipes for chocolate candy. However, a typical eighteenth-century hard chocolate differed substantially from modern chocolate confections. Back then, chocolate candy consisted solely of chocolate paste and sugar held together with plant gums. In addition to being unappealing on its own, the coarse, crumbly texture of this product reduced its ability to hold sugar. Primitive hard chocolate, not surprisingly, was nowhere near as popular as today's improved varieties.

These textural problems were solved in 1828, when a Dutch chocolate maker named Conrad van Houten invented a screw press that could be used to squeeze most of the butter out of cocoa beans. Van Houten's press contributed to the refinement of chocolate by permitting the separation of cocoa beans into cocoa powder and cocoa butter. Dissolved in hot liquid, the powder created a beverage far more palatable than previous chocolate drinks, which were much like blocks of unsweetened baker's chocolate melted in fluid. Blended with regular ground cocoa beans, the cocoa butter made chocolate paste smoother and easier to blend with sugar. Less than twenty years later, an English company introduced the first commercially prepared hard chocolate. In 1876 a Swiss candy maker named Daniel Peter further refined chocolate production, using the dried milk recently invented by the Nestle company to make solid milk chocolate. In 1913 Jules Sechaud, a countryman of Peter's, developed a technique for making chocolate shells filled with other confections. Well before the first World War, chocolate had become one of the most popular confections, though it was still quite expensive.

Hershey Foods, one of a number of American chocolate-making companies founded during the nineteenth and early twentieth centuries, made chocolate more affordable and available. Today the most famous—although not the largest—chocolate producer in the United States, the company was founded by Milton Hershey, who invested the fortune he'd amassed making caramels in a Pennsylvania chocolate factory. Hershey had first become fascinated by chocolate at the 1893 Chicago World's Columbian Exposition, where one of leading attractions was a 2,200-pound (998.8 kilograms), ten-foot (3.05 meters) tall chocolate statue of Germania, the symbol of the Stollwerck chocolate company in Germany (Germania was housed in a 38-foot [11.58 meters] Renaissance temple, also constructed entirely of chocolate). When he turned to chocolate making, Hershey decided to use the same fresh milk that had made his caramels so flavorful. He also dedicated himself to utilizing mass production techniques that would enable him to sell large quantities of chocolate, individually wrapped and affordably priced. For decades after Hershey began manufacturing them in 1904, Hershey bars cost only a nickel.

Another company, M&M/Mars, has branched out to produce dozens of non-chocolate products, thus making the company four times as large as Hershey Foods, despite the fact that the latter firm remains synonymous with chocolate in the eyes of many American consumers. Yet since its founding in 1922, M&M/Mars has produced many of the country's most enduringly popular chocolate confections. M&M/Mars' success began with the *Milky Way* bar, which was cheaper to produce than pure chocolate because its malt flavor derived from nougat, a mixture of egg whites and corn syrup. The *Snickers* and *Three Musketeers* bars, both of which also featured cost-cutting nougat centers, soon followed, and during the 1930s soldiers fighting in the Spanish Civil War suggested the *M&M*. To prevent the chocolate candy they carried in their pockets from melting, these soldiers had protected it with a sugary coating that the Mars company adapted to create its most popular product.

Raw Materials

Although other ingredients are added, most notably sugar or other sweeteners, flavoring agents, and sometimes potassium carbonate (the agent used to make so-called dutch cocoa), cocoa beans are the primary component of chocolate.

Cocoa trees are evergreens that do best within 20 degrees of the equator, at altitudes of between 100 (30.48 centimeters) and 1,000 (304.8 centimeters) feet above sea level. Native to South and Central America, the trees are currently grown on commercial plantations in such places as Malaysia, Brazil, Ecuador, and West Africa. West Africa currently produces nearly three quarters of the world's 75,000 ton annual cocoa bean crop, while Brazil is the largest producer in the Western Hemisphere.

Because they are relatively delicate, the trees can be harmed by full sun, fungi, and insect pests. To minimize such damage, they are usually planted with other trees such as rubber or banana. The other crops afford protection from the sun and provide plantation owners with an alternative income if the cocoa trees fail.

The pods, the fruit of the cocoa tree, are 6-10 inches (15.24-25.4 centimeters) long and 3-4 inches (7.62-10.16 centimeters) in diameter. Most trees bear only about 30 to 40 pods, each of which contains between 20 and 40 inch-long (2.54 centimeters) beans in a gummy liquid. The pods ripen in three to four months, and, because of the even climate in which the trees grow, they ripen continually throughout the year. However, the greatest number of pods are harvested between May and December.

Of the 30 to 40 pods on a typical cacao tree, no more than half will be mature at any given time. Only the mature fruits can be harvested, as only they will produce top quality ingredients. After being cut from the trees with machetes or knives mounted on poles (the trees are too delicate to be climbed), mature pods are opened on the plantation with a large knife or machete. The beans inside are then manually removed.

Still entwined with pulp from the pods, the seeds are piled on the ground, where they are allowed to heat beneath the sun for several days (some plantations also dry the beans mechanically, if necessary). Enzymes from the pulp combine with wild, airborne yeasts

to cause a small amount of fermentation that will make the final product even more appetizing. During the fermenting process, the beans reach a temperature of about 125 degrees Fahrenheit (51 degrees Celsius). This kills the embryos, preventing the beans from sprouting while in transit; it also stimulates decomposition of the beans' cell walls. Once the beans have sufficiently fermented, they will be stripped of the remaining pulp and dried. Next, they are graded and bagged in sacks weighing from 130 to 200 pounds (59.02-90.8 kilograms). They will then be stored until they are inspected, after which they will be shipped to an auction to be sold to chocolate makers.

The Manufacturing Process

Roasting, hulling, and crushing the beans

1 Once a company has received a shipment of cocoa beans at its processing plant, the beans are roasted, first on screens and then in revolving cylinders through which heated air is blown. Over a period of 30 minutes to 2 hours, the moisture in the beans is reduced from about seven percent to about one percent. The roasting process triggers a browning reaction, in which more than 300 different chemicals present in the cocoa beans interact. The beans now begin to develop the rich flavor we associate with chocolate.

2 Roasting also causes the shells to open and break away from the nibs (the meat of the bean). This separation process can be completed by blowing air across the beans as they go through a giant winnowing machine called a cracker and fanner, which loosens the hulls from the beans without crushing them. The hulls, now separated from the nibs, are usually sold as either mulch or fertilizer. They are also sometimes used as a commercial boiler fuel.

3 Next, the roasted nibs undergo *broyage*, a process of crushing that takes place in a grinder made of revolving granite blocks. The design of the grinder may vary, but most resemble old-fashioned flour mills. The final product of this grinding process, made up of small particles of the nib suspended in oil, is a thick syrup known as chocolate liquor.

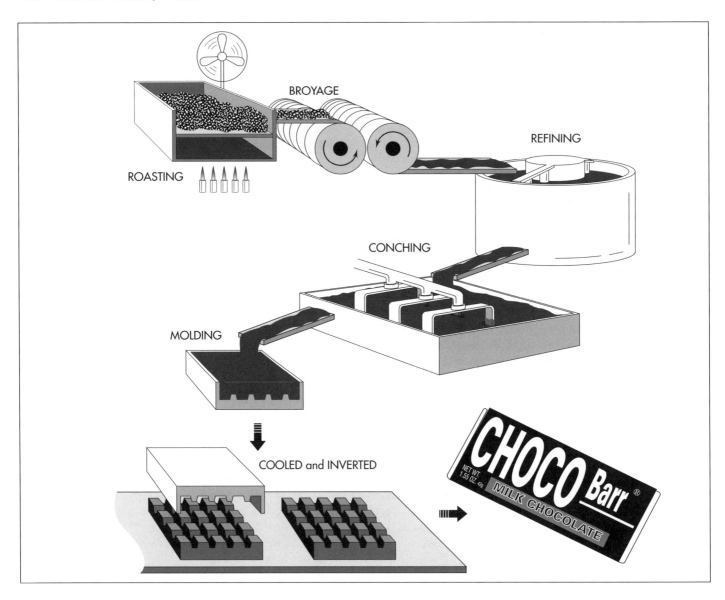

In chocolate manufacture, the cocoa beans are first roasted, during which the bean shells break away from their center (the nibs). Next, the nibs undergo broyage, a crushing process that takes place in a grinder with revolving granite blocks. The following step, refining, further grinds the particles and makes the chocolate mass smoother.

The mass is then conched, or ground and agitated in a huge open vats. During this process, which can take from 3 hours to 3 days, other ingredients such as sugar and vanilla can be added. The mass is then poured into molds of the desired shape, cooled, cut, and wrapped.

4 The next step is refining, during which the liquor is further ground between sets of revolving metal drums. Each successive rolling is faster than the preceding one because the liquor is becoming smoother and flows easier. The ultimate goal is to reduce the size of the particles in the liquor to about .001 inch (.00254 centimeters).

Making cocoa powder

5 If the chocolate being produced is to be cocoa powder, from which hot chocolate and baking mixes are made, the chocolate liquor may be *dutched*, a process so-named because it was invented by the Dutch chocolate maker Conrad van Houten. In the dutching process, the liquor is treated with an alkaline solution, usually potassium carbon-

ate, that raises its pH from 5.5 to 7 or 8. This increase darkens the color of the cocoa, renders its flavor more mild, and reduces the tendency of the nib particles to form clumps in the liquor. The powder that eventually ensues is called dutch cocoa.

6 The next step in making cocoa powder is *defatting* the chocolate liquor, or removing large amounts of butter from it. This is done by further compressing the liquor between rollers, until about half of the fat from its cocoa beans has been released. The resulting solid material, commonly called *press cake*, is then broken, chopped, or crushed before being sifted to produce cocoa powder. When additives such as sugar or other sweeteners have been blended, this cocoa powder becomes a modern version of chocalatl.

Making chocolate candy

7 If the chocolate being produced is to become candy, the press cake is remixed with some of the removed cocoa butter. The restored cocoa butter is necessary for texture and consistency, and different types of chocolate require different amounts of cocoa butter.

8 The mixture now undergoes a process known as *conching*, in which it is continuously turned and ground in a huge open vat. The process's name derives from older vats, which resembled large conch shells. The conching process can last from between three hours to three days (more time is not necessarily better, however). This is the most important step in making chocolate. The speed and temperature of the mixing are critical in determining the quality of the final product.

9 Another crucial aspect of conching is the time and rate at which other ingredients are added. The ingredients added during conching determine what type of chocolate is produced: sweet chocolate consists of chocolate liquor, cocoa butter, sugar, and vanilla; milk chocolate contains sweet chocolate with powdered whole milk or whole liquid milk.

10 At the end of the conching process, the chocolate is poured into molds, cooled, cut, and wrapped.

Quality Control

Proportions of ingredients and even some aspects of processing are carefully guarded secrets, although certain guidelines were set by the 1944 Federal Food, Drug, and Cosmetic Law, as well as more recent laws and regulations. For example, milk chocolate must contain a minimum of 12 percent milk solids and 10 percent chocolate liquor. Sweet chocolate, which contains no milk solids, must contain at least fifteen percent chocolate liquor. The major companies, however, have a reputation for enforcing strict quality and cleanliness standards. Milton Hershey zealously insisted upon fresh ingredients, and the Mars company boasts that its factory floors harbor fewer bacteria than the average kitchen sink. Moreover, slight imperfections are often enough to prompt the rejection of entire batches of candy.

The Future

Although concerns about the high fat and caloric content of chocolate have reduced per capita consumption in the United States from over twenty pounds (9.08 kilograms) per year to around fourteen (6.36 kilograms), chocolate remains the most popular type of confection. In addition, several psychiatrists have recently speculated that, because the substance contains phenylethylamine, a natural stimulant, depressed people may resort to chocolate binges in an unknowing attempt to raise their spirits and adjust their body chemistry. Others have speculated that the substance exerts an amorous effect. Despite reduced levels of consumption and regardless of whether or not one endorses the various theories about its effects, chocolate seems guaranteed to remain what it has been throughout the twentieth century: a perennial American favorite.

Where To Learn More

Books

Chocolate Manufacturers' Association of the U.S.A. *The Story of Chocolate.*

Hirsch, Sylvia Balser and Morton Gill Clark. *A Salute to Chocolate.* Hawthorn Books, 1968.

O'Neill, Catherine. *Let's Visit a Chocolate Factory.* Troll Associates, 1988.

Periodicals

Cavendish, Richard. "The Sweet Smell of Success," *History Today.* July, 1990, pp. 2-3.

"From Xocoatl to Chocolate Bars," *Consumer Reports.* November, 1986, pp. 696-701.

Galvin, Ruth Mehrtens. "Sybaritic to Some, Sinful to Others, but How Sweet it Is!" *Smithsonian.* February, 1986, pp. 54-64.

Marshall, Lydia and Ethel Weinberg. "A Fine Romance," *Cosmopolitan.* February, 1989, pp. 52-4.

—*Lawrence H. Berlow*

Coffee

Background

Coffee is a beverage made by grinding roasted coffee beans and allowing hot water to flow through them. Dark, flavorful, and aromatic, the resulting liquid is usually served hot, when its full flavor can best be appreciated. Coffee is served internationally—with over one third of the world's population consuming it in some form, it ranks as the most popular processed beverage—and each country has developed its own preferences about how to prepare and present it. For example, coffee drinkers in Indonesia drink hot coffee from glasses, while Middle Easterners and some Africans serve their coffee in dainty brass cups. The Italians are known for their *espresso*, a thick brew served in tiny cups and made by dripping hot water over twice the normal quantity of ground coffee, and the French have contributed *café au lait*, a combination of coffee and milk or cream which they consume from bowls at breakfast.

A driving force behind coffee's global popularity is its caffeine content: a six-ounce (2.72 kilograms) cup of coffee contains 100 milligrams of caffeine, more than comparable amounts of tea (50 milligrams), cola (25 milligrams), or cocoa (15 milligrams). Caffeine, an alkaloid that occurs naturally in coffee, is a mild stimulant that produces a variety of physical effects. Because caffeine stimulates the cortex of the brain, people who ingest it experience enhanced concentration. Athletes are sometimes advised to drink coffee prior to competing, as caffeine renders skeletal muscles less susceptible to exhaustion and improves coordination. However, these benefits accrue only to those who consume small doses of the drug.

Excessive amounts of caffeine produce a host of undesirable consequences, acting as a diuretic, stimulating gastric secretions, upsetting the stomach, contracting blood vessels in the brain (people who suffer from headaches are advised to cut their caffeine intake), and causing overacute sensation, irregular heartbeat, and trembling. On a more serious level, many researchers have sought to link caffeine to heart disease, benign breast cysts, pancreatic cancer, and birth defects. While such studies have proven inconclusive, health official nonetheless recommend that people limit their coffee intake to fewer than four cups daily or drink decaffeinated varieties.

Coffee originated on the plateaus of central Ethiopia. By A.D. 1000, Ethiopian Arabs were collecting the fruit of the tree, which grew wild, and preparing a beverage from its beans. During the fifteenth century traders transplanted wild coffee trees from Africa to southern Arabia. The eastern Arabs, the first to cultivate coffee, soon adopted the Ethiopian Arabs' practice of making a hot beverage from its ground, roasted beans.

The Arabs' fondness for the drink spread rapidly along trade routes, and Venetians had been introduced to coffee by 1600. In Europe as in Arabia, church and state officials frequently proscribed the new drink, identifying it with the often-liberal discussions conducted by coffee house habitués, but the institutions nonetheless proliferated, nowhere more so than in seventeenth-century London. The first coffee house opened there in 1652, and a large number of such establishments (*cafés*) opened soon after on both the European continent (*café* derives from the French term for coffee) and in North

America, where they appeared in such Eastern cities as New York, Boston, and Philadelphia in the last decade of the seventeenth century.

In the United States, coffee achieved the same, almost instantaneous popularity that it had won in Europe. However, the brew favored by early American coffee drinkers tasted significantly different from that enjoyed by today's connoisseurs, as nineteenth-century cookbooks make clear. One 1844 cookbook instructed people to use a much higher coffee/water ratio than we favor today (one tablespoon per sixteen ounces); boil the brew for almost a half an hour (today people are instructed never to boil coffee); and add fish skin, isinglass (a gelatin made from the air bladders of fish), or egg shells to reduce the acidity brought out by boiling the beans so long (today we would discard overly acidic coffee). Coffee yielded from this recipe would strike modern coffee lovers as intolerably strong and acidic; moreover, it would have little aroma.

American attempts to create instant coffee began during the mid-1800s, when one of the earliest instant coffees was offered in cake form to Civil War troops. Although it and other early instant coffees tasted even worse than regular coffee of the epoch, the incentive of convenience proved strong, and efforts to manufacture a palatable instant brew continued. Finally, after using U.S. troops as testers during World War II, an American coffee manufacturer (Maxwell House) began marketing the first successful instant coffee in 1950.

At present, 85 percent of Americans begin their day by making some form of the drink, and the average American will consume three cups of it over the course of the day.

Raw Materials

Coffee comes from the seed, or bean, of the coffee tree. Coffee beans contain more than 100 chemicals including aromatic molecules, proteins, starches, oils, and bitter phenols (acidic compounds), each contributing a different characteristic to the unique flavor of coffee. The coffee tree, a member of the evergreen family, has waxy, pointed leaves and jasmine-like flowers. Actually more like a shrub, the coffee tree can grow to more than 30 feet (9.14 meters) in its wild state, but in cultivation it is usually trimmed to between five and 12 feet (1.5 and 3.65 meters). After planting, the typical tree will not produce coffee beans until it blooms, usually about five years. After the white petals drop off, red cherries form, each with two green coffee beans inside. (Producing mass quantities of beans requires a large number of trees: in one year, a small bush will yield only enough beans for a pound of coffee.) Because coffee berries do not ripen uniformly, careful harvesting requires picking only the red ripe berries: including unripened green ones and overly ripened black ones will affect the coffee taste.

Coffee trees grow best in a temperate climate without frost or high temperatures. They also seem to thrive in fertile, well-drained soil; volcanic soil in particular seems conducive to flavorful beans. High altitude plantations located between 3,000 and 6,000 feet (914.4 and 1,828.8 meters) above sea level produce low-moisture beans with more flavor. Due to the positive influences of volcanic soil and altitude, the finest beans are often cultivated in mountainous regions. Today, Brazil produces about half of the world's coffee. One quarter is produced elsewhere in Latin America, and Africa contributes about one sixth of the global supply.

Currently, about 25 types of coffee trees exist, the variation stemming from environmental factors such as soil, weather, and altitude. The two main species are *coffea robusta* and *coffea arabica*. The *robusta* strain produces less expensive beans, largely because it can be grown under less ideal conditions than the *arabica* strain. When served, coffee made from *arabica* beans has a deep reddish cast, whereas *robusta* brews tend to be dark brown or black in appearance. The coffees made from the two commonly used beans differ significantly. *Robusta* beans are generally grown on large plantations where the berries ripen and are harvested at one time, thereby increasing the percentage of under- and over-ripe beans. *Arabica* beans, on the other hand, comprise the bulk of the premium coffees that are typically sold in whole bean form so purchasers can grind their own coffee. Whether served in a coffee house or prepared at home, coffee made from such beans offers a more delicate and less acidic flavor.

Coffee bean harvesting is still done manually. The beans grow in clusters of two; each cluster is called a "cherry." Next, the beans are dried and husked. In one method, the wet method, the beans are put in pulping machines to remove most of the husk. After fermenting in large tanks, the beans are put in hulling machines, where mechanical stirrers remove the final covering and polish the beans to a smooth, glossy finish.

After being cleaned and sorted, the beans are roasted in huge ovens. Only after roasting do the beans emit their familiar aroma. The beans are then cooled.

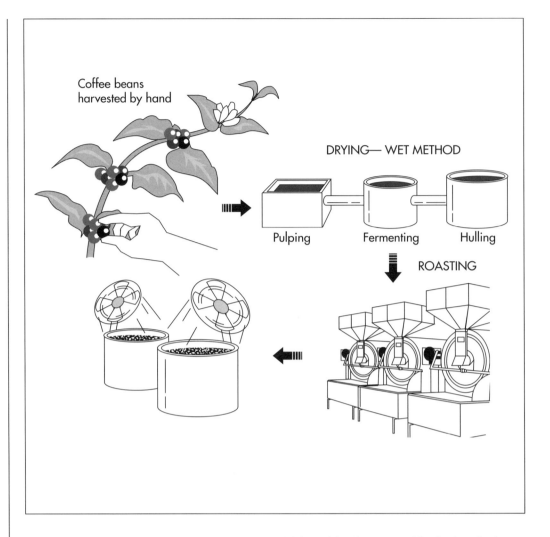

The Manufacturing Process

Drying and husking the cherries

1 First, the coffee cherries must be harvested, a process that is still done manually. Next, the cherries are dried and husked using one of two methods. The dry method is an older, primitive, and labor-intensive process of distributing the cherries in the sun, raking them several times a day, and allowing them to dry. When they have dried to the point at which they contain only 12 percent water, the beans' husks become shriveled. At this stage they are hulled, either by hand or by a machine.

2 In employing the wet method, the hulls are removed before the beans have dried. Although the fruit is initially processed in a pulping machine that removes most of the material surrounding the beans, some of this glutinous covering remains after pulping.

This residue is removed by letting the beans ferment in tanks, where their natural enzymes digest the gluey substance over a period of 18 to 36 hours. Upon removal from the fermenting tank, the beans are washed, dried by exposure to hot air, and put into large mechanical stirrers called *hullers*. There, the beans' last parchment covering, the pergamino, crumbles and falls away easily. The huller then polishes the bean to a clean, glossy finish.

Cleaning and grading the beans

3 The beans are then placed on a conveyor belt that carries them past workers who remove sticks and other debris. Next, they are graded according to size, the location and altitude of the plantation where they were grown, drying and husking methods, and taste. All these factors contribute to certain flavors that consumers will be able to select thanks in part to the grade.

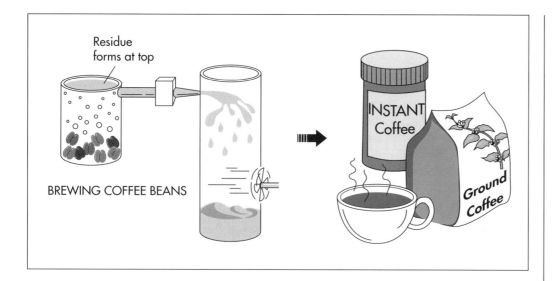

Residue forms at top

INSTANT Coffee

BREWING COFFEE BEANS

Ground Coffee

To make instant coffee, manufacturers grind the beans and brew the mixture in percolators. During this process, an extract forms and is sprayed into a cylinder. As it travels down the cylinder, the extract passes through warm air that converts it into a dry powder.

4 Once these processes are completed, workers select and pack particular types and grades of beans to fill orders from the various roasting companies that will finish preparing the beans. When beans (usually *robusta*) are harvested under the undesirable conditions of hot, humid countries or coastal regions, they must be shipped as quickly as possible, because such climates encourage insects and fungi that can severely damage a shipment.

5 When the coffee beans arrive at a roasting plant, they are again cleaned and sorted by mechanical screening devices to remove leaves, bark, and other remaining debris. If the beans are not to be decaffeinated, they are ready for roasting.

Decaffeinating

6 If the coffee is to be decaffeinated, it is now processed using either a solvent or a water method. In the first process, the coffee beans are treated with a solvent (usually methylene chloride) that leaches out the caffeine. If this decaffeination method is used, the beans must be thoroughly washed to remove traces of the solvent prior to roasting. The other method entails steaming the beans to bring the caffeine to the surface and then scraping off this caffeine-rich layer.

Roasting

7 The beans are roasted in huge commercial roasters according to procedures and specifications which vary among manufacturers (specialty shops usually purchase beans directly from the growers and roast them on-site). The most common process entails placing the beans in a large metal cylinder and blowing hot air into it. An older method, called *singeing*, calls for placing the beans in a metal cylinder that is then rotated over an electric, gas, or charcoal heater.

Regardless of the particular method used, roasting gradually raises the temperature of the beans to between 431 and 449 degrees Fahrenheit (220-230 degrees Celsius). This triggers the release of steam, carbon monoxide, carbon dioxide, and other volatiles, reducing the weight of the beans by 14 to 23 percent. The pressure of these escaping internal gases causes the beans to swell, and they increase their volume by 30 to 100 percent. Roasting also darkens the color of the beans, gives them a crumbly texture, and triggers the chemical reactions that imbue the coffee with its familiar aroma (which it has not heretofore possessed).

8 After leaving the roaster, the beans are placed in a cooling vat, wherein they are stirred while cold air is blown over them. If the coffee being prepared is high-quality, the cooled beans will now be sent through an electronic sorter equipped to detect and eliminate beans that emerged from the roasting process too light or too dark.

9 If the coffee is to be pre-ground, the manufacturer mills it immediately after roasting. Special types of grinding have been developed for each of the different types of coffee makers, as each functions best with coffee ground to a specific fineness.

Instant coffee

10 If the coffee is to be instant, it is brewed with water in huge percolators after the grinding stage. An extract is clarified from the brewed coffee and sprayed into a large cylinder. As it falls downward through this cylinder, it enters a warm air stream that converts it into a dry powder.

Packaging

11 Because it is less vulnerable to flavor and aroma loss than other types of coffee, whole bean coffee is usually packaged in foil-lined bags. If it is to retain its aromatic qualities, pre-ground coffee must be hermetically sealed: it is usually packaged in impermeable plastic film, **aluminum foil**, or cans. Instant coffee picks up moisture easily, so it is vacuum-packed in tin cans or glass jars before being shipped to retail stores.

Environmental Concerns

Methylene chloride, the solvent used to decaffeinate beans, has come under federal scrutiny in recent years. Many people charge that rinsing the beans does not completely remove the chemical, which they suspect of being harmful to human health. Although the Food and Drug Administration has con-sequently ruled that methylene chloride residue cannot exceed 10 parts per million, the water method of decaffeination has grown in popularity and is expected to replace solvent decaffeination completely.

Where To Learn More

Books

Davids, Kenneth. *Coffee.* 101 Productions, 1987.

Pamphlets

"More Fun With Coffee." National Coffee Association.

"The Story of Good Coffee from the Pacific Northwest." Starbucks Coffee Company.

Periodicals

"From Tree to Bean to Cup," *Consumer Reports.* September, 1987, p. 531.

Globus, Paul. "This Little bean is Big Business," *Reader's Digest* (Canadian), March, 1986, p. 35.

—Catherine Kolecki

Combination Lock

Background

The combination lock is one opened not by a key but by the alignment of its interior parts in a definite position. The most common types have an internal mechanism consisting of a series of three or four interconnected rings or discs that are attached to and turned by a central shaft. Manually rotating the outside knob or dial turns the discs, each of which is "programmed" to stop at a notched opening or gate. However, with a four-disc lock, certain preliminary spinning of the dial is necessary to get the lock to move the correct disc. The knob must first be turned to the right and spun past the first number four times before being allowed to stop beneath the marker. Next, rotating in the opposite direction, the knob must pass the second number three times. Reversing directions again, the user must spin the dial past the third number twice, and so on. When the apertures of all the rings align, they enable projections on a spring-loaded bolt to slide through, releasing the bolt and opening the lock.

Combination locks come in two varieties: hand and key change. One kind of hand combination lock that does not use internal wheels is the pushbutton lock, commonly installed in office doors and affording some measure of security. Pushing three or four buttons in order or together releases a shaft or deadbolt, allowing the door to open. The internal mechanism operates similarly to conventional padlocks.

Many people remember the simple padlocks that graced their school lockers. Picking these and other low-priced combination locks was frequently a game—and one often played successfully. With practice, an aspiring lockpicker could actually hear the audible clicks made when the protuberances on the bolt aligned with the notches on the discs. However, manufacturers of better locks design false gates in the discs to make cracking the lock extremely difficult. Only experts can distinguish between the three or more false gates and the true gate, and, since a lock with four discs can use any of 100,000,000 possible combinations, identifying the correct one by chance is unlikely.

The combination lock was invented in China, although historical records provide little specific information about its development. Combination locks came into popular use in the United States in the mid-1800s to secure bank vaults. The locks, integrated into the vault doors, are a colorful footnote to the history of the old West as western films testify. In 1873 James Sargent foiled many a real bank robber by perfecting a time lock that, coupled with a combination lock, kept everyone out of the vault until the clock or clocks that regulated the lock reached the time at which it was set to open, usually once a day.

Raw Materials

A typical combination lock of the padlock variety has twenty component parts, generally made of **stainless steel** or cold-rolled steel that is plated or coated to resist corrosion. Combination locks are constructed to last a lifetime, and their parts are not intended to require repair or replacement. In addition to steel, two other raw materials are essential to the combination lock. Nylon is used for the spacers that separate the discs, enabling them to turn independently, while zamak, a zinc alloy, is molded under pressure to form the bar, shaft, and outside dial.

The various components in a combination lock are made in a variety of ways. Some components, such as those made from zamak, are injection molded—the zamak is heated to a molten state and forced into a mold of the desired shape. Other components, such as the combination cam and disc, are cold rolled—passed between heavy rollers. Still other components are drawn or machined to the proper shape. Most of the components are then plated and finished to protect against corrosion.

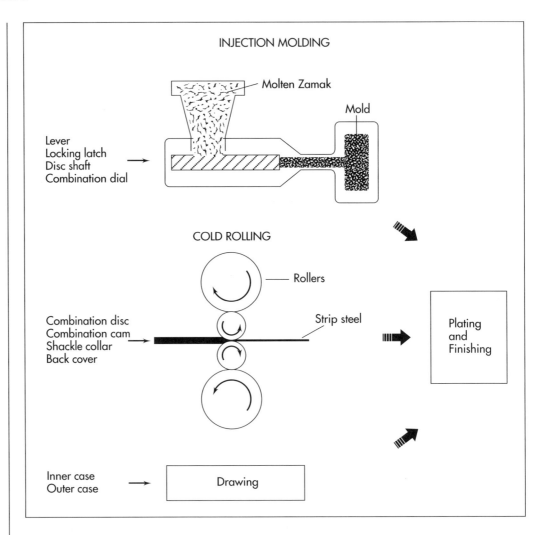

Design

A combination lock's parts can be divided into two categories: internal and external components. Excepting the springs when extended, none of the internal parts exceed two inches (5.08 centimeters) in length. The internal works of the locking mechanism comprise the lever and supporting lever post and a disc shaft about which disc spacers and the combination disc turn. Two, three, or four combination discs are the key precision elements of the mechanism, but it is the combination cam, a notched disc, that generates the combination for the lock mechanism. The cam is also attached to the outside combination dial that is turned by the lock's user. The internal disc spring supports the combination discs under tension, enabling the combination to be dialed. Other internal components in the lock case include a shackle collar that holds the shackle (the U-shaped component that detaches from the case when the lock has been opened) in the locked position with a latch that fits into the shackle notch. An inner case encloses all internal parts and gives the lock body housing strength. External parts include the lock's outer case, the shackle, a back cover, and the combination dial.

The Manufacturing Process

The twenty component parts of the typical combination lock are formed, drawn, cut, pressed, and molded on a variety of machines, both manual and automatic.

Making the internal components

1 The lever, locking latch, and disc shaft are all made by injection molding, a process in which molten zamak is poured into a mold and subjected to heat and pressure until it solidifies into the shape of the mold. Although the post is shaped at room temperature, it is also formed under high pressure.

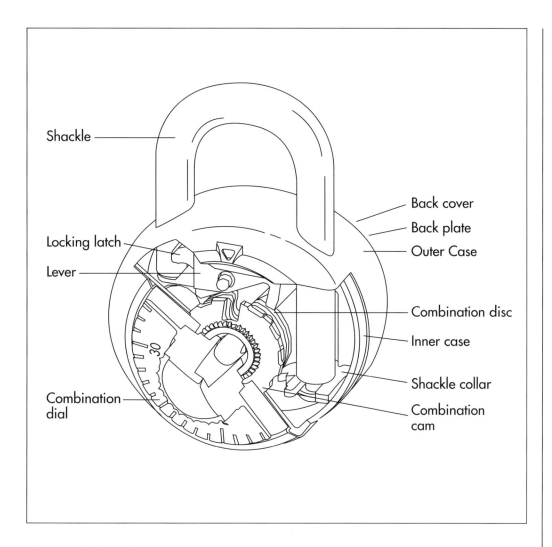

Shackle

Locking latch

Lever

Combination dial

Back cover

Back plate

Outer Case

Combination disc

Inner case

Shackle collar

Combination cam

30

The combination disc and the cam are made of cold-rolled—passed under huge rolls without being heated—flat strip steel; after being cold rolled, the steel is put in a blanking die, a sophisticated cookie cutter, which cuts (or blanks) out the properly shaped piece. The internal disc spring is made from stainless steel round wire and produced on a spring winder that automatically twists and turns the wire to form the traditional coil spring. The shackle collar, like the combination disc and cam, is made from cold-rolled flat strip steel that is blanked in a blanking die. The inner case is produced from flat steel strip and drawn to a cup configuration. This process requires great pressure to stretch and compress the material as it is pressed or drawn around a die, whose shape it takes.

Making the outer parts

2 The outer case is manufactured similarly to the inner case but from stainless steel sheet instead of strip. The back cover, also

stainless steel, is blanked in a blanking die. The durable shackle is made of round bar stock and machined on a screw machine, then formed to its U-shape and notched to accept the locking latch. It is finally annealed (heated to great temperature before being quenched in water) to make it resistant to hacksaws and bolt cutters. The combination dial, also zamak, is injection molded, then chromized. This process involves heating the part in a salt bath rich in chromium. The steel absorbs the chromium, which hardens on the surface as it cools rapidly. The dial is painted black and white wiped, which leaves the numbers highlighted against the black face.

Plating the components

3 Several plating and finishing processes can be used to protect the components against corrosion. The lever, disc shaft, combination cam, and dial are chromized. The inner case, shackle collar, and lever post are all cadmium-plated. The shackle and locking latch are copper nickel-plated. The outer case, of stainless steel, is mechanically polished to enhance luster.

Assembling the lock

4 Assembly of the components is precise with the back plate disc shaft, combination cam, and spacers forming one sub-assembly. The outer and inner cases are riveted together and then pierced at the point where the shackle is inserted. The combination dial, outer and inner case unit, and combination cam are then fastened together. Finally, these sub-assemblies and the remaining parts are fitted together. The lock case is closed and the edges folded over and sealed. Conventional hardware fasteners that can be released with the proper tool are not used.

Labeling and packaging

5 The remaining operation is the application of a removable tag or label to the lock. On this tag is the combination, determined randomly by machine draw. Lock manufacturers today jealously guard their combination setting procedures. A typical combination lock is sold in blister pack, a rigid molded plastic with cardboard backing, although locks may also be individually boxed.

Quality Control

Before any lock is packaged, many manufacturers completely test the locking and unlocking sequence. Other inspections and measurements are performed by individual operators at their stations during both manufacturing and assembly. Combination locks today enjoy a reputation for excellent reliability and durability.

Where To Learn More

Books

All About Locks and Locksmithing. Hawthorne Books, 1972.

Combination Lock Principles. Gordon Press Publishers, 1986.

The Complete Book of Locks and Locksmithing. Tab Books, 1991.

—*Peter Toeg*

Combine

Background

A combine is a large, self-propelled agricultural machine used to harvest grain crops such as wheat, corn, soybeans, milo, rapeseed, and rice. As its name suggests, the combine performs two, and sometimes more, basic functions of harvesting: first it reaps (cuts) the crop, and then it threshes it, separating the kernels of grain from the seed coverings and other debris (*chaff*). Some combines may also bale the straw that remains after threshing; the machines can also be equipped to pick cotton.

Combines are very large pieces of equipment. The operator sits atop the machine in a high cab with full-length windows for a good view. A long, square body, topped with a grain tank and a chute through which the threshed grain can be removed from it, rides on huge, front-mounted drive wheels and smaller, skinnier rear steering wheels. A turbo-charged diesel engine propels the combine and provides power for the header, threshing cylinder, cleaning system, and augers that move the grain from the header through the threshing cylinder to the grain tank and then out to a waiting truck.

As a combine progresses along rows of grain, its front component—the *reel*, a large, hexagonal metal piece set parallel to the ground—rotates, sweeping the grain stalks up into the machine. Different reel designs are required to harvest different crops. For example, while a wheat reel shunts the stalks into a cutting bar that slices them just below the heads of ripe grain, a corn reel strips the ears of corn from the stalks, leaving them flattened against the ground. Today, farmers can choose from many different types and sizes of header models. The explanation below describes the progress of wheat through a combine.

Once inside the body of the combine, the stalks are thrust against the cutter bar, a component that looks something like a comb. With the "tines" of the comb catching the stalks, a knife-like implement slices them near ground level. The stalks are then transported up onto an elevator by means of a stalk auger. Large metal cylinders, augurs feature screw-like projections that trap the grain so that it can be transported. The stalk augur, set parallel to the ground, sweeps the cut stalks onto the elevator—a pair of rollers fitted with conveyor belts that carry the grain upwards into the heart of the combine, the threshing cylinder. This cylinder is a large roller with protuberances. Rotating at high speed over a slitted, half-moon-shaped trough (the *concave*), the cylinder separates the kernels of grain from the heads of the stalks.

Once separated from the kernels, the stalks are swept up by the bars of the threshing cylinder, which deposit them on the first of a series of straw walkers. These are large, slightly overlapping, square platforms that gradually descend toward the rear of the combine. Vibrating slightly, the first walker causes the straw to drop onto the second, and the second shakes until the straw drops onto the third and lowest, at which point it is either dropped through a chute onto the ground or, in a baling machine, packed into bales. Unlike the stalks of grain, the kernels are small enough to fall through the slits in the concave and are caught in the grain pan that lies beneath it. The grain pan vibrates, shaking the kernels, the chaff, and some heads that made it through the threshing cylinder intact into a set of vibrating sieves.

Different reel designs are required to harvest different crops. For example, while a wheat reel shunts the stalks into a cutting bar that slices them just below the heads of ripe grain, a corn reel strips the ears of corn from the stalks, leaving them flattened against the ground.

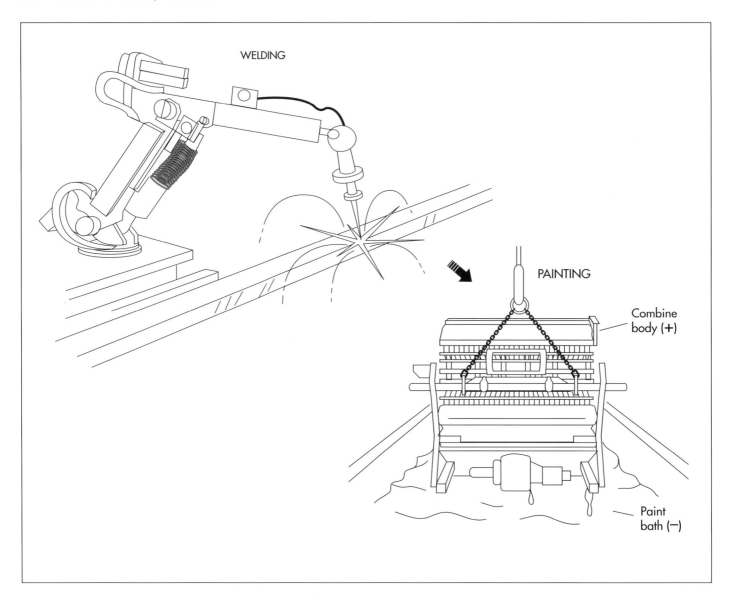

WELDING

PAINTING

Combine
body (+)

Paint
bath (−)

Most combine components are made from sheet steel. Large coils of the steel are delivered to the manufacturer, who then cuts the steel to the proper length, shapes it, and welds it. Welding is done with robots.

After the body is constructed, it is attached to an overhead conveyor, which then transports it to the paint bath. Painting is done electrostatically—the paint is given an opposite charge from the combine body. This technique allows paint to reach every exposed part of metal, providing a corrosion-free surface.

The vibrations cause the kernels to fall through the sieves, while the unthreshed heads are trapped. A fan adjacent to the sieves blows air across them, causing the chaff (which is very light) to blow backwards out the rear of the combine. The unthreshed heads are then routed, via another auger, into the tailings elevator, which transports them back into the threshing cylinder. Meanwhile, the kernels fall into the grain augur and are transported up into the grain elevator, which deposits them in the grain tank. Yet another augur, the unloading augur, is inserted into the grain tank, and grain can be removed from the tank through it.

The combine was developed during the 1800s, when many agricultural processes were being automated. Beginning as early as 1826, individual inventors and businessmen turned out

hundreds of contraptions to aid farmers in harvesting grains. However, these early machines performed only one of two important functions: they were either reapers, which cut the stalks of grain, or threshers, which separated the grain from the chaff.

The first reaper was designed by a Scottish minister, Patrick Bell, in 1826. Of the many others developed during the mid-1800s, the most successful machine was created by an American, Robert McCormick, and perfected by his more famous son, Cyrus. Robert McCormick worked on various reaper designs from 1809 until 1831, and Cyrus McCormick, continuing his father's work, sold the first McCormick Reaper in 1839.

Threshing machines, to separate and clean the kernels of grain, were first assembled in the late 1700s and were in widespread use in England and Scotland by the 1830s. Over the next two decades, several Americans invented threshing machines. The most successful were Hiram and John Pitts, brothers who sold the first "Chicago Pitts" thresher in 1852. Jerome Increase Case also produced an enduringly popular thresher: founded in 1844, the company that bears his name continues to thrive today.

The first farm machine that could do the work of both a reaper and a thresher was patented in 1828, although the first model was not sold until 1838. Both huge and cumbersome, the machine required twenty horses to pull it. For this reason, combines were not used in large numbers until the early twentieth century, when refinements had rendered them easier to use.

Today, modern combines are the most complicated machines produced on an assembly line. While a passenger **automobile** is made up of 6,000 parts, a combine comprises over 17,000. This complexity is reflected in the price: a single combine can cost as much as $100,000. Today, there are two major combine manufacturers in the United States. Both firms, John Deere and J. I. Case, have large, modern manufacturing plants that sit next to one another along the Mississippi River in East Moline, Illinois, and in 1990, they sold about 11,500 combines in the United States and Canada.

Raw Materials

Sheet steel, the main raw material used in manufacturing combines, is delivered to the manufacturing plant in massive rolls, 48 inches (121.92 centimeters) wide and weighing up to 12,000 pounds (5,448 kilograms). After being uncoiled, the rolls are cut into plates that are then cut, drilled, shaped, and welded to make the combine body, external panels, and grain tank. Round steel bars and hollow, square steel channels are also cut and drilled for axles, drive shafts, augers, and supporting structures. Complex subassemblies such as the engine and transmission are either built at other company plants or are purchased from smaller companies. Often, a delivery vehicle transports components to the exact spot along the assembly line where the parts are needed.

After assembly, the combine is painted with water-based **paint** that reaches the factory as a powder and is mixed with highly purified water.

The Manufacturing Process

Cutting the steel into blanks

1 Manufacturing a combine begins with the delivery of large coils of sheet steel to the sheet metal shop. The coil steel is loaded into one of several machines that make up the cut-to-length line in the sheet metal shop. Computer-controlled rollers pull the steel from the coil, flatten it, and feed it into a cutting machine. The steel is cut into blanks, basic rectangular shapes that are later welded together to form the body of the combine and the top-mounted grain tank. For maximum efficiency, the cut-to-length line operates on pre-determined batch schedules. The basic metal shapes cut from the steel coils are used during the day or week that they are cut, so there is no storage of basic components.

2 From the cut-to-length line, the blanks are moved to the cut-to-shape line. In a laser punch press, an industrial laser cuts complex shapes from them and drills holes for shafts, piping, and bolts. Then the press exerts up to 1,000 tons of pressure to bend the steel into final form.

Welding the formed parts

3 Small batches of parts are moved from the sheet metal shop to the welding area, where cellular manufacturing techniques are used for speed and quality control. In cellular manufacturing, several manufacturing functions are grouped in one area so parts can be quickly passed from one operation to the next, and several subcomponents are loaded on a transportation skid before being sent to the next assembly step. Thus, all the parts needed to assemble a batch of components are present when the skid arrives. To further enhance efficiency, much of the welding of sheet steel components is done by powerful, computer-controlled units. Hydraulic lifts properly position components that are then welded by one-armed robots. As the smaller components of the combine are assembled, the body begins to take shape.

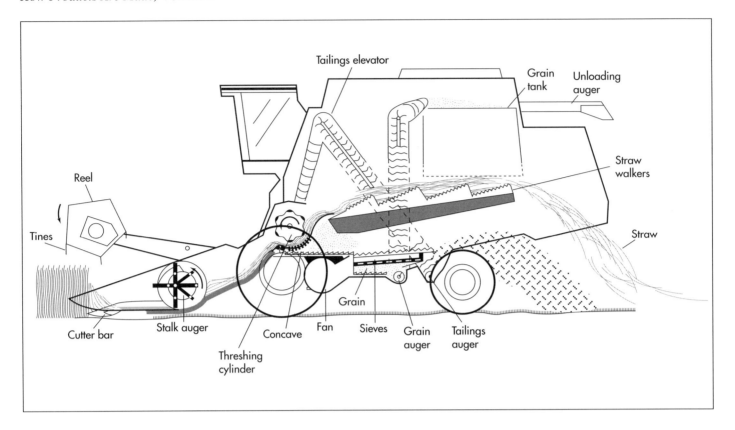

Combines are large, complex, and expensive vehicles—a modern combine contains about 17,000 parts (an automobile contains 6,000) and can cost up to $100,000. Different reel designs allow combines to perform different functions.

In the form of a simple frame, it is now attached to an overhead loadbar conveyor track that carries it through the remainder of the production process.

Painting

4 After the body has been welded, the overhead conveyor transports it to and submerges it in the paint tank, a huge 48,000 gallon (181,776 liters) tank full of electrostatically charged paint. Because combines are used and stored outside, their paint must be able to resist the harmful effects of sunshine and moisture, and the electrostatic process insures that it will. In electrostatic painting, the metal combine body is given a positive electrical charge while the water-based paint is given a negative charge. Because opposite electrical charges are attracted to each other, the positively charged body attracts the negatively charged paint, causing the paint to bond to the combine tightly and completely (only rubber gaskets and other non-metallic parts are not touched by the paint).

5 After the conveyor lifts the combine body from the paint bath, it suspends it over the tank for a few moments so that excess paint can drip off. The body is then moved into a 363 degree Fahrenheit (182

degrees Celsius) oven where the paint is baked to a hard, rust-resistant finish.

6 After painting, the combine body is carried through the assembly line so that other major components may be installed. Where necessary, these components have also been dipped in the electrostatic paint bath. Once the axles, hubs, and **tire**s have been added, the combine is removed from the overhead conveyor and is towed from station to station.

Welding the grain tank

7 After the combine body, the other significant structural assembly is the grain tank. In the grain tank assembly area, skilled workers use a complex positioning and welding system to complete more than 500 separate welds in two, 10-½ minute sequences. Automated sheet metal handling equipment pulls flat sheets from skids fresh from the cut-to-shape line in the sheet metal shop. These sheets are then loaded onto a huge metal table the size of a two-car garage. Next, hydraulic cylinders position the side panels as human welders scramble to secure the corners of the grain tank with tack welds. When the human welders are out of harm's

way, robot arms swing into action, making hundreds of welds in a few minutes.

Final assembly

8 After the body and grain tank have been painted, they are brought to the final assembly line, where 22 different assembly operations are performed. Major components like the engine module are installed, wiring and hydraulic lines are connected, and all systems are tested. Oil, anti-freeze, and gas are added, and the engine is started. On the outside, a final coating of clear polyurethane is applied across the top of the wide, flat surfaces of the cab, grain tank, and engine module, and decals are applied.

Quality Control

Because a combine is an expensive farming implement and is used during the critical days of harvest, each unit must meet the highest standards of operational performance. Failure caused by materials or workmanship cannot be tolerated. Therefore, quality control begins with the suppliers of the raw materials and continues even after final assembly.

Today, combine manufacturers randomly test incoming samples of sheet metal and bar stock to ensure that no weaknesses exist in the metal. In each manufacturing step, workers establish procedures to limit the chance of defects caused by faulty manufacturing methods. Each station in the manufacturing process is responsible for delivering a defect-free component to the next station. Such a manufacturing philosophy drives individual employees to check their own work for defects.

The Future

Over the last few years, combine design has changed, relying less on pulleys, belts, and drive shafts and more on electronic controls, solenoid actuators, and hydraulic power systems. Over the next few years, improvements in the engine and transmission will give farmers even greater power and fuel efficiency. Another area of development is in the threshing cylinder. A new design now being studied features two rotating cages, one inside the other, to clean the grain. Such a design would be more efficient, allowing the combine body to be smaller. Secondary cleaning equipment and fans to blow chaff away from the grain also could be eliminated. These constant efforts to improve design are allowing combine manufacturers to offer units with more power, greater capacity, and greater reliability. Today, combines can offer 5,000 to 10,000 hours between engine overhauls and 25 to 30 percent more power over units just 10 years old.

Where To Learn More

Books

Bell, Brian. *Farm Machinery*, 3rd ed. Diamond Farm Book Publishers, 1989.

Olney, Ross. *The Farm Combine*. Walker and Company, 1984.

Periodicals

"Change Names The Game," *OEM Off-Highway*, May 1992, pp. 8-9.

"Deere: Where There's No Such Thing As The Status Quo," *Production*, June 1991.

—*Robert C. Miller*

Compact Disc

A standard CD can store up to 74 minutes of data. However, most CDs contain only about 50 minutes of music, all of which is recorded on only one side of the CD (the underside).

Background

Ever since the invention of the phonograph in 1876, music has been a popular source of home entertainment. In recent years, the compact disc has become the playback medium of choice for recorded music.

A compact disc, or CD, is an optical storage medium with digital data recorded on it. The digital data can be in the form of audio, video, or computer information. When the CD is played, the information is read or detected by a tightly focused light source called a laser (thus the name optical medium). This article will focus on audio compact discs, which are used to play back recorded music.

The history of the compact disc can be traced back to the development of electronic technology and particularly digital electronic technology in the 1960s. Although the first applications of this technology were not in the recording area, it found increasing use in audio components as the technology evolved.

During the same period, many companies started experimenting with optical information storage and laser technology. Among these companies, electronic giants Sony and Philips made notable progress in this area.

By the 1970s, digital and optical technologies had reached a level where they could be combined to develop a single audio system. These technologies provided solutions to the three main challenges faced by the developers of digital audio.

The first challenge was to find a suitable method for recording audio signals in digital format, a process known as audio encoding. A practical method of audio encoding was developed from the theories published by C. Shannon in 1948. This method, known as pulse code modulation (PCM), is a technique that samples a sound during a short time interval and converts the sample to a numerical value that is then modulated or stored for later retrieval.

The storing of audio signals in digital form requires a large amount of data. For instance, to store one second of music requires one million bits of data. The next challenge, therefore, was to find a suitable storage medium to accommodate any significant amount of sound. The solution to this problem came in the form of optical discs. An optical disc can store large amounts of data tightly compressed together. For example, one million bits of data on a CD can occupy an area smaller than a pinhead. This information is read by means of a laser beam that is capable of focusing on a very narrow area as small as 1/2500th of an inch.

The final challenge of digital audio was to process the densely packed information on compact discs quickly enough to produce continuous music. The solution was provided by the development of integrated circuit technology, which allow the processing of millions of computations in just micro-seconds.

By the late 1970s, a common set of standards for the optical storage discs had been developed by the joint efforts of Sony and Philips. A consortium of 35 hardware manufacturers agreed to adopt this standard in 1981 and the first compact discs and **compact disc player**s were introduced in the market in 1982.

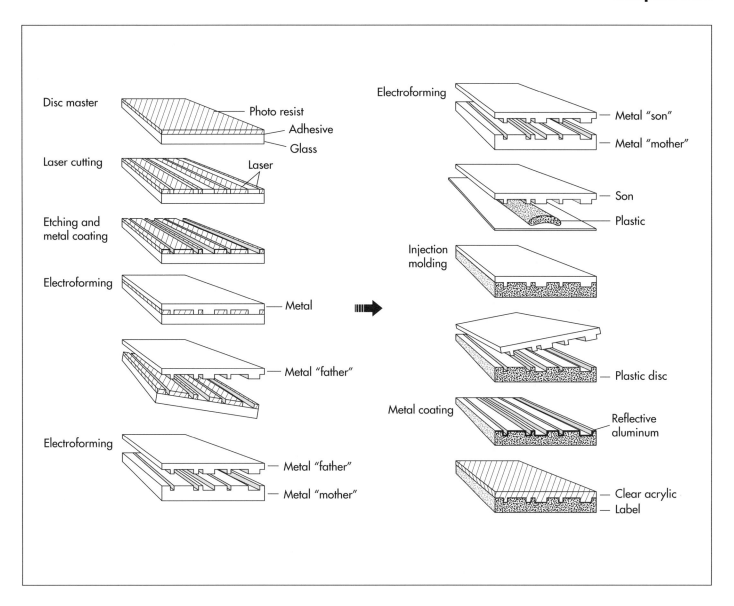

Raw Materials

A compact disc is a deceptively simple looking device considering the technology required to make it. CDs consist of three layers of materials:

- A base layer made of a polycarbonate plastic.

- A thin layer of aluminum coating over the polycarbonate plastic.

- A clear protective acrylic coating over the aluminum layer.

Some manufacturers use a silver or even **gold** layer instead of the aluminum layer in the manufacture of their compact discs.

Design

The compact disc is designed strictly according to the standards established by Sony and Philips in order to maintain universal compatibility. A CD is 4.72 inches (120 millimeters) in diameter and .047 inches (1.2 millimeters) thick. The positioning hole in the middle is .59 of an inch (15 millimeters) in diameter. A CD usually weighs around .53 of an ounce (15 grams).

A standard CD can store up to 74 minutes of data. However, most CDs contain only about 50 minutes of music, all of which is recorded on only one side of the CD (the underside). The recorded data on the CD takes the form of a continuous spiral starting from the inside and moving outward. This spiral or track consists of a series of indentations called pits,

Making a compact disc involves first preparing a glass "disc master." This master is then encoded with the desired information and put through a series of electroforming steps. In electroforming, metal layers are deposited on the glass master using electric currents. When the final master version is ready, its information is transfered onto a plastic disc. A reflective aluminum layer is applied, followed by a clear acrylic protective layer, and finally the label.

separated by sections called lands. A tiny laser beam moving along the track reflects light back to a photo sensor. The sensor sees more light when it is on a land than when it is on a pit, and these variations in light intensity are converted into electrical signals that represent the music originally recorded.

The Manufacturing Process

Compact discs must be manufactured under very clean and dust free conditions in a "clean room," which is kept free from virtually all dust particles. The air in the room is specially filtered to keep out dirt, and occupants of the room must wear special clothing. Because an average dust particle is 100 times larger than the average pit and land on a CD, even the smallest dust particle can render a disc useless.

Preparing the disc master

1 The original music is first recorded onto a digital audio tape. Next, the audio program is transferred to a 3/4-inch (1.9 centimeters) video tape, and then data (called subcodes) used for indexing and tracking the music is added to the audio data on the tape. At this point, the tape is called a pre-master.

2 The pre-master tape will be used to create the disc master (also called the glass master), which is a disc made from specially prepared glass. The glass is polished to a smooth finish and coated with a layer of adhesive and a layer of photoresist material. The disc is approximately 9.45 inches (240 millimeters) in diameter and .24 of an inch (six millimeters) thick. After the adhesive and photoresist are applied, the disc is cured in an oven.

3 Next, both the pre-master tape and the disc master are put into a complex laser cutting machine. The machine plays back the audio program on the pre-master tape. As it does so, the program is transferred to a device called a CD encoder, which in turn generates an electrical signal. This signal powers a laser beam, which exposes or "cuts" grooves into the photoresist coating on the glass disc (the disc master).

4 The grooves that have been exposed are then etched away by chemicals; these etched grooves will form the pits of the CD's surface. A metal coating, usually silver, is then applied to the disc. The disc master now contains the exact pit-and-land track that the finished CD will have.

Electroforming

5 After etching, the disc master undergoes a process called electroforming, in which another metal layer such as nickel is deposited onto the disc's surface. The phrase "electro" is used because the metal is deposited using an electric current. The disc is bathed in an electrolytic solution, such as nickel solphamate, and as the electric current is applied, a layer of metal forms on the disc master. The thickness of this metal layer is strictly controlled.

6 Next, the newly applied metal layer is pulled apart from the disc master, which is put aside. The metal layer, or father, contains a negative impression of the disc master track; in other words, the track on the metal layer is an exact replica, but in reverse, of the track on the disc master.

7 The metal father then undergoes further electroforming to produce one or more mothers, which are simply metal layers that again have positive impressions of the original disc master track. Using the same electroforming process, each mother then produces a son (also called a stamper) with a negative impression of the track. It is the son that is then used to create the actual CD.

8 After being separated from the mother, the metal son is rinsed, dried, polished and put in a punching machine that cuts out the center hole and forms the desired outside diameter.

Replication

9 The metal son is then put into a hollow cavity—a die—of the proper disc shape in an injection molding machine. Molten polycarbonate plastic is then poured into this die to form around the metal son. Once cooled, the plastic is shaped like the son, with the pits and grooves—once again in a positive impression of the original disc master track—formed into one side.

10 The center hole is then punched out of plastic disc, which is transparent at

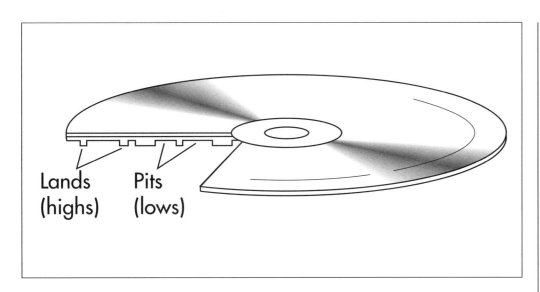

Lands
(highs)

Pits
(lows)

A finished compact disc contains a series of tracks or indentations called "lands" and "pits." A CD player uses a laser beam to read these layers and convert the reflection first into an electrical signal and then into music.

this stage. Next, the disc is scanned for flaws such as water bubbles, dust particles, and warps. If a flaw is found, the disc must be discarded.

11 If the disc meets the quality standards, it is then coated with an extremely thin, reflective layer of aluminum. The coating is applied using vacuum deposition. In this process, aluminum is put into a vacuum chamber and heated to the point of evaporation, which allows it to be applied evenly to the plastic disc.

12 Finally, a clear acrylic plastic is applied to the disc to help protect the underlying layers from physical damage such as scratches. After the label is printed, generally using a silk-screening process, the compact disc is complete and ready for packaging and shipment.

Quality Control

A compact disc is a very precise and accurate device. The microscopic size of the data does not allow for any errors in the manufacturing process. The smallest of dust particles can render a disc unreadable.

The first quality control concern is to ensure that the clean room environment is properly monitored, with controlled temperature, humidity, and filtering systems. Beyond that, quality control checkpoints are built into the manufacturing process. The disc master, for instance, is inspected for smoothness and its photoresist surface for proper thickness by means of laser equipment. At later stages in

the process, such as before and after the aluminum coating is deposited and after the protective acrylic coating is applied, the disc is checked automatically for warps, bubbles, dust particles, and encoding errors on the spiral track. This mechanical checking is combined with human inspection using polarized light, which allows the human eye to spot defective pits in the track.

In addition to checking the discs, the equipment used to manufacture them must be carefully maintained. The laser cutting machine, for instance, must be very stable, because any vibration would make proper cutting impossible. If strict quality control is not maintained, the rejection rate of CDs can be very high.

The Future

The massive storage capabilities, accuracy of data, and relative immunity from wear and tear will continue to make compact discs a popular medium for music and video applications. The hottest new product stirring public interest is CD-Interactive or CD-I, a multimedia system that allows users to interact with computers and television.

Manufacturing techniques will continue to be streamlined and improved, requiring smaller facilities and less human intervention in the process and resulting in lower CD rejection rates. Already in the first decade of CD manufacture, the manufacturing and quality control processes have become almost completely automated.

Where To Learn More

Books

Brewer, Bryan. *The Compact Disc Book: A Complete Guide to the Digital Sound of the Future.* Harcourt Brace, 1987.

Nakajima, H. *Compact Disc Technology.* IOS Press, 1991.

Pohlmann, Ken C. *Principles of Digital Audio.* 1985.

Pohlmann, Ken C. *The Compact Disk Handbook,* 2nd ed., A-R Editions, 1992.

Periodicals

Bernard, Josef. "Compact Discs—Bit by Bit," *Radio-Electronics.* August, 1986, p. 62.

Birchall, Steve. "The Magic of CD Manufacturing," *Stereo Review.* October, 1986, p. 67.

—Rashid Riaz

Compact Disc Player

Background

A **compact disc**, also popularly known simply as a CD, is an optical storage medium with digital data recorded on its surface. A compact disc player is a device that reads the recorded data by means of an optical beam and accurately reproduces the original information (music, pictures, or data). Because the player reads the information by optical means, there is no physical wear and tear on the disc. The basic technology used in all compact disc players is essentially the same, whether the player is designed for audio, video, or computer applications. This article will focus on players designed for audio (specifically, home audio) applications.

The history of the compact disc system can be traced back to the early 1970s, when rapid advancement in digital electronics, laser optics, and large scale integration (LSI) technologies took place. Many companies started exploring the possibility of storing audio signals in optical form using digital rather than analog means. A practical method of modulating the audio signals was found using theories published in 1948 by a scientist named Claude E. Shannon. This method, known as Pulse Code Modulation (PCM), samples audio signals during a short time interval and then converts the samples into numerical values for storage in digital format.

The storage of audio in digital format (known as *audio encoding*) requires large amounts of data. For example, storing one second of audio information requires one million bits of data. Optical discs capable of storing billions of bits of data in a very small area were found ideal for such applications. An optical disc can store up to one million bits of data on an area as small as a pinhead.

Once the technologies for recording and storing digital audio were found, manufacturers started looking for ways to read and process the data stored in such a small area. Experiments with laser devices (a laser emits a very narrow beam of light capable of focusing on a very small area) proved quite successful. The development of LSI techniques meant that the huge amount of data stored on the disc could be processed fast enough to provide continuous music. The stage was now set for the development of a complete compact disc system.

Although many companies participated in early research and experimentation with the various technologies involved in a compact disc system, two companies—Sony of Japan and Philips of the Netherlands—are credited with successfully merging these technologies into a complete system. The two companies collaborated to develop specific standards for the compact disc system, and a consortium of 35 manufacturers agreed to adopt these standards in 1981. The first compact disc players were introduced in the European and Japanese markets in late 1982 and in the United States in early 1983.

Raw Materials

A compact disc player is a very sophisticated piece of electronic equipment. The simple exterior contains complex interior mechanisms to read and process audio signals into very clear and crisp music. The various components include a housing cabinet, an optical pick-up assembly, and printed circuit boards (PCBs), which contain microchips that direct the electronic processes of the system.

The cabinet that houses the maze of components is usually made of light, reinforced alu-

Like a record on a phonograph, the compact disc is rotated on a turntable, and the audio is read by a pick-up device. However, unlike a record player, the pick-up device in a CD player is not a mechanical stylus (a needle) but an optical laser beam that does not come into physical contact with the compact disc.

minum. The laser is a small glass tube filled with gas and a small power supply to generate a laser beam, while the photodiode—a semiconducting part that the light that is reflected from the compact disc into an electrical signal—is generally made of silicon or germanium. The lenses and mirrors in the optical pick-up are made of highly polished glass or plastic. This assembly is housed in its own plastic enclosure. The majority of the electronic components—resistors, transistors, and capacitors—are contained on microchips attached to PCBs. The base material of these components is usually silicon. The hardware that connects the various subassemblies together consists of a variety of metal and plastic nuts, screws, washers, pulleys, motors, gears, belts, and cables.

Design

A compact disc is a 4.75 inch-diameter (12.065 centimeters) polycarbonate plastic disc containing approximately 74 minutes of audio information. Not all the information on the disc is music; some of it is used for error detection, synchronization, and display purposes. Information on a CD is encoded on a spiral track in the form of indentations called *lands* and *pits* that represent binary highs and lows. It is these indentations that the CD player's laser "reads."

Conceptually, the design of a CD player resembles that of a phonograph (record) player. Like a record, the compact disc is rotated on a turntable, and the audio is read by a pick-up device. However, unlike a record player, the motor does not rotate the turntable at a constant speed but adjusts it in accordance with the distance of the pick-up from the center of the turntable. Furthermore, the pick-up device in a CD player is not a mechanical stylus (a needle) but an optical laser beam that does not come into physical contact with the compact disc. This laser focuses its beam on the disc track that contains the lands and pits, and the CD player's detector (the photodiode) senses the difference between the light reflected from the lands and that reflected by the pits. The photodiode turns this reflected light into an electrical signal. Relayed to the electronic circuit board, this signal is then converted back to sound.

There are basically three subassemblies in a compact disc player: the disc drive mecha-

nism assembly; the optical pick-up assembly; and the electronic circuit board assembly, which coordinates the other systems inside the player and which includes the servo mechanism and data decoding circuitry. By sending signals to the servo mechanism, the circuit board adjusts the motor speed, focusing, and tracking of the optical pick-up; manages the flow of data to the decoding circuitry; and provides display information in response to the various buttons on the control panel.

The disc drive mechanism consists of a spindle that holds the CD and a motor that rotates it. The motor, called the *spindle motor,* is mounted underneath the plastic disc loading tray or turntable. A separate motor mounted on the chassis (the base or frame of the CD player) moves the loading tray in and out of the player; this is done by means of a gear that is attached to the motor and that also operates a larger gear to raise and lower a clamp for holding the disc in place.

The optical pick-up consists of a laser, a photodiode, and various lenses and mirrors. The entire subassembly slides back and forth on rails and is controlled by the servo mechanism that receives directing signals from the circuit board. The optical pick-up is usually located underneath the clamp that positions the disc, while the motor that moves the assembly is mounted on the chassis close to the rails. The mechanism works by directing a laser beam through lenses and mirrors onto the underside of the compact disc. The lenses and mirrors keep the beam properly focused. If the beam hits a pit on the disc, no light is reflected and the photodiode remains disengaged. If the beam hits a land, light is reflected back through the lenses and mirrors onto the photodiode, which then generates an electrical signal. This signal is transferred to the electronic circuit board assembly, where it is converted by the data decoding system into audio signals for playback.

The electronic circuit board assembly consists of printed circuit boards that contain the circuitry for the servo mechanism, which operates the optical pick-up system, data decoding, and control system. There are many integrated circuits chips, microprocessors, and large scale integrated components on the board assembly.

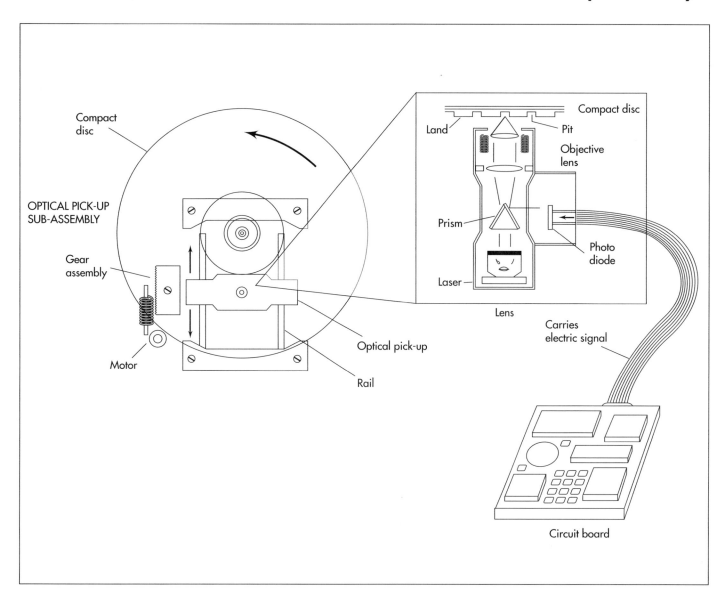

(Diagram labels: Compact disc; OPTICAL PICK-UP SUB-ASSEMBLY; Gear assembly; Motor; Optical pick-up; Rail; Land; Pit; Compact disc; Objective lens; Prism; Photo diode; Laser; Lens; Carries electric signal; Circuit board)

The Manufacturing Process

In today's manufacturing environment there is no single method of manufacture and assembly. Products are increasingly made as subassemblies and brought together as larger subassemblies or as the final product. Robotics and computer run lines allow for virtually any part to be installed in any state of the subassembly at any point in the process. The sequence can be changed in minutes to allow for modifications or quality control check points. The manufacturing process detailed here, therefore, follows a similar approach to the actual manufacturing process used in the industry. The process is first described in terms of the various subassemblies and then the description details how the various subassemblies are brought together to make the final product.

Optical pick-up subassembly

1 Purchased from outside contractors, the laser and the photodiode are installed beneath the disc clamp. The various lenses and mirrors in the assembly must be properly spaced and aligned so that they can focus and direct light as necessary. The whole assembly is then housed in a plastic case. The case is made by the one of the usual plastic forming processes such as extrusion or injection molding, while the lenses and mirrors (usually silicon) are cut into the proper shape and then finely polished with abrasives. The semiconducting photodiode is made by preparing and polishing a substance such as silicon or germanium and then adding impu-

A key assembly in a compact disc player is the optical pick-up assembly. It is situated on rails so that it can move back and forth underneath the compact disc. It works by directing a laser beam at the CD; if the laser hits a land, the reflected light then travels to the photodiode, which generates an electrical signal. In turn, the signal moves to the CD player's circuit board, which converts the signal into music.

rities to create layers. Electrical contacts are then added. After the optical components are in position, the gears and belt that will help to position the optical pick-up are put in place.

Disc drive subassembly

2 Next, the motor that will move the optical pick-up is connected to the gears and belt and placed on the chassis. The loading tray is now centered, and the spindle motor that will rotate the disc is installed. After the clamp to which the optical pick-up has been attached is positioned adjacent to the loading tray, the tray, clamp, and pick-up motor are installed in the loading drawer, which is placed in the CD player's cabinet.

Electronic circuit board subassembly

3 Last to be assembled are the electronic components. Designed by engineers using computer-aided design (CAD) packages, the circuit boards consist of a copper-clad base that has a pattern transferred onto it (*masking*) through screen printing or a similar method. After being coated with a photosensitive material, the patterned areas are etched away chemically to create a multi-layered board—the layers comprise the various transistors and capacitors that make up the circuits. The tiny microchips (usually made of silicon) that are mounted on the board are made in the same way, except on a much smaller scale. Depending on the manufacturer, the CD player may have one large circuit board or several smaller boards. After they have been attached to the panel or panels, the circuits are attached to the CD player's front control panel, the switch assembly, and finally the power supply.

Final assembly

4 Once the various subassemblies are ready, they are connected and interfaced together to complete the final assembly. Most of the work performed at this stage is done by human workers. The CD player is now tested and sent for packaging.

Quality Control

As previously noted, a compact disc player is a very sophisticated device, and strict quality control measures are adopted from the initial to the final stage of the manufacture to ensure the proper functioning of the player in accordance with industry standards.

Because so many of the components in a compact disc player are made by specialized vendors, the player manufacturer must depend on these vendors to produce quality parts. Some of the most crucial elements are those in the optical pick-up assembly. The lenses and mirrors used in the laser pick-up, for instance, are made of high quality glass, and human contact must be avoided during the manufacturing process to keep their surfaces clean and smudge free. Similarly, the electronic circuit components must be made in a "clean room" environment (containing special air filters as well as clothing requirements), because even a single dust particle can cause malfunctioning in the circuitry. The circuit boards and chips are tested at many levels by diagnostic machines to pinpoint faults in the circuits.

As for quality control by the player manufacturer, the disc drive assembly is inspected for proper alignment of the motor, spindle, loading tray, and the various gears. In addition, the optical pick-up is checked for proper alignment of lenses and the laser beam. Once the subassemblies are tied together in the cabinet, all wiring connections are inspected for proper electrical contact and correct interface with the other components. Visual inspections to check belts, pulleys, and gears are an integral part of the quality control process. The final inspection consists of playing a test disc that generates special signals and patterns, enabling workers to track down faults in the system. In addition, the various front panel switches and buttons are checked to ensure that they perform the functions indicated and display the appropriate information on the panel.

The Future

The CD system technology has come a long way in the last few years, and new applications for compact disc systems are being discovered every day. The market has already seen the introduction of CD-ROMs, CD-Videos and CD-Interactive. The latest product to attract consumer attention is Kodak's Photo-CD, which can display photographs on television and computer screens. These pictures can be edited or cropped by the user, just like clip art images.

Audio CD systems will see the introduction of many new features in the coming years. Players featuring advanced remote control functions are now in the development stage.

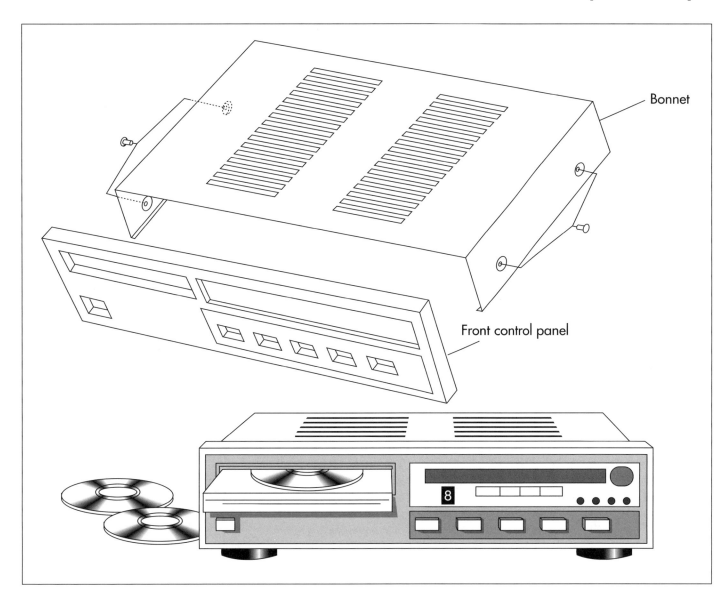

Bonnet

Front control panel

These functions will allow the user to display information on the remote control unit itself, such as song titles, artist names, and the actual lyrics of the songs. Compact discs capable of both recording and playback, like a cassette tape, are also in the works. The CD's vast storage capabilities also lend itself to many broad-based multimedia applications, and it is quite possible that compact discs will become the common medium of data exchange for all audio, video, and computer applications.

Where To Learn More

Books

Brewer, Bryan and Ed Key. *The Compact Disc Book*. 1987.

Davidson, Homer L. *Troubleshooting and Repairing the Compact Disc Player*. 1989.

Pohlman, Ken. *Principles of Digital Audio*. 1985.

Schetina, Erik. *The Compact Disc*. 1989.

Williams, Gene B. *Compact Disk Players*. TAB Books, 1992.

Periodicals

Matzkin, Jonathan, Rock Miller, Gayle C. Ehrenman, et al. "CD-ROM Drives: Finally Up to Speed," *PC Magazine*. October 29, 1991, p. 283.

Ranada, David. "Loose Bits," *High Fidelity*. March, 1986, p. 22.

Shah, Prasanna. "Music of the Bitstream," *Audio*. January, 1991, p. 56.

— *Rashid Riaz*

The housing for a CD player includes a top cover or "bonnet" and a front control panel. The compact disc rests on a loading tray that slides in and out of the player.

Concrete

Although people commonly use the word "cement" as a synonym for concrete, the terms in fact denote different substances: cement, which encompasses a wide variety of fine-ground powders that harden when mixed with water, represents only one of several components in modern concrete.

Background

Concrete is a hardened building material created by combining a chemically inert mineral aggregate (usually sand, gravel, or crushed stone), a binder (natural or synthetic cement), chemical additives, and water. Although people commonly use the word "cement" as a synonym for concrete, the terms in fact denote different substances: cement, which encompasses a wide variety of fine-ground powders that harden when mixed with water, represents only one of several components in modern concrete. As concrete dries, it acquires a stone-like consistency that renders it ideal for constructing roads, bridges, water supply and sewage systems, factories, airports, railroads, waterways, mass transit systems, and other structures that comprise a substantial portion of the U.S. wealth. According to the National Institute of Standards and Technology (NIST), building such facilities is in itself one of the nation's largest industries and represents about 10 percent of the gross national product. Over $4 billion worth of hydraulic cement, a variety which hardens under water, is produced annually in the United States for use in $20 billion worth of concrete construction. The value of all cement-based structures in the United States is in the trillions of dollars—roughly commensurate with the anticipated cost of repairing those structures over the next twenty years.

The words cement and concrete are both of Latin origin, reflecting the likelihood that the ancient Romans were the first to use the substances. Many examples of Roman concrete construction remain in the countries that encircle the Mediterranean, where Roman builders had access to numerous natural cement deposits. Natural cement consists mainly of lime, derived from limestone and often combined with volcanic ash. It formed the basis of most civil engineering until the eighteenth century, when the first synthetic cements were developed.

The earliest manmade cement, called hydraulic lime, was developed in 1756, when an English engineer named John Smeaton needed a strong material to rebuild the Eddystone lighthouse off the coast of Devon. Although the Romans had used hydraulic cement, the formula was lost from the collapse of their empire in the fifth century A.D. until Smeaton reinvented it. During the early nineteenth century several other Englishmen contributed to the refinement of synthetic cement, most notably Joseph Aspdin and Isaac Charles Johnson. In 1824 Aspdin took out a patent on a synthetic blend of limestone and clay which he called Portland cement because it resembled limestone quarried on the English Isle of Portland. However, Aspdin's product was not as strong as that produced in 1850 by Johnson, whose formula served as the basis of the Portland cement that is still widely used today. Concrete made with Portland cement is considered superior to that made with natural cement because it is stronger, more durable, and of more consistent quality. According to the American Society of Testing of Materials (ASTM), Portland cement is made by mixing calcareous (consisting mostly of calcium carbonate) material such as limestone with silica-, alumina-, and iron oxide-containing materials. These substances are then burned until they fuse together, and the resulting admixture, or clinker, is ground to form Portland cement.

Although Portland cement quickly displaced natural cement in Europe, concrete technology in the United States lagged considerably behind. In America, natural cement rock was first discovered during the early 1800s, when it was used to build the Erie Canal. The construction of such inland waterways led to the establishment of a number of American companies producing natural cement. However, because of Portland cement's greater strength, many construction engineers preferred to order it from Europe, despite the additional time and expense involved. Thomas Edison was very interested in Portland cement and even cast phonograph cabinets of the material. When United States industry figured out how to make Portland cement during the early 1870s, the production of natural cement in America began to decline.

After the refinement of Portland cement, the next major innovation in concrete technology occurred during the late nineteenth century, when reinforced concrete was invented. While concrete easily resists compression, it does not tolerate tension well, and this weakness meant that it could not be used to build structures—like bridges or buildings with arches—that would be subject to bending action. French and English engineers first rectified this deficiency during the 1850s by embedding steel bars in those portions of a concrete structure subject to tensile stress. Although the concrete itself is not strengthened, structures built of reinforced concrete can better withstand bending, and the technique was used internationally by the early twentieth century.

Another form of strengthened concrete, prestressed concrete, was issued a U.S. patent in 1888. However, it was not widely used until World War II, when several large docks and bridges that utilized it were constructed. Rather than reinforcing a highly stressed portion of a concrete structure with steel, engineers could now compress a section of concrete before they subjected it to stress, thereby increasing its ability to withstand tension.

Today, different types of concrete are categorized according to their method of installation. Ready- or pre-mixed concrete is batched and mixed at a central plant before it is delivered to a site. Because this type of concrete is sometimes transported in an agitator truck, it is also known as transit-mixed concrete. Shrink-mixed concrete is partially mixed at the central plant, and its mixing is then completed en route to the site.

Raw Materials

Structural concrete normally contains one part cement to two parts fine mineral aggregate to four parts coarse mineral aggregate, though these proportions are often varied to achieve the strength and flexibility required in a particular setting. In addition, concrete contains a wide range of chemicals that imbue it with the characteristics desired for specific applications. Portland cement, the kind most often used in concrete, is made from a combination of a calcareous material (usually limestone) and of silica and alumina found as clay or shale. In lesser amounts, it can also contain iron oxide and magnesia. Aggregates, which comprise 75 percent of concrete by volume, improve the formation and flow of cement paste and enhance the structural performance of concrete. Fine grade comprises particles up to .20 of an inch (five millimeters) in size, while coarse grade includes particles from .20 to .79 of an inch (20 millimeters). For massive construction, aggregate particle size can exceed 1.50 inches (38 millimeters).

Aggregates can also be classified according to the type of rock they consist of: basalt, flint, and granite, among others. Another type of aggregate is *pozzolana*, a siliceous and aluminous material often derived from volcanic ash. Reacting chemically with limestone and moisture, it forms the calcium silicate hydrates that are the basis of cement. Pozzolana is commonly added to Portland cement paste to enhance its densification. One type of volcanic mineral, an aluminum silicate, has been combined with siliceous minerals to form a composite that reduces weight and improves bonding between concrete and steel surfaces. Its applications have included precast concrete shapes and asphalt/concrete pavement for highways. Fly ash, a coal-burning power plant byproduct that contains an aluminosilicate and small amounts of lime, is also being tested as a possible pozzolanic material for cement. Combining fly ash with lime (CaO) in a hydrothermal process (one that uses hot water under pressure) also produces cement.

A wide range of chemicals are added to cement to act as plasticizers, superplasticizers, accelerators, dispersants, and water-reducing agents. Called admixtures, these additives can be used to increase the workability of a cement mixture still in the nonset state, the strength of cement after application, and the material's water tightness. Further, they can decrease the amount of water necessary to obtain workability and the amount of cement needed to create strong concrete. Accelerators, which reduce setting time, include calcium chloride or aluminum sulfate and other acidic materials. Plasticizing or super-plasticizing agents increase the fluidity of the fresh cement mix with the same water/cement ratio, thereby improving the workability of the mix as well as its ease of placement. Typical plasticizers include polycarboxylic acid materials; superplasticizers are sulphanated melamine formaldehyde or sulphanated naph-thalene formaldehyde condensates. Set-retarders, another type of admixture, are used to delay the setting of concrete. These include soluble zinc salts, soluble borates, and carbo-hydrate-based materials. Gas forming admix-tures, powdered zinc or aluminum in combination with calcium hydroxide or hydrogen peroxide, are used to form aerated concrete by generating hydrogen or oxygen bubbles that become entrapped in the cement mix.

Cement is considered a brittle material; in other words, it fractures easily. Thus, many additives have been developed to increase the tensile strength of concrete. One way is to combine polymeric materials such as poly-vinyl alcohol, polyacrylamide, or hydrox-ypropyl methyl cellulose with the cement, producing what is sometimes known as macro-defect-free cement. Another method entails adding fibers made of **stainless steel**, glass, or carbon. These fibers can be short, in a strand, sheet, non-woven fabric or woven fabric form. Typically, such fiber represents only about one percent of the volume of fiber-reinforced concrete.

The Manufacturing Process

The manufacture of concrete is fairly simple. First, the cement (usually Portland cement) is prepared. Next, the other ingredients—aggregates (such as sand or gravel), admix-tures (chemical additives), any necessary fibers, and water—are mixed together with the cement to form concrete. The concrete is then shipped to the work site and placed, compacted, and cured.

Preparing Portland cement

1 The limestone, silica, and alumina that make up Portland cement are dry ground into a very fine powder, mixed together in predetermined proportions, preheated, and calcined (heated to a high temperature that will burn off impurities without fusing the ingredients). Next the material is burned in a large rotary kiln at 2,550 degrees Fahrenheit (1,400 degrees Celsius). At this temperature, the material partially fuses into a substance known as clinker. A modern kiln can produce as much as 6,200 tons of clinker a day.

2 The clinker is then cooled and ground to a fine powder in a tube or ball mill. A ball mill is a rotating drum filled with steel balls of different sizes (depending on the desired fineness of the cement) that crush and grind the clinker. Gypsum is added during the grinding process. The final composition consists of several compounds: tricalcium silicate, dicalcium silicate, tricalcium aluminate, and tetracalcium aluminoferrite.

Mixing

3 The cement is then mixed with the other ingredients: aggregates (sand, gravel, or crushed stone), admixtures, fibers, and water. Aggregates are pre-blended or added at the ready-mix concrete plant under normal operating conditions. The mixing operation uses rotation or stirring to coat the surface of the aggregate with cement paste and to blend the other ingredients uniformly. A variety of batch or continuous mixers are used.

4 Fibers, if desired, can be added by a variety of methods including direct spraying, premixing, impregnating, or hand laying-up. Silica fume is often used as a dispersing or densifying agent.

Transport to work site

5 Once the concrete mixture is ready, it is transported to the work site. There are many methods of transporting concrete, including wheelbarrows, buckets, belt con-

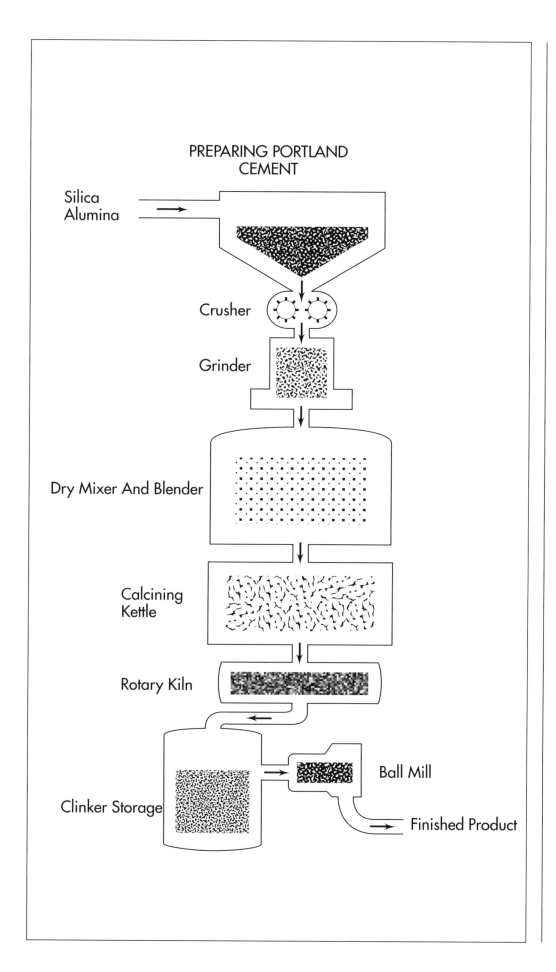

PREPARING PORTLAND
CEMENT

Silica
Alumina

Crusher

Grinder

Dry Mixer And Blender

Calcining
Kettle

Rotary Kiln

Ball Mill

Clinker Storage

Finished Product

The first step in making concrete is to prepare the cement. One type of cement, Portland cement, is considered superior to natural cement because it is stronger, more durable, and of a more consistent quality.

To make it, the raw materials are crushed and ground into a fine powder and mixed together. Next, the material undergoes two heating steps—calcining and burning. In calcining, the materials are heated to a high temperature but do not fuse together. In burning, however, the materials partially fuse together, forming a substance known as "clinker." The clinker is then ground in a ball mill—a rotating steel drum filled with steel balls that pulverize the material.

After the Portland cement is prepared, it is mixed with aggregates such as sand or gravel, admixtures, fibers, and water. Next, it is transferred to the work site and placed. During placing, segregation of the various ingredients must be avoided so that full compaction—elimination of air bubbles—can be achieved.

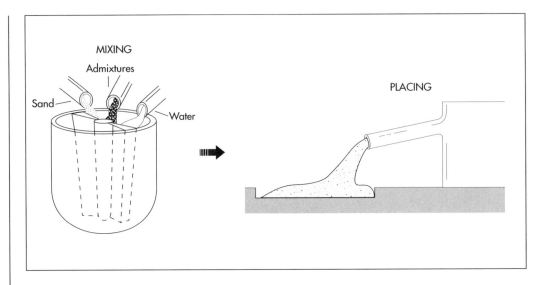

veyors, special trucks, and pumping. Pumping transports large quantities of concrete over large distances through pipelines using a system consisting of a hopper, a pump, and the pipes. Pumps come in several types—the horizontal piston pump with semi-rotary valves and small portable pumps called squeeze pumps. A vacuum provides a continuous flow of concrete, with two rotating rollers squeezing a flexible pipe to move the concrete into the delivery pipe.

Placing and compacting

6 Once at the site, the concrete must be placed and compacted. These two operations are performed almost simultaneously. Placing must be done so that segregation of the various ingredients is avoided and full compaction—with all air bubbles eliminated— can be achieved. Whether chutes or buggies are used, position is important in achieving these goals. The rates of placing and of compaction should be equal; the latter is usually accomplished using internal or external vibrators. An internal vibrator uses a poker housing a motor-driven shaft. When the poker is inserted into the concrete, controlled vibration occurs to compact the concrete. External vibrators are used for precast or thin in situ sections having a shape or thickness unsuitable for internal vibrators. These type of vibrators are rigidly clamped to the formwork, which rests on an elastic support. Both the form and the concrete are vibrated. Vibrating tables are also used, where a table produces vertical vibration by using two shafts rotating in opposite directions.

Curing

7 Once it is placed and compacted, the concrete must cured before it is finished to make sure that it doesn't dry too quickly. Concrete's strength is influenced by its moisture level during the hardening process: as the cement solidifies, the concrete shrinks. If site constraints prevent the concrete from contracting, tensile stresses will develop, weakening the concrete. To minimize this problem, concrete must be kept damp during the several days it requires to set and harden.

Quality Control

Concrete manufacturers expect their raw material suppliers to supply a consistent, uniform product. At the cement production factory, the proportions of the various raw materials that go into cement must be checked to achieve a consistent kiln feed, and samples of the mix are frequently examined using X-ray fluorescence analysis.

The strength of concrete is probably the most important property that must be tested to comply with specifications. To achieve the desired strength, workers must carefully control the manufacturing process, which they normally do by using statistical process control. The American Standard of Testing Materials and other organizations have developed a variety of methods for testing strength. Quality control charts are widely used by the suppliers of ready-mixed concrete and by the engineer on site to continually assess the strength of concrete. Other properties important for compliance include cement content, water/cement ratio, and workability, and standard test methods have been developed for these as well.

The Future

Though the United States led the world in improving cement technology from the 1930s to the 1960s, Europe and Japan have since moved ahead with new products, research, and development. In an effort to restore American leadership, The National Science Foundation has established a Center for Science and Technology of Advanced Cement-Based Materials at Northwestern University. The ACBM center will develop the science necessary to create new cement-based materials with improved properties. These will be used in new construction as well as in restoration and repair of highways, bridges, power plants, and waste-disposal systems.

The deterioration of the U.S. infrastructure has shifted the highway industry's emphasis from building new roads and bridges to maintaining and replacing existing structures. Because better techniques and materials are needed to reduce costs, the *Strategic Highway Research Program* (SHRP), a 5-year $150 million research program, was established in 1987. The targeted areas were asphalt, pavement performance, concrete structures, and highway operations.

The Center for Building Technology at NIST is also conducting research to improve concrete performance. The projects include several that are developing new methods of field testing concrete. Other projects involve computer modeling of properties and models for predicting service life. In addition, several expert systems have been developed for designing concrete mixtures and for diagnosing causes of concrete deterioration.

Another cement industry trend is the concentration of manufacturing in a smaller number of larger-capacity production systems. This has been achieved either by replacing several older production lines with a single, high-capacity line or by upgrading and modernizing an existing line for a higher production yield. Automation will continue to play an important role in achieving these increased yields. The use of waste byproducts as raw materials will continue as well.

Where To Learn More

Books

American Concrete Institute. *Cement and Concrete Terminology.* 1967.

Mindess, S. *Advances in Cementitious Materials.* The American Ceramic Society, 1991. Vol. 16: *Ceramic Transactions.*

Neville, A. M. and J. J. Brooks. *Concrete Technology.* John Wiley & Sons, Inc., 1987.

Skalny, Jan P. *Materials Science of Concrete I.* The American Ceramic Society, 1989.

Skalny, J. and S. Mindess. *Materials Science of Concrete II.* The American Ceramic Society, 1991.

Periodicals

Holterhoff, A. "Implementing SPC in the Manufacture of Calcium Aluminate Cements." *Ceramic Bulletin*, 1991.

Jiang, W. and D. Roy. "Hydrothermal Processing of New Fly Ash Cement." *Ceramic Bulletin*, 1992.

Sheppard, L. "Cement Renovations Improve Concrete Durability." *Ceramic Bulletin*, 1991.

—*L. S. Millberg*

Cooking Oil

The very earliest methods of pressing the vegetable matter probably obtained, at best, 10 percent of the oil available. On the other hand, more modern methods involving solvent extraction can extract all but .5 to 2 percent of the oil.

Background

Cooking oil consists of edible vegetable oils derived from olives, peanuts, and safflowers, to name just a few of the many plants that are used. Liquid at room temperature, cooking oils are sometimes added during the preparation of processed foods. They are also used to fry foods and to make salad dressing.

People in many regions began to process vegetable oils thousands of years ago, utilizing whatever food stuffs they had on hand to obtain oils for a variety of cooking purposes. Early peoples learned to use the sun, a fire, or an oven to heat oily plant products until the plants exuded oil that could then be collected. The Chinese and Japanese produced soy oil as early as 2000 B.C., while southern Europeans had begun to produce olive oil by 3000 B.C. In Mexico and North America, peanuts and sunflower seeds were roasted and beaten into a paste before being boiled in water; the oil that rose to the surface was then skimmed off. Africans also grated and beat palm kernels and coconut meat and then boiled the resulting pulp, skimming the hot oil off the water. Some oils have become available only recently, as extraction technology has improved. Corn oil first became available in the 1960s. Cotton oil, watermelon seed oil, grapeseed oil, and others are now being considered as ways to make use of seeds that were, until recently, considered waste.

The first efforts to increase output were undertaken independently in China, Egypt, Greece, and Rome, among other places. Using a spherical or conical stone mortar and pestle, vertical or horizontal millstones, or simply their feet, people began to crush vegetable matter to increase its available surface area. The ground material would subsequently be placed in sieves such as shallow, flat wicker baskets that were stacked, sometimes as many as 50 high. The matter was then pressed using lever or wedge presses. The Greeks and Romans improved this process by introducing edge runners to grind and a winch or screw to operate a lever press. Their method was used throughout the Middle Ages.

Refinements of this approach included a stamper press that was invented in Holland in the 1600s and used until the 1800s to extract oil, a roll mill invented by English engineer John Smeaton in 1750 to crush vegetable matter more efficiently, and the hydraulic press, invented by Joseph Bramah in England. The first improved screw press was invented by V. D. Anderson in the United States in 1876. His *Expeller* (a trade name) continuously operated a cage press. When vegetable matter was placed in Anderson's closed press, the resultant oil drained out of slots in the side. A screw increased the pressure through the cage toward a restricted opening.

Enhancements in grinding and pressing plant matter were followed by improvements in extracting the oil. In 1856, Deiss of England obtained the first patent for extraction of oil using solvents, following experiments by Jesse Fisher in 1843. At first, solvents such as benzene were pumped through the material and drained through false perforated bottoms. Later, Bollman and Hildebrandt of Germany independently developed continuous systems that sprayed the material with solvent. Both methods were eventually improved, and today solvent extraction is standard in the vegetable oil industry.

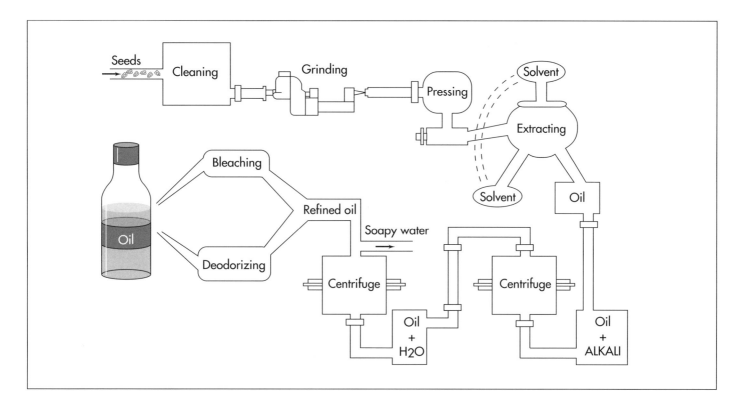

Over time extracting vegetable oils has become more and more efficient. The very earliest methods of pressing the vegetable matter probably obtained, at best, 10 percent of the oil available. On the other hand, more modern methods involving solvent extraction can extract all but .5 to 2 percent of the oil.

Raw Materials

The average bottle of cooking oil contains vegetable oil, with no additives, preservatives, or special flavorings. The oil comes from various parts of plants, in most cases from what are commonly called seeds (including sunflower, palm kernel, safflower, cotton, sesame, and grapeseed oils) or nuts (including peanut, soybean, almond, and walnut oils). A few special cases involve merely squeezing the oil from the flesh of the fruit of the plant. For example, coconut oil comes from the coconut's white meat, palm oil from the pulp of the palm fruit, and olive oil from the flesh of fresh olives. Atypically, corn oil is derived from the germ (embryo) of the kernel.

The Manufacturing Process

Some vegetable oils, such as olive, peanut, and some coconut and sunflower oils, are cold-pressed. This method, which entails minimal processing, produces a light, flavorful oil suitable for some cooking needs. Most oil sources, however, are not suitable for cold pressing, because it would leave many undesirable trace elements in the oil, causing it to be odiferous, bitter tasting, or dark. These oils undergo many steps beyond mere extraction to produce a bland, clear, and consistent oil.

Cleaning and grinding

1 Incoming oil seeds are passed over magnets to remove any trace metal before being dehulled, deskinned, or otherwise stripped of all extraneous material. In the case of cotton, the ginned seeds must be stripped of their lint as well as dehulled. In the case of corn, the kernel must undergo milling to separate the germ.

2 The stripped seeds or nuts are then ground into coarse meal to provide more surface area to be pressed. Mechanized grooved rollers or hammer mills crush the material to the proper consistency. The meal is then heated to facilitate the extraction of the oil. While the procedure allows more oil to be pressed out, more impurities are also pressed out with the oil, and these must be removed before the oil can be deemed edible.

Cooking oil manufacture involves cleaning the seeds, grinding them, pressing, and extracting the oil from them. In extracting, a volatile hydrocarbon such as hexane is used as a solvent.

After extracting, the oil is refined, mixed with an alkaline substance, and washed in a centrifuge. Further washing and refining follows, and then the oil is filtered and/or distilled. It is then ready for packaging.

Pressing

3 The heated meal is then fed continuously into a screw press, which increases the pressure progressively as the meal passes through a slotted barrel. Pressure generally increases from 68,950 to 20,6850 kilopascals as the oil is squeezed out from the slots in the barrel, where it can be recovered.

Extracting additional oil with solvents

4 Soybeans are usually not pressed at all before solvent extraction, because they have relatively little oil, but most oil seeds with more oil are pressed and solvent-treated. After the initial oil has been recovered from the screw press, the *oil cake* remaining in the press is processed by solvent extraction to attain the maximum yield. A volatile hydrocarbon (most commonly hexane) dissolves the oil out of the oil cake, which is then recovered by distilling the light solvent out. The Blaw-Knox Rotocell is used to meet the demands of the United States soybean oil industry. In using this machine, flakes of meal are sent through wedge-shaped cells of a cylindrical vessel. The solvent then passes through the matter to be collected at the bottom. Also still in use by a significant number of manufacturers is the Bollman or Hansa-Muhle unit, in which oilseed flakes are placed in perforated baskets that circulate continuously. The solvent percolates through the matter which is periodically dumped and replaced.

Removing solvent traces

5 Ninety percent of the solvent remaining in the extracted oil simply evaporates, and, as it does, it is collected for reuse. The rest is retrieved with the use of a stripping column. The oil is boiled by steam, and the lighter hexane floats upward. As it condenses, it, too, is collected.

Refining the oil

6 The oil is next refined to remove color, odor, and bitterness. Refining consists of heating the oil to between 107 and 188 degrees Fahrenheit (40 and 85 degrees Celsius) and mixing an alkaline substance such as sodium hydroxide or sodium carbonate with it. Soap forms from the undesired fatty acids and the alkaline additive, and it is usually removed by centrifuge. The oil is further washed to remove traces of soap and then dried.

7 Oils are also degummed at this time by treating them with water heated to between 188 and 206 degrees Fahrenheit (85 and 95 degrees Celsius), steam, or water with acid. The gums, most of which are phosphatides, precipitate out, and the dregs are removed by centrifuge.

8 Oil that will be heated (for use in cooking) is then bleached by filtering it through fuller's earth, activated carbon, or activated clays that absorb certain pigmented material from the oil. By contrast, oil that will undergo refrigeration (because it is intended for salad dressing, for example) is winterized—rapidly chilled and filtered to remove waxes. This procedure ensures that the oil will not partially solidify in the refrigerator.

9 Finally, the oil is deodorized. In this process, steam is passed over hot oil in a vacuum at between 440 and 485 degrees Fahrenheit (225 and 250 degrees Celsius), thus allowing the volatile taste and odor components to distill from the oil. Typically, citric acid at .01 percent is also added to oil after deodorization to inactivate trace metals that might promote oxidation within the oil and hence shorten its shelf-life.

Packaging the oil

10 The completely processed oil is then measured and poured into clean containers, usually plastic bottles for domestic oils to be sold in supermarkets, glass bottles for imports or domestic oils to be sold in specialty stores, or cans for imports (usually olive oil).

Byproducts/Waste

The most obvious byproduct of the oil making process is oil seed cake. Most kinds of seed cake are used to make animal feed and low-grade fertilizer; others are simply disposed of. In the case of cotton, the lint on the seed is used to make yarn and cellulose that go into such products as **mattress**es, **rayon**, and lacquer. Coconut oil generates several byproducts, with various uses: desiccated coconut meat (*copra*) is used in the confectionery industry; coconut milk can be consumed; and *coir*, the fiber from the outer coat, is used to make mats and rope. Since corn oil is derived from a small portion of the entire kernel, it creates corn meal and hominy if it is dry milled, and corn starch and corn syrup if it is wet milled.

Lecithin is a byproduct of the degumming process used in making soybean oil. This industrially valuable product is used to make animal feed, **chocolate**, cosmetics, soap, **paint**, and plastics—to name just a few of its diverse uses. Recent research has focused on utilizing the residual oil seed cake. The cake is high in protein and other nutrients, and researchers are working to develop methods of processing it into a palatable food that can be distributed in areas where people lack sufficient protein in their diets. This goal requires ridding (through additional processing) the oil seed cake of various undesirable toxins (such as gossypol in cotton seed, or aflatoxin in peanut meal). Initial results are promising.

Quality Control

The nuts and seeds used to make oil are inspected and graded after harvest by licensed inspectors in accordance with the United States Grain Standards Act, and the fat content of the incoming seeds is measured. For the best oil, the seeds should not be stored at all, or for a only very short time, since storage increases the chance of deterioration due to mold, loss of nutrients, and rancidity. The seeds should be stored in well-ventilated warehouses with a constantly maintained low temperature and humidity. Pests should be eradicated, and mold growth should be kept to a minimum. Seeds to be stored must have a low moisture content (around 10 percent), or they should be dried until it reaches this level (dryer seeds are less likely to encourage the growth of mold).

Processed oil should be consistent in all aspects such as color, taste, and viscosity. Color is tested using the Lovibund Tintometer or a similar method in which an experienced observer compares an oil's color against the shading of standard colored glasses. Experienced tasters also check the flavor of the oil, and its viscosity is measured using a viscometer. To use this device, oil is poured into a tube that has a bulb at one end

set off by two marks. The oil is then drained, and the time required for the bulb to empty is measured and compared to a chart to determine viscosity.

In addition, the oil should be free of impurities and meet the demands placed upon it for use in cooking. To ensure this, the product is tested under controlled conditions to see at what temperature it begins to smoke (the *smoke point*), flash, and catch on fire; warnings are issued appropriately. To allow its safe use in baking and frying, an oil should have a smoke point of between 402 and 503 degrees Fahrenheit (204 and 260 degrees Celsius). The temperature is then lowered to test the oil's cloud point. This is ascertained by chilling 120 milliliters of salad oil to a temperature of 35 degrees Fahrenheit (zero degrees Celsius) for five and a half hours, during which period acceptable salad oil will not cloud.

Before being filled, the bottles that hold the oil are cleaned and electronically inspected for foreign material. To prevent oxidation of the oil (and therefore its tendency to go rancid), the inert (nonreactive) gas nitrogen is used to fill up the space remaining at the top of the bottle.

Where To Learn More

Books

Hoffman, G. *The Chemistry & Technology of Edible Oils & Fats & Their High Fat Products*. Academic Press, Inc., 1989.

Kirschenbauer, H. G. *Fats and Oils*. Reinhold Publishing, 1960.

Lawson, Harry W. *Standards for Fats and Oils*. Avi Publishing Company, 1985.

Salunkhe, D. K. *World Oilseeds: Chemistry, Technology, and Utilization*. Van Nostrand Reinhold, 1992.

Toussaint-Samat, Maguelonne. *A History of Food*. Blackwell Publishers, 1992.

Periodicals

"A Cook's Tour of Cooking Oils," *Changing Times*, October 1990, pp. 90-1.

Raloff, Janet. "Grape Seeds Sow Cholesterol Benefits," *Science News,* 27 April 1991, p. 268.

Raloff, Janet. "The Positive Side of Palm Oil," *Science News,* 27 April 1991, p. 268.

Simpson, Matthew. "Heart-Healthful Oils: Choosing the Best Fats," *American Health,* October 1990, pp. 88-9.

Sokolov, Raymond. "The Trail of Oil," *Natural History,* May 1989, pp. 82-5.

Stevens, Jane. "The Power of the (Oilseed) Press," *Technology Review.* September, 1992, p. 15.

—*Rose Secrest*

Corrugated Cardboard

Background

Most items at your favorite supermarket, discount store, or shopping mall were safely delivered in boxes made of corrugated cardboard, and many are displayed in the same boxes, which were manufactured so they could be opened and used for this purpose. Other items may arrive in their own corrugated or uncorrugated paperboard boxes. Because corrugated cardboard is such a versatile packaging material, millions of tons are used each year to protect and display products. During 1992, more than 25 million tons of corrugated cardboard were produced in the United States. Another 6 million tons of uncorrugated boxboard or paperboard were also produced for use in folding cartons.

Corrugated cardboard is a stiff, strong, and light-weight material made up of three layers of brown kraft paper. In 1884, Swedish chemist, Carl F. Dahl, developed a process for pulping wood chips into a strong paper that resists tearing, splitting, and bursting. He named it the kraft process because it produces a strong paper that resists tearing, splitting, and bursting.

From the paper mill, rolls of kraft paper are transported to a corrugating, or converting, plant. At the plant, layers of kraft paper are crimped and glued to form corrugated cardboard, which is then cut, printed, folded, and glued to make boxes. At the beginning of this process, kraft rolls from the paper mill are loaded into a huge machine called a corrugator. A typical corrugator is as long as a football field—300 feet (91.44 meters). Some rolls of kraft paper are used as the corrugating medium, and others are used as liners, the layers of kraft paper glued on each side of the medium. After the corrugator has heated, glued, and pressed the kraft paper to form corrugated cardboard, the continuous sheet of cardboard is cut into wide box blanks that then go to other machines for printing, cutting, and gluing. Finally, batches of finished boxes are banded together for shipping to the food processor, toy maker, **automobile** parts distributor, or any of the thousands of businesses that depend on corrugated cardboard packaging.

Raw Materials

Fast-growing pine trees provide the primary raw material used to make corrugated cardboard. The largest packaging companies own thousands of acres of land where trees are matured, harvested, and replaced with seedlings. After the trees are harvested, they are stripped of their limbs; only the trunks will be shipped by truck to a pulp mill. The largest packaging companies also own the mills where trees are converted to kraft paper. At the mill, the harvested tree trunks are subjected to the kraft process, also known as the sulfate process because of the chemicals used to break down wood chips into fibrous pulp. After pulping and other processing, the fibers are sent directly to the paper machine where they are formed, pressed, dried, and rolled into the wide, heavy rolls of kraft paper sent to corrugating plants to be made into cardboard.

At the corrugating plant, only a few other raw materials are needed to make a finished box. Corn starch glue is used to bond the corrugated medium to the liner sheets. Because so much glue is used, rail cars or large tanker trucks deliver it as a dry powder that will be stored in huge silos at the corrugating plant until it is needed. Drawn from the silo, the

A typical corrugator is as long as a football field— 300 feet. Some rolls of kraft paper are used as the corrugating medium, and others are used as liners, the layers of kraft paper glued on each side of the medium.

dry corn starch is mixed with water and other chemicals and pumped into the corrugator to be spread on the corrugated medium as the layers of liner are added. Other raw materials are used to finish the corrugated cardboard after production. Waxes made from paraffin or vegetable oils can be applied to make a water- or grease-resistant container for food products. Brightly colored inks are also applied to create bold graphic designs for self-supporting displays featuring product name, information, and company name and logo. Teams of salespeople and designers work together to create the manufacturing and printing patterns, called dies, that are used to cut and print a specific box design. The dies are created in a pattern shop and transferred to the rotary die-cutting equipment and printers that finish the box blanks.

Design

Kraft paper has been manufactured since 1906. Since then, pulp processing, paper making, and corrugating operations have been developed to a high state of efficiency and productivity. Today, in the corrugated cardboard industry, designers are creating innovative containers that require four-color printing and complex die-cutting. These innovative containers are designed with sophisticated software such as computer-aided design (CAD) programs, allowing a packaging designer to brainstorm different package designs before manufacturing begins. A designer using a CAD program can call up and modify different designs that have been stored in a computer design library. Thus, existing packages can generate new designs. Many retail stores use such light, strong, and colorful containers directly, as point-of-purchase displays.

The Manufacturing Process

Pulping the pine chips

1 Manufacturing a corrugated cardboard box begins with the pulping of wood chips in the kraft (sulfate) process. First, tree trunks are stripped of bark and torn into small chips. Next, these chips are placed in a large, high-pressure tank called a batch digester, where they are cooked in a solution, or liquor, made of sodium hydroxide (NaOH) and several other ionic compounds

such as sulfates, sulfides, and sulfites. These strongly alkaline chemicals dissolve the *lignin*, the glue-like substance that holds the individual wood fibers together in a tree trunk.

2 When the pressure is released after several hours, the wood chips explode like popcorn into fluffy masses of fiber.

Making kraft paper

3 After additional cleaning and refining steps, a consistent slurry of wood pulp is pumped to the paper-making machine, also known as a *Fourdrinier machine*. Gigantic, square structures up to 600 feet long (182.88 meters), these machines contain a wire mesh in which the paper is initially formed. Next, the paper is fed into massive, steam-heated rollers and wide felt blankets that remove the water. At the end, the finished medium, or liner, is rolled for shipment.

Shipping and storing the kraft paper

4 Rolls of kraft paper for corrugating are available in many sizes to fit the production equipment at different corrugating plants. The most common roll sizes are 67 inches (170.18 centimeters) wide and 87 inches (220.98 centimeters) wide. An 87-inch roll of heavier paper can weigh up to 6,000 pounds (2,724 kilograms). As many as 22 rolls of 87-inch paper can be loaded into one railroad boxcar for shipment to a corrugating plant.

5 At the plant, the kraft paper is separated into different grades, which will be used for the medium and the liner. These different grades of corrugated cardboard can be made by combining different grades of kraft paper. A knowledgeable packaging specialist works with a customer to determine the strength required for the corrugated cardboard container being planned. Then, when a plant receives an order for containers, a product engineer specifies the combination of medium and liner to produce a cardboard to match the customer's requirement.

Corrugating the cardboard

6 Using powerful fork-lifts, skilled equipment operators select, move, and load rolls of kraft paper at one end of the corrugator.

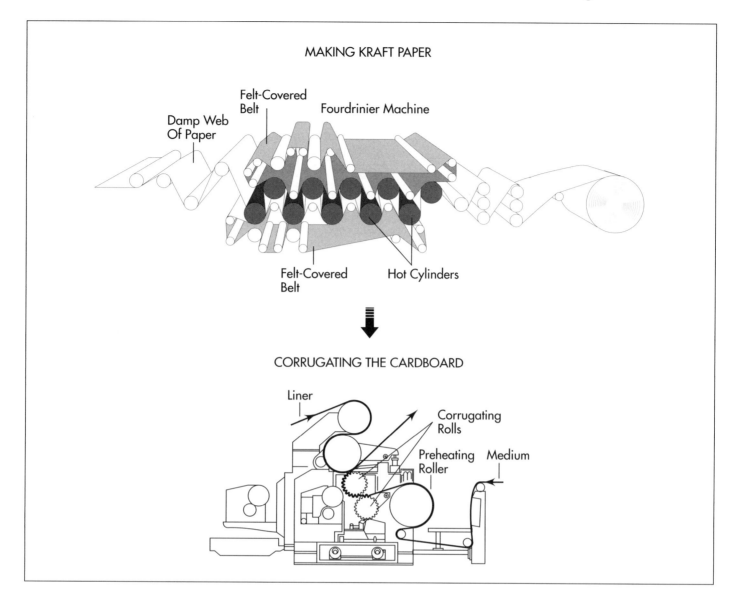

MAKING KRAFT PAPER

Damp Web Of Paper
Felt-Covered Belt
Fourdrinier Machine
Felt-Covered Belt
Hot Cylinders

CORRUGATING THE CARDBOARD

Liner
Corrugating Rolls
Preheating Roller
Medium

7 One roll of medium is loaded to run through the corrugating rolls, and a roll of liner is fed into the corrugator to be joined with the corrugated medium. Liner from another roll travels up over the corrugating rolls along a flat structure called the bridge. This liner will be glued to the corrugated medium later in the process.

8 For a large production run, additional rolls are loaded into automatic splicers. Sensitive detectors check the rolls of paper feeding into the corrugator. When a roll is nearly empty, the corrugator control system starts a splicer, and paper from the new roll is joined to the end of the paper going through the machine. Thus, production of corrugated cardboard is continuous, and no production speed is lost.

9 The medium to be corrugated is fed into the giant, electrically driven rollers of the corrugator, first through the preheating rollers and then into the corrugating rolls. Steam at 175 to 180 pounds of pressure per square inch (psi) is forced through both sets of rollers, and, as the paper passes through them, temperatures reach 350 to 365 degrees Fahrenheit (177 to 185 degrees Celsius).

10 The corrugating rolls are covered with *flutes*—horizontal, parallel ridges like the teeth of massively wide gears. When the hot paper passes between the corrugating rolls, the flutes trap and bend it, forming the middle part of a sheet of corrugated cardboard. Each corrugating machine has interchangeable corrugating rolls featuring different flute sizes. Installing a different

Corrugated cardboard manufacture includes two key steps: making kraft paper and corrugating the cardboard. Kraft paper involves pulping wood chips and then feeding the resulting paper substance through massive steam rollers that remove the water.

Corrugating is also done in a machine that utilizes heavy rollers. One roll of cardboard is corrugated and then glued between two other layers (liners) by the same machine. The glue is then cured by passing the cardboard over heated rolls.

A finished piece of corrugated cardboard consists of a single corrugated layer sandwiched between two liner layers.

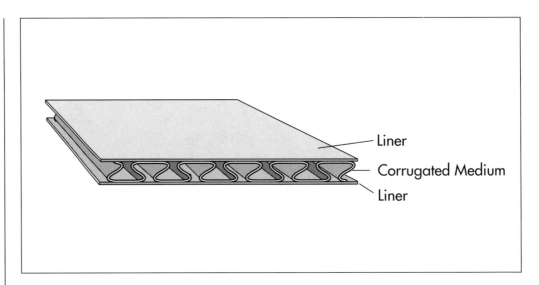

Liner

Corrugated Medium

Liner

flute size in the corrugator changes the width of the corrugated medium.

11 The medium travels next to a set of rollers called the single-facer glue station. Here, one layer of liner is glued to the medium. Starch glue is carefully applied to the corrugated edges of the medium, and the first layer of liner is added. From the single-facer, the medium and liner go to the double-backer glue station where the other layer of liner from the bridge is added following the same procedure. Continuing through the corrugator, the cardboard passes over steam-heated plates that cure the glue.

Forming the blanks into boxes

12 At the end of corrugator, a slitter-scorer trims the cardboard and cuts it into large sheets called *box blanks*. Box blanks pop out of the slitter-scorer like wide slices of toast and slide into an automatic stacker that loads them onto a large, rolling platform. From here, they will be transported to the other machines that will convert them into finished containers. Skilled production workers use a computer terminal and printer to prepare a job ticket for each stack of box blanks produced by the corrugator. With the job ticket, workers can route the stack to the right fabrication machines, called *flexos* (the name is short for flexographic machine). A flexo is a wide, flat machine that processes box blanks.

13 Printing dies and die-cutting patterns are prepared in a pattern shop on large, flexible sheets of rubber or tin. The dies and patterns are loaded onto the large rollers in the flexo, and the box blanks are automatically fed through it. As each blank passes through the rollers of the flexo, it is trimmed, printed, cut, scored, and, in a printer-folder-gluer, folded and glued to form a box. From the flexo, the finished boxes are automatically stacked and sent to a banding machine to be wrapped for shipping. Other equipment in a corrugating plant includes stand-alone die-cutters, die-cutters with print stations, and machines known as curtain coaters that apply a wax coating to fruit, vegetable, and meat containers. Box blanks requiring only simple, one-color printing and die-cutting can be run through a stand-alone die-cutter, print station, and curtain coater to produce water- or grease-resistant containers.

Quality Control

Quality control begins with the suppliers of the kraft paper used to make corrugated cardboard. Kraft paper must be smooth and strong. After the paper passes through the corrugator and is made into box blanks, individual blanks are pulled from a stack and tested. The Cobb test measures moisture in the liner and medium. Glue strength, bursting strength, compression, and highly accurate dimensional tests determine the quality of the manufacturing process. A warp test determines the flatness of the box blank, insuring that each blank will travel smoothly through the flexo machines. As skilled workers run batches of box blanks through the flexo machines, individual boxes are pulled and inspected. Trimming, cutting, and scoring must be correct. No damage to the cardboard is allowed. Also, the different layers of colored ink used in color printing must be perfectly aligned.

The Future

Future corrugated containers will be manufactured using kraft paper produced from recycled packaging rather than trees. Recycling and other environmentally friendly processes will continue to grow in importance in the future of corrugated cardboard. Today, inks based on soybean oil and biodegradable waxes and other coatings are beginning to be used in container manufacturing. Leading packaging companies are already operating paper mills that make fresh, clean kraft paper by de-inking and pulping used containers.

Where To Learn More

Books

Bessen, A. Howard. *Design & Production of Corrugated Packaging & Displays*. Jelmar Publishing Company, Inc., 1991.

The Corrugated & Paperboard Container Industry: An Analysis of Current Markets & Prospects for Future Growth. Business Trend Analysts, Inc., 1991.

Maltenfort, George G. *Corrugated Shipping Containers: An Engineering Approach*. Jelmar Publishing Company, Inc., 1988.

Rohde, Elliot S. *Producing Corrugated Containers Profitably*. Jelmar Publishing Company, Inc., 1993.

Kline, James E. *Paper And Paperboard: Manufacturing and Converting Fundamentals*, 1991.

Periodicals

Carey, Kevin. "The Science of Diecutter Makeready." *Boxboard Containers*. March, 1993.

"Engineers Claim Cardboard Cup," *Design News*. October 6, 1986, p. 51.

"Industry Statistics," *Paperboard Packaging*. March, 1993, p. 16.

Tappi [Technical Association for the Pulp and Paper Industries] Journal.

—*Robert C. Miller*

Cutlery

Forks took about three centuries to gain acceptance, probably because the custom of placing food in one's mouths with both hands, five fingers, or—for the refined few—three fingers, was more expedient than using a new gadget.

Background

Eating or serving with utensils made of silver, silver-plated metals or **stainless steel** is relatively recent. Silver needed to be discovered in sufficient quantities, the smelting processes necessary to hand-craft silver needed to be refined, and in Northern Europe it took several centuries before the more civilized Latin table manners replaced the cruder Anglo-Saxon ones.

Henry VIII, the most famous of England's Tudors, used his hands to tear off large pieces of beef from an entire roast set before him, throw the meat on his trencher board, chop off smaller pieces and shovel them in his mouth. Such table manners were acceptable until the publication of books on manners by Castiglione (1478-1529) and Peacham (1576-1643). Around that time, fine silver table services and eating implements were introduced into English court life. Banquet halls started to use solid silver platters and plates, silver-mounted drinking vessels, silver-handled knives and a variety of spoons. Unassisted bare hands, however, remained the norm for the "lower orders" in England for another century or so.

The spoon was one of man's earliest inventions, possibly as old as the custom of drinking hot liquids. In Northern Europe, the first spoons were carved from wood. Later specimens were fashioned out of horns of cattle, ivory tusks, bronze, and eventually silver and **gold**.

The earliest mention of spoons made from precious metals is found in the Book of Exodus, when Moses is commanded to make dishes and spoons of pure gold for the Tabernacle. Moses asked Bezalel (the first spoon-maker known to us by name in history) to work in gold, silver and brass. Since Bezalel had come with Moses out of Egypt, he must have learned his trade there.

Many Egyptian spoons were cast in the form of handled dishes with a cover and a spout, an elaborate but not very practical design. Greek and Roman spoons, on the other hand, looked much more like the spoons we are used to seeing in modern times. Pan, the patron of shepherds and huntsmen, was honored with spoons in the shape of a goat's foot. The Roman fiddle-patterned spoon, originating in the first or second century A.D., resembles the modern type we know today, except for its squared off stem-head, rather than the arched appearance with which we are familiar.

The first English spoons, made of horn or wood, were probably imitations of those brought in by Roman troops in Britain. The Angles and Saxons introduced a spoon with small, pear-shaped bowl. By the fourteenth century, castings of bronze, brass, pewter and sheet tin were fairly common.

The knife, used by hunters and soldiers for cutting and spearing the meat, was first made of flint, then of metal. Its main characteristic was a sharp edge. Traces of the primitive knife, such as the incurved shape at the top, or the beveling of the metal to achieve an edge, are still present in some of our styles today. Handles at first were only long enough to allow a firm grip for carving.

In the 1630s, the Duke de Richelieu, chief minister to France's Louis XIII, ordered the kitchen staff to file off the sharp points of all house knives and bring them to the royal table, thereby introducing the knife as an every-day eating utensil for the aristocracy.

Forks were introduced at the table around the time of the Crusades, at the beginning of the twelfth century, when Venice's Doge Domenice Silvie and his Dogess placed a fork beside each plate at one of their banquets. The forks took about three centuries to gain acceptance, probably because the custom of placing food in one's mouths with both hands, five fingers, or—for the refined few— three fingers, was more expedient than using a new gadget.

Most dinner guests first carried their own knives. After the introduction of forks, the custom of guests providing their own eating utensils continued, and attention was given to minimize the space occupied by the knife and fork when not in use, with the fork sometimes serving as a handle for the spoon.

The production of tableware on a wide scale in England after 1650 played a large role in improving the dinner-table etiquette. In time, strict laws demanding high standards greatly enhanced the quality of silverware. Silversmiths were required to stamp their name, the place, and the date of their manufactured goods on their pieces. The word "sterling" came to mean "of unexcelled quality." From 1670, English homes of the upper classes had silver spoons as a matter of course, and had already started the custom of passing them on to their heirs. American silversmiths widely copied these spoons. In fact, the colonial craftsmen's first silver goods were spoons. Table knives with steel blades started to appear around this time as well. However, silver forks and sophisticated serving vessels were rare until the late eighteenth century.

Before the seventeenth century, silver could be melted and poured into shaped molds to be cast into a variety of objects, but more often it was hand beaten with sledge hammers on an anvil, or coerced into flatsheets of the required thickness by a version of the old-fashioned laundry mangle with iron instead of wooden rollers. The hammering of the sheet caused it to become brittle after a certain amount of time, and therefore unfit for further working. At that point, it was annealed, or placed under heat of about 1,000 degrees Fahrenheit (540 degrees Celsius), then plunged into cold water, after which the hammering could be resumed.

Workers sit astride their grinding wheels in this photo from the Rockford (Ill.) Cutlery Co., taken about 1900.

First used in the mid-nineteenth century, the term "silverware," referring to Sterling silver or silverplated tableware, has become synonymous with cutlery. Still, cutlery has been made of iron for centuries. In Great Britain, the area of Sheffield has been widely known for producing high-quality cutlery since the thirteenth century. With the introduction of silverplating in the late eighteenth century, the area also became identified with silverplated goods, thus "Sheffield plate."

Not surprisingly, Americans who sought to compete with Sheffield cutlery in the nineteenth century overcame opposition by reducing the cost of their cutlery through the use of powered machinery and simplification of the production process. By 1871, the Russell Manufacturing Company of Turner's Fall, Massachusetts, had reduced the sequence to sixteen steps, each of which might be performed by different individuals. The company consumed annually 700 tons of steel, 200 tons of grindstones, and 22 tons of emery; and for handles, 18 tons of ivory, 56 tons of ebony, 29 tons of rosewood, and 150 tons of cocoawood. Despite the growth, one thing that did not improve for workers in the United States was industrial hygiene. Grinders, especially, were subjected to large doses of metallic dust and commonly succumbed to "grinders' disease," or silicosis.

The most famous product innovation associated with the American cutlery trade was the Bowie knife. With its distinctive long, heavy blade, it was useful for both hunting and fighting. James Bowie, famed frontiersman, designed and popularized this large sheath knife. It became so popular and so commonly associated with violent crime during the 1830s that several states passed laws restricting its use.

William S. Pretzer

Later, the silversmiths (or "flatters") used more sophisticated techniques, such as waterwheels or horse-driven wheels, to pass the metal through the rollers many times until the desired thickness was attained.

These techniques were replaced by the steam engine in the eighteenth century.

Special hammers—without small faces and sharp corners that might cut the metal—were used to raise the flat sheets of metal into hollow forms, such as pots or the bowls of spoons. Handles for spoons, forks, or knives were shaped by casting. The most common method was to embed a pattern (of gunmetal, wood or plaster) in a two-part frame filled with an adhesive loam mixture, bake it hard, open the frame and remove the pattern, then fill the cavity with molten silver, finally breaking the mold to remove the casting. Pieces fashioned this way showed gritty surfaces that required smoothing with file and pumice.

Sheffield plating was the first silverplating technique used. It consisted of attaching a thin skin of sterling to one or both sides of a copper **brick**, rolling it into flatsheets, and then working it in a similar manner as silver. This technique was replaced in 1842, when electroplating (or sterling silver deposited by electrolysis on a base metal) was introduced.

Raw Materials

The raw material of silverware is stainless steel, sterling silver, or, in the case of silverplate, a base metal (such as a high-quality copper alloy) over which a layer of silver is electrically deposited.

Stainless steel is a combination of steel, chrome and nickel. The finest grade of metal used in producing quality lines is 18/8 stainless steel. This means that it contains 18 percent chrome, 8 percent nickel. Stainless steel is very popular because of its easy care, durability, and low price.

The majority of silver is obtained as a byproduct of the extraction of lead, copper and zinc. Silver is separated from smelted lead bullion by the Parkes process, in which zinc is added to the molten bullion that has been heated to above the melting point of zinc. When the zinc has dissolved, the mixture is cooled and a crust of zinc-silver alloy forms on the surface, because the silver combines more readily with zinc than with lead. The crust is removed, pressed to remove excess lead and then processed in a retort to recover the zinc for reuse, leaving a silver-lead bullion with a high silver content. Further refining of the bullion is carried out in a cupellation furnace, where air is blown across the surface of the molten metal to oxidize the lead and other impurities to a slag, leaving the silver, which is cast into anode blocks. Final purification of the silver is made by an electrolytic process. Sterling silver consists of 925 pure silver and 75 parts of an alloy (usually copper). This proportion is fixed by law and therefore never varies. The copper alloy adds durability without sacrificing the natural beauty and workability of silver.

Silverplate is the result of a process that bonds pure silver (silver more pure than sterling) to a strong base metal. The resulting tableware is durable, has the look and feel of silver, but is much less expensive than sterling.

The Manufacturing Process

Blanking

1 Production begins with rectangular, flat blanks of stainless steel, sterling silver, or in the case of plated flatware, an alloy. Large rolls are stamped in individual blanks, which are flat pieces roughly the same shape as the piece to be produced.

Rolling

2 Through a series of rolling operations, these blanks are graded or rolled to the correct thickness and shapes required by the manufacturer's flatware patterns. First the blanks are rolled crosswise from left to right, right to left, and lengthwise, then trimmed to outline. Each spoon, for instance, must be thick at the base of the handle to resist bending. This gives graded pieces the right balance and a good feel in the hand. Each piece is now in the form of a cleanly finished shape in the rough dimension of the utensil.

Annealing

3 Between operations, the blanks must pass through annealing ovens to soften the metal for further machine operations. The annealing, done under great heat, must be very accurately controlled so the final piece will be resistant to bending and to nicks and dents when in use. The last annealing is the most

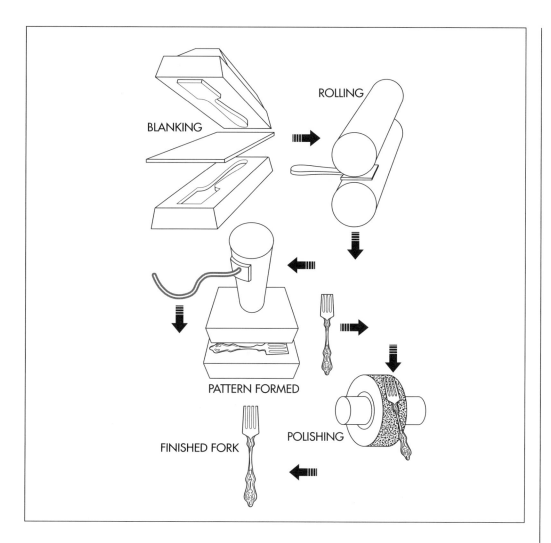

BLANKING

ROLLING

PATTERN FORMED

FINISHED FORK

POLISHING

The first step in cutlery manufacture involves blanking the stainless steel or sterling silver to the proper shape. A series of rolling operations then gives the piece the correct thickness. After heat treatment and trimming, the piece has a pattern embossed on it in a stamping operation. Finally, the piece is buffed and polished.

important, because the pieces must be just the right degree of hardness when they are embossed. Then the metal can be forced easily into all the tiny details in the dies and the ornamentation will be faithfully reproduced.

Cutting to outline

4 The rolled blanks are placed in the cutout press by an operator, to remove the excess metal and to fashion the shape of the piece. This process is similar to cutting shapes from rolled dough. The shape of the piece is cut out of the metal and the excess metal is remelted and transformed back into sheets of metal to be used again. This trimming must ensure an accurate fit of the pieces into the dies when the design is applied.

Forming the pattern

5 The next step is the forming of the pattern. Each pattern has its own hardened steel dies—two dies for each piece, one with

the pattern for the front of the piece, and the other with the pattern for the back of the piece. These are carefully set in the hammers by die setters. The operator quickly places a piece in place under the drop hammer, which descends with a hydraulic pressure of 200 tons. (The bases of the drop hammers are bedded in 160 cubic yards of cement.) The metal is squeezed into every tiny detail of the ornamentation in the die, embossing the pattern on the piece. The blow of the hammer hardens the piece for use in the home. Surplus metal around the outline of the piece is then removed by clipping presses.

Special steps—knife, spoon, and fork

6 Special steps are necessary for the creation of knives, spoons, forks, and holloware pieces. To make the hollow handle for the knife, after two strips of metal are formed to shape, they are then soldered together, buffed and polished until the seam is no longer visible. The blade and handle are

This illustrations shows how a fork looks after each operation is performed. Although the tines are pierced before the pattern is applied, the strip of metal that connects the tines together isn't removed until after the pattern is embossed.

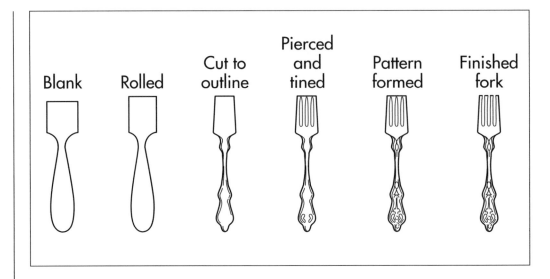

Blank   Rolled   Cut to outline   Pierced and tined   Pattern formed   Finished fork

permanently joined by means of a powerful cement, which bonds with great strength and durability.

7 With the spoon, after the pattern has been embossed upon the front and back of the handle, the next step is the forming of the bowl. The forming is done again under the same powerful drop hammers from accurate steel dies. Each bowl requires two hammer blows. Surplus metal around the outline of the spoon is removed by clipping presses. A small burr still remains to be removed at a later operation.

8 The forming of fork tines is a similar process to that of the forming of the spoon's bowl, but the operation takes place before the pattern is applied to the handle. After a fork is cut to outline, it is pierced and tined: the tines are pieced out, and the small piece of metal that holds the tip of the tines together is removed in another operation after the pattern has been applied.

Silver plating

9 For the silver-plated pieces, the electroplating process is an additional step. The pieces are first prepared by being buffed so that the edges are smooth and the surfaces are free from small holes. When the buffing is completed, the pieces are given a thorough cleaning with as many as 12 different chemical solutions. Finally, they undergo electrolysis, in which a layer of silver is electrically deposited over the base metal.

Buffing and sand polishing

10 The knives, forks and spoons are now buffed, then polished. Depending on the pattern, special finishing processes can give silver-plated and sterling silver pieces a bright, mirror-like finish, a soft, satiny glow, or a brushed or florentine finish.

Quality Control

Final inspection checks the pieces for chafes, scratches, rough spots between a fork's tines, discoloration, or any other flaws that might have occurred when the pieces were stamped, shaped and polished.

The Future

Stainless steel is the preferred tableware for today's customers, and represents the future for flatware manufacturers. According to a senior executive at Oneida, the last major domestic manufacturer of silverware and plated ware in the United States, purchase of sterling and silverplated ware has been declining for the past twenty years, while demand for stainless steel continues to grow.

Where To Learn More

Books

Clayton, Michael. *Christie's Pictorial History of English and American Silver.* Phaidon, 1985.

Ettlinger, Steve. *The Kitchenware Book.* Macmillan Publishing Co., Inc., 1992.

Fennimore, Donald L. *Silver and Pewter*. Knopf, 1984.

Freeman, Dr. Larry. *Victorian Silver: Plated and Sterling Holloware and Flatware*. Century House, 1967.

Giblin, James C. *From Hand to Mouth: Or, How We Invented Knives, Forks, Spoons & Chopsticks & the Table Manners to go with Them*. HarperCollins Children's Books, 1987.

Hamlyn, Paul. *English Silver*. Hamlyn Publishers, 1969.

Hood, Graham. *American Silver: A History of Style, 1650-1900*. Praeger Publishers, 1971.

"Sheet Metal," *How It Works,* Vol. 18. H.S. Stuttman Inc., 1987.

Schwartz, Marvin D. *Collector's Guide to Antique American Silver*. Doubleday, 1975.

Science and Technology Illustrated. Encyclopedia Britannica, 1984.

Watson, Jim. *Sharpening and Knife Making*. Schiffer Publishing Ltd., 1987.

—Eva Sideman

Expanded Polystyrene Foam (EPF)

Although EPF is generally called Styrofoam, Styrofoam is a trademark of Dow Chemical Company and refers specifically to a type of hard, blue EPF used mainly in boating.

Background

Expanded polystyrene foam (EPF) is a plastic material that has special properties due to its structure. Composed of individual cells of low density polystyrene, EPF is extraordinarily light and can support many times its own weight in water. Because its cells are not interconnected, heat cannot travel through EPF easily, so it is a great insulator. EPF is used in flotation devices, insulation, egg cartons, flats for meat and produce, sandwich and hamburger boxes, **coffee** cups, plates, peanut packaging, and picnic coolers. Although it is generally called Styrofoam, Styrofoam is a trademark of Dow Chemical Company and refers specifically to a type of hard, blue EPF used mainly in boating.

During the late 1800s, researchers seeking materials suitable for making film, carriage windshields, and various small items such as combs produced early plastics out of natural substances and chemicals. In making these plastics, the scientists exploited the natural tendency towards polymerization, in which two or more small molecules, or monomers, combine to form chains that are often very long. The resulting molecular chains, or polymers, comprise repeating structural units from the original molecules. One of the most familiar natural polymers is cellulose, the string of glucose molecules that forms a primary component of plant cell walls, cotton, paper, and **rayon**. Polystyrene is among the best-known synthetic polymers (others include polyethylene, polypropylene, and polyester). Styrene, the liquid hydrocarbon from which EPF is made, was derived in the late nineteenth century from storax balsam, which comes from a tree in Asia Minor called the Oriental sweet gum. In the early nineteenth century, completely synthetic plastics were developed from hydrocarbons, whose structure is conducive to easy polymerization. Polystyrene, the polymer from which EPF is made, was invented in 1938.

Foaming plastics were discovered indirectly, because in the beginning no one could see their advantages. Dr. Leo H. Baekeland, the American chemist who developed the first completely synthetic plastic, bakelite, experimented with phenol (an acidic compound) and formaldehyde (a colorless gas) while trying to make a nonporous resin. When one of his mixtures unexpectedly began to foam, Baekeland tried to control the foam before realizing that it could have advantages. Following Baekeland's death in 1944, the first foamed phenolics were developed, soon followed by epoxy foam. A short time later, polystyrene was foamed. At first it was used mainly in insulation and flotation devices for boats, life preservers, and buoys. It was not until EPF replaced paper, kapok (made from the silky fibers that encase ceiba tree seeds), and other natural packaging protection that the substance became as popular as it is today. Its familiarity was furthered by the enormous growth of the fast food and take-out industries, which began to use EPF in burger boxes and coffee cups. Today EPF is easily the most recognized plastic.

However, despite EPF's popularity and unique features, it has recently come under attack because of the gaseous methane derivatives—chlorofluorocarbons (CFCs)—used to foam it. CFCs are inert, and harmless to humans and the environment upon their release. However, long after their first use, scientists realized that CFCs contribute to the depletion of the ozone layer as they decompose. The ozone layer is a layer of the atmos-

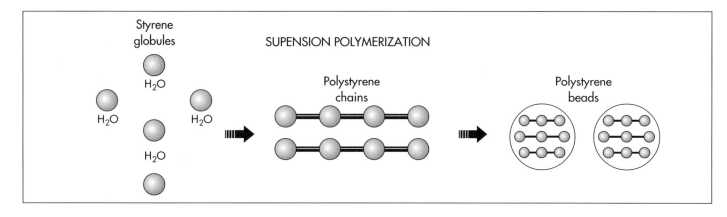

phere that protects the earth against harmful ultraviolet rays from the sun. In 1988 representatives from 31 nations signed the *Montreal Protocol*, a treaty with which they resolved to halve CFC production by 1998. This agreement brought EPF to the world's consciousness as a threat to the ozone layer. While foam packaging is responsible for less than three percent of the CFCs being released into the atmosphere, EPF reduction has been targeted as a way to lower CFC levels, and new technology that explores ways to produce EPF without CFCs has flourished. EPF has also been singled out by environmentalists because it is not being recycled. Action has been taken, however, and programs are under way to see that a greater percentage of EPF will be recycled in upcoming years.

Raw Materials

EPF's main component is styrene (C_8H_8), which is derived from petroleum or natural gas and formed by a reaction between ethylene (C_2H_4) and benzene (C_6H_6); benzene is produced from coal or synthesized from petroleum. Styrene is polymerized either by heat or by an initiator such as benzoyl peroxide. Stopping the polymerization is difficult; however, inhibitors such as oxygen, sulfur, or quinol can be used. To form the low-density, loosely attached cells EPF is noted for, polystyrene must first be suspended in water to form droplets. A suspension agent, such as specially precipitated barium sulfate or copolymers of acrylic and methacrylic acid and their esters (organic product formed by the reaction between of an acid and an alcohol), is then added to the water. Numerous suspension agents are used commercially. All are similarly viscous and serve to hold up the droplets, preventing them from sticking together. The beads of polystyrene produced

by suspension polymerization are tiny and hard. To make them expand, special blowing agents are used, including propane, pentane, methylene chloride, and the chlorofluorocarbons.

Design

Like all plastics, EPF consists of a polymer chain with great molecular weight. A molecule's weight is equivalent to its mass and can be calculated by adding the mass of its constituent atoms. EPF is a linear polymer whose basic unit is styrene (C_8H_8) and whose molecular mass is 104, yet when it is linked together as it is in the plastic, its mass can range between 200,000 and 300,000 (because a polymer chain can contain an indefinite number of molecular links, a terminal mass cannot be determined).

The Manufacturing Process

First, styrene is made by combining ethylene and benzene. Next, the styrene is subjected to suspension polymerization and treated with a polymerization initiator, which together convert it into polystyrene. Once a polymer chain of the desired length has formed, technicians stop the reaction with terminating agents. The resulting polystyrene beads are then cleaned, and anomalous beads filtered out. To make small-cell EPF, workers then melt, add a blowing agent to, and extrude the beads. To produce smooth-skinned EPF, they pre-expand the beads, dramatically reducing their density. Next they heat and expand them before allowing them to sit for 24 hours so that they can cool and harden. The beads are then fed into a mold of the desired shape.

Polystyrene is made in a process known as suspension polymerization. After styrene is produced by combining ethylene and benzene, it is merged with water and a mucilaginous substance to form droplets of polystyrene. Next, the droplets are heated and combined with an initiator, which begins the process of polymerization. The droplets combine to form chains, which in turn combine into beads. Stopping the process with terminators is difficult, since the chains must be of a certain length to be of use.

Making styrene

1 The basic unit of polystyrene is styrene, which is the product of a two-fold reaction. Ethylene and benzene, in the presence of a catalyst such as aluminum chloride, form ethylbenzene (C_8H_8), which is then dehydrogenated (hydrogen is removed) at 1,112-1,202 degrees Fahrenheit (600-650 degrees Celsius) to form styrene (C_8H_8).

Making polystyrene

2 Polystyrene is formed from styrene through suspension polymerization, a process by which tiny drops of the monomer (in this case, styrene) are completely surrounded by water and a mucilaginous substance. Supporting and surrounding the styrene globules, the suspension agent produces uniform droplets of polystyrene.

3 Next, a polymerization initiator is added to the droplets, which are suspended by heat radiation of about 212 degrees Fahrenheit (100 degrees Celsius). This results in free radicals, a group of atoms particularly likely to react with others because they contain unpaired electrons which are available for molecular bonding. Free radicals then combine at randomly to form chains of polystyrene.

4 Stopping the polymerization process is difficult. Terminators are introduced to the process to end it at the appropriate time. Though variable, chain length must fall within a certain range, because polystyrene with overly long chains won't melt readily, and polystyrene with short chains will be brittle.

Preparing the beads

5 After polymerization is complete, the mixture—consisting of beads made up of polystyrene chains—is cooled. These beads are then washed out and dried. Uniform bead size is achieved by sorting the beads through meshes which filter out over- and undersized beads.

Making expanded polystyrene foam

6 First, the beads of polystyrene must be expanded to achieve the proper density. This process is known as pre-expansion, and involves heating the polystyrene either with steam (the most common method) or hot air (for high density foam, such as that used for a coffee cup); the heating is carried out in a vessel holding anywhere from 50 to 500 gallons (189 to 1,892 liters). During pre-expansion, an agitator is used to keep the beads from fusing together. Since expanded beads are lighter than unexpanded beads, they are forced to the top of the vessel's cavity and discharged. This process lowers the density of the beads to three percent of their original value and yields a smooth-skinned, closed cell EPF that is excellent for detailed molding.

7 Next, the pre-expanded beads are usually "aged" for at least 24 hours in mesh storage silos. This allows air to diffuse into the beads, cooling them and making them harder.

Molding

8 After aging, the beads are fed into a mold of the desired shape. Low-pressure steam is then injected into and between the beads, expanding them once more and fusing them together.

9 The mold is then cooled, either by circulating water through it or by spraying water on the outside. EPF is such a good insulator that it is hard to cool the mold down. Using small molds can reduce both the heating and cooling time and thereby speed up the process.

Making extruded, expanded polystyrene foam

10 This process yields EPF with small cell size that can be used to manufacture boards used for insulation. The beads are melted, and a blowing agent is added. The molten polystyrene is then extruded into the proper shape under conditions of high temperature and pressure.

Cutting, bonding, and coating

11 EPF is usually cut with common woodworking tools, which must be kept very sharp at all times to cut smoothly. It can also be bonded with adhesives that do not destroy it. Water-based adhesives are good, as are phenolics, epoxies, resorcinols, and ureas. EPF is not resistant to weathering or

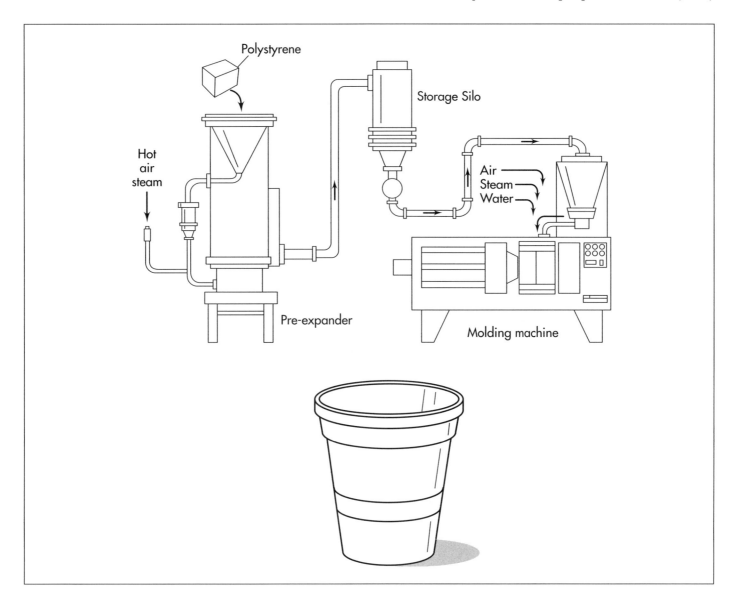

sunlight, and it is flammable, so generally coatings such as epoxy, different kinds of paint, and nonflammable substances are applied to the surface.

Quality Control

EPF is subject to the numerous tests and standards formulated by the American Society for Testing and Materials (ASTM) for plastics in general. Some of these standards concern EPF in particular because of its unique properties, yet some of the tests applied to EPF were developed to measure the properties of other plastics.

The polystyrene melt is tested to determine whether it is sufficiently viscous to produce EPF with the desired properties. Further, the subsequent polystyrene beads must be of uniform size. The standard for perfectly spherical beads is based on those formed in space shuttle experiments under conditions of zero-gravity.

Molded EPF is also tested for strength, flammability, and density, which is particularly important when testing flotation devices. EPF's resiliency is measured by banging a pendulum against the material and observing how far it rebounds. EPF is then tested for porosity. This involves determining how many open and closed cells there are, after considering the surface area of the product and the number of cells cut by fashioning. Permeability is then tested. A simple test involves placing a piece of EPF into a substance and then measuring how much of it is absorbed.

Making EPF involves a number of steps. First, the polystyrene beads undergo pre-expansion, in which they are expanded to give them the proper density. After aging in a storage silo, the beads are fed into a mold and injected with steam, which expands the beads once again and fuses them together. After cooling, the molded EPF is cut to the proper shape and coated with protective epoxy or paint.

Thermal conductivity is important whenever EPF is used for insulation. Cellular plastics have the lowest thermal conductivity (transmission of heat) of any solid material known. They insulate so well that testing for thermal conductivity is time-consuming, even when thin sheets are used. The thin (.79-2 inches or 2-5 centimeters) sheet of EPF is placed next to a heater plate, and both are enclosed by cold plates to minimize heat loss. A controlled, small amount of heat is then applied to one side of the sheet, and, after several hours, the amount of heat penetrating to the other side is measured. Of course, all data must meet the standards for EPF.

The Future

EPF can safely be incinerated and will yield only carbon dioxide and water if the procedure is handled correctly, but the trend has been to recycle it wherever possible. EPF can be recycled into **concrete**, egg cartons, office products, foam insulation, and garbage cans. Unfortunately, only one percent of the 11 billion kilograms of EPF thrown away each year is being recycled. The National Polystyrene Recycling Company, which consists of seven major corporations, including Amoco, Dow, and Mobil, plans to increase this to 25 percent by 1995 by focusing on big users of EPF—fast food outlets and college dining establishments. Since the Montreal Protocol of 1988, new research has focused on ways to reduce CFC use, and on developing alternative blowing agents that will not harm the ozone layer. Recent developments include a process that uses pressurized carbon dioxide to produce smaller, more uniform cells. These in turn provide a foam that is stronger and smoother than earlier foams.

Where To Learn More

Books

Beck, Ronald D. *Plastic Product Design.* Van Nostrand Reinhold Company, 1970.

Concise Encyclopedia of Chemical Technology. John Wiley & Sons, 1985.

Kaufman, Morris. *Giant Molecules: The Technology of Plastics, Fibers, and Rubber.* Doubleday and Company, Inc., 1968.

Modern Plastics Encyclopedia, 1981-1982. McGraw-Hill, 1981.

Richardson, Terry A. *Industrial Plastics: Theory and Application.* South-Western Publishing Co., 1983.

Wolf, Nancy and Ellen Feldman. *Plastics: America's Packaging Dilemma.* Island Press, 1991.

Periodicals

Bak, David J. "Microcells Toughen Foam Sheet," *Design News.* January 23, 1989, p. 170.

"Foam Technologies Eliminate CFCs, reduce VOCs," *Design News.* November 20, 1989, p. 34.

Kirkman, Angela and Charles H. Kline. "Recycling Plastics Today," *Chemtech.* October, 1991, pp. 606-614.

Powell, Corey S. "Plastic Goes Green," *Scientific American.* August 1990, p. 101.

—*Rose Secrest*

Eyeglass Lens

Background

Eyeglass lenses are glass or plastic optical items that fit inside eyewear frames to enhance and/or correct the wearer's vision. The magnifying glass, invented in the early 1200s, was the first optical lens used for enhancing vision. Made from a transparent quartz and beryl lens, the invention revealed the critical discovery that reflective surfaces ground to certain angles could enhance vision. Following this invention, Alessando di Spina introduced eyewear to the general populace. Due to the increasing demand for eyewear, quartz and beryl lenses were virtually replaced by glass lenses. The convex lens was the first optical lens used in glasses to aid the correction of farsightedness, but other corrective lenses followed, including the concave lens for the correction of near-sightedness, and more complex lenses for the correction of astigmatism, as well as the invention of bifocals by Benjamin Franklin in 1784.

More than 80 percent of all eyeglasses worn today have plastic lenses, but plastic lenses have not always been the lens of choice. The glass lens remained dominant until 1952, when plastic lenses were introduced. The plastic lens rapidly grew in popularity because the lens was lighter and less prone to breakage. Today, the manufacture of plastic eyeglass lenses far exceeds the manufacture of glass lenses, but the process has remained much the same for both types. Plastic as well as glass lenses are produced by successive stages of fine grinding, polishing, and shaping. While the same process is used to produce lenses for telescopes, microscopes, binoculars, cameras, and various projectors, such lenses are usually larger and thicker and require greater precision and power. This article will focus on plastic eyeglass lenses.

In the past, opticians relied on separate optical laboratories to produce eyeglass lenses. Today, there are a number of full-service optical outlets that produce lenses for customers on-site. However, optical outlets do receive lens "blanks"—plastic pieces already formed to close-to-exact size with different curves ground into the front of the lens—from optical laboratories. Blanks with different curves are used for specific optical prescriptions.

Raw Materials

The plastic blanks received from optical laboratories are round pieces of plastic such as polycarbonate approximately .75 inch (1.9 centimeters) thick or thicker and similar in size to eyeglass frames, though slightly larger. Most finished eyeglass lenses are ground to at least .25 inch (.63 centimeter), but this thickness may vary depending upon the particular optical prescription or "power" required. Other materials used to produce eyeglass lenses are:

• Adhesive tape

• A liquid with a lead alloy base

• Metal

• Dyes and tints

Design

Eyeglass lenses are designed in a variety of shapes to match eyeglass frames. The thickness and contour of each lens will vary

More than 80 percent of all eyeglasses worn today have plastic lenses, but plastic lenses have not always been the lens of choice. The glass lens remained dominant until 1952, when plastic lenses were introduced. The plastic lens rapidly grew in popularity because the lens was lighter and less prone to breakage.

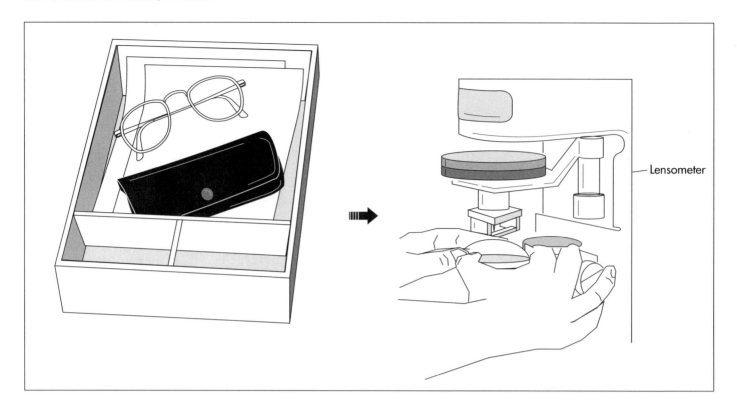

Lensometer

After the lens blanks are received from the factory, the optical laboratory technician selects the appropriate blanks and puts them in a lensometer. This is an instrument used to locate and mark the "optical center"—the point that should be centered over the customer's pupil—of the lens blanks.

depending on the extent and type of correction required. In addition, the bevel surrounding the edge of the lenses will be designed to hold the lenses in the desired eyeglass frames, and some lenses, such as those for metal and rimless frames, will require more detailed edging to fit securely in the frames.

Convex and concave lenses, known as spherical lenses, require one ground curve per lens, while more curves are required to correct astigmatism. The degree and angle of the curve or curves in a lens determines its optical strength.

Various lens treatments and tints are added after the lenses are shaped but before they are inserted in frames. The coatings are added by dipping the lenses into heated metal bins filled with the treatment or tint. The treatments and tints available include various sunglass tints and colors, ultraviolet light tints, durability and impact-resistant treatments, and scratch-resistant treatments. Among the latest advances in tints is the light-sensitive tint, which combines the advantages of regular clear lenses with the protection of sunglasses. These lenses adjust to the amount of sunlight being radiated, thus providing sun protection when needed.

Various grades of plastic are used for eye wear, but the most popular is the "Featherweight," an impact-resistant polycarbonate plastic. This type of plastic lens is more durable and 30 percent thinner and lighter than regular plastic lenses. It is also the more expensive lens. Other lens types include the standard "CR 39" trade name plastic lens—CR 39 is a monomer plastic—and the "High Index" plastic lens, which is 20 percent thinner and lighter than ordinary plastic lenses.

The Manufacturing Process

The following procedure assumes the plastic lenses are being made at an optical laboratory.

1 The optical laboratory technician inputs the optical prescription for a pair of plastic lenses in the laboratory's computer. The computer then provides a printout specifying more information necessary for producing the required prescription.

2 Based on this information, the technician selects the appropriate plastic lens blanks. Each blank is placed in a prescription tray along with the customer's eyeglass frames and the original work order. The prescription tray will remain with the technician throughout the production process.

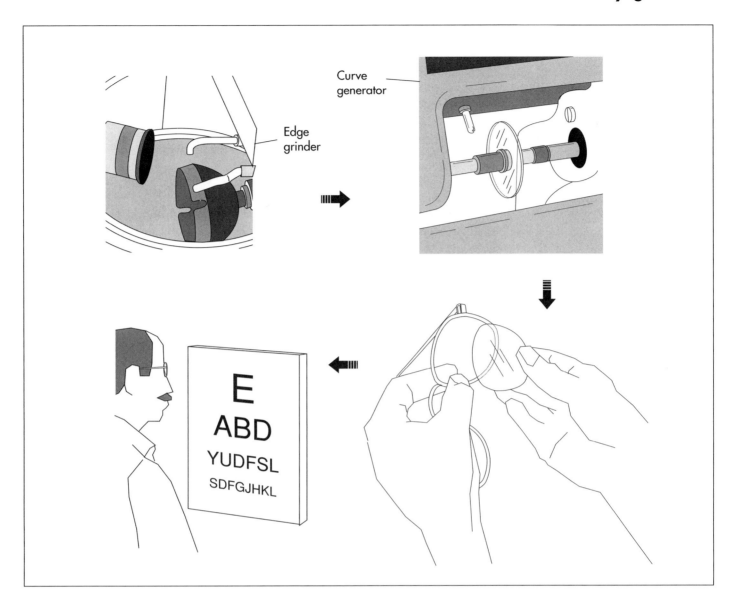

Edge
grinder

Curve
generator

E
ABD
YUDFSL
SDFGJHKL

The plastic blanks have different curves already ground into the front of them; therefore, the technician must select the blank that corresponds to the optical prescription required for each lens. The rest of the optical prescription, or power, must be ground into the back of the lens.

Blocking

3 The technician places the lenses in a lensometer, an instrument used to locate and mark the "optical center"—the point that should be centered over the customer's pupil—of the lens blanks. Next, adhesive tape is affixed to the front of each blank to keep the front from being scratched during the "blocking" process. The technician then places one lens blank at a time in a "blocker" machine, which contains a heated lead alloy

that fuses the block to the front of the blank. The blocks are used to hold each lens in place during the grinding and polishing processes.

4 Next, the technician places each blank into a generator, a grinding machine that is set for the optical prescription. The generator grinds the appropriate optical curves into the back of each lens. After this step, the lenses must be "fined," or polished.

Polishing

5 The technician selects a metal lens *lap*— a mold corresponding to the required optical prescription of the lens, and both lenses are placed in the fining machine with the back of each lens in the appropriate lap. The front of each lens is then polished in a

Although the appropriate curves have already been ground into the front of the lens, the technician must still grind curves into the back of the lens. This is done in a curve generator. After polishing the lenses, they are put in an edge grinder, which grinds each lens to its proper shape and places a bevel around the edge so that the lens will fit the eyeglass frames. Following any necessary tint applications, the lens are put into the frames.

series of fining operations. First, each lens is rubbed against an abrasive fining pad made of soft **sandpaper**. After a second fining pad made of a smooth plastic is placed over the original sandpaper pad, the lens is polished again, as the fining machine rotates the pads in a circular motion while water flows over the lenses. After the initial fining process is completed, the two pads are peeled off and thrown away.

6 Next, the laps are removed from each lens and soaked in hot water for a few moments. The laps are then attached back on the lenses and placed in the fining machine, where the third and final fining pad is attached. The fining machine rotates the pads in a circular motion while a polishing compound consisting of aluminum oxide, water, and polymers flows over the lenses.

7 The lenses are removed from the fining machine, and the block attached to each lens is gently detached with a small hammer. Then, the tape is removed from each lens by hand. The laps are sterilized before they are used to hold other lenses.

8 Each lens is marked "L" or "R" with a red grease **pencil**, indicating which is the left and right lens. After the lenses are again placed in the lensometer to check and mark the optical center and inspect the other curves necessary for the proper optical prescription, a *leap pad*—a small, round metal holder—is then affixed to the back of each lens.

Beveling

9 Next, the technician selects the lens pattern that matches the shape of the eyeglass frames and inserts the pattern and the lenses into an edging machine. The machine grinds each lens to its proper shape and places a bevel around the edge of the lens so that the lens will fit the eyeglass frames. Water flows over the lens throughout this process.

10 If the lenses require additional grinding, the process is done by hand using a mounted power grinder. This step is necessary for lenses to be inserted in metal or rimless frames, which require more precise bevels.

11 Finally, the lenses are dipped into the desired treatment or tint container.

After drying, the eyeglass lenses are ready for insertion in the desired frames. The optical laboratory may send the lenses back to the optical outlet without the frames, in which case the optical outlet will insert the lenses in the frames.

Byproducts

Byproducts or waste from the manufacturing process include plastic dust or fine shavings and a liquid polishing compound consisting of aluminum oxide, water, and polymers. The waste material is placed in metal bins for 48 hours along with sanitation compounds (vermiculite of cat litter) before disposal.

Quality Control

Plastic eyeglass lenses must meet rigid standards set by the American National Standards Institute and the Food and Drug Administration (FDA). In addition, all licensed optical laboratories belong to the National Optical Association, which requires strict adherence to prescribed guidelines regarding quality and safety.

Throughout the normal production process, plastic lenses undergo four basic inspections. Three of these inspections occur in the laboratory and the fourth occurs at the optical outlet before the eyeglasses are given to a customer. Other periodic inspections may also be advised. The four inspections involve checking the optical prescription prior to the production process and verifying the optical center placement; visually checking lenses for scratches, chips, rough edges, or other blemishes; visually checking the optical prescription before the lenses are viewed in the lensometer, and verifying optics while the lenses are in the lensometer; and measuring and verifying frame alignment with a ruler.

Where To Learn More

Books

Impact Resistant Lenses: Questions and Answers. U.S. Department of Health and Human Services, 1987.

Periodicals and Pamphlets

"High-Speed Spindles Aid in Fabricating Plastic Eyeglass Frames with Special Finishes." *Plastics Design & Processing*. December 1983/January 1984, p. 21.

How Your Eyeglasses Are Made. Optical Laboratories Association.

Krasnow, Stefanie. "Athletic Specs: The Eyes Have It." *Sport*. August, 1987, p. 97.

More Than Meets the Eye. Optical Laboratories Association.

"Plastic Beats Acrylic for Lenses." *Design News*. August 18, 1986, p. 29.

—*Greg Ling*

File Cabinet

Background

A file cabinet is a piece of office furniture characterized by drawers that hold papers in vertically placed folders. While such cabinets are mainly used to store documents, they also facilitate organizing, removing, and using such documents.

Since the earliest use of written records, it has been necessary to organize and store information. Ancient methods of filing included clay tablets that were kept in libraries, and leather or papyrus scrolls that were sealed in stone or earthenware vessels. Other filing methods developed later. Sometimes records were simply kept on shelves. During the late Middle Ages, clerks used spindle files. These implements—basically sharp sticks attached to bases—resembled the metal prongs on which today's small businesses might save receipts. Pigeonhole filing, in which bundles of papers were placed on shelves segmented into discrete cubicles, became appropriate for small scale, immediate access filing. In contrast, records not in daily use could be stored in boxes or trunks. People could also use a letterpress to copy receipts and letters into a copybook, and a strongbox to save valuable documents.

To meet the demands of growing businesses during the late 1800s, several methods of filing were developed, among them the bellows, box, and Shannon files. These devices were noted to organize material, either chronologically or alphabetically, in small containers that could be easily opened. In 1868 the first cabinet equipped with drawers became available, but because the papers were laid flat, retrieval was cumbersome.

Vertical files were introduced at the 1893 World's Fair in Chicago. Dr. Nathaniel S. Rosenau is credited with the idea, taken from the already existent vertical method of filing cards. Vertical files are the familiar file cabinets of today. The earliest models were made from wood, but these were gradually replaced by steel vertical files in the twentieth century. While file cabinets are so common and well-known that they are often considered the only or best way to file records, records management experts generally agree that vertical files are useful only for small offices or household records.

Other systems include shorter, wider, vertical files; open shelf files (similar to bookcases); and electronically controlled systems. In the 1940s, the first motorized rotary card file system was invented. Motorized letter-size files soon followed, and a mechanized, horizontal, large wheel version becoming available during the 1950s. In the ensuing decade, prompted by the growing demand for large vertical or open shelf files, a system was developed by which pushing a button could bring a shelf or drawer to eye level. Card files of the time used a system of punched cards: when the appropriate code was punched in, the desired file card would emerge. More recently, electro-optical scanning has made it possible to use scanners to find properly coded folders.

Raw Materials

A typical file cabinet consists of a case whose parts are uniformly made of 18-gauge steel; the bottom of the case may or may not be enclosed. Although some file cabinet cases, usually those produced for individual consumers, are made from oak, steel remains by

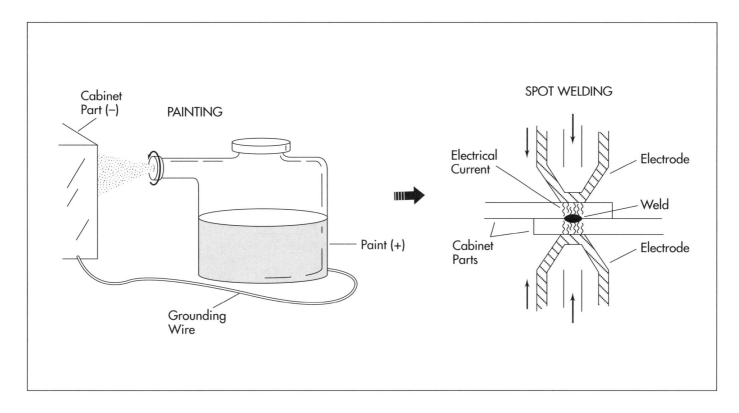

far the most common material used for business file cabinets. Like the case, the compressor (the adjustable mechanism that moves back or forward to hold upright a larger or smaller number of files) is also made from steel, and both are usually painted. To ensure a lasting finish, a special epoxy paint is applied electrostatically. Epoxy **paint** is based on a synthetic resin whose strength derives from condensation polymers, molecules that form tight chains during the condensation process. Electrostatic painting entails applying paint with one charge to an object with the opposite charge; the difference in charges causes the paint to adhere tightly to the object. The cabinet's accessories include handles and card label holders, both of which are likely to be made from anodized aluminum. The sliding mechanism and **ball bearing**s are usually steel, while the rollers are usually made from high density nylon.

Some file cabinets are built to be fireproof. Such cabinets are heavier because their walls are built with special encapsulated chambers filled with vermiculite (a lightweight, highly water-absorbent clay mineral) and several gallons of water. When the file cabinet is heated by the presence of fire, the vermiculite melts and the water turns into steam, thereby accepting the heat and keeping the documents cool.

The Manufacturing Process

Preparing the steel components

1 The 18-gauge steel from which most components of a file cabinet are made is bought in large quantities. It can reach the factory in coils 11.8 to 15.7 inches (.3 to .4 meter) wide, or, for larger components such as the walls of the file cabinet, in sheets of several sizes: 9.8 by 12 feet or 8 by 9.8 feet (3 by 3.66 meters or 2.44 by 3 meters).

2 To make small components such as compressors, a ribbon of steel from a coil is rolled onto a machine that cuts it with a die. To make shelves or dividers, the coils are unrolled and stamped in a press. To make the sides, top, and bottom of the file cabinet, the large sheets of steel are cut to size. Stronger portions of the cabinets, such as gussets, ribs, and end panels, are made simply by folding the steel one, two, or three times, depending on how much strength is desired, and pounding it to form thick, layered parts.

Painting the components

3 Two assembly lines, one for large parts, and the other for small parts, are set up for painting. To produce a superb finish, conven-

After being die-cut or stamped to the proper size, the steel components are painted in an electrostatic process. The paint in the paint gun is given a positive charge, while the cabinet part is given a negative charge. The opposite charges cause the paint to adhere evenly to the cabinet surface.

After painting, the components are welded together in a process known as spot welding. One electrode is placed on each part, and an electric current is passed between them. The heat generated by the current fuses the parts together.

A completed vertical file cabinet includes a compressor, a sliding mechanism, and a handle for each drawer. A quality cabinet will resist rust, drops, and impact.

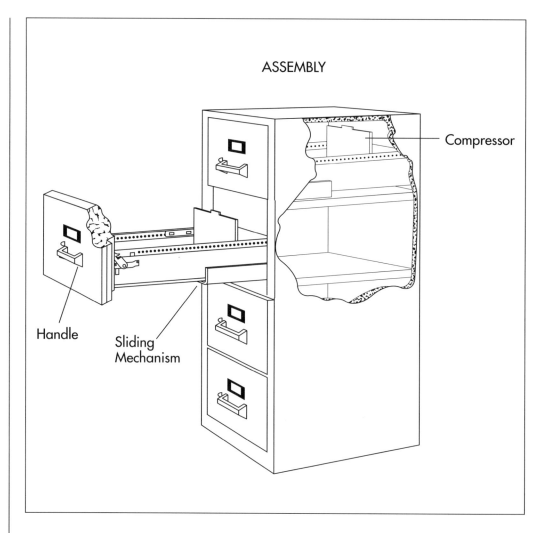

ASSEMBLY

Compressor

Handle

Sliding
Mechanism

tional or, more often, epoxy paints are used in an electrostatic gun. This effective method disperses the paint in powdered form, yielding only one percent waste. Electrostatic painting works best in a vacuum, so a 23-inch (58-centimeter) area around the object to be painted is cleared. An aluminum wire runs from the paint gun to the cabinet in order to ground it. While the paint is given a positive charge, the component to be painted receives a negative charge. The gun then sends the paint out through a small, cupped head that rotates to cover all surfaces, even those that are not flat, evenly. After spraying, the parts are heated to secure the paint. The strong bond that forms between the differently charged paint and part results in a durable finish.

Welding the cabinet components

4 After being painted, the top, bottom, and sides of the cabinet are welded together. The parts are held steady in a jig, a device that resembles a vise. File cabinets are spot welded, meaning that welds are made at regular intervals between two overlapping sheets of metal. During spot welding a low-voltage, high-current power source with two electrodes, one on each side of the joint, is placed on a spot, and pressure is applied. A current is generated between the two electrodes, and the resistance of the metal to the current generates heat that bonds the two sheets together. This method is also known as *electrical resistance welding.*

Assembling the cabinet

5 The slide mechanisms on which the drawers move are usually purchased from a specialty manufacturer and placed within holders that are bolted in place within the cabinet. The drawers are then assembled. Some components, such as the latch or the card label holder, are merely slipped into pre-cut holes in the steel and clamped into place. Other parts, such as the handle, are bolted into place.

6 Placed into **corrugated cardboard** cartons, the completed file cabinets are shipped by common carrier to office supply stores and offices.

Quality Control

A file cabinet's most obvious purpose is to store documents, but another less obvious function is to protect the documents from dust, water, light, drafts, and, in the case of fireproof file cabinets, fire. A quality file cabinet will resist rust, drops, and impact. Long, tightly packed rows of paper can weigh a lot: a full letter size file drawer can weigh approximately 260 to 310 pounds (120 to 140 kilograms). A properly built file cabinet can handle these loads. Drawer mechanisms must be in good working order throughout the lifetime of the file cabinet. The compressor must keep functioning to hold the papers tightly. The drawers must not open inadvertently, but they must open smoothly when unlatched (this requirement usually depends on the slide mechanism being lubricated twice a year).

One method of testing involves the lengthy life-span of a file cabinet. The weight needed to open a drawer is determined using a spring scale. This weight is attached to the door, which is then opened and closed at least 50,000 times to simulate twenty years of use.

Tolerances and dimensions are also important in making file cabinets, because, while height, width, and depth dimensions may vary slightly from manufacturer to manufacturer, the file cabinet must be built to conform to the standard folder sizes. For easy retrieval, the drawer space for folders is usually about one centimeter wider than a standard folder.

Fireproof file cabinets have a rating system that indicates the temperature range within which the documents will remain protected.

At minimum, the documents will be safe at 354 degrees Fahrenheit (177 degrees Celsius). Even at 1704 degrees Fahrenheit (927 degrees Celsius), the documents will be safe for an hour. The ideal climate for documents would offer temperatures between 68 and 78 degrees Fahrenheit (18-24 degrees Celsius) with relative humidity of 50 percent.

The Future

The latest trend in file cabinets is their possible disappearance from computerized offices. Prognosticators of the 1960s and 1970s envisioned paperless offices in which information would be neatly stored on—and easily retrievable from—space-saving computer **floppy disk**s and databases. However, despite the prevalence of computers, as recently as 1990, fully 95 percent of all office documents were on paper, with one million pieces of paper per minute being created in the United States alone. At the present time, computers often seem to function as merely another means of generating paper, or hard copies. This familiarity with and preference for paper documents will, at least in the near future, necessitate the continued use of filing cabinets.

Where To Learn More

Books

Arn, Joseph V. and Paula H. Titlow. *Records Management for an Information Age.* Delmar Publishers, 1991.

Johnson, Mina M. and Norman F. Kallaus. *Records Management.* South-western Publishing, 1967.

Stewart, Jeffrey R., et al. *Filing Systems and Records Management.* McGraw-Hill, 1981.

—Rose Secrest

Fire Extinguisher

Halons are up to ten times more effective in putting out fires than other chemicals. However, in 1992, 87 nations around the world agreed to halt the manufacture of halon fire extinguishers by January 1, 1994. This will eliminate a potential threat to the earth's protective ozone layer, which halon molecules interact with and destroy.

Background

The hand-held fire extinguisher is simply a pressure vessel from which is expelled a material (or agent) to put out a fire. The agent acts upon the chemistry of the fire by removing one or more of the three elements necessary to maintain fire—commonly referred to as the *fire triangle*. The three sides of the fire triangle are fuel, heat, and oxygen. The agent acts to remove the heat by cooling the fuel or to produce a barrier between the fuel and the oxygen supply in the surrounding air. Once the fire triangle is broken, the fire goes out. Most agents have a lasting effect upon the fuel to reduce the possibility of rekindling. Generally, the agents applied are water, chemical foam, dry powder, halon, or carbon dioxide (CO_2). Unfortunately, no one agent is effective in fighting all types (classes) of fires. The type and environment of the combustible material determines the type of extinguisher to be kept nearby.

History

Fire extinguishers, in one form or another, have probably postdated fire by only a short time. The more practical and unitized extinguisher now commonplace began as a pressurized vessel that spewed forth water, and later, a combination of liquid elements. The older extinguishers comprised cylinders containing a solution of **baking soda** (sodium bicarbonate) and water. Inside, a vessel of sulfuric acid was positioned at the top of the body. This design had to be turned upside down to be activated, so that the acid spilled into the sodium bicarbonate solution and reacted chemically to form enough carbon dioxide to pressurize the body cylinder and drive out the water through a delivery pipe.

This volatile device was improved by placing the acid in a glass bottle, designed to be broken by a plunger set on the top of the cylinder body or by a hammer striking a ring contraption on the side to release the acid. Cumbersome and sometimes ineffective, this design also required improvement.

Design

Aside from using different agents, manufacturers of extinguishers generally use some type of pressurized vessel to store and discharge the extinguishing agent. The means by which each agent is discharged varies. Water fire extinguishers are pressurized with air to approximately 150 pounds per square inch (psi)—five times a car **tire** pressure—from a compressor. A squeeze-grip handle operates a spring-loaded valve threaded into the pressure cylinder. Inside, a pipe or "dip tube" extends to the bottom of the tank so that in the upright position, the opening of the tube is submerged. The water is released as a steady stream through a hose or nozzle, pushed out by the stored pressure above it.

Water extinguishers of the "gas cartridge" type operate in much the same manner, but the pressure source is a small cartridge of carbon dioxide gas (CO_2) at 2,000 psi, rather than air. To operate a gas cartridge unit, the end of the extinguisher is struck against the floor, causing a pointed spike to pierce the cartridge, releasing the gas into the pressure vessel. The released CO_2 expands several hundred times its original volume, filling the gas space above the water. This pressurizes the cylinder and forces the water up through a dip-pipe and out through a hose or nozzle to be directed upon the fire. This design proved to be less prone to *leakdown* (loss of pressure over time) than simply pressurizing the entire cylinder.

In foam extinguishers, the chemical agent is generally held under stored pressure. In dry powder extinguishers, the chemicals can either be put under stored pressure, or a gas cartridge expeller can be used; the stored-pressure type is more widely used. In carbon dioxide extinguishers, the CO_2 is retained in liquid form under 800 to 900 psi and is "self-expelling," meaning that no other element is needed to force the CO_2 out of the extinguisher. In halon units, the chemical is also retained in liquid form under pressure, but a gas booster (usually nitrogen) is generally added to the vessel.

Raw Materials

Fire extinguishers can be divided into four classifications: Class A, Class B, Class C, and Class D. Each class corresponds to the type of fire the extinguisher is designed for, and, thus, the type of extinguishing agents used. Class A extinguishers are designed to fight wood and paper fires; Class B units fight contained flammable liquid fires; Class C extinguishers are designed to fight live electrical fires; and Class D units fight burning metal fires.

Water has proven effective in extinguishers used against wood or paper fires (Class A). Water, however, is an electrical conductor. Naturally, for this reason, it is not safe as an agent to fight electrical fires where live circuits are present (Class C). In addition, Class A extinguishers should not to be used in the event of flammable liquid fires (Class B), especially in tanks or vessels. Water can cause an explosion due to flammable liquids floating on the water and continuing to burn. Also, the forceful water stream can further splatter the burning liquid to other combustibles. One disadvantage of water extinguishers is that the water often freezes inside the extinguisher at lower temperatures. For these reasons, foam, dry chemical, CO_2, and halon types were developed.

Foam, although water based, is effective against fires involving contained flammable liquids (Class B). A two-gallon (7.5 liters) extinguisher will produce about 16 gallons (60 liters) of thick, clinging foam that cools and smothers the fire. The agent itself is a proprietary compound developed by the various manufacturers and contains a small amount of propylene glycol to prevent freezing. It is contained as a mixture in a pressurized cylinder similar to the water type. Most aircraft carry this type of extinguisher. Foam can also be used on Class A fires.

The dry powder agent was developed to reduce the electrical hazard of water, and thus is effective against Class C fires. (It can also be used against Class B fires.) The powder is finely divided sodium bicarbonate that is extremely free-flowing. This extinguisher, also equipped with a dip-tube and containing a pressurizing gas, can be either cartridge-operated or of the stored pressure type as discussed above. Many specialized dry chemical extinguishers are also suitable for burning metal fires, or Class D.

Carbon dioxide (CO_2) extinguishers, effective against many flammable liquid and electrical fires (Class B and C), use CO_2 as both the agent and the pressurizing gas. The liquified carbon dioxide, at a pressure that may exceed 800 psi depending on size and use, is expelled through a flared horn. Activating the squeeze-grip handle releases the CO_2 into the air, where it immediately forms a white, fluffy "snow." The snow, along with the gas, substantially reduces the amount of oxygen in a small area around the fire. This suffocates the fire, while the snow clings to the fuel, cooling it below the combustion point. The greatest advantage to the CO_2 extinguisher is the lack of permanent residue. The electrical apparatus that was on fire is then more likely to be able to be repaired. Unlike CO_2 "snow," water, foam, and dry chemicals can ruin otherwise undamaged components.

As extinguishing agents, halons are up to ten times more effective in putting out fires than other chemicals. Most halons are non-toxic and extremely fast and effective. Chemically inert, they are harmless to delicate equipment, including computer circuits, and leave no residue. The advantage of the halon over the CO_2 extinguisher is that it is generally smaller and lighter. Halon is a liquid when under pressure, so it uses a dip-tube along with nitrogen as the pressurizing gas.

Halon, at least in fire extinguishers, may soon become a footnote to history. In 1992, 87 nations around the world agreed to halt the

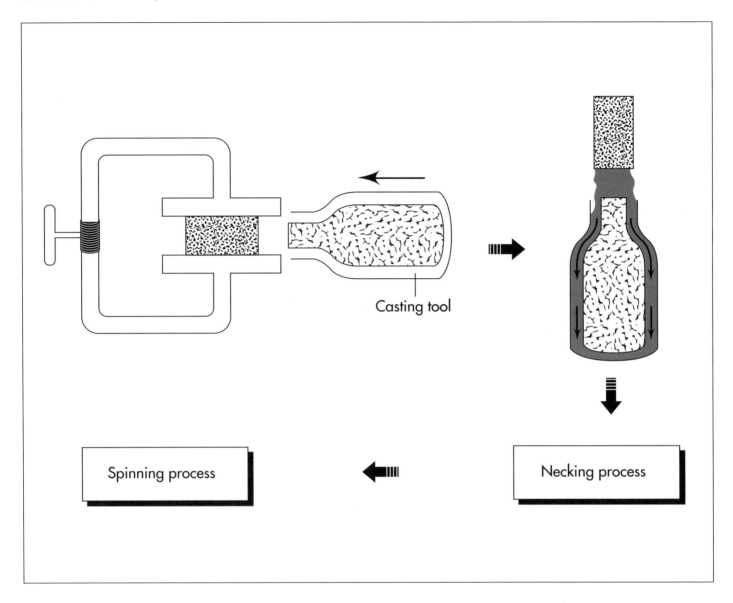

Casting tool

Spinning process

Necking process

The aluminum pressure vessel is made by impact extrusion. In this process, the aluminum block is put into a die and rammed at high velocity with a metal casting tool. The force liquifies the aluminum and causes it to flow into the cavity around the tool, thus forming the open-ended cylinder.

This cylinder is then finished in necking and spinning processes, which form the open end of the cylinder.

manufacture of halon fire extinguishers by January 1, 1994. This will eliminate a potential threat to the earth's protective ozone layer, which halon molecules—highly resistant to decomposition—interact with and destroy.

Most of the other elements of a fire extinguisher are made of metal. The pressure vessel is generally made of an aluminum alloy, while the valve can either be steel or plastic. Other components, such as the actuating handle, safety pins, and mounting bracket, are typically made of steel.

The Manufacturing Process

Manufacture of the tank-type or cylinder fire extinguisher requires several manufacturing operations to form the pressure vessel, load

the chemical agent, machine the valve, and add the hardware, hose, or nozzle.

Creating the pressure vessel

1 Pressure vessels are formed from puck-shaped (disc) blocks of special aluminum alloy. The puck is first impact extruded on a large press under great pressure. In impact extrusion, the aluminum block is put into a die and rammed at very high velocity with a metal tool. This tremendous energy liquifies the aluminum and causes it to flow into a cavity around the tool. The aluminum thus takes the form of an open-ended cylinder with considerably more volume than the original puck.

Necking and spinning

2 The necking process puts a dome on the open end of the cylinder by constricting

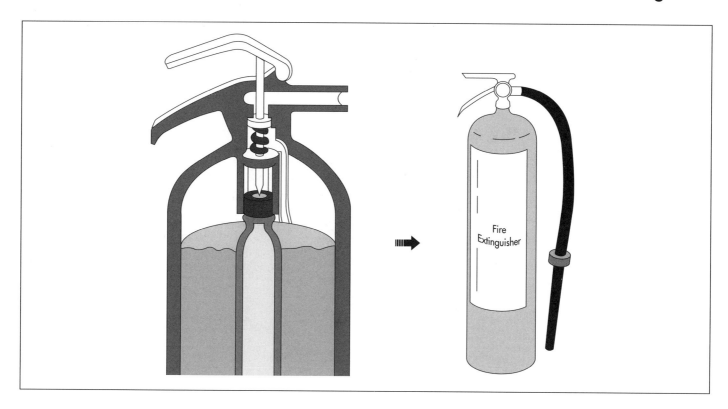

the open end with another operation called *spinning*. Spinning gently rolls the metal together, increasing the wall thickness and reducing the diameter. After spinning, the threads are added.

3 The vessel is hydrostatically tested, cleaned, and coated with a powdered **paint**. The vessel is then baked in an oven where the paint is cured.

Adding the extinguishing agent

4 Next, the extinguishing agent is added. If the vessel is a "stored-pressure" type, the vessel is then pressurized accordingly. If a gas-cartridge is necessary to help expel the extinguishing agent, it is also inserted at this time.

5 After the extinguishing element is added, the vessel is sealed and the valve is added. The valve consists of a machined body made of metal bar stock on a lathe, or a plastic injected molded part on the economy versions. It must be leak free, and it must have provisions for threading into the cylinder.

Final assembly

6 The final manufacturing operation is the assembly of the actuating handle, safety pins, and the mounting bracket. These parts are usually cold formed—formed at low temperatures—steel or sheet metal forms, purchased by the manufacturer from an outside vendor. Identification decals are also placed on the cylinder to identify the proper fire class rating as well as the suitability for recharging. Many of the economy versions are for one time use only and cannot be refilled.

Quality Control

All fire extinguishers in the United States fall under the jurisdiction of the National Fire Protection Association (NFPA), Underwriter's Laboratories, The Coast Guard, and other organizations such as the New York Fire Department. Manufacturers must register their design and submit samples for evaluation before marketing an approved fire extinguisher.

One of the most crucial checkpoints during the manufacturing process occurs after the extinguishing agent is added and the vessel sealed. It is extremely important that the cylinder not leak down the pressurizing gas, because that would render the extinguisher useless. To check for leaks, a boot is placed over the cylinder to serve as an accumulator.

In a typical gas-cartridge extinguisher, a spike pierces the gas cartridge. The released gas expands quickly to fill the space above the water and pressurize the vessel. The water can then be pumped out of the extinguisher with the necessary force.

A trace gas is released inside, and within two minutes any unacceptable rate of leakage can be recorded by sophisticated pressure and gas-detecting equipment. All extinguishers are leak tested.

The Future

With the gradual elimination of halon, a new, non-damaging agent will most likely replace the hazardous chemical within the next few years. In addition, new applications of the old designs are being seen; most prevalent are automatic heat and fire sensors that discharge the extinguisher without the need for an operator.

Where To Learn More

Books

Fire Prevention Handbook. Butterworths, London, 1986.

Mahoney, Gene. *Introduction to Fire Apparatus & Equipment.* 2nd ed., Fire Engineering Books & Videos, 1986.

Pamphlets

Portable Fire Extinguishing Equipment in Family Dwellings & Living Units. National Fire Protection Association, 1992.

—*Douglas E. Betts and Peter Toeg*

Floppy Disk

Background

A floppy disk is a portable computer storage device that permits easy handling of data. Commonly used with personal computers, notebook computers, and word processors, such disks consist of flat, circular plates made of metal or plastic and coated with iron oxide. When a disk is inserted into the disk drive of a computer, information can be magnetically imprinted on this coating, which will thereafter permit easy location and retrieval of the same data.

Magnetic storage can be traced back to the 1900 World's Fair, where a Danish engineer named Valdemar Poulsen displayed a *telegraphone*. This machine contained steel wire on which Poulsen magnetically recorded a speech, thereby generating much interest in the scientific community and inaugurating the use of magnetic storage media. In succeeding decades, a wide variety of magnetic recording devices were developed, including the floppy disk. Magnetic disks, first used to store data in 1962, initially provided supplemental memory in high-speed computer systems. They were considered ideal for this type of retrieval because a user could access information nonsequentially (unlike, for example, a cassette on which a listener has to play through all preceding material to reach a desired point).

Floppy disks—smaller, more flexible, portable versions of the earlier magnetic disks—were introduced during the 1970s. Although they cannot store as much data as convential disks and the data cannot be retrieved as easily, floppy disks have become extremely popular in situations where flexibility, low cost, and easy use are important.

Today, the floppy disk has become an indispensable tool for people working with personal computers and word processors.

The principle of magnetic recording is fairly simple. The magnetic recording (writing) and playback (reading) are carried out by a computer's disk drive, whose function corresponds broadly to that of an audio record player. Data transferred from the computer to the floppy disk is relayed in the form of a binary code and received in the form of magnetic pulses, while the disk in turn conveys magnetic patterns that the computer receives as a binary code. This code uses only 1's and 0's, which the disk represents as single magnetic pulses and the absences of pulses, respectively. Binary code is used because it most effectively utilizes the natural two-state characteristics of electricity and magnetism.

To record information on a disk, a magnetic head contacts the disk's recording surface and magnetically imprints data onto it, translating the computer's binary codes into the disk's magnetic pulses. Once a magnetic pattern consisting of many pulses and absences has been recorded, the disk retains the encoded information just like a permanent magnet. Retrieving info from the disk involves the opposite process. The magnetic head senses the magnetic pattern on the disk's recorded surface and converts it back into an electronic binary code. The computer then "reads" this information, using it to perform calculations or translating it into letters and figures for display on the monitor.

Floppy disks are currently offered in three sizes: an 8-inch (20.32 centimeters) version, a 5 1/4-inch (3.34 centimeters) version, and a 3

A 3 1/2-inch floppy disk contains several layers of liner and recording media sandwiched between two hard plastic cases. The hub is a stainless steel piece that accurately centers the disk on the drive shaft. The shutter, also stainless steel, protects the recording media.

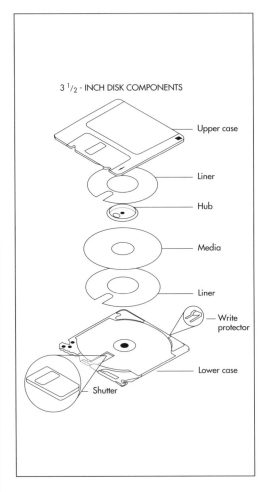

3 1/2 - INCH DISK COMPONENTS

Upper case

Liner

Hub

Media

Liner

Write protector

Lower case

Shutter

1/2-inch (8.89 centimeters) micro-version. The storage capacities on an 8-inch disk range from 250 kilobytes (roughly 250,000 characters) to 1.6 megabytes (roughly 1.6 million characters), on a 5 1/4-inch disk from 250 kilobytes to 1.6 megabytes, and on a 3 1/2-inch disk from 500 kilobytes to 2 megabytes.

Each type of floppy disk is further identified according to its recording density. A *single-sided disk* can store data on one side only, while a *double-sided disk* can store data on both sides. *Double density disks* can store twice as much data as single density disks, and *high density disks* have a special coating that enables them to store even more data.

Raw Materials

All 8-inch and 5 1/4-inch disks have three major components—the *jacket*, the *liner*, and the *recording media*. The jacket is made of a vinyl polymer, polyvinyl chloride (PVC), to protect the media against physical damage that might be caused by handling and storage. Inside the jacket, the liner consists of a spe-

cial-purpose, non-woven, anti-static fabric that is laminated to the PVC during manufacture. The liner continually cleans the disk by removing debris from the surface of the media. The recording media is a pliable layer of Mylar—a polyester film that is a trademark of the Du Pont Corporation—that is only 0.003 inches (0.007 centimeters) thick.

The 3 1/2-inch floppy disk has many different components. It is enclosed in a hard plastic cartridge that protects it from physical damage. The liner consists of a special-purpose fabric similar to that used for 8-inch and 5 1/4-inch disks, and the recording media is likewise a Mylar base 0.003 inches thick. The *hub*, which accurately centers the disk on the drive shaft, is made of **stainless steel** and attached to the media with an adhesive ring. The button that separates the two sides of the shell so the media can move freely inside is made of high-density plastic. The *write protect tab*, which prevents data from being mistakenly recorded or erased, is plastic. The *wiper tab*, also plastic, puts pressure on the liner to allow uniform and continuous cleaning. The *spring-loaded shutter*, which protects the media, is made of stainless steel.

The Manufacturing Process

The manufacture of a floppy disk takes place in three phases. First, the disk itself is made, then the case is made, and finally the two are assembled. The procedure for 8- and 5 1/4-inch disks differs slightly from that for the 3 1/2-inch model.

Disk manufacture

1 First, the recording media (Mylar), in the form of stock roll, is coated with an extremely fine layer of iron oxide. The thickness of this layer depends on the size of the disk and the type of density. For instance, the layer thickness is 110 microinches for 8-inch, high-density diskettes and 35 microinches for 3 1/2-inch high density disks. The coating for standard density diskettes is thicker than that for high density diskettes and is less *coercive*, meaning that it has less magnetic force.

2 Next, the coated film is slit and appropriate size disks are punched out with an automatic device similar to a cookie cutter.

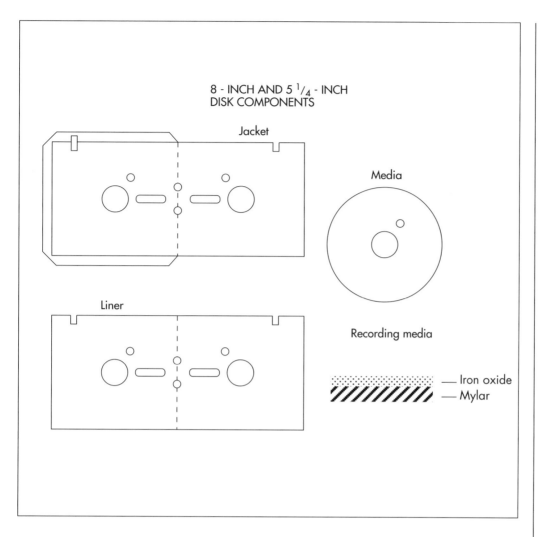

8 - INCH AND 5 ¹/₄ - INCH
DISK COMPONENTS

Jacket

Media

Liner

Recording media

—— Iron oxide
—— Mylar

The makeup of 8-inch and 5 1/4-inch diskettes is the same. Both contain a recording media, a protective liner made of nonwoven fabric, and a soft plastic (PVC) jacket. The recording media consists of Mylar plastic with a coating layer of iron oxide.

Each disk is then burnished or polished according to the required specifications and standards. 8- and 5 1/4-inch disks are now ready for insertion into jackets. For 3 1/2-inch disks, a stainless steel hub is attached to the media with an adhesive ring. 3 1/2-inch disks are now ready for insertion into their plastic cases.

Jacket and case manufacture

3 The jackets of the 8-inch and 5 1/4-inch disks are cut out of polyvinyl chloride (PVC) stock to appropriate size, and the fabric liners laminated to them. Each jacket is then punched to appropriate hole and notch configuration. The *drive spindle hole* in the middle helps to center the disk in the disk drive. The *index hole*, when aligned with an index hole punched in the media, permits the drive to locate the beginning of each segment of data. The long, thin, oval hole, also called the *head access hole*, is used by the magnetic head to come in direct contact with the media.

The write protect notch prevents data from mistakenly being recorded or erased. The *relief notches* keep the lower end of the head access hole from bending. After the apertures have been punched, the jacket is folded three ways, with only the top flap left open. The jackets are now ready for assembly.

4 The case or shell of 3 1/2-inch disks is molded out of hard plastic. It has a rectangular head access slot. The lower shell of the case is assembled with the button, the wiper tab, the write protect tab and the fabric liner. The upper shell is affixed with upper fabric liner. The spring-loaded shutter assembly is now attached and the two shells are connected at the top two corners. The cases are now ready for assembly.

Disk and case assembly

5 For 8- and 5 1/4-inch disks, the media is inserted into the jacket through the top. Each disk then undergoes comprehensive

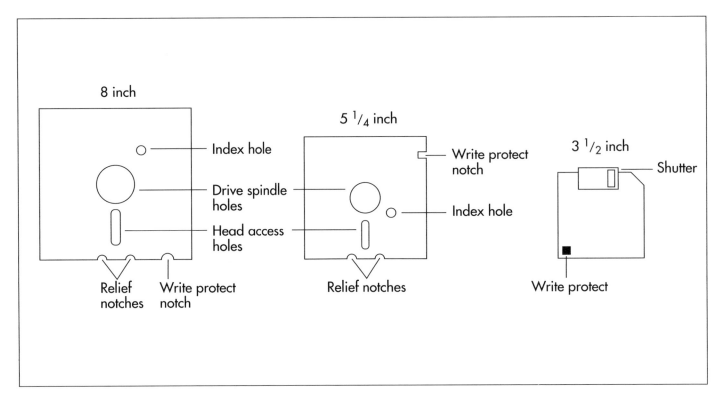

8 inch
— Index hole
— Drive spindle holes
— Head access holes
Relief notches
Write protect notch

5 ¹/₄ inch
— Write protect notch
— Index hole
Relief notches

3 ¹/₂ inch
— Shutter
Write protect

This diagram shows fully assembled floppy disks in all 3 sizes. The relief notches on the 8-inch and 5 1/4-inch disks keep the head access hole from bending. This is important because the computer disk drive uses the head access hole to come in direct contact with the recording media. The index hole allows the disk drive to locate the beginning of each segment of data, while the drive spindle hole is used by the disk drive to center the recording media.

electrical and mechanical testing and certification. After the top of the jacket, which had been left open, is folded, disk assembly is complete. Each disk is then given a final visual inspection before being labeled and packaged for shipment.

6 Assembly of 3 1/2-inch disks is very similar. First, the prepared media is inserted into the shell, and then the disk is tested and certified. The two shells are now welded at the bottom two corners and the assembly is complete. Each disk is given a final visual inspection and then labeled and packaged for shipment.

Quality Control

A floppy disk is a delicate device that must faithfully and accurately record and play back the information stored on its recording media. Dust and scratches on the disk surface must be carefully avoided during the manufacturing process, as even the smallest imperfection can cause writing and reading errors. The manufacturing operation must be performed in a clean environment. As much of the process as possible is performed automatically, to minimize human contact with the disks.

Quality control points are built into the process flow after each major operation.

First, the coating mix is checked for proper viscosity and dispersion. Once the coating is applied, it is checked for thickness, surface tension, durability and coercivity. Punched-out disks are checked for proper dimensions and hole configurations. The semi-assembled cases for 3 1/2-inch disks are checked for proper dimensions, parts placement, shutter assembly function and appearance. The semi-assembled jackets for the 8-inch and 5 1/4-inch disks are checked for proper dimensions, hole and notch configuration, lamination bonds, and appearance.

After the media has been inserted in the case, each disk is rigorously tested and goes through a certification process. Electrical testing checks the various electrical parameters such as the recorded signal variance, recorded frequency and format verification. Mechanical testing checks the various mechanical parameters such as weld strength, jacket durability, media durability, and dimensions. The certification process insures that there are no bad tracks on a disk (a track is the line the magnetic head follows in writing and reading data; collectively, the tracks form concentric circles). A disk that has been 100 percent certified has passed all tests on all tracks. Most manufacturers check every track of every disk and guarantee each disk error free.

The Future

In recent years, optoelectronic memories and storage devices have gained popularity for audio and video recordings, and the same technology is now being applied to computer memories. An optical disk is similar to a conventional disk except that the storage medium is thicker. Because of this difference, it is possible to record multiple images in one location on the disk.

Optical disks capable of storing up to 20 megabytes of data are already available, and research on higher-capacity disk technology is in progress. A recent experiment with a 2 1/2-inch (6.35 centimeters) disk showed that as many as 1000 frames could be superimposed at one location on the disk. The storage capacity of the disk thus approaches about ten pixels, which is the equivalent of about ten hours of regular video.

Such large storage density, combined with high data transfer rate and fast random access, makes optical memory a potential candidate for a wide range of applications such as image processing and database man-agement. The future of floppy disk clearly lies in optical memories. Indications are that practical applications might be available in the next three to five years.

Where To Learn More

Books

Aronson, Susan. *Diskette Reference Manual*. 3M Data Storage Products Division, 1990.

Periodicals

Glass, Brett. "3 1/2-inch Floppy Drives," *PC-Computing*. August, 1990, p. 140.

Gralla, Preston. "Floppy Disks and Drives," *PC-Computing*. October, 1992, p. 324.

Nimersheim, Jack. "Disk Anatomy," *Compute*. January, 1990, p. 58.

Psaltis, Dmitri. "Parallel Optical Memories," *BYTE*. September, 1992, pp. 179-182.

—Rashid Riaz

Gold

About 65 percent of processed gold is used in the arts industry, mainly to make jewelry. Besides jewelry, gold is also used in the electrical, electronic, and ceramics industries. These industrial applications have grown in recent years and now occupy an estimated 25 percent of the gold market.

Background

Gold, recognizable by its yellowish cast, is one of the oldest metals used by humans. As far back as the Neolithic period, humans have collected gold from stream beds, and the actual mining of gold can be traced as far back as 3500 B.C., when early Egyptians (the Sumerian culture of Mesopotamia) used mined gold to craft elaborate jewelry, religious artifacts, and utensils such as goblets.

Gold's aesthetic properties combined with its physical properties have long made it a valuable metal. Throughout history, gold has often been the cause of both conflict and adventure: the destruction of both the Aztec and Inca civilizations, for instance, and the early American gold rushes to Georgia, California, and Alaska.

The largest deposit of gold can be found in South Africa in the Precambrian Witwatersrand Conglomerate. This deposit of gold ore is hundreds of miles across and more than two miles deep. It is estimated that two-thirds of the gold mined comes from South Africa. Other major producers of gold include Australia, the former Soviet Union, and the United States (Arizona, Colorado, California, Montana, Nevada, South Dakota, and Washington).

About 65 percent of processed gold is used in the arts industry, mainly to make jewelry. Besides jewelry, gold is also used in the electrical, electronic, and ceramics industries. These industrial applications have grown in recent years and now occupy an estimated 25 percent of the gold market. The remaining percentage of mined gold is used to make a type of ruby colored glass called purple of Cassius, which is applied to office building windows to reduce the heat in the summer, and to **mirror**s used in space and in electroscopy so that they reflect the infrared spectrum.

Physical Characteristics

Gold, whose chemical symbol is *Au*, is malleable, ductile, and sectile, and its high thermal and electrical conductivity as well as its resistance to oxidation make its uses innumerable. Malleability is the ability of gold and other metals to be pressed or hammered into thin sheets, 10 times as thin as a sheet of paper. These sheets are sometimes evaporated onto glass for infrared reflectivity, molded as fillings for teeth, or used as a coating or plating for parts. Gold's ability to be drawn into thin wire (ductility) enables it to be deposited onto circuits such as transistors and to be used as an industrial solder and brazing alloy. For example, gold wire is often used for integrated circuit electrical connections, for orthodontic and prosthetic appliances, and in **jet engine** fabrication.

Gold's one drawback for use in industry is that it is a relatively soft metal (sectile). To combat this weakness, gold is usually alloyed with another member of the metal family such as silver, copper, platinum, or nickel. Gold alloys are measured by karats (carats). A karat is a unit equal to 1/24 part of pure gold in an alloy. Thus, 24 karat (24K) gold is pure gold, while 18 karat gold is 18 parts pure gold to 6 parts other metal.

Extraction and Refining

Gold is usually found in a pure state; however, it can also be extracted from silver, copper, lead and zinc. Seawater can also contain gold, but in insufficient quantities to

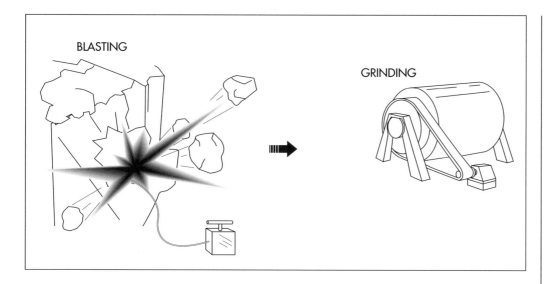

BLASTING

GRINDING

Gold is generally found in two types of deposits: lode (vein) or placer deposits. It is usually extracted from lode deposits by drilling or blasting, whereas placer deposits require hydraulic mining, dredging, or power shoveling. Once extracted, the gold ore is pulverized to prepare it for refining.

be profitably extracted—up to one-fortieth (1/40) of a grain of gold per ton of water. Gold is generally found in two types of deposits: lode (vein) or placer deposits; the mining technique used to extract the gold depends upon the type of deposit. Once extracted, the gold is refined with one of four main processes: floatation, amalgamation, cyanidation, or carbon-in-pulp. Each process relies on the initial grinding of the gold ore, and more than one process may be used on the same batch of gold ore.

Mining

1 In lode or vein deposits, the gold is mixed with another mineral, often quartz, in a vein that has filled a split in the surrounding rocks. Gold is obtained from lode deposits by drilling, blasting, or shoveling the surrounding rock.

Lode deposits often run deep underground. To mine underground, miners dig shafts into the ground along the vein. Using picks and small explosives, they then remove the gold ore from the surrounding rock. The gold ore is then gathered up and taken to a mill for refinement.

2 Placer deposits contain large pieces of gold ore (nuggets) and grains of gold that have been washed downstream from a lode deposit and that are usually mixed with sand or gravel. The three main methods used to mine placer deposits are hydraulic mining, dredging, and power shoveling. All methods of placer deposit mining use gravity as the basic sorting force.

In the first method, a machine called a "hydraulic giant" uses a high pressure stream of water to knock the gold ore off of banks containing the ore. The gold ore is then washed down into sluices or troughs that have grooves to catch the gold.

Dredging and power shoveling involve the same techniques but work with different size buckets or shovels. In dredging, buckets on a conveyor line scoop sand, gravel, and gold ore from the bottom of streams. In power shoveling, huge machines act like shovels and scoop up large quantities of gold-bearing sand and gravel from stream beds.

Hydraulic mining and dredging are outlawed in many countries because they are environmentally destructive to both land and streams.

Grinding

3 Once the gold ore has been mined, it usually is washed and filtered at the mine as a preliminary refinement technique. It is then shipped to mills, where it is first combined with water and ground into smaller chunks. The resulting mixture is then further ground in a ball mill—a rotating cylindrical vessel that uses steel balls to pulverize the ore.

Separating the gold from the ore

4 The gold is then separated from the ore using one of several methods. *Floatation* involves the separation of gold from its ore by using certain chemicals and air. The finely ground ore is dumped into a solution

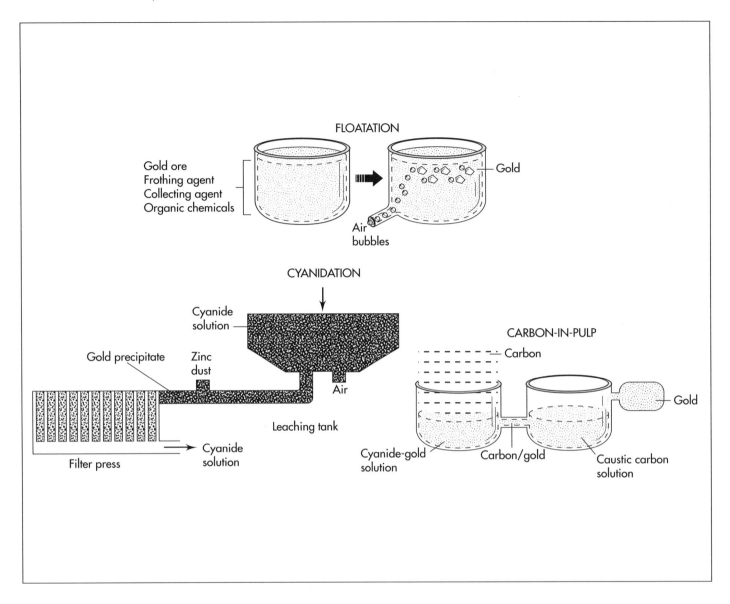

Floatation, cyanidation, and the carbon-in-pulp method are 3 processes used to refine gold. They can be used alone or in combination with one another.

that contains a frothing agent (which causes the water to foam), a collecting agent (which bonds onto the gold, forming an oily film that sticks to air bubbles), and a mixture of organic chemicals (which keep the other contaminants from also bonding to the air bubbles). The solution is then aerated—air bubbles are blown in—and the gold attaches to the air bubbles. The bubbles float to the top, and the gold is skimmed off.

Cyanidation also involves using chemicals to separate the gold from its contaminants. In this process, the ground ore is placed in a tank containing a weak solution of cyanide. Next, zinc is added to the tank, causing a chemical reaction in which the end result is the precipitation (separation) of the gold from its ore. The gold precipitate is then separated from the cyanide solution in a filter press. A similar

method is *amalgamation*, which uses the same process with different chemicals. First, a solution carries the ground ore over plates covered with mercury. The mercury attracts the gold, forming an alloy called an *amalgam*. The amalgam is then heated, causing the mercury to boil off as a gas and leaving behind the gold. The mercury is collected, recycled and used again in the same process.

The *carbon-in-pulp* method also uses cyanide, but utilizes carbon instead of zinc to precipitate the gold. The first step is to mix the ground ore with water to form a pulp. Next, cyanide is added to dissolve the gold, and then carbon is added to bond with the gold. After the carbon particles are removed from the pulp, they are placed in a hot caustic (corrosive) carbon solution, which separates the gold from the carbon.

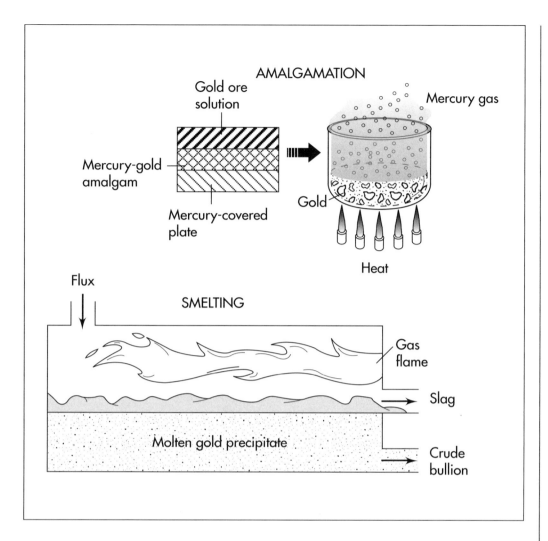

AMALGAMATION

Gold ore solution

Mercury gas

Mercury-gold amalgam

Mercury-covered plate

Gold

Heat

Flux

SMELTING

Gas flame

Slag

Molten gold precipitate

Crude bullion

Two other methods of gold refining are amalgamation and smelting. In amalgamation, the gold ore is dissolved in solution and passed over mercury-covered plates to form a gold/mercury amalgam. When the amalgam is heated, the mercury boils off as a gas and leaves behind the gold.

In smelting, the gold is heated with a chemical substance called "flux." The flux bonds with the contaminants and floats on top of the gold. The flux-contaminant mixture (slag) is hauled away, leaving a gold precipitate.

5 If the gold is still not pure enough, it can be smelted. *Smelting* involves heating the gold with a chemical substance called *flux*. The flux bonds with the contaminants and floats on top of the melted gold. The gold is then cooled and allowed to harden in molds, and the flux-contaminant mixture (*slag*) is hauled away as a solid waste.

The Future

Because gold is a finite resource, its long-term future is limited. In the short term, however, it will continue to find widespread use in jewelry and in industrial applications, especially in the electronics field.

In the last few years, several companies have focused on extracting gold from sulphide ore rather than oxide ore. Previous techniques made such extraction difficult and expensive, but a newer technique called *bioleaching* has made extraction more feasible. The process involves combining the sulphide ore with special bacteria that "eat" the ore or break it down into a more manageable form.

Where To Learn More

Books

Coombs, Charles. *Gold and Other Precious Metals*. Morrow Publishing, 1981.

Gasparrini, Claudia. *Gold & Other Precious Metals: From Ore to Market*. Springer-Verlag, 1993.

Green, Timothy. *The World of Gold*. Walker Publishing, 1968.

Hawkins, Clint. *Gold & Lead*. Harper-Collins, 1993.

Lye, Keith. *Spotlight on Gold*. Rourke Enterprises, 1988.

McCracken, Dave. *Gold Mining in the Nineteen Nineties: The Complete Book of Modern Gold Mining Procedure.* New Era Publications, 1993.

Wise, Edmund, ed. *Gold: Recovery, Properties, and Applications.* Van Nostrand, 1964.

Periodicals

Abelson, Philip H. "Gold." *Science.* July 11, 1986, p. 141.

Dworetzky, Tom. "Gold Bugs." *Discover.* March, 1988, p. 32.

"Some Like It Hot." *Economist.* June 25, 1988, p.88.

"Mining with Microbes: A Labor of Bug." *Science News.* April 14, 1990, p. 236.

—*Alicia Haley and Blaine Danley*

Golf Cart

Background

A golf cart is an electric or gas-powered vehicle used to transport golfers and their equipment around the course during play. Designed to meet golfers' needs, the carts offer a number of specialized safety and comfort features. For example, the fact that they are built low to the ground gives them a low center of gravity, preventing spills when they are driven over uneven terrain. Many electric carts also come with portable **battery** chargers. Often, the center of the steering wheel (where the horn would be in a normal **automobile**) features a metal clipboard to which players can attach their score cards. The vehicles can be ordered with ball and cup holders, plastic enclosures to zip up in case of rain, sun canopies, and racks to hold bags, sweaters, and sand trap rakes. AM/FM radios and cassette players can be built into the dashboard, as can ashtrays and cigarette lighters.

A number of country clubs began to develop private courses during the closing decades of the nineteenth century, and the United States Golf Association (USGA) was founded in 1894. However, those American golfers who did not belong to clubs often played the game without designated courses until after World War II, using such sites as open fields, orchards, and cow pastures. The war's end freed up earth-moving equipment for recreational use, and, as many more private and public courses were constructed, record numbers of Americans took up the game. The self-propelled golf cart as we know it today came into use in the early 1950s. In 1953 only a few of the most exclusive golf clubs owned motor driven carts, but by 1959 the little motor-driven carts could be seen just about everywhere. While caddies are still available at private clubs, and cost- or health-conscious players on public courses often prefer to carry their bags or rent hand-drawn carts, the power-driven cart has superceded both of these options.

Raw Materials

The frames of golf carts are usually made out of steel plates, rods, and tubing. The bodies may be made of sheet aluminum, fiber glass, or sheet steel. Other components, usually plastic or metal, are generally purchased from outside suppliers and assembled to the vehicle. These include components such as **tires**, which are made out of rubber; seat cushions, which typically consist of foam cushion covered by vinyl; steering mechanisms, made of metal; and motors, brakes, batteries, transaxles, suspensions, drive trains, and electrical cables.

Design

There is no standard design for a golf cart. Many choices must be made before the designer draws the first line. Should the body be made from steel, aluminum, fiber glass, or wood? Should it seat two, four, or six passengers? Is it to have an electric or a gasoline engine? Must the cart have a powerful engine and strong brakes to navigate hills, or a small engine to insure efficient operation? Once the capabilities, materials, and appearance are decided upon, a designer uses an integrated CAD/CAM (Computer Aided Design/Computer Aided Manufacturing) system to draw the cart and all its components on the computer screen. Next, the shop makes a prototype cart that will be used to

Manufacturers may soon begin producing carts with video games built into their dashboards, to help players pass time while waiting at the tee. Similarly, video screens featuring a computer-generated layout of each hole with the location of the balls in play are also being examined.

The first step in golf cart manufacture is floor and body panel fabrication, which is done by sheet metal shearing or molding, depending on the material used. Next, the chassis or frame is made by cutting, beveling, and arc-welding the tubular steel pieces.

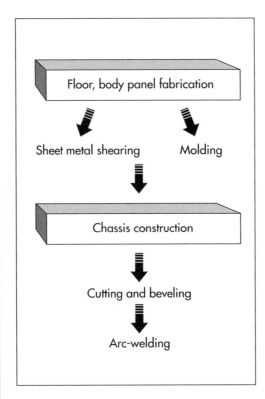

cut, beveled pieces are then placed in a welding fixture, and the chassis, or frame, is arc-welded. In this process, an electric current is fed out of the welding torch through a metal wire that is shielded by a concurrently emitted inert gas (usually argon or helium). As the wire melts, it joins the tubes to form the chassis. Next, the floor is welded in place, and the attaching hardware for the suspension, motor, and body are arc-welded to the frame. At this point, the chassis may need to be straightened to adjust for stresses introduced into the steel tubing during welding. Once it is straight, the chassis and body panels are cleaned and painted with a rust-preventive finish coating.

Transaxle subassembly

3 Next, the right and left side of the transaxle housing are fitted with bearings, gears, seals, and axle housings. Because of the close fits required for the bearings and gears, these parts must be manually installed with special assembly tools. For example, a special gauge is used to determine the size of the spacer required under the pinion gear. These spacers are used to set *preload* (pressure between the gear faces) and *backlash* (spacing between the gear faces). Next, the two mating surfaces of the transaxle housing are coated with an anaerobic sealant, which hardens in the absence of air, and bolted together.

4 The axle shafts and bearings are then slid into the axle housings and locked in place. The transaxle access plate and gasket are positioned and bolted in place. Auto-adjusting, drum type mechanical brakes are then assembled to each end of the axle housings.

Battery charger assembly (electric-powered carts only)

5 The rear cover is snapped into the base plate. The transformer, which adjusts the direct current provided by the battery into an alternating current that is easier for the motor to use, is then bolted to the base plate. Next, the electric cable with plug, thermal switch, and DC Ammeter (used to measure the battery's direct current output) are wired in and attached. Finally, the wrap around and face cover are bolted in place.

test the new design. If the design proves successful, the production system is set up and the manufacturing process begins. Generally, once a design proves to be a good seller it will not be changed from year to year. There are few style trends in golf cart design: the vehicle is, after all, largely utilitarian.

The Manufacturing Process

Fabrication of floor and body panels

1 The floor and body panels are made of sheet steel, aluminum, or fiber glass. If sheet metal is used the metal is cut to size in a sheet metal shear, a machine that cuts it with giant scissors. It is then fed into a roll forming machine, which shapes the metal by passing it over contoured forming rolls. If fiber glass is the chosen material, the floor and body panels are formed as one piece by inserting layers of resin-coated fiber glass in a mold and allowing them to harden.

Chassis construction and painting

2 Tubular steel, which resembles square bicycle handlebars, is cut to size and the edges beveled (cut at an angle of less than 90 degrees) to prepare them for welding. The

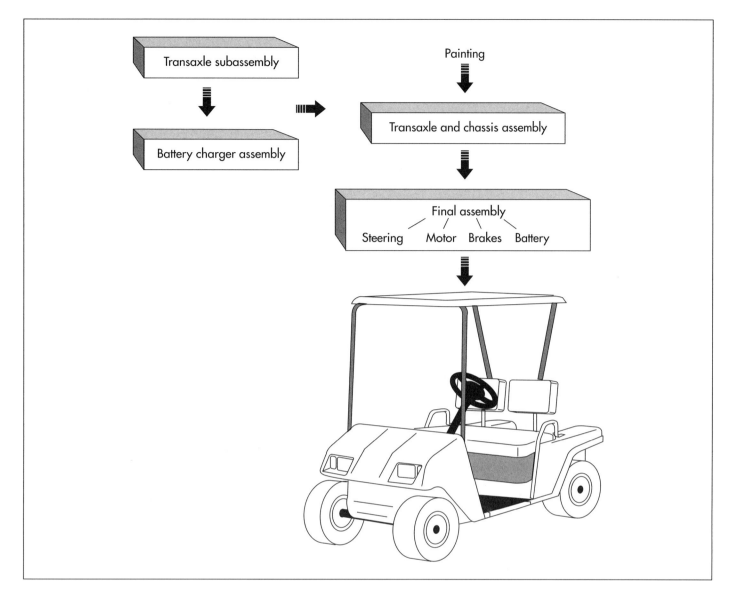

Transaxle and chassis assembly

6 The transaxle subassembly and the welded chassis are placed on a stand that is just the right height to allow the assembly personal to work in a upright position with a minimum of bending. The shock absorbers—oil filled cylinders that cushion the ride by displacing the oil when a bump is hit—are the first components bolted to the chassis, one at each wheel location. Next, the springs are bolted to the chassis, with multiple leaf springs at the front axles and coil springs at the rear. The transaxle and the chassis are joined together by pinning the shock absorbers to the transaxle. Prior to assembly, the coil springs must be compressed using a special fixture. The front axle bar may now be attached to the chassis by bolting the multiple leaf springs to the front axle bar from the

chassis. The front axle shafts are then bolted to each end of the front axle bar. To insure smooth movement, the wheel bearings are packed, meaning that grease is forced into the bearing until it comes out the other side. The wheel plate with studs is then installed.

Installing other components

7 The rack and pinion steering assembly is now bolted to the chassis and attached to the front axle shafts. The steering wheel and steering wheel shaft are then attached to the chassis and rack and pinion steering assembly. Next, the body panels are bolted to the chassis, and then the motor is installed. If the cart is to be electric-powered, a 36-volt direct current electric motor is bolted to the transaxle. If the cart is to be gasoline-powered, an eight-horsepower gasoline engine is

After the chassis and body panels are constructed, they are cleaned and painted. Next, the transaxle subassembly is bolted to the chassis. If the cart is an electric one, the battery charger assembly is also added at this time. Finally, the steering assembly, motor, braking system, and battery are added, and seat cushions and canopy (if necessary) are added.

bolted to the chassis. The continuously variable (CV) transmission is also bolted to the chassis. Belts are then installed to the drive pulleys of the engine, CV transmission, and transaxle.

8 The brake pedal is installed. Brake cables are routed and attached to the pedal and rear brakes. The accelerator pedal is installed, and the accelerator cable is attached to the pedal and the engine. Next, the electrical cables are routed and attached to the chassis.

Fixtures

9 The headlights, stoplights, and on-off key lock are installed and cables connected. Next, the battery rack is bolted in and the batteries installed: six six-volt batteries for the electric drive vehicle, or one twelve-volt battery for the gasoline engine vehicle. A six gallon fuel tank is then installed in the gasoline engine vehicle and a hose routed from the tank to the engine. The batteries are connected and the fuel tank filled.

Final steps

10 The seat cushions are installed and, if ordered, the canopy top, windshield, and storage baskets are attached. For delivery in North America, there are no packaging requirements. Delivery is normally by truck. After being driven onto the truck, the golf carts have their fuel drained, their batteries disconnected, and their wheels blocked in place. Overseas shipments require that the golf cart be placed on a skid—a heavy wood or steel rack—to discourage shifting in transit.

Quality Control

Quality control starts at the design development stage. Structural and fatigue tests are applied to the major components to assure that they will not break or wear out during normal usage. Once a prototype golf cart has been built, it is run on a mechanized track where it is subjected to shocks and severe vibration. Next, it is driven on a test track for hundreds of miles to test its endurance. Finally, the golf cart is placed in an environmental test chamber that is used to simulate actual weather conditions.

Before manufacturing begins, quality assurance personnel visit suppliers to assure that their procedures will enable them to continue supplying high quality parts. Statistical Process Control (SPC) charts are kept and used to show that the processes are under control. These visits have eliminated the need to inspect parts as they are received at the plant.

After the chassis is welded together, it is placed on a special fixture, where it is measured with gauges to assure that it is not warped and checked to verify that all the parts are located properly. The **paint** on the body panels is checked for coating thickness using a contact gauge that will not damage the finished surface. The paint is also optically compared with a standard chip to assure that the color is consistent. The transaxles are placed on a test stand, filled with oil, and run to check for leaks and noise level. After they are assembled, electrical cables are attached to Automatic Test Equipment (ATE) to check for shorts, resistance, and continuity. The battery chargers are checked for output and current draw. Additionally, the battery chargers must go through periodic checks to maintain their Underwriters Laboratory (UL) certification. Each gasoline engine is put on a dynamometer and run to check power output, operating temperature, and leakage. Fuel tanks are pressurized and placed under water to check for leaks. Every finished vehicle is tested for acceleration and breaking.

Waste Disposal

The manufacture of golf carts creates four major types of waste products: metal chips and contaminated coolant from the machining operations, cardboard shipping materials, and paint overspray. Although difficult to collect and sort, metal chips can often be sold to recyclers. Contaminated coolant is just the opposite. It is easy to gather and difficult to dispose of. As the coolant is used it is contaminated with tramp oil, lubricant that leaks out of machines. The coolant also supports bacterial growth. Some companies use holding ponds to break down this bacteria in sunlight; they then recycle the coolant once the tramp oil has been filtered out. Most companies, however, just pay to have the oil hauled away by a waste disposal company.

Cardboard shipping materials are taken to the local landfill, where the landfill operator is paid to bury or burn them. Some companies use recyclable containers made of steel or fiber glass to reduce the amount of cardboard waste, but these become a very expensive alternative when the return shipping costs are taken into account. Paint overspray and paint with an expired shelf life are considered toxic in many cases. To dispose of these materials the golf cart manufacturer must often pay many times the original cost of the paint to have it removed.

The Future

One technical innovation that may become available within the next ten years is a battery that charges in minutes and works for many hours. Manufacturers may also begin producing carts with video games built into their dashboards, to help players pass time while waiting at the tee. Similarly, video screens featuring a computer-generated layout of each hole with the location of the balls in play are also being examined.

Where To Learn More

Books

Peper, George. *Golf in America: The First One Hundred Years*. Harry N. Abrahms, 1988.

Rivele, Richard J. *Chilton's Total Car Care*. Chilton Book Company, 1992.

Shacket, Sheldon R. *The Complete Book of Electric Vehicles*. Domus Books, 1979.

Traister, Robert J. *All About Electric and Hybrid*. TAB Books, 1982.

Periodicals

"Golf Cars." *Golf Magazine*. March, 1989, p. 212.

"Got Anything in a Beemer?" *Los Angeles Magazine*. October, 1988, p. 156.

"Luxury on the Links." *Time*. March 10, 1986, p. 65.

—*Jim Wawrzyniak*

Grinding Wheel

Today, grinding wheels appear in nearly every manufacturing company in the United States, where they are used to cut steel and masonry block; to sharpen knives, drill bits, and many other tools; or to clean and prepare surfaces for painting or plating.

Background

Grinding wheels are made of natural or synthetic abrasive minerals bonded together in a matrix to form a wheel. While such tools may be familiar to those with home workshops, the general public may not be aware of them because most have been developed and used by the manufacturing industry. In this sector, grinding wheels have been important for more than 150 years.

For manufacturers, grinding wheels provide an efficient way to shape and finish metals and other materials. Abrasives are often the only way to create parts with precision dimensions and high-quality surface finishes. Today, grinding wheels appear in nearly every manufacturing company in the United States, where they are used to cut steel and masonry block; to sharpen knives, drill bits, and many other tools; or to clean and prepare surfaces for painting or plating. More specifically, the precision of **automobile** camshafts and **jet engine** rotors rests upon the use of grinding wheels. Quality bearings could not be produced without them, and new materials such as ceramic or material composites would be impossible without grinding wheels to shape and finish parts.

Sandstone, an organic abrasive made of quartz grains held together in a natural cement, was probably the earliest abrasive; it was used to smooth and sharpen the flint on axes. By the early nineteenth century, emery (a natural mineral containing iron and corundum) was used to cut and shape metals. However, emery's variable quality and problems with importing it from India prior to its discovery in the United States prompted efforts to find a more reliable abrasive mineral.

By the 1890s, the search had yielded silicon carbide, a synthetic mineral harder than corundum. Eventually, manufacturers figured out how to produce an even better alternative, synthetic corundum or aluminum oxide. In creating this bauxite derivative, they developed an abrasive material more reliable than both natural minerals and silicon carbide. Research into synthetic minerals also led to production of the so-called superabrasives. Foremost in this category are synthetic diamonds and a mineral known as *cubic boron nitride* (CBN), second in hardness only to the synthetic diamond. Today, development continues, and a seeded-gel aluminum oxide has just been introduced.

Throughout the grinding wheel's history, the bond that holds the abrasive grains together has proven as important as the grains themselves. The success of grinding wheels began in the early 1840s, when bonds containing rubber or clay were introduced, and by the 1870s a bond with a vitrified or glass-like structure was patented. Since then, bonds used in grinding wheels have been continually refined.

Grinding wheels are available in a wide variety of sizes, ranging from less than .25 inch (.63 centimeter) to several feet in diameter. They are also available in numerous shapes: flat disks, cylinders, cups, cones, and wheels with a profile cut into the periphery are just a few. Although many techniques, such as bonding a layer of abrasives to the surface of a metal wheel, are used to make grinding wheels, this discussion is limited to wheels composed of vitrified materials contained in a bonding matrix.

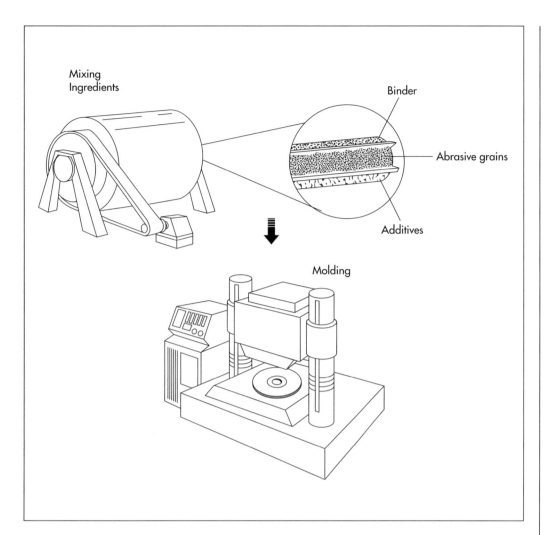

Mixing Ingredients

Binder

Abrasive grains

Additives

Molding

To make a grinding wheel, the ingredients must first be mixed together. Some manufacturers simply mix all materials in a single mixer. Others use separate steps to mix abrasive grains with binder, transfer the wet abrasive to a second mixer containing the powdered bonding materials, and tumble the mixture. Next, the wheel is formed in a molding step: the ingredient mix is poured into the mold and compacted by a hydraulic press.

Raw Materials

Two important components, abrasive grains and bonding materials, make up any grinding wheel. Often, additives are blended to create a wheel with the properties necessary to shape a particular material in the manner desired.

Abrasive grains constitute the central component of any grinding wheel, and the hardness and friability of the grinding materials will significantly affect the behavior of a given wheel. Hardness is measured in terms of a relative scale developed in 1812 by a German mineralogist named Friedrich Mohs. On this scale, extremely soft talc and gypsum represent hardnesses of one and two, and corundum and diamond represent hardness of nine and ten.

Friability refers to how easily a substance can be fractured or pulverized. People who design grinding wheels consider the friability of their abrasives—which can differ with the nature of the materials being ground—very carefully. For example, while diamond is the hardest known material, it is an undesirable steel abrasive because it undergoes a destructive chemical reaction during the cutting process; the same is true of silicon carbide. On the other hand, aluminum oxide cuts irons and steels better than diamond and silicon carbide, but it is less effective for cutting nonmetallic substances.

If selected correctly, an abrasive chosen to shape a particular substance will retain its friability when ground against that substance: because the grinding will cause the abrasive to continue fracturing along clean, sharp lines, it will maintain a sharp edge throughout the grinding process. This gives the grinding wheel the unique characteristic of being a tool that sharpens itself during use.

Although bonded abrasives began as tools made from natural minerals, modern products are made almost exclusively with synthetic materials. A bonding material holds the abrasive grits in place and allows open space between them. Manufacturers of grinding wheels assign a hardness to the wheel, which should not be confused with the hardness of the abrasive grain. Bonds that allow abrasives grains to fracture easily are classified as *soil bonds*. Bonds that restrict the fracturing of the grains and allow a wheel to withstand large forces are classified as *hard bonds*. Generally, soil wheels cut easily, produce poor surface finishes, and have a short useful life. On the other hand, harder wheels last longer and produce finer surface finishes, but cut less well and produce more heat during grinding.

The bonding matrix in which the abrasive grains are fixed may include a variety of organic materials such as rubber, shellac or resin; inorganic materials such as clay are also used. Inorganic bonds with glass-like or vitreous structures are used on the tool-sharpening wheels for the home workshop grinder, while resin bonds are used in masonry or steel-cutting wheels. Generally, vitrified bonds are used with medium to fine grain sizes in wheels needed for precision work. Resin bonds are used generally with coarse grains and for heavy metal removal operations such as foundry work.

In addition to their abrasive and bonding materials, grinding wheels often contain additional ingredients that produce pores within the wheel or assist chemically when a particular abrasive is used to grind a special material. One important aspect of a grinding wheel that can be created or altered through additives is porosity, which also contributes to the cutting characteristics of the grinding wheel. Porosity refers to the open spaces within the bond that allow room for small chips of metal and abrasive generated during the grinding process. Porosity also provides pathways that carry fluids used to control heat and improve the cutting characteristics of the abrasive grains. Without adequate porosity and spacing between abrasive grains, the wheel can become loaded with chips and cease to cut properly.

A variety of products are used as additives to create proper porosity and spacing. In the past, sawdust, crushed nut shells, and coke were used, but today materials that vaporize during the firing step of manufacturing (for example, napthaline-wax) are preferred.

Some grinding wheels receive additional materials that serve as aids to grinding. These include sulfur and chlorine compounds that inhibit microscopic welding of metal particles and generally improve metal-cutting properties.

The Manufacturing Process

Most grinding wheels are manufactured by the cold-press method, in which a mixture of components is pressed into shape at room temperature. The details of processes vary considerably depending upon the type of wheel and the practices of individual companies. For mass production of small wheels, many portions of the process are automated.

Mixing the ingredients

1 Preparing the grinding wheel mixture begins with selecting precise quantities of abrasives, bond materials, and additives according to a specific formula. A binder, typically a water-based wetting agent in the case of vitrified wheels, is added to coat the abrasive grains; this coating improves the grains' adhesion to the binder. The binder also helps the grinding wheel retain its shape until the bond is solidified. Some manufacturers simply mix all materials in a single mixer. Others use separate steps to mix abrasive grains with binder.

Wheel manufacturers often spend considerable effort to develop a satisfactory mixture. The blend must be free-flowing and distribute grain evenly throughout the structure of the grinding wheel to assure uniform cutting action and minimal vibration as the wheel rotates during use. This is particularly important for large wheels, which may be as big as several feet in diameter, or for wheels that have a shape other than the familiar flat disk.

Molding

2 For the most common type of wheel, an annular disc, a predetermined amount of grinding wheel mixture is poured into a mold consisting of four pieces: a circular pin the size of the finished wheel's arbor hole (its center hole); a shell with a 1-inch (2.5-centimeter) wall, about twice as high as the desired grinding wheel is thick; and two flat,

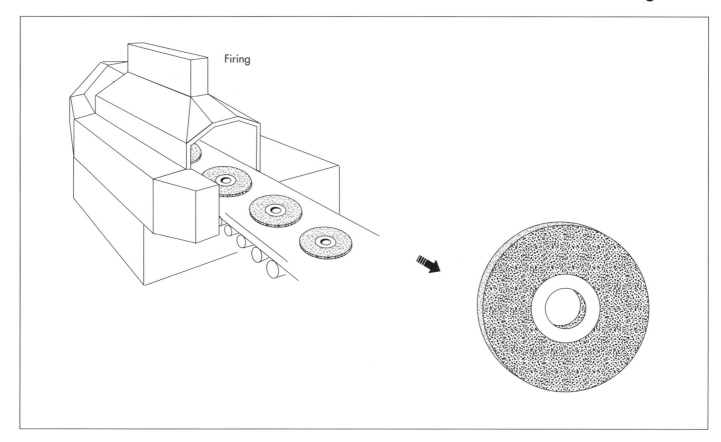

Firing

circular plates with diameter and arbor hole sizes equal to those of the wheel. A variety of methods are used to distribute the mixture evenly. Typically, a straight edge pivots about the center arbor pin to spread the mixture throughout the mold.

3 Using pressures in the range of 100 to 5000 pounds per square inch (psi) for 10 to 30 seconds, a hydraulic press then compacts the mixture into the grinding wheel's final shape. Some manufacturers use gage blocks between the two face plates to limit their movement and establish uniform thickness. Others control wheel thickness by closely monitoring the consistency of the mix and the force of the press.

4 After the mold has been removed from the press and the wheel stripped from the mold, the wheel is placed on a flat, heat-proof carrier. Final shaping of the wheel may take place at this time. All work at this stage has to be done very carefully because the wheel is held together by only the temporary binder. Lighter wheels can be lifted by hand at this stage; heavier ones may be lifted with a hoist or carefully slid on a carrier to be transported to the kiln.

Firing

5 Generally, the purposes of the firing are to melt the binder around the abrasives and to convert it to a form that will resist the heat and solvents encountered during grinding. A wide range of furnaces and kilns are used to fire grinding wheels, and the temperatures vary widely depending upon the type of bond. Wheels with a resin bond are typically fired at a temperature of 300 to 400 degrees Fahrenheit (149 to 204 degrees Celsius), and wheels with vitrified bonds are fired to temperatures between 1700 and 2300 degrees Fahrenheit (927 to 1260 degrees Celsius).

Finishing

6 After firing, wheels are moved to a finishing area, where arbor holes are reamed or cast to the specified size and the wheel circumference is made concentric with the center. Steps may be necessary to correct thickness or parallelism of wheel sides, or to create special contours on the side or circumference of the wheel. Manufacturers also balance large wheels to reduce the vibration that will be generated when the wheel is spun on a grinding machine. Once wheels have

After molding and final shaping, the wheel is fired in an oven or furnace. Firing melts the binder around the abrasives and converts it to a form that will resist the heat and solvents encountered during grinding. Finishing steps that follow firing may include reaming the arbor (center) hole to the proper size, correcting the thickness of the wheel sides, balancing the wheel, and adding labels.

received labels and other markings, they are ready for shipment to the consumer.

Quality Control

There are no clear performance standards for grinding wheels. With the exception of those containing expensive abrasives such as diamonds, grinding wheels are consumable items, and the rates of consumption vary considerably depending on application. However, a number of domestic and global standards are accepted, voluntarily, by manufacturers.

Trade organizations, which represent some manufacturers in the highly competitive U.S. market, have developed standards covering such matters as sizing of abrasive grains, labeling of abrasive products, and the safe use of grinding wheels.

The extent to which grinding wheel quality is checked depends upon the size, cost, and eventual use of the wheels. Typically, wheel manufacturers monitor the quality of incoming raw materials and their production processes to assure product consistency. Special attention is given to wheels larger than six inches in diameter, because they have the potential to harm personnel and equipment if they break during use. Each large vitrified wheel is examined to determine the strength and integrity of the bonding system as well as the uniformity of grain through every wheel. Acoustical tests measure wheel stiffness; hardness tests assure correct hardness of bonds; and spin tests assure adequate strength.

The Future

Changes in manufacturing practices will determine the demand for various types of wheels in the future. For example, the trend in the steel industry towards continuous casting as a way to make steel has greatly reduced that industry's use of some types of grinding wheels. A push for greater productivity by manufacturers is responsible for market projections showing a shift from wheels made of traditional aluminum oxide abrasives to wheels made of newer forms of synthetic abrasives such as the seeded-gel aluminum oxide and cubic boron nitride. Also, the use of advanced materials such as ceramics and composites will increase demands for newer types of grinding wheels. The transition to new abrasive minerals, however, is being impeded by the fact that much manufacturing equipment and many industrial procedures are still unable to make effective use of the newer (and more expensive products). Notwithstanding trends, traditional abrasives are projected to continue serving many uses.

However, competition from several alternative technologies is likely to grow. Advances in cutting tools made of polycrystalline superabrasive materials—fine grain crystalline materials made of diamond or cubic boron nitride—will make such tools a viable option for shaping hard materials. Also, advances in the chemical vapor deposition of diamond films will affect the need for abrasives by lengthening the life of cutting tools and extending their capabilities.

Where To Learn More

Books

Borkowski, J. *Uses of Abrasives & Abrasive Tools*. Prentice Hall, 1992.

Burkar, W. *Grinding & Polishing*. State Mutual Book & Periodical Service, 1989.

Hahn, Robert S. *Handbook of Modern Grinding Technology*. Chapman & Hall, 1986.

Salmon, Stuart C. *Modern Grinding Process Technology*. McGraw-Hill, 1992.

Periodicals

Murray, Charles J. "Retainer System Eases Wheel and Blade Replacement." *Design News*. January 18, 1988, p. 104.

—*Theodore L. Giese*

Guitar

Background

A member of the family of musical instruments called chordophones, the guitar is a stringed instrument with which sound is produced by "plucking" a series of strings running along the instrument's body. While the strings are plucked with one hand, they are simultaneously fingered with the other hand against frets, which are metal strips located on the instrument's neck. The subsequent sound is amplified through a resonating body. There are four general categories of acoustic (non-electric) guitars: flat-top steel-stringed, arched top, classic, and flamenco.

References to guitar-like instruments date back many centuries, and virtually every society throughout history has been found to have used a variation of the instrument. The forerunner of today's guitars were single-string bows developed during early human history. In sections of Asia and Africa, bows of this type have been unearthed in archaeological digs of ancient civilizations. Interestingly, one of these discoveries included an ancient Hittite carving—dating back more than 3,000 years—that depicted an instrument bearing many of the same features of today's guitar: the curves of the body, a flat top with an incurred arc of five sound holes on either side, and a long fretted neck that ran the entire length of the body.

As music technology developed, more strings were added to the early guitars. A four-string variety (named *guitarra latina*) existed in Spain in the late thirteenth century. The guitarra latina closely resembled the ancient Hittite carving except that the instrument now included a bridge that held the strings as they passed over the soundhole. When a fifth string was added in the early sixteenth century, the guitar's popularity exploded. A sixth string (bass E) was added near the end of 1700s, an evolution that brought the instrument closer to its present day functioning. The Carulli guitar of 1810 was one of the first to have six single strings tuned to notes in the present arrangement: E A D G B E.

Guitar technology finally made its way to the United States in the early nineteenth century, with Charles Friedrich Martin, a German guitar maker who emigrated to New York in 1833, leading the way. In the early 1900s, the Martin Company—now located in Nazareth, Pennsylvania—produced larger guitars that still adhered to the design of the classic models, especially the Spanish guitar. Another company, the Gibson company, followed suit and began to produce large steel-string guitars with arched fronts and backs. Known as the cello guitar, this brand of instrument produced a sound more suited for jazz and dance clubs. Another major innovation of the early 1900s was the use of magnetic pickups fitted beneath the strings by which sound traveled through a wire into an amplifier. These instruments would later evolve into electric guitars.

Raw Materials

The guitar industry is in virtual agreement on the woods used for the various parts of the instrument. The back and sides of the guitar's body are usually built with East Indian or Brazilian rosewood. Historically, Brazilian rosewood has been the choice of connoisseurs. However, in an attempt to preserve the wood's dwindling supply, the Brazilian gov-

The back and sides of the guitar's body are usually built with East Indian or Brazilian rosewood. The top (or soundboard) is traditionally constructed of Alpine spruce, although American Sika spruce has become popular among U.S. manufacturers. The neck is constructed from mahogany, while the fingerboard is made of ebony or rosewood.

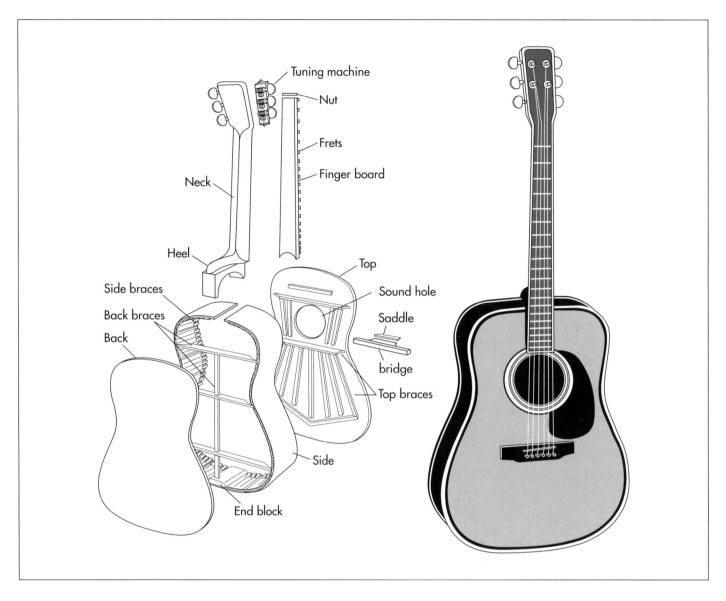

Guitar manufacture generally involves selecting, sawing, and glueing various wood pieces to form the finished instrument. The top and back of the guitar are formed in a process known as "bookmatching," by which a single piece of wood is sliced into two sheets, each the same length and width as the original but only half as thick. This gives the sheets a symmetrical grain pattern. The two sheets are matched to ensure continuity in the grains and glued together.

ernment has placed restrictions on its export, thus raising the price and making East Indian rosewood the current wood of choice. Less expensive brands use mahogany or maple, but the sound quality suffers in guitars constructed with those types of wood.

The top (or soundboard) of the guitar is traditionally constructed of Alpine spruce, although American Sika spruce has become popular among U.S. manufacturers. Cedar and redwood are often substituted for spruce, although these woods are soft and easily damaged during construction.

The neck, which must resist distortion by the pull of the strings and changes in temperature and humidity, is constructed from mahogany and joins the body between the fourteenth

and twelfth frets. Ideally, the fingerboard is made of ebony, but rosewood is often used as a less expensive alternative. Most modern guitars use strings made of some type of metal (usually steel).

The Manufacturing Process

The first and most important step in guitar construction is wood selection. The choice of wood will directly affect the sound quality of the finished product. The wood must be free of flaws and have a straight, vertical grain. Since each section of the guitar uses different types of woods, the construction process varies from section to section. Following is a description of the manufacture of a typical acoustic guitar.

Bookmatching

1 The wood for the top of the guitar is cut from lumber using a process called bookmatching. Bookmatching is a method by which a single piece of wood is sliced into two sheets, each the same length and width as the original but only half as thick. This gives the sheets a symmetrical grain pattern. The two sheets are matched to ensure continuity in the grains and glued together. Once dry, the newly joined boards are sanded to the proper thickness. They are closely inspected for quality and then graded according to color, closeness and regularity of grain, and lack of blemishes.

2 The next step is to cut the top into the guitar shape, leaving the piece of wood oversized until the final trimming. The soundhole is sawed, with slots carved around it for concentric circles that serve as decorative inlays around the soundhole.

Strutting

3 Wood braces are next glued to the underside of the top piece. Strutting, as this process is often called, serves two purposes: brace the wood against the pull of the strings and control the way the top vibrates. An area of guitar construction that differs from company to company, strutting has a great affect on the guitar's tone. Many braces today are glued in an X-pattern originally designed by the Martin Company, a pattern that most experts feel provides the truest acoustics and tone. Although companies such as Ovation and Gibson continue to experiment with improvements on the X-pattern style of strutting, Martin's original concept is widely accepted as producing the best sound.

4 The back, although not as acoustically important as the top, is still critical to the guitar's sound. A reflector of sound waves, the back is also braced, but its strips of wood run parallel from left to right with one cross-grained strip running down the length of the back's glue joint. The back is cut and glued similar to the top—and from the same piece of lumber as the top, to ensure matching grains—using the bookmatch technique.

Constructing the sides

5 Construction of the sides consists of cutting and sanding the strips of wood to the proper length and thickness and then softening the wood in water. The strips are then placed in molds that are shaped to the curves of the guitar, and the entire assembly is clamped for a period of time to ensure symmetry between the two sides. The two sides are joined together with basswood glued to the inside walls. Strips of reinforcing wood are placed along the inner sides so that the guitar doesn't crack if hit from the side. Two endblocks (near the neck and near the bottom of the guitar) are also used to join the top, back and neck.

6 Once the sides are joined and the endblocks are in place, the top and the back are glued to the sides. The excess wood is trimmed off and slots are cut along the side-top and side-back junctions. These slots are for the body bindings that cover the guitar's sides. The bindings are not only decorative, they also keep moisture from entering through the sides and warping the guitar.

Neck and fingerboard

7 The neck is made from one piece of hard wood, typically mahogany or rosewood, carved to exact specifications. A reinforcing rod is inserted through the length of the neck and, after sanding, the fingerboard (often made of ebony or rosewood) is set in place. Using precise measurements, fret slots are cut into the fingerboard and the steel-wired frets are put in place.

8 Once the neck construction is completed, it is attached to the body. Most guitar companies attach the neck and the body by fitting a heel that extends from the base of the neck into a pre-cut groove on the body. Once the glue has dried at the neck-body junction, the entire guitar receives a coat of sealer and then several coats of lacquer. On some models, intricate decorations or inlays are also placed on the guitar top.

Bridge and saddle

9 After polishing, a bridge is attached near the bottom of the guitar below the soundhole, and a saddle is fitted. The saddle is where the strings actually lie as they pass over the bridge, and it is extremely important in the transferring of string vibration to the guitar top. On the opposite end of the guitar,

the nut is placed between the neck and the head. The nut is a strip of wood or plastic on which the strings lie as they pass to the head and into the tuning machine.

Tuning machine

10 The tuning machine is next fitted to the guitar head. This machine is one of the most delicate parts of the guitar and is usually mounted on the back of the head. The pegs that hold each string poke through to the front, and the gears that turn both the pegs and the string-tightening keys are housed in metal casings.

11 Finally, the guitar is strung and inspected before leaving the factory. The entire process of making a guitar can take between three weeks and two months, depending on the amount of decorative detail work on the guitar top.

Electric Guitars

A separate but closely related group of guitars is the electric guitar, which uses a device known as a *pickup*—a magnet surrounded by wire—to convert the energy from string vibrations into an electrical signal. The signal is sent to an amplifier, where it is boosted thousands of times. The body of an electric guitar has little impact on the quality of sound produced, as the amplifier controls both the quality and loudness of the sound. Acoustic guitars can also be fitted with electric pickups, and there are some models available today that already have the pickup built into the body.

Quality Control

Most guitar manufacturers are small, highly personal companies that stress detail and quality. Each company does its own research and testing, which virtually insure the customer of a flawless guitar. During the past few decades, the guitar industry has become more mechanized, allowing for greater speed, higher consistency and lower pricing. Although purists resist mechanization, a well-trained workman using machine tools can usually produce a higher-quality instrument than a craftsman working alone. The final testing procedures at most manufactures are quite stringent; only the best guitars leave the plant, and more than one person makes the final determination as to which instruments are shipped out and which are rejected.

Where To Learn More

Books

Cumpiano, William R. *Guitarmaking: Tradition & Technology.* Rosewood Press, 1987.

Evans, Tom and Mary Anne. *Guitars: Music, History, Construction and Players from the Renaissance to Rock.* Facts on File, 1977.

Hill, Thomas. *The Guitar: An Introduction to the Instrument.* Watts Publishing, 1973.

How It Works: The Illustrated Science and Invention Encyclopedia. Vol. 9. H. S. Stuttman, 1983.

Kamimoto, Hideo. *Complete Guitar Repair.* Oak Publications, 1975.

Wheeler, Thomas. *The Guitar Book.* Harper & Row, 1974.

Periodicals

Del Ray, Tiesco. "Off the Wall: The Theory of Reverse Ergonomics," *Guitar Player.* March, 1986, p. 102.

Sievert, Jon. "Steinberger Factory Tour," *Guitar Player.* December, 1988, p. 38.

Smith, Richard. "Inside Rickenbacker: New Factory, Old Traditions," *Guitar Player.* February, 1990, p. 61.

Widders-Ellis, Andy. "Tomorrow's Acoustics: The Dawning of a New Golden Age," *Guitar Player.* April, 1992, p. 43.

—*Jim Acton*

Helicopter

Background

Helicopters are classified as rotary wing aircraft, and their rotary wing is commonly referred to as the *main rotor* or simply the rotor. Unlike the more common fixed wing aircraft such as a sport biplane or an airliner, the helicopter is capable of direct vertical take-off and landing; it can also hover in a fixed position. These features render it ideal for use where space is limited or where the ability to hover over a precise area is necessary. Currently, helicopters are used to dust crops, apply **pesticide**, access remote areas for environmental work, deliver supplies to workers on remote maritime oil rigs, take photographs, film movies, rescue people trapped in inaccessible spots, transport accident victims, and put out fires. Moreover, they have numerous intelligence and military applications.

Numerous individuals have contributed to the conception and development of the helicopter. The idea appears to have been bionic in origin, meaning that it derived from an attempt to adapt a natural phenomena—in this case, the whirling, bifurcated fruit of the maple tree—to a mechanical design. Early efforts to imitate maple pods produced the whirligig, a children's toy popular in China as well as in medieval Europe. During the fifteenth century, Leonardo da Vinci, the renowned Italian painter, sculptor, architect, and engineer, sketched a flying machine that may have been based on the whirligig. The next surviving sketch of a helicopter dates from the early nineteenth century, when British scientist Sir George Cayley drew a twin-rotor aircraft in his notebook. During the early twentieth century, Frenchman Paul Cornu managed to lift himself off the ground for a few seconds in an early helicopter. However, Cornu was constrained by the same problems that would continue to plague all early designers for several decades: no one had yet devised an engine that could generate enough vertical thrust to lift both the helicopter and any significant load (including passengers) off the ground.

Igor Sikorsky, a Russian engineer, built his first helicopter in 1909. When neither this prototype nor its 1910 successor succeeded, Sikorsky decided that he could not build a helicopter without more sophisticated materials and money, so he transferred his attention to aircraft. During World War I, Hungarian engineer Theodore von Karman constructed a helicopter that, when tethered, was able to hover for extended periods. Several years later, Spaniard Juan de la Cierva developed a machine he called an *autogiro* in response to the tendency of conventional airplanes to lose engine power and crash while landing. If he could design an aircraft in which lift and thrust (forward speed) were separate functions, Cierva speculated, he could circumvent this problem. The autogiro he subsequently invented incorporated features of both the helicopter and the airplane, although it resembled the latter more. The autogiro had a rotor that functioned something like a windmill. Once set in motion by taxiing on the ground, the rotor could generate supplemental lift; however, the autogiro was powered primarily by a conventional airplane engine. To avoid landing problems, the engine could be disconnected and the autogiro brought gently to rest by the rotor, which would gradually cease spinning as the machine reached the ground. Popular during the 1920s and 1930s, autogiros ceased to be produced after the refinement of the conventional helicopter.

The idea for the helicopter appears to have been bionic in origin, meaning that it derived from an attempt to adapt a natural phenomena—in this case, the whirling, bifurcated fruit of the maple tree—to a mechanical design.

The helicopter was eventually perfected by Igor Sikorsky. Advances in aerodynamic theory and building materials had been made since Sikorsky's initial endeavor, and, in 1939, he lifted off the ground in his first operational helicopter. Two years later, an improved design enabled him to remain aloft for an hour and a half, setting a world record for sustained helicopter flight.

The helicopter was put to military use almost immediately after its introduction. While it was not utilized extensively during World War II, the jungle terrain of both Korea and Vietnam prompted the helicopter's widespread use during both of those wars, and technological refinements made it a valuable tool during the Persian Gulf War as well. In recent years, however, private industry has probably accounted for the greatest increase in helicopter use, as many companies have begun to transport their executives via helicopter. In addition, helicopter shuttle services have proliferated, particularly along the urban corridor of the American Northeast. Still, among civilians the helicopter remains best known for its medical, rescue, and relief uses.

Design

A helicopter's power comes from either a piston engine or a gas turbine (recently, the latter has predominated), which moves the rotor shaft, causing the rotor to turn. While a standard plane generates thrust by pushing air behind its wing as it moves forward, the helicopter's rotor achieves lift by pushing the air beneath it downward as it spins. Lift is proportional to the change in the air's momentum (its mass times its velocity): the greater the momentum, the greater the lift.

Helicopter rotor systems consist of between two and six blades attached to a central hub. Usually long and narrow, the blades turn relatively slowly, because this minimizes the amount of power necessary to achieve and maintain lift, and also because it makes controlling the vehicle easier. While lightweight, general-purpose helicopters often have a two-bladed main rotor, heavier craft may use a four-blade design or two separate main rotors to accommodate heavy loads.

To steer a helicopter, the pilot must adjust the pitch of the blades, which can be set three ways. In the *collective* system, the pitch of all the blades attached to the rotor is identical; in the *cyclic* system, the pitch of each blade is designed to fluctuate as the rotor revolves, and the third system uses a combination of the first two. To move the helicopter in any direction, the pilot moves the lever that adjusts collective pitch and/or the stick that adjusts cyclic pitch; it may also be necessary to increase or reduce speed.

Unlike airplanes, which are designed to minimize bulk and protuberances that would weigh the craft down and impede airflow around it, helicopters have unavoidably high drag. Thus, designers have not utilized the sort of retractable landing gear familiar to people who have watched planes taking off or landing—the aerodynamic gains of such a system would be proportionally insignificant for a helicopter. In general, helicopter landing gear is much simpler than that of airplanes. Whereas the latter require long runways on which to reduce forward velocity, helicopters have to reduce only vertical lift, which they can do by hovering prior to landing. Thus, they don't even require shock absorbers: their landing gear usually comprises only wheels or skids, or both.

One problem associated with helicopter rotor blades occurs because airflow along the length of each blade differs widely. This means that lift and drag fluctuate for each blade throughout the rotational cycle, thereby exerting an unsteadying influence upon the helicopter. A related problem occurs because, as the helicopter moves forward, the lift beneath the blades that enter the airstream first is high, but that beneath the blades on the opposite side of the rotor is low. The net effect of these problems is to destabilize the helicopter. Typically, the means of compensating for these unpredictable variations in lift and drag is to manufacture flexible blades connected to the rotor by a hinge. This design allows each blade to shift up or down, adjusting to changes in lift and drag.

Torque, another problem associated with the physics of a rotating wing, causes the helicopter fuselage (cabin) to rotate in the opposite direction from the rotor, especially when the helicopter is moving at low speeds or hovering. To offset this reaction, many helicopters use a tail rotor, an exposed blade or ducted fan mounted on the end of the tail boom typically seen on these craft. Another means of counteracting torque entails installing two rotors, attached to the same engine but rotating in opposite directions, while a third, more space-efficient design features twin rotors that are enmeshed, something like an egg beater. Additional alternatives have been researched, and at least one NOTAR (no tail rotor) design has been introduced.

Raw Materials

The airframe, or fundamental structure, of a helicopter can be made of either metal or organic composite materials, or some combination of the two. Higher performance requirements will incline the designer to favor composites with higher strength-to-weight ratio, often epoxy (a resin) reinforced with glass, aramid (a strong, flexible nylon fiber), or carbon fiber. Typically, a composite component consists of many layers of fiber-impregnated resins, bonded to form a smooth panel. Tubular and sheet metal substructures are usually made of aluminum, though **stainless steel** or titanium are sometimes used in areas subject to higher stress or heat. To facilitate bending during the manufacturing process, the structural tubing is often filled with molten sodium silicate. A helicopter's rotary wing blades are usually made of fiber-reinforced resin, which may be adhesively bonded with an external sheet metal layer to protect edges. The helicopter's windscreen and windows are formed of polycarbonate sheeting.

The Manufacturing Process

Airframe: Preparing the tubing

1 Each individual tubular part is cut by a tube cutting machine that can be quickly set to produce different, precise lengths and specified batch quantities. Tubing requiring angular bends is shaped to the proper angle in a bending machine that utilizes interchangeable tools for different diameters and sizes. For other than minor bends, tubes are filled with molten sodium silicate that hardens and eliminates kinking by causing the tube to bend as a solid bar. The so-called *water glass* is then removed by placing the

Igor Sikorsky pilots his craft, the VS-300, close to the ground in this 1943 demonstration.

In 1939, a Russian emigre to the United States tested what was to become a prominent prototype for later helicopters. Already a prosperous aircraft manufacturer in his native land, Igor Sikorsky fled the 1917 revolution, drawn to the United States by stories of Thomas Edison and Henry Ford.

Sikorsky soon became a successful aircraft manufacturer in his adopted homeland. But his dream was vertical take-off, rotary wing flight. He experimented for more than twenty years and finally, in 1939, flew his first flight in a craft dubbed the *VS 300*. Tethered to the ground with long ropes, his craft flew no higher than 50 feet off the ground on its first several flights. Even then, there were problems: the craft flew up, down, and sideways, but not forward. However, helicopter technology developed so rapidly that some were actually put into use by U.S. troops during World War II.

The helicopter contributed directly to at least one revolutionary production technology. As helicopters grew larger and more powerful, the precision calculations needed for engineering the blades, which had exacting requirements, increased exponentially. In 1947, John C. Parsons of Traverse City, Michigan, began looking for ways to speed the engineering of blades produced by his company. Parsons contacted the International Business Machine Corp. and asked to try one of their new main frame office computers. By 1951, Parsons was experimenting with having the computer's calculations actually guide the machine tool. His ideas were ultimately developed into the computer-numerical-control (CNC) machine tool industry that has revolutionized modern production methods.

William S. Pretzer

bent tube in boiling water, which melts the inner material. Tubing that must be curved to match fuselage contours is fitted over a stretch forming machine, which stretches the metal to a precisely contoured shape. Next, the tubular details are delivered to the machine shop where they are held in clamps so that their ends can be machined to the required angle and shape. The tubes are then deburred (a process in which any ridges or fins that remain after preliminary machining are ground off) and inspected for cracks.

2 Gussets (reinforcing plates or brackets) and other reinforcing details of metal are machined from plate, angle, or extruded profile stock by routing, shearing, blanking, or sawing. Some critical or complex details may be forged or investment cast. The latter process entails injecting wax or an alloy with a low melting point into a mold or die. When the template has been formed, it is dipped in molten metal as many times as necessary to achieve the thickness desired. When the part has dried, it is heated so that the wax or alloy will melt and can be poured out. Heated to a higher temperature to purify it and placed in a mold box where it is supported by sand, the mold is then ready to shape molten metal into reinforcement parts. After removal and cooling, these parts are then finish-machined by standard methods before being deburred once again.

3 The tubes are chemically cleaned, fitted into a subassembly fixture, and MIG (metal-arc inert gas) welded. In this process, a small electrode wire is fed through a welding torch, and an inert, shielding gas (usually argon or helium) is passed through a nozzle around it; the tubes are joined by the melting of the wire. After welding, the subassembly is stress relieved—heated to a low temperature so that the metal can recover any elasticity it has lost during the shaping process. Finally, the welds are inspected for flaws.

Forming sheet metal details

4 Sheet metal, which makes up other parts of the airframe, is first cut into blanks (pieces cut to predetermined size in preparation for subsequent work) by abrasive waterjet, blanking dies, or routing. Aluminum blanks are heat-treated to anneal them (give them a uniform, strain-free structure that will increase their malleability). The blanks are then refrigerated until they are placed in dies where they will be pressed into the proper shape. After forming, the sheet metal details are aged to full strength and trimmed by routing to final shape and size.

5 Sheet metal parts are cleaned before being assembled by riveting or adhesive

bonding. Aluminum parts and welded subassemblies may be anodized (treated to thicken the protective oxide film on the surface of the aluminum), which increases corrosion resistance. All metal parts are chemically cleaned and primer-painted, and most receive finish **paint** by spraying with epoxy or other durable coating.

Making the cores of composite components

6 Cores, the central parts of the composite components, are made of Nomex (a brand of aramid produced by Du Pont) or aluminum "honeycomb," which is cut to size by bandsaw or reciprocating knife. If necessary, the cores then have their edges trimmed and beveled by a machine tool similar to a pizza cutter or meat slicing blade. The material with which each component is built up from its cores (each component may use multiple cores) is called *pre-preg ply*. The plies are layers of oriented fibers, usually epoxy or polyimide, that have been impregnated with resin. Following written instructions from the designers, workers create highly contoured skin panels by setting individual plies on bond mold tools and sandwiching cores between additional plies as directed.

7 Completed *layups*, as the layers of pre-preg affixed to the mold are called, are then transported to an autoclave for curing. An autoclave is a machine that laminates plastics by exposing them to pressurized steam, and "curing" is the hardening that occurs as the resin layers "cook" in the autoclave.

8 Visible trim lines are molded into the panels by scribe lines present in the bond mold tools. Excess material around the edges is then removed by bandsawing. Large panels may be trimmed by an abrasive waterjet manipulated by a robot. After inspection, trimmed panels and other composite details are cleaned and painted by normal spray methods. Surfaces must be well sealed by paint to prevent metal corrosion or water absorption.

Making the fuselage

9 Canopies or windscreens and passenger compartment windows are generally made of polycarbonate sheet. Front panels

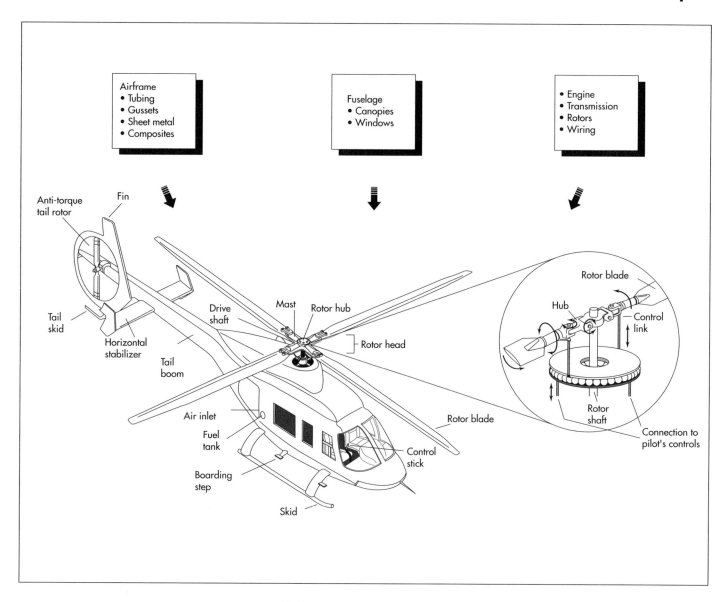

Airframe
• Tubing
• Gussets
• Sheet metal
• Composites

Fuselage
• Canopies
• Windows

• Engine
• Transmission
• Rotors
• Wiring

Anti-torque tail rotor

Fin

Tail skid

Horizontal stabilizer

Tail boom

Drive shaft

Mast

Rotor hub

Rotor head

Air inlet

Fuel tank

Boarding step

Skid

Control stick

Rotor blade

Rotor blade

Hub

Control link

Rotor shaft

Connection to pilot's controls

---

subject to bird strike or other impact may be laminated of two sheets for greater thickness. All such parts are made by placing an oversized blank on a fixture, heating it, and then forming it to the required curvature by use of air pressure in a freeblowing process. In this method, no tool surface touches the optical surfaces to cause defects.

Installing the engine, transmission, and rotors

10 Modern helicopter engines are turbine rather than piston type and are purchased from an engine supplier. The helicopter manufacturer may purchase or produce the transmission assembly, which transfers power to the rotor assembly. Transmission cases are made of aluminum or magnesium alloy.

11 As with the above, the main and tail rotor assemblies are machined from specially selected high-strength metals but are produced by typical machine shop methods. The rotor blades themselves are machined from composite layup shapes. Main rotor blades may have a sheet metal layer adhesively bonded to protect the leading edges.

Systems and controls

12 Wiring harnesses are produced by laying out the required wires on special boards that serve as templates to define the length and path to connectors. Looms, or knitted protective covers, are placed on the wire bundles, and the purchased connectors are soldered in place by hand. Hydraulic tubing is either hand-cut to length and hand-

Most of the crucial components in a helicopter are made of metal and are formed using the usual metal-forming processes: shearing, blanking, forging, cutting, routing, and investment casting. The polycarbonate windscreen and windows are made by laying the sheet over a mold, heating it, and forming it with air pressure in a process called "freeblowing," in which no tool ever touches the part.

formed by craftsmen, or measured, formed, and cut by tube-bending machines. Ends are flared, and tubes are inspected for dimensional accuracy and to ensure that no cracks are present. Hydraulic pumps and actuators, instrumentation, and electrical devices are typically purchased to specification rather than produced by the helicopter manufacturer.

Final assembly

13 Finished and inspected detail airframe parts, including sheet metal, tubular, and machined and welded items, are delivered to subassembly jigs (fixtures that clamp parts being assembled). Central parts are located in each jig, and associated details are either bolted in place or, where rivets are to be used, match-drilled using pneumatically powered drills to drill and ream each rivet hole. For aerodynamic smoothness on sheet metal or composite skin panels, holes are countersunk so that the heads of flat-headed screws won't protrude. All holes are deburred and rivets applied. A sealant is often applied in each rivet hole as the rivet is inserted. For some situations, semi-automated machines may be used for moving from one hole location to the next, drilling, reaming, sealing, and installing the rivets under operator control.

14 After each subassembly is accepted by an inspector, it typically moves to another jig to be further combined with other small subassemblies and details such as brackets. Inspected "top level" subassemblies are then delivered to final assembly jigs, where the overall helicopter structure is integrated.

Upon completion of the structure, the propulsion components are added, and wiring and hydraulics are installed and tested. Canopy, windows, doors, instruments, and interior elements are then added to complete the vehicle. Finish-painting and trimming are completed at appropriate points during this process.

15 After all systems are inspected in final form, along with physical assemblies and appearance aspects, the complete documentation of materials, processes, inspection, and rework effort for each vehicle is checked and filed for reference. The helicopter propulsion system is tested, and the aircraft is flight-tested.

Quality Control

Once tubular components have been formed, they are inspected for cracks. To find defects, workers treat the tubes with a fluorescent liquid penetrant that seeps into cracks and other surface flaws. After wiping off the excess fluid, they dust the coated tube with a fine powder that interacts with the penetrant to render defects visible. After the tubular components have been welded, they are inspected using X-ray and/or fluorescent penetrant methods to discover flaws. Upon completion, the contours of sheet metal details are checked against form templates and hand-worked as required to fit. After they have been autoclaved and trimmed, composite panels are ultrasonically inspected to identify any possible breaks in laminations or gas-filled voids that could lead to structural failure. Prior to installation, both the engine and the transmission subassemblies are carefully inspected, and special test equipment, custom-designed for each application, is used to examine the wiring systems. All of the other components are also tested before assembly, and the completed aircraft is flight-tested in addition to receiving an overall inspection.

The Future

Manufacturing processes and techniques will continue to change in response to the need to reduce costs and the introduction of new materials. Automation may further improve quality (and lower labor costs). Computers will become more important in improving designs, implementing design changes, and reducing the amount of paperwork created, used, and stored for each helicopter built. Furthermore, the use of robots to wind filament, wrap tape, and place fiber will permit fuselage structures to be made of fewer, more integrated pieces. In terms of materials, advanced, high-strength thermoplastic resins promise greater impact resistance and repairability than current thermosets such as epoxy and polyimide. Metallic composites such as aluminum reinforced with boron fiber, or magnesium reinforced with silicon carbide particles, also promise higher strength-to-weight ratios for critical components such as transmission cases while retaining the heat resistance advantage of metal over organic materials.

Where To Learn More

Books

Basic Helicopter Handbook. IAP Inc., 1988.

Seddon, J. *Basic Helicopter Aerodynamics.* American Institute of Aeronautics & Astronautics, 1990.

Periodicals

"Rotary-Wing Technology Pursues Fixed-Wing Performance Capabilities." *Aviation Week & Space Technology.* January 19, 1987, p. 46.

"Advanced Technology Prompts Reevaluation of Helicopter Design." *Aviation Week & Space Technology.* March 9, 1987, p. 252.

Brown, Stuart F. "Tilt-rotor Aircraft." *Popular Science.* July, 1987, p. 46.

"Graphite Tools Produce Volume 'Copter Parts." *Design News.* February 17, 1986, p. 30.

"Researchers Work on Noise Reduction in Helicopters." *Research & Development.* January, 1986, p. 55.

Smith, Bruce A. "Helicoptor Manufacturers Divided on Development of New Aircraft." *Aviation Week & Space Technology.* February 29, 1988, p. 58.

—Phillip S. Waldrop

Jet Engine

Today's commercial jet engines, up to eleven feet in diameter and twelve feet long, can weigh more than 10,000 pounds and produce more than 100,000 pounds of thrust.

Background

The jet engine is the power plant of today's jet aircraft, producing not only the thrust that propels the aircraft but also the power that fuels many of the aircraft's other systems.

Jet engines operate according to Newton's third law of motion, which states that every force acting on a body produces an equal and opposite force. The jet engine works by drawing in some of the air through which the aircraft is moving, compressing it, combining it with fuel and heating it, and finally ejecting the ensuing gas with such force that the plane is propelled forward. The power produced by such engines is expressed in terms of pounds of thrust, a term that refers to the number of pounds the engine can move.

The jet engine, like many technological innovations, took a long time to progress from concept to design to execution. The first attempts to transcend the traditional piston engine were actually modifications of that engine, both heavy and complex. The turbine design was introduced in 1921, and it and the other basic components of the modern jet engine were present in a design for which a Royal Air Force lieutenant named Frank Whittle received an English patent in 1930. Although testing on Whittle's engine began in 1937, it did not fly successfully until 1941. Across the English Channel in a Germany rushing to arm itself for World War II, similar but entirely separate work had begun with a 1935 jet engine patent issued to Hans von Ohain. Four years later, a team of German engineers led by Dr. Max Hahn achieved success, conducting the first entirely jet-powered flight in history. Upon achieving success with the Whittle engine in 1941, the British promptly shipped a prototype to their allies in the United States, where General Electric immediately began producing copies. The first American jet engine, produced by G.E., took flight in a plane constructed by Bell Aircraft late in 1942. Although use of jets was somewhat limited during World War II, by the end of the war all three countries had begun to utilize elite squadrons of jet-powered fighter planes.

Today's commercial engines, up to eleven feet in diameter and twelve feet long, can weigh more than 10,000 pounds and produce more than 100,000 pounds of thrust.

Design

A jet engine is contained within a *cowling*, an external casing that opens outward, somewhat like a rounded **automobile** hood, to permit inspection and repair of the interior components. Attached to each engine (a typical 747 uses four) is a *pylon*, a metal arm that joins the engine to the wing of the plane. Through pumps and feed tubes in the pylons, fuel is relayed from wing tanks to the engine, and the electrical and hydraulic power generated by the engine is then routed back to the aircraft through wires and pipes also contained in the pylons.

At the very front of the engine, a fan helps to increase the flow of air into the engine's first compartment, the *compressor*. As the fan drives air into it, the compressor—a metal cylinder that gradually widens from front to rear—subjects the incoming air to increasing pressure. To accelerate the progress of the air through the engine, the compressor is fitted with blades that rotate like simple household fans. In the incredibly brief time it takes air

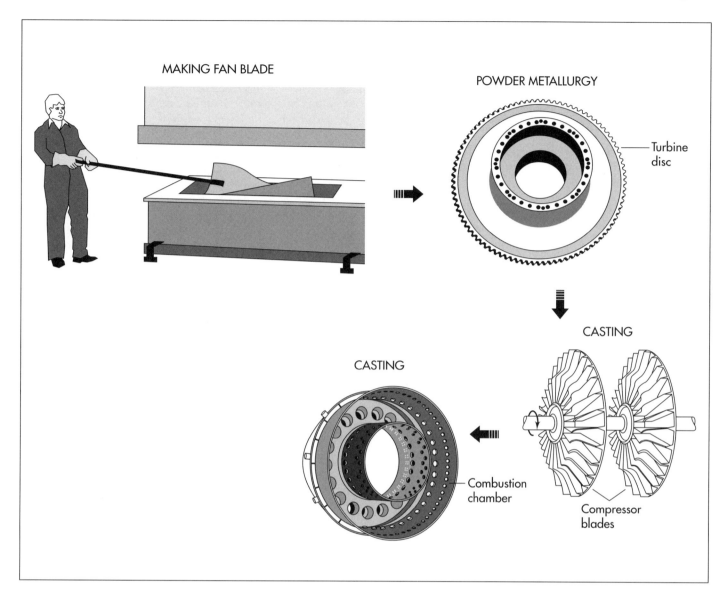

MAKING FAN BLADE

POWDER METALLURGY

Turbine disc

CASTING

CASTING

Combustion chamber

Compressor blades

to reach the inner end of a typical compressor, it has been squeezed into a space 20 times smaller than the intake aperture.

Expanding as it leaves the high-pressure compressor, the air enters the *combustor*, an interior engine cylinder in which the air will be mixed with fuel and burned. The combustion chamber is actually a ring, shaped something like a car's air filter. The air that passes through this ring as it exits the compressor is ignited, while another, larger stream of air merely passes through the center of the ring without being burned. A third stream of air being released from the compressor is passed outside the combustion chamber to cool it.

As the air from the compressor mixes with fuel and ignites in the combustor to produce an incredibly hot volume of gas, some of that

gas leaves the engine through the exhaust system, while another, smaller portion is routed into the engine's *turbine*. The turbine is a set of fans that extend from the same shaft which, further forward in the jet engine, rotates the compressor blades. Its job is to extract enough energy from the hot gases leaving the combustor to power the compressor shaft. In some models, the turbine is also used to generate power for other components of the plane. Because the turbine is subjected to intense heat, each blade has labyrinthine airways cut into it. Cool air from the compressor is routed through these passages, enabling the turbine to function in gas streams whose temperature is higher than the melting point of the alloy from which it is made.

The bulk of the gas that leaves the combustor, however, does so through the exhaust

The parts of a jet engine—they can number 25,000—are made in various ways. The fan blade is made by shaping molten titanium in a hot press. When removed, each blade skin is welded to a mate, and the hollow cavity in the center is filled with a titanium honeycomb. The turbine disc is made by powder metallurgy, while the compressor blades and the combustion chamber are both made by casting.

system, which must be shaped very carefully to insure proper engine performance. Planes flying beneath the speed of sound are equipped with exhaust systems that taper toward their ends; those capable of supersonic travel require exhaust systems that flare at the end but that can also be narrowed to permit the slower speeds desirable for landing. The exhaust system consists of an outer duct, which transmits the cooling air that has been passed along the outside of the combustor, and a narrower inner duct, which carries the burning gases that have been pumped through the combustor. Between these two ducts is a *thrust reverser*, the mechanism that can close off the outer duct to prevent the unheated air from leaving the engine through the exhaust system. Pilots engage reverse thrust when they wish to slow the aircraft.

Raw Materials

Strong, lightweight, corrosion-resistant, thermally stable components are essential to the viability of any aircraft design, and certain materials have been developed to provide these and other desirable traits. Titanium, first created in sufficiently pure form for commercial use during the 1950s, is utilized in the most critical engine components. While it is very difficult to shape, its extreme hardness renders it strong when subjected to intense heat. To improve its malleability titanium is often alloyed with other metals such as nickel and aluminum. All three metals are prized by the aerospace industry because of their relatively high strength/weight ratio.

The intake fan at the front of the engine must be extremely strong so that it doesn't fracture when large birds and other debris are sucked into its blades; it is thus made of a titanium alloy. The intermediate compressor is made from aluminum, while the high pressure section nearer the intense heat of the combustor is made of nickel and titanium alloys better able to withstand extreme temperatures. The combustion chamber is also made of nickel and titanium alloys, and the turbine blades, which must endure the most intense heat of the engine, consist of nickel-titanium-aluminum alloys. Often, both the combustion chamber and the turbine receive special ceramic coatings that better enable them to resist heat. The inner duct of the exhaust sys-

tem is crafted from titanium, while the outer exhaust duct is made from composites—synthetic fibers held together with resins. Although fiberglass was used for years, it is now being supplanted by Kevlar, which is even lighter and stronger. The thrust reverser consists of titanium alloy.

The Manufacturing Process

Building and assembling the components of a jet engine takes about two years, after a design and testing period that can take up to five years for each model. The research and development phase is so protracted because the engines are so complex: a standard Boeing 747 engine, for example, contains almost 25,000 parts.

Building components—fan blade

1 In jet engine manufacture, the various parts are made individually as part of subassemblies; the subassemblies then come together to form the whole engine. One such part is the fan blade, situated at the front of the engine. Each fan blade consists of two blade skins produced by shaping molten titanium in a hot press. When removed, each blade skin is welded to a mate, with a hollow cavity in the center. To increase the strength of the final product, this cavity is filled with a titanium honeycomb.

Compressor disc

2 The disc, the solid core to which the blades of the compressor are attached, resembles a big, notched wheel. It must be extremely strong and free of even minute imperfections, as these could easily develop into fractures under the tremendous stress of engine operation. For a long time, the most popular way to manufacture the disc entailed machine-cutting a metal blank into a rough approximation of the desired shape, then heating and stamping it to precise specifications (in addition to rendering the metal malleable, heat also helps to fuse hairline cracks). Today, however, a more sophisticated method of producing discs is being used by more and more manufacturers. Called *powder metallurgy*, it consists of pouring molten metal onto a rapidly rotating turntable that breaks the metal into millions of microscopic droplets that are flung back up almost imme-

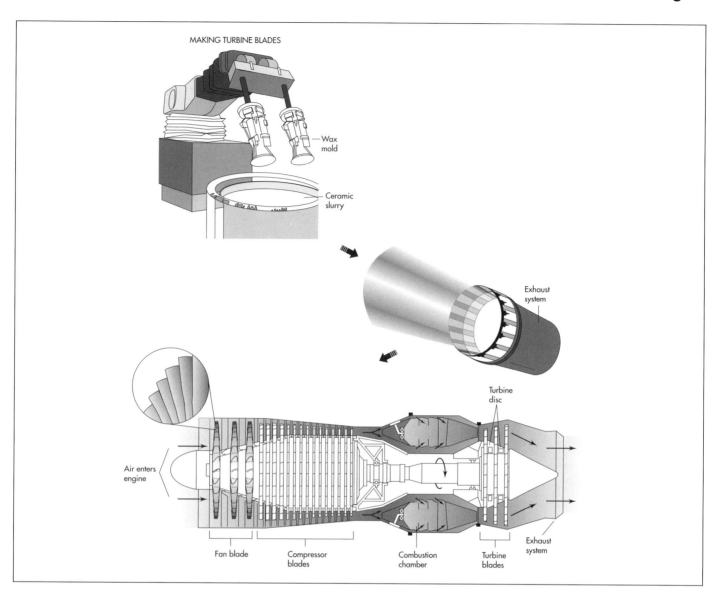

MAKING TURBINE BLADES

Wax mold

Ceramic slurry

Exhaust system

Turbine disc

Air enters engine

Fan blade — Compressor blades — Combustion chamber — Turbine blades — Exhaust system

diately due to the table's spinning. As they leave the table, the droplets' temperature suddenly plummets (by roughly 2,120 degrees Fahrenheit—1,000 degrees Celsius—in half a second), causing them to solidify and form a fine-grained metal powder. The resulting powder is very pure because it solidifies too quickly to pick up contaminants.

3 In the next step, the powder is packed into a forming case and put into a vacuum. Vibrated, the powder sifts down until it is tightly packed at the bottom of the case; the vacuum guarantees that no air pockets develop. The case is then sealed and heated under high pressure (about 25,000 pounds per square inch). This combination of heat and pressure fuses the metal particles into a disc. The disc is then shaped on a large cutting machine and bolted to the fan blades.

Compressor blades

4 Casting, an extremely old method, is still used to form the compressor blades. In this process, the alloy from which the blades will be formed is poured into a ceramic mold, heated in a furnace, and cooled. When the mold is broken off, the blades are machined to their final shape.

Combustion chamber

5 Combustion chambers must blend air and fuel in a small space and work for prolonged periods in extreme heat. To accomplish this, titanium is alloyed to increase its ductility—its ability to formed into shapes. It is then heated before being poured into several discrete, and very complex, segment molds. The sections are removed from their

Turbine blades are made by forming wax copies of the blades and then immersing the copies in a ceramic slurry bath. After each copy is heated to harden the ceramic and melt the wax, molten metal is poured into the hollow left by the melted wax.

A jet engine works by sucking air into one end, compressing it, mixing it with fuel and burning it in the combustion chamber, and then expelling it with great force out the exhaust system.

A jet engine is mounted to the air-plane wing with a pylon. The pylon (and the wing) must be very strong, since an engine can weigh up to 10,000 pounds.

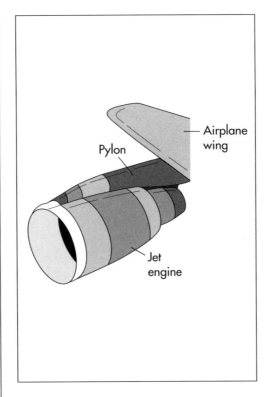

Pylon

Airplane wing

Jet engine

molds, allowed to cool, and welded together before being mounted on the engine.

Turbine disc and blades

6 The turbine disc is formed by the same powder metallurgy process used to create the compressor disc. Turbine blades, however, are made by a somewhat different method than that used to form compressor blades, because they are subjected to even greater stress due to the intense heat of the combustor that lies just in front of them. First, copies of the blades are formed by pouring wax into metal molds. Once each wax shape has set, it is removed from the mold and immersed in a ceramic slurry bath, forming a ceramic coating about .25-inch (.63-centimeter) thick. Each cluster is then heated to harden the ceramic and melt the wax. Molten metal is now poured into the hollow left by the melted wax. The internal air cooling passages within each blade are also formed during this stage of production.

7 The metal grains in the blade are now aligned parallel to the blade by a process called *directional solidifying*. The grain direction is important because the turbine blades are subjected to so much stress; if the grains are aligned correctly, the blade is much less likely to fracture. The solidifying

process takes place in computer-controlled ovens in which the blades are carefully heated according to precise specifications. The metal grains assume the correct configuration as they cool following their removal from the ovens.

8 The next and final stages in preparing tur-bine blades are machine-shaping and either laser drilling or spark erosion. First, the blade is honed to the final, desired shape through a machining process. Next, parallel lines of tiny holes are formed in each blade as a supplement to the interior cooling passageways. The holes are formed by either a small laser beam or by spark erosion, in which carefully controlled sparks are permitted to eat holes in the blade.

Exhaust system

9 The inner duct and the afterburners of the exhaust system are molded from titanium, while the outer duct and the nacelle (the engine casing) are formed from Kevlar. After these three components have been welded into a subassembly, the entire engine is ready to be put together.

Final assembly

10 Engines are constructed by manually combining the various subassemblies and accessories. An engine is typically built in a vertical position from the aft end forward, on a fixture that will allow the operator to manipulate the engine easily during build up. Assembly begins with bolting the high pressure turbine (that closest to the combustor) to the low-pressure turbine (that furthest from the cumbustor). Next, the combustion chamber is fastened to the turbines. One process that is used to build a balanced turbine assembly utilizes a CNC (Computer Numerically Controlled) robot capable of selecting, analyzing, and joining a turbine blade to its hub. This robot can determine the weight of a blade and place it appropriately for a balanced assembly.

11 Once the turbines and combustion chamber have been assembled, the high and low pressure compressors are attached. The fan and its frame comprise the forward most subassembly, and they are connected next. The main drive shaft connecting the low pressure turbine to the low pressure

compressor and fan is then installed, thus completing the engine core.

12 After the final subassembly, the exhaust system, has been attached, the engine is ready to be shipped to the aircraft manufacturer, where the plumbing, wiring, accessories, and aerodynamic shell of the plane will be integrated.

Quality Control

As production begins on a newly designed engine, the first one built is designated a test engine, and numerous experiments are run to test its response to the various situations the engine model will encounter during its service life. These include extreme weather conditions, airborne debris (such as birds), lengthy flights, and repeated starts. The first engine built is always dedicated to quality testing; it will never fly commercially.

Throughout the entire process of building an engine, components and assemblies are inspected for dimensional accuracy, responsible workmanship, and material integrity. Dimensional inspections are undertaken in many different ways. One common method is CNC inspection. A coordinate measuring machine (CMM) will inspect key features of a part and compare them to the designed dimensions. Parts are also inspected for material flaws. One method is to apply a fluorescent liquid over the entire surface of a part. After the liquid has migrated into any cracks or marks, the excess is removed. Under an ultraviolet light any surface imperfections that could cause premature engine failure will illuminate.

All rotating assemblies must be precisely balanced to insure safe extended operation. Prior to final assembly, all rotating subassemblies are dynamically balanced. The balancing process is much like spin-balancing the **tire** on your car. The rotating subassemblies and the completed engine core are computer "spun" and adjusted to insure that they rotate concentrically.

Functional testing of a finished engine takes place in three stages: static tests, stationary operating tests, and flight tests. A static test checks the systems (such as electrical and cooling) without the engine running. Stationary operating tests are conducted with the engine mounted on a stand and running. Flight testing entails a comprehensive exam of all the systems, previously tested or not, in a variety of different conditions and environments. Each engine will continue to be monitored throughout its service life.

Where To Learn More

Books

Moxon, Julian. *How Jet Engines Are Made.* Threshold Books, 1985.

Ott, James. *Jets: Airliners of the Golden Age.* Pyramid Media Group, 1990.

Peace, P. *Jet Engine Manual.* State Mutual Book & Periodical Service, 1989.

Periodicals

Brown, David A. "Norwegians Expect to Develop Family of Radial Inflow Turbine Engines." *Aviation Week & Space Technology.* November 10, 1986, p. 63.

Kandebo, Stanley W. "Engine Makers, Customers to Discuss Powerplants for 130-seat Transports." *Aviation Week & Space Technology.* June 17, 1991, p. 162.

Kandebo, Stanley W. "NASA-Industry Propulsion Team Addressing HSCT Environmental Issues." *Aviation Week & Space Technology.* November 25, 1991, p. 58.

Proctor, Paul. "Advanced Fuel Systems Crucial to High-Speed Transport Progress." *Aviation Week & Space Technology.* February 9, 1987, p. 45.

"Going with the Flow in Jet Engines." *Science News.* July 30, 1988, p. 73.

—*David Harris*

Laboratory Incubator

It is in the field of bio-technology that incubators' greatest potential lies. While such applications as sperm banks, cloning, and eugenics trouble many contemporary observers, genetic material has already been manipulated to measurable positive effect—to make insulin and other biologically essential proteins, for example.

An incubator comprises a transparent chamber and the equipment that regulates its temperature, humidity, and ventilation. For years, the principle uses for the controlled environment provided by incubators included hatching poultry eggs and caring for premature or sick infants, but a new and important application has recently emerged, namely, the cultivation and manipulation of microorganisms for medical treatment and research. This article will focus on laboratory (medical) incubators.

The first incubators were used in ancient China and Egypt, where they consisted of fire-heated rooms in which fertilized chicken eggs were placed to hatch, thereby freeing the hens to continue laying eggs. Later, wood stoves and alcohol lamps were used to heat incubators. Today, poultry incubators are large rooms, electrically heated to maintain temperatures between 99.5 and 100 degrees Fahrenheit (37.5 and 37.8 degrees Celsius). Fans are used to circulate the heated air evenly over the eggs, and the room's humidity is set at about 60 percent to minimize the evaporation of water from the eggs. In addition, outside air is pumped into the incubator to maintain a constant oxygen level of 21 percent, which is normal for fresh air. As many as 100,000 eggs may be nurtured in a large commercial incubator at one time, and all are rotated a minimum of 8 times a day throughout the 21-day incubation period.

During the late nineteenth century, physicians began to use incubators to help save the lives of babies born after a gestation period of less than 37 weeks (an optimal human pregnancy lasts 280 days, or 40 weeks). The first infant incubator, heated by kerosene lamps, appeared in 1884 at a Paris women's hospital.

In 1933, American Julius H. Hess designed an electrically heated infant incubator (most are still electrically heated today). Modern baby incubators resemble cribs, save that they are enclosed. Usually, the covers are transparent so that medical personnel can observe babies continually. In addition, many incubators are made with side wall apertures into which long-armed rubber gloves can be fitted, enabling nurses to care for the babies without removing them. The temperature is usually maintained at between 88 and 90 degrees Fahrenheit (31 to 32 degrees Celsius). Entering air is passed through a HEPA (high efficiency purified air) filter, which cleans and humidifies it, and the oxygen level within the chamber is adjusted to meet the particular needs of each infant. Incubators in neonatal units, centers that specialize in caring for premature infants, are frequently equipped with electronic devices for monitoring the infant's temperature and the amount of oxygen in its blood.

Laboratory (medical) incubators were first utilized during the twentieth century, when doctors realized that they could be could be used to identify pathogens (disease-causing bacteria) in patients' bodily fluids and thus diagnose their disorders more accurately. After a sample has been obtained, it is transferred to a Petri dish, flask, or some other sterile container and placed in a rack inside the incubator. To promote pathogenic growth, the air inside the chamber is humidified and heated to body temperature (98.6 degrees Fahrenheit or 37 degrees Celsius). In addition, these incubators provide the amount of atmospheric carbon dioxide or nitrogen necessary for the cell's growth. As this carefully conditioned air circulates around it, the microorganism multiplies, enabling easier and more certain identification.

A related use of incubators is tissue culture, a research technique in which clinicians extract tissue fragments from plants or animals, place these explants in an incubator, and monitor their subsequent growth. The temperature within the incubator is maintained at or near that of the organism from which the explant was derived. Observing explants in incubators gives scientists insight into the operation and interaction of particular cells; for example, it has enabled them to understand cancerous cells and to develop vaccines for polio, influenza, measles, and mumps. In addition, tissue culture has allowed researchers to detect disorders stemming from the lack of particular enzymes.

Incubators are also used in genetic engineering, an extension of tissue culturing in which scientists manipulate the genetic materials in explants, sometimes combining DNA from discrete sources to create new organisms. While such applications as sperm banks, cloning, and eugenics trouble many contemporary observers, genetic material has already been manipulated to measurable positive effect—to make insulin and other biologically essential proteins, for example. Genetic engineering can also improve the nutritional content of many fruits and vegetables and can increase the resistance of various crops to disease. It is in the field of bio-technology that incubators' greatest potential lies.

Raw Materials

Three main types of materials are necessary to manufacture an incubator. The first is **stainless steel** sheet metal of a common grade, usually .02 to .04 inch (.05 to .1 centimeter) thick. Stainless steel is used because it resists rust and corrosion that might be caused by both naturally occurring environmental agents and by whatever is placed inside the unit. The next category of necessary components includes items purchased from outside suppliers: nuts, screws, insulation, motors, fans, and other miscellaneous items. The third type of necessary material is the electronics package, whose complexity will depend upon the sophistication of the unit in question. Such a package may have simple on/off switches with analog temperature control or a state-of-the-art microprocessor that can be programmed to maintain different temperatures for varying intervals, or to operate various internal light systems.

Design

Like standard refrigerators, incubators are measured in terms of the chamber's volume, which ranges from 5 to 10 cubic feet (1.5 to 3 cubic meters) for countertop models and from 18 to 33 cubic feet (5.5 to 10 cubic meters) for free-standing models.

The sheet metal is used to make two box configurations, an inner chamber and the case that encloses it. Insulation (if the chamber is heated electrically) or a water-jacket (if it is water-heated) surrounds the chamber, and the case supports it, the controls, and the doors. To prevent contamination and avoid fungal or bacterial growth, the chamber must be hermetically sealed, or rendered airtight, as must any apertures built into its walls. A glass door that allows scientists to observe the chamber's contents without disturbing them fits against the chamber's gasket, which helps to keep the incubator airtight. A steel door, solid and insulated, closes over the glass door.

Two types of heat sources are used: electrical heaters that use fans to circulate the warmth they generate, and hot water jackets. In the former design, the inner chamber has an electrical heater mounted on an inside wall and covered by a perforated protective panel. Mounted in the chamber wall just above the heater is a fan whose motor extends through the chamber wall into the control area of the case and whose blades face inward. Other manufacturers heat the chamber by surrounding it with a water-filled jacket.

The dry-wall heater offer several advantages over the water-jacket. First, the former can change temperature within the chamber more quickly. Also, electrically heated units can be thermally decontaminated because the wall heaters not only warm the chamber more quickly but also heat it to higher temperatures (a unit is considered contaminant-free after its chamber temperature has been raised to 212 degrees Fahrenheit or 100 degrees Celsius or above). Water jackets pose another problem wall heaters don't: because they are pressurized, they can develop leaks.

Humidity is generated by heating a small copper bowl that contains limited amounts of purified water; the resulting steam can be introduced into the chamber by means of a control valve. Interior lighting may also be used. Fluorescent and UV (ultra-violet)

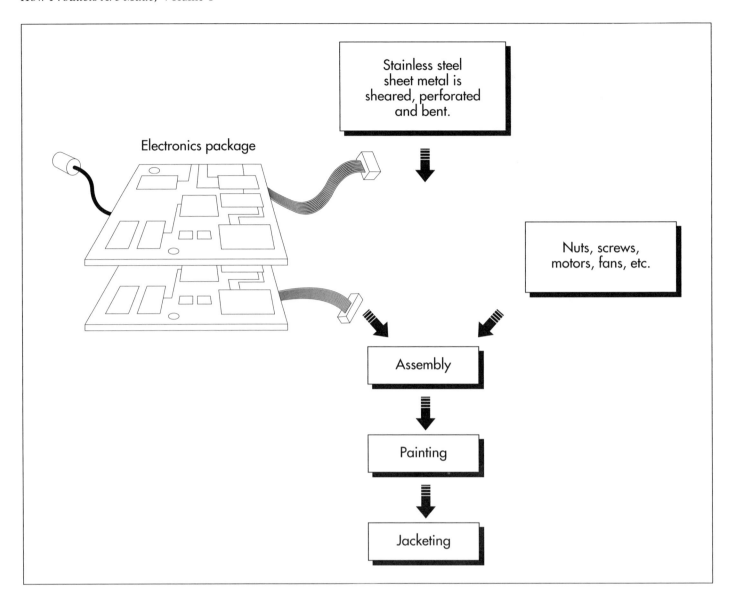

The largest components in a laboratory incubator are made of stainless steel sheet metal that is sheared, perforated, and bent to the proper shape. The pieces are joined together by screws, spot welding, or arc welding. Near the end of the assembly process, either a water jacket or insulation is inserted into the chamber.

lamps can be installed separately or in combination. To adjust temperature, humidity, lights, ventilation, and any other special features, more sophisticated incubators feature control panels on their outer case. However, if the unit is a relatively simple one, it will provide only basic on/off switches with simple analog temperature controls. Inside the chamber, a thermostat or thermocouple is strategically placed so that it can be viewed without difficulty from the outside.

The Manufacturing Process

Cutting, perforating, and bending the sheet metal

1 First, 48 inch by 112 inch (122 centimeter by 284 centimeter) sheets of metal are cut into small, square pieces with a flat shear that resembles a very large, table top paper cutter.

2 A CNC Turret Press is a machine programmed with the dimensions of the sheet metal to be perforated and the location of each hole and notch; the shapes and sizes of each hole and notch also are entered. The machine has a magazine of punches in varying sizes and pre-determined locations in a turret (rotary) holder. An operator places a sheet on the machine bed (table), positions it against three fixed points to insure squareness, and clamps it to the table. The machine will then move the sheet steel over a bed of rollers to different positions under the turret before rotating the turret to the punch programmed for that specific location and triggering the press to punch a hole. Machines of this design can house upwards of 60 dif-

ferent punch geometries and move and strike the sheet metal at high speeds. Most sheet metal cabinetry manufacturers use this technology extensively.

3 Neither computer programmed nor automated, conventional punch presses perform *hard tooling*; in other words, they punch only a particular shape and size hole. Sheet metal is placed into a die by an operator. As the press moves downward the sheet metal is punched. These machines cost less than CNC Presses, but the sheet metal must be placed in numerous presses to obtain the desired configuration of punches.

4 After the sheet metal has been sheared and perforated, some pieces need to be bent in machines known as *power press brakes* or *brakes* for short. Brakes can range in length from 4 to 20 feet (1.2 to 6.1 meters), but they are typically about 10 feet (3 meters) long. Both the stationary bottom, or *bed*, and the moving upper, or *ram*, have slots that run the length of the machine. Because these slots are aligned, any tool placed into them will always be perfectly aligned. The bed has a rectangular block with an open "V" on its topside, while the ram has a knife-edged blade with a radius at its cutting edge. The ram's descent into the open bottom "V" is controlled; the depth at which the blade enters the bed controls the angle at which the sheet metal is bent. A simple straight-edge serves as a back-gauge.

Assembling the cabinets

5 Next, the components of both chamber and case are fitted together, some with sheet metal screws. Others are joined by means of spot welding, a process in which separate pieces of material are fused with pressure and heat.

6 Other components are arc welded using one of three methods. In the first method, known as MIG (metal-arc inert gas) welding, a coil of thin wire is threaded through a hand-held gun. A hose is connected from a tank of inert gas (usually argon) to the tip of the gun's nozzle. A machine generating electrical current is attached to the wire in the gun and the work piece. When the gun's trigger is pulled, the wire rod moves, feeding toward the work piece, and the gas is released, creating an atmosphere at the point where the wire

arcs with the metal. This allows the joining of the parts.

7 The second arc welding method is known as stick welding. In this process, a thin rod approximately 12 inches long, .187 inch thick (30 centimeters long, .47 centimeter thick), and coated with a flux material is placed into a hand-held holder. This holder is attached to a machine generating an electrical charge. Also connected to the machine is a grounding cable that has an end clamped to the part to be welded. When the rod is close to the parts, an arc is struck, generating intense heat that melts the rod and flux. The flux acts as a cleanser, allowing the rod material to adhere to both pieces of metal. The welder drags the rod along the seams of the metal while maintaining its distance from the seam to allow the arc to remain constant.

8 The third arc welding method used to assemble the incubator is TIG (tungsten-arc inert gas) welding, a combination of stick and MIG welding. In this process, a stationary tungsten rod without any flux is inserted into a hand-held gun. Inert gas flows from a tank through the gun's nozzle. When the trigger is pulled, the gas creates an atmosphere; as the tungsten rod strikes its arc, the two parts fuse together without any filler metal.

Painting the incubator

9 At this point, the case may be painted to further provide surface protection, both inside and outside (the inner chamber is never painted). The box is spray painted, usually with an electrostatically charged powder **paint**. This process requires that a small electrical charge be applied so that it will attract the powder particles, which have been given an opposite charge. After the case is sprayed, it is moved into an oven that melts the powder particles, causing them to adhere to the freshly cleaned metal surface. This process is very clean, efficient, and environmentally friendly, and the high-quality paint resists most laboratory spills.

Insulating or jacketing the chamber

10 Next, the inner-chamber is wrapped with insulation (either blanket batting or hard-board), placed inside the case, and secured. If the unit is water-jacketed, the

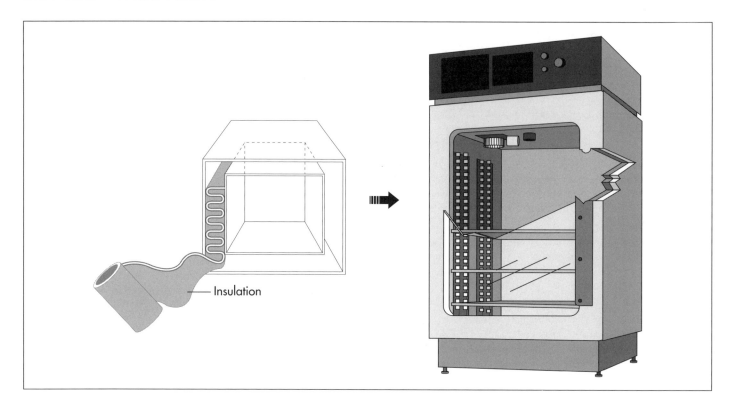

Insulation

In an electrically heated incubator, insulation—either blanket batting or hard-board insulation—is wrapped around the inner chamber and placed inside the case. In water heated incubators, the water jackets are likewise placed within the inside chamber.

The chamber volume for a typical free-standing incubator ranges from 18 to 33 cubic feet.

jacket is placed inside the case and the chamber inside the jacket. A sheet metal door is constructed using methods similar to that mentioned above.

Assembling the control panel

11 While the sheet metal cabinetry is being fabricated, a control panel is being assembled elsewhere in the factory. Following detailed electrical prints, electricians fasten different colored wire of varying thicknesses to electrical devices. The color scheme helps technicians to diagnose problems quickly, and the various thicknesses allow for safe and efficient transfer of lower and higher voltages. Purchased electrical devices such as fuse blocks, switches, terminal blocks, and relays adhere to strict electrical codes. Finally, the wires from the control panel are attached to the control devices (on/off switches or micro-processors) and the electro-mechanical devices (fan motor, lights, and heaters).

Final assembly, testing, and cleaning

12 The incubator now has its inner glass and the outer solid door attached, and shelving and supplemental features are installed. Each unit is 100 percent function-

ally tested. The parameters for each test are set to verify the unit's performance against advertised specifications or the customer's requests, whichever is more stringent. Problems are corrected, and the equipment is re-tested. A copy of the test result is kept on file and the original sent to the customer.

13 The incubator receives a thorough cleaning inside and out. Shelves are removed and packaged separately, and the doors are taped closed. A brace is positioned under the door to help prevent sagging. Next, each unit is secured to a wooden skid and a **corrugated cardboard** box is placed around the case. Packing filler is put in-between the carton and the case. Finally, the product is shipped.

Quality Control

No quality standards are accepted by the entire incubator manufacturing industry. Some areas of the country may require UL (Underwriters Laboratory) Electrical Approval, but those standards apply only to the electro-mechanical devices being used. During the sheet metal work, manufacturers utilize in-house inspection processes that can vary widely, from formal first-piece inspection to random lot sampling inspection. Some companies may keep records of their findings, while others do not. Almost without exception, manufacturers do performance-level testing before shipment as described above.

The Future

While hospitals will always need neonatal incubators, the bio-technological industry is where the growth market lies for this product. Growth chamber type incubators will need to control temperature and relative humidity to more precise settings, as microbiologists and researchers investigate new ways to improve our health and well-being.

Where To Learn More

Books

Coyne, Gary. *The Laboratory Handbook of Materials, Equipment, and Technique*. Prentice Hall, 1991.

—Frank Sokolo

Laser Guided Missile

Future laser guided missile systems will carry their own miniaturized laser on board, doing away with the need for target designator lasers on aircraft. These missiles, currently under development in several countries, are called "fire-and-forget" because a pilot can fire one and forget about it, relying on the missile's internal laser and detecting sensor to guide it towards its target.

Background

Missiles differ from rockets by virtue of a guidance system that steers them towards a pre-selected target. Unguided, or free-flight, rockets proved to be useful yet frequently inaccurate weapons when fired from aircraft during the World War II. This inaccuracy, often resulting in the need to fire many rockets to hit a single target, led to the search for a means to guide the rocket towards its target. The concurrent explosion of radio-wave technology (such as radar and radio detection devices) provided the first solution to this problem. Several warring nations, including the United States, Germany and Great Britain, mated existing rocket technology with new radio- or radar-based guidance systems to create the world's first guided missiles. Although these missiles were not deployed in large enough numbers to radically divert the course of the World War II, the successes that were recorded with them pointed out techniques that would change the course of future wars. Thus dawned the era of high-technology warfare, an era that would quickly demonstrate its problems as well as its promise.

The problems centered on the unreliability of the new radio-wave technologies. The missiles were not able to hone in on targets smaller than factories, bridges, or warships. Circuits often proved fickle and would not function at all under adverse weather conditions. Another flaw emerged as jamming technologies flourished in response to the success of radar. Enemy jamming stations found it increasingly easy to intercept the radio or radar transmissions from launching aircraft, thereby allowing these stations to send conflicting signals on the same frequency, jamming or "confusing" the missile. Battlefield applications for guided missiles, especially those that envisioned attacks on smaller targets, required a more reliable guidance method that was less vulnerable to jamming. Fortunately, this method became available as a result of an independent research effort into the effects of light amplification.

Dr. Theodore Maiman built the first laser (*Light Amplification by Stimulated Emission of Radiation*) at Hughes Research Laboratories in 1960. The military realized the potential applications for lasers almost as soon as their first beams cut through the air. Laser guided projectiles underwent their baptism of fire in the extended series of air raids that highlighted the American effort in the Vietnam War. The accuracy of these weapons earned them the well-known sobriquet of "smart weapons." But even this new generation of advanced weaponry could not bring victory to U.S. forces in this bitter and costly war. However, the combination of experience gained in Vietnam, refinements in laser technology, and similar advances in electronics and computers, led to more sophisticated and deadly laser guided missiles. They finally received widespread use in Operation Desert Storm, where their accuracy and reliability played a crucial role in the decisive defeat of Iraq's military forces. Thus, the laser guided missile has established itself as a key component in today's high-tech military technology.

Raw Materials

A laser guided missile consists of four important components, each of which contains different raw materials. These four components

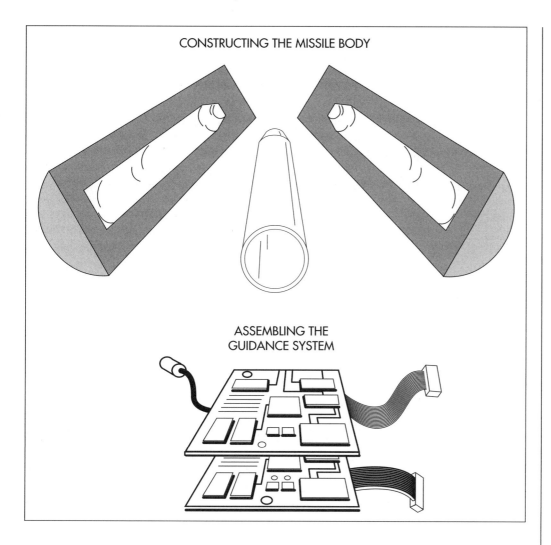

CONSTRUCTING THE MISSILE BODY

ASSEMBLING THE
GUIDANCE SYSTEM

The missile body is die-cast in halves: molten metal (either aluminum or steel) is poured into a metal die and cooled to form the proper shape. The two halves are then welded together.

The principal laser components—the photo detecting sensor and optical filters—are assembled in a series of operations that are separate from the rest of the missile's construction. Circuits that support the laser system are then soldered onto pre-printed boards. The circuit boards for the electronics suite are also assembled independently from the rest of the missile. If called for by the design, microchips are added to the boards at this time.

are the *missile body*, the *guidance system* (also called the *laser and electronics suite*), the *propellant*, and the *warhead*. The missile body is made from steel alloys or high-strength aluminum alloys that are often coated with chromium along the cavity of the body in order to protect against the excessive pressures and heat that accompany a missile launch. The guidance system contains various types of materials—some basic, others high-tech—that are designed to give maximum guidance capabilities. These materials include a photo detecting sensor and optical filters, with which the missile can interpret laser wavelengths sent from a parent aircraft. The photo detecting sensor's most important part is its sensing dome, which can be made of glass, quartz, and/or silicon. A missile's electronics suite can contain gallium-arsenide semiconductors, but some suites still rely exclusively on copper or silver wiring. Guided missiles use nitrogen-based solid propellants as their fuel source. Certain additives (such as graphite or nitroglycerine) can

be included to alter the performance of the propellant. The missile's warhead can contain highly explosive nitrogen-based mixtures, fuel-air explosives (FAE), or phosphorous compounds. The warhead is typically encased in steel, but aluminum alloys are sometimes used as a substitute.

Design

Two basic types of laser guided missiles exist on the modern battlefield. The first type "reads" the laser light emitted from the launching aircraft/helicopter. The missile's electronic suite issues commands to the fins (called *control surfaces*) on its body in an effort to keep it on course with the laser beam. This type of missile is called a *beam rider* as it tends to ride the laser beam towards its target.

The second type of missile uses on-board sensors to pick up laser light reflected from the target. The aircraft/helicopter pilot selects a target, hits the target with a laser beam shot from a target designator, and then launches the missile. The missile's sensor measures the error between its flight path and the path of the reflected light. Correction messages are then passed on to the missile's control surfaces via the electronics suite, steering the missile onto its target.

Regardless of type, the missile designer must run computer simulations as the first step of the design process. These simulations assist the designer in choosing the proper laser type, body length, nozzle configurations, cavity size, warhead type, propellant mass, and control surfaces. The designer then puts together a package containing all relevant engineering calculations, including those generated by computer simulations. The electronics suite is then designed around the capabilities of the laser and control surfaces. Drawings and schematics of all components can now be completed; CAD/CAM (Computer-Aided Design/Manufacture) technology has proven helpful with this task. Electronics systems are then designed around the capabilities of the aircraft's laser and the missile's control surfaces. The following step consists of generating the necessary schematic drawings for the chosen electronics system. Another computer-assisted study of the total guided missile system constitutes the final step of the design process.

The Manufacturing Process

Constructing the body and attaching the fins

1 The steel or aluminum body is die cast in halves. Die casting involves pouring molten metal into a steel die of the desired shape and letting the metal harden. As it cools, the metal assumes the same shape as the die. At this time, an optional chromium coating can be applied to the interior surfaces of the halves that correspond to a completed missile's cavity. The halves are then welded together, and nozzles are added at the tail end of the body after it has been welded.

2 Moveable fins are now added at predetermined points along the missile body. The fins can be attached to mechanical joints that are then welded to the outside of the

body, or they can be inserted into recesses purposely milled into the body.

Casting the propellant

3 The propellant must be carefully applied to the missile cavity in order to ensure a uniform coating, as any irregularities will result in an unreliable burning rate, which in turn detracts from the performance of the missile. The best means of achieving a uniform coating is to apply the propellant by using centrifugal force. This application, called *casting*, is done in an industrial centrifuge that is well-shielded and situated in an isolated location as a precaution against fire or explosion.

Assembling the guidance system

4 The principal laser components—the photo detecting sensor and optical filters—are assembled in a series of operations that are separate from the rest of the missile's construction. Circuits that support the laser system are then soldered onto pre-printed boards; extra attention is given to optical materials at this time to protect them from excessive heat, as this can alter the wavelength of light that the missile will be able to detect. The assembled laser subsystem is now set aside pending final assembly. The circuit boards for the electronics suite are also assembled independently from the rest of the missile. If called for by the design, microchips are added to the boards at this time.

5 The guidance system (laser components plus the electronics suite) can now be integrated by linking the requisite circuit boards and inserting the entire assembly into the missile body through an access panel. The missile's control surfaces are then linked with the guidance system by a series of relay wires, also entered into the missile body via access panels. The photo detecting sensor and its housing, however, are added at this point only for beam riding missiles, in which case the housing is carefully bolted to the exterior diameter of the missile near its rear, facing backward to interpret the laser signals from the parent aircraft.

Final assembly

6 Insertion of the warhead constitutes the final assembly phase of guided missile

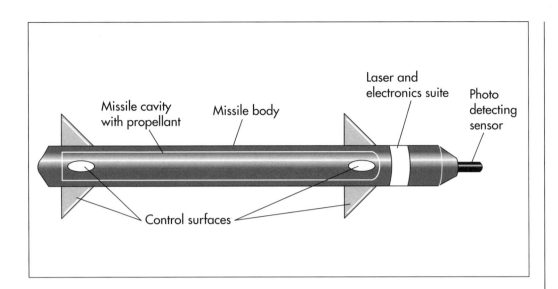

Current laser guided missiles work in one of two ways. The first type, a "beam rider," reads the laser light emitted from the launching aircraft and rides the beam toward the target. The second type uses on-board sensors to pick up laser light sent by the aircraft and reflected from the target. The sensors measure the error between the missile's flight path and the path of the reflected light, and the electronics suite alters the control surfaces as necessary to guide the missile toward the target.

construction. Great care must be exercised during this process, as mistakes can lead to catastrophic accidents. Simple fastening techniques such as bolting or riveting serve to attach the warhead without risking safety hazards. For guidance systems that home-in on reflected laser light, the photo detecting sensor (in its housing) is bolted into place at the tip of the warhead. On completion of this final phase of assembly, the manufacturer has successfully constructed on of the most complicated, sophisticated, and potentially dangerous pieces of hardware in use today.

Quality Control

Each important component is subjected to rigorous quality control tests prior to assembly. First, the propellant must pass a test in which examiners ignite a sample of the propellant under conditions simulating the flight of a missile. The next test is a wind tunnel exercise involving a model of the missile body. This test evaluates the air flow around the missile during its flight. Additionally, a few missiles set aside for test purposes are fired to test flight characteristics. Further work involves putting the electronics suite through a series of tests to determine the speed and accuracy with which commands get passed along to the missile's control surfaces. Then the laser components are tested for reliability, and a test beam is fired to allow examiners to record the photo detecting sensor's ability to "read" the proper wavelength. Finally, a set number of completed guided missiles are test fired from aircraft or helicopters on ranges studded with practice targets.

Byproducts/Waste

Propellants and explosives used in warheads are toxic if introduced into water supplies. Residual amounts of these materials must be collected and taken to a designated disposal site for burning. Each state maintains its own policy pertaining to the disposal of explosives, and Federal regulations require that disposal sites be inspected periodically. Effluents (liquid byproducts) from the chromium coating process can also be hazardous. This problem is best dealt with by storing the effluents in leak-proof containers. As an additional safety precaution, all personnel involved in handling any hazardous wastes should be given protective clothing that includes breathing devices, gloves, boots and overalls.

The Future

Future laser guided missile systems will carry their own miniaturized laser on board, doing away with the need for target designator lasers on aircraft. These missiles, currently under development in several countries, are called "fire-and-forget" because a pilot can fire one of these missiles and forget about it, relying on the missile's internal laser and detecting sensor to guide it towards its target. A further development of this trend will result in missiles that can select and attack targets on their own. Once their potential has been realized, the battlefields of the world will feel the deadly venom of these "brilliant missiles" for years to come. An even more advanced concept envisions a battle rifle for infantry that also fires small, laser guided missiles. Operation Desert Storm clearly showed the need for laser guided accuracy, and, as a result, military establishments dedicated to their missions will undoubtedly invent and deploy ever more lethal versions of laser guided missiles.

Where To Learn More

Books

Bova, Ben. *The Beauty of Light.* John Wiley and Sons, 1988.

Hallmark, Clayton L. and Delton T. Horn. *Lasers: The Light Fantastic.* TAB Books, 1987.

Hecht, Jeff. *Optics: Light for a New Age.* Charles Scribner's Sons, 1987.

Iannini, Robert. E. *Build Your Own Fiberoptic, Infrared, and Laser Space-Age Projects.* TAB Books, 1987.

Laurence, Clifford L. *The Laser Book: A New Technology of Light.* Prentice Hall, 1986.

Von Braun, Wernher, Frederick I. Ordway III, and Dave Dooling. *Space Travel: A History.* Harper & Row, 1985.

Wood, Derek. *Jane's World Aircraft Recognition Handbook.* Jane's Information Group, 1989.

Wulforst, Harry. *The Rocketmakers.* Orion Books, 1990.

Periodicals

"A Dull Scalpel for the Surgical Strike on Libya." *Discover.* June, 1986, p. 8.

Lenorowitz, Jeffrey M. "F-117s Drop Laser-Guided Bombs in Destroying Most Baghdad Targets." *Aviation Week and Space Technology.* Feb. 4, 1991, p. 30.

Magnusson, Paul. "American Smart Bombs, Foreign Brains." *Business Week.* March 4, 1991, p. 18.

—*Robert A. Cortese*

Laundry Detergent

Background

The first soaps were manufactured in ancient times through a variety of methods, most commonly by boiling fats and ashes. Archeologists excavating sites in ancient Babylon have found evidence indicating that such soaps were used as far back as 2800 B.C. By the second century A.D., the Romans were regularly making soap, which they had probably begun to produce even earlier.

In Europe, the use of soap declined during the Middle Ages. However, by the fifteenth century, its use and manufacture had resumed, and an olive-oil based soap produced in Castile, Spain, was being sold in many parts of the known world. Castile soap, which is still available today, has retained its reputation as a high-quality product.

During the colonial period and the eighteenth century, Americans made their own soap at home, where most continued to produce it until soap manufacture shifted away from individual homes to become an industry during the 1930s. The first detergent, or artificial soap, was produced in Germany during World War I. In 1946, the first built detergent appeared, comprising a *surfactant* (a surface-acting agent or soap) and a *builder* (a chemical that enhances the performance of the surfactant as well as rendering the laundering process more effective in other ways). Pushed along by economic prosperity and the development of relatively inexpensive **washing machine**s in the wake of World War II, detergent sales soared; by 1953, they had surpassed soap sales in the United States.

Raw Materials

Although people commonly refer to laundry detergent as "soap," it is actually a synthetic combination that functions much like soap, with certain major improvements. Soap cleans because each soap molecule consists of a hydrocarbon chain and a carboxylic group (fatty acids) that perform two important functions. The carboxylate end of the soap molecule is hydrophilic, meaning that it is attracted to water, while the hydrocarbon end of the molecule is both hydrophobic (repelled by water) and attracted to the oil and grease in dirt. While the hydrophobic end of a soap molecule attaches itself to dirt, the hydrophilic end attaches itself to water. The dirt attached to the carboxylate end of the molecule is chemically dragged away from the clothes being cleaned and into the wash water. Properly agitating and rinsing the clothes furthers the cleansing process.

The major difficulty with using soap to clean laundry shows up when it is used in hard water—water that is rich in natural minerals such as calcium, magnesium, iron, and manganese. When these chemicals react with soap, they form an insoluble curd called a *precipitate*. Difficult to rinse out, the precipitate leaves visible deposits on clothing and makes fabric feel stiff. Even water that is not especially hard will eventually produce precipitates over a period of time.

While the hydrocarbons used in soap generally come from plants or animals, those used in detergent can be derived from crude oil. Adding sulfuric acid to the processed hydrocarbon produces a molecule similar to the fatty acids in soap. The addition of an alkali to the mixture creates a surfactant molecule

In 1946, the first built detergent appeared, comprising a surfactant and a builder. Pushed along by economic prosperity and the development of relatively inexpensive washing machines in the wake of World War II, detergent sales soared; by 1953, they had surpassed soap sales in the United States.

In the blender method of making powder laundry detergent, the ingredients—surfactant, builders, antiredeposition agents, and perfumes—are simply blended together in a mixer, released onto a conveyor belt, and packaged accordingly. This method is favored by smaller companies.

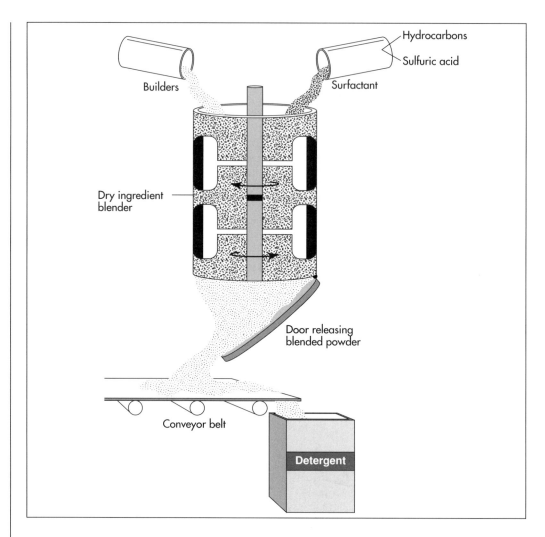

that will not bond with the minerals in hard water, thus avoiding the accumulation of precipitates.

In addition to a surfactant, modern detergent contains several other ingredients. Among the most significant are builders, chemicals which serve several purposes. Most importantly, they increase the efficiency of the surfactant. They also sequester minerals in hard water, meaning that they hold them in solution, preventing them from precipitating out. Furthermore, builders can emulsify oil and grease into tiny globules that can be washed away. Some, like sodium silicate, inhibit corrosion and help assure that the detergent will not damage a washing machine. Still other builders contribute to the chemical balance of the wash water, making sure that it conduces to effective washing.

Modern detergents have several other ingredients including antiredeposition agents, chemicals that help prevent soil from settling back on washed clothes. Fluorescent whitening agents are also common. By converting invisible ultraviolet light into visible blue light, these help to maintain brightness or whiteness. Oxygen bleaches such as sodium perborate improve the detergency of the mixture, especially in low-phosphate or no-phosphate products, as well as helping to remove some types of stains. Processing aids such as sodium sulfate are also used to prevent caking and to standardize product density.

Enzymes and perfumes are also found in commercial detergents. Enzymes (a type of protein) break down some stains to make them easier to remove and are an essential ingredient in various pre-soak products used to treat heavily soiled clothes prior to laundering. Perfumes or fragrances cover the odor of the dirt and any chemical smell from the detergent itself. Suds control agents also have a role in detergents—too many suds can cause mechanical problems with a washing machine.

The Manufacturing Process

Although there are three ways of manufacturing dry laundry detergent, only two are commonly used today. In the blender process favored by smaller companies, the ingredients are mixed in large vats before being packaged. The machines used are very large: a common blender holds 4,000 pounds (1,816 kilograms) of mixed material, but the blenders can accommodate loads ranging from 500 to 10,000 pounds (227 to 4,540 kilograms). By industry standards, these are small batches for which the blender process is ideal. While some settling may occur, the resulting detergent is of high quality and can compete with detergents made by other processes. The second commonly used method of production is called the agglomeration process. Unlike the blender process, it is continuous, which makes it the choice of very large detergent manufacturers. The agglomeration process can produce between 15,000 and 50,000 pounds (6,800 and 22,700 kilograms) of detergent per hour. In the third method, dry ingredients are blended in water before being dried with hot air. Although the resulting product is of high quality, the fuel costs and engineering problems associated with venting, reheating, and reusing the air have led to this method being largely replaced by agglomeration.

The blender process

1 First, ingredients are loaded into one of two machines: a tumbling blender or a ribbon blender. The tumbling blender, shaped like a rectangular box, is turned and shaken from outside by a machine, while the ribbon blender is a cylinder fitted with blades to scrape and mix the ingredients. After the ingredients inside the blender have been mixed, a doorway at the bottom of the bowl is opened. With the blender still agitating the ingredients, the mix is allowed to run out onto a conveyor belt or other channeling device. The belt then moves the detergent to another area of the factory where it can be dropped into boxes or cartons for delivery to wholesalers or distributors.

The agglomeration process

2 In this method, dry ingredients for a detergent are first fed into a large machine known as a *Shuggi agglomerator* (Shuggi is the manufacturer). Inside the agglomerator, sharp, whirling blades mix the material to a fine consistency; the process resembles food being textured inside a food processor.

3 After the dry ingredients have been blended, liquid ingredients are sprayed on the dry mix through nozzles fitted into the agglomerator's walls. The blending continues, causing an exothermic (heat-producing) reaction to occur. The resulting mixture is a hot, viscous liquid similar to gelatin that hasn't hardened.

4 Next, the liquid is allowed to flow out of the agglomerator. As it leaves the machine, it collects on a drying belt where its own heat, exposure to air, and hot air blowers render it friable—easy to crush or crumble. The newly made detergent is then pulverized and pushed through sizing screens that ensure that no large lumps of unmixed product go out to the market. The result of this process is a dry detergent made up of granules of the mixed detergent.

The slurry method

5 In this process, ingredients are dissolved in water to create a slurry. With a pump, the slurry is blown through nozzles inside the top of a cone shaped container as hot, dry air is simultaneously forced into the bottom of the cone. As the slurry dries, "beads" of dry detergent fall to the bottom of the cone, where they can be collected for packaging.

Liquid detergent

6 If the detergent is to be liquid rather than powder, it is simply mixed back in—after all ingredients are blended—with a solution consisting of water and various chemicals known as *solubilizers*. The solubilizers help the water and detergent blend together more fully and evenly.

Quality Control

Manufacturers constantly monitor the quality of their detergents, and they utilize the same testing methods to assess the effectiveness of new products. In one method, light is shined onto a piece of fabric that has been soiled and then washed in the test detergent. The

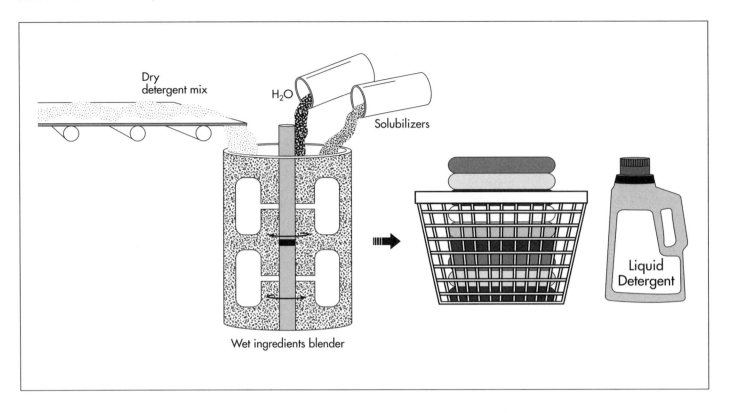

Dry detergent mix

H₂O

Solubilizers

Liquid Detergent

Wet ingredients blender

To make liquid detergent, the dry powder is simply mixed back in with a solution consisting of water and chemicals known as "solubilizers." These chemicals help the water and detergent blend together more evenly.

amount of light reflected, compared to the amount reflected by a sample of the original fabric, is a measure of cleanliness. A reflection rate of 98 percent is considered quite good and indicates that the detergent has cleaned properly.

Another method involves laboratory burning of a small amount of material that has been soiled and then laundered. The weight of the ashes, plus the weight of the gaseous results of the burning, reveal how much of the dirt remained in the fabric after laundering. A result that is much higher than a clean test sample indicates that a significant amount of dirt was retained in the laundered sample. Naturally, the goal is to come as close to the weight of a clean control sample as possible.

Byproducts

In recent years, the laundry detergent industry has been faced with two environmental challenges, both of which have seem to have been dealt with successfully. Environmentalists were concerned that phosphate builders added large amounts of phosphorous compounds to the nation's waterways. Acting as a fertilizer, the phosphorus stimulated the growth of algae, and these unnaturally large crops of algae significantly depleted the amount of dissolved oxygen in water. This

decrease in free oxygen harmed other marine life, thus threatening to disrupt normal ecological patterns.

This problem, and the environmental pressure and legislation it prompted in the late 1960s, led manufacturers to develop effective builders that did not contain phosphates. Today, detergents sold in many states are phosphate-free. Although this adjustment did not entail a change in the manufacturing process, it did require a research effort that took several months to devise a satisfactory alternative.

An earlier environmental problem was that of excess detergent foam appearing in the nation's waterways. In the early 1950s, when home use of washing machines and laundry detergents grew at an explosive rate, there were several instances of large amounts of foam appearing in rivers and streams, although detergent may not have been the only cause of the foaming. Over a period of five years, from 1951 to 1956, it was found that a common surfactant, ABS (alkyl benzene sulfonate), the detergent ingredient that contributed to foaming, was responsible. ABS's complex molecular structure did not biodegrade rapidly enough to keep it from foaming once washing water was discharged. A proven replacement was not immediately available. Beginning in 1956, however, manufacturers replaced ABS with LAS (linear alkylate sulfonate), which biodegrades rapidly, and since that time, LAS has been the primary foaming agent in detergents.

Where To Learn More

Books

De Groot, W. Herman. *Sulphonation Technology in the Detergent Industry.* Kluwer Academic Publishers, 1991.

Periodicals and Pamphlets

Marbach, William D. "Cleaner Clothes from Worms." *Business Week.* December 7, 1992, p. 123.

Pinder, Jeanne B. "Laundry Detergent Takes Formula from Nature." *New York Times.* March 10, 1993, p. C3 (N).

Smith, Emily T. "Fungus around the Collar Could Clean Up Lipstick Stains." *Business Week.* February 15, 1988, p. 107.

Soaps and Detergents. The Soap and Detergent Association, 1981.

—*Lawrence H. Berlow*

Lawn Mower

The first mechanical grass-cutting device was developed in 1830 by Edwin Budding, who created two sizes: large and small. The large mower had to be drawn by horses, whose hooves were temporarily shod with rubber boots to prevent them from damaging the turf; the head gardener at the London Zoo was among the first to purchase this model.

Background

The lawn mower is a mechanical device that literally shaves the surface of the grass by using a rapidly rotating blade or blades.

For centuries, grass was cut by workers who walked through pastures or fields wielding small, sharp scythes. In addition to being tiring and slow, manual cutting was ineffective—the scythes worked well only when the grass was wet. The first mechanical grass-cutting device appeared in 1830, when an English textile worker named Edwin Budding developed a mower allegedly based on a textile machine used to shear the nap off of cloth. Budding's cylindrical mower was attached to a rear roller that propelled it with a chain drive, and it shaved grass with a curved cutting edge attached to the cylinder. He created two sizes, large and small. The large mower had to be drawn by horses, whose hooves were temporarily shod with rubber boots to prevent them from damaging the turf; the head gardener at the London Zoo was among the first to purchase this model. Budding marketed the smaller mower to country gentlemen, who would, he claimed, "find in [his] machine an amusing, useful and healthful exercise."

Mechanized grass cutting was evidently slow to catch on, perhaps because Budding's mower was quite heavy in addition to being inefficiently geared. Only two lawn mower manufacturers exhibited their machines at England's Great Exhibition in 1851. However, several decades later the new machines experienced a surge in popularity due to the interest in lawn tennis that arose in England during the late Victorian period. Before the turn of the century, Budding's initial designs were improved. Weighing considerably less than their predecessors and based on the side wheel design still used in today's most popular mowers, these refined machines were soon visible in yards throughout England.

The earliest gas-driven lawn mowers were designed in 1897 by the Benz Company of Germany and the Coldwell Lawn Mower Company of New York. Two years later an English company developed its own model; however, none of these companies mass produced their designs. In 1902 the first commercially produced power mower, designed by James Edward Ransome, was manufactured and sold. Although Ransome's mower featured a passenger seat, most early mowers did not, and even today the most popular models are pushed from behind.

Power mowers are presently available in four basic designs: the rotary mower, the power reel mower, the riding mower, and the tractor. Because the rotary mower is by far the most common, it is the focus of this entry. Pushed from behind, rotary mowers feature a single rotating blade enclosed in a case and supported by wheels. As the engine turns, it spins the blade. The blade whirls at 3,000 revolutions per minute, virtually 19,000 feet (5,800 meters) per minute at the tip of the blade where the cutting actually occurs. The best rotaries feature a horn of plenty (cornucopia) or wind tunnel shape curving around the front of the housing and ending at the discharge chute through which the mown grass flies out. Self-propelled models are driven by a chain or belt connected to the engine's drive shaft. A gearbox usually turns a horizontal axle which in turn rotates the wheels. Some models have a big chain- or belt-driven movable unit that rises up off and settles down on the wheels.

The power reel mower features several blades attached at both ends to drums that are attached to wheels. The coupled engine drive shaft that spins the reel can also be rigged to propel the mower, if desired. Overlapping the grass, this machine's five to seven blades pull it against a cutting bar at the bottom of the mower. Then one or more rollers smooth and compact the clippings as the mower goes over them. Reel mowers are more efficient than rotary mowers because the latter actually use only the end of the blade to do most of the cutting, whereas the fixed blades in a reel mower cut with the entire length of both edges. However, rotary mowers are easier to manufacture because the basic design is simpler, and they are also favored over reel mowers on most types of turf. By industry estimates, most of the 40 million mowers in use on any given summer Saturday are rotary mowers.

Raw Materials

The typical gas-powered walk-behind mower may have as many as 270 individual parts, including a technologically advanced two- or four-cycle engine, a variety of machined and formed parts, various subassemblies purchased from outside contractors, and many pieces of standard hardware. Most of these pieces are metal, including the major components: mower pan, handlebar, engine, and blades. A few, however, are made of plastic, such as side discharge chutes, covers, and plugs.

The Manufacturing Process

Manufacturing the conventional rotary lawn mower requires precision inventory control, strategic placement of parts and personnel, and synchronization of people and tasks. In some instances, robotic cells are used in conjunction with a trained labor force.

Unloading and distributing the components

1 Trucked into the plant's loading dock, the components are moved by forklifts or overhead trolleys to other centers for forming, machining, painting, or, if they require no additional work upon arrival, assembly.

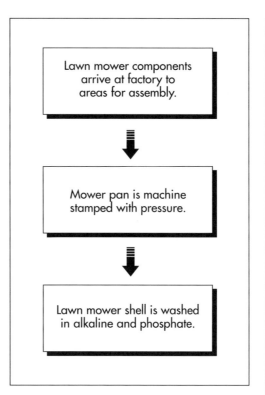

The mower pan

2 The steel mower pan, the largest single part and one used in various models, is first machine-stamped under great heat and pressure. The pan is then transported to a robotic cell, where a plasma cutter creates apertures in it. The term *plasma* refers to any of a number of gases (argon is commonly used) that can be raised to high temperature and highly ionized by being passed through a constricted electrical arc. When directed through the narrow opening of a torch, this hot, ionized gas can be used for both cutting and welding.

3 After other elements such as baffles (deflecting plates) are welded on, the finished pan and a number of other exposed parts are powder painted in a sealed room. Powder painting entails thoroughly washing the parts in alkaline and phosphate solutions and rinsing them to seal the surfaces. The parts are then attached to overhead conveyors and run through a **paint** booth. Fine paint particles are sprayed from a gun that imbues them with an electrostatic charge—opposite to the charge given to the part being painted—that causes the paint to adhere to the surface of the parts evenly. Next, the parts are baked in ovens to produce a permanently fixed, enamel-like coating. The pan

After arrival at the factory, the various parts are formed, painted, and assembled. The mower pan is machine-stamped before undergoing plasma cutting, which creates apertures in the pan. Other parts are welded to the pan, and then the entire shell is prepared for an electrostatic paint coating.

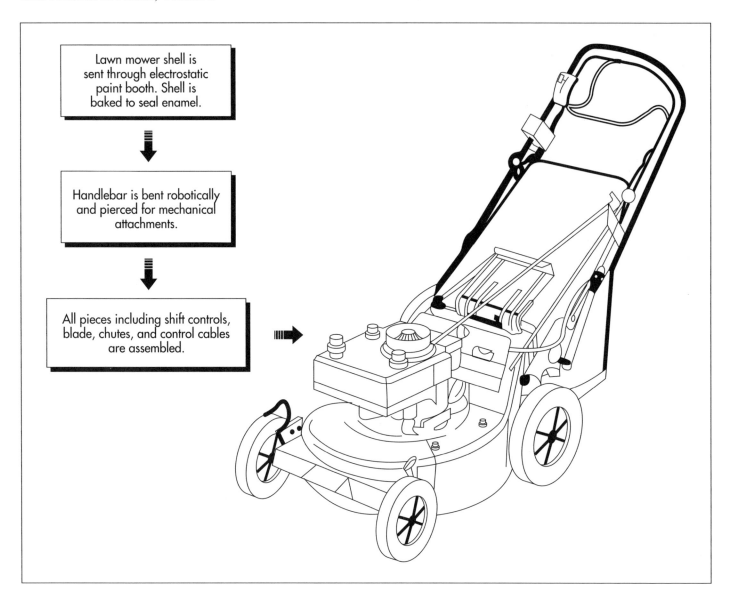

Lawn mower shell is sent through electrostatic paint booth. Shell is baked to seal enamel.

Handlebar is bent robotically and pierced for mechanical attachments.

All pieces including shift controls, blade, chutes, and control cables are assembled.

The shell is painted electrostatically and then baked to seal the paint. Meanwhile, the handlebar is bent and pierced by robots, and then the remaining components are assembled.

and other parts are now ready to withstand years of exposure to corrosive grass fluids and the constant peppering from dirt and debris kicked up in the cutting process.

Shaping the handlebar

4 The handlebar is created in a robotic cell whose mechanical arms perform three operations. In a bender, the tubing is first bent in at least four places. A second press operation flattens the ends, and a third pierces fourteen or so round and square holes in the tubing. These holes will accommodate the starting mechanism, blade and wheel drive control, and the pan attachment. The finished handlebar is then transported to a subassembly station, where many of the controls are added.

Other subassemblies

5 The other major subassemblies are also created at various plant centers using formed, machined, or purchased materials and standard hardware. Parts purchased from outside suppliers include engines built to manufacturer's physical and performance specifications, **tire**s, shift mechanisms, wiring harnesses, and bearings. Injection-molded plastic parts are purchased for use in side discharge chutes, covers, and plugs. Injection molding refers to a process in which molten plastic is squirted into a mold and then allowed to cool. As it cools, the plastic assumes the shape of the mold.

6 Assembly teams put the six or more major subassemblies together on a rolling line at a pace determined by the task and

skills required. The engine is first placed upside down in a frame fixture, and the mower pan is bolted down along with the drive mechanism. Then come the rear axle, brackets, and rods to secure the shift controls. The blade and accompanying clutch wheels and parts are fastened to the engine through the pan opening with preset air-driven torque wrenches. After another team member adds hardware and wheels, the unit is flipped onto its wheels. The handlebar is attached, and control cables are secured and set. Finally, the mower—each mower—is performance-tested before shipment to dealers, where some final set-up adjustments are made.

Quality Control

Inspectors monitor the manufacturing process throughout the production run, checking fits, seams, tolerances, and finishes. In particular, the paint operation is scrutinized. Samples of each painted part are regularly pulled off the line for ultrasonic testing, a process that utilizes the corrosion activity created in a salt bath to simulate 450 hours of continuous exposure to the natural environment. Painted parts are also scribed and the deterioration of the exposed surface watched for tell-tale signs of rust. If needed, the paint or cleaning cycles are adjusted to assure high quality and durable finishes.

Final performance testing—the last step in the assembly sequence—guarantees reliability and safety for users. A small quantity of a gas/oil mixture is added to each engine. A technician cranks the engine and checks its rpm with a gauge; drive elements and safety switches are also checked. As required by current Consumer Product Safety Commission regulations, the mower blade, when running, must stop within three seconds after the control handle is released.

The Future

Like many other machines, the lawn mower will benefit from the development of new and more efficient power sources. A recent invention is the solar-powered lawn mower, which uses energy from the sun rather than gasoline as fuel. It needs no tuneups or oil changes, and it operates very quietly. Perhaps its biggest drawback is the amount of energy its **battery** can store: only enough for two hours of cutting, which must be followed by three days of charging. However, as batteries with more storage capabilities are developed, this drawback will disappear.

Where To Learn More

Books

Davidson, Homer L. *Care and Repair of Lawn and Garden Tools*. TAB Books, 1992.

Hall, Walter. *Parp's Guide to Garden and Power Tools*. Rodale Press, 1983.

Nunn, Richard. *Lawn Mowers and Garden Equipment*. Creative Homeowner Press, 1984.

Peterson, F. *Handbook of Lawn Mower Repair*. Putnam, 1984.

Periodicals

Buderi, Robert. "Now, You Can Mow the Lawn from Your Hammock." *Business Week*. May 14, 1990, p. 64.

"Robo-Mower." *The Futurist*. January-February, 1989, p. 39.

Kimber, Robert. "Pushing toward Safety: The Evolution of Lawn-Mower Design." *Horticulture*. May, 1990, p. 70.

Murray, Charles J. "Riding Mower's Design Reduces Turning Radius." *Design News*. April 5, 1993, p. 81.

Smith, Emily T. "A Lawn Mower That Gets Its Power from the Sun." *Business Week*. February 11, 1991, p. 80.

—*Peter Toeg*

Light Bulb

On October 19, 1879, Thomas Edison ran his first test of this new lamp. It ran for two days and 40 hours; October 21—the day the filament finally burned out—is the usual date given for the invention of the first commercially practical lamp.

Background

From the earliest periods of history until the beginning of the 19th century, fire was man's primary source of light. This light was produced through different means—torches, **candle**s, oil and gas lamps. Besides the danger presented by an open flame (especially when used indoors), these sources of light also provided insufficient illumination.

The first attempts at using electric light were made by English chemist Sir Humphry Davy. In 1802, Davy showed that electric currents could heat thin strips of metal to white heat, thus producing light. This was the beginning of incandescent (defined as glowing with intense heat) electric light. The next major development was the arc light. This was basically two electrodes, usually made of carbon, separated from each other by a short air space. Electric current applied to one of the electrodes flowed to and through the other electrode resulting in an arc of light across the air space. Arc lamps (or light bulbs) were used mainly in outdoor lighting; the race was still on among a large group of scientists to discover a useful source of indoor illumination.

The primary difficulty holding back the development of a commercially viable incandescent light was finding suitable glowing elements. Davy found that platinum was the only metal that could produce white heat for any length of time. Carbon was also used, but it oxidized quickly in air. The answer was to develop a vacuum that would keep air away from the elements, thus preserving the light-producing materials.

Thomas A. Edison, a young inventor working in Menlo Park, New Jersey, began working on his own form of electric light in the 1870s. In 1877 Edison became involved with the rush for a satisfactory electric light source, devoting his initial involvement to confirming the reasons for his competitors' failures. He did, however, determine that platinum made a much better burner than carbon. Working with platinum, Edison obtained his first patent in April of 1879 on a relatively impractical lamp, but he continued searching for an element that could be heated efficiently and economically.

Edison also tinkered with the other components of the lighting system, including building his own power source and devising a breakthrough wiring system that could handle a number of lamps burning at the same time. His most important discovery, however, was the invention of a suitable filament. This was a very thin, threadlike wire that offered high resistance to the passage of electric currents. Most of the early filaments burned out very quickly, thus rendering these lamps commercially useless. To solve this problem, Edison began again to try carbon as a means of illumination.

He finally selected carbonized cotton thread as his filament material. The filament was clamped to platinum wires that would carry current to and from the filament. This assembly was then placed in a glass bulb that was fused at the neck (called *sealing-in*). A vacuum pump removed the air from the bulb, a slow but crucial step. Lead-in wires that would be connected to the electrical current protruded from the glass bulb.

On October 19, 1879, Edison ran his first test of this new lamp. It ran for two days and 40 hours (October 21—the day the filament finally burned out—is the usual date given for the invention of the first commercially practical lamp). Of course, this original lamp underwent a number of revisions. Manufacturing plants were set up to mass produce light bulbs and great advances were made in wiring and electrical current systems. However, today's incandescent light bulbs greatly resemble Edison's original lamps. The major differences are the use of tungsten filaments, various gases for higher efficiency and increased lumination resulting from filaments heated to higher temperatures.

Although the incandescent lamp was the first and certainly the least expensive type of light bulb, there are a host of other light bulbs that serve myriad uses:

- Tungsten halogen lamps

- Fluorescent lamps are glass tubes that contain mercury vapor and argon gas. When electricity flows through the tube, it causes the vaporized mercury to give off ultraviolet energy. This energy then strikes phosphors that coat the inside of the lamp, giving off visible light.

- Mercury vapor lamps have two bulbs—the arc tube (made of quartz) is inside a protecting glass bulb. The arc tube contains mercury vapor at a higher pressure than that of the fluorescent lamp, thus allowing the vapor lamp to produce light without using the phosphor coating.

- Neon lamps are glass tubes, filled with neon gas, that glow when an electric discharge takes place in them. The color of the light is determined by the gas mixture; pure neon gas gives off red light.

- Metal halide lamps, used primarily outdoors for stadiums and roadways, contain chemical compounds of metal and halogen. This type of lamp works in much the same fashion as the mercury vapor lamps except that metal halide can produce a more natural color balance when used without phosphors.

- High-pressure sodium lamps are also similar to mercury vapor lamps; however, the arc tube is made of aluminum oxide instead of quartz, and it contains a solid mixture of sodium and mercury.

Thomas A. Edison (center, with cap) with workers in his laboratory in Menlo Park, New Jersey. The photo was taken in 1880.

More than twenty inventors, dating back to the 1830s, had produced incandescent electric lights by the time Thomas Edison entered the search. The 1870s was the crucial decade, as the technologies of production and the forces of demand combined to make the search for a commercially feasible electric light the high-tech, high-stakes race of the era. Edison had established his research laboratory in rural Menlo Park, New Jersey, midway between New York City and Philadelphia. The laboratory building and several outbuildings were constructed in 1876 with profits Edison had made with his telegraph inventions. He initially intended to take projects from any investor who wanted his help and to continue working on his own ideas in telegraph and telephone systems. He said he thought the laboratory could produce a new invention every ten days and a major breakthrough every six months.

In 1877, Edison decided to enter the highly publicized race for a successful light bulb and enlarged his laboratory facilities with a machine shop and an office and research library. The staff grew from 12 to over 60 as Edison tackled the entire lighting system, from generator to insulator to incandescent bulb. Along the way, Edison created a new process of invention, orchestrating a team approach that brought financing, materials, tools, and skilled workers together into an "invention factory." Thus, the search for the light bulb illustrated new forms of research and development that were later developed by General Electric, Westinghouse, and other companies.

William S. Pretzer

Raw Materials

This section as well as the following one (The Manufacturing Process) will focus on incandescent light bulbs. As mentioned earlier, many different materials were used for the filament until tungsten became the metal of choice during the early part of the twentieth century. Although extremely fragile,

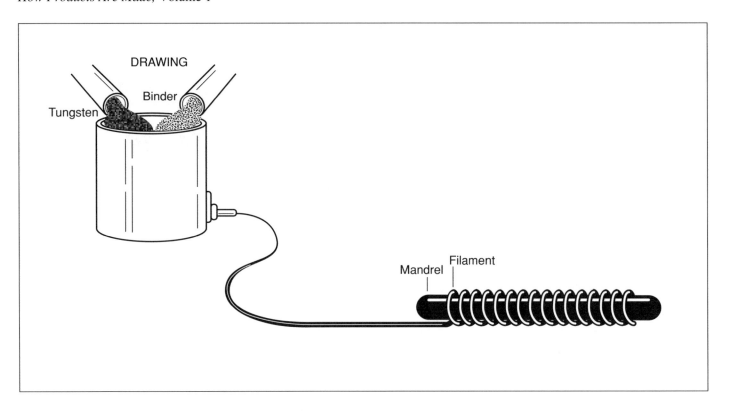

One of the main components in a light bulb, the filament, is prepared by mixing tungsten and binder and then drawing the mixture into a fine wire around a steel mandrel. After heating the wire and then dissolving the mandrel with acid, the filament assumes its proper coiled shape.

tungsten filaments can withstand temperatures as high as 4500 degrees Fahrenheit (2480 degrees Celsius) and above. The development of the tungsten filaments is considered the greatest advancement in light bulb technology because these filaments could be produced cheaply and last longer than any of the previous materials.

The connecting or lead-in wires are typically made of nickel-iron wire (called *dumet* because it uses two metals). This wire is dipped into a borax solution to make the wire more adherent to glass. The bulb itself is made of glass and contains a mixture of gases, usually argon and nitrogen, which increase the life of the filament. Air is pumped out of the bulb and replaced with the gases. A standardized base holds the entire assembly in place. The base, known as the "Edison screw base," was originally made of brass and insulated with plaster of paris and, later, **porcelain**. Today, aluminum is used on the outside and glass is used to insulate the inside of the base, producing a stronger base.

The Manufacturing Process

The uses of light bulbs range from street lights to **automobile** headlights to flashlights. For each use, the individual bulb dif-

fers in size and wattage, which determine the amount of light the bulb gives off (*lumens*). However, all incandescent light bulbs have the three basic parts—the filament, the bulb and the base. Originally produced by hand, the light bulb manufacture is now almost entirely automated.

Filament

1 The filament is manufactured through a process known as *drawing*, in which tungsten is mixed with a binder material and pulled through a die—a shaped orifice—into a fine wire. Next, the wire is wound around a metal bar called a *mandrel* in order to mold it into its proper coiled shape, and then it is heated in an process known as *annealing*. This process softens the wire and makes its structure more uniform. The mandrel is then dissolved in acid.

2 The coiled filament is attached to the lead-in wires. The lead-in wires have hooks at their ends which are either pressed over the end of the filament or, in larger bulbs, spot-welded.

Glass bulb

3 The glass bulbs or casings are produced using a ribbon machine. After heating in

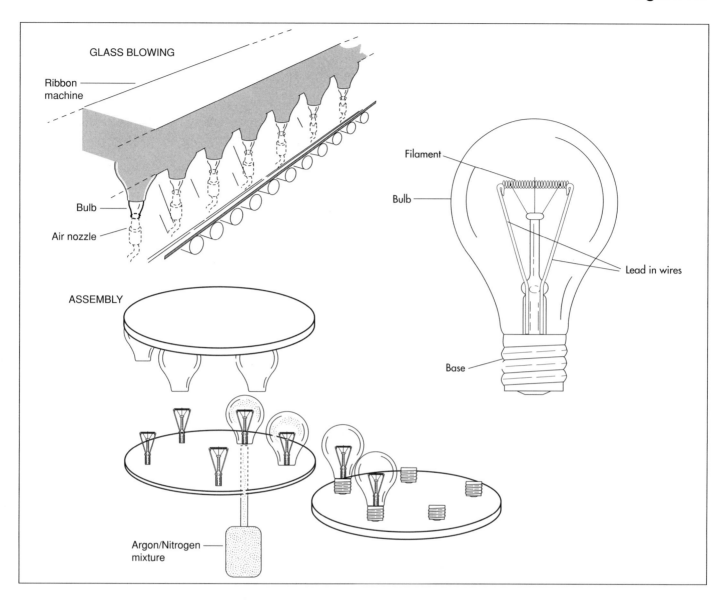

GLASS BLOWING

Ribbon machine

Bulb

Air nozzle

ASSEMBLY

Argon/Nitrogen mixture

Filament

Bulb

Lead in wires

Base

a furnace, a continuous ribbon of glass moves along a conveyor belt. Precisely aligned air nozzles blow the glass through holes in the conveyor belt into molds, creating the casings. A ribbon machine moving at top speed can produce more than 50,000 bulbs per hour. After the casings are blown, they are cooled and then cut off of the ribbon machine. Next, the inside of the bulb is coated with silica to remove the glare caused by a glowing, uncovered filament. The company emblem and bulb wattage are then stamped onto the outside top of each casing.

Base

4 The base of the bulb is also constructed using molds. It is made with indentations in the shape of a screw so that it can easily fit into the socket of a light fixture.

Assembly

5 Once the filament, base, and bulb are made, they are fitted together by machines. First, the filament is mounted to the stem assembly, with its ends clamped to the two lead-in wires. Next, the air inside the bulb is evacuated, and the casing is filled with an argon and nitrogen mixture. These gases ensure a longer-life for the filament. The tungsten will eventually evaporate and break. As it evaporates, it leaves a dark deposit on the bulb known as *bulb-wall blackening.*

6 Finally, the base and the bulb are sealed. The base slides onto the end of the glass bulb such that no other material is needed to keep them together. Instead, their conforming shapes allow the two pieces to be held

Virtually the entire light bulb manufacturing process is automated. The glass bulbs are blown by a ribbon machine that can produce more than 50,000 bulbs per hour. After the filament and stem assembly are inserted into the bulb, the air inside the bulb is evacuated and an argon/nitrogen mixture is pumped in. Finally, the base is sealed on.

together snugly, with the lead-in wires touching the aluminum base to ensure proper electrical contact. After testing, bulbs are placed in their packages and shipped to consumers.

Quality Control

Light bulbs are tested for both lamp life and strength. In order to provide quick results, selected bulbs are screwed into life test racks and lit at levels far exceeding their normal burning strength. This provides an accurate reading on how long the bulb will last under normal conditions. Testing is performed at all manufacturing plants as well as at some independent testing facilities. The average life of the majority of household light bulbs is 750 to 1000 hours, depending on wattage.

The Future

The future of the incandescent light bulb is uncertain. While heating a filament until it glows is certainly a satisfactory way to produce light, it is extremely inefficient: about 95 percent of the electricity supplied to a typical light bulb is converted to heat, not light. In a world with dwindling resources, where energy conservation is increasingly vital, this inefficiency may eventually make the incandescent light bulb impractical.

There are other light sources already in use that could supplant the incandescent bulb. Fluorescent tubes, for instance, already dominate the industrial market, and undoubtedly they will find increasing use as a domestic light source as well. Fluorescent bulbs use at least 75 percent less energy than incandescent bulbs and can last twenty times longer. The recent development of "compact" fluo-

rescent bulbs, which unlike the standard fluorescent tube can screw into a typical domestic lamp, may expand the domestic market for fluorescent lighting.

Another recent development is the "radio-wave bulb," a bulb that creates light by transmitting energy from a radio-wave generator to a mercury cloud, which in turn produces ultraviolet light. A phosphor coating on the bulb then converts the ultraviolet light into visible light. Such bulbs use only 25 percent as much energy as incandescent bulbs, and they can last a decade or more. They are also completely interchangeable with incandescent bulbs.

Where To Learn More

Books

Friedel, Robert. *Edison's Electric Light: Biography of an Invention.* Rutgers University Press, 1987.

Periodicals

Adler, Jerry. "At Last, Another Bright Idea." *Newsweek.* June 15, 1992, p. 67.

Coy, Peter. "Light Bulbs to Make America Really Stingy with the Juice." *Business Week.* March 29, 1993, p. 91.

Miller, William H. "The 20-Year Light Bulb Clicks On." *Industry Week.* November 16, 1992, p. 41.

Pargh, Andy. "Light Bulbs Shed New Light." *Design News.* June 22, 1992, p. 164.

—*Jim Acton*

Light–Emitting Diode (LED)

Background

Light–emitting diodes (LEDs)—small colored lights available in any electronics store—are ubiquitous in modern society. They are the indicator lights on our stereos, **automobile** dashboards, and **microwave ovens**. Numeric displays on clock radios, digital **watch**es, and calculators are composed of bars of LEDs. LEDs also find applications in telecommunications for short range optical signal transmission such as TV remote controls. They have even found their way into jewelry and clothing—witness sun visors with a series of blinking colored lights adorning the brim. The inventors of the LED had no idea of the revolutionary item they were creating. They were trying to make lasers, but on the way they discovered a substitute for the **light bulb**.

Light bulbs are really just wires attached to a source of energy. They emit light because the wire heats up and gives off some of its heat energy in the form of light. An LED, on the other hand, emits light by electronic excitation rather than heat generation. Diodes are electrical valves that allow electrical current to flow in only one direction, just as a one-way valve might in a water pipe. When the valve is "on," electrons move from a region of high electronic density to a region of low electronic density. This movement of electrons is accompanied by the emission of light. The more electrons that get passed across the boundary between layers, known as a junction, the brighter the light. This phenomenon, known as *electroluminescence*, was observed as early as 1907. Before working LEDs could be made, however, cleaner and more efficient materials had to be developed.

LEDs were developed during the post-World War II era; during the war there was a potent interest in materials for light and microwave detectors. A variety of semiconductor materials were developed during this research effort, and their light interaction properties were investigated in some detail. During the 1950s, it became clear that the same materials that were used to detect light could also be used to generate light. Researchers at AT&T Bell Laboratories were the first to exploit the light-generating properties of these new materials in the 1960s. The LED was a forerunner, and a fortuitous byproduct, of the laser development effort. The tiny colored lights held some interest for industry, because they had advantages over light bulbs of a similar size: LEDs use less power, have longer lifetimes, produce little heat, and emit colored light.

The first LEDs were not as reliable or as useful as those sold today. Frequently, they could only operate at the temperature of liquid nitrogen (-104 degrees Fahrenheit or -77 degrees Celsius) or below, and would burn out in only a few hours. They gobbled power because they were very inefficient, and they produced very little light. All of these problems can be attributed to a lack of reliable techniques for producing the appropriate materials in the 1950s and 1960s, and as a result the devices made from them were poor. When materials were improved, other advances in the technology followed: methods for connecting the devices electronically, enlarging the diodes, making them brighter, and generating more colors.

The advantages of the LED over the light bulb for applications requiring a small light source encouraged manufacturers like Texas Instru-

Sudden widespread market acceptance in the 1970s was the result of the reduction in production costs and also of clever marketing, which made products with LED displays (such as watches) seem "high tech" and, therefore, desirable.

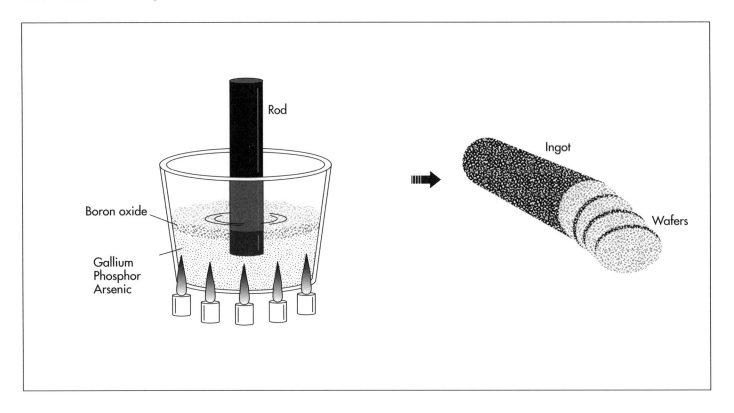

To make the semiconductor wafers, gallium, arsenic, and/or phosphor are first mixed together in a chamber and forced into a solution. To keep them from escaping into the pressurized gas in the chamber, they are often covered with a layer of liquid boron oxide. Next, a rod is dipped into the solution and pulled out slowly. The solution cools and crystallizes on the end of the rod as it is lifted out of the chamber, forming a long, cylindrical crystal ingot. The ingot is then sliced into wafers.

ments and Hewlett Packard to pursue the commercial manufacture of LEDs. Sudden widespread market acceptance in the 1970s was the result of the reduction in production costs and also of clever marketing, which made products with LED displays (such as watches) seem "high tech" and, therefore, desirable. Manufacturers were able to produce many LEDs in a row to create a variety of displays for use on clocks, scientific instruments, and computer card readers. The technology is still developing today as manufacturers seek ways to make the devices more efficiently, less expensively, and in more colors.

Raw Materials

Diodes, in general, are made of very thin layers of semiconductor material; one layer will have an excess of electrons, while the next will have a deficit of electrons. This difference causes electrons to move from one layer to another, thereby generating light. Manufacturers can now make these layers as thin as .5 micron or less (1 micron = 1 ten-thousandth of an inch).

Impurities within the semiconductor are used to create the required electron density. A semiconductor is a crystalline material that conducts electricity only when there is a high density of impurities in it. The slice, or

wafer, of semiconductor is a single uniform crystal, and the impurities are introduced later during the manufacturing process. Think of the wafer as a cake that is mixed and baked in a prescribed manner, and impurities as nuts suspended in the cake. The particular semiconductors used for LED manufacture are gallium arsenide (GaAs), gallium phosphide (GaP), or gallium arsenide phosphide (GaAsP). The different semiconductor materials (called *substrates*) and different impurities result in different colors of light from the LED.

Impurities, the nuts in the cake, are introduced later in the manufacturing process; unlike imperfections, they are introduced deliberately to make the LED function correctly. This process is called *doping*. The impurities commonly added are zinc or nitrogen, but silicon, germanium, and tellurium have also been used. As mentioned previously, they will cause the semiconductor to conduct electricity and will make the LED function as an electronic device. It is through the impurities that a layer with an excess or a deficit of electrons can be created.

To complete the device, it is necessary to bring electricity to it and from it. Thus, wires must be attached onto the substrate. These wires must stick well to the semiconductor and be strong enough to withstand subse-

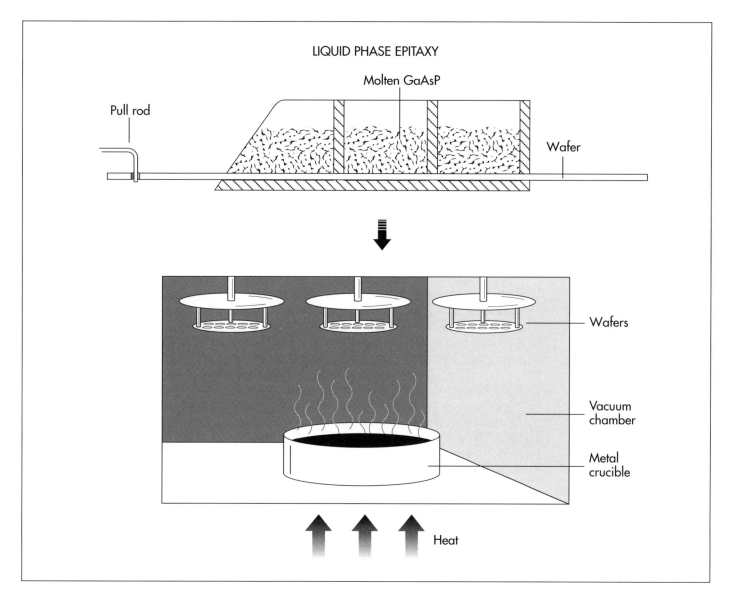

LIQUID PHASE EPITAXY

Pull rod

Molten GaAsP

Wafer

Wafers

Vacuum chamber

Metal crucible

Heat

quent processing such as soldering and heating. **Gold** and silver compounds are most commonly used for this purpose, because they form a chemical bond with the gallium at the surface of the wafer.

LEDs are encased in transparent plastic, rather like the lucite paperweights that have objects suspended in them. The plastic can be any of a number of varieties, and its exact optical properties will determine what the output of the LED looks like. Some plastics are diffusive, which means the light will scatter in many directions. Some are transparent, and can be shaped into lenses that will direct the light straight out from the LED in a narrow beam. The plastics can be tinted, which will change the color of the LED by allowing more or less of light of a particular color to pass through.

Design

Several features of the LED need to be considered in its design, since it is both an electronic and an optic device. Desirable optical properties such as color, brightness, and efficiency must be optimized without an unreasonable electrical or physical design. These properties are affected by the size of the diode, the exact semiconductor materials used to make it, the thickness of the diode layers, and the type and amount of impurities used to "dope" the semiconductor.

The Manufacturing Process

Making semiconductor wafers

1 First, a semiconductor wafer is made. The particular material composition—GaAs,

One way to add the necessary impurities to the semiconductor crystal is to grow additional layers of crystal onto the wafer surface. In this process, known as "Liquid Phase Epitaxy," the wafer is put on a graphite slide and passed underneath reservoirs of molten GaAsP.

Contact patterns are exposed on the wafer's surface using photoresist, after which the wafers are put into a heated vacuum chamber. Here, molten metal is evaporated onto the contact pattern on the wafer surface.

GaP, or something in between—is determined by the color of LED being fabricated. The crystalline semiconductor is grown in a high temperature, high pressure chamber. Gallium, arsenic, and/or phosphor are purified and mixed together in the chamber. The heat and pressure liquify and press the components together so that they are forced into a solution. To keep them from escaping into the pressurized gas in the chamber, they are often covered with a layer of liquid boron oxide, which seals them off so that they must "stick together." This is known as *liquid encapsulation*, or the *Czochralski crystal growth method*. After the elements are mixed in a uniform solution, a rod is dipped into the solution and pulled out slowly. The solution cools and crystallizes on the end of the rod as it is lifted out of the chamber, forming a long, cylindrical crystal ingot (or *boule*) of GaAs, GaP, or GaAsP. Think of this as baking the cake.

2 The boule is then sliced into very thin wafers of semiconductor, approximately 10 mils thick, or about as thick as a garbage bag. The wafers are polished until the surfaces are very smooth, so that they will readily accept more layers of semiconductor on their surface. The principle is similar to sanding a table before painting it. Each wafer should be a single crystal of material of uniform composition. Unfortunately, there will sometimes be imperfections in the crystals that make the LED function poorly. Think of imperfections as unmixed bits of flower or **sugar** suspended in the cake during baking. Imperfections can also result from the polishing process; such imperfections also degrade device performance. The more imperfections, the less the wafer behaves like a single crystal; without a regular crystalline structure, the material will not function as a semiconductor.

3 Next, the wafers are cleaned through a rigorous chemical and ultrasonic process using various solvents. This process removes dirt, dust, or organic matter that may have settled on the polished wafer surface. The cleaner the processing, the better the resulting LED will be.

Adding epitaxial layers

4 Additional layers of semiconductor crystal are grown on the surface of the wafer, like adding more layers to the cake. This is one way to add impurities, or dopants, to the crystal. The crystal layers are grown this time by a process called *Liquid Phase Epitaxy* (LPE). In this technique, epitaxial layers—semiconductor layers that have the same crystalline orientation as the substrate below—are deposited on a wafer while it is drawn under reservoirs of molten GaAsP. The reservoirs have appropriate dopants mixed through them. The wafer rests on a graphite slide, which is pushed through a channel under a container holding the molten liquid (or *melt*, as it is called). Different dopants can be added in sequential melts, or several in the same melt, creating layers of material with different electronic densities. The deposited layers will become a continuation of the wafer's crystal structure.

LPE creates an exceptionally uniform layer of material, which makes it a preferred growth and doping technique. The layers formed are several microns thick.

5 After depositing epitaxial layers, it may be necessary to add additional dopants to alter the characteristics of the diode for color or efficiency. If additional doping is done, the wafer is again placed in a high temperature furnace tube, where it is immersed in a gaseous atmosphere containing the dopants—nitrogen or zinc ammonium are the most common. Nitrogen is often added to the top layer of the diode to make the light more yellow or green.

Adding metal contacts

6 Metal contacts are then defined on the wafer. The contact pattern is determined in the design stage and depends on whether the diodes are to be used singly or in combination. Contact patterns are reproduced in photoresist, a light-sensitive compound; the liquid resist is deposited in drops while the wafer spins, distributing it over the surface. The resist is hardened by a brief, low temperature baking (about 215 degrees Fahrenheit or 100 degrees Celsius). Next, the master pattern, or mask, is duplicated on the photoresist by placing it over the wafer and exposing the resist with ultraviolet light (the same way a photograph is made from a negative). Exposed areas of the resist are washed away with developer, and unexposed areas remain, covering the semiconductor layers.

7 Contact metal is now evaporated onto the pattern, filling in the exposed areas. Evaporation takes place in another high temperature chamber, this time vacuum sealed. A chunk of metal is heated to temperatures that cause it to vaporize. It condenses and sticks to the exposed semiconductor wafer, much like steam will fog a cold window. The photoresist can then be washed away with acetone, leaving only the metal contacts behind. Depending on the final mounting scheme for the LED, an additional layer of metal may be evaporated on the back side of the wafer. Any deposited metal must undergo an annealing process, in which the wafer is heated to several hundred degrees and allowed to remain in a furnace (with an inert atmosphere of hydrogen or nitrogen flowing through it) for periods up to several hours. During this time, the metal and the semiconductor bond together chemically so the contacts don't flake off.

8 A single 2 inch-diameter wafer produced in this manner will have the same pattern repeated up to 6000 times on it; this gives an indication of the size of the finished diodes. The diodes are cut apart either by cleaving (snapping the wafer along a crystal plane) or by sawing with a diamond saw. Each small segment cut from the wafer is called a die. A difficult and error prone process, cutting results in far less than 6000 total useable LEDs and is one of the biggest challenges in limiting production costs of semiconductor devices.

Mounting and packaging

9 Individual dies are mounted on the appropriate package. If the diode will be used by itself as an indicator light or for jewelry, for example, it is mounted on two metal leads about two inches long. Usually, in this case, the back of the wafer is coated with metal and forms an electrical contact with the lead it rests on. A tiny gold wire is soldered to the other lead and wire-bonded to the patterned contacts on the surface of the die. In wire bonding, the end of the wire is pressed down on the contact metal with a very fine needle. The gold is soft enough to deform and stick to a like metal surface.

10 Finally, the entire assembly is sealed in plastic. The wires and die are suspended inside a mold that is shaped accord-

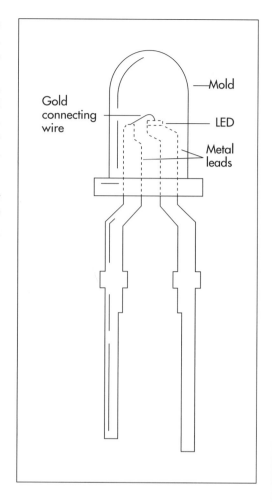

Gold connecting wire — Mold — LED — Metal leads

ing to the optical requirements of the package (with a lens or connector at the end), and the mold is filled with liquid plastic or epoxy. The epoxy is cured, and the package is complete.

Quality Control

Quality in semiconductor manufacturing takes two forms. The first concern is with the final produced product, and the second with the manufacturing facility. Every LED is checked when it is wire bonded for operation characteristics. Specific levels of current should produce specific brightness. Exact light color is tested for each batch of wafers, and some LEDs will be pulled for stress testing, including lifetime tests, heat and power breakdown, and mechanical damage.

In order to produce products consistently, the manufacturing line has to operate reliably and safely. Many of the processing steps above can be automated, but not all are. The general cleanliness of the facility and incoming blank wafers is monitored closely. Spe-

A typical LED indicator light shows how small the actual LED is. Although the average lifetime of a small light bulb is 5-10 years, a modern LED should last 100 years or more before it fails.

cial facilities ("clean rooms") are built that keep the air pure up to one part in 10,000 for particular processing steps (particularly numbers 1-5 above). All of these checks arise from a desire to improve the yield, or the number of successful LEDs per wafer.

The Future

Optoelectronics is blossoming with the advent of better and better processing techniques. It is now possible to make wafers with a purity and uniformity unheard of 5 years ago. This will effect how bright and how efficient LEDs can be made, and how long they will last. As they get better, they are appropriate for increasingly demanding applications, such as communications. The average lifetime of a small light bulb is 5-10 years, but the average modern LED should last 100 years before failure. This makes them suitable for applications where it is difficult or impossible to replace parts, such as undersea or outerspace electronics. Although LEDs are inappropriate for long-range **optical fiber** transmission, they are often useful for short range optical transmission such as remote controls, chip to chip communication, or excitation of optical amplifiers.

Other materials are being developed that will allow fabrication of blue and white light LEDs. In addition to making possible a wider variety of indicators and toys with more colors, blue light is preferable for some applications such as optical storage and visual displays. Blue and white light are easier on the eyes. Additional colors would certainly open up new applications.

Finally, as process technology advances and it becomes possible to incorporate more devices on a single chip, LED displays will become more "intelligent." A single microchip will hold all the electronics to cre-

ate an alphanumeric display, and will make instrumentation smaller and more sophisticated.

Where To Learn More

Books

Bergh, A. A. and P. J Dean. *Light–Emitting Diodes.* Clarendon Press, 1976.

Gillessen, Klaus. *Light–Emitting Diodes: An Introduction.* Prentice Hall, 1987.

Optoelectronics/Fiber-Optics Applications Manual. McGraw-Hill, 1981.

Understanding Solid State Electronics. Radio Shack/Texas Instruments Learning Center, 1978.

Williams, E. W. and R. Hall. *Luminescence and the Light–Emitting Diode.* Pergamon Press, 1978.

Periodicals

Cole, Bernard C. "Now a LED Can Take On the Light Bulb." *Electronics.* October, 1988, p. 41.

Iversen, Wesley R. "Would You Believe LED Brake Lights." *Electronics.* September 18, 1986.

Marston, Ray. "Working with LED's." *Radio-Electronics.* January, 1992, p. 50; February, 1992, p. 69.

Weisburd, Stefi. "Silicon Devices: LED There Be Light." *Science News.* May 9, 1987, p. 294.

—*Leslie G. Melcer*

Lipstick

Background

Cosmetics can be traced back to ancient civilizations. In particular, the use of lip color was prevalent among the Sumerians, Egyptians, Syrians, Babylonians, Persians, and Greeks. Later, Elizabeth I and the ladies of her court colored their lips with red mercuric sulfide. For years, rouge was used to color both the lips and the cheeks, depending on the fashion of the times.

In Western society during the latter half of the nineteenth century, it was generally believed only promiscuous women wore lipstick—or makeup at all. It was not until the twentieth century that lipstick, and cosmetics in general, gained true societal acceptance.

Improvements in the manufacture of applicators and metal tubes reduced the cost of the cosmetic. This combined with newfound acceptance by the general population caused widespread use and popularity to increase. By 1915 push up tubes were available, and the first claims of "indelibility" were made.

Lipsticks are made to appeal to the current fashion trend and come in a wide range of colors. Lipstick is made of dyes and pigments in a fragranced oil-wax base. Retail prices for lipsticks are relatively low, with quality products priced at less than $4.00. More expensive products are available, with prices ranging up to nearly $50.00 for exclusive products. Lip balms, by contrast, generally retail for less than $1.00.

The tubes that hold lipstick range from inexpensive plastic dispensers for lip balms to ornate metal for lipsticks. Sizes are not uniform, but generally lipstick is sold in a tube 3 inches (7.6 centimeters) in length and about .50 inch (1.3 centimeters) in diameter. (Lip balms are generally slightly smaller in both length and diameter.) The tube has two parts, a cover and a base. The base is made up of two components, the twisting or sliding of which will push the lipstick up for application. Since the manufacture of the tube involves completely different technologies, we will focus here on the manufacture of lipstick only.

Raw Materials

The primary ingredients found in lipstick are wax, oil, alcohol, and pigment. The wax used usually involves some combination of three types—beeswax, candelilla wax, or the more expensive carnauba. Wax enables the mixture to be formed into the easily recognized shape of the cosmetic. Oils such as mineral, caster, lanolin, or vegetable are added to the wax. Fragrance and pigment are also added, as are preservatives and antioxidants, which prevent lipstick from becoming rancid. And while every lipstick contains these components, a wide variety of other ingredients can also be included to make the substance smoother or glossy or to moisten the lips.

Just as there is no standard to the lipstick size and container shape, there are no standard types of, or proportions for, ingredients used. Beyond the base ingredients (wax, oil, and antioxidants) supplemental material amounts vary greatly. The ingredients themselves range from complex organic compounds to entirely natural ingredients, the proportions of which determine the characteristics of the lipstick. Selecting lipsticks is, as with all cosmetics, an individual choice, so manufactur-

Sizes are not uniform, but generally lipstick is sold in a tube 3 inches in length and about .50 inch in diameter. The tube has two parts, a cover and a base. The base is made up of two components, the twisting or sliding of which will push the lipstick up for application.

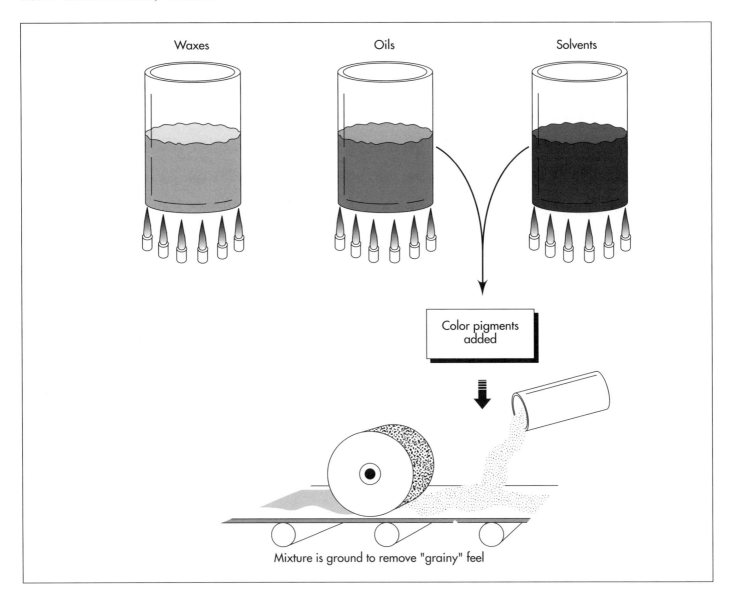

Waxes   Oils   Solvents

Color pigments
added

Mixture is ground to remove "grainy" feel

To make lipstick, the various raw ingredients are first melted separately, and then the oils and solvents are ground together with the desired color pigments.

ers have responded by making a wide variety of lipsticks available to the consumer.

In general, wax and oil make up about 60 percent of the lipstick (by weight), with alcohol and pigment accounting for another 25 percent (by weight). Fragrance is always added to lipstick, but accounts for one percent or less of the mixture. In addition to using lipstick to color the lips, there are also lip liners and **pencil**s. The manufacturing methods described here will just focus on lipstick and lip balms.

The Manufacturing Process

The manufacturing process is easiest to understand if it is viewed as three separate steps: melting and mixing the lipstick; pouring the

mixture into the tube; and packaging the product for sale. Since the lipstick mass can be mixed and stored for later use, mixing does not have to happen at the same time as pouring. Once the lipstick is in the tube, packaging for retail sale is highly variable, depending on how the product is to be marketed.

Melting and mixing

1 First, the raw ingredients for the lipstick are melted and mixed—separately because of the different types of ingredients used. One mixture contains the solvents, a second contains the oils, and a third contains the fats and waxy materials. These are heated in separate **stainless steel** or ceramic containers.

2 The solvent solution and liquid oils are then mixed with the color pigments. The

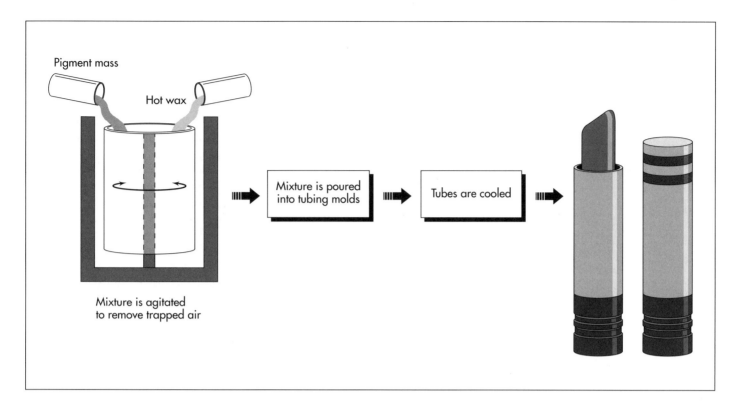

Pigment mass

Hot wax

Mixture is agitated
to remove trapped air

Mixture is poured
into tubing molds

Tubes are cooled

mixture passes through a roller mill, grinding the pigment to avoid a "grainy" feel to the lipstick. This process introduces air into the oil and pigment mixture, so mechanical working of the mixture is required. The mixture is stirred for several hours; at this point some producers use vacuum equipment to withdraw the air.

3 After the pigment mass is ground and mixed, it is added to the hot wax mass until a uniform color and consistency is obtained. The fluid lipstick can then be strained and molded, or it may be poured into pans and stored for future molding.

4 If the fluid lipstick is to be used immediately, the melt is maintained at temperature, with agitation, so that trapped air escapes. If the lipstick mass is stored, before it is used it must be reheated, checked for color consistency, and adjusted to specifications, then maintained at the melt temperature (with agitation) until it can be poured.

As expected, lipsticks are always prepared in batches because of the different color pigments that can be used. The size of the batch, and the number of tubes of lipstick produced at one time, will depend on the popularity of the particular shade being produced. This will determine the manufactur-

ing technique (automated or manual) that is used. Lipstick may be produced in highly automated processes, at rates of up to 2,400 tubes an hour, or in essentially manual operations, at rates around 150 tubes per hour. The steps in the process basically differ only in the volume produced.

Molding

5 Once the lipstick mass is mixed and free of air, it is ready to be poured into the tube. A variety of machine setups are used, depending on the equipment that the manufacturer has, but high volume batches are generally run through a melter that agitates the lipstick mass and maintains it as a liquid. For smaller, manually run batches, the mass is maintained at the desired mix temperature, with agitation, in a melter controlled by an operator.

6 The melted mass is dispensed into a mold, which consists of the bottom portion of the metal or plastic tube and a shaping portion that fits snugly with the tube. Lipstick is poured "up-side down" so that the bottom of the tube is at the top of the mold. Any excess is scraped from the mold.

7 The lipstick is cooled (automated molds are kept cold; manually produced molds

After the pigment mass is prepared, it is mixed with the hot wax. The mixture is agitated to free it of any air bubbles. Next, the mixture is poured into tubing molds, cooled, and separated from the molds. After final touch-up and visual inspection, the lipstick is ready for packaging.

are transferred to a refrigeration unit) and separated from the mold, and the bottom of the tube is sealed. The lipstick then passes through a flaming cabinet (or is flamed by hand) to seal pinholes and improve the finish. The lipstick is visually inspected for air holes, mold separation lines, or blemishes, and is reworked if necessary.

8 For obvious reasons, rework of the lipstick must be limited, demonstrating the importance of the early steps in removing air from the lipstick mass. Lipstick is reworked by hand with a spatula. This can be done inline, or the tube can be removed from the manufacturing process and reworked.

Labeling and packaging

9 After the lipstick is retracted and the tube is capped, the lipstick is ready for labeling and packaging. Labels identify the batch and are applied as part of the automated operation. While there is a great deal of emphasis on quality and appearance of the finished lipstick product, less emphasis is placed on the appearance of lip balms. Lip balms are always produced in an automated process (except for experimental or test batches). The heated liquid is poured into the tube in the retracted position; the tube is then capped by machine—a far less laborious process.

10 The final step in the manufacturing process is the packaging of the lipstick tube. There are a variety of packaging options available, ranging from bulk packs to individual packs, and including packaging as a component in a makeup kit or special promotional offering. Lip balms are packaged in bulk, generally with minimum protection to prevent shipping damage. Packaging for lipsticks varies, depending on what will happen at the point of sale in the retail outlet. Packaging may or may not be highly automated, and the package used depends on the end use of the product rather than on the manufacturing process.

Byproducts

There is little or no waste in the manufacture of lipstick. Product is reused whenever possible, and since the ingredients are expensive they are seldom thrown out, unless no other alternative presents itself. In the normal manufacturing process there are no byprod-

ucts, and waste portions of lipstick will be thrown out with the disposal of cleaning materials.

Quality Control

Quality control procedures are strict, since the product must meet Food and Drug Administration (FDA) standards. Lipstick is the only cosmetic ingested, and because of this strict controls on ingredients, as well as the manufacturing processes, are imposed. Lipstick is mixed and processed in a controlled environment so it will be free of contamination. Incoming material is tested to ensure that it meets required specifications. Samples of every batch produced are saved and stored at room temperature for the life of the product (and often beyond that) to maintain a control on the batch.

As noted above, appearance of lipstick as a final product is very important. For this reason everyone involved in the manufacture becomes an inspector, and non-standard product is either reworked or scrapped. Final inspection of every tube is performed by the consumer, and if not satisfactory, will be rejected at the retail level. Since the retailer and manufacturer are often times not the same, quality problems at the consumer level have a major impact on the manufacturer.

Color control of lipstick is critical, and one only has to see the range of colors available from a manufacturer to be aware of this. The dispersion of the pigment is checked stringently when a new batch is manufactured, and the color must be carefully controlled when the lipstick mass is reheated. The color of the lipstick mass will bleed over time, and each time a batch is reheated, the color may be altered. Colorimetric equipment is used to provide some numerical way to control the shades of lipstick. This equipment gives a numerical reading of the shade, when mixed, so it can identically match previous batches. Matching of reheated batches is done visually, so careful time and environment controls are placed on lipstick mass when it is not immediately used.

There are two special tests for lipstick: the *Heat Test* and the *Rupture Test*. In the Heat Test, the lipstick is placed in the extended position in a holder and left in a constant temperature oven of over 130 degrees

Fahrenheit (54 degrees Celsius) for 24 hours. There should be no drooping or distortion of the lipstick. In the Rupture Test, the lipstick is placed in two holders, in the extended position. Weight is added to the holder on the lipstick portion at 30-second intervals until the lipstick ruptures. The pressure required to rupture the lipstick is then checked against the manufacturer's standards. Since there are no industry standards for these tests, each manufacturer sets its own parameters.

The Future

Lipstick is the least expensive and most popular cosmetic in the world today. In 1986 lipstick sales in the United States were more than $720,000,000. There are no accurate figures for current sales of lip balm, since the market is expanding. Manufacturers continue to introduce new types and shades of lipstick, and there is a tremendous variety of product available at moderate cost. As long as cosmetics remain in fashion (and there is no indication that they will not) the market for lipstick will continue to be strong, adding markets in other countries as well as diversifying currently identified markets.

Where To Learn More

Books

Brumber, Elaine. *Save Your Money, Save Your Face*. Facts on File Publications, 1986.

Donsky, Howard. *Beauty Is Skin Deep*. Rodale Press, 1985.

Schoen, Linda Allen, ed. *The AMA Book of Skin and Hair Care*. J.B. Lippincott Company, 1976.

—Peter S. Lucking

Liquid Crystal Display (LCD)

The basis of LCD technology is the liquid crystal, a substance made of complicated molecules. Like water, liquid crystals are solid at low temperatures, and they melt as you heat them. But when liquid crystals melt, they change not into a clear liquid but into a cloudy one. At slightly higher temperatures, the cloudiness disappears, and they look much like any other liquid.

Background

Liquid crystal displays (LCDs) consist of liquid crystals that are activated by electric current. They are used most frequently to display one or more lines of alpha-numeric information in a variety of devices: fax machines, laptop computer screens, answering machine call counters, scientific instruments, portable **compact disc player**s, clocks, and so forth. The most expensive and advanced type—active matrix displays—are even being used as screens for handheld color TVs. Eventually, they may be widely used for large screen, high-definition TVs.

The basis of LCD technology is the liquid crystal, a substance made of complicated molecules. Like water, liquid crystals are solid at low temperatures. Also like water, they melt as you heat them. But when ice melts, it changes into a clear, easily flowing liquid. Liquid crystals, however, change into a cloudy liquid very different from liquids like water, alcohol, or **cooking oil**. At slightly higher temperatures, the cloudiness disappears, and they look much like any other liquid.

When the liquid crystal is a solid, its molecules are lined up parallel to one another. In the intermediate cloudy phase (liquid), the molecules still retain this more or less parallel orientation. As in any liquid, the molecules are free to move around, but they tend to "line up" in one direction, reflecting light and causing a cloudy appearance. Higher temperatures tend to agitate the molecules and thus make the liquid clear.

In an LCD, an electric current is used to switch segments of liquid crystals from a transparent phase to a cloudy phase, each segment forming part of a number or letter. The segments can also be in the shape of tiny dots or pixels, and the can be arranged in rows and columns. They are turned on and off individually to either block or allow polarized light to pass through. When the light is blocked, a dark spot is created on the reflecting screen.

There are two general types of LCDs: passive matrix, and the newer active matrix (AMLCDs). Brighter and easier to read, active matrix displays use transistors behind each pixel to boost the image. The manufacturing process for AMLCDs, however, is much trickier than that for passive matrix LCDs. As many as 50 percent of those made must now be thrown out because of imperfections. One imperfection is enough to ruin an AMLCD. This makes them very expensive to manufacture.

Raw Materials

A working LCD consists of several components: display glass, drive electronics, control electronics, mechanical package, and power supply. The *display glass*—between which the liquid crystals lie—is coated with row and column electrodes and has contact pads to connect drive electronics (electric current) to each row and column electrode. The *drive electronics* are integrated circuits that supply current to "drive" the row and column electrodes. The *control electronics* are also integrated circuits. They decode and interpret the incoming signals—from a laptop computer, for example—and send them to the drive electronics. The *mechanical package* is the frame that mounts the printed circuit boards for the drive and control electronics to the display glass. This package

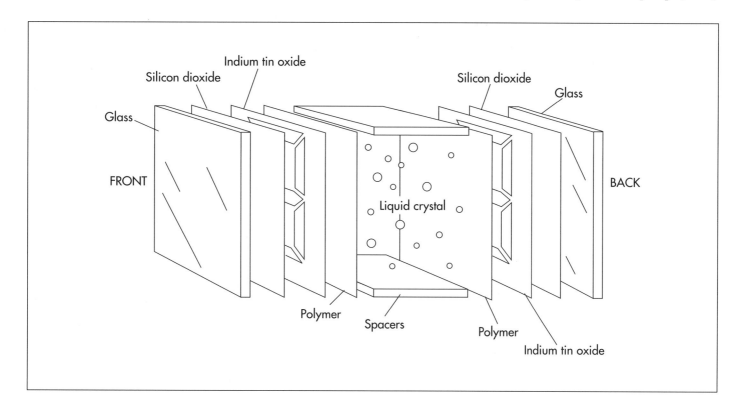

also strengthens and protects the display glass and anchors the entire display to the device using the LCD, whether it is a laptop computer, a fax machine, or another device. Finally, the *power supply* is an electronic circuit that supplies current to the LCD. Equipment makers who use LCDs often purchase the power supplies separately.

In all LCDs, the liquid crystal is sandwiched between two pieces of glass or transparent plastic called *substrates*. Just any glass will not do. If the glass has many sodium or other alkali ions, they can move to the glass surface, combine with any moisture that is there, and alter the electric field pattern and liquid crystal alignment. To eliminate that, LCD makers either use borosilicate glass, which has few ions, or they apply a layer of silicon dioxide to the glass. The silicon dioxide prevents the ions from touching any moisture. An even simpler solution is to use plastic instead of glass. Using plastic also makes the display lighter. However, inexpensive plastics scatter light more than glass, and they may react chemically with liquid crystal substances.

Most LCDs today also use a source of light coming from the rear of the display (backlight), such as a fluorescent light, to make the liquid crystal appear darker against the

screen when in its cloudy phase. LCD makers also use sheets of polarizer material to enhance this effect.

The Manufacturing Process

Making passive matrix LCDs is a multi-step process. The surface and rear glass of the display is first polished, washed, and coated with silicon dioxide (SiO_2). Next, a layer of indium tin oxide is evaporated onto the glass and etched into the desired pattern. A layer of long chain polymer is then applied to allow the liquid crystals to align properly, followed by a sealing resin. The spacers next are put into place, and the glass sandwich is filled with the liquid crystal material.

Preparing the glass substrates

1 First, the two glass substrates must be cut to the proper size, polished, and washed. Cutting can be done with a diamond saw or scribe, while polishing involves a process called *lapping*, in which the glass is held against a rotating wheel that has abrasive particles embedded in it. After being washed and dried, the substrates are coated with a layer of silicon dioxide.

In all LCDs, the liquid crystal is sandwiched between 2 pieces of glass or transparent plastic called substrates. If glass is used, it is often coated with silicon dioxide to improve liquid crystal alignment. Transparent electrode patterns are then made by applying a layer of indium tin oxide to the glass and using a photolithography or silk-screening process to produce the pattern.

Making the electrode pattern

2 Next, the transparent electrode pattern must be made on the substrates. This is done by completely coating both front and rear glass surfaces with a very thin layer of indium tin oxide. Manufacturers then make a mask of the desired pattern, using either a silk-screening or photolithography process. They apply the finished mask to the fully coated glass, and areas of indium tin oxide that are not needed are etched away chemically.

3 Alternatively, finer definition can be achieved by using glass that has a layer of etching-resistant, light-sensitive material (called *photoresist*) above the indium tin oxide film. A mask with the desired pattern is placed over the glass, and the glass is bombarded with ultraviolet light. This light causes the resistive layer it shines on to lose its resistance to etching, allowing the chemicals to eat away both the exposed photoresist and the indium tin oxide below it, thus forming the pattern. The unnecessary photoresist that remains can then be removed with other chemicals. A second variety of resistive film resists etching only *after* it is exposed to ultraviolet light; in this case, a negative mask of the pattern must be used. Regardless of which method is used, the patterns on the two substrates are designed to overlap only in specific places, a design that ensures that the thin strips of indium tin oxide conveying voltage to each element have no electrode positioned directly opposite that might show up while the cell is working.

Applying the polymer

4 After the electrode pattern is in place, the substrates must be coated with a polymer. The polymer allows the liquid crystals to align properly with the glass surface. Polyvinyl alcohol, polyamides, and some silanes can be used. Polyamides are the most popular agents, because polyvinyl alcohol is subject to moisture problems, and silanes produce a thin, unreliable coating.

5 After coating the glass, manufacturers then stroke the polymer coat in a single direction with soft material. This can result in small parallel grooves being etched into the polymer, or it may simply stretch the polymer coat. In any case, this process forces the liquid crystals to lie parallel to the direction of the stroke. The crystals may be aligned another way, by evaporating silicon oxide onto the glass surface at an oblique angle. This procedure is used to make most digital **watch** displays but is not convenient for making large-scale displays. It also does not yield the low-tilt angle possible with the previous method.

6 If LCD makers want to align liquid crystals perpendicular to the glass surface, another technique is used: coating the glass with an amphophilic material. This is material whose molecules display affinity for water at one end of the molecule and repulsion from water at the other end. One end—the affinity end—adheres to the glass surface while the other end—the repulsing end—points into the liquid crystal area, repelling the liquid crystals and forming them into an alignment that is perpendicular to the glass surface.

Applying the sealant and injecting the liquid crystal

7 A sealing resin is next applied to the substrates, followed by plastic spacers that will give the liquid crystal cell the proper thickness. Next, the liquid crystal material is injected into the appropriate area between the two glass substrates. The thickness of the LCD cell is usually restricted to 5-25 micrometers. Because proper thickness is crucial for cell operation and because spacers don't always achieve uniform thickness, LCD makers sometimes put appropriately sized glass fibers or beads in the liquid crystal material. The beads or fibers cannot be seen by the naked eye. They help hold the cell at the proper thickness while the sealant material is setting.

8 To make LCDs more visible, polarizers are added. These are usually made from stretched polyvinyl alcohol films that have iodine in them and that are sandwiched between cellulose acetate layers. Colored polarizers, made using dye instead of iodine, are also available. Manufacturers glue the polarizer to the glass using an acrylic adhesive and cover it with a plastic protective film. They can make reflective polarizers, which also are used in LCDs, by incorporating a simple metal foil reflector.

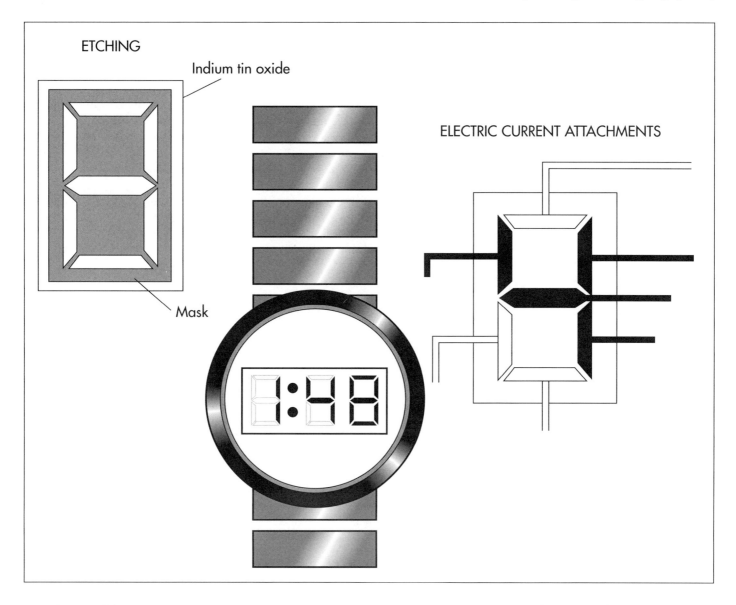

ETCHING

Indium tin oxide

Mask

ELECTRIC CURRENT ATTACHMENTS

Final assembly

9 After the polarizer film is attached, the unit is allowed to age. Finally, the finished glass display assembly is mounted to the circuit boards containing the control and drive electronics. Then, the entire package is ready to be mounted to the device using the LCD—laptop computer, fax machine, clock, etc.

Active Matrix LCD Manufacture

The process used to make an active matrix LCD (AMLCD) is quite similar to that used for passive matrix LCDs, although it is more complex and more difficult. Generally, the steps of SiO₂ coating, indium tin oxide application, and the photoresist etching are replaced by a host of other steps.

In the case of AMLCDs, each LCD component has to be changed to work properly with the thin film transistor and electronics used to boost and clarify the LCD image. Like their passive matrix brethren, active matrix displays are sandwiches consisting of several layers: a polarizing film; a sodium barrier film (SiO₂), a glass substrate incorporating a black matrix, and a second sodium barrier film; a color filter and a color filter overcoat made of acrylic/urethane; a transparent electrode; an orientation film made of polyamide; and the actual liquid crystal material incorporating plastic/glass spacers to maintain proper LCD cell thickness.

Quality Control

LCDs—especially those for laptop computer displays—are made under highly controlled

In a typical LCD watch assembly, the shaded areas are etched away chemically to form the electrode pattern. The segments are turned on and off individually to either block or allow polarized light to pass through. When electric current is applied to a segment, the light is blocked and a dark spot is created on the reflecting screen.

conditions in a clean room environment to maximize yield. "Clean rooms" have special air filtering devices designed to keep all dust particles out of the room, and workers inside the room must wear special clothing. Nonetheless, many LCDs have to be discarded because of imperfections. This is particularly true of AMLCDs, which currently have a rejection rate of approximately 50 percent. To minimize the rejection rate, each active device is inspected and as many are repaired as possible. In addition, active matrix assemblies are inspected immediately after the photoresist etching step and again after the liquid crystal material is injected.

The Future

The future is clearly with active matrix LCDs, even though the current rejection rate is very high and the manufacturing process is so expensive. Gradual improvements are expected in the manufacturing process of AMLCDs, and in fact companies are already beginning to offer inspection and repair equipment that may cut the current rejection rate from 50 percent down to around 35 percent.

But the real boost to LCD manufacturing technology may come from all the money that companies are pouring into the research and development process on large screen, AMLCD displays for the long-awaited high-definition television technology.

Where To Learn More

Books

Chandrasekhar, S. *Liquid Crystals*, 2nd ed. Cambridge University Press, 1993.

Collins, Peter J. *Liquid Crystals: Nature's Delicate Phase of Matter.* Princeton University Press, 1991.

Doane, J. W., ed. *Liquid Crystal Displays and Applications.* SPIE-International Society for Optical Engineering, 1990.

Drzaic, P. S., ed. *Liquid Crystal Materials, Devices, and Applications.* SPIE-International Society for Optical Engineering, 1992.

Kaneko, D. *Liquid Crystal TV Displays.* Kluwer Academic Publishers, 1987.

O'Mara, William C. *Liquid Crystal Flat Panel Display: Manufacturing Science and Technology.* Van Nostrand Reinhold, 1993.

Periodicals

Curran, Lawrence. "Kopin, Sarnoff Team in Advanced LCD Effort." *Electronics.* August 10, 1992, p. 11.

Fitzgerald, Michael. "Display Standards Elusive." *Computerworld.* December 21, 1992, p. 27.

Fleischmann, Mark. "Wall-Size TV from Tiny LCDs." *Popular Science.* June, 1991, p. 94.

Kinnaman, Daniel E. "LCD Panels: The Next Generation." *Technology & Learning.* March, 1993, p. 44.

Robinson, Gail M. "Display Systems Leap Forward: New Technologies Offer Designers More Choices Than Ever in CRTs, LCDs, EL and More." *Design News.* February 13, 1989, p. 52.

Woodard, Ollie C., Sr. and Tom Long. "Display Technologies." *Byte.* July, 1992, p. 158.

—*Edward J. Stone*

Lubricating Oil

Background

Since the Roman era, many liquids, including water, have been used as lubricants to minimize the friction, heat, and wear between mechanical parts in contact with each other. Today, lubricating oil, or lube oil, is the most commonly used lubricant because of its wide range of possible applications. The two basic categories of lube oil are *mineral* and *synthetic*. Mineral oils are refined from naturally occurring petroleum, or crude oil. Synthetic oils are manufactured polyalphaolefins, which are hydrocarbon-based polyglycols or ester oils.

Although there are many types of lube oils to choose from, mineral oils are the most commonly used because the supply of crude oil has rendered them inexpensive; moreover, a large body of data on their properties and use already exists. Another advantage of mineral-based lube oils is that they can be produced in a wide range of viscosities—viscosity refers to the substance's resistance to flow—for diverse applications. They range from low-viscosity oils, which consist of hydrogen-carbon chains with molecular weights of around 200 atomic mass units (amu), to highly viscous lubricants with molecular weights as high as 1000 amu. Mineral-based oils with different viscosities can even be blended together to improve their performance in a given application. The common 10W-30 motor oil, for example, is a blend of low viscous oil (for easy starting at low temperatures) and highly viscous oil (for better motor protection at normal running temperatures).

First used in the aerospace industry, synthetic lubricants are usually formulated for a specific application to which mineral oils are ill-suited. For example, synthetics are used where extremely high operating temperatures are encountered or where the lube oil must be fire resistant. This article will focus on mineral-based lube oil.

Raw Materials

Lube oils are just one of many fractions, or components, that can be derived from raw petroleum, which emerges from an oil well as a yellow-to-black, flammable, liquid mixture of thousands of hydrocarbons (organic compounds containing only carbon and hydrogen atoms, these occur in all fossil fuels). Petroleum deposits were formed by the decomposition of tiny plants and animals that lived about 400 million years ago. Due to climatic and geographical changes occurring at that time in the Earth's history, the breakdown of these organisms varied from region to region.

Because of the different rates at which organic material decomposed in various places, the nature and percentage of the resulting hydrocarbons vary widely. Consequently, so do the physical and chemical characteristics of the crude oils extracted from different sites. For example, while California crude has a specific gravity of 0.92 grams/milliliter, the lighter Pennsylvania crude has a specific gravity of 0.81 grams/milliliter. (*Specific gravity*, which refers to the ratio of a substance's weight to that of an equal volume of water, is an important aspect of crude oil.) Overall, the specific gravity of crudes ranges between 0.80 and 0.97 grams/milliliter.

Depending on the application, chemicals called additives may be mixed with the

Lube oils are just one of many fractions, or components, that can be derived from raw petroleum, which emerges from an oil well as a yellow-to-black, flammable, liquid mixture of thousands of hydrocarbons (organic compounds containing only carbon and hydrogen atoms, these occur in all fossil fuels).

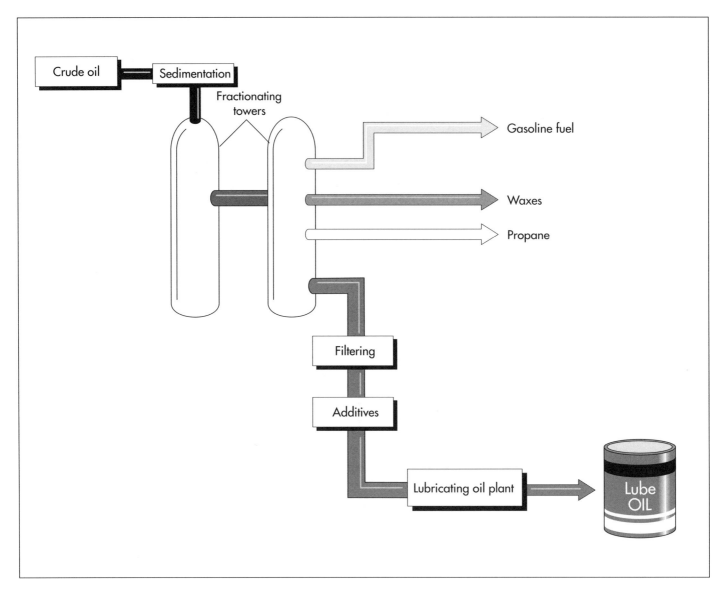

Lubricating oil is refined from crude oil. After undergoing a purifying process called sedimentation, the crude oil is heated in huge fractionating towers. The various vapors—which can be used to make fuel, waxes, or propane, among other substances—boil off and are collected at different points in the tower. The lube oil that is collected is filtered, and then additives are mixed in.

refined oil to give it desired physical properties. Common additives include metals such as lead or metal sulphide, which enhance lube oil's ability to prevent galling and scoring when metal surfaces come in contact under extremely high pressures. High-molecular weight polymerics are another common additive: they improve viscosity, counteracting the tendency of oils to thin at high temperatures. Nitrosomines are employed as antioxidants and corrosion inhibitors because they neutralize acids and form protective films on metal surfaces.

The Manufacturing Process

Lube oil is extracted from crude oil, which undergoes a preliminary purification process

(sedimentation) before it is pumped into fractionating towers. A typical high-efficiency fractionating tower, 25 to 35 feet (7.6 to 10.6 meters) in diameter and up to 400 feet (122 meters) tall, is constructed of high grade steels to resist the corrosive compounds present in crude oils; inside, it is fitted with an ascending series of condensate collecting trays. Within a tower, the thousands of hydrocarbons in crude oil are separated from each other by a process called *fractional distillation.* As the vapors rise up through the tower, the various fractions cool, condense, and return to liquid form at different rates determined by their respective boiling points (the lower the boiling point of the fraction, the higher it rises before condensing). Natural gas reaches its boiling point first, followed by gasoline, kerosene, fuel oil, lubricants, and tars.

Sedimentation

1 The crude oil is transported from the oil well to the refinery by pipeline or tanker ship. At the refinery, the oil undergoes sedimentation to remove any water and solid contaminants, such as sand and rock, that may be suspended in it. During this process, the crude is pumped into large holding tanks, where the water and oil are allowed to separate and the contaminants settle out of the oil.

Fractionating

2 Next, the crude oil is heated to about 700 degrees Fahrenheit (371 degrees Celsius). At this temperature it breaks down into a mixture of hot vapor and liquid that is then pumped into the bottom of the first of two fractionating towers. Here, the hot hydrocarbon vapors float upward. As they cool, they condense and are collected in different trays installed at different levels in the tower. In this tower, normal atmospheric pressure is maintained continuously, and about 80 percent of the crude oil vaporizes.

3 The remaining 20 percent of the oil is then reheated and pumped into a second tower, wherein vacuum pressure lowers the residual oil's boiling point so that it can be made to vaporize at a lower temperature. The heavier compounds with higher boiling points, such as tar and the inorganic compounds, remain behind for further processing.

Filtering and solvent extraction

4 After further processing to remove unwanted compounds, the lube oil that has been collected in the two fractionating towers is passed through several ultrafine filters, which remove remaining impurities. Aromatics, one such contaminant, contain six-carbon rings that would affect the lube oil's viscosity if they weren't removed in a process called *solvent extraction*. Solvent extraction is possible because aromatics are more soluble in the solvent than the lube oil fraction is. When the lube oil is treated with the solvent, the aromatics dissolve; later, after the solvent has been removed, the aromatics can be recovered from it.

Additives, inspection, and packaging

5 Finally, the oil is mixed with additives to give it the desired physical properties (such as the ability to withstand low temperatures). At this point, the lube oil is subjected to a variety of quality control tests that assess its viscosity, specific gravity, color, flash, and fire points. Oil that meets quality standards is then packaged for sale and distribution.

Quality Control

Most applications of lube oils require that they be nonresinous, pale-colored, odorless, and oxidation-resistant. Over a dozen physical and chemical tests are used to classify and determine the grade of lubricating oils. Common physical tests include measurements for viscosity, specific gravity, and color, while typical chemical tests include those for flash and fire points.

Of all the properties, viscosity, a lube oil's resistance to flow at specific temperatures and pressures, is probably the single most important one. The application and operating temperature range are key factors in determining the proper viscosity for an oil. For example, if the oil is too viscous, it offers too much resistance to the metal parts moving against each other. On the other hand, if it not viscous enough, it will be squeezed out from between the mating surfaces and will not be able to lubricate them sufficiently. The Saybolt Standard Universal Viscometer is the standard instrument for determining viscosity of petroleum lubricants between 70 and 210 degrees Fahrenheit (21 and 99 degrees Celsius). Viscosity is measured in the *Saybolt Universal second*, which is the time in seconds required for 50 milliliters of oil to empty out of a Saybolt viscometer cup through a calibrated tube orifice at a given temperature.

The specific gravity of an oil depends on the refining method and the types of additives present, such as lead, which gives the lube oil the ability to resist extreme mating surface pressure and cold temperatures. The lube oil's color indicates the uniformity of a particular grade or brand. The oil's flash and fire points vary with the crude oil's origin. The *flash point* is the temperature to which an oil has to be heated until sufficient flammable vapor is driven off so that it will flash when brought into contact with a flame. The *fire point* is the higher temperature at which the oil vapor will continue to burn when ignited.

Common engine oils are classified by viscosity and performance according to specifications established by the Society of Automotive Engineers (SAE). Performance factors include wear prevention, oil sludge deposit formation, and oil thickening.

The Future

The future of mineral-based lubricating oil is limited, because the natural supplies of petroleum are both finite and non-renewable. Experts estimate the total recoverable light to medium petroleum reserves at 1.6 trillion barrels, of which a third has been used. Thus, synthetic-based oils will probably be increasingly important as natural reserves dwindle. This is true not only for lubricating oil but also for the other products that result from petroleum refining.

Where To Learn More

Books

Fuels, Lubricants, and Coolants, 7th ed. Deere & Company Service Publications, 1992.

Malone, L. J. *Basic Concepts of Chemistry.* John Wiley & Sons, Inc., 1989.

Nadkarni, R. A., ed. *Analysis of Petroleum Products & Lubricants.* American Society for Testing & Materials, 1991.

Seal, Shirley C., ed. *Fluids, Lubricants & Sealing Devices.* National Fluid Power Association, 1989.

Periodicals

Bienkowski, Keith. "Coolants and Lubricants: The Truth." *Manufacturing Engineering.* March, 1993.

"System Provides Real-Time Lube Oil Blending." *Design News.* February 26, 1990, p. 39.

O'Lenick, Anthony and Raymond E. Bilbo. "Saturated Liquid Lubricant Withstands Aluminum Forming." *Research & Development.* February, 1989, p. 162.

Peterson, Ivars. "Friction Features." *Science News.* April 30, 1988, p. 283.

Templeton, Fleur. "The Right Lube Job for Superhot Ceramic Engines?" *Business Week.* May 18, 1992, p. 113.

Vogel, Todd, John Rossant, and Sarah Miller. "Oil's Rude Awakening." *Business Week.* September 26, 1988, p. 44.

—*Craig F. Whitlow*

Mattress

Background

From the available evidence, it seems fairly certain that the concept of the mattress originated during prehistoric times. By lying on piles of leaves, straw, and animal skins, early humans were able to sleep more comfortably and more soundly than they could have on hard surfaces. As greater numbers of people left a nomadic, hunting existence for a settled, agrarian lifestyle, primitive furnishings, including the bed, began to develop.

To a large extent the development of the mattress is closely linked with that of the bed. In many ancient societies, the bed was considered the most important piece of furniture in the household; often, it provided a central gathering place for dining and relaxing as well as sleeping. Over the centuries, bed frames became more elaborate for those who could afford luxury; however, mattresses themselves remained unsophisticated—and uncomfortable. Until the twentieth century, they generally consisted of lumpy pads filled with horse hair, cotton, or rags. Poorer people relied on *ticks*—fabric sacks stuffed with straw, corn cobs, or other crop debris. In addition to offering an inconsistent texture, such primitive mattresses were difficult to clean—and they generally started out dirty, stuffed as they were with agricultural debris that often entered the pad or ticking with soil and insects. However, they offered one concrete advantage: made at home from cast-off farm goods, they were cheap. Even late in the nineteenth century when small local manufacturers began to produce mattresses commercially, the items remained inexpensive because early mattress makers continued to rely on extremely inexpensive stuffing (usu-ally, unusable fabric remnants discarded by second-hand tailors).

Mattresses with stabilizing interior springs, probably the single most significant advance in mattress design, were first developed during the mid-1800s. By placing a set of uniform springs inside layers of upholstery, mattress manufacturers could imbue their product with a firm, resilient, and uniform texture. However, because so-called innerspring mattresses were expensive to manufacture, only luxury ships and hotels that could pass the cost along to their affluent patrons purchased them initially. It was not until after World War I that innerspring mattresses were mass-produced by Zalmon Simmons, Jr., the president of a company that had theretofore produced bedsteads. Despite the fact that Simmons asked 40 dollars—more than twice the cost of the finest horse hair mattress available at that time—for his innerspring mattress in 1926, his products proved so comfortable that millions of Americans purchased them.

To render potential customers more willing to spend what must have struck many as a small fortune on his innerspring mattress, Simmons promoted the advantages of a good night's sleep. The effectiveness of this marketing strategy has only increased over the years, as subsequent research has confirmed that abundant, high-quality sleep constitutes a fundamental component of good health. Today's sophisticated mattresses improve sleeping comfort in several ways. First, through a variety of enhanced innerspring designs, modern mattresses distribute the weight of the body over a broad area; this also helps to prevent differential wear on the mattress. In addition, mattresses offer sur-

Until the twentieth century, mattresses generally consisted of lumpy pads filled with horse hair, cotton, or rags. Poorer people relied on ticks—fabric sacks stuffed with straw, corn cobs, or other crop debris.

faces of appropriate softness and flexibility to help keep the spine in its naturally curved position. However, contemporary mattress manufacturers carefully avoid excessively soft surfaces that would distort the position of the sleeper's spine, resulting in discomfort or even pain.

Presently, the consumer demand for mattresses is fairly consistent. In 1990, approximately 16 million mattresses were sold in the United States. Together with foundations, mattresses accounted for about $4 billion in retail sales. With the exception of a few large companies, most mattress manufacturers are fairly small, community-based operations. Of the approximately 825 mattress factories across the United States, most are still owned and operated by the founding families.

Design

Today, most mattresses are manufactured according to standard sizes. This standardization was initiated by the industry to resolve any dimensional discrepancies that might occur between companies that manufacture beds and companies that make mattresses. The sizes include the twin bed, 39 inches wide and 74 inches long; the double bed, 54 inches wide and 74 inches long; the queen bed, 60 inches wide and 80 inches long; and the king bed, 78 inches wide and 80 inches long.

The "core" of a typical mattress is the innerspring unit, a series of wire coils that are attached to one another with additional wire. The upholstery layers are affixed to the innerspring: the first, called the *insulator*, is fitted directly onto the innerspring and prevents the next layer, the *cushioning*, from molding to the coils. While the insulator is fairly standard, the number of cushioning layers can vary widely in number, ranging from two to eight layers and from 1/4 inch to 2 inches (.63 to 5 centimeters) in thickness. Moving outward, the next component is the *flanges*, connecting panels that are attached to the mattress's quilted cover with large, round staples called *hogs rings*. The top, bottom, and side panels of the mattress are stitched together with border tape.

While a wide variety of springs are designed to accommodate special needs and situations, the four most commonly used coils are the *Bonnell*, the *Offset*, the *Continuous*, and the *Pocket System*. The Bonnell springs are hourglass-shaped and knotted at both ends. The Offset design is similarly hourglass-shaped, but its top and bottom are flattened to facilitate a hinging action between the coils. The Continuous innerspring consists of one extremely long strand of steel wire configured into S-shaped units. Finally, in the Pocket System, each coil is encased in a fabric casing that also connects it to neighboring coil-casing units.

A typical mattress contains between 250 and 1,000 coil springs, and mattresses that use fewer coils normally require a heavier gauge of wire. It is not uncommon for an innerspring unit to require as much as 2,000 linear feet (610 meters) of steel wire. The individual coils can be joined in several ways. One common method is to use helicals—corkscrew-shaped wires that run along the top and bottom of the springs, lacing the coils together. Rigid border wires are sometimes attached around the perimeters to stabilize the unit.

Most manufacturers also produce foundation mattresses or boxsprings that lie directly beneath the mattress, resting on the frame of the bed. One of the most common types of box spring foundations uses a spiked coil configuration, in which the springs are narrow at the bottom but spiral to a wider diameter at the top. While a spring system provides the most common type of boxspring support, torsion bars are also sometimes used. Other foundation mattresses contain no springs at all but consist of a built-up wooden frame.

Raw Materials

Mattresses are presently made of many materials, both natural and synthetic. The innerspring, helical, and boxspring components are made from wire; the boxspring wire is usually of a heavier gauge than that used in the innerspring. The insulator consists of semi-rigid netting or wire mesh, and the cushioning layers can comprise a number of different materials including natural fiber, polyurethane foam, and polyester. The flanges are made of fabric, and the hogs rings of metal. Top, bottom, and side panels consist of a durable fabric cover quilted over a backing of foam or fiber, and the binding

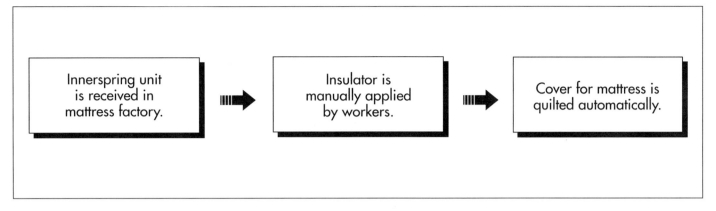

| Innerspring unit is received in mattress factory. | → | Insulator is manually applied by workers. | → | Cover for mattress is quilted automatically. |

tape that holds the ticking together is made of heavy-duty, fibrous, synthetic material. The underlying boxspring may consist of either a wooden frame with slats or of metal coils similar to those used in the mattress itself. The boxspring may be upholstered, but, even if it is not, it always receives a fabric covering.

The Manufacturing Process

Building mattress layers

1 Most mattress manufacturers subcontract the production of the innerspring unit to an outside firm that specializes in making springs. Once the completed spring unit is received and inspected, the workers manually apply the insulator. Next, they apply the cushioning layers that will determine the feel and comfort of the final product.

2 While the mattress is being "built up" in one part of the plant, the decorative cover that will serve as the exterior for the top, bottom and sides is being made in another part. Usually this cover is made on a giant quilting machine, which controls a multitude of needles that stitch the cover to a layer of backing material. The stitching chosen serves both useful and ornamental purposes, as it must prevent the mattress cover from slipping or creeping over the layers of cushioning in addition to creating a visually pleasing exterior.

3 Once the fabric is quilted, it is cut into panels that will fit the top and bottom of the mattress. The side panels are often cut from this same composite or made separately on a border machine. If side handles or vents are to be added, they are attached to the side panels before these are applied to the mattress.

Attaching the flanges

4 Specially modified sewing machines are used to attach the flanges to the top and bottom panels, and the hogs rings are stapled to the flanges. Everything is now ready for the closing operation, during which the hogs rings will be secured to the innerspring unit.

Completing the mattress

5 The closing operation is of one of the most highly skilled and critical procedures in the entire process. It is done with a movable sewing head that is mounted on a track. Tape edge operators manually feed the top, bottom, and side panels and a heavy duty binding tape into the sewing machine as it moves around the mattress. As this combination of materials is fed into the machine, the operators uses their skill to feed the proper amount of each material into the machine to produce a professionally tailored product.

6 Some of the highest quality mattresses may also feature a pillowtop, a panel filled with soft upholstery and attached to the top and bottom panels of the mattress for a more luxurious feel and appearance. Prequilted, the pillowtop is then taped to the mattress.

Boxsprings

7 If the desired boxspring has a spiked coil design, it is made by stapling the bottom of each coil to a flat wooden frame. A wire grid is then placed on top of the springs and, once aligned, manually locked to them. A thin layer of upholstery is applied to the top. If the desired boxspring contains no springs,

Once the completed innerspring unit is received, workers manually apply the insulator. Next, they apply the cushioning layers that will determine the feel and comfort of the final product. Meanwhile, the decorative cover that will serve as the exterior for the top, bottom, and sides is made on a giant quilting machine, which controls a multitude of needles that stitch the cover to a layer of backing material.

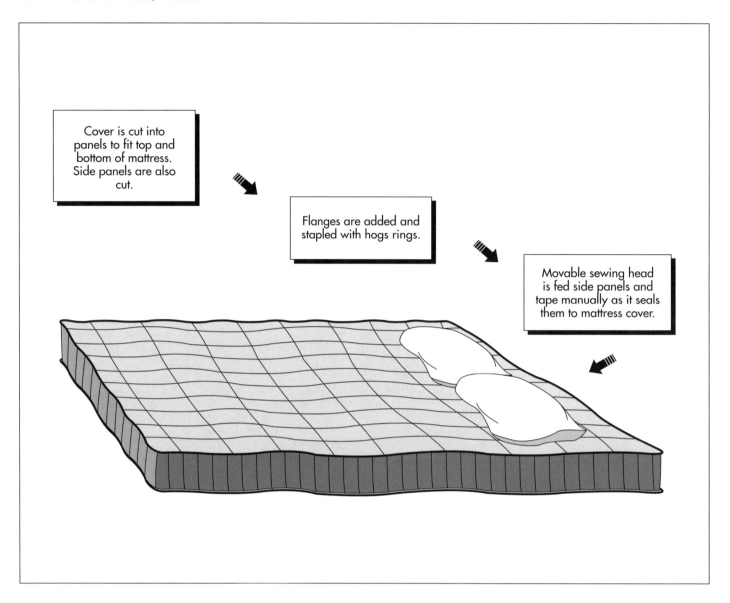

Cover is cut into panels to fit top and bottom of mattress. Side panels are also cut.

Flanges are added and stapled with hogs rings.

Movable sewing head is fed side panels and tape manually as it seals them to mattress cover.

Once the cover is quilted, it is cut into top, bottom, and side panels. Next, flanges are added, and hogs rings are stapled to them. Finally, in the closing operation, workers use a movable sewing head mounted on a track to feed the top, bottom, and side panels and a heavy duty binding tape into the sewing machine as it moves around the mattress. The mattress is then ready for packaging.

it consists of a wooden frame that may or may not have a layer of upholstery attached to its top. Regardless of the internal composition, the frame is usually inserted into a pre-sewn cover that encases the top and sides of the unit. A border fabric that matches the mattress exterior is applied to the sides, and a dust cover is added to the face.

Inspection, labeling, and packing

8 Once the units are complete, they are inspected for quality. If every thing is in order, they are labeled with the content and the contingent "do not remove" tag, required by law to ensure the consumer that the contents are properly represented in the labeling. The finished product is then transported to the packing area. Here it is inserted by hand or by automated machinery into protective

plastic or paper covers. Additional information about the warranty, safety, and care of the product is also included in the packaging.

Quality Control

During the manufacturing phase most quality control procedures are carried out by sight. The majority of manufacturers implement inspections at critical points in the production process: after receiving the innerspring, before the closing, and before packing.

Fire is a very real danger with all conventional mattresses, and the industry and the federal government have long sought ways to limit that danger. Since 1973, manufacturers selling in the United States have been required by law to make mattresses that resist ignition by cigarettes. In 1987, the industry voluntarily began to include tags on mattresses that warn consumers of potential fire hazards.

The Future

In recent years a great deal of research has been done on the relationship between effective sleep and the sleeping environment. Since comfort and sleep are to a great extent subjective, it is often difficult to quantify the results of such studies. However, many of the larger companies continue to spend a considerable amount of money on research, especially on the design of the innerspring. In these studies quality and comfort are key considerations.

While traditional innerspring construction continues to account for the lion's share of the mattresses produced in this country, both the water bed and the air mattress are gaining in popularity. While these unique designs require many different skills and production technologies, the growing demand for them over the last 20 years indicates a significant new trend.

Where To Learn More

Associations

American Innerspring Manufacturers, 1918 North Parkway, Memphis, Tennessee, 38112.

International Sleep Products Association, 333 Commerce St., Alexandria, Virginia, 22314.

National Home Furnishings Association, P.O. Box 2396, High Point, North Carolina, 27261.

—*Dan Pepper*

Microwave Oven

Microwaves can pass through plastic, glass, and paper materials; metal surfaces reflect them, and foods (especially liquids) absorb them. Microwaves heat food very quickly because they penetrate all layers simultaneously. Inside a piece of food or a container filled with liquid, the microwaves agitate molecules, thereby heating the substance.

Background

Microwaves are actually a segment of the electromagnetic wave spectrum, which comprises forms of energy that move through space, generated by the interaction of electric and magnetic fields. The spectrum is commonly broken into subgroups determined by the different wavelengths (or frequencies) and emission, transmission, and absorption behaviors of various types of waves. From longest to shortest wavelengths, the spectrum includes electric and radio waves, microwaves, infrared (heat) radiation, visible light, ultraviolet radiation, X-rays, gamma rays, and electromagnetic cosmic rays. Microwaves have frequencies between approximately .11 and 1.2 inches (0.3 and 30 centimeters).

Microwaves themselves are used in many different applications such as telecommunication products, radar detectors, wood curing and drying, and medical treatment of certain diseases. However, certain of their properties render them ideal for cooking, by far the most common use of microwave energy. Microwaves can pass through plastic, glass, and paper materials; metal surfaces reflect them, and foods (especially liquids) absorb them. A meal placed in a conventional oven is heated from the outside in, as it slowly absorbs the surrounding air that the oven has warmed. Microwaves, on the other hand, heat food much more quickly because they penetrate all layers simultaneously. Inside a piece of food or a container filled with liquid, the microwaves agitate molecules, thereby heating the substance.

The ability of microwave energy to cook food was discovered in the 1940s by Dr. Percy Spencer, who had conducted research on radar vacuum tubes for the military during World War II. Spencer's experiments revealed that, when confined to a metal enclosure, high-frequency radio waves penetrate and excite certain type of molecules, such as those found in food. Just powerful enough to cook the food, the microwaves are not strong enough to alter its molecular or genetic structure or to make it radioactive.

Raytheon, the company for which Dr. Spencer was conducting this research, patented the technology and soon developed microwave ovens capable of cooking large quantities of food. Because manufacturing costs rendered them too expensive for most consumers, these early ovens were used primarily by hospitals and hotels that could more easily afford the $3,000 investment they represented. By the late 1970s, however, many companies had developed microwave ovens for home use, and the cost had begun to come down. Today, microwaves are a standard household appliance, available in a broad range of designs and with a host of convenient features: rotating plates for more consistent cooking; digital timers; autoprogramming capabilities; and adjustable levels of cooking power that enable defrosting, browning, and warming, among other functions.

Design

The basic design of a microwave oven is simple, and most operate in essentially the same manner. The oven's various electronic motors, relays, and control circuits are located on the exterior casing, to which the oven cavity is bolted. A front panel allows the user to program the microwave, and the

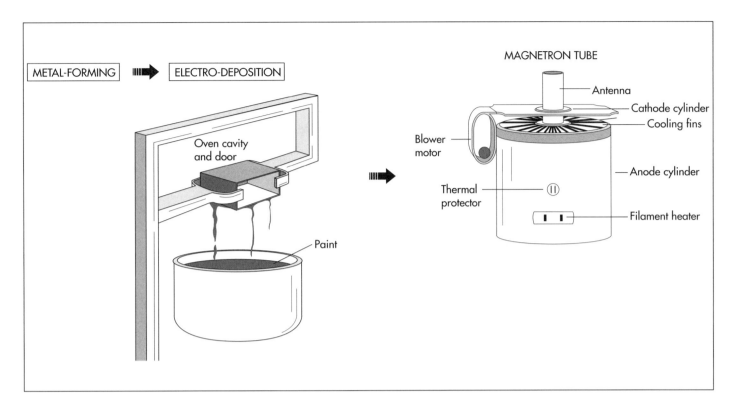

METAL-FORMING ➤ ELECTRO-DEPOSITION

Oven cavity and door

Paint

MAGNETRON TUBE

Antenna
Cathode cylinder
Cooling fins
Blower motor
Anode cylinder
Thermal protector
Filament heater

door frame has a small window to enable the cook to view the food while it is cooking.

Near the top of the steel oven cavity is a magnetron—an electronic tube that produces high-frequency microwave oscillations—which generates the microwaves. The microwaves are funneled through a metal waveguide and into a stirrer fan, also positioned near the top of the cavity. The fan distributes the microwaves evenly within the oven. Manufacturers vary the means by which they disburse microwaves to achieve uniform cooking patterns: some use dual stirrer fans located on opposite walls to direct microwaves to the cavity, while others use entry ports at the bottom of the cavity, allowing microwaves to enter from both the top and bottom. In addition, many ovens rotate food on a turntable.

Raw Materials

The cover or outer case of the microwave oven is usually a one-piece, wrap-around metal enclosure. The oven's inside panels and doors are made of galvanized or **stainless steel** and are given a coating of acrylic enamel, usually light in color to offer good visibility. The cooking surface is generally made of ceramic or glass. Inside the oven,

electromechanical components and controls consist of timer motors, switches, and relays. Also inside the oven are the magnetron tube, the waveguide, and the stirrer fan, all made of metal. The hardware that links the various components consists of a variety of metal and plastic parts such as gears, pulleys, belts, nuts, screws, washers, and cables.

The Manufacturing Process

Oven cavity and door manufacture

1 The process of manufacturing a microwave oven starts with the cavity and the door. First, the frame is formed using automatic metal-forming presses that make about 12 to 15 parts per minute. The frame is then rinsed in alkaline cleaner to get rid of any dirt or oil and further rinsed with water to get rid of the alkaline solution.

2 Next, each part is treated with zinc phosphate, which prepares it for electro-deposition. Electro-deposition consists of immersing the parts in a **paint** tank at 200 volts for 2.5 minutes. The resulting coating is about 1.5 mils thick. The parts are then moved through a paint bake operation where the paint is cured at 300 degrees Fahrenheit (149 degrees Celsius) for 20 minutes.

The oven cavity and door are made using metal-forming techniques and then painted using electro-deposition, in which electric current is used to apply the paint.

The magnetron tube subassembly includes several important parts. A powerful magnet is placed around the anode to provide the magnetic field in which the microwaves will be generated, while a thermal protector is mounted directly on the magnetron to prevent damage to the tube from overheating. An antenna enclosed in a glass tube is mounted on top of the anode, and the air within the tube is pumped out to create a vacuum. Also, a blower motor used to cool the metal fins of the magnetron is attached directly to the tube.

The chassis or frame is mounted in a pallet for the main assembly operation. A pallet is a vise-like device used in conjunction with other tools.

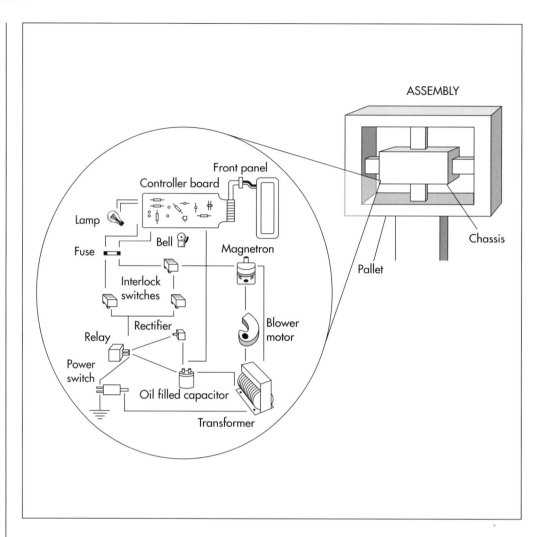

ASSEMBLY

Front panel
Controller board
Lamp
Bell
Fuse
Magnetron
Interlock switches
Blower motor
Rectifier
Relay
Power switch
Oil filled capacitor
Transformer
Pallet
Chassis

3 After the door has been painted, a perforated metal plate is attached to its window aperture. The plate reflects microwaves but allows light to enter the cavity (the door will not be attached to the cavity until later, when the chassis is assembled).

The magnetron tube subassembly

4 The magnetron tube assembly consists of a cathode cylinder, a filament heater, a metal anode, and an antenna. The filament is attached to the cathode, and the cathode is enclosed in the anode cylinder; this cell will provide the electricity that will help to generate the microwaves. Metal cooling fins are welded to the anode cylinder, and a powerful magnet is placed around the anode to provide the magnetic field in which the microwaves will be generated. A metal strap holds the complete assembly together. A thermal protector is mounted directly on the magnetron to prevent damage to the tube from overheating.

5 An antenna enclosed in a glass tube is mounted on top of the anode, and the air within the tube is pumped out to create a vacuum. The waveguide is connected to the magnetron on top of the protruding antenna, while a blower motor used to cool the metal fins of the magnetron is attached directly to the tube. Finally, a plastic fan is attached to the motor, where it will draw air from outside the oven and direct it towards the vanes. This completes the magnetron subassembly.

Main chassis assembly

6 The chassis assembly work is performed on a pallet—a work-holding device used in conjunction with other tools—located at the station. First, the main chassis is placed on the pallet, and the cavity is screwed on to the chassis. Next, the door is attached to the cavity and chassis by means of hinges. The magnetron tube is then bolted to the side of the cavity and the main chassis.

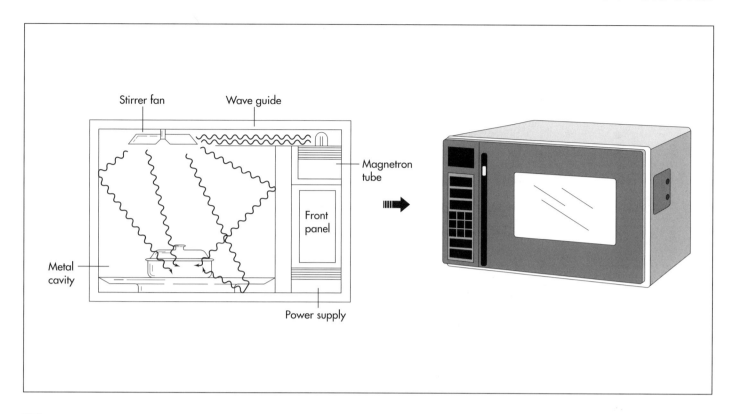

Stirrer fan

Wave guide

Magnetron tube

Front panel

Metal cavity

Power supply

7 The circuit that produces the voltage required to operate the magnetron tube consists of a large transformer, an oil-based capacitor, and a high voltage rectifier. All of these components are mounted directly on the chassis, close to the magnetron tube.

Stirrer fan

8 The stirrer fan used to circulate the microwaves is mounted on top of the cavity. Some manufacturers use a pulley to drive the fan from the magnetron blower motor; others use a separate stirrer motor attached directly to the fan. Once the stirrer fan is attached, a stirrer shield is screwed on top of the fan assembly. The shield prevents dirt and grease from entering the waveguide, where they could produce arcing and damage the magnetron.

Control switches, relays, and motors

9 The cook switch provides power to the transformer by energizing a relay and a timer. The relay is mounted close to the power transformer, while the timer is mounted on the control board. The defrost switch works like the cook switch, activating a motor and timer to operate the defrost cycle. Also mounted on the control board are a timer bell that rings when the cooking cycle is complete and a light switch that allows viewing of the cavity. A number of interlocking switches are mounted near the top and bottom of the door area. The interlocking switches are sometimes grouped together with a safety switch that monitors the other switches and provides protection if the door accidently opens during oven operation.

Front panel

10 A front panel that allows the operator to select the various settings and features available for cooking is attached to the chassis. Behind the front panel, the control circuit board is attached. The board, which controls the various programmed operations in their proper sequence when the switches are pushed on the front panel, is connected to the various components and the front panel by means of plug-in sockets and cables.

Making and assembling the case

11 The outer case of the microwave is made of metal and is assembled on a roll former. The case is slipped onto the pre-assembled microwave oven and bolted to the main chassis.

In a completed microwave oven, the magnetron tube creates the microwaves, and the waveguide directs them to the stirrer fan. In turn, this fan points the waves into the oven cavity where they heat the food inside.

Testing and packaging the oven

12 The power cords and dial knobs are now attached to the oven, and it is sent for automatic testing. Most manufacturers run the oven from 50-100 hours continuously as part of the testing process. After testing is complete, a palletizer robot records the model and serial data of the oven for inventory purposes, and the oven is sent for packaging. This completes the manufacturing process.

Quality Control

Extensive quality control during the manufacture of microwave ovens is essential, because microwave ovens emit radiation that can burn anyone exposed at high levels for prolonged periods. Federal regulations, applied to all ovens made after October 1971, limit the amount of radiation that can leak from an oven to 5 milliwatts of radiation per square centimeter at approximately 2 inches from the oven surface. The regulations also require all ovens to have two independent, interlocking switches to stop the production of microwaves the moment the latch is released or the door is opened.

In addition, a computer controlled scanner is used to measure emission leaks around the door, window, and back of the oven. Other scanners check the seating of the magnetron tube and antenna radiation. Each scanner operation relays data to the next-on-line operation so that any problems can be corrected.

The Future

Because of their speed and convenience, microwave ovens have become an indispensable part of modern kitchens. Many developments in the microwave market and allied industries are taking place fairly rapidly. For example, foods and utensils designed specially for microwave cooking have become a huge business. New features will also be introduced in microwaves themselves, including computerized storage of recipes that the consumer will be able to recall at the touch of a button. The display and programmability of the ovens will also be improved, and combination ovens capable of cooking with microwaves as well as by conventional methods will become a standard household product.

Where To Learn More

Books

Davidson, Homer L. *Microwave Oven Repair*, 2nd edition. Tab Books Inc., 1991.

Gallawa, J. Carlton. *The Complete Microwave Oven Service Handbook: Operation, Maintenance.* Prentice Hall, 1989.

Microwave Oven Radiation. U.S. department of Health and Human Services, 1986.

Pickett, Arnold and John Ketterer. *Household Equipment in Residential Design.* John Wiley and Sons, 1986.

Raytheon Company. *Appliance Manufacturer.* Cahners Publishing, 1985.

Periodicals

Klenck, Thomas. "How It Works: Microwave Oven." *Popular Mechanics.* September, 1989, p. 78.

Roman, Mark. "The Little Waves That Could." *Discover.* November, 1989, p. 54.

—*Rashid Riaz*

Mirror

Background

From the earliest recorded history, humans have been fascinated by reflections. Narcissus was supposedly bewitched by his own reflection in a pool of water, and magic powers are ascribed to mirrors in fairy tales. Mirrors have advanced from reflective pools and polished metal surfaces to clear glass hand-held and bathroom mirrors. They have been used in interior decoration since the 17th century, and reflective surfaces on cars and in hotel lobbies are still popular in modern design. Mirrors are used for practical purposes as well: examining our appearance, examining what is behind us on the road, building skyscrapers, and making scientific research instruments, such as microscopes and lasers.

The nature of modern mirrors is not fundamentally different from a pool of water. When light strikes any surface, some of it will be reflected. Mirrors are simply smooth surfaces with shiny, dark backgrounds that reflect very well. Water reflects well, glass reflects poorly, and polished metal reflects extremely well. The degree of reflectivity—how much light bounces off of a surface—and the diffusivity of a surface—what direction light bounces off of a surface—may be altered. These alterations are merely refinements, however. In general, all reflective surfaces, and hence, all mirrors, are really the same in character.

Man-made mirrors have been in existence since ancient times. The first mirrors were often sheets of polished metal and were used almost exclusively by the ruling classes. Appearance often reflected, and in some cases determined, position and power in society, so the demand for looking glasses was high, as was the demand for the improvement of mirror-making techniques. Silvering—the process of coating the back of a glass sheet with melted silver—became the most popular method for making mirrors in the 1600s. The glass used in these early mirrors was often warped, creating a ripple in the image. In some severe cases, the images these mirrors reflected were similar to those we'd see in a fun-house mirror today. Modern glassmaking and metallurgical techniques make it easy to produce sheets of glass that are very flat and uniformly coated on the back, improving image clarity tremendously. Still, the quality of a mirror depends on the time and materials expended to make it. A handheld purse mirror may reflect a distorted image, while a good bathroom mirror will probably have no noticeable distortions. Scientific mirrors are designed with virtually no imperfections or distorting qualities whatsoever.

Materials technology drastically affects the quality of a mirror. Light reflects best from surfaces that are non-diffusive, that is, smooth and opaque, rather than transparent. Any flaw in this arrangement will detract from the effectiveness of the mirror. Innovations in mirror making have been directed towards flattening the glass used and applying metal coatings of uniform thickness, because light traveling through different thicknesses of glass over different parts of a mirror results in a distorted image. It is due to these irregularities that some mirrors make you look thinner and some fatter than normal. If the metal backing on a mirror is scratched or thin in spots, the brightness of the reflection will also be uneven. If the coating is very thin, it may be possible to see through the mirror. This is how one-way

Silvering—coating the back of a glass sheet with melted silver—was the most popular method for making mirrors in the 1600s. The glass used in these early mirrors was often warped, creating a ripple in the image. Modern glassmaking techniques make it easy to produce sheets of glass that are very flat and uniformly coated on the back, improving image clarity tremendously.

mirrors are made. Non-opaque coating is layered over the thin, metal backing and only one side of the mirror (the reflecting side) is lit. This allows a viewer on the other side, in a darkened room, to see through.

Raw Materials

Glass, the main component of mirrors, is a poor reflector. It reflects only about 4 percent of the light which strikes it. It does, however, possess the property of uniformity, particularly when polished. This means that the glass contains very few pits after polishing and will form an effective base for a reflective layer of metal. When the metal layer is deposited, the surface is very even, with no bumps or wells. Glass is also considered a good material for mirrors because it can be molded into various shapes for specialty mirrors. Glass sheets are made from silica, which can be mined or refined from sand. Glass made from natural crystals of silica is known as fused quartz. There are also synthetic glasses, which are referred to as synthetic fused silica. The silica, or quartz, is melted to high temperatures, and poured or rolled out into sheets.

A few other types of glass are used for high-quality scientific grade mirrors. These usually contain some other chemical component to strengthen the glass or make it resistant to certain environmental extremes. Pyrex, for example, is a borosilicate glass—a glass composed of silica and boron—that is used when mirrors must withstand high temperatures.

In some cases, a plastic substrate will do as well as a glass one. In particular, mirrors on children's toys are often made this way, so they don't break as easily. Plastic polymers are manufactured from petroleum and other organic chemicals. They can be injection molded into any desired shape, including flat sheets and circles, and can be opaque or transparent as the design requires.

These base materials must be coated to make a mirror. Metallic coatings are the most common. A variety of metals, such as silver, **gold**, and chrome, are appropriate for this application. Silver was the most popular mirror backing one hundred years ago, leading to the coinage of the term "silvering." Old silver-backed mirrors often have dark lines behind the glass, however, because the material was coated very thinly and unevenly, causing it to flake off, scratch or tarnish. More recently, before 1940, mirror manufacturers used mercury because it spread evenly over the surface of the glass and did not tarnish. This practice was also eventually abandoned, for it posed the problem of sealing in the toxic liquid. Today, aluminum is the most commonly used metallic coating for mirrors.

Scientific grade mirrors are sometimes coated with other materials, like silicon oxides and silicon nitrides, in up to hundreds of layers of, each a 10,000th of an inch thick. These types of coatings, referred to as *dielectric coatings,* are used both by themselves as reflectors, and as protective finishes on metallic coatings. They are more scratch resistant than metal. Scientific mirrors also use silver coatings, and sometimes gold coatings as well, to reflect light of a particular color of light more or less well.

Design

Surface regularity is probably the most important design characteristic of mirrors. Mirrors for household use must meet roughly the same specifications as window panes and picture frame glass. The glass sheets used must be reasonably flat and durable. The designer need only specify the thickness required; for example, thicker mirrors are more durable, but they are also heavier. Scientific mirrors usually have specially designed surfaces. These surfaces must be uniformly smooth within several 1000ths of an inch, and can be designed with a specific curvature, just like **eyeglass lens**es. The design principle for these mirrors is the same as that of eyewear: a mirror may be intended to focus light as well as reflect it.

The mirror design will also specify the type of coating to be used. Coating material is chosen based on required durability and reflectivity and, depending on the intended purpose of the mirror, it may be applied on the front or back surface of the mirror. Any subsequent layers of protective coatings must also be specified at this stage. For most common mirrors, the reflective coating will be applied on the back surface of the glass because it is less likely to be harmed there. The back side is then frequently mounted in a

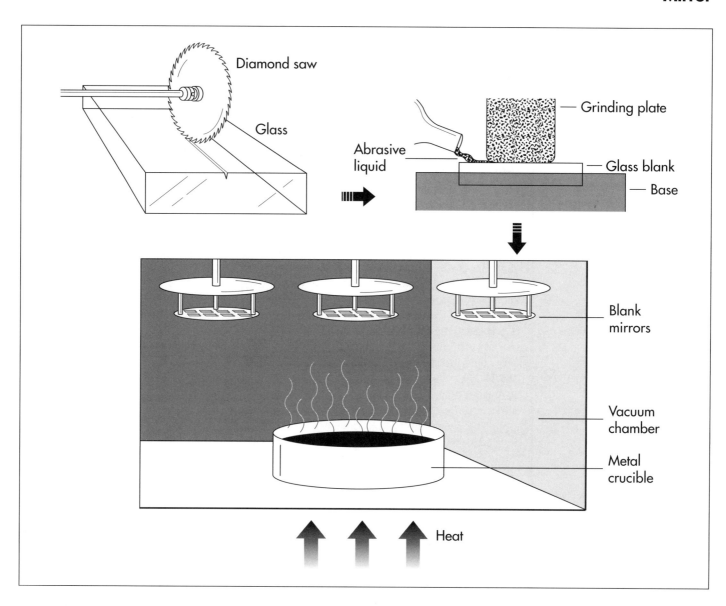

plastic or metal frame so as to entirely seal the coating from the air and sharp objects.

For scientific use, the color, or wavelength of light, which the mirror will reflect must be considered. For standard visible light or ultraviolet light mirrors, aluminum coatings are common. If the mirror is to be used with infrared light, a silver or gold coating is best. Dielectric coatings are also good in the infrared range. Ultimately, however, the choice of coating will depend on durability as well as wavelength range, and some reflectivity may be sacrificed for resilience. A dielectric coating, for example, is much more scratch resistant than a metallic coating and, despite the additional cost, these coatings are often added on top of metal to protect it. Coatings on scientific grade mirrors are usually applied on the front surface of the glass,

because light which travels through glass will always distort to a small degree. This is undesirable in most scientific applications.

The Manufacturing Process

Cutting and shaping the glass

1 The first step in manufacturing any mirror is cutting the outline of the glass "blank" to suit the application. If the mirror is for an **automobile**, for example, the glass will be cut out to fit in the mirror mount on the car. Although some mirror manufacturers cut their own glass, others receive glass that has already been cut into blanks. Regardless of who cuts the glass, very hard, finely pointed blades are used to do the cutting. Diamond scribes or saws—sharp metal points or saws

The initial step in mirror manufacture involves cutting and shaping the glass blanks. Cutting is usually done with a saw with diamond dust embedded in the tips. Next, the blanks are put in optical grinding machines, which use abrasive liquid plus a grinding plate to produce a very even, smooth finish on the blanks. The reflective material is then applied in an evaporator, which heats the metal coating until it evaporates onto the surface of the blanks.

with diamond dust embedded in them—are often used because the diamond will wear down the glass before the glass wears down the diamond. The cutting method used depends entirely on the final shape the mirror will take. In one method, the blades or scribes may be used to cut partway through the glass; pressure can then be used to break the glass along the score line. In another method, a machine uses a diamond saw to cut all the way through the glass by drawing the blade back and forth or up and down multiple times, like an automated bandsaw. Cutting is usually done before the metal coating is applied, because the coating may flake off the glass as a result of the cut. An alternative to cutting the glass to form blanks is to mold the glass in its molten state.

2 Blanks are then placed in optical grinding machines. These machines consist of large base plates full of depressions that hold the blanks. The blank-filled base is placed against another metal plate with the desired surface shape: flat, convex, or concave. A grinding compound—a gritty liquid—is spread over the glass blanks as they are rubbed or rolled against the curved surface. The action is similar to grinding spices with a mortar and pestle. The grit in the compound gradually wears away the glass surface until it assumes the same shape as the grinding plate. Finer and finer grits are used until the surface is very smooth and even.

Hand grinding techniques exist as well, but they are extremely time-consuming and difficult to control. They are only used in cases where mechanical grinding would be impossible, as is the case with very large or unusually shaped surfaces. A commercial optical grinder can accommodate 50 to 200 blanks, which are all polished simultaneously. This is much more efficient than hand grinding. Even specialty optics can be made mechanically in adjustable equipment.

Applying the reflective material

3 When the glass surfaces are shaped appropriately and polished to a smooth finish, they are coated with whatever reflective material the designer has chosen. Regardless of the coating material, it is applied in an apparatus called an evaporator. The evaporator is a large vacuum chamber with an upper plate for supporting the blank

mirrors, and a lower crucible for melting the coating metal. It is so called because metal is heated in the crucible to the point that it evaporates into the vacuum, depositing a coating on the surface of the glass much like hot breath will steam a cold window. Blanks are centered over holes in the upper plate that allow the metal vapor to reach the surface of the glass. Metals can be heated to several hundreds or thousands of degrees (depending on the boiling point of the metal), before they vaporize. The temperature and timing for this procedure are controlled very precisely to achieve exactly the right thickness of metal.This method of coating creates very uniform and highly reflective surfaces.

4 The shape of the holes in the upper plate will be transferred to the glass in metal, like **paint** through a stencil. This effect is often used to intentionally pattern the mirror. Metal stencils, or masks, can be applied to the surface of the glass to create one or more patterns.

5 Dielectric coatings—either as reflective layers or as protective layers over metal ones—are applied in much the same way, except that gases are used instead of metal chunks. Silicon oxides and silicon nitrides are typically used as dielectric coatings. When these gases combine in extreme heat, they react to form a solid substance. This reaction product forms a coating just like metal does.

6 Several evaporation steps may be combined to make a multiple-layer coating. Clear dielectric materials may be evaporated on top of metal or other dielectrics to change the reflective or mechanical properties of a surface. Mirrors with silvering on the back of the glass, for instance, often have an opaque dielectric layer applied to improve the reflectivity and keep the metal from scratching. One-way mirrors are the exception to this procedure, in which case great care must be taken not to damage the thin metal coating.

7 Finally, when the proper coatings have been applied, the finished mirror is mounted in a base or packed carefully in a shock resistant package for shipping.

Quality Control

How good does a mirror have to be? Is it sufficient to have 80 percent of the light bounce off? Does all 80 percent have to bounce in exactly the same direction? The answer is dependent on the application. A purse mirror might only be 80 or 90 percent reflective, and might have some slight irregularity in the thickness of the glass (like ripples on the surface of a pond). The image would be slightly distorted in this case, but the distortion would be barely visible to the naked eye. If, however, a mirror is to be used for a scientific application, for example in a telescope, the shape of the surface and the reflectivity of the coating must be known to a very specific degree, to insure the reflected light goes exactly where the telescope designer wants it, and at the right intensity. The tolerances on the mirror will affect the cost and ease with which it can be manufactured.

Batch mirror uniformity is the first and foremost job of quality assurance. Mirrors on the edge of a grinding plate or evaporator chamber may not have the same surface or coating as those in the center of the apparatus. If there is a wide range of metal thicknesses or surface flatnesses in a single batch of mirrors, the process must be adjusted to improve uniformity.

Several methods are employed to test the integrity of a mirror. The surface quality is examined first visually for scratches, unevenness, pits, or ripples. This can be done with the unaided eye, with a microscope, or with an infrared photographic process designed to show differences in metal thicknesses.

For more stringent surface control, a profile of the mirror can be measured by running a stylus along the surface. The position of the stylus is recorded as it is dragged across the mirror. This is similar to the way a record player works. Like the record player, the drawback to a mechanical stylus is that it can damage the surface it is detecting. Mirror manufacturers have come to the same solution as the recording industry: use a laser. The laser can be used for non-destructive testing in the same way a **compact disc player** reads the music from a disc without altering its surface.

In addition to these mechanical tests, mirrors may be exposed to a variety of environmental conditions. Car mirrors, for example, are taken through extremes of cold and heat to

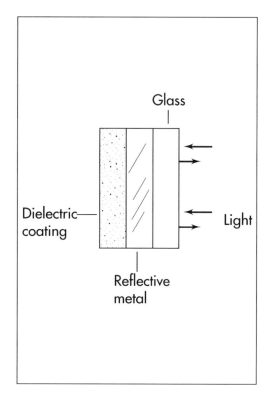

A typical mirror can include a metal reflective layer and one or more dielectric coatings—as protective layers over the metal one. Dielectric coatings are applied in much the same way as metal layers, except that gases such as silicon oxides and silicon nitrides are used instead of metal chunks.

insure that they will withstand weather conditions, while bathroom mirrors are tested for water resistance.

The Future

As glassmaking techniques improve, mirrors find a more elaborate place in art and architecture. Stronger, lighter glasses are more attractive to designers. Some one-way mirror manufacturing techniques allow windows to be manufactured that are mirrored on the outside. This creates a distinctive appearance on a building and also makes the building's air conditioning system more efficient by deflecting heat during the summer. This type of mirror is now commonly seen on office buildings.

Mirrors will also continue to be used in sophisticated optical applications, from microscopes and telescopes to laser-based reading systems such as compact disc players and **bar code scanner**s.

Where To Learn More

Books

Hecht, Eugene. *Optics.* Addison-Wesley Publishing Co., 1974.

Korsch, Dietrich. *Reflective Optics.* Academic Press, 1991.

Londono, ed. *Recent Trends in Optical Systems Design: Computer Lens Design.* SPIE-International Society for Optical Engineering, 1987.

Periodicals

Derra, Skip. "Spin Casting Method Makes the Grade for Telescopic Mirrors." *Research & Development.* August, 1989, p. 24.

Folger, Tim and Roger Ressmeyer. "The Big Eye." *Discover.* November, 1991, p. 40.

Hogan, Brian J. "Astronomy Gets a Sharper Vision." *Design News.* August 26, 1991, p. 110.

"Custom Optics." *Laser Focus World.* December, 1992.

Nash, J. Madeline. "Shoot for the Stars." *Time.* April 27, 1992, p. 56.

Walker, Jearl. "Wonders with the Retroreflector, a Mirror That Removes Distortion from a Light Beam." *Scientific American.* April, 1986, p. 118.

—*Leslie G. Melcer*

Nail Polish

Background

Unlike many other cosmetics that have a history of hundreds or even thousands of years, nail polish (or lacquer, or enamel) is almost completely an invention of twentieth century technology. Nail coverings were not unknown in ancient times—the upper classes of ancient Egypt probably used henna to dye both hair and fingernails—but essentially, its composition, manufacture and handling reflect developments in modern chemical technology.

Modern nail polish is sold in liquid form in small bottles and is applied with a tiny brush. Within a few minutes after application, the substance hardens and forms a shiny coating on the fingernail that is both water- and chip-resistant. Generally, a coating of nail polish may last several days before it begins to chip and fall off. Nail polish can also be removed manually by applying nail polish "remover," a substance designed to break down and dissolve the polish.

Raw Materials

There is no single formula for nail polish. There are, however, a number of ingredient types that are used. These basic components include: film forming agents, resins and plasticizers, solvents, and coloring agents. The exact formulation of a nail polish, apart from being a corporate secret, greatly depends upon choices made by chemists and chemical engineers in the research and development phase of manufacturing. Additionally, as chemicals and other ingredients become accepted or discredited for some uses, adjustments are made. For example, formaldehyde was once frequently used in polish production, but now it is rarely used.

The primary ingredient in nail polish is nitrocellulose (cellulose nitrate) cotton, a flammable and explosive ingredient also used in making dynamite. Nitrocellulose is a liquid mixed with tiny, near-microscopic cotton fibers. In the manufacturing process, the cotton fibers are ground even smaller and do not need to be removed. The nitrocellulose can be purchased in various viscosities to match the desired viscosity of the final product.

Nitrocellulose acts as a film forming agent. For nail polish to work properly, a hard film must form on the exposed surface of the nail, but it cannot form so quickly that it prevents the material underneath from drying. (Consider commercial puddings or gelatin products that dry or film on an exposed surface and protect the moist product underneath.) By itself or used with other functional ingredients, the nitrocellulose film is brittle and adheres poorly to nails.

Manufacturers add synthetic resins and plasticizers (and occasionally similar, natural products) to their mixes to improve flexibility, resistance to soap and water, and other qualities; older recipes sometimes even used nylon for this purpose. Because of the number of desired qualities involved, however, there is no single resin or combination of resins that meets every specification. Among the resins and plasticizers in use today are castor oil, amyl and butyl stearate, and mixes of glycerol, fatty acids, and acetic acids.

The colorings and other components of nail polish must be contained within one or more solvents that hold the colorings and other materials until the polish is applied. After application, the solvent must be able to evaporate. In many cases, the solvent also acts a

The primary ingredient in nail polish is nitrocellulose cotton, a flammable and explosive ingredient also used in making dynamite. Nitrocellulose is a liquid mixed with tiny, near-microscopic cotton fibers. In the manufacturing process, the cotton fibers are ground even smaller and do not need to be removed.

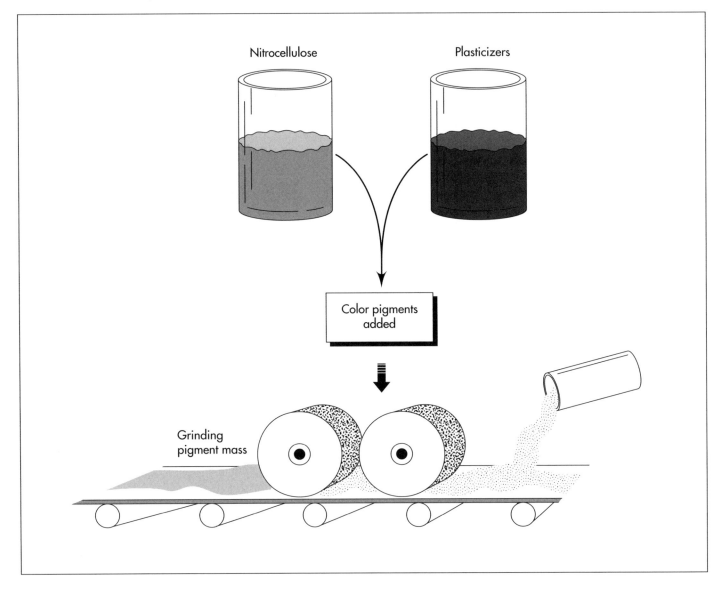

Nail polish is made by combining nitrocellulose and plasticizers with color pigments. The mixing is done in a "two-roll" differential speed mill, which grinds the pigment between a pair of rollers that are able to work with increasing speed as the pigment is ground down. The goal is to produce fine dispersion of the color.

plasticizer. Butyl stearate and acetate compounds are perhaps the most common.

Finally, the polish must have a color. Early polishes used soluble dyes, but today's product contains pigments of one type or another. Choice of pigment and its ability to mix well with the solvent and other ingredients is essential to producing a good quality product.

Nail polish is a "suspension" product, in which particles of color can only be held by the solvent for a relatively short period of time, rarely more than two or three years. Shaking a bottle of nail polish before use helps to restore settled particles to the suspension; a very old bottle of nail polish may have so much settled pigment that it can never be restored to the solvent. The problem of settling is perhaps the most difficult to be addressed in the manufacturing process.

In addition to usual coloring pigments, other color tones can be added depending upon the color, tone, and hue of the desired product. Micas (tiny reflective minerals), also used in **lipstick**s, are a common additive, as is "pearl" or "fish scale" essence. "Pearl" or "guanine" is literally made from small fish scales and skin, suitably cleaned, and mixed with solvents such as castor oil and butyl acetate. The guanine can also be mixed with **gold**, silver, and bronze tones.

Pigment choices are restricted by the federal Food and Drug Administration (FDA), which maintains lists of pigments considered acceptable and others that are dangerous and cannot be used. Manufacturing plants are inspected regularly, and manufacturers must be able to prove they are using only FDA approved pigments. Since the FDA lists of ac-

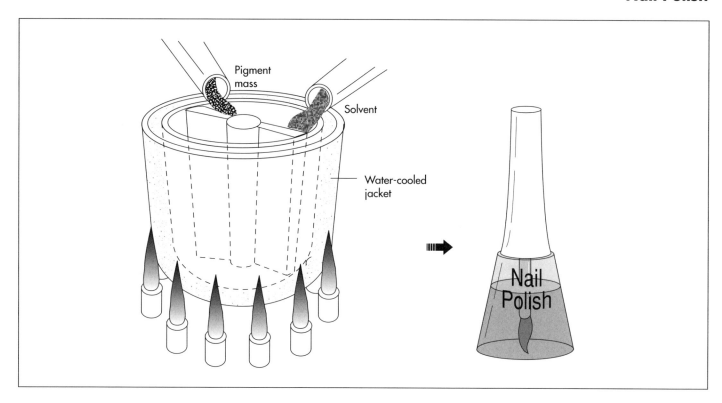

Pigment mass

Solvent

Water-cooled jacket

Nail Polish

ceptable and unacceptable pigments change with new findings and reexaminations of colors, manufacturers occasionally have to reformulate a polish formula.

The Manufacturing Process

Early methods of making nail polish used a variety of methods that today look charmingly amateurish. One common technique was to mix cleaned scraps of movie film and other cellulose with alcohol and castor oil and leave the mixture to soak overnight in a covered container. The mixture was then strained, colored, and perfumed. Though recognizable as nail polish, the product was far from what we have available today.

The modern manufacturing process is a very sophisticated operation utilizing highly skilled workers, advanced machinery, and even robotics. Today's consumers expect a nail polish to apply smoothly, evenly, and easily; to set relatively quickly; and to be resistant to chipping and peeling. In addition, the polish should be dermatologically innocuous.

Mixing the pigment with nitrocellulose and plasticizer

1 The pigments are mixed with nitrocellulose and plasticizer using a "two-roll" dif-

ferential speed mill. This mill grinds the pigment between a pair of rollers that are able to work with increasing speed as the pigment is ground down. The goal is to produce fine dispersion of the color. A variation of this mill is the Banbury Mixer (used also in the production of rubber for **rubber band**s).

2 When properly and fully milled, the mixture is removed from the mill in sheet form and then broken up into small chips for mixing with the solvent. The mixing is performed in **stainless steel** kettles that can hold anywhere from 5 to 2,000 gallons. Stainless steel must be used because the nitrocellulose is extremely reactive in the presence of iron. The kettles are jacketed so that the mixture can be cooled by circulating cold water or another liquid around the outside of the kettle. The temperature of the kettle, and the rate of cooling, are controlled by both computers and technicians.

This step is performed in a special room or area designed to control the hazards of fire and explosion. Most modern factories perform this step in an area with walls that will close in if an alarm sounds and, in the event of explosion, with ceilings that will safely blow off without endangering the rest of the structure.

Once the pigment mass is prepared, it is mixed with solvent in a stainless steel kettle. The kettle has a water-jacket to facilitate cooling of the mixture.

Adding other ingredients

3 Materials are mixed in computerized, closed kettles. At the end of the process, the mix is cooled slightly before the addition of such other materials as perfumes and moisturizers.

4 The mixture is then pumped into smaller, 55 gallon drums, and then trucked to a production line. The finished nail polish is pumped into explosion proof pumps, and then into smaller bottles suitable for the retail market.

Quality Control

Extreme attention to quality control is essential throughout the manufacturing process. Not only does quality control increase safety in the process, but it is the only way that a manufacturer can be assured of consumer confidence and loyalty. A single bottle of poor quality polish can lose a customer forever. Regardless of quality control, however, no single nail polish is perfect; the polish always represents a chemical compromise between what is desired and what the manufacturer is able to produce.

The nail polish is tested throughout the manufacturing process for several important factors (drying time, smoothness of flow, gloss, hardness, color, abrasion resistance, etc.). Subjective testing, where the mixture or final product is examined or applied, is ongoing. Objective, laboratory testing of samples, though more time consuming, is also necessary to ensure a usable product. Laboratory tests are both complicated and unforgiving, but no manufacturer would do without them.

The Future

Perhaps the major problem with nail polishes—from the consumer's point of view—is the length of the drying time. Various methods of producing fast-drying polish have recently been patented, and these methods, along with others that are still being developed, may result in marketable products.

Of all the different types of cosmetics, nail polish is the one that is most likely to continue to be positively affected by advancements and developments in the chemistry field.

Where To Learn More

Books

Balsam, M. S., ed. *Cosmetics: Science & Technology.* Krieger Publishing, 1991.

Chemistry of Soap, Detergents, & Cosmetics. Flinn Scientific, 1989.

Flick, Ernest W. *Cosmetic & Toiletry Formulations.* 2nd ed., Noyes Press, 1992.

Meyer, Carolyn. *Being Beautiful: The Story of Cosmetics From Ancient Art to Modern Science.* William Morrow and Company, 1977.

Wells, F. V. and Irwin I. Lubowe, M.D., eds. *Cosmetics and The Skin.* Reinhold Publishing Corp., 1964.

Periodicals

Andrews, Edmund L. "Patents: A Nail Polish That Dries Fast." *New York Times,* March 7, 1992, p. 40.

Andrews, Edmund L. "Patents: Quick-Dry Coating for Nail Polish." *New York Times,* June 13, 1992, p. 36.

"Makeup Formulary." *Cosmetics & Toiletries,* April, 1986, pp. 103-22.

Ikeda, T., T. Kobayashi, and C. Tanaka. "Development of Highly Safe Nail Enamel." *Cosmetics & Toiletries,* April, 1988, pp. 59-60+.

Schlossman, Mitchell L. "Nail Cosmetics." *Cosmetics & Toiletries,* April, 1986, pp. 23-4+.

—*Lawrence H. Berlow*

Necktie

Background

Neckwear dates back 30,000 years when primitive peoples adorned their chests with beads and bangles. Throughout the ages, people continued to wear wood, metal, pearls, feathers, glass, or cloth around their necks. Perhaps the superstition widely believed in the Middle Ages that bodily ills entered one through the throat had something to do with the continued popularity of a protective neckcloth, or perhaps soldiers felt more secure in having their neck covered in battle.

The first neckties, known as cravats, were worn by soldiers in the seventeenth century. According to legend, Croatian mercenaries, after having fought over Turkey, visited Louis XIV in Paris to celebrate their victory. The Sun King was so impressed by the colored silk scarfs the soldiers wore around their necks that he adopted the fashion himself. The mercenaries, called the Royal Cravattes (from the Croatian word *kravate*), lent their name to what became a popular fashion accessory. The style quickly spread to England after exiled Charles II returned from France, bringing with him his interest in cravats, and they have continued to be a part of men's neckwear since then.

The stock tie, which appeared to be a well-tied knot in the front but was actually fastened at the back of the neck, was an alternative to the cravat for almost two hundred years, only to be forgotten by the early 1900s. The modern necktie became the norm in the twentieth century. Ninety-five million ties are sold in the United States annually, generating more than $1.4 billion in retail sales, according to *MR Magazine* and the Neckwear Association of America's 1992 Handbook.

Raw Materials

The most commonly used fibers for the manufacturing of neckties are silk, polyester, **wool** and wool blends, acetate, **rayon**, nylon, cotton, linen, and ramie. Neckties made from silk represent about 40 percent of the market. Raw silk is primarily imported from China and, to a far lesser extent, Brazil. Domestic weavers of tie fabrics buy their silk yarn in its natural state and have it finished and dyed by specialists. Technological advances have made possible the use of microfiber polyesters, which produce a rich, soft fabric resembling silk and which can be combined with natural or other artificial fibers to produce a wide range of effects.

Design

The design of neckties is an interactive process between weavers and tie manufacturers. Because small quantities in any given pattern and color are produced, and because fabrics can be so complex, tie fabric weaving is seen as an art form by many in the industry.

Much of neckwear design is done in Como, Italy. If a new design is requested, time is spent developing ideas, producing sample goods, and booking orders against the samples. Most of the time, however, weavers work with open-stock items (designs that have been previously used and have a lasting appeal). Weavers use computerized silk screens, a process that has replaced the more time and labor-intensive manual silk-screening. When working with a standard design, the designer fills in each year's popular colors, changing both background and foreground colors, making it broader or narrower, larger or smaller, according to demand. The

The first neckties, known as cravats, were worn by soldiers in the seventeenth century. According to legend, Croatian mercenaries, after having fought over Turkey, visited Louis XIV in Paris to celebrate their victory. The Sun King was so impressed by the colored silk scarfs the soldiers wore that he adopted the fashion himself.

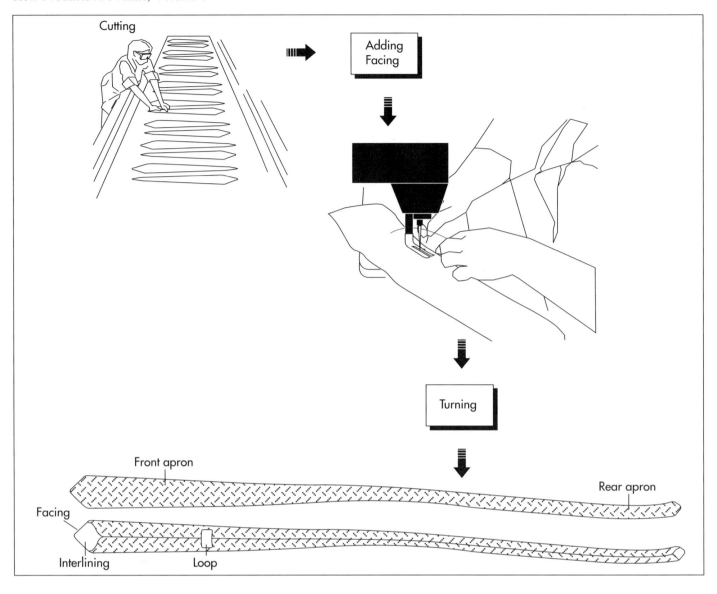

Cutting

Adding Facing

Turning

Front apron

Rear apron

Facing

Interlining

Loop

The first step in the manufacture of neckties is cutting the pieces from 40-yard bolts of cloth. Next, using a sewing machine, workers join the tie's 3 sections on the bias in the neckband area and then add the facing to the back of the tie's ends. At this point, the tie is inside out. After the interlining is stitched to the tie, the tie is turned right-side out.

manufacturer offers input and refinements in coloration and patterns. If willing to commit to a large amount of yardage, a manufacturer can also develop his or her own design and commission a weaver to produce it.

Once the design is complete, it is sent to mills where it is imprinted onto 40-yard bolts of silk. The bolts of silk are then sent to the United States for manufacturing.

The main components of a necktie are the outer fabric, or shell, the interlining (both cut on the bias), and the facing or tipping, which is stitched together by a resilient slip-stitch so that the finished tie can "give" while being tied and recover from constant knotting. The quality of the materials and construction determines if a tie will drape properly and hold its shape without wrinkling.

A well-cut lining is the essence of a good necktie. This interlining determines not only the shape of the tie but also how well it will wear. Therefore, it must be properly coordinated in blend, nap, and weight to the shell fabric. Lightweight outer material may require heavier interlining, while heavier outer fabrics need lighter interlining to give the necessary hand, drape, and recovery. Most interlining manufacturers use a marking system to identify the weight and content of their cloths, usually colored stripes, with one stripe being the lightest and six stripes being the heaviest. This facilitates inventory control and manufacturing.

A completed tie measures from 53 to 57 inches in length. Extra-long ties, recommended for tall men or men with large necks, are 60 to 62 inches long, and student ties are between 48 and 50 inches in length.

The Manufacturing Process

Cutting the outer fabric

1 In the workroom, an operator first spreads the 40-yard bolts of cloth on a long cutting table. Cutting the outer fabric is done by a skilled hand to maximize the yield, or the number of ties cut from the piece of goods. If the fabric has a random design, the operator stacks between 24 and 72 plies of fabric pieces in preparation for cutting the fabric. If pattern of the fabric (or of the "goods") consists of panels, such as stripes with a medallion at the bottom, these panels are then stacked according to the pattern.

Adding the facing

2 Using the chain stitch of a sewing machine, sewing operators join the tie's three sections on the bias in the neckband area. The operator now adds the facing, or tipping (an extra piece of silk, nylon, rayon, or polyester), to the back of the tie's ends. Facing gives a crisp, luxurious hand to the shell. Two types of facing are currently utilized. Three-quarter facing extends six to eight inches upward from the point of the tie, while full facing extends even higher, ending just under the knot.

3 A quarter to a half of an inch of the shell of the fabric is now turned under, to form a point. The point is then machine-hemmed by the sewing operator.

Piece pressing

4 Quality silk ties are pocket or piece-pressed. This means that the joint at the neck (the piecing) is pressed flat so the wearer will not be inconvenienced by any bulkiness.

Interlining

5 The interlining is slip-stitched to the outer shell with resilient nylon thread, which runs through the middle of the tie. Most ties are slip-stitched with a Liba machine, a semi-automated machine that closely duplicates the look and resiliency of hand stitching. Hand stitching is often used in the manufacture of high-quality neckties because it offers maximum resiliency and draping qualities.

The technique is characterized by the irregularly spaced stitches on the reverse of the tie when the seam is spread slightly apart; by the dangling, loose thread with a tiny knot at the end of the reverse of the front apron; and by the ease with which the tie can slide up and down this thread.

Turning the lining

6 Using a turning machine or a manual turner (with a rod about 9 1/2 inches long), an operator turns the tie right-side out by pulling one end of the tie through the other. While not yet pressed, the tie is almost complete. On silk ties only, the lining is then tucked by hand into the bottom corner of the long end of the tie. If necessary, the operator hand-trims the lining to fit the point of the long end. (In all other ties, the lining does not reach all the way to the bottom corner.)

7 A final piece to be sewn on is the loop, which serves both as a holder for the thin end of the tie when it's being worn and as the manufacturer's label.

The Future

Relatively recent disruptions in the supply of raw silk from China, in addition to technological advancements, have highlighted the advantages of using man-made fiber yarns. These artificial fibers are readily and dependably synthesized from domestic resources and are also usually yarn-dyed. Microfiber polyester or nylon fibers (with a denier per filament count of one or less) can be bundled into yarn finer than cotton and silk and can be combined with natural or other man-made fibers to produce a wide range of effects. Introduced into fabrics as air textured, false twist textured, or fully-drawn flat yarns, they produce a rich, soft, silk-like hand.

Where To Learn More

Books

Boucher, Francois. *20,000 Years of Fashion: The History of Costume and Personal Adornment.* Harry N. Abrams, Inc., Publishers, 1966.

Gibbings, Sarah. *The Tie: Trends and Traditions.* Barron's, 1990.

History of Costume from Ancient Egypt to the Twentieth Century. Harper and Row Publishers, Inc., 1965.

Schoeffler, O. E. and William Gale. *Esquire's Encyclopedia of 20th Century Men's Fashions*. McGraw Hill, Inc., 1973.

Yarwood, Doreen. *The Encyclopedia of World Costume*. Charles Scribner's and Sons, 1978.

—*Eva Sideman*

Optical Fiber

Background

An optical fiber is a single, hair-fine filament drawn from molten silica glass. These fibers are replacing metal wire as the transmission medium in high-speed, high-capacity communications systems that convert information into light, which is then transmitted via fiber optic cable. Currently, American telephone companies represent the largest users of fiber optic cables, but the technology is also used for power lines, local access computer networks, and video transmission.

Alexander Graham Bell, the American inventor best known for developing the telephone, first attempted to communicate using light around 1880. However, light wave communication did not become feasible until the mid-twentieth century, when advanced technology provided a transmission source, the laser, and an efficient medium, the optical fiber. The laser was invented in 1960 and, six years later, researchers in England discovered that silica glass fibers would carry light waves without significant attenuation, or loss of signal. In 1970, a new type of laser was developed, and the first optical fibers were produced commercially.

In a fiber optic communications system, cables made of optical fibers connect datalinks that contain lasers and light detectors. To transmit information, a datalink converts an analog electronic signal—a telephone conversation or the output of a video camera—into digital pulses of laser light. These travel through the optical fiber to another datalink, where a light detector reconverts them into an electronic signal.

Raw Materials

Optical fibers are composed primarily of silicon dioxide (SiO_2), though minute amounts of other chemicals are often added. Highly purified silica powder was used in the now-outmoded crucible manufacturing method, while liquid silicon tetrachloride ($SiCl_4$) in a gaseous stream of pure oxygen (O_2) is the principal source of silicon for the vapor deposition method currently in widespread use. Other chemical compounds such as germanium tetrachloride ($GeCl_4$) and phosphorus oxychloride ($POCl_3$) can be used to produce core fibers and outer shells, or *claddings,* with function-specific optical properties.

Because the purity and chemical composition of the glass used in optical fibers determine the most important characteristic of a fiber—degree of attenuation—research now focuses on developing glasses with the highest possible purity. Glasses with a high fluoride content hold the most promise for improving optical fiber performance because they are transparent to almost the entire range of visible light frequencies. This makes them especially valuable for multimode optical fibers, which can transmit hundreds of discrete light wave signals concurrently.

Design

In a fiber optic cable, many individual optical fibers are bound together around a central steel cable or high-strength plastic carrier for support. This core is then covered with protective layers of materials such as aluminum, Kevlar, and polyethylene (the cladding). Because the core and the cladding are constructed of slightly differing materials, light

Because the purity and chemical composition of the glass used in optical fibers determine the most important characteristic of a fiber—degree of attenuation—research now focuses on developing glasses with the highest possible purity. Glasses with a high fluoride content hold the most promise for improving optical fiber performance because they are transparent to almost the entire range of visible light frequencies.

To make an optical fiber, layers of silicon dioxide are first deposited on the inside surface of a hollow substrate rod. This is done using Modified Chemical Vapor Deposition, in which a gaseous stream of pure oxygen combined with various chemical vapors is applied to the rod. As the gas contacts the hot surface of the rod, a glassy soot several layers thick forms inside the rod.

After the soot is built up to the desired thickness, the substrate rod is moved through other heating steps to drive out any moisture and bubbles trapped in the soot layers. During heating, the substrate rod and internal soot layers solidify to form the boule or preform of highly pure silicon dioxide.

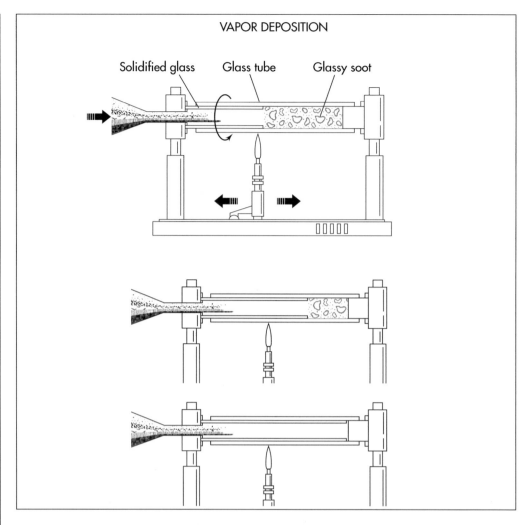

VAPOR DEPOSITION

Solidified glass Glass tube Glassy soot

travels through them at different speeds. As a light wave traveling in the fiber core reaches the boundary between the core and cladding, these compositional differences between the two cause the light wave to bend back into the core. Thus, as a pulse of light travels through an optical fiber, it is constantly bouncing away from the cladding. A pulse moves through the optical fiber at the speed of light—186,290 miles per second (299,340 kilometers per second) in a vacuum, somewhat slower in practice—losing energy only because of impurities in the glass and because of energy absorption by irregularities in the glass structure.

Energy losses (attenuation) in an optical fiber are measured in terms of loss (in decibels, a unit of energy) per distance of fiber. Typically, an optical fiber has losses as low as 0.2 decibels per kilometer, meaning that after a certain distance the signal becomes weak and must be strengthened, or *repeated.* With current datalink technology, laser sig-

nal repeaters are necessary about every 30 kilometers (18.5 miles) in a long-distance cable. However, on-going research in optical material purity is aimed at extending the distance between repeaters of an optical fiber up to 100 kilometers (62 miles).

There are two types of optical fibers. In a single-mode fiber, the core is smaller, typically 10 micrometers (a micrometer is one-millionth of a meter) in diameter, and the cladding is 100 micrometers in diameter. A single-mode fiber is used to carry just one light wave over very long distances. Bundles of single-mode optical fibers are used in long-distance telephone lines and undersea cables. Multimode optical fibers, which have a core diameter of 50 micrometers and a cladding diameter of 125 micrometers, can carry hundreds of separate light wave signals over shorter distances. This type of fiber is used in urban systems where many signals must be carried to central switching stations for distribution.

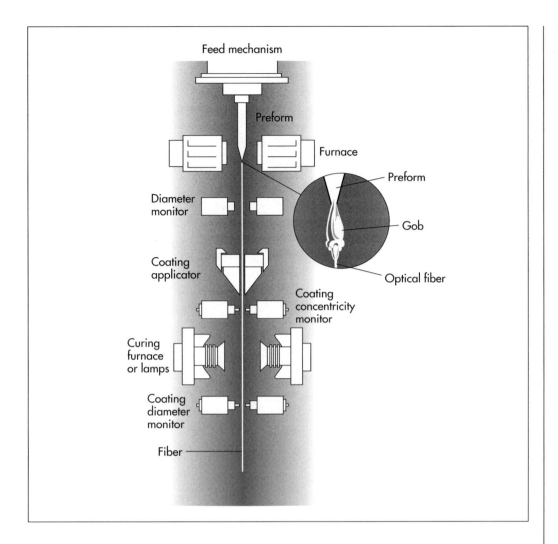

Feed mechanism

Preform

Furnace

Preform

Gob

Diameter
monitor

Optical fiber

Coating
applicator

Coating
concentricity
monitor

Curing
furnace
or lamps

Coating
diameter
monitor

Fiber

After the solid glass preform is prepared, it is transferred to a vertical drawing system. In this system, the preform is first heated. As it does so, a gob of molten glass forms at its end and then falls away, allowing the single optical fiber inside to be drawn out.

The fiber then proceeds through the machine, where its diameter is checked, a protective coating is applied, and it is cured by heat. Finally, it is wound on a spool.

The Manufacturing Process

Both the core and the cladding of an optical fiber are made of highly purified silica glass. An optical fiber is manufactured from silicon dioxide by either of two methods. The first, the crucible method, in which powdered silica is melted, produces fatter, multimode fibers suitable for short-distance transmission of many light wave signals. The second, the vapor deposition process, creates a solid cylinder of core and cladding material that is then heated and drawn into a thinner, single-mode fiber for long-distance communication.

There are three types of vapor deposition techniques: Outer Vapor Phase Deposition, Vapor Phase Axial Deposition, and Modified Chemical Vapor Deposition (MCVD). This section will focus on the MCVD process, the most common manufacturing technique now in use. MCVD yields a low-loss fiber well-suited for long-distance cables.

Modified Chemical Vapor Deposition

1 First, a cylindrical preform is made by depositing layers of specially formulated silicon dioxide on the inside surface of a hollow substrate rod. The layers are deposited by applying a gaseous stream of pure oxygen to the substrate rod. Various chemical vapors, such as silicon tetrachloride ($SiCl_4$), germanium tetrachloride ($GeCl_4$), and phosphorous oxychloride ($POCl_3$), are added to the stream of oxygen. As the oxygen contacts the hot surface of the rod—a flame underneath the rod keeps the walls of the rod very hot—silicon dioxide of high purity is formed. The result is a glassy soot, several layers thick, deposited inside the rod. This soot will become the core. The properties of these layers of soot can be altered depending on the types of chemical vapors used.

2 After the soot is built up to the desired thickness, the substrate rod is moved through other heating steps to drive out any

A typical optical fiber cable usually includes several optical fibers around a central steel cable. Various protective layers are applied, depending on the harshness of the environment where the cable will be situated.

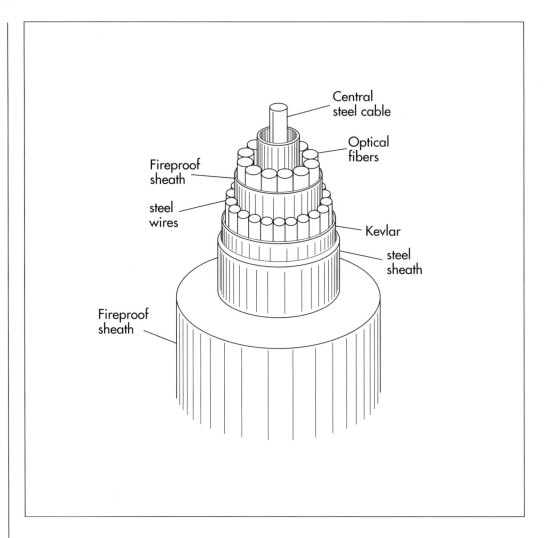

moisture and bubbles trapped in the soot layers. During heating, the substrate rod and internal soot layers solidify to form the boule or preform of highly pure silicon dioxide. A preform usually measures 10 to 25 millimeters (.39 to .98 inch) in diameter and 600 to 1000 millimeters (23.6 to 39.37 inches) in length.

Drawing the fibers

3 The solid preform is then automatically transferred to a vertical fiber drawing system. The machines that make up a typical vertical drawing system can be two stories high and are able to produce continuous fibers up to 300 kilometers (186 miles) long. This system consists of a furnace to melt the end of the preform, sensors to monitor the diameter of the fiber being pulled from the preform, and coating devices to apply protective layers over the outer cladding.

4 The preform first passes through a furnace, where it is heated to about 3600 de-

grees Fahrenheit (about 2000 degrees Celsius). Next, a drop of molten glass called a "gob" forms at the end of the preform, much like a droplet of water that collects at the bottom of a leaky faucet. The gob then falls away, and the single optical fiber inside is drawn out of the preform. As the optical fiber is pulled from the preform, the material in the original substrate rod forms the cladding, and the silicon dioxide deposited as soot forms the core of the optical fiber.

5 As the fiber is drawn out, measuring devices monitor its diameter and its concentricity, while another device applies a protective coating. The fiber then passes through a curing furnace and another measuring device that monitors diameter, before being wound on a spool.

Quality Control

Quality control begins with the suppliers of the chemical compounds used as the raw materials for the substrate rods, chemical reactants, and fiber coatings. Specialty chemical suppliers provide detailed chemical analyses of the constituent compounds, and these analyses are constantly checked by computerized on-stream analyzers connected to the process vessels.

Process engineers and highly trained technicians closely watch the sealed vessels as preforms are being created and fibers drawn. Computers operate the complex control schemes necessary to manage the high temperatures and high pressures of the manufacturing process. Precise measurement devices continuously monitor fiber diameter and provide feedback for control of the drawing process.

The Future

Future optical fibers will come from ongoing research into materials with improved optical properties. Currently, silica glasses with a high fluoride content hold the most promise for optical fibers, with attenuation losses even lower than today's highly efficient fibers. Experimental fibers, drawn from glass containing 50 to 60 percent zirconium fluoride (ZrF_4), now show losses in the range of 0.005 to 0.008 decibels per kilometer, whereas earlier fibers often had losses of 0.2 decibels per kilometer.

In addition to utilizing more refined materials, the producers of fiber optic cables are experimenting with process improvement. Presently, the most sophisticated manufacturing processes use high-energy lasers to melt the preforms for the fiber draw. Fibers can be drawn from a preform at the rate of 10 to 20 meters (32.8 to 65.6 feet) per second, and single-mode fibers from 2 to 25 kilometers (1.2 to 15.5 miles) in length can be drawn from one preform. At least one company has reported creating fibers of 160 kilometers (99 miles), and the frequency with which fiber optics companies are currently retooling—as often as every eighteen months—suggests that still greater innovations lie ahead. These advances will be driven in part by the growing use of optical fibers in computer networks, and also by the increasing demand for the technology in burgeoning international markets such as Eastern Europe, South America, and the Far East.

Where To Learn More

Books

Yeh, Chai. *Handbook of Fiber Optics.* Academic Press, 1990.

Periodicals

Jungbluth, Eugene D. "How Do They Make Those Marvelous Fibers?" *Laser Focus World.* March, 1992, p. 165.

Ketron, Lisa A. "Fiber Optics: The Ultimate Communications Media." *Ceramic Bulletin.* Volume 66, number 11, 1987, p. 1571.

Shuford, Richard S. "An Introduction to Fiber Optics," *Byte.* December, 1984, p. 121.

Soja, Thomas A. "Worldwide Telecom Demand Spurs Fiber Optics Market." *Laser Focus World.* December, 1992, p. 83.

Wire Journal International. October, 1992 (entire issue devoted to fiber optics).

—Robert C. Miller

Paint

In Boston around 1700, Thomas Child built the earliest American paint mill, a granite trough within which a 1.6 foot granite ball rolled, grinding the pigment. The first paint patent was issued for a product that improved whitewash, a water-slaked lime often used during the early days of the United States.

Background

Paint is a term used to describe a number of substances that consist of a pigment suspended in a liquid or paste vehicle such as oil or water. With a brush, a roller, or a spray gun, paint is applied in a thin coat to various surfaces such as wood, metal, or stone. Although its primary purpose is to protect the surface to which it is applied, paint also provides decoration.

Samples of the first known paintings, made between 20,000 and 25,000 years ago, survive in caves in France and Spain. Primitive paintings tended to depict humans and animals, and diagrams have also been found. Early artists relied on easily available natural substances to make paint, such as natural earth pigments, charcoal, berry juice, lard, blood, and milkweed sap. Later, the ancient Chinese, Egyptians, Hebrews, Greeks, and Romans used more sophisticated materials to produce paints for limited decoration, such as painting walls. Oils were used as varnishes, and pigments such as yellow and red ochres, **chalk**, arsenic sulfide yellow, and malachite green were mixed with binders such as gum arabic, lime, egg albumen, and beeswax.

Paint was first used as a protective coating by the Egyptians and Hebrews, who applied pitches and balsams to the exposed wood of their ships. During the Middle Ages, some inland wood also received protective coatings of paint, but due to the scarcity of paint, this practice was generally limited to store fronts and signs. Around the same time, artists began to boil resin with oil to obtain highly miscible (mixable) paints, and artists of the fifteenth century were the first to add drying oils to paint, thereby hastening evaporation. They also adopted a new solvent, linseed oil, which remained the most commonly used solvent until synthetics replaced it during the twentieth century.

In Boston around 1700, Thomas Child built the earliest American paint mill, a granite trough within which a 1.6 foot (.5 meter) granite ball rolled, grinding the pigment. The first paint patent was issued for a product that improved whitewash, a water-slaked lime often used during the early days of the United States. In 1865 D. P. Flinn obtained a patent for a water-based paint that also contained zinc oxide, potassium hydroxide, resin, milk, and linseed oil. The first commercial paint mills replaced Child's granite ball with a buhrstone wheel, but these mills continued the practice of grinding only pigment (individual customers would then blend it with a vehicle at home). It wasn't until 1867 that manufacturers began mixing the vehicle and the pigment for consumers.

The twentieth century has seen the most changes in paint composition and manufacture. Today, synthetic pigments and stabilizers are commonly used to mass produce uniform batches of paint. New synthetic vehicles developed from polymers such as polyurethane and styrene-butadene emerged during the 1940s. Alkyd resins were synthesized, and they have dominated production since. Before 1930, pigment was ground with stone mills, and these were later replaced by steel balls. Today, sand mills and high-speed dispersion mixers are used to grind easily dispersible pigments.

Perhaps the greatest paint-related advancement has been its proliferation. While some wooden houses, stores, bridges, and signs

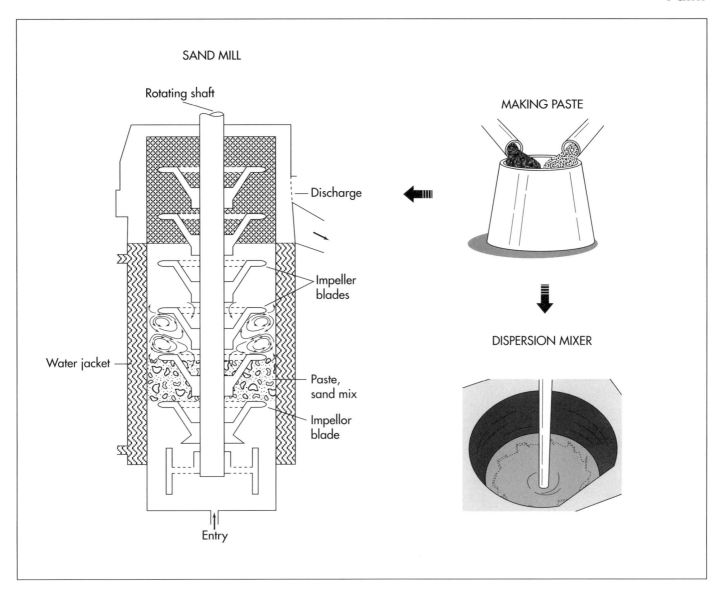

SAND MILL

Rotating shaft

Discharge

Impeller blades

Water jacket

Paste, sand mix

Impellor blade

Entry

MAKING PASTE

DISPERSION MIXER

---

were painted as early as the eighteenth century, it wasn't until recently that mass production rendered a wide variety of paints universally indispensable. Today, paints are used for interior and exterior housepainting, boats, **automobile**s, planes, appliances, furniture, and many other places where protection and appeal are desired.

Raw Materials

A paint is composed of pigments, solvents, resins, and various additives. The pigments give the paint color; solvents make it easier to apply; resins help it dry; and additives serve as everything from fillers to antifungicidal agents. Hundreds of different pigments, both natural and synthetic, exist. The basic white pigment is titanium dioxide, selected for its excellent concealing properties,

and black pigment is commonly made from carbon black. Other pigments used to make paint include iron oxide and cadmium sulfide for reds, metallic salts for yellows and oranges, and iron blue and chrome yellows for blues and greens.

Solvents are various low viscosity, volatile liquids. They include petroleum mineral spirits and aromatic solvents such as benzol, alcohols, esters, ketones, and acetone. The natural resins most commonly used are linseed, coconut, and soybean oil, while alkyds, acrylics, epoxies, and polyurethanes number among the most popular synthetic resins. Additives serve many purposes. Some, like calcium carbonate and aluminum silicate, are simply fillers that give the paint body and substance without changing its properties. Other additives produce certain desired char-

The first step in making paint involves mixing the pigment with resin, solvents, and additives to form a paste. If the paint is to be for industrial use, it usually is then routed into a sand mill, a large cylinder that agitates tiny particles of sand or silica to grind the pigment particles, making them smaller and dispersing them throughout the mixture. In contrast, most commercial-use paint is processed in a high-speed dispersion tank, in which a circular, toothed blade attached to a rotating shaft agitates the mixture and blends the pigment into the solvent.

Paint canning is a completely auto-mated process. For the standard 8 pint paint can available to con-sumers, empty cans are first rolled horizontally onto labels, then set up-right so that the paint can be pumped into them. One machine places lids onto the filled cans while a second machine presses on the lids to seal the cans. From wire that is fed into it from coils, a bailometer cuts and shapes the handles before hooking them into holes precut in the cans.

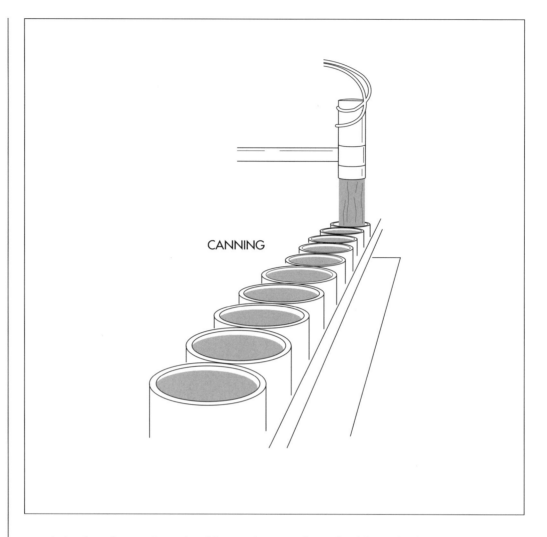

CANNING

acteristics in paint, such as the thixotropic agents that give paint its smooth texture, dri-ers, anti-settling agents, anti-skinning agents, defoamers, and a host of others that enable paint to cover well and last long.

Design

Paint is generally custom-made to fit the needs of industrial customers. For example, one might be especially interested in a fast-drying paint, while another might desire a paint that supplies good coverage over a long lifetime. Paint intended for the consumer can also be custom-made. Paint manufacturers provide such a wide range of colors that it is impossible to keep large quantities of each on hand. To meet a request for "aquamarine," "canary yellow," or "maroon," the manufac-turer will select a base that is appropriate for the deepness of color required. (Pastel paint bases will have high amounts of titanium dioxide, the white pigment, while darker tones will have less.) Then, according to a

predetermined formula, the manufacturer can introduce various pigments from calibrated cylinders to obtain the proper color.

The Manufacturing Process

Making the paste

1 Pigment manufacturers send bags of fine grain pigments to paint plants. There, the pigment is premixed with resin (a wetting agent that assists in moistening the pigment), one or more solvents, and additives to form a paste.

Dispersing the pigment

2 The paste mixture for most industrial and some consumer paints is now routed into a sand mill, a large cylinder that agitates tiny particles of sand or silica to grind the pig-ment particles, making them smaller and dis-persing them throughout the mixture. The

mixture is then filtered to remove the sand particles.

3 Instead of being processed in sand mills, up to 90 percent of the water-based latex paints designed for use by individual home-owners are instead processed in a high-speed dispersion tank. There, the premixed paste is subjected to high-speed agitation by a circular, toothed blade attached to a rotating shaft. This process blends the pigment into the solvent.

Thinning the paste

4 Whether created by a sand mill or a dispersion tank, the paste must now be thinned to produce the final product. Transferred to large kettles, it is agitated with the proper amount of solvent for the type of paint desired.

Canning the paint

5 The finished paint product is then pumped into the canning room. For the standard 8 pint (3.78 liter) paint can available to consumers, empty cans are first rolled horizontally onto labels, then set upright so that the paint can be pumped into them. A machine places lids onto the filled cans, and a second machine presses on the lids to seal them. From wire that is fed into it from coils, a bailometer cuts and shapes the handles before hooking them into holes precut in the cans. A certain number of cans (usually four) are then boxed and stacked before being sent to the warehouse.

Quality Control

Paint manufacturers utilize an extensive array of quality control measures. The ingredients and the manufacturing process undergo stringent tests, and the finished product is checked to insure that it is of high quality. A finished paint is inspected for its density, fineness of grind, dispersion, and viscosity. Paint is then applied to a surface and studied for bleed resistance, rate of drying, and texture.

In terms of the paint's aesthetic components, color is checked by an experienced observer and by spectral analysis to see if it matches a standard desired color. Resistance of the color to fading caused by the elements is de-termined by exposing a portion of a painted surface to an arc light and comparing the amount of fading to a painted surface that was not so exposed. The paint's hiding power is measured by painting it over a black surface and a white surface. The ratio of coverage on the black surface to coverage on the white surface is then determined, with .98 being high-quality paint. Gloss is measured by determining the amount of reflected light given off a painted surface.

Tests to measure the paint's more functional qualities include one for mar resistance, which entails scratching or abrading a dried coat of paint. Adhesion is tested by making a crosshatch, calibrated to .07 inch (2 millimeters), on a dried paint surface. A piece of tape is applied to the crosshatch, then pulled off; good paint will remain on the surface. Scrubbability is tested by a machine that rubs a soapy brush over the paint's surface. A system also exists to rate settling. An excellent paint can sit for six months with no settling and rate a ten. Poor paint, however, will settle into an immiscible lump of pigment on the bottom of the can and rate a zero. Weathering is tested by exposing the paint to outdoor conditions. Artificial weathering exposes a painted surface to sun, water, extreme temperature, humidity, or sulfuric gases. Fire retardancy is checked by burning the paint and determining its weight loss. If the amount lost is more than 10 percent, the paint is not considered fire-resistant.

Byproducts/Waste

A recent regulation (California Rule 66) concerning the emission of volatile organic compounds (VOCs) affects the paint industry, especially manufacturers of industrial oil-based paints. It is estimated that all coatings, including stains and varnishes, are responsible for 1.8 percent of the 2.3 million metric tons of VOCs released per year. The new regulation permits each liter of paint to contain no more than 250 grams (8.75 ounces) of solvent. Paint manufacturers can replace the solvents with pigment, fillers, or other solids inherent to the basic paint formula. This method produces thicker paints that are harder to apply, and it is not yet known if such paints are long lasting. Other solutions include using paint powder coatings that use no solvents, applying paint in closed systems from which VOCs can be retrieved, using water as a solvent, or using acrylics that dry under ultraviolet light or heat. A consumer with some unused paint on hand can return it to the point of purchase for proper treatment.

A large paint manufacturer will have an in-house wastewater treatment facility that treats all liquids generated on-site, even storm water run-off. The facility is monitored 24 hours a day, and the Environmental Protection Agency (EPA) does a periodic records and systems check of all paint facilities. The liquid portion of the waste is treated on-site to the standards of the local publicly owned wastewater treatment facility; it can be used to make low-quality paint. Latex sludge can be retrieved and used as fillers in other industrial products. Waste solvents can be recovered and used as fuels for other industries. A clean paint container can be reused or sent to the local landfill.

Where To Learn More

Books

Flick, Ernest W. *Handbook of Paint Raw Materials*, 2nd ed. Noyes Data Corp., 1989.

Martens, Charles R. *Emulsion and Water-Soluble Paints and Coatings*. Reinhold Publishing Company, 1964.

Morgans, W. M. *Outlines of Paint Technology*, 3rd ed. John Wiley & Sons, 1990.

The Paints and Coatings Industry. Business Trend Analysts, 1990.

Paints and Protective Coatings. Gordon Press, 1991.

Turner, G. P. A. *Introduction to Paint Chemistry and Principles of Paint Technology*, 3rd ed. Chapman & Hall, 1988.

Weismantel, Guy E. *Paint Handbook*. McGraw-Hill, 1981.

Periodicals

Levinson, Nancy. "Goodbye, Old Paint." *Architectural Record*. January, 1992, pp. 42-43.

Scott, Susan. "Painting with Pesticides: the Controversial Organoxin Paints." *Sea Frontiers*. November/December, 1987, pp. 415-421.

—*Rose Secrest*

Pantyhose

Background

Pantyhose are a form of sheer women's hosiery that extend from the waist to the toes. The terms *hosiery* and *stocking* derive from the Anglo-Saxon words *hosa,* meaning "tight-legged trouser," and *stoka,* meaning "stump." When the upper part of a trouser leg was cut off, the remaining stoka became "stocking," and hosa became "hosiery." For centuries, sheer stockings and hose were worn as separate leg and foot coverings. However, after World War II, fashion designers began to attach panties to stockings, creating the form of hosiery currently favored by most women. Although their most basic purpose is to protect and beautify the feet and legs of female consumers, nylons are also put to other uses, including supporting the legs of football players and protecting crops from dust storms. Pantyhose have even been recycled in the arts and crafts industry, where they are cut up and stuffed with fiberfill to become the arms and legs of dolls and stuffed animals.

Few early references to women's hosiery exist because any public mention of women's legs was considered improper until the twentieth century. The first extant discussion of a garment resembling today's pantyhose concerns the "tight-fitting hose" young Venetian men wore beneath short jackets during the fourteenth century. Made of silk, these leggings were often brightly colored and embroidered; older Venetians considered them extremely immodest. One of the earliest mentions of women wearing stockings appears in the records of Queen Elizabeth I, whose "silk woman" presented her with a pair of knitted black silk stockings. Admiring their softness and comfort, the Queen requested more, and wore only silk stockings for the rest of her life.

In 1589, when the Reverend William Lee attempted to patent the first knitting machine, Queen Elizabeth denied his request because, she contended, the coarse stockings produced by Lee's machine were inferior to the silk hose she had shipped from Spain. Lee improved his machine, enabling it to manufacture softer stockings, but Elizabeth's successor, James I, denied his second patent application as well, this time out of fear that the machine would endanger the livelihood of English hand knitters. After Lee's death, his brother built a framework knitting machine that remained unrivalled for several hundred years.

When William Cotton invented the first automated knitting machine in 1864, he incorporated the key features of Lee's design, notably the spring-beard needle that is still used in many contemporary knitting machines. Named for the fine, open hook that projects from the needle at an angle like that of the hair in a man's beard, the spring-beard needle must be used with a pressing device to close the hook as it forms a loop. This type of needle is ideal for hosiery because it produces smaller loops and, consequently, a finer weave. Cotton's straight-bar machine created flat sheets of fabric using a weft stitch whereby a continuous yarn was fed to needles that sewed back-and-forth horizontal rows. By increasing or reducing the number of needles used to knit different portions of a stocking, workers could vary the thickness of the garment: more needles produced thicker fabric. Stitching began at the top of the stocking with a welt, or thick strip to which women could attach garters. To accommo-

Few early references to women's hosiery exist because any public mention of women's legs was considered improper until the twentieth century. The first extant discussion of a garment resembling today's pantyhose concerns the "tight-fitting hose" young Venetian men wore during the fourteenth century. Made of silk, these leggings were often brightly colored and embroidered; older Venetians considered them extremely immodest.

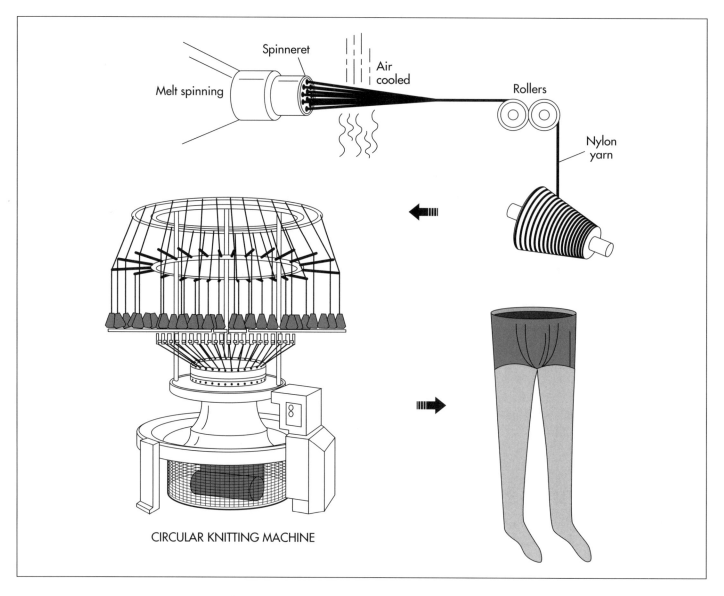

Melt spinning

Spinneret

Air cooled

Rollers

Nylon yarn

CIRCULAR KNITTING MACHINE

Nylon is made in a process known as "melt spinning." First, a syrupy polymer solution is produced and then extruded through a spinneret. As the nylon strings emerge, they are cooled by air and stretched over rollers to stabilize the molecular chains and strengthen the fibers. The yarn is then wound on spools.

Next, the yarn is fed into a computer-controlled circular knitting machine, which uses its 300 to 420 needles to convert the nylon into a series of loops. It takes about 90 seconds to knit a full-length stocking leg.

date the feet and ankles, the stocking fabric was thinned at the bottom, although the fabric at the heel remained thick, for cushioning purposes. After it was removed from Cotton's machine, the fabric was manually shaped and seamed up the back to produce so-called full-fashioned stockings.

Also produced during the mid-nineteenth century, the first seamless stockings were made on circular machines that knitted tubes of fabric to which separate foot and toe pieces were subsequently attached. Although these stockings were more attractive in that they featured no visible seams, they bagged at the knees and ankles because circular machines could not add or drop stitches like the Lee and Cotton machines. It was not until the World War II era that two developments made possible better-fitting stockings. First, circular

machines were improved so that they could knit stockings in one piece. Still more significant was the DuPont Company's invention of a synthetic fiber called nylon. After being sewn into a tube, nylon fabric could be heated and formed into a shape that it would thereafter retain through numerous stretchings and washings. Hosiery made from this revolutionary fabric was introduced to the general population in 1940, and its immediate popularity soon rendered the word "nylons" synonymous with hosiery.

However, the war that had accelerated the development of nylon also increased the demand for it, so, during the early forties, the hosiery industry offered socks instead of stockings. The anklet, a short cotton sock, became the temporary replacement favored by most women, particularly the young consumers known as "bobby-soxers." Yet, when the war ended and nylon was once again available for consumer uses, most women returned to nylon stockings. During the sixties, decreasing skirt lengths necessitated longer stockings, and fashion designers created what we now know as pantyhose by attaching panties to hosiery. In addition to accommodating all hemline fluctuations, pantyhose don't need to be held up with the garters and garter belts previously used to secure stockings. Nylons have become a fashion accessory that few women are willing to do without. This is especially true in the white-collar workforce, where they are considered an essential part of appropriate office attire.

Raw Materials

Pantyhose are generally made from a nylon-based blend of synthetic fibers. The nylon most commonly used—Nylon 6,6—is made from adipic acid, an organic acid, and hexamethylene diamine, an organic base, which are chemically combined to form a nylon salt. Because nylon is a plastic material—actually the first thermoplastic fiber ever used—the salt must undergo polymerization. In this process, different molecules are combined to form longer molecular chains. These chains result in a smooth, thick substance that is then cut into small shapes or pellets, before being spun into yarn. The nylon fiber's size, strength, weight, elasticity, and luster are determined during its preparation by controlling the number and type of filaments used. For example, luster is produced by adding titanium dioxide (TiO_2). The resulting fiber is highly elastic and retains its shape after repeated washings and stretchings. Its resistance to wrinkles and creases, its durability, and the fact that it dries quickly make it a desirable fabric for busy women.

Today, filaments of another synthetic fiber, *spandex*, are frequently combined with nylon filaments to increase elasticity and achieve a snugger fit. More recently, other new fibers known as *microfibers* or *microdeniers* have been blended with nylon. A denier is a unit of measure that indicates the thickness of nylon yarn. The denier scale ranges from 7 to 80 denier, with smaller numbers indicating finer yarn and higher numbers denoting heavier yarn that will be used to make stronger fabrics. When blended with nylon, microdeniers enhance softness, hold color more evenly, and provide a better fit.

Design

Pantyhose are usually classified as sheer, semisheer, or service weight, with the weight determined by the denier and the number of needles used during production. Although stockings do not differ in shape, fashion designers will vary the color, texture and pattern of their hosiery. Much as the fashion industry offers different types of clothing appropriate for specific functions and occasions, it designs hosiery tailored to particular purposes. For example, heavier knit and natural colored pantyhose are considered more practical for daytime and office wear while sheer hosiery is saved for evening affairs and special occasions. Similarly, darker nylons are generally found on retail shelves during the winter, while paler shades are displayed in the spring and summer. In addition, some designers offer hose with extra elastic sewn in to the midriff to serve as "tummy control"; still others produce nylons with lightweight girdles instead of panties. Because nylon does not "breathe" well, some manufacturers offer hosiery with cotton crotch panels, and both toes and heels can be reinforced to deter runs.

The Manufacturing Process

Making nylon yarn

1 Nylon yarn is made in a process known as *melt spinning*. First, the chemicals involved—adipic acid and hexamethylene diamine—must be polymerized to form a thick resin that is then cut into chips or pellets. These pellets are then heated and pressurized in an autoclave into a syrupy solution. Next, the solution is extruded through a spinneret—a device that looks and works like a shower head, with long strings of nylon solution coming out of the holes in the device. The number of holes depends on the type of yarn desired: one hole produces monofilament yarn, which is very thin and sheer; several holes produce multifilament yarn, which is denser and less sheer. As the fibers emerge from the spinneret, they are cooled by air and then stretched over rollers to stabilize the molecular chains and strengthen the fibers. The yarn is then wound on spools.

After the legs are seamed together and the toe openings closed, the pantyhose garments are immersed in a dyeing machine. A modern dye machine can color about 3,500 dozen pairs of hose a day. After drying and boarding—steaming the hose to the proper shape—the garments are ready for packaging.

DYEING · Nylon net with knitted pantyhose · Dye-filled tub

Knitting

2 Yarn is fed into a circular knitting machine, which converts it into a series of loops. Usually computer-controlled, the machine contains 300 to 420 needles and rotates at speeds up to 1,200 RPM; it takes about 90 seconds to knit a full-length stocking leg.

Seaming

3 Next, openings at the toes are seamed together, and two stocking legs are seamed together to form pantyhose. Sometimes they are seamed together with a crotch. Like the other steps in pantyhose manufacture, seaming is almost completely automated.

Dyeing and drying

4 The sewn product then goes to a dye machine where it will be dyed to one of more than 100 different shades. The dye machine can color about 3,500 dozen pairs a day. Once dyed, the pantyhose are taken to a compartment dryer which dries them.

Boarding

5 This next step, boarding, is sometimes done before the dyeing process, depending on the desired final product. Boarding is the process of placing the pantyhose over leg forms where they are steamed and heated to the desired shape. With less expensive hosiery, this step may be completely bypassed and the pantyhose packaged in their relaxed state.

Inspecting

6 Throughout the manufacturing process, quality checks are performed on the pantyhose. A statistical method is used for inspection.

Packaging

7 Pantyhose that meet the inspection guidelines are packaged in a box or paperboard envelope, either manually or automatically.

Filling orders: Picking and shipping

8 After they leave the manufacturing plant, the pantyhose are stored in warehouses and organized according to size, style, and color for efficient order-filling. Customer orders are filled by personnel at various "picking" stations positioned alongside a conveyor belt that carries the filled cases to a staging area for final shipping to retail markets.

Byproducts/Waste

The hosiery industry must confront the problems all textile mills face in producing a fabric. In particular, hosiery mills must treat the wastewater generated during the dyeing phase to prevent contamination. Many of the dyes used to tint pantyhose contain toxic substances such as ammonium sulfate. To minimize harmful wastewater, manufacturers must adhere to guidelines set by the U.S. government's Environmental Protection Agency (EPA). Treating the water before it is dumped into rivers has alleviated some of the wastewater concerns. Another approach has been to control the amounts of various chemicals used during the manufacturing process. Failure to measure chemicals properly can create an over-abundance of some of the materials, thereby causing harmful waste. A third idea has been to substitute less harmful chemicals when possible.

The Future

The hosiery industry currently produces almost 2 billion pairs of women's sheer hose annually. Industry analysts predict that consumers will continue to demand high-quality nylons in a variety of shades, styles, and degrees of sheerness. Manufacturers will strive to meet the consumer's need by experimenting with hybrid fabrics that combine synthetic fibers with natural fibers such as cotton.

Where To Learn More

Books

Corbman, Bernard P. *Textiles: Fiber to Fabric*, 6th ed. McGraw-Hill, 1983.

Farrell, Jeremy. *Socks and Stockings*. Drama Book Publishers, 1992.

Grass, Milton N. *History of Hosiery*. Fairchild Publications, 1955.

Wingate, Isabel B. and June F. Mohler. *Textile Fabrics and Their Selection*, 8th ed. Prentice-Hall, Inc. 1984.

Pamphlets

National Association of Hosiery Manufacturers. *Hosiery, The Opportunity Industry*.

—Catherine Kolecki

Peanut Butter

Around 1925, peanut butter was sold from an open tub, with half an inch of oil on the surface. While the paste was sticky and produced considerable thirst, consumers were ready for such an economical and nutritious staple.

Background

Wild peanuts originated in Bolivia and northeastern Argentina. The cultivated species, *Arachis hypogaea*, was grown by Indians in pre-Columbian times. The peanut plant is a vinelike plant whose flowerstalks wither and bow to the ground after fertilization, burying the young pods, which come to maturity underground.

Peanuts were introduced to the United States from Africa, but were not considered a staple crop until the 1890s, when they were promoted as a replacement for the cotton crop destroyed by the boll weevil.

The three types of domestic peanuts are the Virginia, Spanish, and Runner-type peanuts. It is mostly the Runner-type peanuts, grown in Alabama, Florida, and Georgia, that are used in the manufacture of peanut butter. While Runner peanuts offer a higher yield, they also require more moisture than the Spanish or Virginia peanuts.

Around the end of the seventeenth century, Haitians made peanut butter by using a heavy wood mortar and a wood pestle with a metal cap. The mortar—featuring a metal bottom and weighing about 20 pounds—and the 5-pound pestle were used to pound the peanuts into a paste. During the nineteenth century in the United States, shelled, roasted peanuts were chopped or pounded into a creamy paste in a cloth bag and eaten fresh. American botanist and inventor George Washington Carver experimented with soybeans, sweet potatoes, and other crops, eventually deriving 300 products from the peanut alone—among the most notable was peanut butter.

A physician in St. Louis, Missouri started manufacturing peanut butter commercially in 1890. Featured at the St. Louis World's Fair as a health food, peanut butter was recommended for infants and invalids because of its high nutritional value. Sanitariums, particularly one in Battle Creek, Michigan, used it for their patients because of its high protein content.

Around 1925, peanut butter was sold from an open tub, with half an inch of oil on the surface. While the paste was sticky and produced considerable thirst, consumers were ready for such an economical and nutritious staple.

Realizing that the financial rewards from pig feed were beginning to dwindle, farmers began investing in the new cash crop. Thus, with increased harvest and availability of peanuts, the development and production of peanut butter grew. Most recently, peanut butter has been used primarily as a sandwich spread, although it also appears in prepared dishes and confections.

Originally, the process of peanut butter manufacturing was entirely manual. Until about 1920, the peanut farmer shelled the seed by hand, cultivated by hand hoeing about four times, and plowed with a single furrow plow, also four times. The farmer dug the vines with a single row plow, manually stacked the vines in the field for drying, and then hand-picked the nuts or beat them from the vines. A mule, a plow, and two hoes were all that was needed as far as peanut cultivation equipment was concerned. To produce peanut butter, small batches of peanuts were roasted, blanched, and ground as needed for sale or consumption. Salt and/or **sugar** was added upon request, and the product was eaten fresh. Mechanized cultivation and harvesting increased the yield of the harvest. Milling plants became larger, and consumption soared.

Raw Materials

The peanut, rich in fat, protein, vitamin B, phosphorus, and iron, has significant food value. In its final form, peanut butter consists of about 90 to 95 percent carefully selected, blanched, dry-roasted peanuts, ground to a size to pass through a 200-mesh screen. To improve smoothness, spreadability and flavor, other ingredients are added, including include salt (1.5 percent), hydrogenated vegetable oil (0.125 percent), dextrose (2 percent), and corn syrup or honey (2 to 4 percent). To enhance peanut butter's nutritive value, ascorbic acid and yeast are also added. The amounts of other ingredients can vary as long as they do not add up to more than 10 percent of the peanut butter. Peanut butter contains 50 to 52 percent fat, 28 to 29 percent protein, 2 to 5 percent carbohydrate, and 1 to 2 percent moisture.

The Manufacturing Process

Planting and harvesting peanuts

1 Peanuts are planted in April or May, depending upon the climate. The peanut emerges as a plant followed by a yellow flower. After blooming and then wilting, the flower bends over and penetrates the soil. The peanut is formed underground. Peanuts are harvested beginning in late August, but mostly in September and October, during clear weather, when the soil is dry enough so it will not adhere to the stems and pods. The peanuts are removed from vines by portable, mechanical pickers and transported to a peanut sheller for mechanical drying.

2 Peanuts from the pickers are delivered to warehouses for cleaning. Blowers remove dust, sand, vines, stems, leaves, and empty shells. Screens, magnets, and size graders remove trash, metal, rocks, and clods. After the cleaning process, the peanuts weigh 10 to 20 percent less. The raw, cleaned peanuts are stored unshelled in silos or warehouses.

George Washington Carver, left, and industrialist Henry Ford share a weed sandwich in this 1942 photograph.

For George Washington Carver, peanuts were a means to several ends. Throughout his career, Carver searched for ways to make small Southern family farms, often African-American owned, self-sufficient. Carver's popularization of peanuts and peanut products was part of his effort to free small farmers from dependence on commercial products and debt. It was also part of his effort to wean farmers away from the annual production of soil-depleting staple crops like cotton and tobacco. Carver's list of peanut products—from peanut milk and makeup to paint and soap—represented a wide range of household activities.

Carver's interest in peanuts began in the mid-1910s, after he had pursued much research and education about other crops, especially sweet potatoes. A well-organized peanut industry lobby heard of Carver's work and capitalized on their mutual interest in the promotion of peanuts. Carver became the unofficial spokesman and publicist for the industry, especially after his 1921 appearance at tariffs hearings conducted by the U.S. House of Representatives' Ways and Means Committee. Facing alternatively bemused and hostile questioning from legislators, the African-American scientist eloquently and humorously explained the social, economic, and nutritional benefits of the domestic cultivation and consumption of peanuts. What evolved into a lunchtime favorite for kids was thrust into national prominence through one industry's search for growth and one man's search for economic independence for his people.

William S. Pretzer

Shelling and processing

3 Shelling consists of removing the shell (or hull) of peanuts with the least damage to the seed or kernels. The moisture of the

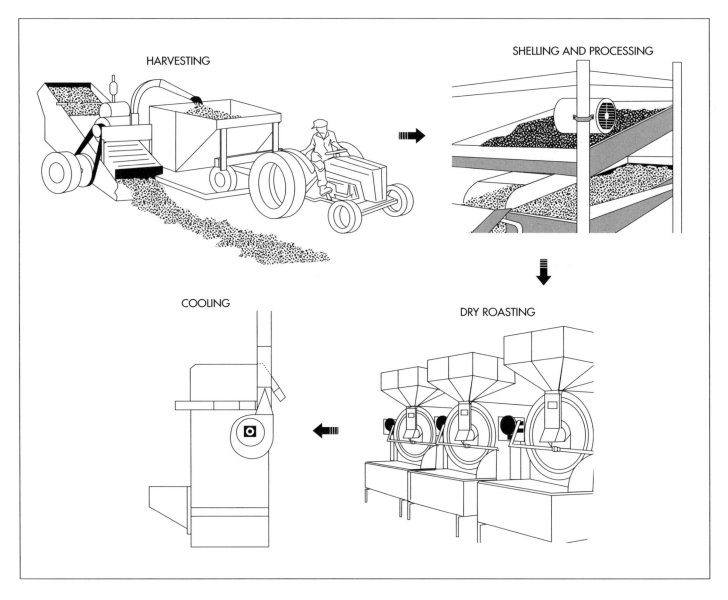

HARVESTING

SHELLING AND PROCESSING

COOLING

DRY ROASTING

The first several steps in peanut butter manufacture involve processing the main ingredient: the peanuts. After harvesting, the peanuts are cleaned, shelled, and graded for size. Next, they are dry roasted in large ovens, and then they are transferred to cooling machines, where suction fans draw cooling air over the peanuts.

unshelled peanuts is adjusted to avoid excessive brittleness of the shells and kernels and to reduce the amount of dust in the plant. The size-graded peanuts are passed between a series of rollers adjusted to the variety, size, and condition of the peanuts, where the peanuts are cracked. The cracked peanuts then repeatedly pass over screens, sleeves, blowers, magnets, and destoners, where they are shaken, gently tumbled, and air blown, until all the shells and other foreign material (rocks, mudballs, metal, shrivels) are removed.

4 The shelled peanuts are graded for size in a size grader. The peanuts are lifted and then oriented on the perforations of the size grader. The larger peanuts (the "overs") are sent to one trough, while the "troughs" are guided towards another trough. The peanuts

are then graded for color, defects, spots, and broken skins.

5 The peanuts are shipped in large bulk containers or sacks to peanut butter manufacturers. (Inedible peanuts are diverted as oil stock in semibulk form.) To ensure proper size and grading, the truckloads transporting peanuts to peanut manufacturers are sampled mechanically. The sampler, testing two truckloads simultaneously, can quickly and accurately assess size and grading by examining 10 samples per truckload.

If edible peanuts need to be stored for more than 60 days, they are placed in refrigerated storage at 34 to 40 degrees Fahrenheit (2 to 6 degrees Celsius), where they may be held for as long as 25 months. Shelled, the remaining peanuts weigh 30 to 60 percent less, occupy

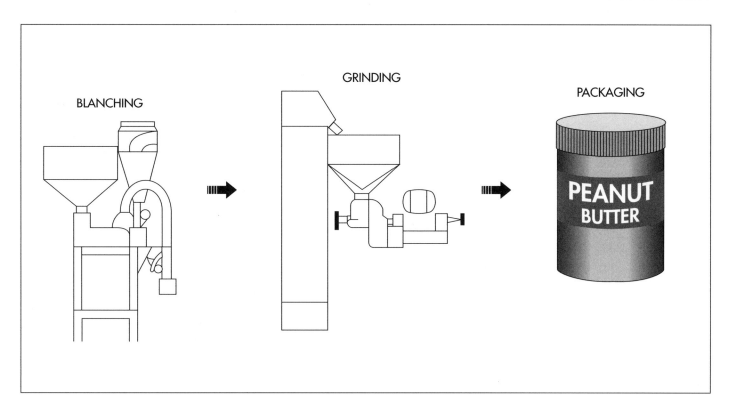

BLANCHING

GRINDING

PACKAGING

PEANUT BUTTER

60 to 70 percent less space, and have a shelf life about 60 to 75 percent shorter than unshelled peanuts.

Making peanut butter

6 The peanut butter manufacturers first dry roast the peanuts. *Dry roasting* is done by either the batch or continuous method. In the batch method, peanuts are roasted in 400-pound lots in a revolving oven heated to about 800 degrees Fahrenheit (426.6 degrees Celsius). The peanuts are heated at 320 degrees Fahrenheit (160 degrees Celsius) and held at this temperature for 40 to 60 minutes to reach the exact degree of doneness. All the nuts in each batch must be uniformly roasted.

Large manufacturers prefer the continuous method, in which peanuts are fed from the hopper, roasted, cooled, ground into peanut butter and stabilized in one operation. This method is less labor-intensive, creates a more uniform roasting, and decreases spillage. Still, some operators believe that the best commercial peanut butter is obtained by using the batch method. Since peanut butter may call for a blending of peanuts, the batch method allows for the different varieties to be roasted separately. Furthermore, since peanuts frequently come in lots of different moisture content which may need special at-

tention during roasting, the batch method can also meet these needs readily. The steps outlined below apply to peanut butter manufacturing that uses the batch method of roasting.

Cooling and blanching

7 A photometer indicates when the cooking is complete. At the exact time cooking is completed, the roasted peanuts are removed from heat as quickly as possible in order to stop cooking and produce a uniform product. The hot peanuts then pass from the roaster directly to a perforated metal cylinder (or blower-cooler vat), where a large volume of air is pulled through the mass by suction fans. The peanuts are brought to a temperature of 86 degrees Fahrenheit (30 degrees Celsius). Once cooled, the peanuts pass through a gravity separator that removes foreign materials.

8 The skins (or seed coats) are now removed with either heat or water. The heat blanching method has the advantage of removing the hearts of the peanuts, which contain a bitter principle.

Heat blanching: Depending on the variety and degree of doneness desired, the peanuts are exposed to a temperature of 280 degrees Fahrenheit (137.7 degrees Celsius) for up to

After the peanuts are roasted and cooled, they undergo blanching—removal of the skins by heat or water. The heat method has the advantage of removing the bitter heart of the peanut. Next, the blanched peanuts are pulverized and ground with salt, dextrose, and hydrogenated oil stabilizer in a grinding machine. After cooling, the peanut butter is ready to be packaged.

20 minutes to loosen and crack the skins. After cooling, the peanuts are passed through the blancher in a continuous stream and subjected to a thorough but gentle rubbing between brushes or ribbed rubber belting. The skins are rubbed off, blown into porous bags, and the hearts are separated by screening.

Water blanching: A newer process than heat blanching, water blanching was introduced in 1949. While the kernels are not heated to destroy natural antioxidants, drying is necessary in this process and the hearts are retained. The first step is to arrange the kernels in troughs, then roll them between sharp stationary blades to slit the skins on opposite sides. The skins are removed as a spiral conveyor carries the kernels through a one-minute scalding water bath and then under an oscillating canvas-covered pad, which rubs off their skins. The blanched kernels are then dried for at least six hours by a current of 120 degrees Fahrenheit (48.8 degrees Celsius) air.

9 The blanched nuts are mechanically screened and inspected on a conveyor belt to remove scorched and rotten nuts or other undesirable matter. Light nuts are removed by blowers, discolored nuts by a high-speed electric color sorter, and metal parts by magnets.

Grinding

10 Most of the devices used for grinding peanuts into butter are built so they can be adjusted over a wide range—permitting the variation in the quantity of peanuts ground per hour, the fineness of the product, and the amount of oil freed from the peanuts. Most grinding mills also have an automatic feed for peanuts and salt, and are easy to clean. To prevent overheating, grinding mills are cooled by a water jacket.

Peanut butter is usually made by two grinding operations. The first reduces the nuts to a medium grind and the second to a fine, smooth texture. For fine grinding, clearance between plates is about .032 inch (.08 centimeter). The second milling uses a very high-speed comminutor that has a combination cutting-shearing and attrition action and operates at 9600 rpm. This milling produces a very fine particle with a maximum size of less than 0.01 inch (.025 centimeter).

To make chunky peanut butter, peanut pieces approximately the size of one-eighth of a kernel are mixed with regular peanut butter, or incomplete grinding is used by removing a rib from the grinder.

At the same time the peanuts are fed into the grinder to be milled, about 2 percent salt, dextrose, and hydrogenated oil stabilizer are fed into the grinder in a continuous, horizontal operation, with about plus or minus 2 percent accuracy, and are thoroughly dispersed.

11 Peanuts are kept under constant pressure from the start to the finish of the grinding process to assure uniform grinding and to protect the product from air bubbles. A heavy screw feeds the peanuts into the grinder. This screw may also deliver the deaerated peanut butter into containers in a continuous stream under even pressure. From the grinder, the peanut butter goes to a **stainless steel** hopper, which serves as an intermediate mixing and storage point. The stabilized peanut butter is cooled in this rotating refrigerated cylinder (called a *votator*), from 170 to 120 degrees Fahrenheit (76.6 to 48.8 degrees Celsius) or less before it is packaged.

Packaging

12 The stabilized peanut butter is automatically packed in jars, capped, and labeled. Since proper packaging is the main factor in reducing oxidation (without oxygen no oxidation can occur), manufacturers use vacuum packing. After it is put into final containers, the peanut butter is allowed to remain undisturbed until crystallization throughout the mass is completed. Jars are then placed in cartons and placed in product storage until ready to be shipped out to retail or institutional customers.

Quality Control

Quality control of peanut butter starts on the farm through harvesting and curing, and is then carried through the steps of shelling, storing, and manufacturing the product. All these steps are handled by machines. While complete mechanical harvesting, curing, and shelling may have some disadvantages, the end result is a brighter, cleaner, and more uniform peanut crop.

In the United States, strict quality control has been maintained on peanuts for many years with cooperation and approval from both the

U.S. Department of Agriculture (USDA) and the Food and Drug Administration (FDA). Quality control is handled by the Peanut Administrative Committee, which is an arm of the USDA. Raw peanut responsibility rests with the Department of Agriculture. During and after manufacture, quality control is under the supervision of the FDA.

In its definition of peanut butter, the FDA stipulates that seasoning and stabilizing ingredients must not "exceed 10 percent of the weight of the finished food." Furthermore, the FDA states that "artificial flavorings, artificial sweeteners, chemical preservatives, added vitamins, and color additives are not suitable ingredients of peanut butter." A product that does not conform to the FDA's standards must be labeled "imitation peanut butter."

Byproducts

Peanut vines and leaves are used for feed for cattle, sheep, goats, horses, mules, and other livestock because of high nutritional value. Peanut shells accumulate in great quantities at shelling plants. They contain stems, peanut pops, immature nuts and dirt. These shells are used mainly for fuel for the boiler generating steam for making electricity to operate the shelling plant. Limited markets exist for peanut shells for roughage in cattle feed, poultry litter, and filler in artificial fire logs. Potential additional uses are pet litter, mushroom-growing medium, and floor-sweeping compounds.

The Future

In the United States and most of the 53 peanut-producing countries in the world, the production and consumption of peanuts, including peanut butter, is increasing. The quality of peanuts continues to improve to meet higher standards. The convenience peanut butter offers its users and its high nutritional value meet the demands of contemporary lifestyles.

The use of peanuts as food is being introduced to remote parts of the world by American ambassadors, missionaries and Peace Corps volunteers. Some developing countries, understanding that their food protein scarcity will not be solved through animal proteins alone, are interested in growing the protein-rich peanut crop.

Where To Learn More

Books

Coyle, L. Patrick, Jr. *The World Encyclopedia of Food*. Facts on File, 1982.

Erlbach, Arlene. *Peanut Butter*. Lerner Publications, 1993.

Lapedes, Daniel, ed. *McGraw Hill Encyclopedia of Food*, 4th ed: *Agriculture and Nutrition*. McGraw-Hill, 1977.

Woodroof, Jasper Guy, ed. *Peanuts: Production, Processing, Products*. Avi Publishing Company, 1983.

Zisman, Honey. *The Great American Peanut Butter Book: A Book of Recipes, Facts, Figures, and Fun*. St. Martin's Press, 1985.

Periodicals

"The Nuttiest Peanut Butter." *Consumer Reports*. September, 1990, p. 588.

"PBTV." *Environment*. November, 1987, p. 23.

—Eva Sideman

Pencil

The hardness of a pencil is designated by numbers or letters. Most manufacturers use the numbers 1 to 4, with 1 being the softest and making the darkest mark. Number 2 pencils (medium soft) are used for normal writing. Pencils are also sometimes graded by letters, from 6B, the softest, to 9H, the hardest.

Background

One of the oldest and most widely used writing utensils, the pencil originated in pre-historic times when chalky rocks and charred sticks were used to draw on surfaces as varied as animal hides and cave walls. The Greeks and Romans used flat pieces of lead to draw faint lines on papyrus, but it was not until the late 1400s that the earliest direct ancestor of today's pencil was developed. About one hundred years later graphite, a common mineral occurring as soft, lustrous veins in rocks, was discovered near Borrowdale in northwestern England. The Borrowdale mine supplied Europe with graphite for several hundred years; however, because people could not then differentiate between graphite and lead, they referred to the former as "black lead." Cut into rods or strips, graphite was heavily wrapped in twine to provide strength and a comfortable handle. The finished product, called a lead pencil, was quite popular. In the late sixteenth century, a method for gluing strips of wood around graphite was discovered in Germany, and the modern pencil began to take form. In 1779, scientists determined that the material they had previously thought was lead was actually a form of microcrystalline carbon that they named graphite (from the Greek "graphein" meaning "to write"). Graphite is one of the three natural forms of pure carbon—the others are coal and diamond.

In the late eighteenth century the Borrowdale mine was depleted, and, as graphite was now less plentiful, other materials had to be mixed with it to create pencils. A Frenchman chemist, Nicolas Jacques Conté, discovered that when powdered graphite, powdered clay, and water were mixed, molded, and baked, the finished product wrote as smoothly as pure graphite. Conté also discovered that a harder or softer writing core could be produced by varying the proportion of clay and graphite—the more graphite, the blacker and softer the pencil. In 1839, Lothar von Faber of Germany developed a method of making graphite paste into rods of the same thickness. He later invented a machine to cut and groove the pencil wood. Following the depletion of the once-abundant graphite source at Borrowdale, other graphite mines were gradually established around the world.

A number of these mines were set up in the United States, and the first American pencils were manufactured in 1812, after the War of 1812 ended English imports. William Monroe, a cabinet maker in Concord, Massachusetts, invented a machine that cut and grooved wood slats precisely enough to make pencils. Around that time, American inventor Joseph Dixon developed a method of cutting single cedar cylinders in half, placing the graphite core in one of the halves, and then gluing the two halves back together. In 1861, Eberhard Faber built the United States' first pencil-making factory in New York City.

Today, the hardness of a pencil is designated by numbers or letters. Most manufacturers use the numbers 1 to 4, with 1 being the softest and making the darkest mark. Number 2 pencils (medium soft) are used for normal writing. Pencils are also sometimes graded by letters, from 6B, the softest, to 9H, the hardest. The idea of attaching an eraser to a pencil is traced to Hyman W. Lipman, an American whose 1858 U.S. patent was bought by Joseph Rechendorfer in 1872 for a reported $100,000.

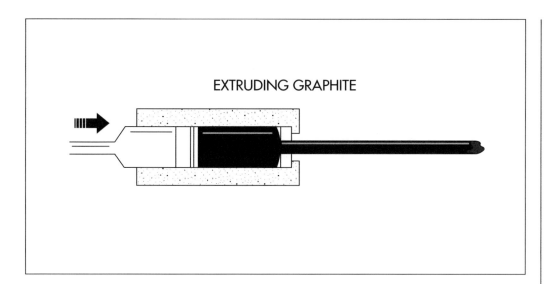

EXTRUDING GRAPHITE

The first step in pencil manufacture involves making the graphite core. One method of doing this is extrusion, in which the graphite mixture is forced through a die opening of the proper size.

In addition to the conventional wood pencil, a number of other pencils are widely used. In the early 1880s, the search for a pencil that didn't require sharpening led to the invention of what has variously been termed the automatic, propelling, or repeating pencil. These instruments have a metal or plastic case and use leads similar to those found in wood cased pencils. The lead, lodged in a metal spiral inside the case, is held in place by a rod with a metal stud fastened to it. When the cap is twisted, the rod and stud move downward in the spiral, forcing the lead toward the point. The early twentieth century saw the development of colored pencils in which the graphite core was replaced by a combination of pigments or dyes and a binder. Today, colored pencils are available in more than 70 colors, with 7 different yellows and 12 different blues. However, the cedar-casing lead pencil—manufactured at a pace of 6 billion per year in 40 different countries—continues to outsell all of its competitors, including the ballpoint pen.

Raw Materials

The most important ingredient in a pencil is the graphite, which most people continue to call lead. Conté's method of combining graphite with clay is still used, and wax or other chemicals are sometimes added as well. Virtually all graphite used today is a manufactured mixture of natural graphite and chemicals.

The wood used to manufacture pencils must be able to withstand repeated sharpening and cut easily without splintering. Most pencils are made from cedar (specifically, California cedar), the choice wood for many years. Cedar has a pleasant odor, does not warp or lose its shape, and is readily available. Some pencils have erasers, which are held on with a ferrule, a metal case that is either glued or held on with metal prongs. The erasers themselves consist of pumice and rubber.

The Manufacturing Process

Now that most commercially used graphite is made in factories rather than mined, manufacturers are able to easily control its density. The graphite is mixed with clay according to the type of pencil being made—the more graphite used, the softer the pencil, and the darker its line. For colored pencils, pigments are added to the clay, and virtually no graphite is used.

Processing the graphite

1 Two methods are used to form the graphite into its finished state. The first is an extrusion method in which the graphite and wax mixture is forced through a mold to create a spaghetti-like string, which is then cut to precise measurements and dried in ovens. In the second method, the graphite and clay mixture is poured into a machine called a *billet press*. A plug is placed over the top of the press, and a metal ram ascends from the bottom to squash the mixture into a hard, solid cylinder called a "billet." The billet is then removed from the top of the machine and placed into an extrusion press that forces it through a mold, slicing off strips the

To make the wood casings for the pencils, square slats are formed, and then grooves are cut into the slats. Next, graphite sticks are inserted into the grooves on one slat, and then a second slat with empty grooves is glued on top of the graphite-filled slat. Correctly sized pencils are cut out of the sandwich, and the eraser and metal ferrule are attached.

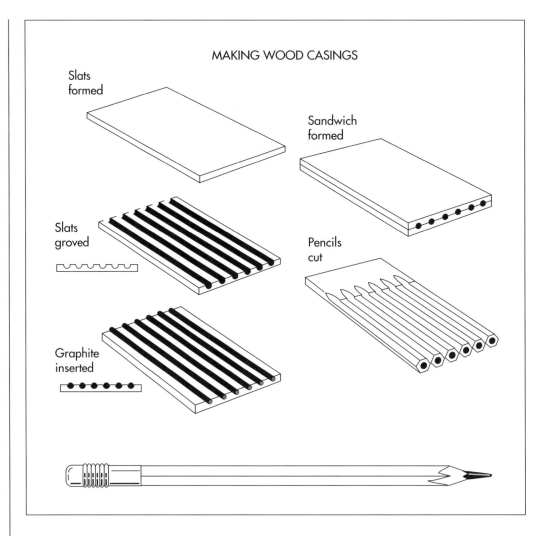

MAKING WOOD CASINGS

Slats formed

Slats groved

Graphite inserted

Sandwich formed

Pencils cut

size of the pencil core. After being cut to size, the cores pass along a conveyor belt and are collected in a trough to await insertion in the pencil wood.

Making the wood casings

2 The cedar usually arrives at the factory already dried, stained, and waxed, to prevent warping. Logs are then sawed into narrow strips called "slats"; these are about 7.25 inches (18.4 centimeters) long, .25 inch (.635 centimeter) thick, and 2.75 inches (6.98 centimeters) wide. The slats are placed into a feeder and dropped, one-by-one, onto a conveyor belt which moves them along at a constant rate.

3 The slats are then planed to give them a flat surface. Next, they pass under a cutter head that makes parallel semicircular grooves—one half as deep as the graphite is thick—along the length of one side of each slat. Continuing along the conveyor belt, half

of the slats are coated with a layer of glue, and the cut graphite is laid in the grooves of these slats.

4 The slats without glue—and without graphite in the grooves—are placed on another belt that carries them to a machine that picks them up and turns them over, so they are laying on the belt with the grooves facing down. The two conveyor belts then meet, and each unglued slat is placed over a slat with glue and graphite, forming a sandwich. After the sandwiches have been removed from the conveyor belt, they are placed into a metal clamp and squeezed by a hydraulic press and left clamped together until the glue is dried. When the pencils are dried, the ends are trimmed to remove excess glue.

Shaping the pencils

5 The next step is shaping, when the sandwiches actually become pencils. The

sandwiches are placed on a conveyor belt and moved through two sets of cutters, one above and one below the belt. The cutters above the sandwiches cut around the top half, while the lower set cuts around the bottom half and separates the finished pencils. The majority of pencils are hexagonal, so designed to keep the pencils from rolling off surfaces; a single sandwich yields six to nine hexagonal pencils.

Final steps

6 After the pencils have been cut, their surfaces are smoothed by sanders, and varnish is applied and dried. This is done with varnishing machines, in which the pencils are immersed in a vat of varnish and then passed through a felt disk, which removes the excess varnish. After drying, the pencils are put through the process again and again until the desired color is achieved. Finally, the pencils receive a finishing coat.

7 The pencils once again are sent on a conveyor belt through shaping machines, which remove any excess varnish that has accumulated on the ends of the pencils. This step also ensures that all of the pencils are the same length.

8 Erasers are then attached, held to the pencil by a round, metal case called a "ferrule." The ferrule first attaches to the pencil either with glue or with small metal prongs, and then the eraser is inserted and the ferrule clamped around it. In the final step, a heated steel die presses the company logo onto each pencil.

Colored pencils

Colored pencils are produced in much the same way as black-writing pencils, except that their cores contain coloring materials such as dyes and pigments instead of graphite. First, clay and gum are added to pigment as bonding agents, and then the mixture is soaked in wax to give the pencils

smoothness. When the pencils have been formed, the outsides are painted according to the color of the center mixture.

Quality Control

Because they travel along a conveyor belt during the manufacturing process, pencils are thoroughly scrutinized before they are distributed to the public. Workers are trained to discard pencils that appear dysfunctional, and a select number are sharpened and tested when the process is complete. A common problem is that the glue of the sandwiches sometimes doesn't adhere, but this nuisance is usually caught when the sandwiches are being cut.

Where To Learn More

Books

Fischler, George. *Fountain Pens and Pencils*. Schiffer Publishing, 1990.

Petroski, Henry. *The Pencil: A History of Design and Circumstance*. Knopf, 1990.

Thomson, Ruth. *Making Pencils*. Franklin Watts, 1987.

Periodicals

Leibson, Beth. "A Low-Tech Wonder." *Reader's Digest*. July, 1992, p. 92.

Lord, Lewis J. "The Little Artifact that Could." *U.S. News & World Report*. January 22, 1990, p. 63.

Sprout, Alison. "Recycled Pencil." *Fortune*. June 15, 1992, p. 113.

Urbanski, Al. "Eberhard Faber: the Man, the Pencil, the Born-Again Marketing Company." *Sales & Marketing Management*. November, 1986, p. 44.

—Jim Acton

Pesticide

All attempts at pest control were pretty much individual affairs until the 1840s, when a North American fungus called powdery mildew *invaded Britain, and the epidemic was controlled with large-scale applications of sulfur. The Colorado beetle in the western United States was the next target: by 1877 western settlers had learned to protect their potato crop by using water-insoluble chemicals such as paris green.*

Background

The word "pesticide" is a broad term that refers to any device, method, or chemical that kills plants or animals that compete for humanity's food supply or are otherwise undesirable. Pesticides include insecticides, fungicides, herbicides, nematocides (used to kill nematodes, elongated cylindrical worms), and rodenticides. Of these various pesticides, insecticides have a longer and more noteworthy history, perhaps because the number of insects labeled "pests" greatly exceeds the number of all other plant and animal "pests" combined. Hence, this article focuses on the use of agricultural insecticides.

Since they first began cultivating crops (around 7000 B.C.) if not before, humans have devised methods to prevent insects from eating or otherwise destroying precious crops. Some cultures relied on the practice of planting during certain phases of the moon. Other early agricultural practices that indirectly kept insect populations low were rotating crops; planting small, varied crops; and selecting naturally resistant plants. People picked bugs off plants by hand and made noise to ward off grasshoppers. Chemicals were also used early on. The crushed petals of the pyrethrum (a type of chrysanthemum), sulfur, and arsenic were used in the Middle East, Rome, and China, respectively. The Chinese also used natural predators such as ants to eat undesirable insects.

All attempts at pest control were pretty much individual affairs until the 1840s, when a North American fungus called *powdery mildew* invaded Britain, and the epidemic was controlled with large-scale applications of sulfur. The Colorado beetle in the western United States was the next target: by 1877 western settlers had learned to protect their potato crop by using water-insoluble chemicals such as paris green. Other pesticides such as derria, quassia, and tar oil followed, but nineteenth-century pesticides were weak. They had to be supplemented by introducing natural predators, or, in some cases, by grafting threatened plants onto more resistant rootstock.

By World War II, only about 30 pesticides existed. Research during the war yielded DDT (dichloro-diphenyl-trichloro-ethane), which had been synthesized in 1874 but wasn't recognized as an insecticide until 1942. Other strong pesticides soon followed, such as chlordane in 1945 and endrin in 1951. Poison gas research in Germany yielded the organophosphorus compounds, the best known of which is parathion. These new pesticides were very strong. Further research yielded hundreds of organophosphorus compounds, the most noteworthy being malathion, which was recently used in California against the medfly.

Until the 1800s, when people began to spray personal gardens using fairly large machines, pesticides were generally applied by hand. Airplanes were not used until the 1920s, and slow, well-controlled, low-level flights were not implemented until the 1950s. The first aerial spraying of synthetic pesticides used large amounts of inert materials, 4000 liters per hectare (a hectare equals 2.47 acres). This quantity was rapidly reduced to 100 to 200 liters/hectare, and by the 1970s the amount had been reduced (in some cases) to .3 liters per hectare of the ingredient itself (for example, malathion) applied directly to the fields.

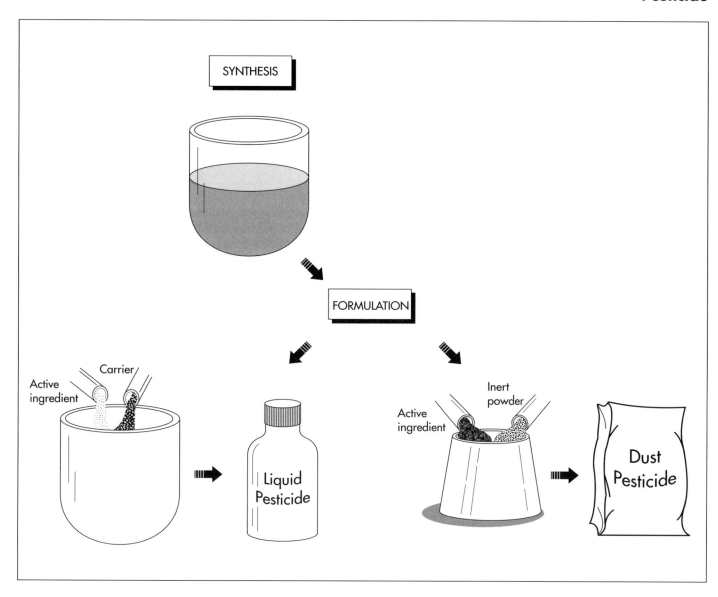

Today, some 900 active chemical pesticides are used to manufacture 40,000 commercial preparations. The Environmental Protection Agency (EPA) estimates that the use of pesticides doubled between 1960 and 1980. Currently, over 372 million kilograms a year are used in the United States, with over 1.8 billion kilograms a year used worldwide.

Raw Materials

A pesticide consists of an active ingredient coupled with inert ingredients. The active ingredient kills the pests, while the inert ingredients facilitate spraying and coating the target plant; they can also contribute other advantages that are not conferred by the active ingredient alone.

Active ingredients were once distilled from natural substances; now they are largely syn-

thesized in a laboratory. Almost all are hydrocarbons derived from petroleum. Most pesticides contain other elements, the type and number of which depend on the pesticide desired. Chlorine, oxygen, sulfur, phosphorus, nitrogen, and bromine are most common. Inert ingredients can be many substances, dependent on the type of pesticide. Liquid pesticides have traditionally used kerosene or some other petroleum distillate as a carrier, though water has recently begun to replace kerosene. Emulsifiers (such as soap) are also added to distribute the active ingredient evenly throughout the solvent. A powder or dust pesticide will typically contain vegetable matter such as ground up nut shells or corn cobs, clays such as diatomite or attapulgite, or powdered minerals such as talc or calcium carbonate as a base. To cause the pesticide to adhere bet-

In pesticide manufacturing, an active ingredient is first synthesized in a chemical factory. Next, a formulator mixes the active ingredient with a carrier (for liquid pesticide) or with inert powders or dry fertilizers (for dust pesticide), then bottles or packages it. Liquid pesticides are packaged in 200-liter drums for large-scale operations or 20-liter jugs for small-scale operations, while dry formulations can be packaged in 5 to 10 kilogram plastic or plastic-lined bags.

After receiving the pesiticide, farmers dilute it with water before applying it. Application can involve crop dusting with small airplanes or using sprinklers or tractors. Small farmers may even use hand-held sprayers.

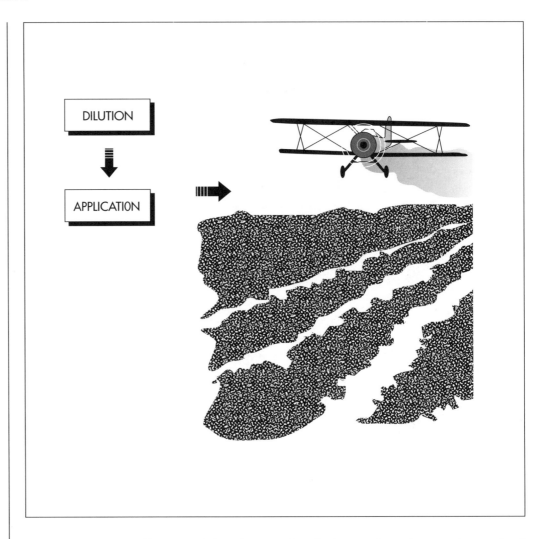

DILUTION

APPLICATION

ter to the plant or soil, a material such as cornstarch or flour may be added.

The Manufacturing Process

Manufacturing a pesticide involves at least three separate activities. The active ingredient is first synthesized in a chemical factory, then formulated in the same place or sent to a formulator, who prepares the liquid or powder form. The pesticide is then sent to the farmer or other certified applicator, who dilutes it before applying it to the fields.

Synthesizing the pesticide

1 When a new pesticide is first developed, it is manufactured on a small scale in a laboratory. If the substance proves viable, production begins in the factory. Batch or continuous manufacturing insures a high volume, perhaps as much as 500 kilograms per cycle. Synthesizing a pesticide is a complex chemical procedure that requires trained chemists and a large, sophisticated laboratory. The basic procedure entails altering an organic molecule to form a pesticide. This may involve any of a number of specific reagents and catalysts and often must take place in a controlled climate (within a certain temperature range, for example). Once synthesized, the active ingredient is packaged and sent to a formulator. Liquid insecticides can be shipped in tank trucks or 200-liter drums. Transport of the active ingredient follows all regulations for hazardous materials transportation.

Formulating the pesticide

2 A formulator accepts the active ingredient, measures out the proper amount, mixes it with carrier if it is to be a liquid pesticide or with inert powders or dry fertilizers if it is to be a dust pesticide, then bottles or packages it. Liquid pesticides are packaged in 200-liter drums if a large-scale farmer is

the anticipated customer or 20-liter jugs for small-scale operations. Dry formulations can be packaged in 5 to 10 kilogram plastic or plastic-lined bags. An emulsified formulation is usually concentrated to render transport easier (the active ingredient typically makes up 50 percent of the emulsified concentrate), but granulated and dry pesticides are ready to use.

Diluting the pesticide

3 The pesticide might be stored a short time before it is requested. When it is ready for transport, the estimated necessary amount is sent to the farmer, who dilutes the emulsified concentrate to create the amount of pesticide desired. In most instances, the final product consists of only .5 to 1 percent of the original active ingredient. The pesticide is now ready to be applied.

Applying the pesticide

4 There are several ways to apply a pesticide. The method with which Americans are most familiar is crop dusting, though its use is generally limited to large, flat areas. A plane loaded with 2000-liter (or larger) tanks flies over a field and sprays out the pesticide from booms. Booms are long, horizontal rods from which several sprinklers spray down. Another method is to attach the tanks and booms to a tractor and spray closer to the ground. For small farmers, the most economical method of spraying is to use one or more workers with hand-held sprayers attached to small tanks. A hand pump can be carried on the shoulder; its tank capacity is only about 3 to 12 liters. Small tanks with a capacity of around 200 liters are also used. The pesticides are applied with a hand gun. A rough estimate of the amount applied is 150 to 300 liters per hectare.

Quality Control

Pesticides are by their very nature toxic substances; hence, a great deal of concern has centered on safety. The laws dealing with pesticide safety are very strict and will become even stricter in the future. Besides legal restrictions, pesticides are also subject to stringent quality control standards like any other manufactured product.

Most large pesticide manufacturers have highly developed quality control laboratories that test each pesticide for potency, emulsification, density, color, pH, particle size (if a dust), and suspension (if a liquid). If the company makes more than one pesticide, the product's identity must also be verified. A pesticide must be stable, easy to apply, and easy to store. Shelf-life must extend past one year. In accelerated tests, the pesticide is subjected to high temperatures for a short period, then checked for effectiveness. A typical pesticide is 95 percent pure. Labels must be easy to read and meet all regulations. The manufacturer keeps files for each raw material, active ingredient, formulation, and packaged item, and samples are stored for three years.

Today's pesticides, when used properly, are very safe. Farmers who apply their own pesticides must be trained by the U.S. Agricultural Extension Service and certified by the state department of agriculture before they can purchase pesticides. Commercial applicators must also undergo training and pass a written test.

When preparing a formulation for application, which in most cases means diluting it, the applicator should wear protective clothing as directed by the label. Often, this protective garb includes an apron or coveralls, a broad-brimmed hat, long-sleeved shirt, long socks, unlined neoprene or rubber gloves, long pants, and unlined neoprene or rubber boots worn over shoes. For some pesticides, applicators must also wear goggles and/or a respirator.

As an additional precaution, application equipment is calibrated before each use. To calibrate a sprayer, the applicator measures off a distance in the field, then sprays it with a neutral substance such as water. The amount of water used is then checked to see if it is appropriate. All equipment is also checked to see if spraying is even, and worn equipment is replaced promptly.

Byproducts/Waste

When they were introduced, pesticides were seen as a wonderful technology that would increase crop yields and reduce insect-borne diseases. The first sign that this was a hopeful myth was the discovery in the 1950s that pesticide volume must be increased to have the same effect it once had. With the publication of *Silent Spring* by Rachel Carson in 1962, an awareness of the danger of unrestricted pesticide use grew.

Pesticides kill the pests they are aiming for most of the time, yet often they also kill the pests' natural predators, thereby exacerbating the problem. In some cases, exterminating a pest merely allows another pest to take its place. After a period of pesticide use, the insects become resistant to the pesticide, and stronger or more pesticides must be used to control the population. There is evidence that pesticides are misused, that their effect in some cases is negligible, and that applicators are not aware of the proper use of pesticides. Coupled with these concerns is the worry over blanket spraying of residential areas and contaminated food.

DDT is the most widely noted case of a pesticide that caused damage far from the farm. High levels of DDT have been found in birds of prey, causing them to become endangered because of the effect it has on their eggs. DDT becomes more concentrated the higher it climbs in the food chain, and many people have voiced their concern about its possible presence in humans. In 1972, the Environmental Protection Agency (EPA) announced a ban on almost all uses of DDT.

Several dozen other pesticides have also been banned, or their use restricted by the EPA. Ironically, these pesticides are still being exported to assist developing countries, where it is estimated that three million acute cases of pesticide poisoning occur per year, along with 20,000 deaths directly related to the misuse of pesticides. Because many of these countries export produce to the United States, the possibility of American contamination is high.

Integrated pest management (IPM) was begun in the 1960s in response to the pesticides dilemma. The idea behind IPM was to use a variety of insect controls instead of relying solely on chemical insecticides. The methods include introducing natural predators, parasites, and bacterial, viral, and fungal insecticides to the fields. Workers may simply vacuum up the insects, or introduce certain plants to ward off pests that attack a particular crop. Farmers may plow at the most effective time, plow their crop residue under, or strip harvest. They may plant pest-resistant plants. Sexual attractant traps may pull pests away from crops. Sterilized males can be released into the field. Insects can be engineered to remain juvenile and never reproduce, molt too rapidly and therefore die rapidly, or become too confused to locate crop foods. Other possibilities are being tested at present. It is possible that in the future pesticide use will diminish as research leads to ways to combat pests with more knowledge and planning and less reliance on chemical intervention.

Where To Learn More

Books

Carson, Rachel. *Silent Spring.* Houghton Mifflin Company, 1962.

Lee, Sally. *Pesticides.* Franklin Watts, 1991.

Ware, George W. *Pesticides: Theory and Application.* W.H. Freeman, 1983.

Periodicals

Gibbons, Ann. "Overkilling the Insect Enemy." *Science.* August 10, 1990, p. 621.

Holmes, Bob. "The Joy Ride Is Over." *U.S. News and World Report.* September 14, 1992, pp. 73-74.

Reganold, John P., Robert I. Papendick, and James F. Parr. "Sustainable Agriculture." *Scientific American.* June, 1990, pp. 112-120.

Richmond, Suzan. "Making Sure It's Organic." *Changing Times.* October, 1990, p. 102.

Satchell, Michael. "A Vicious 'Circle of Poison.'" *U.S. News and World Report.* June 10, 1991, pp. 31-32.

—*Rose Secrest*

Porcelain

Background

The term porcelain refers to a wide range of ceramic products that have been baked at high temperatures to achieve vitreous, or glassy, qualities such as translucence and low porosity. Among the most familiar porcelain goods are table and decorative china, chemical ware, dental crowns, and electrical insulators. Usually white or off-white, porcelain comes in both glazed and unglazed varieties, with bisque, fired at a high temperature, representing the most popular unglazed variety.

Although porcelain is frequently used as a synonym for china, the two are not identical. They resemble one another in that both are vitreous wares of extremely low porosity, and both can be glazed or unglazed. However, china, also known as soft-paste or tender porcelain, is softer: it can be cut with a file, while porcelain cannot. This difference is due to the higher temperatures at which true porcelain is fired, 2,650 degrees Fahrenheit (1,454 degrees Celsius) compared to 2,200 degrees Fahrenheit (1,204 degrees Celsius) for china. Due to its greater hardness, porcelain has some medical and industrial applications which china, limited to domestic and artistic use, does not. Moreover, whereas porcelain is always translucent, china is opaque.

Hard-paste or "true" porcelain originated in China during the T'ang dynasty (618-907 A.D.); however, high quality porcelain comparable to modern wares did not develop until the Yüan dynasty (1279-1368 A.D.). Early Chinese porcelain consisted of kaolin (china clay) and pegmatite, a coarse type of granite. Porcelain was unknown to European potters prior to the importation of Chinese wares during the Middle Ages. Europeans tried to duplicate Chinese porcelain, but, unable to analyze its chemical composition, they could imitate only its appearance. After mixing glass with tin oxide to render it opaque, European craftspeople tried combining clay and ground glass. These alternatives became known as soft-paste, glassy, or artificial porcelains. However, because they were softer than genuine porcelain, as well as expensive to produce, efforts to develop true porcelain continued. In 1707 two Germans named Ehrenfried Walter von Tschirnhaus and Johann Friedrich Böttger succeeded by combining clay with ground feldspar instead of the ground glass previously used.

Later in the eighteenth century the English further improved upon the recipe for porcelain when they invented bone china by adding ash from cattle bones to clay, feldspar, and quartz. Although bone china is fired at lower temperatures than true porcelain, the bone ash enables it to become translucent nonetheless. Because it is also easier to make, harder to chip, and stronger than hard porcelain, bone china has become the most popular type of porcelain in the United States and Britain (European consumers continue to favor hard porcelain).

Raw Materials

The primary components of porcelain are clays, feldspar or flint, and silica, all characterized by small particle size. To create different types of porcelain, craftspeople combine these raw materials in varying proportions until they obtain the desired green (unfired) and fired properties.

Although the composition of clay varies depending upon where it is extracted and how it

Although porcelain is frequently used as a synonym for china, the two are not identical. They resemble one another in that both are vitreous wares of extremely low porosity, and both can be glazed or unglazed. However, china, also known as soft-paste or tender porcelain, is softer: it can be cut with a file, while porcelain cannot.

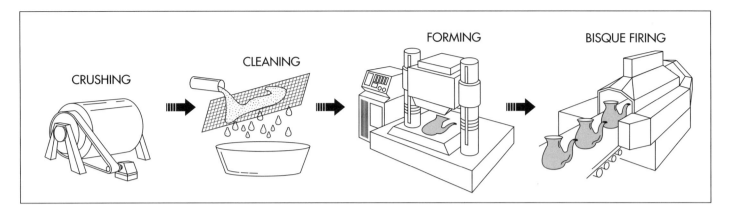

CRUSHING → CLEANING → FORMING → BISQUE FIRING

To make porcelain, the raw materials—such as clay, felspar, and silica—are first crushed using jaw crushers, hammer mills, and ball mills. After cleaning to remove improperly sized materials, the mixture is subjected to one of four forming processes—soft plastic forming, stiff plastic forming, pressing, or casting—depending on the type of ware being produced. The ware then undergoes a preliminary firing step, bisque-firing.

is treated, all clays vitrify (develop glassy qualities), only at extremely high temperatures unless they are mixed with materials whose vitrification threshold is lower. Unlike glass, however, clay is refractory, meaning that it holds its shape when it is heated. In effect, porcelain combines glass's low porosity with clay's ability to retain its shape when heated, making it both easy to form and ideal for domestic use. The principal clays used to make porcelain are china clay and ball clay, which consist mostly of kaolinate, a hydrous aluminum silicate.

Feldspar, a mineral comprising mostly aluminum silicate, and flint, a type of hard quartz, function as fluxes in the porcelain body or mixture. Fluxes reduce the temperature at which liquid glass forms during firing to between 1,835 and 2,375 degrees Fahrenheit (1,000 and 1,300 degrees Celsius). This liquid phase binds the grains of the body together.

Silica is a compound of oxygen and silicon, the two most abundant elements in the earth's crust. Its resemblance to glass is visible in quartz (its crystalline form), opal (its amorphous form), and sand (its impure form). Silica is the most common filler used to facilitate forming and firing of the body, as well as to improve the properties of the finished product. Porcelain may also contain alumina, a compound of aluminum and oxygen, or low-alkali containing bodies, such as steatite, better known as soapstone.

The Manufacturing Process

After the raw materials are selected and the desired amounts weighed, they go through a series of preparation steps. First, they are

crushed and purified. Next, they are mixed together before being subjected to one of four forming processes—soft plastic forming, stiff plastic forming, pressing, or casting; the choice depends upon the type of ware being produced. After the porcelain has been formed, it is subjected to a final purification process, bisque-firing, before being glazed. Glaze is a layer of decorative glass applied to and fired onto a ceramic body. The final manufacturing phase is firing, a heating step that takes place in a type of oven called a *kiln.*

Crushing the raw materials

1 First, the raw material particles are reduced to the desired size, which involves using a variety of equipment during several crushing and grinding steps. Primary crushing is done in jaw crushers which use swinging metal jaws. Secondary crushing reduces particles to 0.1 inch (.25 centimeter) or less in diameter by using mullers (steel-tired wheels) or hammer mills, rapidly moving steel hammers. For fine grinding, craftspeople use ball mills that consist of large rotating cylinders partially filled with steel or ceramic grinding media of spherical shape.

Cleaning and mixing

2 The ingredients are passed through a series of screens to remove any under- or over-sized materials. Screens, usually operated in a sloped position, are vibrated mechanically or electromechanically to improve flow. If the body is to be formed wet, the ingredients are then combined with water to produce the desired consistency. Magnetic filtration is then used to remove iron from the slurries, as these watery mixtures of insoluble material are called. Because iron occurs so pervasively in most clays and will impart

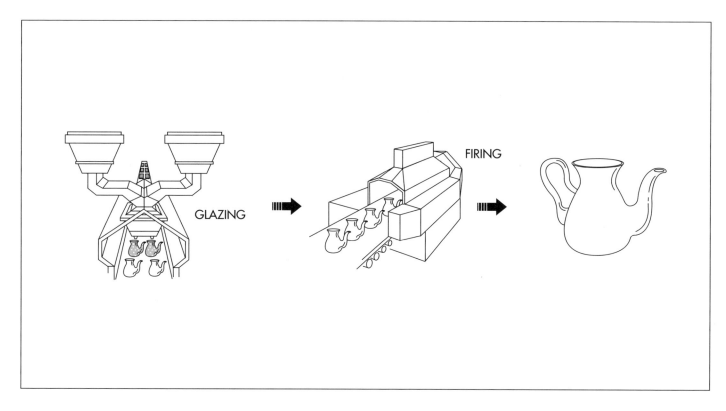

GLAZING

FIRING

an undesirable reddish hue to the body if it oxidizes, removing it prior to firing is essential. If the body is to be formed dry, shell mixers, ribbon mixers, or intensive mixers are typically used.

Forming the body

3 Next, the body of the porcelain is formed. This can be done using one of four methods, depending on the type of ware being produced:

- *soft plastic forming,* where the clay is shaped by manual molding, wheel throwing, jiggering, or ram pressing. In wheel throwing, a potter places the desired amount of body on a wheel and shapes it while the wheel turns. In jiggering, the clay is put on a horizontal plaster mold of the desired shape; that mold shapes one side of the clay, while a heated die is brought down from above to shape the other side. In ram pressing, the clay is put between two plaster molds, which shape it while forcing the water out. The mold is then separated by applying vacuum to the upper half of the mold and pressure to the lower half of the mold. Pressure is then applied to the upper half to free the formed body.

- *stiff plastic forming,* which is used to shape less plastic bodies. The body is forced through a steel die to produce a column of uniform girth. This is either cut into the desired length or used as a blank for other forming operations.

- *pressing,* which is used to compact and shape dry bodies in a rigid die or flexible mold. There are several types of pressing, based on the direction of pressure. Uniaxial pressing describes the process of applying pressure from only one direction, whereas isostatic pressing entails applying pressure equally from all sides.

- *slip casting,* in which a slurry is poured into a porous mold. The liquid is filtered out through the mold, leaving a layer of solid porcelain body. Water continues to drain out of the cast layer, until the layer becomes rigid and can be removed from the mold. If the excess fluid is not drained from the mold and the entire material is allowed to solidify, the process is known as *solid casting.*

Bisque-firing

4 After being formed, the porcelain parts are generally bisque-fired, which entails heating them at a relatively low temperature to vaporize volatile contaminants and minimize shrinkage during firing.

After bisque firing, the porcelain wares are put through a glazing operation, which applies the proper coating. The glaze can be applied by painting, dipping, pouring, or spraying. Finally, the ware undergoes a firing step in an oven or kiln. After cooling, the porcelain ware is complete.

Glazing

5 After the raw materials for the glaze have been ground they are mixed with water. Like the body slurry, the glaze slurry is screened and passed through magnetic filters to remove contaminants. It is then applied to the ware by means of painting, pouring, dipping, or spraying. Different types of glazes can be produced by varying the proportions of the constituent ingredients, such as alumina, silica, and calcia. For example, increasing the alumina and decreasing the silica produces a matte glaze.

Firing

6 Firing is a further heating step that can be done in one of two types of oven, or kiln. A periodic kiln consists of a single, refractory-lined, sealed chamber with burner ports and flues (or electric heating elements). It can fire only one batch of ware at a time, but it is more flexible since the firing cycle can be adjusted for each product. A tunnel kiln is a refractory chamber several hundred feet or more in length. It maintains certain temperature zones continuously, with the ware being pushed from one zone to another. Typically, the ware will enter a preheating zone and move through a central firing zone before leaving the kiln via a cooling zone. This type of kiln is usually more economical and energy efficient than a periodic kiln.

7 During the firing process, a variety of reactions take place. First, carbon-based impurities burn out, chemical water evolves (at 215 to 395 degrees Fahrenheit or 100 to 200 degrees Celsius), and carbonates and sulfates begin to decompose (at 755 to 1,295 degrees Fahrenheit or 400 to 700 degrees Celsius). Gases are produced that must escape from the ware. On further heating, some of the minerals break down into other phases, and the fluxes present (feldspar and flint) react with the decomposing minerals to form liquid glasses (at 1,295 to 2,015 degrees Fahrenheit or 700 to 1,100 degrees Celsius). These glass phases are necessary for shrinking and bonding the grains. After the desired density is achieved (greater than 2,195 degrees Fahrenheit or 1,200 degrees Celsius), the ware is cooled, which causes the liquid glass to solidify, thereby forming a strong bond between the remaining crystalline grains. After cooling, the porcelain is complete.

Quality Control

The character of the raw materials is important in maintaining quality during the manufacturing process. The chemical composition, mineral phase, particle size distribution, and colloidal surface area affect the fired and unfired properties of the porcelain. With unfired body, the properties evaluated include viscosity, plasticity, shrinkage, and strength. With fired porcelain, strength, porosity, color, and thermal expansion are measured. Many of these properties are monitored and controlled during manufacturing using statistical methods. Both the raw materials and the process parameters (milling time and forming pressure, for example) can be adjusted to achieve desired quality.

The Future

High-quality porcelain art and dinnerware will continue to enhance the culture. Improvements in manufacturing will continue to increase both productivity and energy efficiency. For instance, a German kiln manufacturer has developed a prefabricated tunnel kiln for fast firing high-quality porcelain in less than 5 hours. Firing is achieved by partly reducing atmosphere at a maximum firing temperature of 2,555 degrees Fahrenheit (1,400 degrees Celsius). The kiln uses high-velocity burners and an automatic control system, producing 23,000 pounds (11,500 kilograms) of porcelain in 24 hours.

Manufacturers of porcelain products may also have to increase their recycling efforts, due to the increase in environmental regulations. Though unfired scrap is easily recycled, fired scrap poses a problem: mechanically strong and therefore hard to break down, it is usually dumped into landfills. However, preliminary research has shown that fired scrap can be reused after thermal quenching (where the scrap is reheated and then quickly cooled), which makes it weaker and easier to break down. The scrap can then be used as a raw material.

Porcelain appears to be playing a more important role in technical applications. Recent patents have been issued to Japanese and American companies in the area of electrical insulators and dental prostheses. NGK Insulators, Ltd., a Japanese manufacturer, has developed high-strength porcelain for electrical insulators, whereas Murata Manufacturing Co. has developed low-temperature-sintering porcelain components for electronic applications.

Where To Learn More

Books

Campbell, James E. *The Art and Architecture Information Guide Series*, vol. 7: *Pottery and Ceramics, A Guide to Information Sources*. Gale Research, 1978.

Camusso, Lorenzo, ed. *Ceramics of the World: From Four Thousand B.C. to the Present*. Harry N. Abrams, 1992.

Charles, Bernard H. *Pottery and Porcelain*. Hippocrene Books, 1974.

Jones, J. T. and M. F. Bernard. *Ceramics, Industrial Processing and Testing*. Iowa State University Press, 1972.

Periodicals

Shashidhar, N. and J. S. Reed. "Recycling Fired Porcelain." *Ceramic Bulletin*. Vol. 69, No. 5, 1990, pp. 834-841.

Wilson, Lana. "Charcoal and Metallic Salts." *Ceramics Monthly*. October, 1987, p. 36.

—*L. S. Millberg*

Postage Stamp

The penny black and other early stamps needed to be separated with a scissors; perforated stamps did not appear until 1854 in England and 1857 in the United States. However, though larger stamps are occasionally produced, the penny black's original size, .75 by .875 inch, has remained standard.

Background

The postage stamp is a relatively modern invention, first proposed in 1837 when Sir Rowland Hill, an English teacher and tax reformer, published a seminal pamphlet entitled *Post Office Reform: Its Importance and Practicability*. Among other reforms, Hill's treatise advocated that the English cease basing postal rates on the distance a letter traveled and collecting fees upon delivery. Instead, he argued, they should assess fees based on weight and require prepayment in the form of stamps. Hill's ideas were accepted almost immediately, and the first English adhesive stamp, which featured a portrait of Queen Victoria, was printed in 1840. This stamp, called the "penny black," provided sufficient postage for letters weighing up to .5 ounce (14 grams), regardless of distance. To encourage widespread use of stamps, letters mailed without them were now charged double at the point of delivery. After Britain, Brazil became the next nation to produce postage stamps, issuing stamps made by its currency engraver in 1843. Various cantons in what later became Switzerland also produced stamps in 1843. United States postage stamps (in five and ten cent denominations) were first authorized by Congress in 1847 and came on the market on July 1 of the same year. By 1860, more than 90 countries, colonies, or districts were issuing postage stamps.

Most early stamps were of a single color—the United States, for example, did not produce multicolored stamps until 1869, and they did not become common until the 1920s. The penny black and other early stamps needed to be separated with a scissors; perforated stamps did not appear until 1854 in England and 1857 in the United States. However, though larger stamps are occasionally produced, the penny black's original size, .75 by .875 inch (1.9 by 2.22 centimeters), has remained standard.

Initially, stamps were manufactured by the same businesses that provided a country with currency, or by a country's mint. Yet it soon became apparent that printing stamps is unlike minting money in that the different paper types call for different printing pressures. Consequently, printing stamps became a discrete activity, though one still sometimes carried out by companies that made currency. In ensuing years, methods of producing stamps mirrored the development of modern printing processes. Today, stamp making processes utilize much of the finest printing technology available.

In the United States, the decision to produce a stamp is made by a Citizens' Stamp Advisory Committee, which meets regularly in conjunction with staff from the Post Office. The committee is responsible for determining what stamps will be produced, in what denominations, and at what time. Suggestions for stamps come from throughout the country, although the committee itself might recommend a particular design. Most frequently, however, there is a large pool of recommendations with which to work. In some cases, suggestions are accompanied by drawings and pictures which might form the basis for the stamp being considered.

Once the committee decides that a particular stamp will be produced, it commissions an artist to design it or modify a submitted design. It then decides, primarily on the basis of workload, whether the stamp should be produced by the Bureau of Engraving and

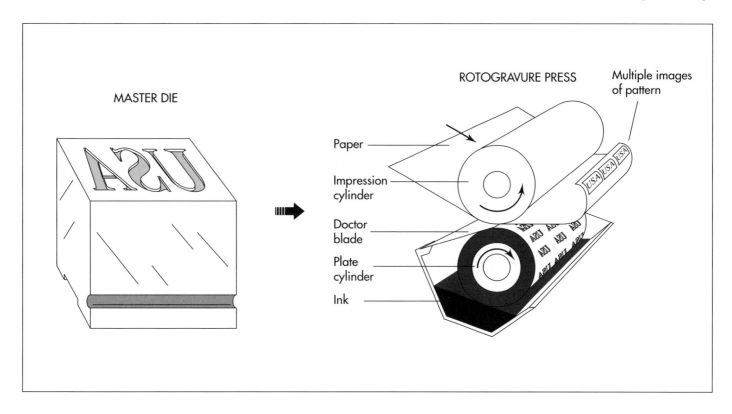

MASTER DIE

ROTOGRAVURE PRESS

Multiple images of pattern

Paper

Impression cylinder

Doctor blade

Plate cylinder

Ink

Printing or by outside contractors, who have been used much more extensively since the late 1980s. It's possible for a common stamp in great demand (such as an everyday first class mail stamp) to be made by the Bureau of Engraving and Printing and by several contractors. Currently, perhaps ten to fifteen American firms are capable of manufacturing stamps that meet Post Office standards.

Specifications for the stamp, such as color, size, design, and even the printing process itself are then drawn up in consultation with the original artist or designer. If the stamp is to be contracted out, a "request for proposal" appears in the *Commerce Business Daily*, a U.S. government publication which lists contracts available to non-government firms. After the stamp is printed, samples will be sent to the International Bureau of the Universal Postal Union in Switzerland, where they are marked as samples (commonly perforated with a word such as "specimen") and then distributed to member nations to help postal workers recognize other countries' legitimate postage.

In addition to requirements for the picture or design on a stamp, other requirements, all of which can be met at a printing plant, are sometimes added to a stamp's specification. The most common one is phosphor tagging,

in which an invisible mark that can be read only by a special machine is placed on a stamp. The tagging facilitates the automated sorting of mail.

Other requirements might be for such things as printing the stamp on chalked paper to prevent reuse of a stamp by cleaning or washing off a cancellation. When a canceled stamp printed on chalked paper is wetted, the picture will blur as the cancellation mark is wiped off, cuing postal workers to the fact that the stamp is no longer valid.

Raw Materials

Although stamps were originally printed on sheets of paper that were fed into presses individually, the paper now used comes on a roll. The two kinds of paper most commonly used to print stamps are laid and wove paper, the former with ribbed lines and the latter without. While other nations use both types, the United States presently uses only wove. Either laid or wove paper might feature watermarks, faint designs that result from differences in the pressure applied to various parts of a roll of paper during the production process. Commonly used in other counties, watermarked paper has not been utilized in the United States since 1915.

The engraving method of intaglio printing begins with the creation of a master die on which the design of the stamp is engraved, in reverse. The design is in the lowered portion of the die—the raised portion will not be reproduced in the final product. This is an exacting hand process, in which the engraver carefully cuts a mirror image of the original drawing for the stamp.

The master die impression is then copied onto a transfer roll, and in turn onto a printing plate. The impression on the plate is in the form of grooves rather than a raised image. Next, the plate is fastened into the printing press and coated with ink, and the appropriate paper is fed through the press.

The Manufacturing Process

At the printing plant, the process begins with the delivery of paper for stamps, with the glue already applied to the back. Two printing processes are most often used in making stamps, the intaglio process (which includes the gravure process), and the offset process. It is not unusual, however, for a particular stamp's specifications to call for the use of both methods.

Intaglio, perhaps the oldest means of producing stamps, is also the most time-consuming. However, because this method creates stamps with more distinct images, the process has not been pushed aside by newer, faster, and less expensive methods. Intaglio involves engraving, scratching, or etching an image onto a printing plate, which in turn transfers that image onto paper. In one well-known intaglio process, called *gravure,* the image is first transferred onto the plate photographically, and then etched into the plate. This section, however, will focus on an engraving process.

Creating the master die

1 The engraving method of intaglio begins with the creation of a "master die" in which the design of the stamp is engraved, in reverse. The design is in the lowered portion of the die—the raised portion of the die will not be reproduced in the final product. This is an exacting hand process, in which the engraver is carefully cutting a mirror image of the original drawing for the stamp. It might be several weeks before the engraver is satisfied that he or she has created the perfect duplicate.

2 After the die has been completed, it is heated to harden the engraved image. In the next step, the hardened intaglio is transferred to a transfer roll, which consists of soft steel wrapped around a rod-shaped carrier, or mandrel, and which resembles a shortened rolling pin. The transfer roll is machine-pressed against the master die, and rocked back and forth until the master die has created a relief impression on the transfer roll. At this point, the relief is a positive impression (no longer in reverse). The process is repeated until the desired number of reliefs has been created on the transfer roll.

Preparing the printing plate

3 Like the master die, the transfer roll is hardened by heating. It is then pressed against a printing plate, leaving another relief, again in reverse, on the printing plate. If there are several reliefs on a transfer roll, all can be passed to the printing plate. Several printing plates can be made from the same transfer roll if the decision is made to use more than one machine to produce a particular stamp. The impression on the plate is in the form of grooves rather than a raised image.

4 Once the plate is ready for use, it is fastened into the printing press and coated with ink. Inking is done automatically by several processes including spraying ink through small jets or moving an ink-covered roller across a plate. The plate is then wiped by a blade called the *doctor blade,* leaving ink only in the grooves.

5 The plate then presses against the paper, leaving a positive impression of the reverse image that was originally copied onto the master die.

6 If more than one color is involved, separate colors are handled by a process known as *selective inking.* A particular color of ink is applied by a piece of hard rubber that comes in contact with only the section of the stamp that is to receive that color. After the ink is applied in one area, another piece of rubber, with another color for another area, is used to ink another portion of the plate.

Offset lithography

7 The offset method of printing is less expensive than intaglio and also can produce very fine results, and it is a common choice for many stamps. In this method, a picture or design is first made photochemically on an aluminum plate. Once attached to the printing press, the plate is alternately bathed in ink and water: the photochemical image gets ink, while the non-image parts are dampened with water, which acts as a repellent to the ink and ensures that only the image will be transferred to the paper. Next, the plate presses against a rubber "blanket," which carries a reverse image of the final picture. In turn, the rubber blanket contacts the paper, producing the final positive image.

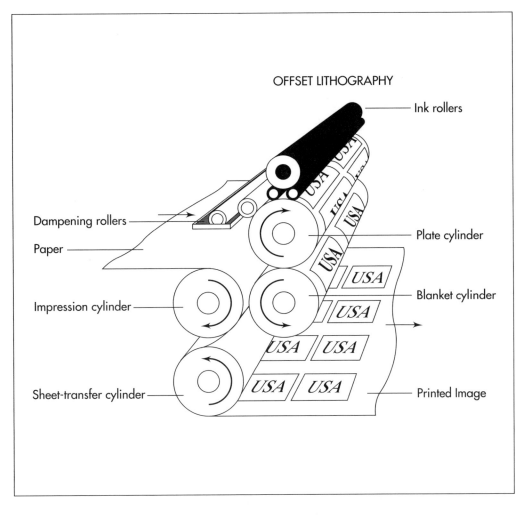

OFFSET LITHOGRAPHY

Ink rollers

Dampening rollers

Paper

Impression cylinder

Sheet-transfer cylinder

Plate cylinder

Blanket cylinder

Printed Image

In offset lithography, a picture or design is first made photochemically on an aluminum plate. Once attached to the printing press, the plate is alternately bathed in ink and water: the photochemical image gets ink, while the non-image parts are dampened with water, which acts as a repellent to the ink and ensures that only the image will be transferred to the paper. Next, the plate presses against a rubber "blanket," which carries a reverse image of the final picture. In turn, the rubber blanket contacts the paper, producing the final positive image.

Perforation

8 Perforations can be made either during the printing process by an adjacent machine or, less commonly, by a separate machine afterwards. In the first method, the sheet of paper is passed through a machine which uses little pins to punch the perforation holes through the paper in a horizontal and vertical grid. After pushing through the paper, the pins meet a matching metal indentation on the other side. After being perforated, the stamps move out of the press. In the other method of producing perforations, called *rouletting*, a wheel similar to a pizza cutter but with pins is rolled across one side of the stamped paper after it has been removed from the printing press, laying down a row of holes. Though originally a hand-operation, this method of perforation is now automated.

Quality Control

Stamps are inspected at every stage of the printing process, by the people who are running the stamps and by inspectors whose only responsibility is to observe the process and remove errors before the stamps proceed to the next step.

Printing machines are hugely complex, and errors in the printing process are a fact of life. Misfed paper, clogged inking apparatus, variations in pressure, changes in ink quality, incorrectly adjusted mechanisms, and a host of other problems can be minimized but not always eliminated. Even changes in the humidity of the pressroom can affect the press and the paper enough to produce less-than-perfect results.

Several of the most spectacular errors of the past occurred because presses were manually fed; in other words, individual sheets of paper were inserted into the press by hand. If a sheet of paper required an impression from a second press (to add a second color), and the sheet was turned accidentally, the resulting stamps featured misplaced blotches of color. This type of error does not occur today because presses are roll-fed: rather than being fed into a press sheet by sheet, paper is fed in from a continuous roll.

Most errors are detected, and the flawed stamps destroyed, under tight security controls in the printing plant. Enough errors slip through, however, to make the collecting of "error stamps" an interesting specialty for some stamp collectors.

The Future

One twentieth-century innovation that has significantly diminished the use of stamps is the postage meter. Developed in New Zealand in 1902, meters were introduced in the United States twelve years later. In addition to their use by the federal Post Office, meters are now leased by private companies that send out large amounts of mail. These meters allow companies to post and mail letters without using stamps. Particularly popular with businesses that send out bulk mailings, meters now "stamp" over one half of the mail posted in the United States. However, individuals continue to use postage stamps, which remain not only functional but popular, as can be seen in the excitement generated by such recent stamps as those commemorating World War II, Elvis Presley, and Princess Grace of Monaco.

Where To Learn More

Books

Lewis, Brenda Ralph. *Stamps! A Young Collector's Guide.* Lodestar Books, 1991.

Olcheski, Bill. *Beginning Stamp Collecting.* Henry Z. Walck, 1991.

Scott 1993 Standard Postage Stamp Catalogue. Vol. 1: *Basic Stamp Information,* pp. 20A-26A. Scott Publishing Co., 1992.

Periodicals

Healey, Barth. "Tactical Technology Fights Counterfeiters." *New York Times.* May 16, 1993, p. N22.

Patota, Anne. "Coil Stamp Provides Test for Pre-Phosphored Paper." *Stamps.* May 16, 1987, p. 458.

Schiff, Jacques C., Jr. "Much to Learn about Printing." *Stamps.* July 4, 1992, p. 10.

"Computer Enhances National Guard Color." *Stamps.* November 8, 1986, p. 418.

"Postage Stamp Design: Creating Art Works the Size of Your Thumb." *Stamps.* November 5, 1988, p. 217.

—*Lawrence H. Berlow*

Pressure Gauge

Background

Many of the processes in the modern world involve the measurement and control of pressurized liquid and gas systems. This monitoring reflects certain performance criteria that must be controlled to produce the desirable results of the process and insure its safe operation. Boilers, refineries, water systems, and compressed gas systems are but a few of the many applications for pressure gauges.

The mechanical pressure indicating instrument, or gauge, consists of an elastic pressure element; a threaded connection means called the "socket"; a sector and pinion gear mechanism called the "movement"; and the protective case, dial, and viewing lens assembly. The elastic pressure element is the member that actually displaces or moves due to the influence of pressure. When properly designed, this pressure element is both highly accurate and repeatable. The pressure element is connected to the geared "movement" mechanism, which in turn rotates a pointer throughout a graduated dial. It is the pointer's position relative to the graduations that the viewer uses to determine the pressure indication.

The most common pressure gauge design was invented by French industrialist Eugene Bourdon in 1849. It utilizes a curved tube design as the pressure sensing element. A less common pressure element design is the diaphragm or disk type, which is especially sensitive at lower pressures. This article will focus on the Bourdon tube pressure gauge.

Design

In a Bourdon tube gauge, a "C" shaped, hollow spring tube is closed and sealed at one end. The opposite end is securely sealed and bonded to the socket, the threaded connection means. When the pressure medium (such as air, oil, or water) enters the tube through the socket, the pressure differential from the inside to the outside causes the tube to move. One can relate this movement to the uncoiling of a hose when pressurized with water, or the party whistle that uncoils when air is blown into it. The direction of this movement is determined by the curvature of the tubing, with the inside radius being slightly shorter than the outside radius. A specific amount of pressure causes the "C" shape to open up, or stretch, a specific distance. When the pressure is removed, the spring nature of the tube material returns the tube to its original shape and the tip to its original position relative to the socket.

Raw Materials

Pressure gauge tubes are made of many materials, but the common design factor for these materials is the suitability for *spring tempering*. This tempering is a form of heat treating. It causes the metal to closely retain its original shape while allowing flexing or "elasticity" under load. Nearly all metals have some degree of elasticity, but spring tempering reinforces those desirable characteristics. Beryllium copper, phosphor bronze, and various alloys of steel and **stainless steel** all make excellent Bourdon tubes. The type of material chosen depends upon its corrosion properties with regards to the process media (water, air, oil, etc). Steel has a limited service life due to corrosion but is adequate for oil; stainless steel alloys add cost if specific corrosion resistance is not required; and beryllium copper is usually reserved for high pressure applications. Most gauges in-

The most common pressure gauge design was invented by French industrialist Eugene Bourdon in 1849. It utilizes a curved tube design (called a "Bourdon tube") as the pressure sensing element.

MAKING THE
BOURDON TUBE

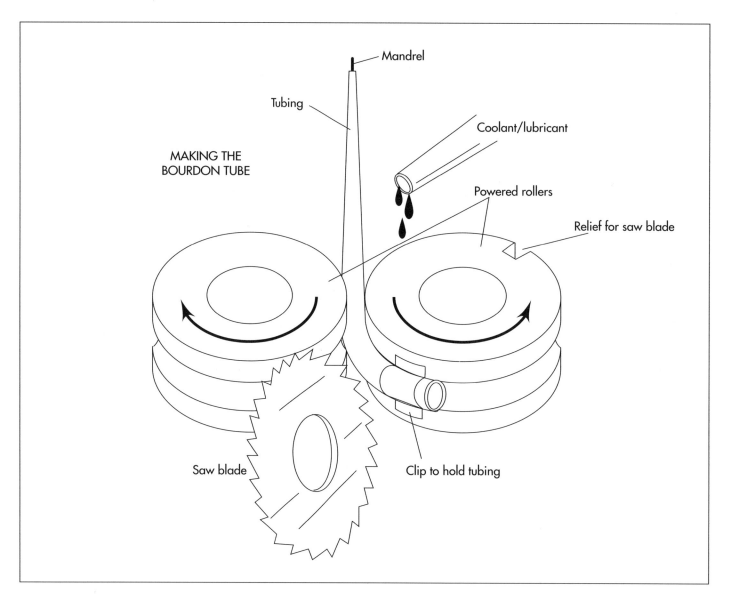

Mandrel

Tubing

Coolant/lubricant

Powered rollers

Relief for saw blade

Saw blade

Clip to hold tubing

A crucial step in the manufacture of a pressure gauge is making the C-shaped bourdon tube. In this step, a metal tube is pulled through grooved rollers on an automatic rolling machine. One roller grasps the tubing end and forms the inside radius, while the other provides outside pressure to maintain uniform contact with the tubing. The same roller that grabs and bends the tubing also contains a saw blade. As the roller continues turning after creating the bend, the saw blade on it cuts the tubing to the proper length.

tended for general use of air, light oil, or water utilize phosphor bronze. The pressure range of the tubes is determined by the tubing wall thickness and the radius of the curvature. Instrument designers must use precise design and material selection, because exceeding the elastic limit will destroy the tube and accuracy will be lost.

The socket is usually made of brass, steel, or stainless steel. Lightweight gauges sometimes use aluminum, but this material has limited pressure service and is difficult to join to the Bourdon tube by soldering or brazing. Extrusions and rolled bar stock shapes are most commonly used.

The movement mechanism is made of glass filled polycarbonate, brass, nickel silver, or stainless steel. Whichever material is used, it must be stable and allow for a friction-free assembly. Brass and combinations of brass and polycarbonate are most popular.

To protect the Bourdon tube and movement, the assembly is enclosed within a case and viewing lens. A dial and pointer, which are used to provide the viewer with the pressure indication, are made from nearly all basic metals, glass, and plastics. Aluminum, brass, and steel as well as polycarbonate and polypropylene make excellent gauge cases and dials. Most lenses are made of polycarbonate or acrylic, which are in favor over glass for obvious safety reasons. For severe service applications, the case is sealed and filled with glycerine or silicone fluid. This fluid cushions the tube and movement against damage from impact and vibration.

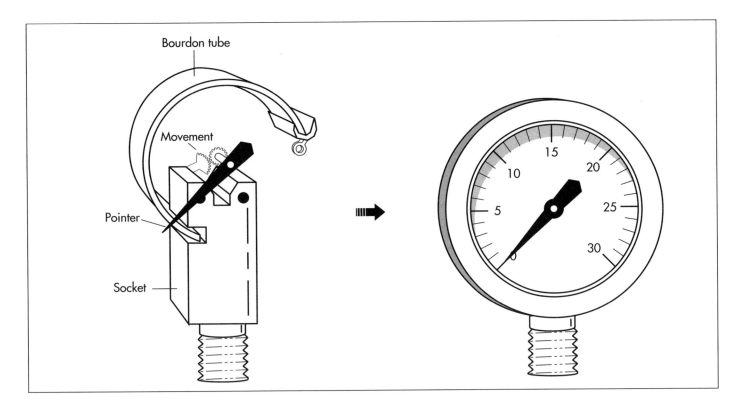

The Manufacturing Process

Making the Bourdon tube

1 The Bourdon tube is the most important part of the instrument. The tube may be made from solid bar stock by drilling the length to the desired inside diameter and turning the outside diameter on a lathe to achieve the appropriate wall thickness. However, most general purpose gauges utilize preformed tubing purchased from a metals supplier. The gauge builder specifies the desired wall thickness, material, configuration, and diameter. The supplier provides the material in 10- to 12-foot (3- to 3.65-meter) lengths, ready for production.

2 Most manufacturers have closely guarded proprietary rolling methods for rolling the tubing into the "C" shape. The "C" shape of the tube is generally formed in an automatic rolling machine. This machine contains two precision, powered rollers, through which the tubing passes. One roller grasps the tubing end and forms the inside radius, while the other provides outside pressure to maintain uniform contact with the tubing. Each roller contains a groove that fits around the outside of the tubing; these grooves allow the tubing to maintain its circular shape rather than

being flattened. In the rolling process, a steel mandrel—a bar that guides the tubing into the rollers and helps it keep its shape—is first inserted though the free end of the tubing and positioned just before the rollers. This lubricated mandrel is of the desired interior shape of the oval. The tubing then passes over the mandrel and between the rollers. One roller contains a clip that grabs the tubing; as the roller turns, it pulls the tubing and bends it into the "C" shape.

3 The same roller that grabs and bends the tubing also contains a saw blade. As the roller continues turning after creating the bend, the saw blade on it cuts the tubing to the proper length. The tubing is then heat treated in ovens.

Other components

4 The socket is basically a block of metal that serves as a connector to the source of the pressure medium; a mount for the case, dial, and movement; and as an attachment slot for the Bourdon tube. One end of the socket is threaded, which allows it to be screwed into the pressure-providing apparatus. The socket may be cast, forged, extruded, or machined from bar stock. Most sockets are made on automated machining centers that turn, drill, mill, and thread all in

After the Bourdon tube is made, its closed end is attached to the socket by soldering, brazing, or welding. The free end of the Bourdon tube is precisely located during this assembly operation, and then sealed, usually by the same means used to join the tube to the socket.

Once the Bourdon tube and socket assembly is secure, the tip of the unsupported end of the "C" is attached to an endpiece. This endpiece contains a small hole that connects the tip to the geared movement mechanism. The other components—the movement, pointer, and dial—are then assembled onto the socket as a group.

one cycle. General machining practices apply to most socket manufacture.

5 Movements are geared mechanisms that contain a pinion (a rotating shaft), sector, support plates, hairspring, and spacer columns. The mechanism converts the somewhat linear displacement of the Bourdon tip into rotary movement, as well as providing a means for calibration adjustment. The pointer is fastened to the rotating shaft, or pinion, and sweeps across the graduated dial indicating the pressure amount. Most movements are supplied to the gauge builder ready to use. Many types of manufacturing processes are used to produce the movement components, and the workmanship of the mechanism closely resembles a clockwork when completed.

6 The case, dial, and pointer may be sheet metal stampings, plastic moldings, or castings. Stampings and moldings require little further processing, but castings will require some machining—trimming off excess material, for instance—to meet the final requirements. These components are painted as required, and the dials are printed with the appropriate artwork. Common printing practice, utilizing both offset and direct methods, is used. The lens most commonly is a plastic part made by injection molding, whereby the plastic is heated into a molten state and then poured into a mold of the desired shape. The attachment feature that secures and seals the lens to the case is designed into the mold. Glass lenses are still used, but must be retained by a ring of some type. Glass has fallen out of favor because of the safety problems of breakage.

Final assembly

7 After the Bourdon tube is made, its closed end is attached to the socket by soldering, brazing, or welding. The free end of the Bourdon tube is precisely located during this assembly operation, and then sealed, usually by the same means used to join the tube to the socket. Once the Bourdon tube and socket assembly is secure, the tip of the unsupported end of the "C" is attached to an endpiece. This endpiece contains a small hole that connects the tip to the geared movement mechanism. The Bourdon tip doesn't move a great distance within its pressure range, typically .125 to .25 inch (.31 to .63 centimeter).

Understandably, the greater the pressure, the farther the tip moves. The other components—the movement, pointer, and dial—are then assembled onto the socket as a group.

Calibration

Calibration occurs just before the final assembly of the gauge to the protective case and lens. The assembly consisting of the socket, tube, and movement is connected to a pressure source with a known "master" gauge. A "master" gauge is simply a high accuracy gauge of known calibration. Adjustments are made in the assembly until the new gauge reflects the same pressure readings as the master. Accuracy requirements of 2 percent difference are common, but some may be 1 percent, .5 percent, or even .25 percent. Selection of the accuracy range is solely dependant upon how important the information desired is in relationship to the control and safety of the process. Most manufacturers use a graduated dial featuring a 270 degree sweep from zero to full range. These dials can be from less than 1 inch (2.5 centimeters) to 3 feet (.9 meter) in diameter, with the largest typically used for extreme accuracy. By increasing the dial diameter, the circumference around the graduation line is made longer, allowing for many finely divided markings. These large gauges are usually very fragile and used for master purposes only. Masters themselves are inspected for accuracy periodically using dead weight testers, a very accurate hydraulic apparatus that is traceable to the National Bureau of Standards in the United States.

It is interesting to note that when the gauge manufacturing business was in its infancy, the theoretical design of the pressure element was still developing. The Bourdon tube was made with very general design parameters, because each tube was pressure tested to determine what range of service it was suitable for. One did not know exactly what pressure range was going to result from the rolling and heat treating process, so these instruments were sorted at calibration for specific application. Today, with the development of computer modeling and many decades of experience, modern Bourdon tubes are precisely rolled to specific dimensions that require little, if any, calibration. Modern calibration can be performed by computers using electronically controlled mechanical adjusters to adjust the components. This unfortunately eliminates the image of the master craftsman sitting at the calibration bench, finely tuning a delicate, watch-like movement to extreme precision. Some instrument repair shops still perform this unique work, and these beautiful pressure gauges stand as equals to the clocks and timepieces created by master craftsmen years ago.

Applications and Future

Once the calibrated gauge is assembled and packaged, it is distributed to equipment manufacturers, service companies, and testing laboratories for use in many different applications. These varied applications account for the wide range in design of the case and lens enclosure. The socket may enter the case from the back, top, bottom or side. Some dials are illuminated by the luminescent inks used to print the graduations or by tiny lamps connected to an outside electrical source. Gauges intended for high pressure service usually are of "dead front" safety design, a case design feature that places a substantial thickness of case material between the Bourdon tube and the dial. This barrier protects the instrument viewer from gauge fragments should the Bourdon tube rupture due to excess pressure. The internal case design directs these high velocity pieces out the back of the gauge, away from the viewer. Many applications involve mounting the gauge directly to the running machinery, resulting in the need for liquid filling. Unfilled gauges quickly succumb to the destructive effects of vibration. Special mounting flanges are secured to the cases to allow for panel and surface mounting independent of the pressure plumbing. Case and lens materials are chosen to cope with a variety of abusive or contaminated environments, and are sealed by various means to keep moisture and contaminants out of the movement mechanism.

The use of pressure gauges in the future appears to be dependant on the quickly growing electronic sensor industry. These sensors are electronic components that provide an electrical signal and have essentially no moving parts. Many gauges today already have these sensors mounted within the case to send information to process control computers and controllers. These sensors are intrinsically safe, allowing their use in flammable or explosive environments. The whole process control issue has grown in recent years as a result of the need to prevent accidental releases of the process media, many of which are harmful to the environment. As environmental concerns grow, this interface will be in demand and the mechanical gauge may fall out of favor. However, the mechanical gauge does not require the electrical power source or the computer equipment needed by the electronic sensor. That makes the gauge cost effective for most general uses, and it is in this area that industry expects to continue to thrive.

Where To Learn More

Books

Kardos, Geza, ed. *Bourdon Tubes and Bourdon Tube Gauges: An Annotated Bibliography*. Books on Demand, 1989.

Pressure Gauge Handbook. M. Dekker, 1985.

Periodicals

Arslanian, Russ. "How to Select a Pressure Calibration Device." *InTech*. June, 1989, pp. 84-85.

Garrett, D. Dewayne and M. C. Banta. "A Suggested Improvement for the Fabrication of Low-Cost Manometers." *Journal of Chemical Education*. June, 1990, p. 523.

Jimenez-Dominguez, H., F. Figueroa-Lara, and S. Galindo. "Bourdon Gauge Absolute Manometer." *Review of Scientific Instruments*. March, 1986, p. 499.

—*Douglas E. Betts*

Rayon

Rayon is a natural-based material made from the cellulose of wood pulp or cotton. This natural base gives it many of the characteristics—low cost, diversity, and comfort—that have led to its popularity and success. Today, rayon is considered to be one of the most versatile and economical man-made fibers available. It has been called "the laboratory's first gift to the loom."

Background

For centuries humankind has relied upon various plants and animals to provide the raw materials for fabrics and clothing. Silkworms, sheep, beaver, buffalo deer, and even palm leaves are just some of the natural resources that have been used to meet these needs. However, in the last century scientists have turned to chemistry and technology to create and enhance many of the fabrics we now take for granted.

There are two main categories of man-made fibers: those that are made from natural products (cellulosic fibers) and those that are synthesized solely from chemical compounds (noncellulosic polymer fibers). Rayon is a natural-based material that is made from the cellulose of wood pulp or cotton. This natural base gives it many of the characteristics—low cost, diversity, and comfort—that have led to its popularity and success. Today, rayon is considered to be one of the most versatile and economical man-made fibers available. It has been called "the laboratory's first gift to the loom."

In the 1860s the French silk industry was being threatened by a disease affecting the silkworm. Louis Pasteur and Count Hilaire de Chardonnet were studying this problem with the hope of saving this vital industry. During this crisis, Chardonnet became interested in finding a way to produce artificial silk. In 1885 he patented the first successful process to make a useable fiber from cellulose. Even though other scientists have subsequently developed more cost-effective ways of making artificial silk, Chardonnet is still considered to be the father of rayon.

For the next forty years this material was called *artificial* or *imitation silk*. By 1925 it had developed into an industry unto itself and was given the name *rayon* by the Federal Trade Commission (FTC). The term *rayon* at this time included any man-made fiber made from cellulose. In 1952, however, the FTC divided rayons into two categories: those fibers consisting of pure cellulose (rayon) and those consisting of a cellulose compound (acetate).

By the 1950s, most of the rayon produced was being used in industrial and home furnishing products rather than in apparel, because regular rayon (also called *viscose rayon*) fibers were too weak compared to other fibers to be used in apparel. Then, in 1955, manufacturers began to produce a new type of rayon—high-wet-modulus (HWM) rayon—which was somewhat stronger and which could be used successfully in sheets, towels, and apparel. The advent of HWM rayon (also called *modified rayon*) is considered the most important development in rayon production since its invention in the 1880s.

Today rayon is one of the most widely used fabrics in our society. It is made in countries around the world. It can be blended with natural or man-made fabrics, treated with enhancements, and even engineered to perform a variety of functions.

Raw Materials

Regardless of the design or manufacturing process, the basic raw material for making rayon is cellulose. The major sources for natural cellulose are wood pulp—usually from pine, spruce, or hemlock trees—and

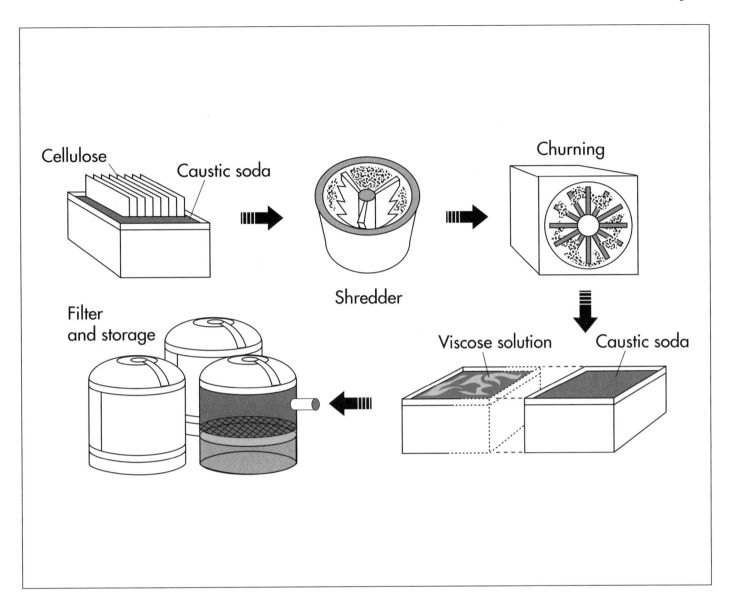

Cellulose

Caustic soda

Churning

Shredder

Filter
and storage

Viscose solution

Caustic soda

cotton linters. Cotton linters are residue fibers which cling to cotton seed after the ginning process.

Strictly defined, rayon is a manufactured fiber composed of regenerated cellulose. The legal definition also includes manufactured fibers in which substitutes have not replaced more than 15 percent of the hydrogens.

While the basic manufacturing process for all rayon is similar, this fabric can be engineered to perform a wide range of functions. Various factors in the manufacturing process can be altered to produce an array of designs. Differences in the raw material, the processing chemicals, fiber diameter, post treatments and blend ratios can be manipulated to produce a fiber that is customized for a specific application.

Regular or viscose rayon is the most prevalent, versatile and successful type of rayon. It can be blended with man-made or natural fibers and made into fabrics of varying weight and texture. It is also highly absorbent, economical and comfortable to wear.

Regular viscose rayon does have some disadvantages. It's not as strong as many of the newer fabrics, nor is it as strong as natural cotton or flax. This inherent weakness is exacerbated when it becomes wet or overexposed to light. Also, regular rayon has a tendency to shrink when washed. Mildew, acid and high temperatures such as ironing can also result in damage. Fortunately, these disadvantages can be countered by chemical treatments and the blending of rayon with other fibers of offsetting characteristics.

To make rayon, sheets of purified cellulose are steeped in caustic soda, dried, shredded into crumbs, and then aged in metal containers for 2 to 3 days. The temperature and humidity in the metal containers are carefully controlled.

After ageing, the crumbs are combined and churned with liquid carbon disulfide, which turns the mix into orange-colored crumbs known as sodium cellulose xanthate. The cellulose xanthate is bathed in caustic soda, resulting in a viscose solution that looks and feels much like honey.

High-wet-modulus rayon is a stronger fiber than regular rayon, and in fact is more similar in performance to cotton than to regular rayon. It has better elastic recovery than regular rayon, and fabrics containing it are easier to care for—they can be machine-washed, whereas fabrics containing regular rayon generally have to be dry-cleaned.

The Manufacturing Process

While there are many variations in the manufacturing process that exploit the versatility of the fiber, the following is a description of the procedure that is used in making regular or viscose rayon.

Regardless of whether wood pulp or cotton linters are used, the basic raw material for making rayon must be processed in order to extract and purify the cellulose. The resulting sheets of white, purified cellulose are then treated to form regenerated cellulose filaments. In turn, these filaments are spun into yarns and eventually made into the desired fabric.

Processing purified cellulose

1 Sheets of purified cellulose are steeped in sodium hydroxide (caustic soda), which produces sheets of alkali cellulose. These sheets are dried, shredded into crumbs, and then aged in metal containers for 2 to 3 days. The temperature and humidity in the metal containers are carefully controlled.

2 After ageing, the crumbs are combined and churned with liquid carbon disulfide, which turns the mix into orange-colored crumbs known as sodium cellulose xanthate. The cellulose xanthate is bathed in caustic soda, resulting in a viscose solution that looks and feels much like honey. Any dyes or delusterants in the design are then added. The syrupy solution is filtered for impurities and stored in vats to age, this time between 4 and 5 days.

Producing filaments

3 The viscose solution is next turned into strings of fibers. This is done by forcing the liquid through a spinneret, which works like a shower-head, into an acid bath. If staple fiber is to be produced, a large spinneret with large holes is used. If filament fiber is being produced, then a spinneret with smaller holes is used. In the acid bath, the acid coagulates and solidifies the filaments, now known as regenerated cellulose filaments.

Spinning

4 After being bathed in acid, the filaments are ready to be spun into yarn. Depending on the type of yarn desired, several spinning methods can be used, including Pot Spinning, Spool Spinning, and Continuous Spinning. In Pot Spinning, the filaments are first stretched under controlled tension onto a series of offsetting rollers called *godet wheels.* This stretching reduces the diameter of the filaments and makes them more uniform in size, and it also gives the filaments more strength. The filaments are then put into a rapidly spinning cylinder called a *Topham Box,* resulting in a cake-like strings that stick to the sides of the Topham Box. The strings are then washed, bleached, rinsed, dried, and wound on cones or spools.

Spool Spinning is very similar to Pot Spinning. The filaments are passed through rollers and wound on spools, where they are washed, bleached, rinsed, dried, and wound again on spools or cones.

In Continuous Spinning, the filaments are washed, bleached, dried, twisted, and wound at the same time that they are stretched over godet wheels.

5 Once the fibers are sufficiently cured, they are ready for post-treatment chemicals and the various weaving processes necessary to produce the fabric. The resulting fabric can then be given any of a number of finishing treatments. These include calendaring, to control smoothness; fire resistance; pre-shrinking; water resistance; and wrinkle resistance.

High-Wet-Modulus Rayon Manufacture

The process for manufacturing high-wet-modulus rayon is similar to that used for making regular rayon, with a few exceptions. First, in step #1 above, when the purified cellulose sheets are bathed in a caustic soda so-

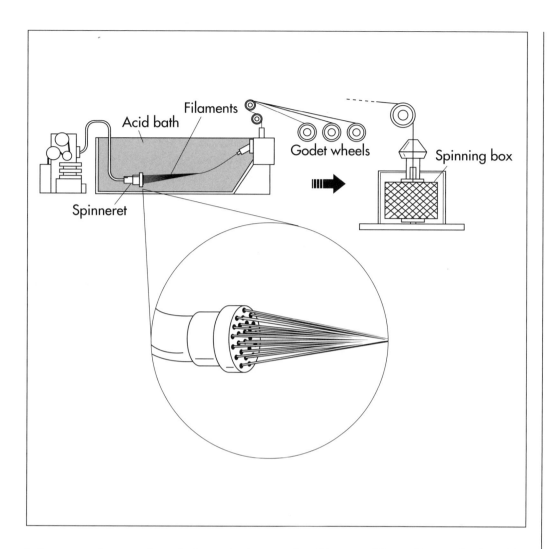

Acid bath

Filaments

Godet wheels

Spinning box

Spinneret

After the syrupy viscose solution is prepared, it is forced through a spinneret into an acid bath. The resulting strings or filaments are then stretched on godet wheels to strengthen them and put into a spinning Topham box. This method produces cake-like strings of rayon, which are washed, rinsed, and dried before being wound on spools or cones.

lution, a weaker caustic soda is used when making HWM rayon. Second, neither the alkali crumbs (#1 above) nor the viscose solution (step #2) is aged in the HWM process. Third, when making HWM rayon, the filaments are stretched to a greater degree than when making regular rayon.

Quality Control

As with most chemically oriented processes, quality control is crucial to the successful manufacture of rayon. Chemical make-up, timing and temperature are essential factors that must be monitored and controlled in order to produce the desired result.

The percentages of the various fibers used in a blended fabric must be controlled to stay within in the legal bounds of the Textile Fiber Identification Act. This act legally defines seventeen groups of man-made fibers. Six of these seventeen groups are made from natural material. They include rayon, acetate,

glass fiber, metallics, rubber, and azion. The remaining eleven fabrics are synthesized solely from chemical compounds. They are nylon, polyester, acrylic, modacrylic, olefin, spandex, anidex, saran, vinal, vinyon, and nytril.

Within each generic group there are brand names for fibers which are produced by different manufacturers. Private companies often seek patents on unique features and, as could be expected, attempt to maintain legal control over their competition.

Byproducts

As one of the industry's major problems, the chemical by-products of rayon have received much attention in these environmentally conscious times. The most popular method of production, the viscose method, generates undesirable water and air emissions. Of particular concern is the emission of zinc and hydrogen sulfide.

At present, producers are trying a number of techniques to reduce pollution. Some of the techniques being used are the recovery of zinc by ion-exchange, crystallization, and the use of a more purified cellulose. Also, the use of absorption and chemical scrubbing is proving to be helpful in reducing undesirable emissions of gas.

The Future

The future of rayon is bright. Not only is there a growing demand for rayon worldwide, but there are many new technologies that promise to make rayon even better and cheaper.

For a while in the 1970s there was a trend in the clothing industry toward purely synthetic materials like polyester. However, since purely synthetic material does not "breath" like natural material, these products were not well received by the consumer. Today there is a strong trend toward blended fabrics. Blends offer the best of both worlds.

With the present body of knowledge about the structure and chemical reactivity of cellulose, some scientist believe it may soon be possible to produce the cellulose molecule directly from sunlight, water and carbon dioxide. If this technique proves to be cost effective, such hydroponic factories could represent a giant step forward in the quest to provide the raw materials necessary to meet the world wide demand for man-made fabric.

Where To Learn More

Books

Corbman, Bernard P. *Textiles: Fiber to Fabric*, 6th ed. McGraw-Hill, 1983.

Hollen, Norma, Jane Saddler, Anna Langford, and Sara Kadolph. *Textiles*, 6th ed. Macmillan, 1988.

Periodicals

Foley, Theresa M. "Rayon Fiber Manufacturer Shuts Down, Threatening U.S. Booster Production." *Aviation Week & Space Technology*. November 7, 1988, p. 29.

Smith, Emily T. "A Safe Shortcut around the Toxic Road to Rayon." *Business Week*. February 11, 1991, p. 80.

Templeton, Fleur. "From Log to Lingerie in a Few Easy Steps." *Business Week*. April 6, 1992, p. 95.

"Turning Corn and Paper into Rayon." *USA Today*. June, 1991, p. 7.

—Dan Pepper

Refrigerator

Background

Prior to the development of artificial refrigeration techniques during the 1800s, people utilized a variety of means to chill and preserve foodstuffs. For centuries, ice served as the principal refrigerant. Ironically, the ancient Indians and Egyptians pioneered an ice-making technique that served as the conceptual basis for the first "modern" refrigerators developed during the nineteenth century: evaporation. The relatively quick evaporation of a liquid creates an expanding volume of gas. As water vapor rises, its kinetic energy increases dramatically, in part because the warm vapor is drawing in energy from its surroundings, which are cooled by this process. The Indians and Egyptians took advantage of this phenomenon by placing wide, shallow bowls filled with water outside during the cool nights. As some water quickly evaporated, the remaining water cooled, forming ice. With this method, it was possible to create sizeable chunks of ice that could then be used to cool food.

Using a more primitive means of procuring ice, the ancient Chinese simply transported it from the mountains to cool their food; later, the Greeks and Romans adopted this practice. To preserve the ice itself, people stored it in pits or caves insulated with straw and wood, by which means they could maintain a supply of ice for months. In industrialized nations, ice served as the primary method of chilling food through the nineteenth century, when people inserted blocks of ice in insulated cabinets alongside the food they wished to store. Even today, in many developing nations ice remains the sole available refrigerant.

The first known attempt to develop an artificial refrigerator took place in Scotland at the University of Glasgow. There, in 1748, William Cullen revived the ancient Indian-Egyptian practice of freezing liquid by means of evaporation, although he accelerated the process by boiling ethyl ether into a partial vacuum (ethyl evaporates more quickly than water). Cullen attempted this merely as an experiment, as did American Oliver Evans, who designed another refrigerator in 1805. Evans's machine, based on a closed cycle of compressed ether, represented the first effort to use simple vapor instead of vaporizing a liquid. While Evans never developed his machine beyond the prototype stage, in 1844 an American doctor named John Gorrie actually built a very similar machine to provide ice for the hospital in which he worked. Gorrie's machine compressed air that was next cooled with water. The cooled air was then routed into an engine cylinder, and, as it re-expanded, its temperature dropped enough so that ice could be made.

In 1856 another American, Alexander Twinning, began selling a refrigeration machine based on the same vapor-compression principle, and soon after that Australian James Harrison enlarged the American design (meant to be used in individual homes) for the meat-packing and beer-making industries. Three years later, Ferdinand Carré refined the basic concept underlying all of these refrigerators when he introduced ammonia as a coolant. Ammonia represented an advance because it expands more rapidly than water and can thus absorb more heat from its environs. Carré also contributed other innovations. His refrigerator operated by means of a cycle in which a refrigerant vapor (ammonia) was absorbed in a liquid (a mixture of ammonia and water) that was subsequently heated. The heat caused the refrig-

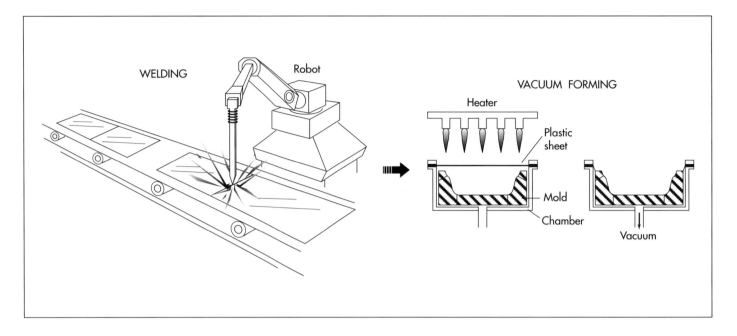

WELDING   Robot

VACUUM FORMING

Heater

Plastic sheet

Mold

Chamber

Vacuum

The outer cabinet and door, made of sheet metal, are either welded or clinched together. While some manufacturers also use sheet metal for the inner cabinet, some manufacturers and some models use plastic for inner liners. The plastic liners are made by vacuum forming. In this process, a thick piece of plastic slightly larger than the finished part has its outer edges clamped and is then heated. The hot plastic is next pulled by vacuum into a mold and cooled. After trimming, the resulting part is ready for assembly.

erant to vaporize, thereby creating a cooling effect (after it vaporized, the refrigerant was condensed so that it could once again be absorbed in the liquid, repeating the cycle). Carré's machine not only sold extremely well, it also inaugurated modern refrigeration by upgrading Evans's compression concept and adding a more sophisticated refrigerant. These components remain the basis of most refrigerators used today.

Ammonia itself posed several problems, however. While it served as a very effective coolant, it was both odiferous and poisonous when it leaked, and it quickly disappeared from refrigeration after synthetic alternatives were developed during the 1920s. The best known of these, patented by Du Pont under the name *freon*, was created by chemically altering the methane molecule, substituting two chlorine and two fluorine atoms for its four hydrogen atoms. The resulting gas (technically, dichlorofluoromethane) was hailed because its low boiling point, surface tension, and viscosity rendered it an ideal—and ostensibly problem-free—refrigerant. Later, in the 1970s, scientists realized that freon posed problems of its own related to the environment (see "Environmental Concerns" section below) and began searching for new agents to use in refrigeration.

Raw Materials

Refrigerators today consist of several basic components: the exterior cabinet and door,

the inner cabinet or liner, the insulation inserted between the two, the cooling system, the refrigerant, and the fixtures. The cabinet and door are made of aluminum or steel sheet metal that is sometimes prepainted. The metal is generally purchased in a coil that is either fed directly into the manufacturing process or cut to size and fed sheet by sheet. The inner cabinet is made of sheet metal, like the outer cabinet, or of plastic. The insulation that fills the gap between the inner and outer cabinets consists of fiberglass or polyfoam. The components of the cooling system (compressor, condenser, coils, fins) are made of aluminum, copper, or an alloy. The tubing is usually copper, because of that metal's ductility—its ability to bend without breaking. Freon remains the most commonly used refrigerant, and almost all of the large interior fixtures (door and cabinet liners) are made from vacuum-formed plastic; smaller fixtures (butter compartments, egg trays, salad crispers) are purchased as small plastic blanks or in pre-formed pieces.

Design

The contemporary refrigerator is based on two basic laws of physics: one, that heat flows from warmer material to cooler materials and never the reverse; two, that decreasing the pressure of a gas also decreases its temperature. Although refinements have been made since Carré introduced his model during the late nineteenth century, these basic principles are still visible in today's refrigerators.

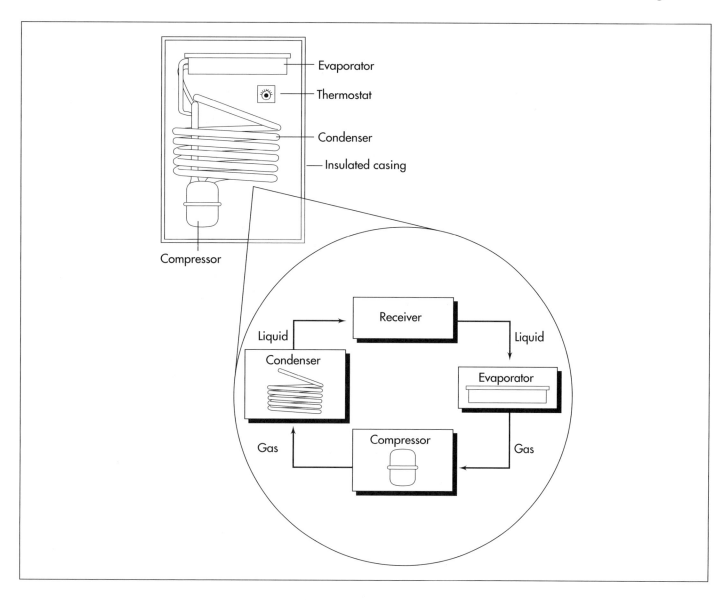

Refrigerators work by removing the warmth from the air within their interior compartments and relaying that heat to the air outside. The coolant (freon) accomplishes this transfer as it passes through a circuit, moving from the evaporator to the condenser. Beginning in the evaporator, which lies inside an insulated cabinet, the freon is heated. Because it has been made to boil, the freon draws heat from the air within the refrigerator. Having absorbed this heat, the freon is then routed to the condenser. In this set of copper coils (usually mounted at the back or on the bottom of the refrigerator), the freon condenses—returns to a liquid state—transferring its heat into the outside air as it does so. After cooling, the freon then returns to the evaporator, where it is once again heated and begins to absorb heat from the food stored within the refrigerator. Sometimes, to increase their surface area (and thus facilitate thermal transfer), the evaporator and the condenser are fitted with metal fins.

For defrosting, a coil is wrapped around the freezer unit. When the timer reaches defrost, the refrigerant is passed through this coil while it is hot to raise the temperature and melt the ice. The coil is generally positioned away from any ice makers to prevent the ice cubes from melting and freezing together.

The Manufacturing Process

Outer cabinet and door

1 Pieces of sheet metal are either welded or clinched together. Clinching is a process closely resembling stapling in that the two

A refrigerator works by removing the warmth from the air within its interior compartments and relaying that heat to the air outside. Beginning in the evaporator, the freon is heated and begins to draw heat from the air within the refrigerator. Having absorbed this heat, the freon is then routed to the condenser by the compressor. In this set of copper coils (usually mounted at the back or on the bottom of the refrigerator), the freon returns to a liquid state, transferring its heat into the outside air as it does so. After cooling, the freon returns to the evaporator, where the cycle begins again.

pieces are crimped together under pressure, though no additional pieces such as staples are added. If the part of the cabinet is to be visible, it will be welded and ground down to appear as one piece. The extent to which the welding process is automated depends on the company and the number of refrigerators being produced.

2 If the sheet metal was not purchased in precoated form, it is now painted. Some manufacturers use spray equipment to lay a uniform coat of **paint** on the metal. Others dip the parts in a paint/solvent mixture before heating them to bake the paint onto the surface.

Inner cabinet

3 The inner cabinet is sometimes made from sheet metal very similar to the outer shell. Any seams are caulked to improve insulation and looks. Some manufacturers and some models use plastic for inner liners; for example, the inner door is almost exclusively made from plastic today. The plastic liners are vacuum formed. In this process, a thick piece of plastic slightly larger than the finished part has its outer edges clamped and is then heated. The hot plastic is next pulled by vacuum into a mold and cooled. After trimming, the resulting part is ready for assembly.

4 The inner cabinet is inserted into the outer cabinet, and the two are snapped together before the fixtures are inserted. Some tubes and wires are run through the gap between the two before it is filled with insulation. A dispensing device (sometimes robotically operated, sometimes a manually operated long 'gun') inserts foam between the walls. When heated in an oven, this foam expands to add rigidity and insulation to the cabinet. A similar process is used for the doors.

Cooling system

5 The refrigeration components are attached to the cabinet using screws and clips. The tubing is soldered together, and a protective coating is sprayed on the joints. The order of this assembly varies between manufacturers and models. The copper tubing from which the coils (condensers and evaporators) have separately been cut, bent, and soldered is then attached to the refrigerator as a unit.

6 The seal on the refrigerator door is created by means of magnet laden gaskets that are attached to the doors with screws. Handles and hinges are also screwed onto the door before its hinges are screwed onto the cabinet. Some adjustment is allowed for proper operation of the door.

Testing and adding accessories

7 Most manufacturers mix testing with manufacturing from this point on. The unit is leak tested with nitrogen (a safe gas that makes up about 79 percent of the air); if it passes, it is charged with refrigerant and subjected to further testing. Next, the accessories (shelves, crispers, ice trays, etc.) are added and taped down for shipping. The unit is given a final look and then packaged for shipping.

Quality Control

As mentioned above, all subassemblies of tubing that will contain refrigerant are pressure-tested with nitrogen, which will reveal any flaws in the tubing and in the soldering that joins it. The entire unit is also leak-tested prior to charging with freon. Once charged, the unit is tested as a whole to ensure that it is capable of reaching design temperatures including those necessary during the defrost cycle. The unit is operated with sensors inside that determine the temperature changes over time. Sometimes the refrigerant pressures are also measured. The unit is then subjected to a final 'sniff' test by a machine that detects refrigerant to ensure that no leaks have developed during testing.

Byproducts/Waste

Metal components that are rejected are sold to metal recycling companies. Plastic components are ground into small pieces and either reused as raw material or returned to the vendor for reuse. If a unit is rejected after it has been charged, the refrigerant is drained by special equipment and reused.

Environmental Concerns

In the mid-1970s, scientists began to understand that as gases in the chlorofluorocarbon (CFC) group, which includes freon, waft upward into the stratosphere (the upper layer of the atmosphere), they gradually decompose,

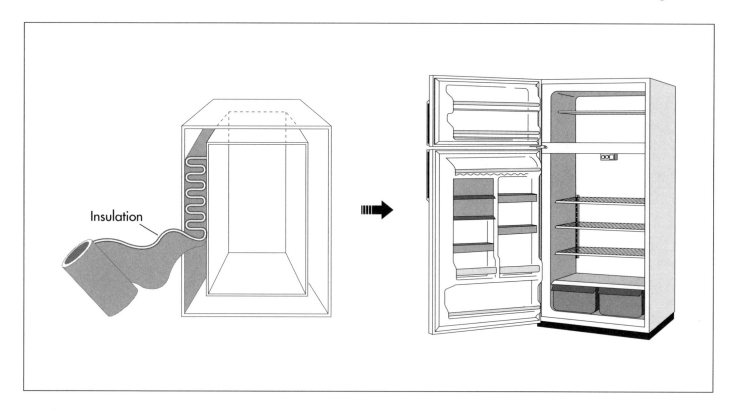

Insulation

releasing chlorine atoms as they do so. The problem with this is that each chlorine atom can destroy tens of thousand of ozone molecules, ozone being the triatomic form of oxygen that comprises a protective layer in the stratosphere, absorbing much solar ultraviolet radiation that would harm animal life if it reached the earth's surface. As researchers realized that CFC emissions were exacerbating the hole in the ozone layer over the Antarctic continent, public pressure to limit emissions mounted. In 1987, representatives from nations around the globe signed an agreement, the *Montreal Protocol on Substances that Deplete the Ozone Layer*, in which they agreed to phase out production of the chemicals known to deplete the ozone layer, including freon. Unfortunately, chlorofluorocarbons are also present in the polystyrene foam that some manufacturers use as an insulator between the external case and the interior lining of their refrigerators. So, efforts to reduce the CFC emissions from refrigerators are presently continuing on two fronts, as manufacturers attempt to find alternatives to both the coolant freon and the insulator polystyrene.

The Future

In terms of freon, several intermediate steps have been taken to minimize CFC emission

as researchers attempt to identify safe coolant alternatives. Refrigerator designs have been improved to reduce the amount of freon needed; leak detection systems have been installed; maintenance has been limited to trained, authorized personnel; and refrigerant is recovered and recycled whenever possible. Moreover, long-term replacements for freon are being explored. Thus far, the most promising among them is HCFC-22, which, although still a chlorofluorocarbon, contains an additional hydrogen atom that reduces the molecule's ozone-depletion capacity by 95 percent. While its cost (three to five times greater than that of freon) is problematic, HCFC-22 is presently undergoing tests to determine its toxicity.

CFC-containing insulation may be replaced by the same kind of vacuum insulation that is used in thermos bottles. Research indicates that vacuum insulation is more efficient in terms of both space and energy, so, at present, it appears that insulation alternatives will become viable well before freon substitutes.

Where To Learn More

Books

Boast, Michael F. *Newnes Refrigeration Pocket Book.* Butterworth-Heinemann, 1991.

The space between the inner and outer cabinets is filled with foam insulation, usually polystyrene, which can be inserted manually or automatically by a robot. When heated in an oven, this foam expands to add rigidity and insulation to the cabinet.

Because this insulation releases CFCs, which contribute to the destruction of the ozone layer, researchers are searching for substitutes. The polystyrene may be replaced by the same kind of vacuum insulation that is used in thermos bottles, since vacuum insulation is more efficient in terms of both space and energy.

Cerepnalkovski, I. *Modern Refrigerating Machines.* Elsevier Science Publishing, 1991.

Dellino, Clive V. *Cold and Chilled Storage Technology.* Van Nostrand Reinhold, 1989.

Marsh, R. Warren and Olive C. Throats. *Principles of Refrigeration.* Delmar Publishers Inc., 1979.

Stoecker, W. F. and J. W. Jones. *Refrigeration & Air Conditioning.* McGraw-Hill, 1982.

Periodicals

"Refrigeration's Revitalization." *Appliance,* February 1993, pp. 54-58.

"Refrigerator Doors Have a 'Clear' Edge." *Design News.* January 7, 1991, p. 33.

"A $30-million Super-Efficient Refrigerator." *Electrical World.* July, 1992, p. 30.

Marbach, William D. "Now, An Icebox That's Cool for the Environment." *Business Week.* July 22, 1991, p. 65.

Murray, Charles J. "Plastic Welding Technique Aids Refrigerator Assembly: Special Parts Replace Metal Anchors on Refrigerator Liners." *Design News.* February 15, 1988, p. 230.

—*Barry M. Marton*

Revolver

Background

The term "handgun" refers to any small firearm intended for use with one hand only. Currently, the two most important types of handguns are revolvers and automatic pistols. The key distinction between the two is that the former contains a cylindrical magazine (the firearm compartment from which cartridges, or bullets, are fed into the barrel) with multiple chambers that enable the shooter to fire repeated shots without pausing to reload. An automatic (self-loading) pistol feeds cartridges into the barrel from a detachable magazine that is inserted through the bottom of the butt (the gun's handle). This type of pistol utilizes some of the recoil force from each cartridge firing to feed the next cartridge into its single chamber. As the two varieties differ widely in design and production, this article will concentrate on the revolver.

The earliest firearms ensued from the invention of black powder, a precursor of gunpowder developed in China during the ninth century A.D.; among other things, the Chinese apparently used their invention to propel primitive rockets. The recipe and uses for black powder were eventually transmitted to Europe by Mongol conquerors, and it was the Europeans who perfected the substance during the fourteenth century. Within one hundred years, the first small arms were being developed. However, early handguns remained troublesome for several centuries. For one thing, very few people could shoot them accurately (sighting targets proved easier with the long barrel of a musket to serve as a guide). Another problem was that their firepower had to be minimal if soldiers were to fire them with one hand. Until the mid-eighteenth century, most handguns could hold only one cartridge at a time, and this had to be loaded through the gun's muzzle (barrel).

The handgun became vastly improved in 1835, when Samuel Colt patented the first workable revolver, which became known as the *cap-and-ball*. Although Colt's handgun still had to be front-loaded, its revolving cylinder contained five or six chambers, and the shooter advanced it automatically by cocking the hammer (earlier models had required shooters to align each chamber and depress the hammer separately). Later improvements yielded a cartridge revolver that did not have to be loaded through the muzzle, better ejection designs, and double-action cocking mechanisms.

By the end of the nineteenth century, when handguns incorporating these innovations were being mass produced, the revolver had reached its mature form. It remained the weapon of choice for military personnel until the second decade of the twentieth century, when it was replaced by automatic pistols. Although many predicted that the advent of the automatic model would render the revolver obsolete, it has remained popular. Today, revolvers continue to be used alongside automatic pistols by police officers, members of the armed forces, and target shooters throughout the world.

Design

To understand how a revolver is made, it is important to know how each subsystem functions within the weapon. A revolver contains four main subsystems: the Frame Group; the Cylinder, Extractor, and Crane Group; the Barrel and Sight Group; and the Trigger, Timing Hand, and Hammer Group.

In 1835, Samuel Colt patented the first workable revolver, which became known as the cap-and-ball. Although Colt's handgun had to be front-loaded, its revolving cylinder contained five or six chambers, and the shooter advanced it automatically by cocking the hammer (earlier models had required shooters to align each chamber and depress the hammer separately).

361

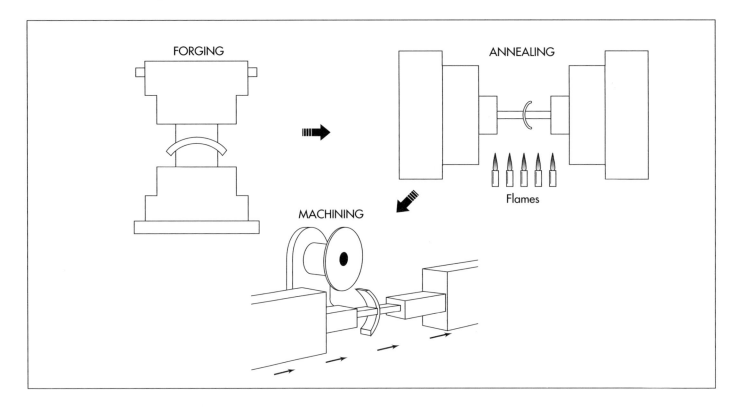

FORGING

ANNEALING

Flames

MACHINING

Most revolver parts begin as steel or stainless steel blanks that are forged into close approximations of the desired parts. In forging, a heated blank is put into a forging press and impacted with several hundred tons of force. This impact forces the metal into the forging die, a steel block with a cavity shaped like the part being produced. After annealing or heat treating the parts, they undergo basic machining processes such as milling, drilling, and tapping. Modern machining centers are automated, computer-controlled devices.

The *Frame Group* consists of the main frame, the trigger guard, and the hand grip. Its purpose is to provide a strong frame to contain the powerful force of the cartridge discharge, position the shooter's hand correctly, and insure that the trigger functions precisely. Designs vary slightly due to manufacturers' patents, but the operation is basically the same. Some frames have a removable sideplate that provides access to the trigger group, while others insert the trigger group as a separate assembly though the bottom of the frame. All modern revolvers utilize a frame design incorporating a solid top strap that connects the top of the grip area to the barrel mounting area, reinforcing the structural integrity of the frame.

The *Cylinder, Extractor, and Crane Group* consists of the cylinder itself, the shaft upon which it rotates, the extractor, the extractor shaft, a return spring, and the crane. The cylinder commonly contains six chambers for six cartridges of the correct caliber arranged in a circle. The rim, or outer edge of the cartridge base, rests upon a semicircular ledge formed by the extractor, which contains six small depressions in the center. The outside of the cylinder has six corresponding locking grooves. The cylinder rotates on the cylinder pin, which locks into the frame on one end and the crane on the other end.

While the inside of the frame supports the base of the cartridge, the forcing cone on the barrel helps the bullet accurately jump the gap between the cylinder face and the barrel.

The *Barrel and Sight Group* is very important to the accuracy of the weapon. Threaded onto the frame, the barrel receives the bullet from the chamber upon firing. Inside, the barrel is rifled, or inscribed with a series of grooves that impart a stabilizing spin to bullets as they leave the gun. The sights consist of a Rear Sight with its groove or notch and a Front Sight which is typically shaped like a blade or post. The notch and the top of the blade, which can be adjusted, are aligned to help shooters aim. Most high quality revolvers feature sights purchased from companies whose specialty is fine mechanisms. Optical sights, low-and no-light sights, and lasers are also available.

The *Trigger Group* is best explained by describing the firing sequence, initiated when the shooter pulls back on the hammer spur. This action compresses, or cocks, the hammer spring and pushes the timing hand connecting the hammer to the trigger group into an extractor depression, rotating the cylinder to align that chamber and the barrel. The trigger mechanism latch engages the locking grooves, stopping further rotation and secur-

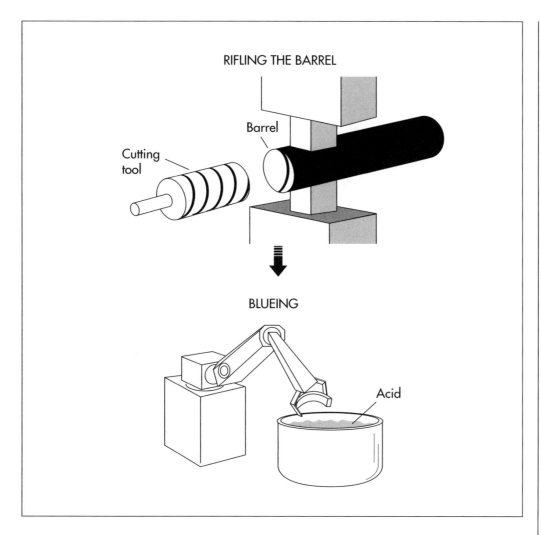

RIFLING THE BARREL

Cutting tool

Barrel

BLUEING

Acid

The barrel of the revolver contains rifling—a series of grooves with a precise twist that cause the bullet to spin as it exits the gun. To produce the rifling, a worker draws a broach-like cutting tool through the barrel blank repeatedly, removing metal to approximately .01 inch deep. In an alternative method called "button rifling," a hardened form tool is drawn through the barrel blank under high force, displacing the metal in the grooves without cutting. This is similar in some respects to the forging operation, only it is done without heating the barrel.

ing the cylinder for firing. At the end of the travel, the hammer is latched by the trigger sear and held ready for firing. When the trigger is fully depressed, the hammer unlatches from the trigger sear and is propelled forward by the hammer spring. This energy is transmitted to the firing pin, which strikes the primer of the cartridge, firing the weapon. This sequence of firing is called *single action*.

With the advent of the *double action design*, a connection bar was used to allow the trigger to rotate the cylinder, cock the hammer, and complete the firing in one motion. This design promoted an increase in rate of firepower and simplified the draw and fire situation. Most modern revolvers are of the double action design. After firing, the shooter releases the trigger. The trigger spring then returns the trigger to the forward position and forces the hand and latch to retract within the frame in preparation for the next shot. Once the cartridges have been fired, the cylinder latch on the side of the frame is pressed, disengaging

the cylinder pin from the frame. This allows the entire assembly to swing out of the frame on the crane for reloading. The extractor shaft is pressed, lifting the cartridge cases out of their chambers, after which the cylinder spring returns the extractor to the cylinder. Live cartridges are again loaded and the cylinder is then simply pushed back into the frame, where the cylinder pin spring latches it back into place.

Raw Materials

With the exception of the grips, which may be wood or plastic, nearly all components of the revolver are metal. Steel was the primary metal until changes in its availability and advances in other metals rendered them more desirable. For example, during the 1860s, the disruption in the steel supply caused by the Civil War led to the use of brass for revolver frames. During World War II, the need for a lightweight weapon for use by aircraft crews brought about the use of a aluminum alloy frame. The **stainless steel** frame and barrel soon followed, improving corrosion resistance and reducing maintenance.

The Manufacturing Process

Forging the components

1 The major components of most revolvers begin as a group of steel or stainless steel blanks that are forged into close approximations of the desired parts. The basic shape of each part is formed by placing a heated blank of material into a forging press and impacting it with several hundred tons of force. This impact forces the metal into the forging die, a steel block with a cavity shaped like the part being produced. Sometimes, multiple strikes by the press are required, each with a more precise die than the previous step. The resulting part is both extremely strong and very similar to final shape.

Annealing and machining

2 After forging, the flow patterns of the metal must be stabilized by heat treating. This procedure consists of reheating the parts in a controlled atmosphere to relieve internal stresses without reducing the metal's inherent strength.

3 Machining can now begin on the frame, cylinder, and other component parts. Most modern revolvers are manufactured on automated, computer-controlled machining centers and lathes. However, a number of manufacturers have had such excellent service and results with some of their machines that they continue to utilize fifty-year-old equipment. Regardless of whether older or modern equipment is used, the basic process actions of milling, drilling, and tapping are essentially the same. The tolerances on this machining must be held within one or two thousandths of an inch. All of the components, from the screws to the trigger, are machined using similar processes.

4 To effectively machine the raw forging, a worker clamps it into a holding apparatus that secures the part during machining. Properly designed fixtures also contain tool guides and bushings to support the cutting tool and increase accuracy. Many of the operations performed will require several specialized fixtures. Cylinders, screws, shafts, and barrels are made on lathes while frames, sideplates, sights, and triggers are made on a milling and machining center.

Rifling the barrel

5 One of the most unique processes is the rifling of the barrel. Rifling is essentially a series of grooves within the barrel. These grooves have a precise twist that, through contact with the bullet circumference, causes the bullet to spin during firing. This rate of twist is about 1 turn in 16 inches (40.6 centimeters). To produce the rifling, a worker subjects the barrel to either the cutting or the button rifling process. Cutting is accomplished by drawing a broach-like cutting tool through the barrel blank repeatedly, removing metal to approximately .010 inch (.025 centimeter) deep. Cutting marks and other scratches within the rifling can impair accuracy by damaging the bullet, which throws it out of balance. However, one advantage of these marks is that they are different in every gun barrel, producing unique rifling imprints on the bullets they fire. This is how law enforcement specialists match bullets to the gun that fired them.

6 Button rifling refers to an operation in which a hardened form tool is drawn through the barrel blank under high force, displacing the metal in the grooves without cutting. This is similar in some respects to the forging operation, only it is done without heating the barrel. The advantages of button rifling are increased production, no chip formation, and improved surface quality.

Applying protective coatings

7 After machining, the metal surfaces of most steel or aluminum weapons receive a protective coating to reduce corrosion. Commonly referred to as *blueing*, this process entails submersing the parts in tanks of acid and other chemicals. In these vats, the chemicals react with the metal to produce a durable barrier against the elements. Chrome and **gold** plating, parkerizing, and anodizing (for aluminum) are some variants of the blueing process, while plating, another means of applying a protective coat, is accomplished by setting up an electric current between the parts and the supply anode, which consists of another type of metal. The

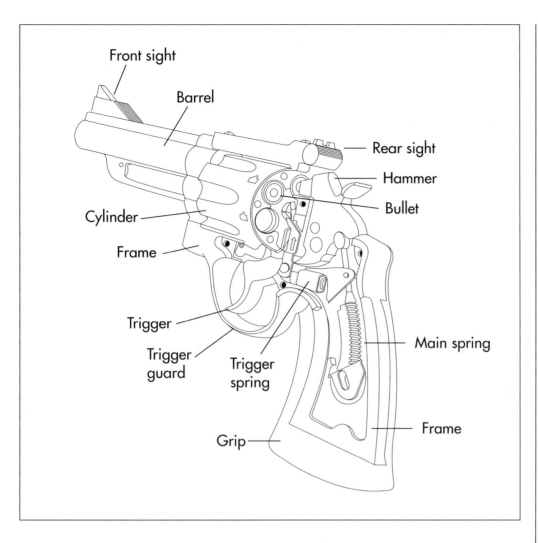

Front sight

Barrel

Rear sight

Hammer

Bullet

Cylinder

Frame

Trigger

Trigger
guard

Trigger
spring

Main spring

Frame

Grip

A revolver contains 4 main subsystems: the Frame Group; the Cylinder, Extractor, and Crane Group; the Barrel and Sight Group; and the Trigger, Timing Hand, and Hammer Group. Most modern revolvers are of the double action design, in which the trigger rotates the cylinder, cocks the hammer, and completes the firing in one motion.

electrical path carries molecules of the plating metal to the component, where they bond very tightly to the surface.

Assembly

8 The entire weapon is assembled by one person who fits all of the components, many of them manually. While dimensional control has improved significantly over the past twenty years, the timing of the trigger and hand mechanism and the crispness of the trigger pull are still set by hand. Most manufacturers have grades of fitting quality; for example, the trigger pull of a service weapon that will be used by police is set heavier than that of a target or specialty handgun. One would expect to exert a more determined effort to discharge a weapon in a law enforcement setting, while at the target range the lighter trigger pull is desirable to increase accuracy. Once the weapon has been put together, any necessary filing, polishing, and tuning will be performed before testing.

Quality Control

After assembly and fine tuning, the weapon is dry fired (without ammunition) and checked for function before being sent to the firing line for proof firing. The first phase of the proof firing process entails inspecting and recording the gun's trigger weighting, sights, and cylinder spacing. Next, the gun is loaded with special ammunition and fired. Industry standards dictate the types and relative power of the proofing cartridges. They are typically heavier charged than the service cartridge, assuring that any weakness in the gun will be detected before it is placed into service. The gun is then packaged and shipped to law enforcement agencies, military contractors, and federally licensed weapons dealers.

The Future

From the manufacturing standpoint, the handgun is still making use of new materials and processes, even though the design is quite mature. With the advent of investment castings, net shape forgings, and lightweight alloys, revisions to the standard design will continue. From a social perspective, the handgun has been the center of increasing debate since the 1960s. Many people have contended that limiting access to guns and ammunition would reduce violence in the United States. However, such proposals have been counterbalanced by a popular interpretation of the Second Amendment to the Constitution, which many believe guarantees individual citizens the right to bear arms. This debate continues in both the media and various state and federal legislatures. As of today, revolvers remain popular with law enforcement officers and military personnel. In addition, ordinary citizens can purchase and utilize them with relative ease, as the constraints that some states have recently imposed upon gun purchasers are generally limited to mandatory waiting periods that enable salespeople to perform background checks.

Where To Learn More

Books

Gould, A. C. *Modern American Pistols and Revolvers.* Wolfe Publishing, 1987.

Grennell, Dean A. *Handgun Digest,* 2nd ed. DBI Books, 1991.

Long, Duncan. *Combat Revolvers: The Best (and Worst) Modern Wheelguns.* Paladin Press, 1989.

Newton, Michael. *Armed and Dangerous: A Writer's Guide to Weapons.* Writer's Digest Books, 1990.

Pistols and Revolvers: A Handbook. Gordon Press, 1989.

Wood, J. B. *Gun Digest Book of Firearms Assembly—Disassembly,* Part II: *Revolvers.* DBI Books, 1990.

—Douglas E. Betts

Rubber Band

Background

Rubber bands are one of the most convenient products of the twentieth century, used by numerous individuals and industries for a wide variety of purposes. The largest consumer of rubber bands in the world is the U.S. Post Office, which orders millions of pounds a year to use in sorting and delivering piles of mail. The newspaper industry also uses massive quantities of rubber bands to keep individual newspapers rolled or folded together before home delivery. Yet another large consumer is the agricultural products industry. The flower industry buys rubber bands to hold together bouquets or uses delicate bands around the petals of flowers (especially tulips) to keep them from opening in transit. Vegetables such as celery are frequently bunched together with rubber bands, and the plastic coverings over berries, broccoli, and cauliflower are often secured with rubber bands. All in all, more than 30 million pounds of rubber bands are sold in the United States alone each year.

Rubber, which derives from plants that grow best in an equatorial climate, was first discovered by European explorers in the Americas, where Christopher Columbus encountered Mayan indians using water-proof shoes and bottles made from the substance. Intrigued, he carried several Mayan rubber items on his return voyage to Europe. Over the next several hundred years, other European explorers followed suit. The word rubber was born in 1770, when an English chemist named Joseph Priestley discovered that hardened pieces of rubber would rub out **pencil** marks. By the late eighteenth century, European scientists had discovered that dissolving rubber in turpentine produced a liquid that could be used to waterproof cloth.

However, until the beginning of the 19th century, natural rubber presented several technical challenges. While it clearly had the potential for useful development, no one was able to get it to the point where it could be used commercially. Rubber rapidly became dry and brittle during cold European winters. Worse, it became soft and sticky when warm.

The American inventor Charles Goodyear had been experimenting with methods to refine natural rubber for nearly a decade before an accident enabled him to overcome these problems with unprocessed rubber. One day in 1839, Goodyear accidentally left a piece of raw rubber on top of a warm stove, along with some sulfur and lead. On discovering his "mistake," Goodyear delightedly realized that the rubber had acquired a much more usable consistency and texture. Over the next five years, he perfected the process of converting natural rubber into a usable commodity. This process, which Goodyear dubbed *vulcanization* after the Roman god of fire, enabled the modern rubber industry to develop.

The first rubber band was developed in 1843, when an Englishman named Thomas Hancock sliced up a rubber bottle made by some New World Indians. Although these first rubber bands were adapted as garters and waistbands, their usefulness was limited because they were unvulcanized. Hancock himself never vulcanized his invention, but he did advance the rubber industry by developing the *masticator* machine, a forerunner of the modern rubber milling machine used to manufacture rubber bands as well as other rubber products. In 1845, Hancock's countryman Thomas Perry patented the rubber band and opened the first rubber-band factory. With the combined contributions of

The first rubber band was developed in 1843, when an Englishman named Thomas Hancock sliced up a rubber bottle made by some New World Indians. Although these first rubber bands were adapted as garters and waistbands, their usefulness was limited because they were unvulcanized (uncured).

After the latex has been harvested and purified, it is combined with acetic or formic acid to form rubber slabs. Next, the slabs are squeezed between rollers to remove excess water and pressed into bales or blocks, usually 2 or 3 square feet.

The rubber is then shipped to a rubber factory, where the slabs are machine cut into small pieces and mixed in a Banbury mixer with other ingredients—sulfur to vulcanize it, pigments to color it, and other chemicals to increase or diminish the elasticity of the resulting rubber bands. After being milled, the heated rubber strips are fed into an extruding machine that forces the rubber out in long, hollow tubes.

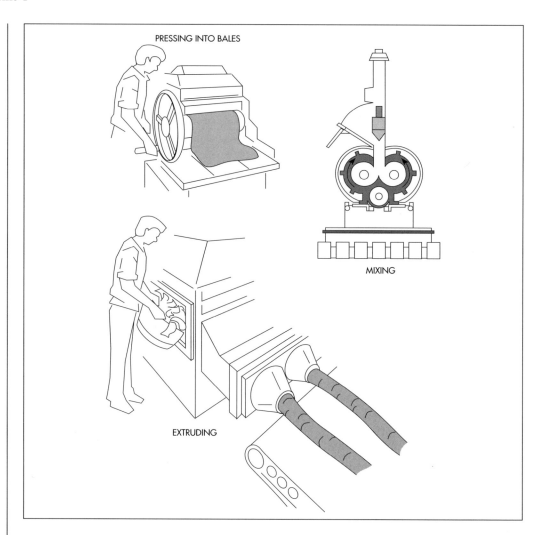

PRESSING INTO BALES

MIXING

EXTRUDING

Goodyear, Hancock, and Perry, manufacturing effective rubber bands became possible.

In the late nineteenth century, British rubber manufacturers began to foster the development of rubber plantations in British colonies like Malaya and Ceylon. Rubber plantations thrived in the warm climate of Southeast Asia, and the European rubber industry thrived as well, because now it could avoid the expense of importing rubber from the Americas, which lay beyond Britain's political and economic control.

Raw Materials

Although 75 percent of today's rubber products are made from the synthetic rubber perfected during World War II, rubber bands are still made from organic rubber because it offers superior elasticity. Natural rubber comes from *latex,* a milky fluid composed primarily of water with a smaller amount of rubber and trace amounts of resin, protein,

sugar, and mineral matter. Most non-synthetic industrial latex derives from the rubber tree (*Hevea brasiliensis*), but various equatorial trees, shrubs, and vines also produce the substance.

Within the rubber tree, latex is found between the external bark and the Cambium layer, through which the tree's sap flows. Distinct from the sap, latex serves as a protective agent, seeping out of and sealing over wounds in the tree's bark. To "tap" the substance, rubber harvesters cut a "V"-shaped wedge in the bark. They have to be careful to make their cuts at a depth of between .25 and .5 inch (.635 and 1.2 centimeters) in a mature tree (7 to 10 inches or 17.7 to 25.4 centimeters in diameter), because they must reach the latex without cutting into the sap vessels. They must also take care to tap each tree in a slightly different place every time. At the end of the nineteenth century botanist Henry Ridley began recommending this measure, having noted that repeated tapping in the same

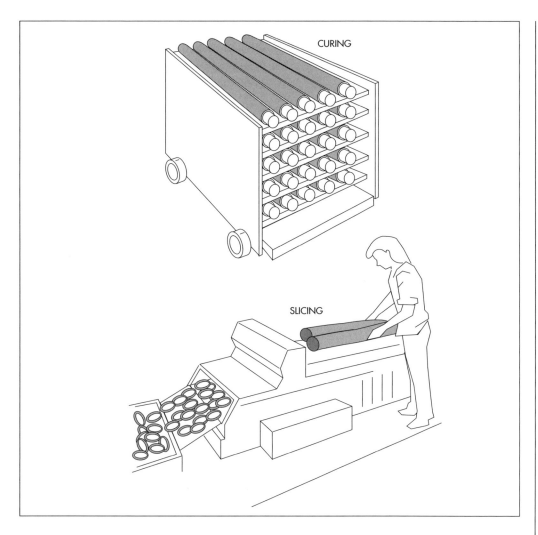

CURING

SLICING

After being extruded, the rubber tubes are forced over aluminum poles called *mandrels* and cured in large ovens. Finally, the tubes are removed from the mandrels and fed into a cutting machine that slices them into finished rubber bands.

spot swiftly killed rubber trees. After workers make a cut, latex oozes out and collects in a container attached to the tree. Tapping takes place every other day, and each tapping yields about 2 ounces (56 grams) of the substance. After tapping, the cut dries, and latex stops flowing in an hour or two.

The Manufacturing Process

Processing the natural latex

1 The initial stage of manufacturing the harvested latex usually takes place on the rubber plantation, prior to packing and shipping. The first step in processing the latex is purification, which entails straining it to remove the other constituent elements apart from rubber and to filter out impurities such as tree sap and debris.

2 The purified rubber is now collected in large vats. Combined with acetic or formic acid, the rubber particles cling together to form slabs.

3 Next, the slabs are squeezed between rollers to remove excess water and pressed into bales or blocks, usually 2 or 3 square feet (.6 or .9 square meter), ready for shipping to factories. The size of the blocks depends on what the individual plantation can accommodate.

Mixing and milling

4 The rubber is then shipped to a rubber factory. Here, the slabs are machine cut (or chopped) into small pieces. Next, many manufacturers use a Banbury Mixer, invented in 1916 by Fernely H. Banbury. This machine mixes the rubber with other ingredients—sulfur to vulcanize it, pigments to color it, and other chemicals to increase or diminish the elasticity of the resulting rubber bands. Although some companies don't add these ingredients until the next stage

(milling), the Banbury machine integrates them more thoroughly, producing a more uniform product.

5 Milling, the next phase of production, entails heating the rubber (a blended mass if it has been mixed, discrete pieces if it has not) and squeezing it flat in a milling machine.

Extrusion

6 After the heated, flattened rubber leaves the milling machine, it is cut into strips. Still hot from the milling, the strips are then fed into an extruding machine which forces the rubber out in long, hollow tubes (much as a meat grinder produces long strings of meat). Excess rubber regularly builds up around the head of each extruding machine, and this rubber is cut off, collected, and placed back with the rubber going into the milling machine.

Curing

7 The tubes of rubber are then forced over aluminum poles called *mandrels*, which have been covered with talcum powder to keep the rubber from sticking. Although the rubber has already been vulcanized, it's rather brittle at this point, and needs to be "cured" before it is elastic and usable. To accomplish this, the poles are loaded onto racks that are steamed and heated in large machines.

8 Removed from the poles and washed to remove the talcum powder, the tubes of rubber are fed into another machine that slices them into finished rubber bands. Rubber bands are sold by weight, and, because they tend to clump together, only small quantities can be weighed accurately by machines. Generally, any package over 5 pounds (2.2 kilograms) can be loaded by machine but will still require manual weighing and adjusting.

Quality Control

Sample rubber bands from each batch are subjected to a variety of quality tests. One such test measures *modulus*, or how hard a band snaps back: a tight band should snap back forcefully when pulled, while a band made to secure fragile objects should snap back more gently. Another test, for *elongation*, determines how far a band will stretch, which depends upon the percentage of rubber in a band: the more rubber, the further it should stretch. A third trait commonly tested is *break strength*, or whether a rubber band is strong enough to withstand normal strain. If 90 percent of the sample bands in a batch pass a particular test, the batch moves on to the next test; if 90 percent pass all of the tests, the batch is considered market-ready.

The Future

Rubber bands are a "mature product," for which the market is not growing as quickly as it did several years ago. Nevertheless, the demand for rubber bands is steady, and not at all likely to fall off dramatically in the predictable future.

Where To Learn More

Books

Cobb, Vicki. *The Secret Life of School Supplies.* J.B. Lippincott, 1981.

Graham, Frank and Ada Graham. *The Big Stretch: The Complete Book of the Amazing Rubber Band.* Knopf, 1985.

McCafferty, Danielle. *How Simple Things Are Made.* Subsistence Press, 1977.

Wulffson, Don. L. *Extraordinary Stories Behind the Invention of Ordinary Things.* Lothrop, Lee & Shepard Books, 1981.

—*Lawrence H. Berlow*

Running Shoe

Background

While most footwear protects and supports the foot, the running shoe goes beyond what one would expect of the ordinary shoe. Its advantages have been the subject of intense scrutiny in recent years, a focus that results from an increasingly health- and leisure-conscious population in general, and from the popularity of running in particular. As more people have become involved in the sport, more and more varied equipment has become available to runners. Consequently, the running shoe has evolved quite dramatically over the past 15 years.

Running as a sport can be traced back to the ancient Greeks, who advocated a culture based on sound bodies and sound minds. During Greek athletic contests, runners competed barefoot and often naked. Later, the Romans mandated that their messengers wear thin-soled sandals. As shoemaking evolved through the centuries, leather became and remained the favored material because of its durability. However, the first references to shoes designed specifically for running don't appear until 1852, when historians noted a race in which runners wore shoes with spiked soles. In 1900, the first sneaker, or all-purpose athletic shoe, was designed. Made primarily of canvas, this sneaker featured a rubber rim made possible by Charles Goodyear's 1839 discovery of vulcanized rubber. Known about for 1,000 years, rubber was finally rendered commercially useful when Goodyear heated and combined it with sulphur, thereby preventing it from hardening and losing its elasticity. In athletic shoes, rubber helped to cushion the impact of running on hard surfaces. However, it did not last as a shoemaking ma-

terial: it was not durable, and leather returned as the preferred material for running shoes. Yet leather wasn't the ideal fabric, either. In addition to being expensive, leather shoes caused chafing, and runners had to purchase chamois liners to protect their feet. A Scotsman known as "Old Man" Richings provided some relief when he invented a customized shoe designed with a seamless toe box (a piece of material inserted between the toe cap and the shoe lining and treated with a hardening agent, the toe box protects the toes against rubbing).

In 1925, Adolph Dassler, a German shoemaker, decided to concentrate on athletic shoes, and founded a business with his brother, Rudolph, to do so. The Dasslers' running shoes provided both arch support and speed lacing, and their high-quality products attracted prominent athletes including some Olympians: Jesse Owens is reported to have worn Dassler shoes during the 1936 games in Munich. The brothers later formed separate companies—Adolph, the Adidas company and Rudolph, the Puma company. Another manufacturer of running shoes during the mid-twentieth century was Hyde Athletic of New England, although the company specialized in football shoes. A 1949 description of Hyde's running shoe said that it featured kangaroo leather, a welt construction (a welt is a strip used to connect the upper to the sole—see "Design" section below), an elastic gore closure (a triangular piece of leather on the upper part of the shoe), and a leather sole covered in crepe rubber, a crinkly form of the material used especially for shoe soles. One of the most unusual running shoes of the mid-twentieth century was worn by the Japanese runner who won the 1951 Boston Marathon. Called

One of the most unusual running shoes of the mid-twentieth century was worn by the Japanese runner who won the 1951 Boston Marathon. Called the Tiger, his shoe was modeled after a traditional Japanese shoe that enclosed the big toe separately from the other toes.

the Tiger, his shoe was modeled after a traditional Japanese shoe that enclosed the big toe separately from the other toes.

During the 1960s, a company called New Balance began to examine how running impacts the foot. As a result of this research, New Balance developed an orthopedic running shoe with a rippled sole and wedge heel to absorb shock. As running became more popular and joggers more knowledgeable, the demand for footwear that would help prevent injuries increased. Many runners also began to request shoes that provided support in a lightweight construction, and nylon, invented during World War II, consequently began to replace the heavier leather and canvas materials previously used to make running shoes. Today, however, the comfort of the running shoe isn't known only to the jogger. Running shoes can be spotted on just about anyone who wants comfort in a shoe. In fact, running shoes have ceased to surprise when they appear on the feet of otherwise formally-attired office workers en route to work. In 1990, consumers spent $645 million for 15 million pairs of running shoes, and experts note that the majority bought were used for comfort rather than running.

Raw Materials

Running shoes are made from a combination of materials. The sole has three layers: insole, midsole, and outsole. The insole is a thin layer of man-made ethylene vinyl acetate (EVA). The components of the midsole, which provides the bulk of the cushioning, will vary among manufacturers. Generally it consists of polyurethane surrounding another material such as gel or liquid silicone, or polyurethane foam given a special brand name by the manufacturer. In some cases the polyurethane may surround capsules of compressed air. Outsoles are usually made of carbon rubber, which is hard, or blown rubber, a softer type, although manufacturers use an assortment of materials to produce different textures on the outsole.

The rest of the covering is usually a synthetic material such as artificial suede or a nylon weave with plastic slabs or boards supporting the shape. There may be a leather overlay or nylon overlay with leather attachments. Cloth is usually limited to the laces fitted

through plastic eyelets, and nails have given way to an adhesive known as cement lasting that bonds the various components together.

Design

The last 15 years have witnessed great changes in the design of the running shoe, which now comes in all styles and colors. Contemporary shoe designers focus on the anatomy and the movement of the foot. Using video cameras and computers, they analyze such factors as limb movement, the effect of different terrains on impact, and foot position on impact. Runners are labeled *pronators* if their feet roll inward or *supinators* if their feet roll to the outside. Along with pressure points, friction patterns, and force of impact, this information is fed into computers which calculate how best to accommodate these conditions. Designers next test and develop prototypes based on their studies of joggers and professional runners, readying a final design for mass production.

A running shoe may have as many as 20 parts to it, and the components listed below are the most basic. The shoe has two main parts: the upper, which covers the top and sides of the foot, and the bottom part, which makes contact with the surface.

As we work our way around the shoe clockwise, starting at the front on the upper part is the featherline, which forms the edge where the mudguard (or toeguard) tip meets the bottom of the shoe. Next is the vamp, usually a single piece of material that gives shape to the shoe and forms the toe box. The vamp also has attachments such as the throat, which contains the eyestay and lacing section. Beneath the lacing section is the tongue, protecting the foot from direct contact with the laces. Also attached to the vamp along the sides of the shoe are reinforcements. If sewn on the outside of the shoe these reinforcements are called a *saddle*; if sewn on the inside, they are called an *arch bandage.* Further towards the back of the shoe is the collar, which usually has an Achilles tendon protector at the top back of the shoe. The foxing shapes the rear end of the shoe. Underneath it is a plastic cup that supports the heel, the heel counter.

The bottom has three main parts, outsole, midsole, and wedge. The outsole provides

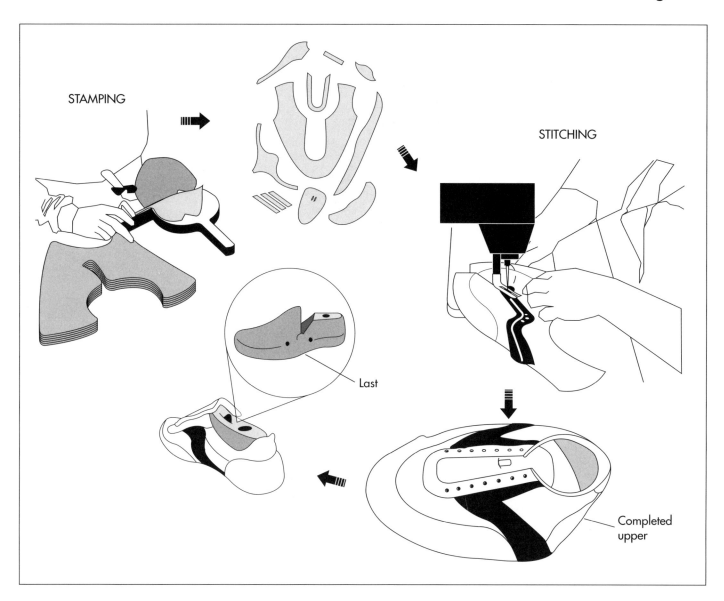

STAMPING

STITCHING

Last

Completed upper

traction and absorbs shock. The midsole is designed specifically for shock absorption, and the wedge supports the heel. Located inside the shoe, the insole also contains the arch support (sometimes called the *arch cookie*).

The Manufacturing Process

Shoemaking is a labor-intensive process, and the cost of producing the many components of the running shoe reflect the skilled labor necessary. Each phase of production requires precision and skills, and taking shortcuts to reduce costs can result in an inferior shoe. Some running shoes (known as *sliplasted shoes*) have no insole board. Instead, the single-layer upper is wrapped around both

the top and the bottom portions of the foot. Most running shoes, however, consist of an insole board that is cemented to the upper with cement. This section will focus on cement-lasted shoes.

Shipping and stamping the fabric

1 First, prepared rolls of synthetic material and rolls of dyed, split, and suede leather (used as part of the foxing) are sent to the factory.

2 Next, die machines stamp the shoe shapes, which are then cut out in cookie cutter fashion with various markings to guide the rest of the assembly. After being bundled and labeled, these pieces are sent to another part of the factory where they'll be stitched.

The first step in running shoe manufacture involves die cutting the shoe parts in cookie cutter fashion. Next, the pieces that will form the upper part of the shoe are stitched or cemented together. At this point, the upper looks not like a shoe but like a round hat; the extra material is called the *lasting margin*. After the upper is heated and fitted around a plastic mold called a *last*, the insole, midsole, and outsole are cemented to the upper.

Completed running shoes are quality tested using procedures developed by the Shoe and Allied Trades Research Association. Defects that are checked for include poor lasting, incomplete cement bonding, and stitching errors.

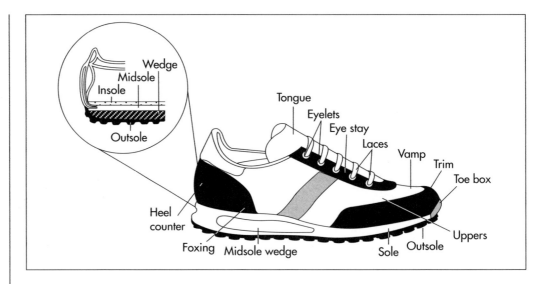

Assembling the upper and the insole

3 The pieces that will form the upper part of the shoe are stitched or cemented together and the lace holes punched out. These pieces include the featherline, the vamp, the mudguard, the throat (with eyestay and lacing section), the tongue, reinforcements such as the saddle or arch bandage, the collar (with Achilles tendon protector), the foxing, and the logo. At this point, the upper looks not like a shoe but like a round hat, because there is extra material—called the *lasting margin*—that will be folded underneath the shoe when it gets cemented to the sole.

4 Next, the insole is stitched to the sides of the upper. Stiffening agents are then added to the heel region and toe box, and an insole board is inserted.

Attaching the upper and bottom parts

5 The completed upper is heated and fitted around a last, a plastic mold that forms the final shape of the shoe. An automatic lasting machine then pulls the upper down over the last. Finally, a cement nozzle applies cement between the upper and insole board, and the machine presses the two pieces together to bond them. The upper now has the exact shape of the finished shoe.

6 Pre-stamped and cutout forms of the midsole and outsole or wedge are layered and cemented to the upper. First, the outsole and midsole are aligned and bonded together. Next, the outsole and midsole are aligned with the upper and placed over a heater to re-activate the cement. As the cement cools, the upper and bottom are joined.

7 The shoe is removed from the last and inspected. Any excess cement is scraped off.

Quality Control

Manufacturers can test their materials using procedures developed by the Shoe and Allied Trades Research Association (SATRA), which provides devices designed to test each element of the shoe. Once the shoe is complete, an inspector at the factory checks for defects such as poor lasting, incomplete cement bonding, and stitching errors. Because running can cause a number of injuries to the foot as well as to tendons and ligaments in the leg, another test is currently being developed to evaluate a shoe's shock absorption properties.

The Future

In the near future, experts predict refinements of current designs and manufacturing processes rather than radical breakthroughs. Within the next ten years, athletic shoe sizing should become standard worldwide. Designers will continue to seek lighter weight materials that provide better support and stability with further use of gels and air systems. Electronic components will also be built into the running shoe, so that information about physical characteristics and developments can be measured with a micro chip and later downloaded into a computer. Another feature that is already beginning to appear is the **battery**-operated lighting systems to accommodate the evening jogger. As consumers continue to spend millions for the comfort of running shoes, manufacturers of the ordinary shoe will continue to compete for these dollars by applying running shoe design principles to everyday shoes.

Where To Learn More

Books

Cavanagh, Peter R. *The Running Shoe Book.* Macmillan, 1980.

Cheskin, Melvyn P. *The Complete Handbook of Athletic Footwear.* Fairchild Books, 1986.

Nigg, Benno M. *Biomechanics of Running Shoes.* Human Kinetics Publishers, Inc., 1986.

Rossi, William A., ed. *The Complete Footwear Dictionary.* Krieger Publishing, 1993.

The Shoe in Sport. Mosby-Year Book, 1989.

Periodicals

Begley, Sharon. "The Science in Sports." *Newsweek.* July 27, 1992, p. 58.

"Running Shoes: The Sneaker Grows Up." *Consumer Reports.* May, 1992, pp. 308-314.

Ireland, Donald R. "The Shocking Truth about Athletic Footwear." *ASTM Standardization News.* June, 1992, pp. 42-45.

Murray, Charles J. "Composite Insole Absorbs Shock in Running Shoes." *Design News.* May 2, 1988, p. 100.

Wolkomir, Richard. "The Race to Make a 'Perfect' Shoe Starts in the Laboratory." *Smithsonian.* September, 1989, p. 94.

—Catherine Kolecki

Saddle

The first saddles were simply animal skins or cloths thrown over the backs of horses, offering only a small measure of comfort to the riders. About 2,000 years ago, the Sarmatians, a nomadic tribe who lived around the Black Sea region, designed a saddle based on a shaped wooden foundation, or tree.

Background

A saddle is a seat for the rider of an animal, usually a horse. A well-made saddle gives the horse rider the necessary support, security, and control over the animal. The saddle makes it possible for the rider to keep in balance with the horse by allowing him or her to sit over the horse's point of balance.

The first saddles were simply animal skins or cloths thrown over the backs of horses, offering only a small measure of comfort to the riders. About 2,000 years ago, the Sarmatians, a nomadic tribe who lived around the Black Sea region, designed a saddle based on a shaped wooden foundation, or tree. The tree had front and rear arches joined by wooden bars on each side of the horse's spine. This design, improved upon during the medieval era with the advent of the dip-seated saddle, survives in an adapted form as the Western saddle.

A typical saddle includes a base frame or "tree"; a seat for the rider; skirts, panels, and flaps that protect the horse from the rider's legs and vice versa; a girth that fits around the stomach of the horse and keeps the saddle stable; and stirrups for the rider's feet.

The saddle tree is the frame on which the saddle is built. Its shape determines the shape of the saddle, which varies from the flat-race tree weighing only a few ounces to the modern dip-seated spring tree.

Ideally, the tree should be built to fit the back of the horse for which the saddle is intended. Most of the time, however, saddles are manufactured for certain sizes and shapes and will fit most horses of equivalent sizes and shapes. Trees are usually made in three width fittings: narrow, medium, and broad, and four lengths: 15 inches, 16 inches, 16 1/2 inches and 17 1/2 inches (38.1, 40.64, 41.9, and 44.45 centimeters respectively).

Panels are cushions divided by a channel that gives a comfortable padded surface to the horse's back while raising the tree high enough to give easy clearance of the animal's spine. The panels also disperse the rider's weight over a larger surface, thereby protecting the horse from the weight of the rider. These panels also protect the horse's back from the hardness of the saddle. The purpose of the skirts is to protect the rider's legs from the sweat of the horse, and to cover the girths and girth straps. Saddles also include D-rings, small leather straps with strings attached that can hold canteens, jackets, food pouches, and other items.

Modern horse saddles are divided into two broad categories: the English and Western saddle. Originally designed for show jumping, the English saddle has a deep seat and sloped back. Its design was derived in part from the crouched-forward position adopted by Tod Sloan, an American jockey, and the subsequent Italian design introduced by Caprilli in 1906. Sloan's forward crouch placed the rider's weight forward, thus freeing the horse's loins and hindquarters. Because professional jockeys had previously positioned their weight on the loins and behind the movement of the horse, Sloan's technique revolutionized professional horse racing.

One type of English saddle, the "jumping saddle," is designed to position the rider more forward. It is almost always built on a spring tree and generally has a deep seat. In

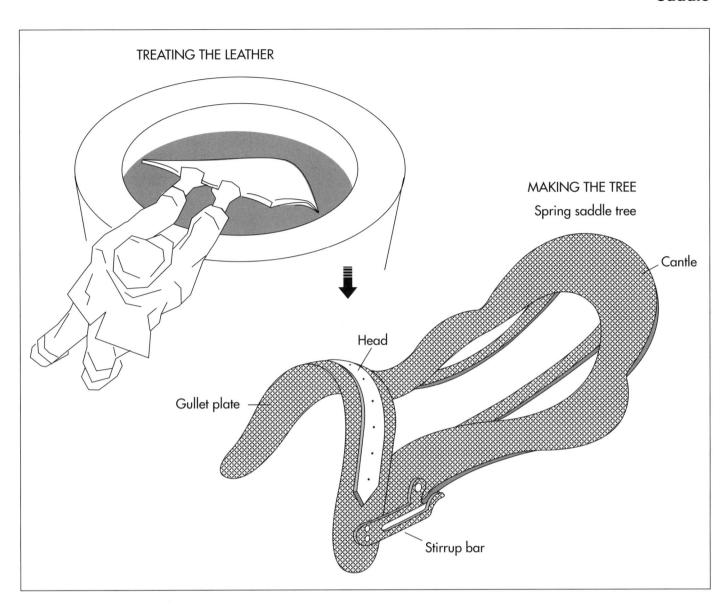

TREATING THE LEATHER

MAKING THE TREE
Spring saddle tree

Cantle

Head

Gullet plate

Stirrup bar

contrast, the "dressage saddle" is designed to position the rider more to the center of the horse, allowing him or her to use the leg and weight aids with greater precision. Only the sweat flap separates the rider's leg from the horse. Today, English saddles are used for sport and general purposes.

Traditionally, the Western saddle has been used primarily for work. It has a wider and longer panel than the English saddle and disperses more of the rider's weight over the back of the horse. Western saddles also have a roping horn on the pommel to facilitate the roping of cattle, and are equipped with extra D-rings, or tie-downs, to hold ropes and other items.

There are four types of Western saddles. The pleasure or "ranch saddle," which weighs

approximately 25 pounds (11.35 kilograms), and the "equitation saddle," weighing about 25 to 30 pounds (11.35 to 13.62 kilograms), are suitable for general riding. The "roping saddle" (about 40 to 50 pounds [18 to 23 kilograms) is designed for use in cattle roping. Because of the comfort it provides, many find it suitable for general riding as well. The "cutting saddle" is slightly lighter, about 30 pounds, and is used in cow cutting competitions. Because its light weight allows for greater movement, some riders also find the cutting saddle suitable for general purposes.

Raw Materials

Flaps, girth straps, and stirrup leathers are typically made from animal skins taken from cattle, pig, sheep, or deer; cowhide is the

The first step in saddle manufacture is treating the leather. This involves soaking the hide in a lime solution to loosen the outer layer of skin and the hair, and then removing the hair.

The frame of the saddle is the tree. One typical tree type, the spring tree, is shaped out of thin plywood. Fiberglass material (the fiberglass looks like a white screen mesh) is then stretched over this plywood, and liquid resin is hand-brushed or sprayed on top, resulting in a very strong and durable product.

most common skin used in saddle making. Saddle trees can be composed of several materials, including beech wood, fiberglass, plastic, laminated wood, steel, aluminum, and iron. Seats are usually made from canvas, felt, and **wool**, while panels can include plastic foam, rubber, and linen.

The Manufacturing Process

Treating the leather

1 After the hide or skin is removed from the animal's carcass, it is soaked in drums containing lime and other chemicals to loosen the hair and outer layer of the skin. The inside flesh layer is also removed, either by machine or hand with a special knife. The remaining hide is soaked in lime and bacteria solutions to remove residue. Next, the hair is removed, either by machine or manually with a special knife. The hide is soaked again, this time in an acid solution in order to remove the lime left by the previous soakings. Because it is important that the fleshy side is left smooth with no loose fibers, the hide undergoes a final treatment called *scudding*, which involves hanging the hide over a beam and removing any bits of remaining hair, tissue, and dirt with a blunt knife. The hide is then thoroughly washed.

2 To prevent hides from decaying, they are immersed in a diluted solution of tanning acid. Over several months, they are gradually treated with stronger solutions. Oil tanning, or chamoising, is still used sometimes by rubbing animal or fish grease into the hide.

3 At this point, the leather has two sides, the flesh side and the grain side. The hides are now given to a currier, who manually rubs a mixture of tallow, cod oil, and other greases, plus wax, into the leather over a period of time. This process gives the leather color, makes it flexible, durable, and waterproof. The most common and popular colors for saddles are golden yellow, also known as the London color, and Havana, which is of a darker shade. Warwick, a much darker color that turns black with use, is applied in the making of frizzing harness as opposed to riding tack. (This color is produced by staining with aniline dye.) The currier then allows the hides to mature for several weeks.

Making the saddle tree

4 There are two basic saddle tree designs: the rigid and spring tree, both of which can accommodate either a straight or dipped seat. The modern English saddle usually has a spring tree, while the Western saddle has a rigid tree.

The spring tree is first shaped out of thin plywood. Fiberglass material (the fiberglass looks like a white screen mesh) is then stretched over this plywood, and liquid resin is hand-brushed or sprayed on top, resulting in a very strong and durable product. Two "springs" made of lightweight steel strips are then inserted under the tree running from front to the rear along the widest part of the seat, and set about two inches (five centimeters) from the outside. The springs provide greater comfort and more flexibility to the rider by allowing the pressure exerted through the seat bones to be transmitted to the horse.

5 The rigid saddle tree is made by molding it out of fiberglass, by combining wood shavings with resin in a mold under pressure, or by creating a wooden tree around which wet leather strips are wrapped and allowed to dry.

6 To reinforce the saddle tree, steel plates are placed underneath the tree from the pommel (the head) to the cantle (the rear part of the saddle, which projects upward). The steel plates are secured above and below the pommel at the head and gullet of the tree.

Stirrups

7 The stirrup bars are attached next. A prong-line metal bracket measuring three inches wide is bolted onto the tree below the head on the point of the tree (the forward-most point of the saddle). Bars are made of two pieces: the bar itself, and a movable catch or "thumb piece," which is set into the bar. This catch works on the premise that it can be opened when the stirrup leather is put in position and will, in theory, open and release the leather if the rider should fall. The bars are always forged (hammered or squeezed into the proper shape) or cast (put into a liquid state and forced into a shaped mold), and the word "forged" or "cast" is always stamped on the bar.

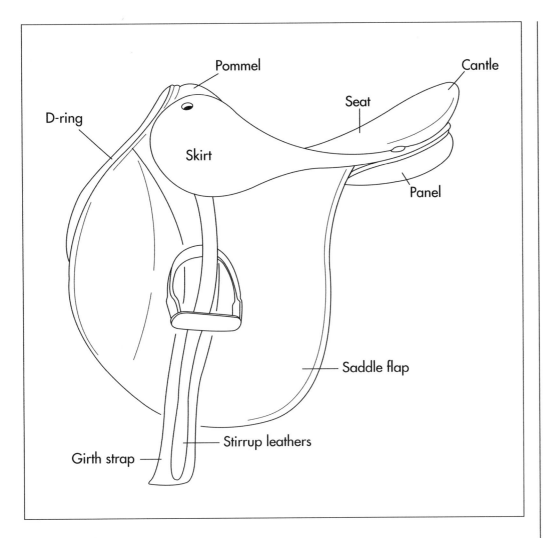

Pommel

Cantle

Seat

D-ring

Skirt

Panel

Saddle flap

Girth strap

Stirrup leathers

A typical saddle includes a seat for the rider; skirts, panels, and flaps that protect the horse from the rider's legs and vice versa; a girth that fits around the stomach of the horse and keeps the saddle stable; and stirrups for the rider's feet. D-rings are used to hold items such as canteens or ropes.

8 The stirrup leathers, about 7/8 inch (2.2 centimeters) wide, are made from "read leather": cowhide, rawhide, or buffalo hide. They go over the top of the bar and back down to the stirrups.

The seat

9 A strong muslin cloth is placed over the tree from the pommel to the cantle, to form a foundation. Pitch **paint** is then applied to waterproof it. Next, strips of white serge, a woolen material, are stretched and fastened tightly with small nails from the head of the tree at the pommel to the cantle. Stretch canvas is then positioned over the serge and nailed in place. This forms the base of the seat.

10 Small pieces of shaped felt and leather (called *bellies*) are placed on the edges of the tree at the broadest part of the seat so that when the seat is eventually made, it will

not drop away at the edges. A piece of serge is then tightly stretched and stitched down to the canvas layer to make the shape of the seat. Next, a small slit is made so that the space between the serge and canvas can be lightly stuffed with wool to give the seat resilience and to prevent the tree itself being felt through the leather seat.

11 Pigskin is now dampened and stretched tightly, and is then stretched over the seat. (The pigskin is dampened and stretched so that when it dries and shrinks, a neat and tight final product will be achieved.) The under panel, which protects the horse from the girths, is stitched and nailed into place on the tree. The under panel is usually made of pigskin leather or grained cowhide.

Girths

12 Girth straps are attached to the saddle next. Made of soft leather, these straps are very short. Attached to them are the girths, whose purpose is to hold the saddle firmly in place by fastening them around the horse's belly. These girths are made in 7/8-inch or one-inch (2.54 centimeters) thick sizes, and they can range in length from 36 inches (91.44 centimeters) for a tiny pony to 54 inches (137 centimeters) for a large horse (these measurements include the buckles). Girths are made of soft leather, mohair, or nylon.

Panels

13 The outer panels, made of leather, are stuffed with felt, wool, or plastic foam and are covered in either leather, serge, or linen. They are attached underneath the saddle. Leather skirts are then sewn just above the outer panel. D-rings (also known as tie-downs) are now attached to the saddle. Usually about one inch wide, the D-rings are made of rawhide and have strings attached to them.

Byproducts

Byproducts of saddle manufacturing include saddle and bridle accessories such as bit guards, lip straps, leather straps for the nose nets, breastplates, and girth safes, which prevent the buckles from wearing a hole in the panel.

Where To Learn More

Books

Baker, Jennifer. *Saddlery and Horse Equipment: A Practical Horse Guide.* Arco Publishing, 1982.

Beatie, Russel H. *Saddles.* University of Oklahoma Press, 1981.

The Complete Book of Riding: A Guide to Saddlery, Care and Management, International Breeds, Riding Techniques and Competitive Riding. Gallery Books, 1989.

Crabtree, Helen K. *Saddle Equitation.* Doubleday, 1982.

Sherer, Richard L. *Horseman's Handbook of Western Saddles.* Sherer Custom Saddles, 1988.

—Eva Sideman

Salsa

Background

Salsa is the Spanish word for sauce, and in Mexico it refers to sauces that are used as an ingredient for a variety of dishes and as a condiment. Most salsas are especially spicy, due to the prominence of hot chili peppers in their ingredients. Literally hundreds of such sauces exist, including piquant fruit salsas. In the United States, salsa resembles a spicy tomato sauce from Mexico called salsa cruda, or raw salsa, and is used primarily as a condiment, especially with **tortilla chips**. In 1991, salsa outsold ketchup as the most popular condiment in America. Today, salsas account for almost half of the sauces sold in the United States. In 1992, salsa accounted for $802 million in sales; that figure is expected to reach $1 billion by 1995.

Salsas have been know for a thousand years in Mexico, yet salsa as we know it today is a fairly well-balanced blend of both Old World and New World ingredients. The tomatoes, tomatillos, and chilies found in salsa are native to this hemisphere, while all the other ingredients, such as onions, garlic, and other spices, are Old World in origin. Mexican cuisine has traces of Aztec, Spanish, French, Italian, and Austrian influences. The ingredients of salsa began in places as diverse as India and the Near East, yet most of them had established firm footholds in Europe before Spain's conquest of Mexico in the early sixteenth century. Hence, most of the ingredients can be attributed to Spain's influence on Mexico.

Mexican cuisine is traditionally noteworthy for its time-consuming preparation. Foods such as mole are complex blends of pulverized spices, fruits, **chocolate**, or other ingredients that can take days to prepare. Fresh salsa used to be made using a *molcajete* and a *tejolote*, or mortar and pestle. This device, originally made from black basalt, has been in use for 3,500 years to prepare a variety of foods.

Raw Materials

Mass-produced salsas come in different varieties. The basic formula for salsa consists of tomatoes and/or tomato paste, water, chili peppers (green, yellow, serrano, and/or anaheim), optional jalapeño peppers, vinegar, onions, garlic, green bell peppers, and spices, including black pepper, cilantro, paprika, cumin, and oregano. The most common alternative salsa is salsa verde, made with tomatillos. Of the same genus (*Physalis*) as the ground cherry grown in the southern United States, tomatillos are tart, green fruits grown inside papery pods that replace red tomatoes in the basic salsa recipe. Other special formulas may have green tomatoes, carrots, black-eyed peas, or even cactus as ingredients.

Most commercially prepared salsas also contain additives. These include salt, **sugar**, vegetable oil, calcium chloride, pectin, modified food starch, xanthum gum, guar gum, dextrose, and potassium sorbate. Beet powder and canthaxanthin can be added for color, and sodium benzoate or citric acid can be added as preservatives.

The Manufacturing Process

Selecting the produce

1 The salsa manufacturer purchases fresh, frozen, or dehydrated produce, such as

Most salsas are especially spicy, due to the prominence of hot chili peppers in their ingredients. Literally hundreds of such sauces exist, including piquant fruit salsas. In the United States, salsa resembles a spicy tomato sauce from Mexico called salsa cruda, or raw salsa, and is used primarily as a condiment.

The initial steps in making salsa involve inspecting, peeling, and stemming tomatoes; roasting, washing, and blanching chili peppers; and cleaning other produce. The vegetables are then cut using standard machines pre-set to the desired level of fineness. To make chunky salsa, the vegetables are usually diced while the fresh cilantro is minced. To make smoother salsa, all the vegetables are processed to the same consistency as the tomatoes.

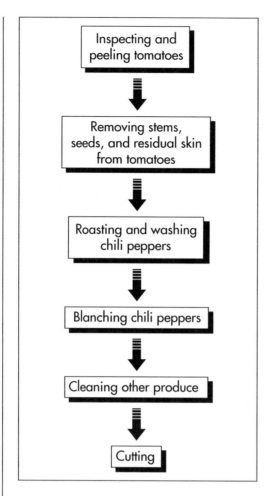

Inspecting and peeling tomatoes

Removing stems, seeds, and residual skin from tomatoes

Roasting and washing chili peppers

Blanching chili peppers

Cleaning other produce

Cutting

tomatoes, peppers, and onions, from growers. Other ingredients, such as vinegar, tomato paste, spices, or additives, are purchased from manufacturers in processed form.

Preparing the produce

2 The tomatoes are first inspected, then peeled using lye. The stems, seeds, and any residual skin are then removed. Some salsa manufacturers roast their green chili peppers before washing them. Next, the stem, seeds, and calyx are removed. The chili peppers are then blanched, and the pH value, or acid count, is adjusted using citric acid.

3 All other produce is cleaned by passing the vegetables through tanks of water or by spraying under high water pressure. The inedible parts of these vegetables (such as garlic peel, stems, or onion skins) are removed by processing machines. The vegetables are then cut using standard machines that are pre-set to the desired level of fineness. To make chunky salsa, the vegetables are usually diced while the fresh cilantro is

minced. To make smoother salsa, all the vegetables are processed to the same consistency as the tomatoes.

Cooking the salsa

4 Most salsa is not fresh due to long-distance transport of the product from manufacturing plants to retail outlets. Because it is important for the product to have a long shelf-life, heating the salsa is necessary to prohibit the growth of mold within the container before purchase. Most salsa, however, is minimally processed. The tomato paste or processed tomatoes, water, vinegar, and spices are placed in a pre-mix kettle that is large enough to hold several batches of salsa. This mixture is then placed in a batch kettle along with the other ingredients such as onions and chili peppers. Salsa may be slow or fast cooked, or, in the case of fresh salsa, steam cooked. Cooking time and temperature vary; the slow method subjects the salsa to a low temperature of 163 degrees Fahrenheit (71 degrees Celsius) for 45 minutes, while the fast method subjects the salsa to a high temperature of 253 degrees Fahrenheit (121 degrees Celsius) for 30 seconds under pressure.

Vacuum-sealing the salsa

5 After cooking, the salsa is ladled into glass jars, plastic bottles, or other containers that are usually made from heat-resistant polyethylene or polypropylene. Fresh salsa is placed into the container cold and then steam heated, while cooked salsa is placed into the container while it is still warm. The machine that fills the containers does so by volume. The jars or containers are then sealed and cooled in cold water or air. This process vacuum-seals the product because the heated salsa cools and contracts, producing a partial vacuum under the seal.

Packaging

6 Jars and plastic containers that are not preprinted with product information are labeled and then packed in **corrugated cardboard** boxes to be shipped to stores.

Quality Control

As a food for human consumption, salsa must undergo rigorous testing to insure that

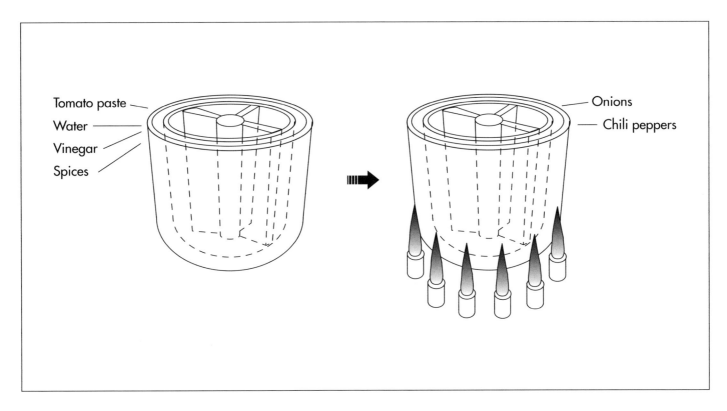

Tomato paste
Water
Vinegar
Spices

Onions
Chili peppers

each batch is sterile and safe. Salsa manufacturers that do not use preservatives in their product must be even more careful that mold does not grow during its shelf-life.

All incoming produce and spices must first be inspected for quality. To mass-produce salsa, an important criterion is that the vegetables be consistent so that batches will not differ in quality, color, or flavor. Consistency is very important in the case of chili peppers, as the degree of hotness must be in a stringently determined range. A jar of salsa labeled "mild" should have a slightly piquant flavor that does not overwhelm the timid salsa consumer. Conversely, a jar of salsa labeled "hot" should not disappoint the braver salsa consumer.

Chili peppers are selected by choosing specifically categorized seeds or germ plasm to be grown into the chili peppers intended for salsa. Chili peppers range in hotness—from the mild bell pepper to the hottest known pepper, the Scotch bonnet—although most salsa manufacturers will only go as high as jalapeño. The system used to classify chili pepper hotness is the Scoville Units method. It determines the amount of water and time needed to neutralize the heat of the pepper after ingestion. The higher the Scov-

ille Unit, the hotter the pepper. The hotter chili peppers are easily measured in the hundreds of thousands Scoville Units. Each type of pepper has several different levels of hotness to choose from, and the salsa manufacturer selects the peppers that will provide the necessary degree of hotness for each blend. Once the salsa is prepared, it is tasted by experienced tasters to see that it meets acceptable standards of flavor and hotness.

The equipment used to prepare salsa is cleaned and inspected daily. Equipment is cleaned with chlorides, quaternary ammonias, or any substance that is effective against bacteria, then rinsed thoroughly. A swab test, which consists of rubbing a cotton swab over a small surface area of the kettle, is then done for each kettle. The sample is then placed in a solution of known dilution, put on a dish, and placed in an **laboratory incubator**. After one or two days, the sample is checked for microbes. The number of harmful organisms is multiplied by the total affected surface area of the kettle to arrive at the total number of microbes. Many samples of finished salsa are taken, and the samples undergo the same treatment and testing as those samples taken from the equipment. Salsa factories are regularly inspected by the Food and Drug Administration (FDA), as well as state food regulatory inspectors.

Once prepared, the tomato paste or processed tomatoes, water, vinegar, and spices are placed in a pre-mix kettle that is large enough to hold several batches of salsa. This mixture is then placed in a batch kettle for cooking along with the other ingredients such as onions and chili peppers. Cooking time and temperature vary; the slow method subjects the salsa to a low temperature of 163 degrees Fahrenheit for 45 minutes, while the fast method subjects the salsa to a high temperature of 253 degrees Fahrenheit for 30 seconds under pressure.

Salsa is packaged automatically using large machines that vacuum-seal the glass or plastic jars after filling them with the appropriate amount of salsa. Salsa's surging popularity has made it the most popular condiment in the United States.

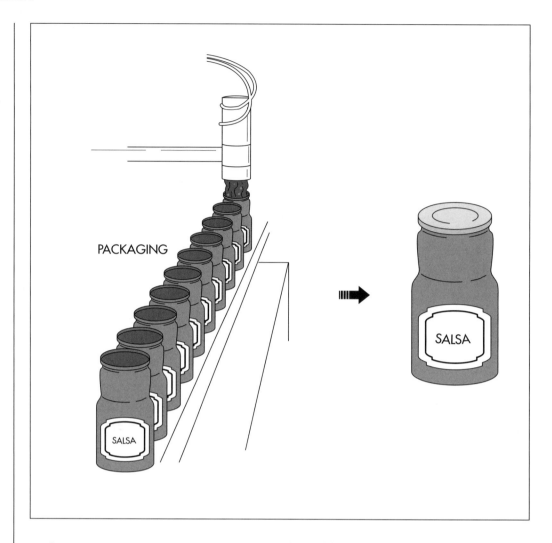

PACKAGING

SALSA

Where To Learn More

Books

Birosik, P. J. *Salsa*. Macmillan Publishing, 1993.

Esquivel, Laura. *Like Water for Chocolate*. Doubleday, 1992.

Fischer, Lee. *Salsa Lover's Cook Book*. Golden West Publishers, n.d.

Leonard, Jonathan Norton. *Latin American Cooking*. Time-Life Books, 1968.

McMahan, Jacqueline H. *The Salsa Book*. The Olive Press, 1989.

Miller, Mark. *The Great Salsa Book*. Ten Speed Press, 1993.

Petroski, Henry. *The Evolution of Useful Things*. Alfred A. Knopf, 1992.

Periodicals

O'Neill, Molly. "Salsa Nova," *New York Times Magazine*. June 14, 1992, p. 61.

Sokolov, Raymond. "Before the Conquest: Thousands of 'Mexican' Dishes Could Not Have Existed Before Cortes," *Natural History*. August, 1989, p. 76.

Stern, Gabriella. "Yanquis Are Finding Wide-Ranging Uses for Salsa and Picante," *Wall Street Journal*. January 19, 1993, pp. B1, B8.

—Rose Secrest

Sandpaper

Background

Although the most familiar types of coated abrasives are probably the individual sheets of sandpaper with which home woodworkers prepare furniture or crafts for painting, the trade term "coated abrasives" actually encompasses a much wider array of products for both individual and industrial use. While these products assume many forms, all are essentially a single layer of abrasive grit attached to a flexible backing. In addition to their best-known form, sandpapers are also available to consumers on belts, rolls, and disks. However, the biggest users of coated abrasives are manufacturers who employ large-scale abrasives in various phases of industrial production. For example, coated abrasives are critical in both the furniture and automotive industries.

Coated abrasives date as far back as the thirteenth century, when the Chinese used crushed shells and seeds glued with natural gum to parchment. By 1769 coated abrasive paper was being sold on the streets of Paris. An 1808 article describes a process for making coated abrasives, and in 1835 a United States patent was issued for a machine that produced coated abrasives.

Not always a highly versatile tool, coated abrasives were originally restricted to finishing applications such as polishing or preparing surfaces for painting or plating. Through improvements in the strength of backings and the properties of abrasive minerals, coated abrasives now can be used for heavy-duty applications. Today, industrial uses for coated abrasives range from hand polishing with sheets of coated abrasive to grinding steel with large machines that use 300-horse-power electric motors to drive belts several feet wide.

Currently, approximately forty companies manufacture or import jumbo rolls in the United States. The size of the industry is limited because it requires a substantial investment in equipment, raw materials, energy, and labor. A larger number of companies convert the jumbo rolls into useable products such as disks and belts.

Raw Materials

The name "sandpaper" is actually a misnomer, as most coated adhesive products contain neither sand nor paper. Generally, they consist of some type of abrasive mineral, which can be organic or synthetic; flexible backings; and adhesives. Other materials may be added for special applications. Most companies that manufacture jumbo rolls of coated abrasives purchase minerals and backing materials from independent companies that specialize in making these items. Natural minerals come from companies that mine and process the minerals, synthetic minerals come from companies that specialize in such refractory materials, and most backings come from fabric manufacturers.

The abrasive grain, the key part of coated abrasive products, may be either a natural or synthetic mineral. Due to their extreme hardness, natural minerals such as garnet or emery (corundum with iron impurities) find limited use in products for wood-related applications, while crocus mineral (natural iron oxide) is limited to use as a polishing agent because of its softness. However, such natural minerals comprise less than one percent of the abrasives market. Metalworking applications require synthetic minerals exclusively because such minerals offer consistent quality and can be specially manufactured with an elongated structure that bonds well to flexible backings.

The use of a particular coated abrasive product determines the mineral that will be used in that product. Aluminum oxide is the most common abrasive, followed by silicon carbide. Because silicon carbide is harder and sharper, it is used for applications involving glass and other nonmetal materials. Aluminum oxide, which is the tougher abrasive, is used for metalworking applications where high forces are common. Minerals containing zirconium alumina and alumina are typically used where extremely rugged abrasives are needed, such as in foundries. Expensive and extremely hard minerals such as diamond or cubic boron nitride are restricted to special polishing processes.

The sizes of abrasive grains range from fine particles that look like flour (2,000 grit) to large particles that look like granulated **sugar** (60 grit). Finer grains are used for surface finishing applications and larger grains for shaping and material removal applications. Recent developments in making uniform and extremely small grain abrasives with particles the size of air-born particulate in smoke have created applications in fine polishing known as *superfinishing*. Other improvements include patented technology to cluster fine minerals into small hollow spheres or conglomerates the size of conventional grains. Such refinements have improved cutting ability and extended the useful life of coated abrasive products.

The backing is the flexible platform to which the abrasive mineral is attached. The development of coated abrasives as a versatile manufacturing tool can in part be attributed to improvements in backing materials. Without a strong and flexible backing, coated abrasives could not survive rough handling or the effects of liquids that are often used as grinding aids.

Backings come in four basic materials, each with unique attributes. Paper is the lightest of the backing materials and also the weakest. Although its lack of material strength limits paper's usefulness for hand applications, its flexibility makes it ideal for applications in which the coated abrasive must fit closely to the contour of a work piece. Graded on a scale that increases with the physical weight of a ream, paper backings come in weights rated A to F. Unless specially treated, paper cannot be used with water or other fluids.

Backings made from woven fibers come in progressively heavier weight designations of J, X, Y, M, and H and are typically made of cotton, polyester, or **rayon**. The pattern of weave in the backing varies from fibers woven at 90 degree angles to fibers overlaid at 90 degree angles and stitched together. A less-common mesh or screen patten is used for backings in materials needed in wet, low-pressure applications. Fiber backings are made of multiple layers of resin-impregnated cloth fibers that are used in some dry, high-pressure applications. Film backings, a recent development, have improved the effectiveness of coated abrasives in precision finishing. Uniformly thick synthetic film can be used with special micron-sized minerals to produce highly reflective finishing and precision dimensions on parts.

The bond or adhesive is applied to the backing in two layers, each of which serves a different purpose. The first layer of adhesive, called the *make coat*, holds the abrasive mineral to the backing. After the first layer of adhesive and grain have been applied, a second adhesive, the *size coat*, is applied in varying thicknesses depending upon the kind of product being manufactured. A thin layer of size coat leaves more of the abrasive mineral exposed, yielding a product that cuts more aggressively. Thicker layers of size coats, which cover more of the mineral, create a product that cuts less aggressively but creates finer finishes.

The Manufacturing Process

Applying the make coat to the backing

1 A typical sanding belt originates with the manufacture of a large roll of coated abrasive containing an "X" weight cotton fabric backing, 100 grit aluminum oxide, and resin bond. Production starts when the make coat is applied to one side of the backing material.

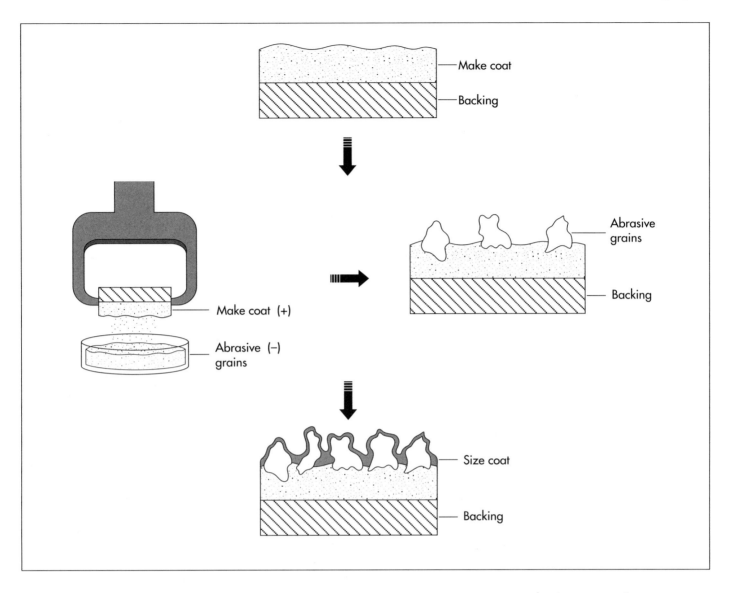

Make coat

Backing

Make coat (+)

Abrasive (−)
grains

Abrasive
grains

Backing

Size coat

Backing

Applying the abrasive to the make coat

2 The next step, applying the abrasive mineral, is the most important in the manufacturing process because it determines the orientation and density of the mineral. In the past, the backing with the first layer of adhesive passed under a controlled stream of abrasive, which applied a thin layer of randomly oriented grit. Today, the backing is passed, adhesive side down, over a pan of abrasives that have been electrostatically charged—given an electric charge opposite to the backing. The opposite charge causes the abrasive to adhere evenly to the backing, resulting in a very sharp, fast-cutting coated abrasive tool with the maximum life possible.

3 Controlling mineral density on the flexible backing gives rise to two important variations in product design: open- and closed-coat abrasives. An open-coat product contains abrasives grains that cover from 50 to 70 percent of the surface area of the backing. This lower density allows the finished product to be flexible and prevents it from clogging or loading with bits of work material. In closed-coat products, the mineral covers 100 percent of the available surface area, making the finished products better for finishing applications and more suitable for rougher handling than open-coat products.

Applying the size coat

4 Once the grain has been imbedded in the make coat, the roll is dried and moved on for application of the size coat. Following application of the size coat, the roll is dried again and cured under carefully controlled temperature and humidity conditions. The

The term "sandpaper" is a misnomer, since most coated abrasives contain neither sand nor paper. Instead, a typical coated abrasive contains a backing of cotton, polyester, or rayon, with an initial layer of adhesive backing—the make coat—applied to it. The abrasive grains are then applied using an electrostatic deposition process, in which the grains are given an electric charge. Finally, another layer of adhesive—the size coat—is applied.

Sandpaper can take any number of sizes and shapes and can be used for a variety of applications, from the common hand-held sheet shown here to huge machines that use 300-horsepower electric motors to drive belts several feet wide.

finished product is then wound on a large spool and shipped to the companies that will convert it into sanding belts or other items.

5 Additional materials and processes may be included to give the converted product special characteristics. One such treatment is the addition of a grinding aid in the size coat that improves grinding of some metals in high-pressure applications. Another treatment entails applying a pressure-sensitive adhesive to the nonabrasive side of the backing to make some types of sanding disks. Material may be also added to reduce the static electricity that is generated when a belt is used on wood. Passing the roll through two closely spaced steel rollers in a process called *satining* crushes protruding minerals and leaves a product with uniform thickness designed for fine finishing applications.

Flexing the roll

6 Before the coated abrasive roll is converted into a belt or other product, it is systematically flexed or bent to break the continuous layer of adhesive bond. This flexing is necessary because the freshly manufactured roll is so stiff that it otherwise would not perform properly when converted into other products. Flexing can be applied in either a single direction or in multiple directions. Single direction flexing breaks the bond usually at a 90 degree angle to the edge of the roll. For special applications in which the belt must accurately conform to contours of a part surface, single direction flexing is applied along lines parallel to the sides of the belt. Multiple flexing breaks the bond at 45 degree angles to the sides of the belt in a criss-cross pattern or in a combination of 90 degree and 45 degree directions. Although the latter produces a very flexible belt, such flexing greatly reduces the useful life of the product.

Conversion

7 Converting roll material into abrasive belts starts with cutting strips of coated abrasives to the desired width. Each strip is then cut to the proper length, and the ends are joined together. The joint in common belts is an overlapping splice at 45 degrees. Narrow belts are spliced at a more acute angle and wide belts at a greater angle. A variety of splicing techniques can be applied depending upon the importance of changes in belt thickness at the slice and the amount of stress the belt will receive during use. One common practice in preparing a splice for joining is *skiving*, a process that removes a layer of abrasive or backing from the ends of the belt. To minimize thickness of joints in products used for finishing applications, both ends are skived. Coarse-grained products, which are used for less precise applications, are skived on one end only. Conversion of other products proceeds similarly. For example, sanding disks begin with a properly sized section of roll material, and a machine punches out the individual disks complete with the hole in the center.

Quality Control

The quality of coated abrasive products is controlled by various government and voluntary standards established by trade organizations within the abrasive industry. These standards are primarily concerned with safety and with the consistent grading and identification of products. Safety standards appear in American National Standards Institute (ANSI) publication B7.7, and grain sizing and identification standards are in ANSI publication B74. 18.

The Future

Coated abrasives will continue as reliable and useful tools for the consumer and the manufacturing industry, although changes in the use of some products are likely. For example, as nonwoven abrasive products are improved and become better recognized, they may replace some coated abrasives products. Continuing development of minerals and backings will improve the performance of existing coated abrasive products. New film backing and ultra-fine abrasive minerals will enable new approaches to highly reflective and precision finishes. Also, coated abrasives will be used more with automated equipment as designs are improved and better computer controls become available.

Where To Learn More

Books

Borkowski, J. *Uses of Abrasives and Abrasive Tools*. Prentice Hall, 1992.

King, Robert I. and Robert S. Hahn. *Handbook of Modern Grinding Technology*. Chapman and Hall, 1984.

McKee, Richard L. *Machining with Abrasives*. Van Nostrand Reinhold, 1982.

Periodicals

Capotosto, Roberto. "Reusable Sanding Sheets," *Popular Mechanics*. June, 1991, p. 73.

Flexner, Bob. "Fine Grit," *Workbench*. January, 1992, p. 18.

Whiteley, Peter O. "What You Really Need to Know About Sandpaper," *Sunset*. October, 1992, p. 148.

—*Theodore L. Giese*

Satellite Dish

Taylor Howard, an employee at Stanford University who was well-versed in the usefulness of satellites as relayers of data, is credited with designing the first satellite dish for personal use. Howard's dish, which was placed into operation on September 14, 1976, was made of aluminum mesh and was about 16 feet wide.

Background

A satellite dish is a parabolic television antenna that receives signals from communication satellites in orbit around the earth. Its sole function is to provide the television viewer with a wider variety of channels.

The first communications satellite—*Echo I*—was launched by the United States in 1960, transmitting telephone signals. In 1961 *Relay* began transmitting television signals, and in the same year *Syncom* established itself as the first geosynchronous satellite capable of transmitting signals to one particular section of the earth's surface continuously.

The rapid advances in communication satellite technology were not simultaneously matched by advances in satellite dish use and technology. Television broadcasting began with individual stations that could only serve a limited area. Television networks had to provide their affiliate stations with recordings of programs if they wished to provide nationwide service. Satellite television was not widely available until the 1970s, when cable television stations equipped with satellite dishes received signals that were then sent to subscribers by coaxial cable. By 1976, there were 130 satellite dishes owned by cable companies, and by 1980, every cable television station had at least one satellite dish.

About that time personal satellite dish earth stations were selling for approximately $35,000 per unit. Taylor Howard, an employee at Stanford University who was well-versed in the usefulness of satellites as relayers of data, is credited with designing the first satellite dish for personal use. Howard's dish, which was placed into opera-tion on September 14, 1976, was made of aluminum mesh and was about 16 feet (5 meters) wide. By 1980, 5,000 satellite dishes had been purchased for home use. In 1984 alone 500,000 were installed. Recent reports state that there are 3.7 million owners of home satellite dishes worldwide, and the number will continue to grow.

A typical commercial satellite dish of the 1970s was made of heavy fiberglass, and the dish itself, at its smallest size, had a diameter of about ten feet (three meters). Since then, satellite dish design has shifted toward light-weight, aluminum mesh dishes (similar to Howard's homemade dish), some of which are inexpensive and small (three feet, or one meter, in diameter is typical), with many sections (petals) that can be easily assembled. England, Japan, and Germany, have led the way with direct broadcast TV, which sends signals directly to the viewer's dish, but the United States has yet to do so. This trend would yield smaller, more affordable satellite dishes and regulated satellite programming.

Raw Materials

The basic satellite dish consists of the following materials:

- A parabolic reflector made of fiberglass or metal, usually aluminum, with a protruding steel feed horn and amplifier in its middle.

- A steel actuator that enables the dish to receive signals from more than one satellite.

- A metal (usually aluminum) shroud measuring about 6 to 18 inches (15 to 45 centimeters) in height. It is installed on the dish's circumference perpendicularly to reduce side interference.

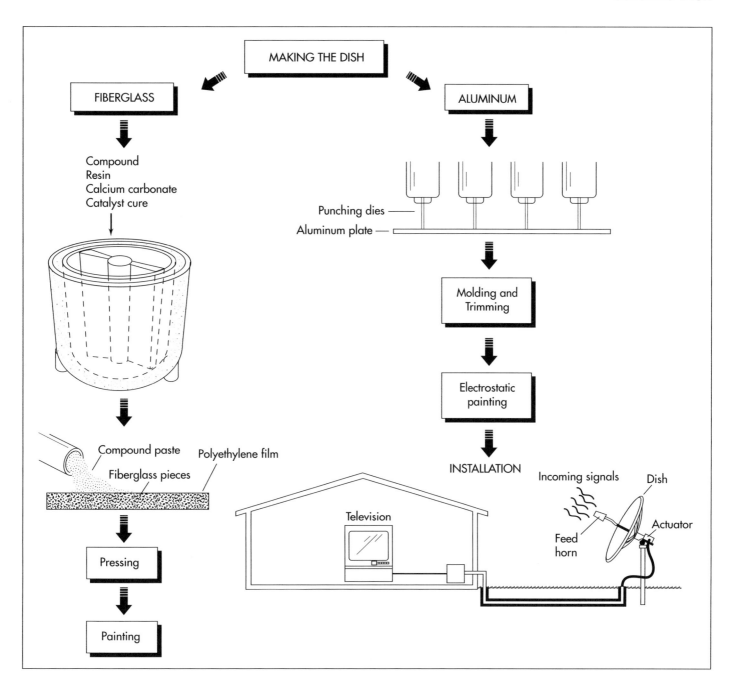

- Cables, most likely made from vinyl tubing and copper wiring.

The Manufacturing Process

1 To make fiberglass suitable for dish manufacture, a sheet molding compound mixture that includes reflective metallic material and ultraviolet scattering compositions is mixed with resin, calcium carbonate, and a catalyst cure. This mixture forms a paste that is poured onto a sheet of polyethylene film that has fiberglass added in chopped form.

The result is a sheet layered with the compound paste, fiberglass, and the polyethylene film.

2 This sheet is then pressed at 89 degrees Fahrenheit (30 degrees Celsius) to mature. To shape the sheet into the desired parabolic shape, it is pressed at high pressure (of 1,400-2,200 metric tons). The dish is then trimmed, cooled, and painted. After the **paint** has dried, the dish is packed for shipment in sturdy boxes.

3 For metallic dishes, the common metal of choice is aluminum. This type of dish can

The manufacture of fiberglass dishes involves first preparing a compound paste that contains resin and calcium carbonate and pouring it onto a polyethylene film with fiberglass bits embedded in it. The material is then pressed into shape. In contrast, aluminum dishes are perforated with punching dies and molded into shape.

Although some current home satellite dishes are very small—only about 3 feet in diameter—manufacturers have begun to introduce even smaller dishes that have a diameter of only 18 inches and can fit on a window sill or a porch.

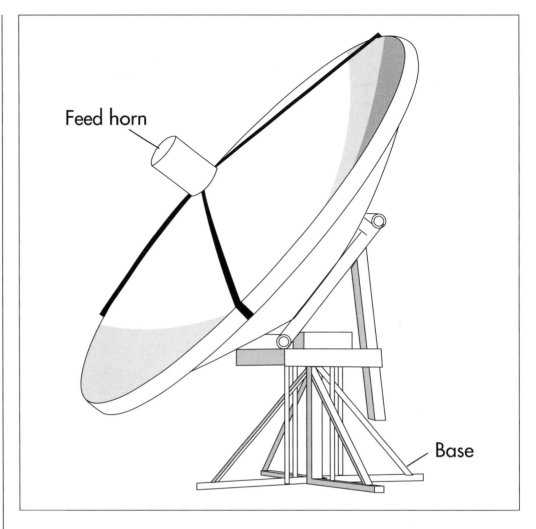

Feed horn

Base

be assembled in sections called petals, or all at once. An aluminum plate is perforated with a punching die, creating tiny holes. The size of these holes are contingent on the manufacturer's preference. Larger holes mean greater loss of the signal, so fairly small holes are selected. Another factor in the selection of hole size is the power of the broadcasting satellite. Newer, more powerful satellites require a hole size that is approximately half that required for older, less powerful satellites. The newly perforated aluminum plate is then heated, stretched over a mold, cooled, and trimmed. A paint powder coating for protection is then applied using an electrostatic charge, in which the paint is given an opposite electrical charge from the plate. The dish or petal is then heated to melt the powder and seal the paint on. The petals are usually sealed together with ribs in the factory.

4 Mesh petals are made from aluminum that is extruded—forced into a die of the proper shape. They are usually joined together on site by sliding them into aluminum ribs that attach to the hub and then securing them with metal pins.

Installation

5 All dishes, when complete, will have the necessary equipment (the feed horn, the amplifier, etc.) installed in the factory. When the dish has been set up at the local dealer, it is transported to the site location on a open trailer. Satellite dishes can be installed either by professionals or by the purchaser, with assistance from the retailer if necessary. The method selected depends upon the size of the dish and the mechanical expertise of the purchaser.

6 An installation site reasonably clear of obstructions not more than 246 feet (75 meters) from the house is selected. Site selection is also contingent on local building codes and the possibility of microwave interference from radio and television towers in the vicinity. Once a site is selected, the base must be installed first. The base of most satellite dishes consists of a **concrete** foundation that extends below the frost line. A clayey soil is excellent, while sandy or rocky soil requires more concrete. A base tube filled with concrete is then set into the concrete foundation.

Some satellite dishes require a slab mount installation, a method considered to be more stable than typical base construction. In some cases, slab mount installation is necessary since the site selected for the placement of the satellite dish is unstable. The slab is generally 1.6 feet (.5 meter) square and 3.2 feet (1 meter) deep. Soil is excavated to the proper depth and the concrete is poured. A triangular steel mount fixture is then embedded into the concrete.

7 Next, the pedestal is attached to either the base tube or the triangular steel mount fixture. The elevation arm is then attached to the pedestal.

Alignment

8 The mounted satellite dish must be aligned in order to point toward the satellite. The angle at which the dish is eventually situated will vary according to which satellite is selected and at what latitude the dish is located. Coaxial cables connect the satellite to the receiver that is located in the house near the television. A trench must be dug for these cables, which are placed into a pipe before being buried.

Quality Control

Satellite dishes for consumer use are not usually required to undergo rigorous tests with set standards, but some parameters are generally met. For example, so that the microwaves are received properly, the surface of the dish should be as smooth as possible and its parabolic shape should be exact. It must also be composed at least partially of metal, otherwise the microwaves will not reflect. If the dish is either mesh or perforated aluminum, the holes must be relatively tiny to minimize loss. Dish size is important; it should match that appropriate to the latitude. The mount should be sturdy, and the dish aligned properly for maximum reception.

Members and joints are tested and compared to the American Steel Construction Institute or the American Aluminum Association methods rules, whichever apply. The satellite dish should be built to withstand high winds, snow, ice, rain, and extreme temperatures.

After the dish is installed, the owner is generally responsible for cleaning it twice a year, more if necessary, tightening and lubricating all bolts once a year, and trimming obstructive weeds and trees from around it. In rare occasions, the owner must adjust the alignment to correct bad reception.

The Future

Satellite dishes will become ubiquitous in upcoming years. More communication satellites will certainly be launched, and the growth explosion in individual satellite dish ownership will continue. One factor that should affect home satellite dish ownership in the near future is the switchover to more powerful satellites that will transmit signals in the K band (12 GHz). Because most of the present satellite dishes accept signals in the C band (3.7 to 4.2 GHz), owners of C band satellite dishes will have to convert them to K band. Researchers and designers are contemplating even smaller dishes that could be placed on a rooftop or outside a window and still function as well as the larger satellite dishes of today.

Some experts see the growth of satellite television as a revolution that is less concerned with crystal clear images of old sitcoms than with the possibilities of two-way communication that universal dish ownership would promote. Satellite television will be used to pay bills, shop, and participate in game shows. It can also be used to communicate over long distances, perhaps to play interactive video games with someone halfway across the continent. Some visionaries see the revolution as the return of one-on-one communication like that of a town meeting. In any case, it is almost certain that satellite television will continue to proliferate in upcoming years.

Manufacturers will continue to make smaller and less costly satellite dishes. Recently, for instance, 18-inch (45.7-centimeter) diameter dishes have been introduced into the market in Japan, Europe, and the United States. These dishes are small enough to fit on a windowsill or a porch railing. Manufacturers are also working on producing a flat-plate dish for satellite signal reception.

Where To Learn More

Books

Baylin, Frank, and Amy Toner. *Satellites Today.* ConSol Network, Inc., 1984.

Clifford, Martin. *The Complete Guide to Satellite TV.* Tab Books, 1984.

Easton, Anthony T. *The Home Satellite TV Book.* Wideview Books, 1982.

Prentiss, Stan. *Satellite Communications.* Tab Books, 1987.

Sutphin, S. E. *Understanding Satellite Television Reception.* Prentice-Hall, 1986.

Traister, John E. *Guide to Satellite Television Installation.* Prentice-Hall, 1987.

Traister, Robert J. *Build a Personal Earth Station for Worldwide Satellite TV Reception.* Tab Books, 1985.

Periodicals

Booth, Stephen A. "Signals from Space," *Popular Mechanics.* April, 1992, p. 60.

Elrich, David. "Satellite TV: It's Worth a Closer Look," *Home Mechanix.* September, 1990, p. 78.

—*Rose Secrest*

Screwdriver

Background

It would be very difficult to find an American household that did not have at least one screwdriver. Perhaps the most ubiquitous of hand tools, the screwdriver has a long genealogy, the result of a complicated manufacturing process. Archimedes is considered to have invented the screw in the third century B.C., though his invention was designed to transfer motion (as in the continuous worm of a worm and gear assembly) rather than to fasten things together.

By the first century B.C., large wooden screws were used in presses for producing **wine** and olive oil, and were turned with spikes stuck into or through a handle that resembled a modern corkscrew used for opening wine bottles, although larger. These were made of wood with a flat rather than a pointed end, and a container to hold the material being pressed.

Metal screws and nuts seem to have been used as fasteners in the fifteenth century, although the heads of these screws were turned with a wrench and not a screwdriver—the screw heads were either square or hexagonal. Screws with slots in their heads were found in armor in the following century, although the design of the tool used to work the screws, the screwdriver, is unknown.

The modern screwdriver descends directly from a flat-bladed bit used in a carpenter's brace circa 1750. Woodworkers were using hand screwdrivers in the early 1800s, and they became more common after 1850, when machines made the automatic production of screws possible. These early screwdrivers were flat throughout the length of their shaft; the current design of a rounded bar that is flattened or shaped only at the working end makes the tool much stronger and takes advantage of the round wire used in its manufacture. The oldest and most common type of screwdriver is the slotted screwdriver, which fits a screw with a single slot in the head. There are perhaps thirty different types of screwdrivers available today in a variety of sizes, all with different purposes and all designed to fit into special screws.

The second most widely used screwdriver, the "Phillips," was invented in the late 1920s by Henry Phillips. Soon after its introduction, the tool posed a dilemma for its user—the head of the driver pulls away from the screw as it is fastened, or "cam-out," leading to stripped screw heads and assemblies that are difficult to take apart. However, cam-out became a virtue; the screws were meant to be driven with a power tool, and the assembler would know that the screw was completely driven when his power tool slid out of the screw head. A screw head that could accept the greater torque (turning power) of a power tool was an advantage over hand-turned, slotted screw heads. Today, manufacturers are producing or gearing up production of Phillips screwdrivers that eliminate cam-out. Possible solutions (although details of some systems are company secrets) focus on the angle of the edges that fit into the Phillips screw, or using a better gripping material to coat or plate the screwdriver tip.

The torx screwdriver, widely used for **automobile** repair and other applications, was designed to take the torque that a Phillips screw can while eliminating the cam-out problem. It has six edges in a star pattern on its flat point, and fits flat into the screw head.

Early screwdrivers were flat throughout the length of their shaft; the current design of a rounded bar that is flattened or shaped only at the working end makes the tool much stronger and takes advantage of the round wire used in its manufacture.

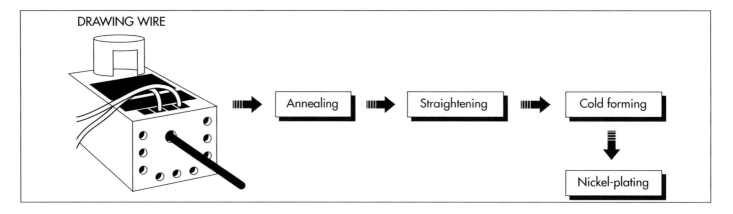

DRAWING WIRE

Annealing → Straightening → Cold forming → Nickel-plating

To make the steel rod, wire is machine-drawn to the appropriate diameter, annealed (heat-treated), straightened, and then cold-formed to the proper shape. The cold forming press cuts the wire to the desired length and forms the tip of the screwdriver and the "wings" that will fit into the handle. The rod is then nickel-plated to give it a protective finish.

It is not unusual to find torx drivers sold in a set with slotted and Phillips screwdrivers.

Other types of screwdrivers have been designed for special uses, and a well-stocked hardware store will have slotted, Phillips, torx, Robertson (a square shaft that fits into a corresponding square cut out in the head of the screw), and other more obscure types of screwdrivers. Some screwdrivers have not found a ready market, such as one that was designed to fit into special screws that have slots both on the top of the screw and on the side of the screw head, with corresponding grippers on the point of the screwdriver. There are so many screwdrivers and types of screws available that even a high quality of design innovation is overcome by consumer resistance to purchasing new types of screwdrivers and corresponding screws.

Raw Materials

The raw materials for most screwdrivers are very basic: steel wire for the bar and plastic (usually cellulose acetate) for the handle. In addition, the steel tips are generally plated with nickel or chromium.

The Manufacturing Process

Making a flat-tip or slotted screwdriver is not very different than making any other configuration. Variations between a flat-tip and a Phillips screwdriver will be discussed later in this entry.

Making the steel bar

1 First, coils of green wire (wire that has not yet been drawn to final size) are delivered to a factory in large coils, some as heavy as

3,000 pounds (1,362 kilograms). The wire is usually about .375 inch (.95 centimeter) in diameter. The wire is then machine-drawn to the diameter necessary for the production run; one adjustable drawing machine can produce any required diameter. In drawing, wire is fed through a die with a reducing aperture until it assumes the proper size.

2 After the wire is drawn, it is annealed (heat treated) to obtain the correct tensile strength in the metal. This process involves baking the wire at a temperature of about 1,350 degrees Fahrenheit (732 degrees Celsius) for 12 hours.

3 Next, the wire is straightened by a string forge and then transferred to a cold forming press, which cuts the wire to the appropriate length and forms the tip of the screwdriver and the "wings" that will fit into the handle. These wings can be seen through a clear or semi-clear plastic handle. The newly formed "bar" (the actual screwdriver without its handle) is then heat treated in an in-line furnace at approximately 1,555 degrees Fahrenheit (846 degrees Celsius). This is a continuous flow process, and as the bars come through the furnace they fall into an oil quench for cooling. The bars are then placed in a draw back oven (450 to 500 degrees Fahrenheit or 232 to 259 degrees Celsius) and baked to a specified hardness.

4 Consumer model screwdrivers are nickel-plated—covered with a protective coating of nickel—before assembly. If the screwdriver is designated for professional use, it is transferred to a hand-grinding department, where the tip is ground to size. The shank is chemically milled and then polished. The screwdriver then goes to a nickel flash bath and is electrically chrome plated.

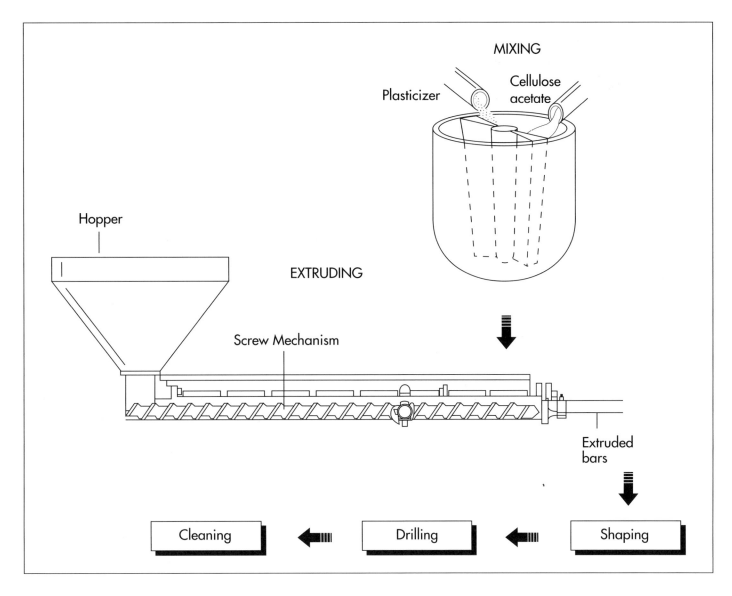

MIXING

Plasticizer

Cellulose acetate

Hopper

EXTRUDING

Screw Mechanism

Extruded bars

Cleaning

Drilling

Shaping

Phillips screwdrivers

5 After the cold forming press (step #3 above) cuts the wire, the screwdriver is sent to a "swage and grind" operation, where dies form blades for the tip from the heated wire. The tool is then ground and the wings are formed.

6 If a professional model is being produced, the bar goes to a tipping operation (an automatic tipping machine that creates the bullet point), and then to a profilator machine (a machine that cuts a "profile"). This latter machine cuts the four grooves or slots on the sides above the point. The wire is then winged, and heat-treated in the same way as the flat-tip screwdriver bars. Consumer model Phillips screwdrivers are nickel plated, while the professional model is polished and nickel/chrome plated.

Handles

7 The handles of a screwdriver are usually made of cellulose acetate; it is delivered to the factory in powder form (cellulose acetate rosin) and then mixed with a liquid plasticizer in a giant blender that holds approximately 1,000 pounds (454 kilograms) of the mixed material. If a colored handle is desired, pigments are added into the blender. The resulting paste, which has the consistency of thick cake batter, then goes to an extruder (a machine that forces a material out through an opening, the way a meat grinder forces out strings of meat), which extrudes a solid piece of cellulose acetate. The cellulose acetate is then cut into small pellets.

8 Next, the pellets are fed into another extruder that extrudes the materials for the handles in bars that are 8 to 10 feet (2.4 to

The plastic handles are made by mixing cellulose acetate with a plasticizer and then extruding the mixture into bar form. After further shaping, the bars are drilled so that the rods can be inserted, cleaned to remove dirt, and dipped in an acetone vapor bath, which melts and smooths the outside of the handle.

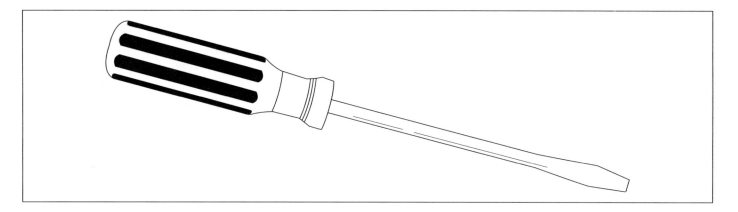

The oldest and most common type of screwdriver is the slotted screwdriver, which fits a screw with a single slot in the head. There are perhaps thirty different types of screwdrivers available today in a variety of sizes, all with different purposes and all designed to fit into special screws.

3 meters) in length. If a two-color handle is desired, a second extruding machine can be attached to the first to extrude a single, two-color rod. The rods are then put into an automatic turning machine, which shapes the handles and cuts them to the final length. A hole is then drilled in the handle where the bar will be inserted.

9 The handles are machine washed and dried to remove grease, oil, and excess scraps from the turning machine and the extruder. Next, the handles are immersed in an acetone vapor bath, which melts and smooths the outside of the handle. The acetone vapor is highly flammable, and this process takes place inside an explosion-proof room.

Assembly

10 The method of final assembly depends on the quality of the tool being produced. Professional models are assembled individually on a horizontal assembly machine that hydraulically forces the bar into the plastic handle. The handles are branded by a hot stamp immediately before going into the assembly machine. This assembly process requires one skilled operator for each machine.

Other models might be assembled on hydraulic presses, three at a time. The least expensive models are assembled six at a time on one machine and placed by robot on a skin card machine that packages the screwdrivers for mass-market sale.

11 Before packaging, the screwdrivers might be fitted with a special handle cover, depending on need. A rubber cap fitted over a screwdriver handle, for example,

might be more comfortable for a professional using his tool five or six hours a day. A large handle with deep grooves might be ideal for some workers, while the home handyman who assembles a lamp or cabinet once every six months may not need or want to pay for the extra comfort.

Quality Control

Consumer Reports magazine found, in 1983 tests, that the type of finish had little effect on the quality of screwdrivers, although most of their tested screwdrivers were plated. Poor-quality plating, on the other hand, might indicate that not enough care was paid to the tool in the manufacturing process. Similarly, poor-quality grinding can lead to rounded edges and corners which will not be as efficient as they could be; a tip that was burned during the grinding process may not be as hard as it should be.

Where To Learn More

Books

Hoffman, E. *Fundamentals of Tool Design.* T/C Publications, 1984.

Pollack, Herman W. *Tool Design.* Prentice Hall, 1988.

Self, Charles R. *Fasten It.* TAB Books, 1984.

Watson, Aldren A. *Hand Tools: Their Ways and Workings.* Portland House, 1982.

Periodicals

Bailey, Jeff. "Does Henry Phillips, Bane of Handymen, Really Rest in Peace?" *Wall Street Journal,* September 15, 1988, p. 4.

"Screwdrivers," *Consumer Reports*. January, 1983, pp. 44-7.

Kinghorn, Bob. "The New Age of Screwdriving," *Family Handyman*. October, 1989, p. 12.

Pierson, John. "Screwdriver Redesign Aims to Lock Out Slips," *Wall Street Journal*. January 22, 1991, pp. 1-2.

Yeaple, Frank. "Zinc's Properties Enhance Hand Tool's Producibility," *Design News*. January 22, 1990, p. 115.

—*Lawrence H. Berlow*

Seismograph

The earliest known device used to detect earthquakes was a Chinese device consisting of a copper cylinder with eight dragon heads positioned around its upper circumference; directly beneath the dragon heads were eight copper frogs. In its mouth, each dragon held a small ball that dropped into the mouth of the frog below it when a weighted rod inside the cylinder was triggered by an earthquake.

Background

Seismographs are instruments designed to detect and measure vibrations within the earth, and the records they produce are known as *seismograms*. Like the many other terms beginning with this prefix, these words derive from the Greek *seismos*, meaning "shock" or "earthquake." Although certain types of seismographs are used for underground surveying, the devices are best known for studying earthquakes.

A seismograph consists of a pendulum mounted on a support base. The pendulum in turn is connected to a recorder, such as an ink pen. When the ground vibrates, the pendulum remains still while the recorder moves, thus creating a record of the earth's movement. A typical seismograph contains 3 pendulums: one to record vertical movement and two to record horizontal movement.

Seismographs evolved from seismoscopes, which can detect the direction of tremors or earthquakes but cannot determine the intensity or the pattern of the vibration. The earliest known device used to detect earthquakes was created by a Chinese scholar, Chang Heng, around A.D. 132. Detailed accounts reveal that it was a beautiful and ingenious apparatus consisting of a richly decorated copper cylinder with eight dragon heads positioned around its upper circumference, facing outwards. Fixed around the lower circumference, directly beneath the dragon heads, were eight copper frogs. In its mouth, each dragon held a small ball that dropped into the mouth of the frog below it when a rod inside the cylinder, flexible and weighted at its upper end, was triggered by an earthquake. The particular frog that captured a fallen ball indicated the general direction of the earthquake.

For over seventeen hundred years the study of earthquakes depended on imprecise instruments such as Chang Heng's. Over the centuries a wide variety of seismoscopes were constructed, many relying on the detection of ripples in a pool of water or liquid mercury. One such device, similar to the frog and dragon mechanism, featured a shallow dish of mercury that would spill into little dishes placed around it when a tremor occurred. Another type of seismoscope, developed during the eighteenth century, consisted of a pendulum suspended from the ceiling and attached to a pointer that dragged in a tray of fine sand, moving when vibrations swayed the pendulum. During the nineteenth century, the first seismometer was constructed; it used various types of pendulums to measure the size of underground vibrations.

The first true seismograph may have been a complex mechanism designed by the Italian scientist Luigi Palmieri in 1855. This machine used tubes filled with mercury and fitted with electrical contacts and floats. When tremors disturbed the mercury, the electrical contacts concurrently stopped a clock and triggered a device that recorded the movements of the floats, roughly indicating both the time and the intensity of the earthquake. The first accurate seismographs were developed in Japan in 1880 by the British geologist John Milne, often known as the father of seismology. Together with fellow expatriate scientists James Alfred Ewing and Thomas Gray, Milne invented many different seismological devices, one of which was the horizontal pendulum seismograph. This sophisticated instrument consisted of a weighted rod that, when disturbed by tremors, shifted a slitted plate. The plate's movement permitted a reflected light to shine through the slit, as well as through another stationary slit below it. Falling onto light-sensitive paper, the light then inscribed a record of the tremor. Today most seismographs still rely on the basic designs introduced by Milne and his associates, and scientists continue to evaluate tremors by studying the movement of the earth relative to the movement of a pendulum.

The first electromagnetic seismograph was invented in 1906 by a Russian Prince, Boris Golitsyn, who adapted the principle of electromagnetic induction developed by the English physicist Michael Faraday during the nineteenth century. Faraday's law of induction postulated that changes in magnetic intensity could be used to generate electric currents. Incorporating this precept, Golitsyn built a machine in which tremors cause a coil to move through magnetic fields, thereby producing an electrical current which is fed into a galvanometer, a device that measures and directs the current. The current then fluctuates a mirror similar to the one that directed the light in Milne's apparatus. The advantage of this electronic system is that the recorder can be set up in a convenient place such as a laboratory, while the seismograph itself can be installed in a remote location.

During the twentieth century, the Nuclear Test Detection Program has made modern seismology possible. Despite the real danger of earthquakes, seismology could not command a large number of seismographs until the threat of subterranean nuclear explosions prompted the establishment of the World-Wide Standardized Seismograph Network (WWSSN) in 1960. The Network set up 120 seismographs in 60 countries, and, under its auspices, seismographs became much more sophisticated. Developed after World War II, the Press-Ewing seismograph enabled researchers to record so-called long period seismic waves, vibrations that travel long distances at relatively slow speeds. This seismograph uses a pendulum like that used in the Milne model, but replaces the pivot supporting the rod with an elastic wire to reduce friction. Other post-war innovations included atomic clocks to make timings more accurate, and digital readouts that could be fed into a computer. However, the most important

```
┌─────────────────────┐
│   Choosing site     │
└─────────────────────┘
          ▼
┌─────────────────────┐
│     Assembly        │
└─────────────────────┘
          ▼
┌─────────────────────┐
│ Making component parts │
└─────────────────────┘
          ▼
┌──────────────────────────────┐
│ Attaching pendulum to spring or wire │
└──────────────────────────────┘
          ▼
┌──────────────────────────────┐
│ Suspending pendulum between coils │
└──────────────────────────────┘
          ▼
┌─────────────────────┐
│  Wiring coils to PCBs │
└─────────────────────┘
          ▼
┌──────────────────────────┐
│ Connecting unit to recorder │
└──────────────────────────┘
          ▼
┌─────────────────────┐
│   Installation      │
└─────────────────────┘
```

This flow chart shows the steps involved in seismograph manufacture and installation. The main material used is aluminum, followed by normal electrical equipment composed of copper, steel, glass, and plastic. The basic unit comprises a pendulum inside an airtight container that is attached by a hinge and a wire (for horizontal units) or a spring (for vertical units) to a supporting frame set firmly in the ground.

development during modern times has been the implementation of seismograph arrays. These arrays, some consisting of hundreds of seismographs, are linked to a single central recorder. By comparing the discrete seismograms produced by various stations, researchers can determine the earthquake's epicenter (the point on the earth's surface directly above the origin of the quake).

Today, three types of seismographs are used in earthquake research, each with a period corresponding to the scale of the vibrations it will measure (the period is the length of time a pendulum requires to complete one full oscillation). Short-period seismographs are used to study primary and secondary vibrations, the fastest-moving seismic waves. Because these waves move so quickly, the short-period seismograph takes less than a second to complete one full oscillation; it also magnifies the resulting seismograms so that scientists can perceive the pattern of the earth's swift motions. The pendulums in long (intermediate) period seismographs generally take up to twenty seconds to oscillate, and they are used to measure slower-moving waves such as Love and Rayleigh waves, which follow primary and secondary waves. The WWSSN currently uses this type of instrument. The seismographs whose pendulums have the longest periods are called *ultra-long* or *broad-band* instruments. Broad-band seismographs are used increasingly often to develop a more comprehensive understanding of global vibrations.

Raw Materials

The components of a seismograph are standard. The most important material is aluminum, followed by normal electrical equipment composed of copper, steel, glass, and plastic. A modern seismograph consists of one or more seismometers that measure the vibrations of the earth. A seismometer comprises a pendulum (an inert mass) inside an airtight container that is attached by a hinge and a wire (for horizontal units) or a spring (for vertical units) to a supporting frame set firmly in the ground. One or more electric coils is attached to the pendulum and placed within the field of a magnet. Even miniscule movements of the coil will generate electrical signals that are then fed into an amplifier and a filter and stored in computer memory for later printing. A less sophisticated seismograph will have either a **mirror** that shines light onto light-sensitive paper (as in Milne's seismograph), a pen that writes with quick-drying ink upon a roll of paper, or a heat pen that marks thermal paper.

Design

The demand for earthquake seismographs is not that high; it can be met by a few manufacturers who design custom-made seismographs to meet the needs of particular researchers. Thus, while the basic compo-

nents of the seismograph are standard, certain features can be adapted to serve specific purposes. For instance, someone might need a more sensitive instrument to study seismic events thousands of miles away. Another seismologist might select an instrument whose pendulum has a short period of only a few seconds so as to observe the earliest tremors of an earthquake. For underwater studies, the seismograph would have to be submersible.

The Manufacturing Process

Choosing a site

1 A site might interest a seismologist for a number of reasons. The most obvious one is that the region is earthquake-prone, perhaps because it is adjacent to a fault or fracture in the earth's crust. Such fractures dislodge one of the blocks of earth adjoining them, causing the block to shift higher, lower, or horizontally parallel to the fault, and leaving the area vulnerable to further instability. A seismograph might also be installed in a region currently without one, so that seismologists can gather data for a more complete picture of the area.

2 Although some seismographs are placed in university or museum basements for educational purposes, the ideal location for earthquake research would be more remote. To record the earth's seismic movements more accurately, a seismograph should be placed where traffic and other vibrations are minimal. In some cases, an unused tunnel can be appropriated. Other times, a natural underground cavern is available. Seismological researchers may even choose to dig a well and place the instrument inside if no other underground hole exists where a seismograph is deemed desirable. An above-ground seismograph is also possible, but it must rest above a solid rock foundation.

Assembling the seismometer unit

3 At a specialized factory the component parts of the seismograph are assembled and prepared for shipment. First, the pendulum is attached to either a soft spring (if it's a vertical unit) or a wire (if it's a horizontal unit) and suspended within a cylinder

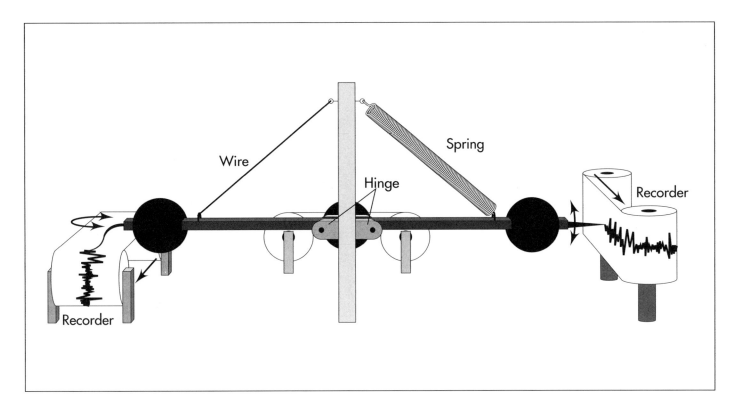

between electric coils. Next, the coils are wired to printed circuit boards and placed inside the seismograph body. The whole unit can in turn be connected to a digital audio tape recorder, which receives the current generated by the coils and transferred to the circuit boards. If the data recording equipment consists of more traditional equipment, such as a roll of paper and a pen, these are now attached to the unit. Depending on the final destination, the seismograph is shipped by truck or plane in a cushioned crate by transporters experienced in moving delicate electronic equipment.

Installing the seismometer unit

4 A seismograph intended for educational purposes might be bolted into the **concrete** floor of a basement, but research seismographs are best situated far from the inevitable vibrations of a building. They are either installed directly onto the bedrock in instances where great precision is required, or in a bed of concrete. In both cases, earth is removed and the ground leveled. In the second instance, a bed of concrete is poured and allowed to set.

5 After the base has been prepared, the seismometer unit is bolted into place. In some instances where great sensitivity is required, it will be housed in a vault where the temperature and humidity are controlled. The seismometer unit is usually installed in the chosen field, cavern, or vault, while the amplifiers, filters, and recording equipment are housed separately.

6 In modern seismology, it is typical to have several seismometer units arrayed at a distance from one another. Each seismometer unit sends signals to a central location, where the data can be printed out and studied. The signals may be broadcast from an antenna built into the unit, or, in more sophisticated units, beamed up to a satellite.

Quality Control

Seismographs are designed to withstand the elements. They are waterproof and dust-proof, and many are designed to function despite extreme temperatures and high humidity, depending on where they will be installed. Despite their sensitivity and protection requirements, many seismographs have been known to last 30 years. Quality control workers in the factory check the design and the final product to see if they meet the customer's demands. All parts are checked for tolerance and fit, and the seismograph is tested to see if it works properly. In addition, most seismographs have built-in testing devices so that they can be tested after

While horizontal seismometers contain a pendulum attached to a wire, vertical units use a spring instead. When the ground vibrates during an earthquake, the pendulum remains still while the recorder moves, thus creating a record of the earth's movement.

Some recorders consist of a coil that generates an electrial signal, which in turn is stored in computer memory for later printing. A less sophisticated seismograph will have either a mirror that shines light onto light-sensitive paper, a pen that writes with quick-drying ink upon a roll of paper, or a heat pen that marks thermal paper.

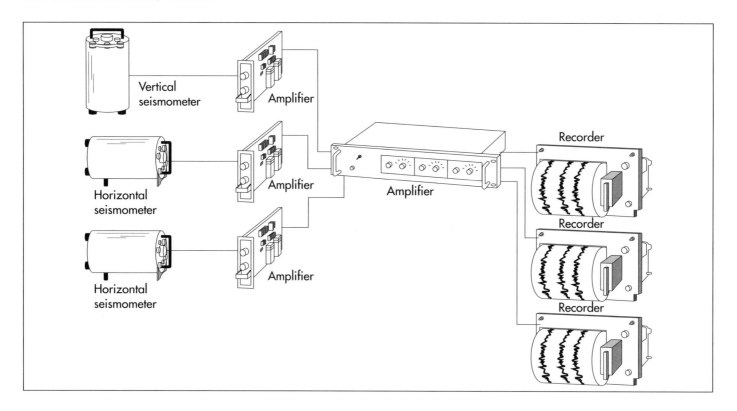

A typical seismograph contains 3 pendulums: one to record vertical movement and two to record horizontal movement. The seismometer unit is usually installed in a field, cavern, or vault, while the amplifiers and recording equipment are housed separately.

being installed and before being put to work. Qualified computer programmers also test the software for bugs before shipment. While sensitivity and accuracy are important, timing is also critical, particularly in earthquake prediction. Most modern seismographs are connected to an atomic clock that is calibrated to Universal Time (formerly called Greenwich Time), thus insuring highly accurate information that all researchers can understand.

Another critical aspect of quality control with modern seismographs is minimizing human error. While earlier seismographs were simple, and practically anyone could learn how to use them, contemporary seismographs are precise, sensitive devices that are complex and difficult to use. Today, seismograph researchers and workers must be trained by engineers and scientists from the manufacturing facility if they are not already qualified engineers and scientists themselves. They must learn how to run and maintain the seismograph as well as all auxiliary equipment such as a computer.

The Future

Seismology is best known for the study of earthquakes. Its emphasis has not been on theoretical study of the earth's structure, but rather on predicting and lessening the impact of earthquakes in vulnerable regions. Study of the earth's interior has been directed towards searching for oil deposits, testing for ground instabilities before construction, and tracking down subterranean nuclear explosions. Earthquake prediction, however, is foremost. If researchers can determine beforehand that a quake will take place, precautions such as increasing hospital and safety personnel can be scheduled. The first official earthquake prediction issued by the United States government took place only in 1985. Hence, earthquake prediction is in its infancy. Recent major earthquakes such as the one that occurred in San Francisco in 1989 have intensified study of the San Andreas fault. Currently, a team of seismologists is studying the Parkfield segment of that fault to determine if they can predict a minor earthquake. The data from this attempt could come in handy to predict major earthquakes in more heavily populated areas. Other developments include more sensitive and more durable seismographs that can record both long and short period waves. One earth scientist believes that an earthquake warning system could be set up. Such a system would require a seismograph to pick up the vibrations, a computer to interpret them as an imminent earthquake, and a communication system to warn emergency personnel in time. Some experts envision large arrays of seismographs in earthquake-prone areas, where individual seismograph owners could collect and transmit data to seismologists.

Where To Learn More

Books

Bolt, Bruce A. *Earthquakes: A Primer*. W. H. Freeman and Company, 1978.

Eiby, George A. *Earthquakes*. Van Nostrand Reinhold, 1980.

Golden, Frederic. *The Trembling Earth: Probing and Predicting Quakes*. Charles Scribner's Sons, 1983.

Iacopi, Robert. *Earthquake Country*. Lane Books, 1971.

Vogt, Gregory. *Predicting Earthquakes*. Franklin Watts, 1989.

Walker, Bruce. *Earthquake*. Time-Life Books, 1982.

Periodicals

Lindh, Allan G. "Earthquake Prediction Comes of Age," *Technology Review*. February/March 1990, pp. 42-51.

"[Interview with] Allan Lindh," *Omni*. March, 1991, pp. 68-71.

"The Amateur Scientist," *Scientific American*. July, 1957, pp. 152-162.

Van Dam, Laura. "Reducing Disasters During Earthquakes," *Technology Review*. February/March 1990, pp. 12-13.

—*Rose Secrest*

Shaving Cream

Soap was used for shaving through the early 1800s. In 1840, a concentrated soap that foamed was sold in tablets by Vroom and Fowler, whose Walnut Oil Military Shaving Soap was probably the first soap made especially for shaving.

Background

Shaving cream is a substance applied to the skin to facilitate removal of hair. Shaving cream softens and moistens the skin and the hair, thus making shaving more comfortable and contributing to smoother skin. The advantages of using shaving cream, rather than soap, oil, or just water, are many. Shaving with a modern bar of soap approximates shaving with cream but doesn't provide all of the benefits: soap is only one element of many in a modern shaving preparation.

According to Burma Shave chronicler Frank Rowsome, Jr., modern shaving cream began with Burma Shave, which achieved high sales volume almost immediately after it was introduced. Prior to that time, lather was produced from a bar, and was basically another form of soap.

Manufacturing soap itself is an ancient craft—the word comes from the Old English word *sape*. By the seventh century, Italian soapmakers were organized in a guild, and, in the next century, the Holy Roman Emperor Charlemagne recognized soapmakers as craftsman. In the fourteenth and fifteenth centuries soap was made at Savona, Italy. The modern French, Spanish and German words for soap (*savon, jabon,* and *seife,* respectively) are cognates of the name of that town.

The early American settlers manufactured soap at home, using a method which called for mixing and heating animal fat with lye in a pot set over a fire, usually outdoors. This "open kettle" method of soap making was popular for years. Later adapted for large scale production, its use continued through the first half of the twentieth century.

By the eighteenth century, soap makers realized that they could enhance their product by improving the quality of the fat and the purity of the lye they used. Castile soap, made in Spain and still available today, soon achieved eminence as a face soap because of its smoothness and quality. Castile soap originally used olive oil rather than animal fat, and the modern version uses other fats and oils in addition to olive oil.

Although Americans continued to make their own soap at home for many years, they also began to manufacture soap commercially during the late seventeenth and early eighteenth centuries. Because they utilized similar materials and methods, soap makers were frequently in partnership with **candle** and tallow makers. The first soap maker to render (purify by melting) fats at his own operation was William Colgate, who had learned his trade in the early 1800s in New York City. The company that today bears his name is a major producer of soap and other cosmetic preparations. In the nineteenth century storekeepers purchased soap from manufacturers in large blocks, from which their customers in turn cut smaller chunks. Jesse Oakley of Newburgh, New York, became the first manufacturer to sell wrapped soap in a cake form that was a good size for home use.

Soap was used for shaving through the early 1800s. In 1840, a concentrated soap that foamed was sold in tablets by Vroom and Fowler, whose Walnut Oil Military Shaving Soap was probably the first soap made especially for shaving. A century later, as the United States entered World War II, animal fats of relatively uncontrolled type and quality were still being used to make soap. To help supply American troops with soap,

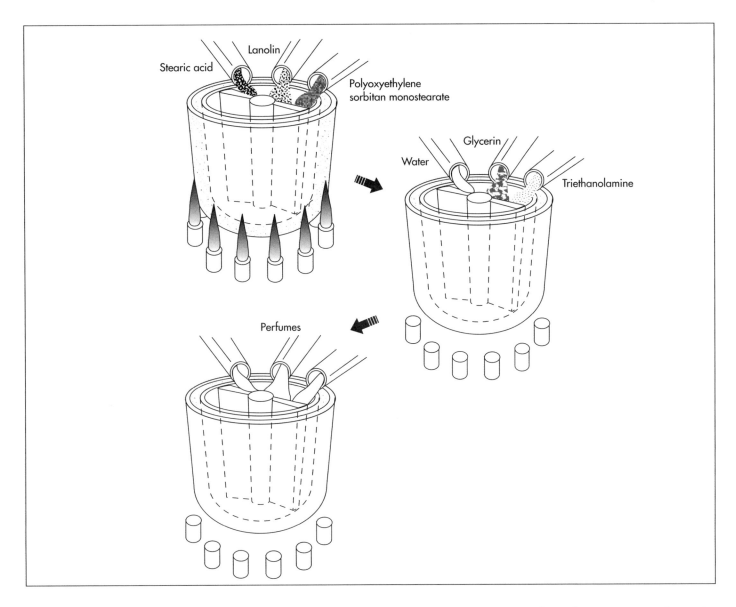

Stearic acid
Lanolin
Polyoxyethylene
sorbitan monostearate

Water
Glycerin
Triethanolamine

Perfumes

women were urged to save cans of cooking fat, and then bring them to local butchers who collected and delivered the fat to soap manufacturers. Because contaminants were inevitable in ingredients collected so haphazardly, the soap makers had to heat, strain, and reheat the fats—a process both inefficient and expensive. However, by the end of the war, mounting questions about purity and consistency led to the creation of the modern, regulated soap and cosmetic industry.

In addition to raising concerns about the quality of soap, World War II contributed to the invention of the spray can. Aerosol containers were first invented during the war as a device for dealing with insects carrying malaria and other diseases. Initially assigned to the Secretary of Agriculture, the patent for this "bug bomb" was released to American

industry after the war. When the first aerosol shaving cream appeared in 1950, it captured almost one fifth of the market for shaving preparations within a short time. Today, aerosol preparations dominate the shaving cream market.

Raw Materials

The goal of any shaving preparation is to wet and soften the hair to be shaved, cushion the effect of the razor, and provide a residual film to soothe the skin. This film should be of the proper pH value: neither excessively alkaline nor overly acidic, it should correspond to the skin's pH level.

Many manufacturers would have us believe that the recipes for shaving cream are carefully guarded secrets. However, the secrecy

In shaving cream manufacture, the fatty or oily materials are first combined and heated in a jacketed kettle, and then most of the remaining ingredients are added. The mixing continues while the mass cools, and then any desired perfumes are added.

revolves mostly around the quantities in which standard ingredients are used, and the choice of substitutes for the few ingredients that are variable. By law, ingredients are listed right on the container, except for perfumes. Actual recipes are easily found in industrial chemistry textbooks available at many libraries. A standard recipe contains approximately 8.2 percent stearic acid, 3.7 percent triethanolamine, .5 percent lanolin, 2 percent glycerin, 6 percent polyoxyethylene sorbitan monostearate, and 79.6 percent water.

Two major ingredients in this formula are common in many of today's preparations. Stearic acid is one of the main ingredients in soap making, and triethanolamine is a surfactant, or surface-acting agent, which does the job of soap, albeit much better. While one end of a surfactant molecule attracts dirt and grease, the other end attracts water. Lanolin and polyoxyethylene sorbitan monostearate are both emulsifiers which hold water to the skin, while glycerin, a solvent and an emollient, renders skin softer and more supple.

Common substitutes for the third, fourth, and fifth ingredients listed above include laureth 23 and lauryl sulfate (both sudsing and foaming agents), waxes, cocamides (which cleanse and aid foaming), and lanolin derivatives (emulsifiers). Most ingredients are powdered or flaked, although lanolin, lanolin derivatives, and cocamides are liquids.

The differences between one brand of shaving cream and another amount to adjustments in the proportions of ingredients and in the processing method (longer or shorter heating times, storage of the finished product, and so on), and choice of ingredients such as emulsifiers or perfumes. Also important is the choice of aerosol propellant. Some mixtures contain more than one propellant; most common are butane, isobutane, and propane. Though the wide range of choices for ingredients is well known, the exact combinations of ingredients represent the highest level of "magic" in modern chemistry.

The Manufacturing Process

The modern manufacture of shaving cream is a carefully controlled process. Although carried out on a large scale, its manufacture resembles a laboratory procedure involving only small quantities of ingredients. There are two main phases to the manufacturing process.

1 In the first phase, the fatty or oily portions of the formula—stearic acid, lanolin, and polyoxyethylene sorbitan monostearate—are heated in a jacketed kettle to a temperature of approximately 179 to 188 degrees Fahrenheit (80 to 85 degrees Celsius). The jacketed kettle, which can hold as little as 300 gallons or as much as 10,000 gallons, resembles a double boiler: one container, placed inside another, is heated when steam is circulated through the outer container. Inside the interior kettle are blades that revolve to mix the oils as they are heated.

2 After the first group of ingredients has turned smooth over a period of roughly 40 minutes, the steam is released from the outer container of the kettle, and the mixture is allowed to cool.

3 The second phase of manufacture begins when the mixture has cooled to about 152 degrees Fahrenheit (65 degrees Celsius). Most of the remaining ingredients—water, glycerin, and triethanolamine—are added now, and mixing continues for approximately 40 minutes.

4 When the mixture reaches a temperature of 125 to 134 degrees Fahrenheit (50 to 55 degrees Celsius), perfumes or other scents can be added. Because perfumes consist primarily of highly volatile oils, they would evaporate if added when the blend was still warm. The formulas for perfumes, which can contain more than 200 different ingredients, come closer to being trade secrets than information about shaving cream itself (though textbook and handbook formulas for perfume are not hard to come by). In recognition of this, manufacturers do not have to disclose information about fragrances.

5 The mixture, still being stirred, is allowed to cool further, until it reaches a temperature of 89 degrees Fahrenheit (30 degrees Celsius). Now a thickening white mass of highly viscous liquid, it is forced through a silk or **stainless steel** screen to eliminate any lumps that may have formed in the mixing

process, and to catch the rare impurity or foreign object such as a small wood splinter.

6 If this particular mixture is designated for tube packaging, it is now placed in a tube and fitted with a cap. After the bottom of the tube has been crimped, the product is ready for shipment and stocking on a store shelf.

7 When the desired product is an aerosol spray, the shaving cream is poured into an open can. Next a valve and a cover are fitted onto the can and forced downward to form a seal. Propellant is then forced into the can through the valve. Most shaving preparations contain between four and five percent propellant; a larger amount would dry the shaving cream as it came out of the can, rendering it unusable. A small amount of material is intentionally released (purged) to relieve excess pressure, and the can is tested in water to make sure that the valve is holding tightly. The can is now ready to be shipped.

Quality Control

Today's soaps, shaving creams, and lotions are all manufactured under strict quality control, and regulated by various federal agencies including the Food and Drug Administration (FDA). Some states have their own regulatory agencies, though state agencies are more likely to focus on environmental concerns than product safety. Batches of shaving cream are examined and analyzed both at the manufacturing site and in the laboratory. Individual containers of shaving preparations are coded so that a manufacturer knows exactly which batch any given can or tube came from, and can identify its distribution history.

A manufacturer of shaving cream needs to be certain that each batch meets quality standards. Among the things tested for are pH value (the acidity or alkalinity of the product), the height of the foam when sprayed, and its absorption rate (spray the foam on a piece of paper—how long does it take till the bottom of the paper shows moisture?).

Water quality must also be checked carefully. Most manufacturers make sure the water they use is pure by exposing the water to ultraviolet light or using distilled water. Having a microbiologist on site to test the water and the final product is common in the industry.

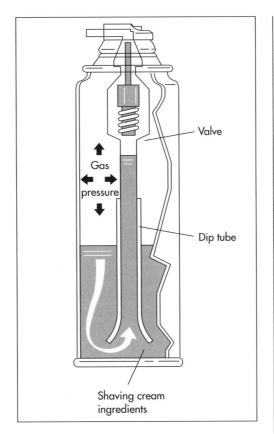

Valve

Gas pressure

Dip tube

Shaving cream ingredients

In a typical aerosol can, the shaving cream ingredients occupy only a small portion of the can. The propellant or gas occupies 4 to 5 percent of the can; a larger amount would dry the shaving cream as it came out of the can, rendering it unusable.

Where To Learn More

Books

DeNavarre, M. G. *The Chemistry and Manufacture of Cosmetics.* Van Nostrand, 1962.

Lubowe, Irwin I. *Cosmetics and the Skin.* Reinhold Publishing Corp., 1964.

Men's Shaving Products Market. Frost & Sullivan, 1990.

Winter, Ruth. *A Consumer's Dictionary of Cosmetic Ingredients,* Crown, 1989.

Periodicals

Brooks, Geoffrey J. and Fred Burmeister. "Preshave and Aftershave Products." *Cosmetics and Toiletries.* April, 1990, pp. 67-69.

"Creams and Lotions Formulary." *Cosmetics and Toiletries.* November, 1986, pp. 139-70.

"Deodorants, Antiperspirants and Shaving Products Formulary." *Cosmetics and Toiletries.* April, 1990, pp. 75-87.

—*Lawrence H. Berlow*

Soda Bottle

PET was developed in 1941, but it wasn't until the early 1970s that the plastic soda bottle became a reality. Nathaniel C. Wyeth, son of well-known painter N. C. Wyeth and an engineer for the Du Pont Corporation, finally developed a usable bottle after much experimentation. Wyeth's crucial discovery was a way to improve the blow-molding technique of making plastic bottles.

Background

The soda bottle so common today is made of polyethylene terephthalate (PET), a strong yet lightweight plastic. PET is used to make many products, such as polyester fabric, cable wraps, films, transformer insulation, generator parts, and packaging. It makes up 6.4 percent of all packaging and 14 percent of all plastic containers, including the popular soft drink bottle. Accounting for 43 percent of those sold, PET is the most widely used soft drink container. Aluminum, a close second, is 34 percent, while glass, which used to be 100 percent of the bottles, is only a small percentage of those sold today.

Plastics were first made in the 1800s from natural substances that were characterized by having chains of molecules. When these substances were combined with other chemicals in the laboratory, they formed products of a plastic nature. While hailed as a revolutionary invention, early plastics had their share of problems, such as flammability and brittleness. Polyesters, the group of plastics to which PET belongs, were first developed in 1833, but these were mostly used in liquid varnishes, a far cry from the solid, versatile form they took later.

Purely synthetic plastics that were a vast improvement on earlier plastics arrived in the early 1900s, yet they still had limited applications. Experimentation continued, with most of the hundreds of new plastics created over the next several decades failing commercially. PET was developed in 1941, but it wasn't until the early 1970s that the plastic soda bottle became a reality. Nathaniel C. Wyeth, son of well-known painter N. C. Wyeth and an engineer for the Du Pont Cor-

poration, finally developed a usable bottle after much experimentation.

Wyeth's crucial discovery was a way to improve the blow-molding technique of making plastic bottles. Blow molding is ancient, having been used in glass-making technology for approximately two thousand years. Making plastic bottles by blow molding didn't happen until suitable plastics were developed around 1940, but production of these bottles was limited because of inconsistent wall thickness, irregular bottle necks, and difficulty in trimming the finished product. Wyeth's invention of stretch blow molding in 1973 solved these problems, yielding a strong, lightweight, flexible bottle.

The overwhelming success of PET soda bottles—in 1991, more than eight billion bottles were manufactured in the U.S.—has resulted in a disposal problem, but recycling of the bottles is growing, and manufacturers are finding new ways to use recycled PET.

Raw Materials

PET is a polymer, a substance consisting of a chain of repeating organic molecules with great molecular weight. Like most plastics, PET is ultimately derived from petroleum hydrocarbons. It is created by a reaction between terephthalic acid ($C_8H_6O_4$) and ethylene glycol ($C_2H_6O_2$).

Terephthalic acid is an acid formed by the oxidation of para-xylene (C_8H_{10}), an aromatic hydrocarbon, using just air or nitric acid. Para-xylene is derived from coal tar and petroleum using fractional distillation, a process that utilizes the different boiling points of compounds to cause them to "fall out" at different points of the process.

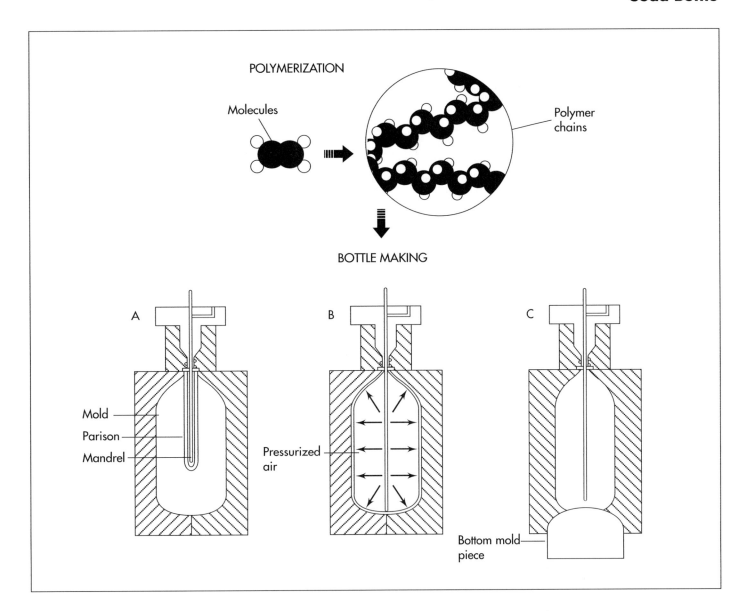

POLYMERIZATION

Molecules

Polymer chains

BOTTLE MAKING

A

B

C

Mold
Parison
Mandrel

Pressurized air

Bottom mold piece

Ethylene glycol is derived from ethylene (C_2H_4) indirectly through ethylene oxide (C_2H_4O), a substance also found in antifreeze. Ethylene is a gaseous hydrocarbon that is present in petroleum and natural gas, but is usually derived industrially by heating ethane or an ethane-propane mixture.

The Manufacturing Process

Polymerization

1 Before the bottles can be made, the PET itself must be manufactured, or polymerized. In polymerization, smaller molecules are combined to form larger substances. To make PET, terephthalic acid is first combined with methanol (CH_3OH). This reaction yields dimethyl terephthalate and water.

Next, the dimethyl terephthalate is combined with an excess of ethylene glycol at 305 degrees Fahrenheit (150 degrees Celsius) to yield another substance, bis 2-hydroxyethyl terephthalate and methanol.

2 The final step of polymerization involves the condensation polymerization of the bis 2-hydroxyethyl terephthalate. In this process, a polymer is formed while another molecule is released, or "falls out." The condensation polymerization of bis 2-hydroxyethyl terephthalate is carried out in a vacuum at 530 degrees Fahrenheit (275 degrees Celsius) and results in chains of PET and ethylene glycol (see step #1 above); the latter substance is continuously removed during polymerization and used to make more PET. After the PET mixture reaches the required viscosity (thickness), it is cooled to avoid

In plastic soda bottle manufacture, the plastic—polyethylene terephthalate (PET)—is first polymerized, which involves creating long strings of molecules. Once the plastic is prepared, it undergoes stretch blow molding. In this process, a long tube (parison) of PET is put into a mold, and a steel rod (mandrel) is inserted into it. Next, highly pressurized air shoots through the mandrel and forces the parison against the walls of the mold. A separate bottom piece is inserted into the mold to shape the bottle so that it can stand on a flat surface.

degradation and discoloration. Later, it can be reheated for its various uses.

Bottle-making

3 PET beverage bottles are made using a process known as *stretch blow molding* (also called *orientation blow molding*). First, PET pellets are injection molded—heated and put into a mold—into a thin walled tube of plastic, called a *parison*. The parison is then cooled and cut to the proper length.

4 Next, the parison tube is re-heated and placed into another mold, which is shaped like a soda bottle, complete with screwtop. A steel rod (a mandrel) is slid into the parison. Highly pressurized air then shoots through the mandrel and fills the parison, pressing it against the inside walls of the mold. The pressure of the air stretches the plastic both radially ("out") and axially ("down"). The combination of high temperature and stretching in the desired direction causes the molecules to polarize, line up and essentially crystallize to produce a bottle of superior strength. The entire procedure must be done quickly, and the plastic must be pressed firmly against the wall, or the bottle will come out misshapen. In order to give the bottom of the bottle its proper concave shape—so that it can stand upright—a separate bottom piece is attached to the mold during the blowing process.

5 The mold must then be cooled. Different cooling methods are used. Water in pipes may flow around the mold, or liquid carbon dioxide, highly pressurized moist air, or room air is shot into the bottle to cool it more directly. The procedure is preferably done quickly, to set the bottle before creep (flow) occurs.

6 The bottle is then removed from the mold. In mass production, small bottles are formed continuously in a string of attached bottles that are separated and trimmed. Other trimming must be done wherever the plastic leaked through the cracks of the mold (like the way pancake batter does when squeezed in a waffle maker). Ten to 25 percent of the plastic is lost this way, but it can be reused.

7 Some soft drink producers make their own bottles, but usually finished bottles

are sent from specialty manufacturers to soft drink companies in trucks. Plastic is cheap to transport because it is light. Accessories such as lids and labels are manufactured separately. Occasionally, the plastic bottle manufacturer will put labels supplied by the soft drink company on the bottles before shipping them.

Quality Control

Polymerization is a delicate reaction that is difficult to regulate once the conditions are set and the process is set into motion. All molecules produced during the reaction, some of which might be side effects and impurities, remain in the finished product. Once the reaction gets going, it's impossible to stop it at mid-point and remove impurities, and it is also difficult and expensive to eliminate unwanted products when the reaction is complete. Purifying polymers is an expensive process, and quality is hard to determine. Variations in the polymerization process could make changes that are undetectable in routine control tests.

The polymerization of terephthalic acid and ethylene glycol can yield two impurities: diethylene glycol and acetaldehyde. The amount of diethylene glycol is kept to a minimum, so that PET's final properties are not affected. Acetaldehyde, which is formed during the polymerization as well as during the production of the bottle, will give a funny taste to the soft drink if it occurs in large enough amounts. By using optimum injection-molding techniques that expose the polymer to heat for a short time, very low concentrations of acetaldehyde appear and the taste of the beverage will be unaffected.

Testing is performed on those specific characteristics of PET that make it perfect for beverage bottles. Numerous standards and tests have been developed for plastics over the years. For instance, PET must be shatterproof under normal conditions, so bottles undergo impact resistance tests that involve dropping them from a specific height and hitting them with a specified force. Also, the bottle must hold its shape as well as resist pressure while stacked, so resistance to creep is measured by testing for deformity under pressure. In addition, soft drinks contain carbon dioxide; that's what gives them their fizz. If carbon dioxide were able to escape through the bottle's plastic walls, most beverages bought would have already gone flat. Hence, the bottle's permeability to carbon dioxide is tested. Even its transparency and gloss are tested. All tests aim for consistency of size, shape, and other factors.

Recycling

A large number of the billions of PET bottles produced every year are thrown away, producing a serious environmental concern. Action has already been taken to stem the waste flow, mainly in the area of recycling. Only aluminum fetches a higher price at the recycling center than PET, so, at a one to two pecent recovery rate, PET is the most extensively recycled plastic. Products made from recycled PET bottles include carpeting, **concrete**, insulation, and **automobile** parts. Still, it wasn't until 1991 that the first PET soda bottle using recycled PET appeared. Consisting of 25 percent recycled PET, the bottle was introduced by Coca-Cola and Hoechst Celanese Corporation for use in North Carolina. By 1992, this bottle was being used in 14 other states, and other manufacturers (such as Pepsi, in partnership with Constar International Inc.) had produced a similar bottle.

Despite PET's high recycling rate compared to other plastics, many companies and officials want to make it even higher. Current plans are to look into PET incineration, in which it is claimed that, if done properly, the products of complete combustion are merely carbon dioxide and water. Current goals of state and federal governments are that 25 to 50 percent of PET be recycled, that recycling of PET be made available to one-half of the United States population, and that 4000 curbside recycling programs be implemented in the near future. In 1990, according to the National Association for Plastic Container Recovery, there were 577 curbside programs for PET.

Where To Learn More

Books

Beck, Ronald D. *Plastic Product Design.* Van Nostrand Reinhold, 1970.

Kaufman, Morris. *Giant Molecules: The Technology of Plastics, Fibers, and Rubber.* Doubleday, 1968.

Modern Plastics Encyclopedia, 1981-82. McGraw-Hill, 1981.

Richardson, Terry A. *Industrial Plastics: Theory and Application.* South-Western Publishing, 1983.

Wolf, Nancy and Ellen Feldman. *Plastics: America's Packaging Dilemma.* Island Press, 1991.

Periodicals

"Picked Up, Dropped Off." *Beverage World.* August, 1992, p. 16.

Kirkman, Angela and Charles H. Kline. "Recycling Plastics Today." *Chemtech.* October, 1991, pp. 606-614.

Sfiligoj, Eric. "Answering the Critics: Recyclable Polyethylene Terephthalate Beverage Containers Are Replacing Glass Bottles." *Beverage World.* June, 1992, p. 34.

—*Rose Secrest*

PET bottles now account for 43 percent of the soft drink container market. The overwhelming success of PET soda bottles—in 1991, more than eight billion bottles were manufactured in the U.S.—has resulted in a disposal problem, but recycling of the bottles is growing, and manufacturers are finding new ways to use recycled PET.

Solar Cell

When research into electricity began and simple batteries were being made and studied, research into solar electricity followed amazingly quickly. As early as 1839, Antoine-César Becquerel exposed a chemical battery to the sun to see it produce voltage. This first conversion of sunlight to electricity was one percent efficient—one percent of the incoming sunlight was converted into electricity.

Background

Photovoltaic solar cells are thin silicon disks that convert sunlight into electricity. These disks act as energy sources for a wide variety of uses, including: calculators and other small devices; telecommunications; rooftop panels on individual houses; and for lighting, pumping, and medical refrigeration for villages in developing countries. Solar cells in the form of large arrays are used to power satellites and, in rare cases, to provide electricity for power plants.

When research into electricity began and simple batteries were being made and studied, research into solar electricity followed amazingly quickly. As early as 1839, Antoine-César Becquerel exposed a chemical **battery** to the sun to see it produce voltage. This first conversion of sunlight to electricity was one percent efficient. That is, one percent of the incoming sunlight was converted into electricity. Willoughby Smith in 1873 discovered that selenium was sensitive to light; in 1877 Adams and Day noted that selenium, when exposed to light, produced an electrical current. Charles Fritts, in the 1880s, also used gold-coated selenium to make the first solar cell, again only one percent efficient. Nevertheless, Fritts considered his cells to be revolutionary. He envisioned free solar energy to be a means of decentralization, predicting that solar cells would replace power plants with individually powered residences.

With Albert Einstein's explanation in 1905 of the photoelectric effect—metal absorbs energy from light and will retain that energy until too much light hits it—hope soared anew that solar electricity at higher efficiencies would become feasible. Little progress was made, however, until research into diodes and transistors yielded the knowledge necessary for Bell scientists Gordon Pearson, Darryl Chapin, and Cal Fuller to produce a silicon solar cell of four percent efficiency in 1954.

Further work brought the cell's efficiency up to 15 percent. Solar cells were first used in the rural and isolated city of Americus, Georgia as a power source for a telephone relay system, where it was used successfully for many years.

A type of solar cell to fully meet domestic energy needs has not as yet been developed, but solar cells have become successful in providing energy for artificial satellites. Fuel systems and regular batteries were too heavy in a program where every ounce mattered. Solar cells provide more energy per ounce of weight than all other conventional energy sources, and they are cost-effective.

Only a few large scale photovoltaic power systems have been set up. Most efforts lean toward providing solar cell technology to remote places that have no other means of sophisticated power. About 50 megawatts are installed each year, yet solar cells provide only about .1 percent of all electricity now being produced. Supporters of solar energy claim that the amount of solar radiation reaching the Earth's surface each year could easily provide all our energy needs several times over, yet solar cells have a long way to go before they fulfill Charles Fritts's dream of free, fully accessible solar electricity.

Raw Materials

The basic component of a solar cell is pure silicon, which is not pure in its natural state.

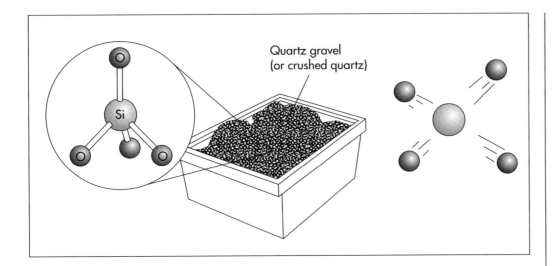

Quartz gravel
(or crushed quartz)

To make solar cells, the raw materials—silicon dioxide of either quartzite gravel or crushed quartz—are first placed into an electric arc furnace, where a carbon arc is applied to release the oxygen. The products are carbon dioxide and molten silicon. At this point, the silicon is still not pure enough to be used for solar cells and requires further purification.

Pure silicon is derived from such silicon dioxides as quartzite gravel (the purest silica) or crushed quartz. The resulting pure silicon is then doped (treated with) with phosphorous and boron to produce an excess of electrons and a deficiency of electrons respectively to make a semiconductor capable of conducting electricity. The silicon disks are shiny and require an anti-reflective coating, usually titanium dioxide.

The solar module consists of the silicon semiconductor surrounded by protective material in a metal frame. The protective material consists of an encapsulant of transparent silicon rubber or butyryl plastic (commonly used in **automobile windshield**s) bonded around the cells, which are then embedded in ethylene vinyl acetate. A polyester film (such as mylar or tedlar) makes up the backing. A glass cover is found on terrestrial arrays, a lightweight plastic cover on satellite arrays. The electronic parts are standard and consist mostly of copper. The frame is either steel or aluminum. Silicon is used as the cement to put it all together.

The Manufacturing Process

Purifying the silicon

1 The silicon dioxide of either quartzite gravel or crushed quartz is placed into an electric arc furnace. A carbon arc is then applied to release the oxygen. The products are carbon dioxide and molten silicon. This simple process yields silicon with one percent impurity, useful in many industries but not the solar cell industry.

2 The 99 percent pure silicon is purified even further using the floating zone technique. A rod of impure silicon is passed through a heated zone several times in the same direction. This procedure "drags" the impurities toward one end with each pass. At a specific point, the silicon is deemed pure, and the impure end is removed.

Making single crystal silicon

3 Solar cells are made from silicon boules, polycrystalline structures that have the atomic structure of a single crystal. The most commonly used process for creating the boule is called the *Czochralski method*. In this process, a seed crystal of silicon is dipped into melted polycrystalline silicon. As the seed crystal is withdrawn and rotated, a cylindrical ingot or "boule" of silicon is formed. The ingot withdrawn is unusually pure, because impurities tend to remain in the liquid.

Making silicon wafers

4 From the boule, silicon wafers are sliced one at a time using a circular saw whose inner diameter cuts into the rod, or many at once with a multiwire saw. (A diamond saw produces cuts that are as wide as the wafer—.5 millimeter thick.) Only about one-half of the silicon is lost from the boule to the finished circular wafer—more if the wafer is then cut to be rectangular or hexagonal. Rectangular or hexagonal wafers are sometimes used in solar cells because they can be fitted together perfectly, thereby utilizing all available space on the front surface of the solar cell.

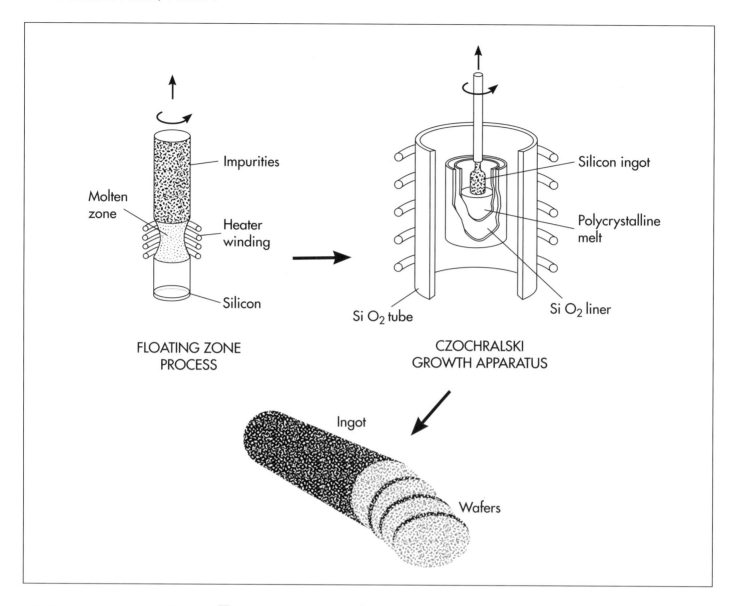

Molten zone

Impurities

Heater winding

Silicon

FLOATING ZONE PROCESS

Silicon ingot

Polycrystalline melt

Si O$_2$ tube

Si O$_2$ liner

CZOCHRALSKI GROWTH APPARATUS

Ingot

Wafers

After the initial purification, the silicon is further refined in a floating zone process. In this process, a silicon rod is passed through a heated zone several times, which serves to "drag" the impurities toward one end of the rod. The impure end can then be removed.

Next, a silicon seed crystal is put into a Czochralski growth apparatus, where it is dipped into melted polycrystalline silicon. The seed crystal rotates as it is withdrawn, forming a cylindrical ingot of very pure silicon. Wafers are then sliced out of the ingot.

5 The wafers are then polished to remove saw marks. (It has recently been found that rougher cells absorb light more effectively, therefore some manufacturers have chosen not to polish the wafer.)

Doping

6 The traditional way of doping (adding impurities to) silicon wafers with boron and phosphorous is to introduce a small amount of boron during the Czochralski process in step #3 above. The wafers are then sealed back to back and placed in a furnace to be heated to slightly below the melting point of silicon (2,570 degrees Fahrenheit or 1,410 degrees Celsius) in the presence of phosphorous gas. The phosphorous atoms "burrow" into the silicon, which is more porous because it is close to becoming a liq-

uid. The temperature and time given to the process is carefully controlled to ensure a uniform junction of proper depth.

A more recent way of doping silicon with phosphorous is to use a small particle accelerator to shoot phosphorous ions into the ingot. By controlling the speed of the ions, it is possible to control their penetrating depth. This new process, however, has generally not been accepted by commercial manufacturers.

Placing electrical contacts

7 Electrical contacts connect each solar cell to another and to the receiver of produced current. The contacts must be very thin (at least in the front) so as not to block sunlight to the cell. Metals such as palladium/silver, nickel, or copper are vacuum-evaporated

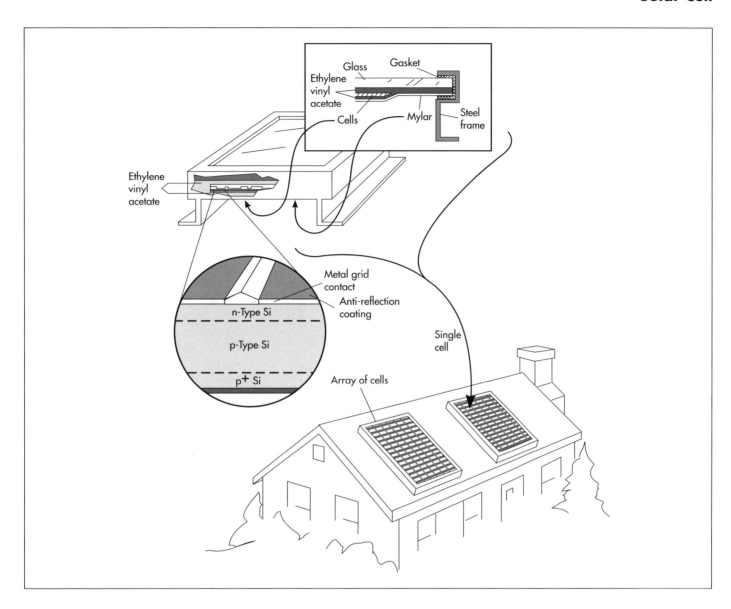

Ethylene vinyl acetate

Glass Gasket

Cells Mylar Steel frame

Metal grid contact

Anti-reflection coating

n-Type Si

p-Type Si

p+ Si

Single cell

Array of cells

This illustration shows the makeup of a typical solar cell. The cells are encapsulated in ethylene vinyl acetate and placed in a metal frame that has a mylar backsheet and glass cover.

through a photoresist, silkscreened, or merely deposited on the exposed portion of cells that have been partially covered with wax. All three methods involve a system in which the part of the cell on which a contact is not desired is protected, while the rest of the cell is exposed to the metal.

8 After the contacts are in place, thin strips ("fingers") are placed between cells. The most commonly used strips are tin-coated copper.

The anti-reflective coating

9 Because pure silicon is shiny, it can reflect up to 35 percent of the sunlight. To reduce the amount of sunlight lost, an anti-reflective coating is put on the silicon wafer. The most commonly used coatings are titanium dioxide and silicon oxide, though others are used. The material used for coating is either heated until its molecules boil off and travel to the silicon and condense, or the material undergoes sputtering. In this process, a high voltage knocks molecules off the material and deposits them onto the silicon at the opposite electrode. Yet another method is to allow the silicon itself to react with oxygen- or nitrogen-containing gases to form silicon dioxide or silicon nitride. Commercial solar cell manufacturers use silicon nitride.

Encapsulating the cell

10 The finished solar cells are then encapsulated; that is, sealed into silicon rubber or ethylene vinyl acetate. The encapsulated solar cells are then placed into an

aluminum frame that has a mylar or tedlar backsheet and a glass or plastic cover.

Quality Control

Quality control is important in solar cell manufacture because discrepancy in the many processes and factors can adversely affect the overall efficiency of the cells. The primary research goal is to find ways to improve the efficiency of each solar cell over a longer lifetime. The Low Cost Solar Array Project (initiated by the United States Department of Energy in the late 1970s) sponsored private research that aimed to lower the cost of solar cells. The silicon itself is tested for purity, crystal orientation, and resistivity. Manufacturers also test for the presence of oxygen (which affects its strength and resistance to warp) and carbon (which causes defects). Finished silicon disks are inspected for any damage, flaking, or bending that might have occurred during sawing, polishing, and etching.

During the entire silicon disk manufacturing process, the temperature, pressure, speed, and quantities of dopants are continuously monitored. Steps are also taken to ensure that impurities in the air and on working surfaces are kept to a minimum.

The completed semiconductors must then undergo electrical tests to see that the current, voltage, and resistance for each meet appropriate standards. An earlier problem with solar cells was a tendency to stop working when partially shaded. This problem has been alleviated by providing shunt diodes that reduce dangerously high voltages to the cell. Shunt resistance must then be tested using partially shaded junctions.

An important test of solar modules involves providing test cells with conditions and intensity of light that they will encounter under normal conditions and then checking to see that they perform well. The cells are also exposed to heat and cold and tested against vibration, twisting, and hail.

The final test for solar modules is field site testing, in which finished modules are placed where they will actually be used. This provides the researcher with the best data for determining the efficiency of a solar cell under ambient conditions and the solar cell's effective lifetime, the most important factors of all.

The Future

Considering the present state of relatively expensive, inefficient solar cells, the future can only improve. Some experts predict it will be a billion-dollar industry by the year 2000. This prediction is supported by evidence of more rooftop photovoltaic systems being developed in such countries as Japan, Germany, and Italy. Plans to begin the manufacture of solar cells have been established in Mexico and China. Likewise, Egypt, Botswana, and the Philippines (all three assisted by American companies) are building plants that will manufacture solar cells.

Most current research aims for reducing solar cell cost or increasing efficiency. Innovations in solar cell technology include developing and manufacturing cheaper alternatives to the expensive crystalline silicon cells. These alternatives include solar windows that mimic photosynthesis, and smaller cells made from tiny, amorphous silicon balls. Already, amorphous silicon and polycrystalline silicon are gaining popularity at the expense of single crystal silicon. Additional innovations including minimizing shade and focusing sunlight through prismatic lenses. This involves layers of different materials (notably, gallium arsenide and silicon) that absorb light at different frequencies, thereby increasing the amount of sunlight effectively used for electricity production.

A few experts foresee the adaptation of hybrid houses; that is, houses that utilize solar water heaters, passive solar heating, and solar cells for reduced energy needs. Another view concerns the space shuttle placing more and more solar arrays into orbit, a solar power satellite that beams power to Earth solar array farms, and even a space colony that will manufacture solar arrays to be used on Earth.

Where To Learn More

Books

Bullock, Charles E. and Peter H. Grambs. *Solar Electricity: Making the Sun Work for You.* Monegon, Ltd., 1981.

Komp, Richard J. *Practical Photovoltaics.* Aatec Publications, 1984.

Making and Using Electricity from the Sun. Tab Books, 1979.

Periodicals

Crawford, Mark. "DOE's Born-Again Solar Energy Plan," *Science.* March 23, 1990, pp. 1403-1404.

"Waiting for the Sunrise," *Economist.* May 19, 1990, pp. 95+.

Edelson, Edward. "Solar Cell Update," *Popular Science.* June, 1992, p. 95.

Murray, Charles J. "Solar Power's Bright Hope," *Design News.* March 11, 1991, p. 30.

—*Rose Secrest*

Spark Plug

Spark plugs are under constant attack by corrosive gases at 4,500 degrees Fahrenheit, crushing pressures of 2,000 pounds per square inch, and electrical discharges of up to 18,000 volts. This unrelenting assault under the hood of a typical automobile occurs dozens of times per second and over a million times in a day's worth of driving.

Background

The purpose of a spark plug is to provide a place for an electric spark that is hot enough to ignite the air/fuel mixture inside the combustion chamber of an internal combustion engine. This is done by a high voltage current arcing across a gap on the spark plug.

A spark plug is made of a center electrode, an insulator, a metal casing or shell, and a side electrode (also called a ground electrode). The center electrode is a thick metal wire that lies lengthwise within the plug and conducts electricity from the ignition cable hooked to one end of the plug to the electrode gap at the other end. The insulator is a ceramic casing that surrounds much of the center electrode; both the upper and lower portions of the center electrode remain exposed. The metal casing or shell is a hexagon-shaped shell with threads, which allow the spark plug to be installed into a tapped socket in the engine cylinder head. The side electrode is a short, thick wire made of nickel alloy that is connected to the metal shell and extends toward the center electrode. The tips of the side and center electrodes are about 0.020 - 0.080 inch apart from each other (depending on the type of engine), creating the gap for the spark to jump across.

The several hundred types of spark plugs available cover a variety of internal-combustion engine-driven transportation, work, and pleasure vehicles. Spark plugs are used in **automobile**s, trucks, buses, tractors, boats (inboard and outboard), aircraft, motorcycles, scooters, industrial and oil field engines, oil burners, power mowers and chain saws. Turbine igniters, a type of spark plug, help power the **jet engine**s in most large commercial aircraft today while glowplugs are used in diesel engine applications.

The heat range or rating of a spark plug refers to its thermal characteristics. It is the measure of how long it takes heat to be removed from the tip of the plug, the firing end, and transferred to the engine cylinder head. At the time of the spark, if the plug tip temperature is too cold, carbon, oil, and combustion products can cause the plug to "foul out" or fail. If the plug tip temperature is too hot, preignition occurs, the center electrode burns, and the piston may be damaged. Heat range is changed by altering the length of the insulator nose, depending on the type of engine, the load on the engine, the type of fuel, and other factors. For a "hot" plug, an insulator with a long conical nose is used; for a "cold" plug, a short-nosed insulator is used.

Spark plugs are under constant chemical, thermal, physical, and electrical attack by corrosive gases at 4,500 degrees Fahrenheit, crushing pressures of 2,000 pounds per square inch (PSI), and electrical discharges of up to 18,000 volts. This unrelenting assault under the hood of a typical automobile occurs dozens of times per second and over a million times in a day's worth of driving.

History

The spark plug evolved with the internal combustion engine, but the earliest demonstration of the use of an electric spark to ignite a fuel-air mixture was in 1777. In that year, Alessandro Volta loaded a toy pistol with a mixture of marsh gas and air, corked the muzzle, and ignited the charge with a spark from a Leyden jar.

In 1860, French engineer Jean Lenoir created what most closely resembles the spark plug

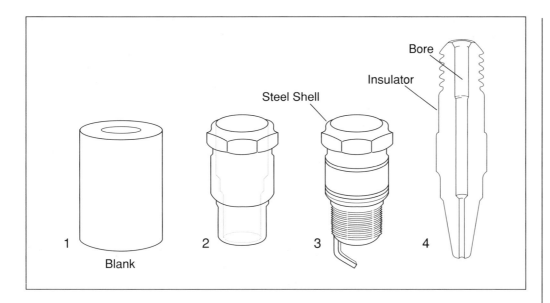

1 Blank
2
3
4

Bore
Insulator
Steel Shell

To make spark plugs, manufacturers first extrude or cold-form steel to the proper hollow shape (1). At this point, the steel forms are called "blanks." Next, these blanks undergo further forming operations such as machining and knurling (2), and then the side electrode—with only a partial bend—is attached (3). The ceramic insulator, with a hollow bore through its center, is molded under pressure (4).

of today. He combined an insulator, electrodes, and spark gap in a single unit. As part of his patent application for the internal combustion engine that year, he devoted one sentence to describing the spark plug. He refined this spark plug in 1885.

In the early 1900s, Robert and Frank Stranahan, brothers and partners in an automobile parts importing business, set out to produce a more efficient and durable spark plug. They added gaskets between the metal shell and **porcelain** insulator, made manufacturing easier, and reduced the possibility of gas leakage past the gaskets. In 1909, Robert Stranahan sold the plug to one automobile manufacturer and went into the spark plug manufacturing business, cornering the market at that time.

The industry exploded as the age of the automobile opened. Eventually, variations in ignition systems, fuel, and performance requirements placed new demands on spark plugs. Although the basic design and function of the plug has changed little since its inception, a staggering variety and number of electrode and insulator materials have been tried.

Raw Materials

The electrodes in a spark plug typically consist of high-nickel alloys, while the insulator is generally made of aluminum oxide ceramic and the shell is made of steel wire.

Selection of materials for both the electrodes and the insulator have consumed much research and development time and cost. One

major spark plug manufacturer claims to have tested 2,000 electrode materials and over 25,000 insulator combinations. As electrodes erode, the gap between them widens, and it takes more voltage than the ignition system can provide to fire them. High-nickel alloys have been improved and thicker electrodes have been used to reduce engine performance loss. In addition, precious and exotic metals are increasingly being used by manufacturers. Many modern plugs feature silver, **gold**, and platinum in the electrodes, not to mention center electrodes with copper cores. Silver has superior thermal conductivity over other electrode metals, while platinum has excellent corrosion resistance.

Insulator material also can have a dramatic effect on spark plug performance. Research continues to find a material that better reduces flashover, or electrical leakage, from the plug's terminal to the shell. The breakthrough use of Sillimanite, a material that is found in a natural state and also produced artificially, has been succeeded by the use of more heat-resistant aluminum oxide ceramics, the composition of which are manufacturers' secrets.

One major manufacturer's process for making the insulator involves wet grinding batches of ceramic pellets in ball mills, under carefully controlled conditions. Definite size and shape of the pellets produce the free-flowing substance needed to make a quality insulator. The pellets are obtained through a rigid spray-drying operation that removes the water from the ceramic mixture, until it is ready for pouring into molds.

The Manufacturing Process

Each major element of the spark plug—the center electrode, the side electrode, the insulator, and the shell—is manufactured in a continuous in-line assembly process. Then, the side electrode is attached to the shell and the center electrode is fitted inside the insulator. Finally, the major parts are assembled into a single unit.

Shell

1 The one-piece spark plug shells can be made in several ways. When solid steel wire is used, the steel can be cold-formed, whereby coils of steel are formed and molded at relatively low temperatures. Or, the steel can be extruded, a process in which the metal is heated and then pushed through a shaped orifice (called a *die*) to produce the proper hollow shape. Shells can also be made from bars of steel that are fed into automatic screw machines. These machines completely form the shell, drill the hole through it, and ream it—a process that improves the finish of the drilled hole and makes the size of the hole more exact.

2 The formed or extruded shells—called *blanks* until they're molded into their final shapes—require secondary operations to be performed on them, such as machining and knurling. Knurling a shell blank involves passing it through hard, patterned rollers, which form a series of ridges on the outside of the blank. Similarly, machining—in which machine tools cut into the exterior of the shell blank—generates shapes and contours on the outside of the shell. The shells are now in their final shape and are complete except for threads and side electrodes.

Side electrode

3 The side electrode is made of a nickel alloy wire, which is fed from rolls into an electric welder, straightened, and welded to the shell. It is then cut to the proper length. Finally, the side electrode is given a partial bend; it is given its final bend after the rest of the plug assembly is in place.

4 The threads are then rolled on the shells. Now complete, the shells are usually given a permanent and protective silvery finish by an electrolytic process. In this process, the shell is placed in a solution of acids, salts, or alkalis, and an electrical current is passed through the solution. The result is a thin metal coating applied evenly over the shell.

Insulator

5 Insulators are supplied from stock storage. Ceramic material for the insulator in liquid form is first poured into rubber molds. Special presses automatically apply hydraulic pressure to produce unfired insulator blanks. The dimensions of the bore—the hollow part of the insulator—into which the center electrodes will be pressed are rigidly controlled.

6 Special contour grinding machines give the pressed insulator blanks their final exterior shape before the insulators are fired in a tunnel kiln to temperatures in excess of 2,700 degrees Fahrenheit. The computer-controlled process produces insulators that are uniformly strong, dense, and resistive to moisture. The insulators may be fired again after identifying marks and a glaze are applied.

Center electrode

7 The nickel alloy center electrode is first electrically welded to the basic steel terminal stud, a narrow metal wire that runs from the middle of the plug to the lower end (the opposite end from the electrode gap). The terminal stud is attached to a nut, which in turn is attached to the ignition cable that supplies the electric current to the plug.

8 The center electrode/terminal stud assembly is sealed into the insulator and tamped under extreme pressure. Insulator assemblies are then sealed in the metal shell under 6,000 pounds pressure. After reaming to correct depth and angle, the rim or edge of the shell—called the *flange*—is bent or crimped to complete a gas-tight seal. Spark plug gaskets from stock are crimped over the plug body so that they won't fall off.

9 To form the proper gap between the two electrodes, the center electrode of the now completely assembled spark plug is machine-trimmed to specifications, and the ground electrode is given a final bend.

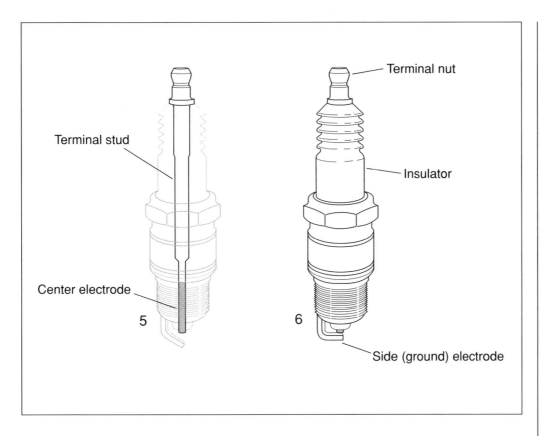

Terminal stud

Center electrode

5

Terminal nut

Insulator

6

Side (ground) electrode

The terminal stud and center electrode are electrically welded together and then inserted through the bore inside the insulator (5). This assembly is then sealed under extreme pressure. Finally, the center electrode is machined to its exact shape, and the side electrode is given its final bend (6).

Packaging

10 After a final inspection, the spark plugs are placed in open cartons that have been automatically formed. The plugs are generally wrapped in plastic film, placed first in a carton, and then prepared for shipping in quantity to users.

Quality Control

Inspections and measurements are performed throughout the manufacturing and assembly operations. Both incoming parts and tooling are inspected for accuracy. New gauges are set up for use in production while other gauges are changed and calibrated.

Detailed inspections of shells from each machine are constantly made for visible flaws. The ceramic insulator contour can be checked by projecting its silhouette onto a screen at a magnification of 20 times actual size and matching the silhouette to tolerance lines. In addition, regular statistical inspections can be made on insulators coming off the production line.

During spark plug assembly, a random sampling are pressure tested to check that the center electrode is properly sealed inside the insulator. Visual inspections assure that assembly is in accordance with design specifications.

Where To Learn More

Books

Heywood, John. *Internal Combustion Engine Fundamentals.* McGraw-Hill, 1988.

Schwaller, Anthony. *Motor Automotive Mechanics.* Delmar Publishers, 1988.

Periodicals

Davis, Marlan. "Fire in the Hole: Spark-plug Design Heats up with New High-tech Materials and Design Concepts." *Hot Rod.* February, 1990.

"Spark Plug 'Sees' Inside Engines." *Design News.* October 17, 1989.

"Hot Spark Basics." *Popular Mechanics.* May, 1989.

—*Peter Toeg*

Stainless Steel

Japanese researchers have recently developed a corrosion-resistant stainless steel that displays the shape-memory effect. This type of material returns to its original shape upon heating after being plastically deformed. Potential applications include assembly components, temperature sensing (circuit breakers and fire alarms), and springs.

Background

Stainless steel is an iron-containing alloy—a substance made up of two or more chemical elements—used in a wide range of applications. It has excellent resistance to stain or rust due to its chromium content, usually from 12 to 20 percent of the alloy. There are more than 57 stainless steels recognized as standard alloys, in addition to many proprietary alloys produced by different stainless steel producers. These many types of steels are used in an almost endless number of applications and industries: bulk materials handling equipment, building exteriors and roofing, **automobile** components (exhaust, trim/decorative, engine, chassis, fasteners, tubing for fuel lines), chemical processing plants (scrubbers and heat exchangers), pulp and paper manufacturing, petroleum refining, water supply piping, consumer products, marine and shipbuilding, pollution control, sporting goods (snow skis), and transportation (rail cars), to name just a few.

About 200,000 tons of nickel-containing stainless steel is used each year by the food processing industry in North America. It is used in a variety of food handling, storing, cooking, and serving equipment—from the beginning of the food collection process through to the end. Beverages such as milk, **wine**, beer, soft drinks and fruit juice are processed in stainless steel equipment. Stainless steel is also used in commercial cookers, pasteurizers, transfer bins, and other specialized equipment. Advantages include easy cleaning, good corrosion resistance, durability, economy, food flavor protection, and sanitary design. According to the U.S. Department of Commerce, 1992 shipments of all stainless steel totaled 1,514,222 tons.

Stainless steels come in several types depending on their microstructure. Austenitic stainless steels contain at least 6 percent nickel and austenite—carbon-containing iron with a face-centered cubic structure—and have good corrosion resistance and high ductility (the ability of the material to bend without breaking). Ferritic stainless steels (ferrite has a body-centered cubic structure) have better resistance to stress corrosion than austenitic, but they are difficult to weld. Martensitic stainless steels contain iron having a needle-like structure.

Duplex stainless steels, which generally contain equal amounts of ferrite and austenite, provide better resistance to pitting and crevice corrosion in most environments. They also have superior resistance to cracking due to chloride stress corrosion, and they are about twice as strong as the common austenitics. Therefore, duplex stainless steels are widely used in the chemical industry in refineries, gas-processing plants, pulp and paper plants, and sea water piping installations.

Raw Materials

Stainless steels are made of some of the basic elements found in the earth: iron ore, chromium, silicon, nickel, carbon, nitrogen, and manganese. Properties of the final alloy are tailored by varying the amounts of these elements. Nitrogen, for instance, improves tensile properties like ductility. It also improves corrosion resistance, which makes it valuable for use in duplex stainless steels.

The Manufacturing Process

The manufacture of stainless steel involves a series of processes. First, the steel is melted,

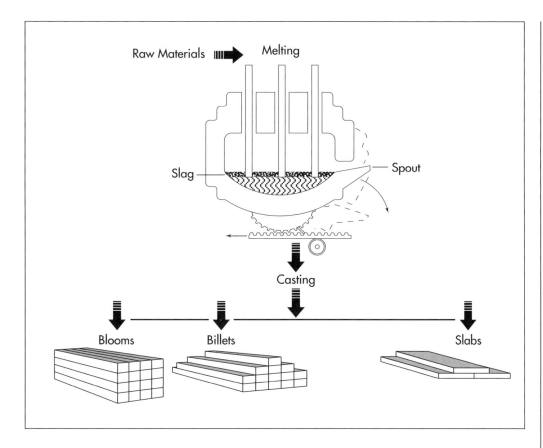

Raw Materials ➡ Melting

Slag — Spout

Casting

Blooms Billets Slabs

To make stainless steel, the raw materials—iron ore, chromium, silicon, nickel, etc.—are melted together in an electric furnace. This step usually involves 8 to 12 hours of intense heat. Next, the mixture is cast into one of several shapes, including blooms, billets, and slabs.

and then it is cast into solid form. After various forming steps, the steel is heat treated and then cleaned and polished to give it the desired finish. Next, it is packaged and sent to manufacturers, who weld and join the steel to produce the desired shapes.

Melting and casting

1 The raw materials are first melted together in an electric furnace. This step usually requires 8 to 12 hours of intense heat. When the melting is finished, the molten steel is cast into semi-finished forms. These include blooms (rectangular shapes), billets (round or square shapes 1.5 inches or 3.8 centimeters in thickness), slabs, rods, and tube rounds.

Forming

2 Next, the semi-finished steel goes through forming operations, beginning with hot rolling, in which the steel is heated and passed through huge rolls. Blooms and billets are formed into bar and wire, while slabs are formed into plate, strip, and sheet. Bars are available in all grades and come in rounds, squares, octagons, or hexagons 0.25 inch (.63 centimeter) in size. Wire is usually available

up to 0.5 inch (1.27 centimeters) in diameter or size. Plate is more than 0.1875 inch (.47 centimeter) thick and over 10 inches (25.4 centimeters) wide. Strip is less than 0.185 inch (.47 centimeter) thick and less than 24 inches (61 centimeters) wide. Sheet is less than 0.1875 (.47 centimeter) thick and more than 24 (61 centimeters) wide.

Heat treatment

3 After the stainless steel is formed, most types must go through an annealing step. Annealing is a heat treatment in which the steel is heated and cooled under controlled conditions to relieve internal stresses and soften the metal. Some steels are heat treated for higher strength. However, such a heat treatment—also known as *age hardening*—requires careful control, for even small changes from the recommended temperature, time, or cooling rate can seriously affect the properties. Lower aging temperatures produce high strength with low fracture toughness, while higher-temperature aging produces a lower strength, tougher material.

Though the heating rate to reach the aging temperature (900 to 1000 degrees Fahrenheit or 482 to 537 degrees Celsius) does not effect the properties, the cooling rate does. A post-aging quenching (rapid cooling) treatment can increase the toughness without a significant loss in strength. One such process involves water quenching the material in a 35-degree Fahrenheit (1.6-degree Celsius) ice-water bath for a minimum of two hours.

The type of heat treatment depends on the type of steel; in other words, whether it is austenitic, ferritic, or martensitic. Austenitic steels are heated to above 1900 degrees Fahrenheit (1037 degrees Celsius) for a time depending on the thickness. Water quenching is used for thick sections, whereas air cooling or air blasting is used for thin sections. If cooled too slowly, carbide precipitation can occur. This buildup can be eliminated by thermal stabilization. In this method, the steel is held for several hours at 1500 to 1600 degrees Fahrenheit (815 to 871 degrees Celsius). Cleaning part surfaces of contaminants before heat treatment is sometimes also necessary to achieve proper heat treatment.

Descaling

4 Annealing causes a scale or build-up to form on the steel. The scale can be removed using several processes. One of the most common methods, pickling, uses a nitric-hydrofluoric acid bath to descale the steel. In another method, electrocleaning, an electric current is applied to the surface using a cathode and phosphoric acid, and the scale is removed. The annealing and descaling steps occur at different stages depending on the type of steel being worked. Bar and wire, for instance, go through further forming steps (more hot rolling, forging, or extruding) after the initial hot rolling before being annealed and descaled. Sheet and strip, on the other hand, go through an initial annealing and descaling step immediately after hot rolling. After cold rolling (passing through rolls at a relatively low temperature), which produces a further reduction in thickness, sheet and strip are annealed and descaled again. A final cold rolling step then prepares the steel for final processing.

Cutting

5 Cutting operations are usually necessary to obtain the desired blank shape or size to trim the part to final size. Mechanical cutting is accomplished by a variety of methods, including straight shearing using guillotine knives, circle shearing using circular knives horizontally and vertically positioned, sawing using high speed steel blades, blanking, and nibbling. Blanking uses metal punches and dies to punch out the shape by shearing. Nibbling is a process of cutting by blanking out a series of overlapping holes and is ideally suited for irregular shapes.

Stainless steel can also be cut using flame cutting, which involves a flame-fired torch using oxygen and propane in conjunction with iron powder. This method is clean and fast. Another cutting method is known as *plasma jet cutting*, in which an ionized gas column in conjunction with an electric arc through a small orifice makes the cut. The gas produces extremely high temperatures to melt the metal.

Finishing

6 Surface finish is an important specification for stainless steel products and is critical in applications where appearance is also important. Certain surface finishes also make stainless steel easier to clean, which is obviously important for sanitary applications. A smooth surface as obtained by polishing also provides better corrosion resistance. On the other hand, rough finishes are often required for lubrication applications, as well as to facilitate further manufacturing steps.

Surface finishes are the result of processes used in fabricating the various forms or are the result of further processing. There are a variety of methods used for finishing. A dull finish is produced by hot rolling, annealing, and descaling. A bright finish is obtained by first hot rolling and then cold rolling on polished rolls. A highly reflective finish is produced by cold rolling in combination with annealing in a controlled atmosphere furnace, by grinding with abrasives, or by buffing a finely ground surface. A mirror finish is produced by polishing with progressively finer abrasives, followed by extensive buffing. For grinding or polishing, **grinding wheel**s or abrasive belts are normally used. Buffing uses cloth wheels in combination with cutting compounds containing very fine abrasive particles in bar or stick forms. Other finishing methods include tumbling, which forces

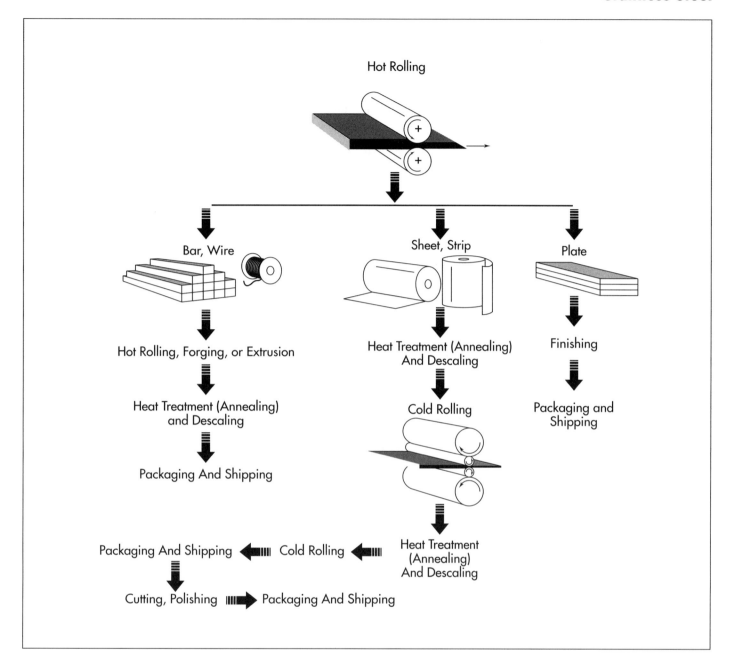

Hot Rolling

Bar, Wire

Sheet, Strip

Plate

Hot Rolling, Forging, or Extrusion

Heat Treatment (Annealing) And Descaling

Finishing

Heat Treatment (Annealing) and Descaling

Cold Rolling

Packaging and Shipping

Packaging And Shipping

Packaging And Shipping ◄ Cold Rolling ◄ Heat Treatment (Annealing) And Descaling

Cutting, Polishing ▶ Packaging And Shipping

movement of a tumbling material against surfaces of parts, dry etching (sandblasting), wet etching using acid solutions, and surface dulling. The latter uses sandblasting, wire brushing, or pickling techniques.

Manufacturing at the fabricator or end user

7 After the stainless steel in its various forms are packed and shipped to the fabricator or end user, a variety of other processes are needed. Further shaping is accomplished using a variety of methods, such as roll forming, press forming, forging, press drawing, and extrusion. Additional heat treating

(annealing), machining, and cleaning processes are also often required.

There are a variety of methods for joining stainless steel, with welding being the most common. Fusion and resistance welding are the two basic methods generally used with many variations for both. In fusion welding, heat is provided by an electric arc struck between an electrode and the metal to be welded. In resistance welding, bonding is the result of heat and pressure. Heat is produced by the resistance to the flow of electric current through the parts to be welded, and pressure is applied by the electrodes. After

The initial steel shapes—blooms, billets, slabs, etc.—are hot rolled into bar, wire, sheet, strip, and plate. Depending on the form, the steel then undergoes further rolling steps (both hot and cold rolling), heat treatment (annealing), descaling (to remove buildup), and polishing to produce the finished stainless steel. The steel is then sent the end user.

parts are welded together, they must be cleaned around the joined area.

Quality Control

In addition to in-process control during manufacture and fabrication, stainless steels must meet specifications developed by the American Society for Testing and Materials (ASTM) with regard to mechanical properties such as toughness and corrosion resistance. Metallography can sometimes be correlated to corrosion tests to help monitor quality.

The Future

Use of stainless and super stainless steels is expanding in a variety of markets. To meet the requirements of the new Clean Air Act, coal-fired power plants are installing stainless steel stack liners. Other new industrial applications include secondary heat exchangers for high-efficiency home furnaces, service-water piping in nuclear power plants, ballast tanks and fire-suppression systems for offshore drilling platforms, flexible pipe for oil and gas distribution systems, and heliostats for solar-energy plants.

Environmental legislation is also forcing the petrochemical and refinery industries to recycle secondary cooling water in closed systems rather than simply discharge it. Reuse results in cooling water with elevated levels of chloride, resulting in pitting-corrosion problems. Duplex stainless steel tubing will play an increasingly important role in solving such industrial corrosion problems, since it costs less than other materials. Manufacturers are developing highly corrosion-resistant steels in respond to this demand.

In the automotive industry, one steel manufacturer has estimated that stainless-steel usage per vehicle will increase from 55 to 66 pounds (25 to 30 kilograms) to more than 100 pounds (45 kilograms) by the turn of the century. New applications include metallic substrates for catalytic converters, **air bag** components, composite bumpers, fuel line and other fuel-system parts compatible with alternate fuels, brake lines, and long-life exhaust systems.

With improvements in process technology, superaustenitic stainless steels (with nitrogen contents up to 0.5 percent) are being developed. These steels are used in pulp-mill bleach plants, sea water and phosphoric-acid handling systems, scrubbers, offshore platforms, and other highly corrosive applications. A number of manufacturers have begun marketing such materials in sheet, plate, and other forms. Other new compositions are being developed: ferritic iron-base alloys containing 8 and 12 percent Cr for magnetic applications, and austenitic stainless with extra low sulfur content for parts used in the manufacture of semiconductors and pharmaceuticals.

Research will continue to develop improved and unique materials. For instance, Japanese researchers have recently developed several. One is a corrosion-resistant stainless steel that displays the shape-memory effect. This type of material returns to its original shape upon heating after being plastically deformed. Potential applications include assembly components (pipe fittings, clips, fasteners, clamps), temperature sensing (circuit breakers and fire alarms), and springs. An improved martensitic stainless steel has also been developed for precision miniature and instrument rolling-contact bearings, which has reduced vibration levels, improved life expectancy, and better surface finish compared to conventional materials.

Where To Learn More

Books

Cleaning and Descaling Stainless Steels. American Iron and Steel Institute, 1982.

Finishes for Stainless Steel. American Iron and Steel Institute, June, 1983.

Llewellyn, D. T. *Steels: Metallurgy & Applications.* Butterworth-Heinemann, 1992.

MacMillan, Angus, ed. *The Steel-Alloying Handbook.* Elkay Publishing Services, 1993.

Stainless Steel & Heat Resisting Steels. Iron & Steel Society, Inc., 1990.

Periodicals

Davison, Ralph M. and James D. Redmond. "Practical Guide to Using Duplex Stainless

Steels." *Materials Performance*. January, 1990, pp. 57-62.

Hasimoto, Misao. "Combined Deposition Processes Create New Composites." *Research & Development*. October, 1989.

Tuthill, Arthur and Richard Avery. "Specifying Stainless Steel Surface Treatments." *Advanced Materials & Processes*. December, 1992, pp. 34-38.

—*L. S. Millberg*

Stapler

The basic household stapler uses a staple with a wire size of .017 of an inch in diameter, while multi-use staplers operate with wire sizes averaging .050 of an inch in diameter. Staplers used in the construction industry utilize what resemble nails that come in preloaded magazines—similar to firearm ammunition and probably almost as deadly at short range.

Background

There are virtually as many types of staplers as there are uses for them. Staplers are produced for use in: the manufacture of furniture; medical fields; carpet tacking; electrical wire and insulation installation; picture frame manufacture and, of course, in the home or office.

The size of staplers ranges as well—from a mini stapler (as small a finger) to one requiring two hands to use. And while there is no specific standard size of staple, the basic household (office) type—with a wire size of .017 of an inch in diameter—is generally accepted as typical. The average multi-use stapler operates with wire sizes averaging .050 of an inch in diameter. Staplers used in the construction industry utilize what resemble nails that come in preloaded magazines (packets)—similar to firearm ammunition and probably almost as deadly at short range.

Even with the potential of dozens of uses, staplers are most frequently used in binding multi-page documents and other such related office tasks. They are extremely inexpensive: a "typical" home or office stapler costs less than $10.00, and a packet of 5,000 staples, less than $2.00.

Raw Materials

A stapler comprises many components, most of which are metal stampings and spring type parts. Main components of a typical home or office stapler include the base; the anvil (the metal plate over which you put the document that you want to staple); the magazine (which holds the staples); the metal head (which covers the magazine); and the hanger (which is welded to the base and holds the pin that connects the magazine and base). Rivets are used to keep the parts together, and a pin is the hinge point for the top and bottom half. There are also rubber and plastic materials used both in enhancing the product and in making the stapler cosmetically appealing. The springs in a stapler typically perform two separate jobs: they keep the row of staples lined up in the track and ready to be used, and they return the plunger blade to its original up position. (The plunger blade acts as a guillotine, in that it separates one single staple from the row of staples each time it is forced down.)

The most recent staplers are being made almost entirely of plastic. Currently, however, the most popularly used staplers are still those made of metal. Thus, the following focuses solely on the metal stapler and how it is manufactured.

The Manufacturing Process

While staplers are produced for a number of different uses and in just as many sizes, the basic principles behind the workings of each remain the same, and the chief components (springs, stampings, rivets, moldings, and pins), once completed, are assembled to create similar finished products.

Forming the springs

1 Two types of springs are used in the basic stapler: the coil and the leaf. A coil spring is made from metal that has the ability to withstand a constant pressure and release and still maintain its shape. The coil spring material is wound around an appropriately

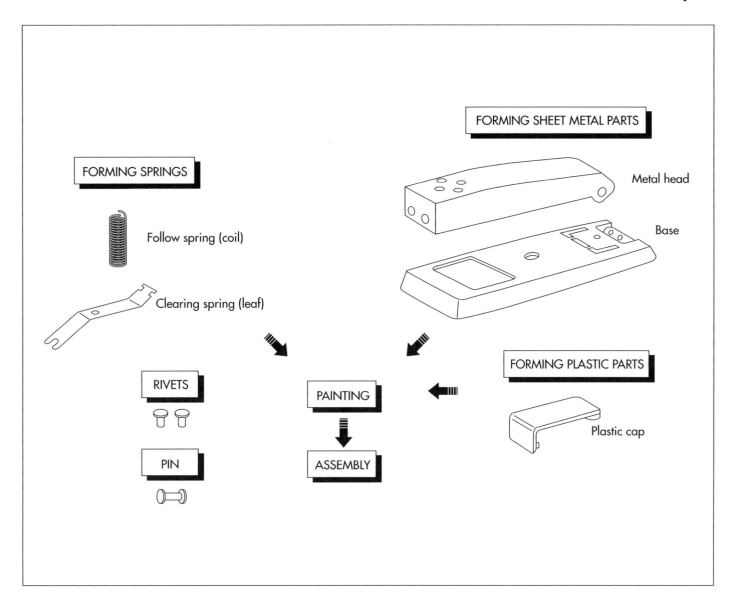

FORMING SHEET METAL PARTS

Metal head

Base

FORMING SPRINGS

Follow spring (coil)

Clearing spring (leaf)

RIVETS

PIN

PAINTING

ASSEMBLY

FORMING PLASTIC PARTS

Plastic cap

sized rod (similar to winding a thin wire around a pencil) and is then heat-treated to a produce changes in the metal's characteristics—changes that give the metal "elasticity." The heat-treated coil spring can be pulled apart and pressed together, within reason, and still return to its original wound up condition. A good example of a coil spring is the *follow spring*, which connects the case to the *follow block*—the metal piece in the magazine that holds the staples toward one end of the magazine.

2 Leaf springs, which resemble a diving board, are typically made by either bending or rolling (slightly curling) a thin piece of steel and then carefully heating it to a temperature that will cause internal stresses. Thinly slicing a carrot lengthwise into strips and then placing them in ice water causes the strips to curl up; this is the same effect observed when springs are properly heat-treated. The steel maintains either a curled or flat position and resists any bending motion applied to it. One example of a leaf spring is the *clearing spring*, the part on the underside of the stapler that allow you to unlatch the base from the upper assembly (the magazine and metal head).

Stamping of parts

3 Stampings are typically made of flat sheet metal material of varying thicknesses that are sandwiched between a punch and die. When the punch pushes on the material, it "shears" a piece of material (the shape of the punch) out of the sheet. A similar principle is applied when using a cookie cutter on rolled-out dough. Stamping material can also be in

The parts of a stapler are formed in various ways before coming together to form the finished item. Coil springs such as the follow spring are wound around rods and heat-treated, while leaf springs such as the clearing spring are rolled or bent to their proper shape. Sheet metal parts such as the head and base are typically stamped between a punch and die, while plastic parts can be injection molded.

The pins, stampings, and springs are subassembled in stages and then assembled together with the upper and lower halves of the stapler frame. The last items to be assembled are the feet (anti-skid rubber pads) and the snap-on plastic cap.

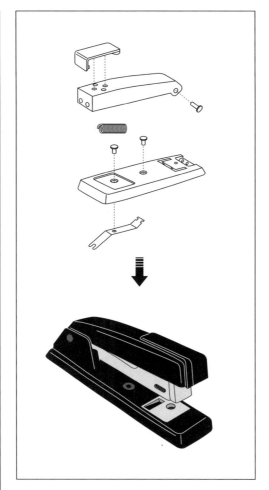

the form of a coil of material that looks something like a roll of paper towel. (The material type and thickness depends on the configuration of the part being made). The coil allows automatic feeding of the material across a punch and die using a coil feeder. The coil is gradually unwound as parts are stamped out of it. This is a very cost-efficient way of mass producing stampings because it does not require an operator to hold the material between the punch and die. Most of the major metal components besides springs and rivets, such as the base, metal head, and anvil, are made in this way.

Brake forming

4 After a part is stamped, it is usually then formed into a shape. If the shape is an intricate one, another type of punch and die is used. The material may also be heated in order to soften it, allowing the material to bend more easily. Most stapler parts have somewhat square corners, so typically the material is bent at 90 degree angles. There are now machines that perform stamping and

brake forming processes during the same operation; they simultaneously punch out shapes and bend them to make the appropriate parts. This eliminates the amount of setups and different machines required to make all of the parts.

Rivets

5 A rivet is usually made of a fairly strong steel material, but it must also have some elasticity. A rivet is designed to hold parts in place just like a screw and nut, except that the rivet is one piece and cannot be easily disassembled. One end typically has a head on it (like a nail or a screw), and the other end is usually hollow (either partially or along the whole length). Rivets are made by cutting off a piece of bar stock and forging it to obtain the desired configuration. Forging is a process similar to stamping, except that the starting material is almost to size already. Forging will minimally change the size and shape; the strength of the material, however, is significantly increased.

Creating plastic moldings

6 Plastic parts of staplers are made by injection molding, in which a liquified plastic is injected into a die. The liquid flows into the open void and is then cooled. As the die cools, the plastic solidifies and takes on the shape of the die. The die is opened and the part is removed.

Making the pin

7 The pin is little more than a piece of bar stock, cut off to a certain length either with a saw or on a machining center. Because the pin is used as a hinge point for the top and bottom half of the stapler, it is usually made from a strong, heat-treatable metal.

Painting

8 As required to prevent rust, or for cosmetic reasons, some of the components are painted. The parts are hung on small racks, set on a conveyor and passed by a spray nozzle. Some automatic painting operations employ electrostatic spraying, wherein the parts and **paint** are electrically charged. The paint and the parts are given opposite charges—for instance, the paint will be given a negative charge while the part will be given

a positive charge—because opposite electrical charges attract each other. Electrostatic painting ensures that every possible space on the part will be evenly painted. This method also eliminates wasted paint (overspray).

Assembly

9 The pins, stampings, and springs are sub-assembled in stages and then assembled together with the upper and lower halves of the stapler frame. For the bottom subassembly, consisting of the base, hanger, anvil, and clearing spring, the parts are placed in an assembly jig that holds them in position to allow the rivets to be placed in the correct holes. Once the rivets are locked in place, a tool called an *orbital riveter* spins the hollow end of the rivet until it collapses outward and captures the parts together. The top half, consisting of the magazine subassembly, the case, the follow spring, the driver-ram spring, and the metal head, is assembled the same way in it's own assembly jig.

10 The top and bottom halves come together in another jig, and the pin that connects the two is riveted into place. Finally, the finishing touches such as the feet (anti-skid rubber pads) and the plastic cap are then snapped on.

Quality Control

Samples of all the components are tested individually as they are manufactured. A certain percentage of parts are thoroughly checked as they come off of the automatic machines. Critical dimensions are scrutinized and adjustments are made to the machines or the tools are repaired/replaced as they wear out.

Once the parts are assembled, they are sample inspected for functionality and again a small number of units are continuously cycled until they wear out. The component that wears out is checked for conformity to determine whether it was normal wear or a design flaw.

An important item determining longevity and product warranty is the use of factory recommended staples. The use of incorrect staples is said to be attributed to cause the majority of stapler malfunctions. It should be noted that some stapler companies will service their staplers (for free or a nominal fee) only if their staples, exclusively, are used in the unit.

The Future

Staplers, like most other mechanisms, are continually adjusted and improved upon. As new materials and processes are developed, many uses become incorporated into all kinds of products, the stapler is no exception. Likewise the use for staplers will continue to increase as one of the latest uses is in the medical field as a substitute for stitches.

Where To Learn More

Books

Ewers, William. *The Staple Gun in Home and Industry*. Sincere Press, 1971.

Periodicals

Capotosto, Rosario. "Pop Goes the Stapler." *Popular Mechanics*. August, 1987, p. 19.

"Now, a Stapler Can Become a Riveting Tool." *Consumer Reports*. February, 1987, p. 73.

McCafferty, Phil. "Plastic Nails." *Popular Science*. April, 1987, p. 66.

—William L. Ansel

Stethoscope

The universally acknowledged inventor of the stethoscope is René-Théophile-Hyacinthe Laënnec, who, finding it difficult to listen to a patient's heartbeat unaided, rolled up a cylinder of paper, thereby amplifying the sound. Laënnec had noticed, as others such as Leonardo da Vinci had before him, that sound becomes amplified to the human ear as it passes through wood.

Background

A stethoscope is a medical instrument used to listen to sounds produced in the body, especially those that emanate from the heart and lungs. Most modern stethoscopes are binaural; that is, the instrument is intended for use with both ears. Stethoscopes comprise two flexible rubber tubes running from a valve to the earpieces. The valve also connects the tubes to the chestpiece, which can be either a bell-shaped piece to pick up low sounds or a flat disk for higher frequencies. The stethoscope is used mainly for the detection of heart murmurs, irregular heart rhythms, or abnormal heart sounds. It is also used to listen to the sound of air moving through the lungs in order to detect abnormalities in the air tubes and sacs found in the lung walls.

The universally acknowledged inventor of the stethoscope is René-Théophile-Hyacinthe Laënnec, who, finding it difficult to listen to a patient's heartbeat unaided, rolled up a cylinder of paper, thereby amplifying the sound. Laënnec had noticed, as others such as Leonardo da Vinci had before him, that sound becomes amplified to the human ear as it passes through wood. He observed children holding a piece of wood to their ears and scratching the other end. The wood increased the sound of the scratching. In 1819, Laënnec provided physicians with what he originally called a baton, a hollow cylinder made from wood (walnut or such light woods as fir or boxwood) perhaps as short as 5.9 inches (15 centimeters) in length. The bore was shaped like a **trumpet**, but for listening to the heart, a stopper could be inserted to make the bore merely cylindrical.

The first true stethoscopes (based on Laënnec's "baton") were made of wood (usually cedar or pine) tubes that ranged in shape from cylinder- to goblet- or hourglass-shaped. The lengths ranged from 5.90 to 8.86 inches (15 to 22.5 centimeters). Unlike those of today, these stethoscopes were monaural; that is, they were held to one ear and had no ear plugs. This type of stethoscope is still used in some places in Europe. Stethoscopes of varying materials (such as hard rubber or aluminum) were common during the mid-nineteenth century. A few telescoped to provide a stethoscope of varying length. The first innovation was not at first applied to the stethoscope, but to conversation tubes and hearing aids produced by many manufacturers in the late 1800s. These items were at first horn-shaped, yet eventually included earplugs connected to rubber tubes. Designers of stethoscopes adapted such devices, and the stethoscope of the time consisted of an earplug, a flexible rubber tube, and a bell-shaped chestpiece. Despite its shortcomings in the conductance of all chest sounds equally, this early stethoscope was commended for its convenient shape and flexibility.

Binaural stethoscopes increased in popularity fairly rapidly. As early as 1829 a trumpet-shaped mahogany chestpiece was screwed into a joint from which two lead pipes led to the ears. The device, invented by medical student Nicholas P. Comins, was deemed flexible (despite the rigidity of the wooden and metallic parts), because unlike the earlier monaural stethoscopes, it had movable parts.

The 1840s and 1850s saw the development of prototypes that closely resembled the stethoscope of today. In 1841 Marc-Hector Landouzy of Paris introduced a stethoscope made partly of gum elastic tubes; this proto-

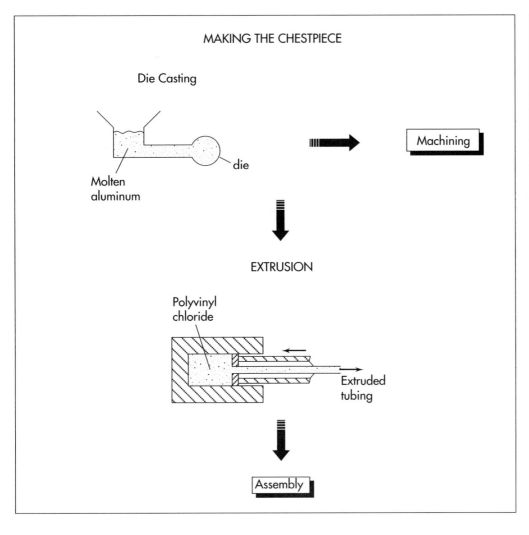

MAKING THE CHESTPIECE

Die Casting

Molten aluminum

die

Machining

EXTRUSION

Polyvinyl chloride

Extruded tubing

Assembly

The aluminum chestpiece is die cast into an approximation of its round shape before being machined to its exact form. The flexible tubing, which can be made of polyvinyl chloride or latex rubber, is extruded into shape.

type was improved slightly in 1851 by Arthur Leared of Dublin. The main problem with many early designs was the inferior earpieces that provided muffled sound. George Cammann of New York perfected the nineteenth century stethoscope in 1852. His instrument, considered to be the best of the time, had ivory or ebony knobs as earpieces, and these had springs attached to hold them more securely in the ear. The tubes were made of coils of wires sandwiched between rubber that was then coated with silk or cotton. The chestpiece was surrounded by a ring of rubber, creating a suction cup that more easily adhered to the skin.

Another type of stethoscope was developed in 1859. Designed by Scott Alison, the differential stethoscope had two separate chestpieces, allowing the user to hear and compare sounds in two different places. This stethoscope also allowed the physician to better pinpoint the source of the sound through the natural process of triangulation our ears normally use to discover the direction of sounds.

The first electronic stethoscopes became available as early as the 1890s; by 1902, Albert Abrams developed a truly useable one. With it, he was able to amplify the sounds made by the heart. By applying resistance gradually to the circuit, he could eliminate certain sounds, thereby differentiating between the heart's muscular and valvular movements.

The basic form of the binaural stethoscope has remained virtually unchanged since the beginning of the twentieth century. Major advancements have been made in the type of materials used—plastics such as polyvinyl chloride and Bakelite became available; the manufacturing processes that increase the airtightness and flexibility of the stethoscope have been refined; and large scale production has been streamlined, ensuring that medical practitioners can obtain sufficient stetho-

Although the stethoscope is a simple device, it is typical for its metal parts and plastic parts to be manufactured at separate locations, and for the entire device to be assembled at yet another location. It is also common for inexpensive models to be sold disassembled.

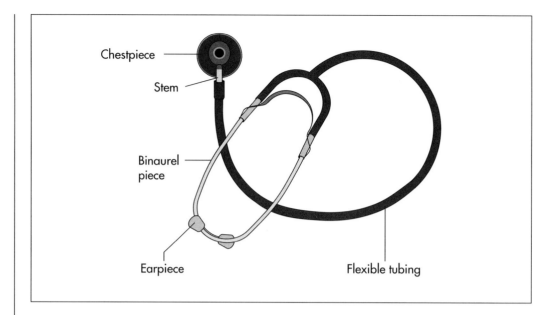

Chestpiece

Stem

Binaurel piece

Earpiece

Flexible tubing

scopes from a wide range of choices, and that consumers can purchase stethoscopes for home use.

Raw Materials

A binaural stethoscope consists of earplugs, binaural pieces, flexible tubing, a stem, and a chestpiece. The earplugs are attached to springs made of steel so that they fit firmly in the ears, while the earplugs themselves are made from either Delrin (a trademark plastic that is white, rigid, and similar to nylon) or softer molded silicone rubber. The binaural pieces that run from the earplugs to the flexible tubing, the stem that runs from the flexible tubing to the chestpiece, and the chestpiece itself are made from metal (aluminum, chrome-plated brass, or **stainless steel**). The flexible tubing is either polyvinyl chloride or latex rubber. The stem for stethoscopes with dual diaphragms has a valve with a steel **ball bearing** and a steel spring inside. This type of stethoscope can switch from a flat diaphragm to a cupped one when turned by shifting the ball bearing to cover up the pathway to the diaphragm that is not in use. The flat diaphragm is formed from a flat, thin, rigid plastic disk that can be Bakelite, an epoxy-fiberglass compound, or other suitable plastic. Today, most stethoscopes have an anti-chill ring attached to both sides of the diaphragm. The anti-chill ring, besides being more comfortable for the patient, allows better suction and thus allows sounds to be heard more clearly. The rings are made from either silicone rubber or polyvinyl chloride.

The Manufacturing Process

Although the stethoscope is a simple device, it is typical for its metal parts and plastic parts to be manufactured at separate locations, and for the entire device to be assembled at yet another location. It is also common for inexpensive models to be sold disassembled. Stethoscopes are rarely custom-made. If there is a large volume sold to one customer, the manufacturer can make a certain specified color or put the name of the hospital onto the stethoscopes.

Making the metal chestpiece

1 Aluminum is typically die cast. In this process, pressured molten aluminum is injected into molds, forming a slug in the form of a crude binaural piece or chestpiece. The slug is then machined to form its proper shape. Stainless steel arrives in huge rods that are machined on lathes using a semi-automatic process. Brass is also machined before being sent out for electroplating.

The machining process consists of cutting excess metal from the slug or rod according to a plan that will yield a correctly shaped binaural piece or chestpiece. The binaural piece is then threaded at the top for the earplugs, and barbs are cut into the bottom to allow for the tubing connection. The chestpiece is also barbed at the top to allow for the connection. The metal springs are then connected and sealed to the binaural pieces.

Forming the tubes

2 More expensive stethoscopes have tubing that is "dipped." The binaural pieces are repeatedly dipped into a liquid latex until the tubes are of the correct thickness. Tubes intended for inexpensive or disassembled models are molded or extruded using standard methods. To attach the separate tubing, it is first heated by placing it in warm water; next, it is pushed onto the binaural pieces, wrapping snugly around the barbs. Another less-common method of attaching the tubing is to place the binaural pieces in a mold and then place the tubing around them to form a seal.

Assembly

3 Stethoscopes are hand assembled. Once the binaural pieces have tubes, the diaphragm is placed in the chestpiece and sealed. Next, the anti-chill ring is put on both sides of the chestpiece. This can be done by cutting a recess in a circular track around the rim and slipping the ring inside. The preferred method is to stretch the ring around the rim of the diaphragm or bell, making a secure fit. The earplugs are then screwed on.

Packaging

4 Inexpensive stethoscopes, which may be disassembled, are placed in bags and sealed. Mid-range stethoscopes are boxed. Quality stethoscopes are placed in sturdy boxes that have spaces die-cut in the packaging into which the stethoscope and accessories fit snugly. The stethoscopes are then placed in cases that hold 20 to 50 boxes each and shipped to medical supply dealers, or, if there is a large volume, directly to a hospital. The medical supply dealers then provide stethoscopes to private practice, hospitals, medical supply stores, and drug stores.

Quality Control

A stethoscope must be able to pick up incredibly subtle, quiet sounds at such a level that a person of normal hearing can detect them using the instrument. Air leaks can decrease the volume of sound by as much as 10 to 15 decibels, as well as allow ambient noise to enter the stethoscope; therefore airtightness is imperative. Even inexpensive, disassembled stethoscopes available in drug stores easily disclose recognizable sounds (such as a heartbeat), while the highest quality instrument must meet tolerances of approximately 2.5×10^{-6} meters to ensure that all the pieces fit snugly and the junctions are airtight.

Air leaks are almost inevitable, and are caused by cracking, punctures, weakness of metal, or pinhole formation during the manufacturing process. To detect any problems before shipping, the manufacturer places the stethoscopes in a machine that blows a steady stream of air through each instrument. There are also tug tests for stethoscopes. The instrument is placed on a machine that pulls at a certain level of force to check whether normal use will separate the pieces.

All raw materials are also inspected, and each piece manufactured at a place other than the assembly plant is inspected for quality. Specific tolerances and procedures are checked at each step of the manufacturing and assembly process to see that the work is done correctly. The inspection consists of visually examining the stethoscope and testing the mechanical parts for proper fit and function. Every single assembled stethoscope is then checked to see if it is acoustically reliable.

Nurses, doctors, and other health care professionals undergo extensive training in auscultation so that they can interpret the sounds they hear, though most might specialize in only one or a few types of readings. For instance, somebody listening to a patient breathe must know the sounds of a healthy lung system, as well as the sounds of each type of lung dysfunction so the patient can be diagnosed correctly.

Maintenance and proper use of the stethoscope is just as important as the quality of manufacture. The stethoscope should be inspected periodically for air leaks and for defective parts that need replacing. To remove earwax and lint, the earplugs and chestpiece should be carefully wiped with rubbing alcohol, and the rest should be washed in mild, soapy water. If hospital procedure requires it, and the stethoscope can handle it, it should undergo standard sterilization procedures.

Where To Learn More

Books

Davis, Audrey B. *Medicine and Its Technology*. Greenwood Press, 1981.

Reiser, Stanley Joel. *Medicine and the Reign of Technology.* Cambridge University Press, 1978.

Periodicals

Bak, David J. "Stethoscope Allows Electronic Amplification," *Design News.* December 15, 1986, p. 50.

Beaumont, Estelle. "For the Latest Word on Stethoscopes: Listen Here!" *Nursing78.* November, 1978, pp. 33-37.

Jaffe, Joe. "Build This Doppler-Ultrasound Heart Monitor," *Radio-Electronics.* November, 1991, p. 49.

Reiser, Stanley Joel. "The Medical Influence of the Stethoscope," *Scientific American.* February, 1979, pp. 148-156.

Stone, John. "Cadence of the Heart," *The New York Times Magazine.* April 24, 1988, pp. 61-62.

—*Rose Secrest*

Sugar

Background

Before the birth of Jesus of Nazareth, sugarcane (from which sugar is made) was harvested on the shores of the Bay of Bengal; it spread to the surrounding territories of Malaysia, Indonesia, Indochina, and southern China. The Arabic people introduced "sugar" (at that point a sticky paste, semi-crystallized and believed to have medicinal value) to the Western world by bringing both the reed and knowledge for its cultivation to Sicily and then Spain in the eighth and ninth centuries. Later, Venice—importing finished sugar from Alexandria—succeeded in establishing a monopoly over this new spice by the fifteenth century; at that point, it started buying raw sugar, and even sugarcane, and treating it in its own refineries. Venice's monopoly, however, was short-lived. In 1498, Portuguese navigator Vasco da Gama returned from India bringing the sweet flavoring to Portugal. Lisbon started to import and refine raw sugar, and, in the sixteenth century, it became the European sugar capital. It was not long before the sweetener was available in France, where its primary function continued to be medicinal, and during the reign of Louis XIV, sugar could be bought by the ounce at the apothecary. By the 1800s, sugar (though still expensive) was widely available to both upper and middle classes.

Raw Materials

Sugar is a broad term applied to a large number of carbohydrates present in many plants and characterized by a more or less sweet taste. The primary sugar, glucose, is a product of photosynthesis and occurs in all green plants. In most plants, the sugars occur as a mixture that cannot readily be separated into the components. In the sap of some plants, the sugar mixtures are condensed into syrup. Juices of sugarcane (*Saccharum officinarum*) and sugar beet (*Beta vulgaris*) are rich in pure sucrose, although beet sugar is generally much less sweet than cane sugar. These two sugar crops are the main sources of commercial sucrose.

The sugarcane is a thick, tall, perennial grass that flourishes in tropical or subtropical regions. Sugar synthesized in the leaves is used as a source of energy for growth or is sent to the stalks for storage. It is the sweet sap in the stalks that is the source of sugar as we know it. The reed accumulates sugar to about 15 percent of its weight. Sugarcane yields about 2,600,000 tons of sugar per year.

The sugar beet is a beetroot variety with the highest sugar content, for which it is specifically cultivated. While typically white both inside and out, some beet varieties have black or yellow skins. About 3,700,000 tons of sugar are manufactured from sugar beet.

Other sugar crops include sweet sorghum, sugar maple, honey, and corn sugar. The types of sugar used today are white sugar (fully refined sugar), composed of clear, colorless or crystal fragments; or brown sugar, which is less fully refined and contains a greater amount of treacle residue, from which it obtains its color.

The Manufacturing Process

Planting and harvesting

1 Sugarcane requires an average temperature of 75 degrees Fahrenheit (23.9 degrees

Sugarcane is a perennial grass that flourishes in tropical or subtropical regions. Sugar synthesized in the leaves is used as energy for growth or sent to the stalks for storage—the stored sap in the stalks is the source of sugar as we know it. Sugar beet is a beetroot typically white both inside and out, although some beet varieties have black or yellow skins.

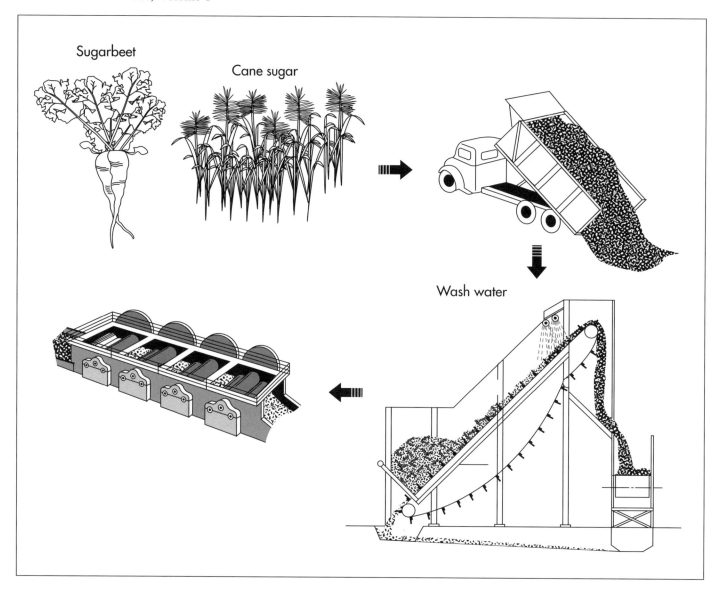

Sugarbeet

Cane sugar

Wash water

In the United States, harvesting of both cane and sugar beet is done primarily by machine, although in some states it is also done by hand. The harvested cane stalks and beets are loaded mechanically into trucks or railroad cars and taken to mills for processing into raw sugar. Once there, they are cleaned, washed, milled to extract juice, filtered, and purified. The result is a clear, sugar-filled juice.

Celsius) and uniform rainfall of about 80 inches (203 centimeters) per year. Therefore, it is grown in tropical or subtropical areas.

Sugarcane takes about seven months to mature in a tropical area and about 12-22 months in a subtropical area. At this time, fields of sugarcane are tested for sucrose, and the most mature fields are harvested first. In Florida, Hawaii, and Texas, standing cane is fired to burn off the dry leaves. In Louisiana, the six- to ten-feet (1.8- to 3-meter) tall cane stalks are cut down and laid on the ground before burning.

2 In the United States, harvesting (of both cane and sugar beet) is done primarily by machine, although in some states it is also done by hand. The harvested cane stalks are loaded mechanically into trucks or railroad

cars and taken to mills for processing into raw sugar.

Preparation and processing

3 After the cane arrives at the mill yards, it is mechanically unloaded, and excessive soil and rocks are removed. The cane is cleaned by flooding the carrier with warm water (in the case of sparse rock and trash clutter) or by spreading the cane on agitating conveyors that pass through strong jets of water and combing drums (to remove larger amounts of rocks, trash, and leaves, etc.). At this point, the cane is clean and ready to be milled.

When the beets are delivered at the refinery, they are first washed and then cut into strips. Next, they are put into diffusion cells with

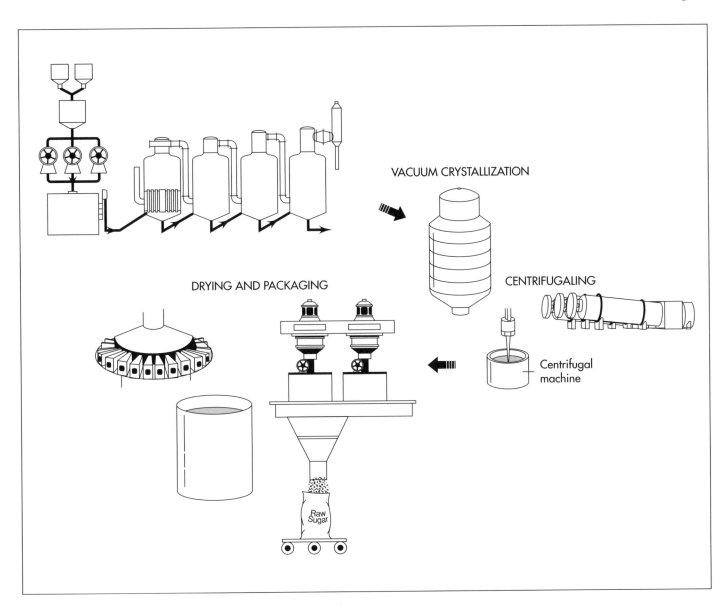

VACUUM CRYSTALLIZATION

DRYING AND PACKAGING

CENTRIFUGALING

Centrifugal machine

Raw Sugar

water at about 175 degrees Fahrenheit (79.4 degrees Celsius) and sprayed with hot water countercurrently to remove the sucrose.

Juice extraction pressing

4 Two or three heavily grooved crusher rollers break the cane and extract a large part of the juice, or swing-hammer type shredders (1,200 RPM) shred the cane without extracting the juice. Revolving knives cutting the stalks into chips are supplementary to the crushers. (In most countries, the shredder precedes the crusher.) A combination of two, or even all three, methods may be used. The pressing process involves crushing the stalks between the heavy and grooved metal rollers to separate the fiber (*bagasse*) from the juice that contains the sugar.

5 As the cane is crushed, hot water (or a combination of hot water and recovered impure juice) is sprayed onto the crushed cane countercurrently as it leaves each mill for diluting. The extracted juice, called *vesou*, contains 95 percent or more of the sucrose present. The mass is then diffused, a process that involves finely cutting or shredding the stalks. Next, the sugar is separated from the cut stalks by dissolving it in hot water or hot juice.

Purification of juice—clarification and evaporation

6 The juice from the mills, a dark green color, is acid and turbid. The clarification (or defecation) process is designed to remove both soluble and insoluble impurities (such as sand, soil, and ground rock) that

After being purifed, the clear juice undergoes vacuum evaporation to remove most of the water. In this process, four vacuum-boiling cells are arranged in series so that each succeeding cell has a higher vacuum. The vapors from one body can thus boil the juice in the next one, a method called *multiple-effect evaporation*. Next, the syrupy solution is vacuum-crystallized to form sugar crystals. The remaining liquid is removed using centrifugaling and drying, and the sugar is packaged.

have not been removed by preliminary screening. The process employs lime and heat as the clarifying agents. Milk of lime (about one pound per ton of cane) neutralizes the natural acidity of the juice, forming insoluble lime salts. Heating the lime juice to boiling coagulates the albumin and some of the fats, waxes, and gums, and the precipitate formed entraps suspended solids as well as the minute particles.

The sugar beet solution, on the other hand, is purified by precipitating calcium carbonate, calcium sulfite, or both in it repeatedly. Impurities become entangled in the growing crystals of precipitate and are removed by continuous filtration.

7 The muds separate from the clear juice through sedimentation. The non-sugar impurities are removed by continuous filtration. The final clarified juice contains about 85 percent water and has the same composition as the raw extracted juice except for the removed impurities.

8 To concentrate this clarified juice, about two-thirds of the water is removed through vacuum evaporation. Generally, four vacuum-boiling cells or bodies are arranged in series so that each succeeding body has a higher vacuum (and therefore boils at a lower temperature). The vapors from one body can thus boil the juice in the next one—the steam introduced into the first cell does what is called *multiple-effect evaporation.* The vapor from the last cell goes to a condenser. The syrup leaves the last body continuously with about 65 percent solids and 35 percent water.

The sugar beet sucrose solution, at this point, is also nearly colorless, and it likewise undergoes multiple-effect vacuum evaporation. The syrup is seeded, cooled, and put in a centrifuge machine. The finished beet crystals are washed with water and dried.

Crystallization

9 Crystallization is the next step in the manufacture of sugar. Crystallization takes place in a single-stage vacuum pan. The syrup is evaporated until saturated with sugar. As soon as the saturation point has been exceeded, small grains of sugar are

added to the pan, or "strike." These small grains, called *seed,* serve as nuclei for the formation of sugar crystals. (Seed grain is formed by adding 56 ounces [1,600 grams] of white sugar into the bowl of a slurry machine and mixing with 3.3 parts of a liquid mixture: 70 percent methylated spirit and 30 percent glycerine. The machine runs at 200 RPM for 15 hours.) Additional syrup is added to the strike and evaporated so that the original crystals that were formed are allowed to grow in size.

The growth of the crystals continues until the pan is full. When sucrose concentration reaches the desired level, the dense mixture of syrup and sugar crystals, called *massecuite,* is discharged into large containers known as crystallizers. Crystallization continues in the crystallizers as the massecuite is slowly stirred and cooled.

10 Massecuite from the mixers is allowed to flow into centrifugals, where the thick syrup, or molasses, is separated from the raw sugar by centrifugal force.

Centrifugaling

11 The high-speed centrifugal action used to separate the massecuite into raw sugar crystals and molasses is done in revolving machines called centrifugals. A centrifugal machine has a cylindrical basket suspended on a spindle, with perforated sides lined with wire cloth, inside which are metal sheets containing 400 to 600 perforations per square inch. The basket revolves at speeds from 1,000 to 1,800 RPM. The raw sugar is retained in the centrifuge basket because the perforated lining retains the sugar crystals. The mother liquor, or molasses, passes through the lining (due to the centrifugal force exerted). The final molasses (*blackstrap molasses*) containing sucrose, reducing sugars, organic nonsugars, ash, and water, is sent to large storage tanks.

Once the sugar is centrifuged, it is "cut down" and sent to a granulator for drying. In some countries, sugarcane is processed in small factories without the use of centrifuges, and a dark-brown product (noncentrifugal sugar) is produced. Centrifugal sugar is produced in more than 60 countries while noncentrifugal sugar in about twenty countries.

Drying and packaging

12 Damp sugar crystals are dried by being tumbled through heated air in a granulator. The dry sugar crystals are then sorted by size through vibrating screens and placed into storage bins. Sugar is then sent to be packed in the familiar packaging we see in grocery stores, in bulk packaging, or in liquid form for industrial use.

Byproducts

The bagasse produced after extracting the juice from sugar cane is used as fuel to generate steam in factories. Increasingly large amounts of bagasse are being made into paper, insulating board, and hardboard, as well as furfural, a chemical intermediate for the synthesis of furan and tetrahydrofuran.

The beet tops and extracted slices as well the molasses are used as feed for cattle. It has been shown that more feed for cattle and other such animals can be produced per acre-year from beets than from any other crop widely grown in the United States. The beet strips are also treated chemically to facilitate the extraction of commercial pectin.

The end product derived from sugar refining is blackstrap molasses. It is used in cattle feed as well as in the production of industrial alcohol, yeast, organic chemicals, and rum.

Quality Control

Mill sanitation is an important factor in quality control measures. Bacteriologists have shown that a small amount of sour bagasse can infect the whole stream of warm juice flowing over it. Modern mills have self-cleaning troughs with a slope designed in such a way that bagasse does not hold up but flows out with the juice stream. Strict measures are taken for insect and pest controls.

Because cane spoils relatively quickly, great steps have been taken to automate the methods of transportation and get the cane to the mills as quickly as possible. Maintaining the high quality of the end-product means storing brown and yellow refined sugars (which contain two percent to five percent moisture) in a cool and relatively moist atmosphere, so that they continue to retain their moisture and do not become hard.

Most granulated sugars comply with standards established by the National Food Processors Association and the pharmaceutical industry (U.S. Pharmacopeia, National Formulary).

Where To Learn More

Books

Clarke, M. A., ed. *Chemistry & Processing of Sugarbeet & Sugarcane.* Elsevier Science Publishing Co., Inc., 1988.

Hugot, E. *Handbook of Cane Sugar Engineering.* 3rd ed. Elsevier Science Publishing Co., Inc., 1986.

Lapedes, Daniel, ed. *McGraw Hill Encyclopedia of Food, Agriculture and Nutrition.* McGraw Hill, 1977.

McGee, Harold. *On Food and Cooking: The Science and Lore of the Kitchen.* Collier Books, 1984.

Meade, G. P. *Cane Sugar Handbook: A Manual for Cane Sugar Manufacturers and Their Chemists.* John Wiley and Sons, 1977.

Pennington, Neil L. and Charles Baker, eds. *Sugar: A Users' Guide to Sucrose.* Van Nostrand Reinhold, 1991.

Rost, Waverly. *Food.* Simon & Schuster, 1980.

Periodicals

"Sugar: Can We Make It On the Homestead?" *Countryside & Small Stock Journal.* May-June, 1987, p. 9.

Hayes, Joanne L. "Sugarloaf Lore," *Country Living.* March, 1989, p. 132.

"Squeezing All the Sweetness Out of Sugarcane—and More," *Chemical & Engineering News.* May 12, 1986, pp. 38-9.

—*Eva Sideman*

Super Glue

Cyanoacrylate glues are often called super glue. Usually referred to as C.A.s, these glues typify the newest and strongest of modern glues. Although well known for home uses, C.A.s have found industrial applications in construction, medicine, and dentistry.

Background

Glue is a gelatinous adhesive substance used to form a surface attachment between discrete materials. Currently, there are five basic types of glue. Solvent glues comprise an adhesive base mixed with a chemical solvent that makes the glue spreadable; the glue dries as the solvent evaporates. Most solvents are flammable, and they evaporate quickly; toluene, a liquid hydrocarbon made from fossil fuels, is often used. Included in this category are glues sold as liquid solders and so-called contact cements.

Water-based glues use water as a solvent instead of chemicals. They work slower than chemical solvent glues; however, they are not flammable. This category comprises such glues as white glue and powdered casein glue, made from milk protein and mixed at home or in the shop.

Two part glues include epoxy and resorcinol, a crystalline phenol that can be synthesized or made from organic resins. One part contains the actual glue; the other part is a catalyst or hardener. Two part glue is very useful for working with metals (**automobile** dent filler is a two part glue) but must be mixed properly to work well.

Animal hide glues are useful for woodworking and veneer work. Made from the hides as well as the bones and other portions of animals, the glue is sold either ready-made or as a powder or flake that can be mixed with water, heated, and applied hot.

Cyanoacrylate glues, usually referred to as *C.A.s*, typify the newest and strongest of modern glues, which are made from synthetic polymers. A polymer is a complex molecule made up of smaller, simpler molecules (monomers) that attach to form repeating structural units. Once a polymeric reaction has been catalyzed, it can be difficult to halt: the natural impulse to form polymeric chains is very strong, as are the resulting molecular bonds—and the glues based upon them. In the home and office, small quantities of C.A.s are useful for an almost infinite number of repairs such as mending broken pottery, repairing joints, and even holding together split fingernails. In industry, C.A.s have become important in construction, medicine, and dentistry.

Cyanoacrylate glues were discovered at a Kodak lab in 1951 when two chemists, Dr. Harry Coover and Dr. Fred Joyner, tried to insert a film of ethyl cyanoacrylate between two prisms of a refractometer to determine the degree to which it refracted, or bent, light passing through it. Though the first conclusion of Coover, Joyner, and the other members of the lab team was only that an expensive piece of laboratory equipment had been ruined, they soon realized that they had stumbled upon a new type of adhesive.

Moving from a lab accident to a marketable product is not easy; Kodak did not begin selling the first cyanoacrylate glue, Eastman 910, until 1958 (the company no longer makes C.A. adhesives). Today, several companies make C.A. glues in a variety of formulations. Some large manufacturers operate research laboratories to respond to new demands for special formulations and to develop new and better C.A.s.

The method by which polymers act as a glue is not completely understood. Most other glues work on a hook and eye principle—the

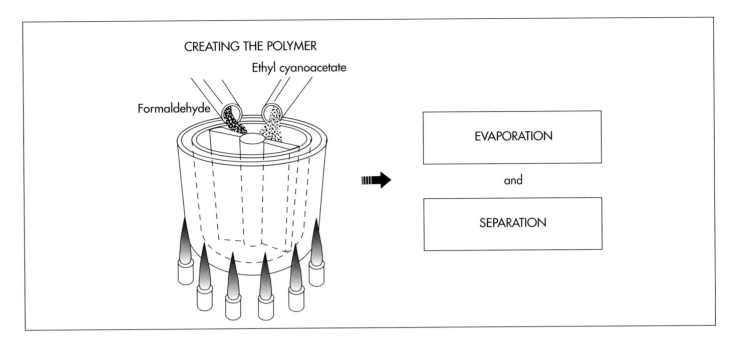

CREATING THE POLYMER

Formaldehyde

Ethyl cyanoacetate

EVAPORATION

and

SEPARATION

glue forms into microscopic hooks and eyes that grab onto each other, a sort of molecular velcro. With glues that work this way, the thicker the application, the more effective the bond. However, cyanoacrylate glues appear to bond differently. Current theory attributes the adhesive qualities of the cyanoacrylate polymer to the same electromagnetic force that holds all atoms together. Although a sizeable mass of one substance will electronically repel any other substance, two atoms of different substances placed in very close proximity will exert a mutually attractive force. Experiments with several substances have shown that two pieces of the same experimental material (**gold**, for example) can be made to adhere to each other without benefit of an added adhesive if forced into close proximity.

This phenomenon explains why a thin film of C.A. glue works better than a thicker one. A thinner glue can be squeezed so close to the material it is bonding that the electromagnetic force takes over. A thicker film permits enough space between the materials it is bonding so that the molecules can repel one another, and the glue will consequently not hold as well.

Raw Materials

The chemicals necessary to form cyanoacrylate polymer include ethyl cyanoacetate, formaldehyde, nitrogen or some other nonre-active gas, free radical inhibitors, and base scavengers. Ethyl cyanoacetate comprises ethyl, a hydrocarbon radical (a radical is an atom or group of atoms that, because it contains an unpaired electron, is more likely to react with other atoms), cyanide, and acetate, an ester produced by mixing acetic acid with alcohol and removing the water. Formaldehyde is a colorless gas often used in the manufacture of synthetic resins. Nitrogen is an the most abundant gas in the earth's atmosphere, comprising 78 percent of by volume and occurring as well in all living tissue. Because it does not react with other substances, it is commonly used to buffer highly reactive elements that would otherwise engage in undesired reactions with contiguous substances. Free radical inhibitors and base scavengers both serve to remove substances that would otherwise sabotage the product.

The Manufacturing Process

C.A.s are produced in heated kettles that can hold from a few gallons to several thousand gallons; the size depends upon the scale of the particular manufacturing operation.

Creating the polymer

1 The initial ingredient is ethyl cyanoacetate. Placed into a glass-lined kettle with revolving mixing blades, this material is then mixed with formaldehyde. The mixing of the two chemicals triggers condensation, a

The initial ingredient in super glue, ethyl cyanoacetate, is placed into a kettle with revolving blades and mixed with formaldehyde. The mixing triggers condensation, a chemical reaction that produces water; this water is then evaporated as the kettle is heated. When the water has evaporated, what remains in the kettle is the C.A. polymer. Next, the kettle is heated again, causing thermal cracking of the polymer and creating reactive monomers that separate out. When the finished glue is applied, these monomers recombine to form a bond.

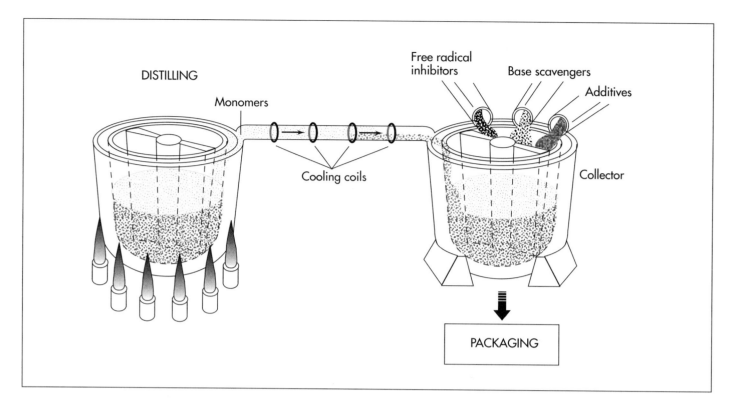

DISTILLING

Monomers

Cooling coils

Free radical inhibitors

Base scavengers

Additives

Collector

PACKAGING

The separated monomers are piped to a second kettle. In going from one vessel to the other, the monomers move through a series of cooling coils that allow them to become liquid. The contents of the second collecting container (the one holding the liquid monomers) are effectively the C.A. glue, although they still need to be protected against curing. Various chemicals called free radical inhibitors and base scavengers are added to precipitate out impurities that would otherwise harden the mixture. After receiving any necessary additives, the glue is packaged accordingly.

chemical reaction that produces water that is then evaporated as the kettle is heated. When the water has evaporated, what remains in the kettle is the C.A. polymer.

2 Because the C.A. will begin to cure, or harden, on contact with any moisture, the kettle space left empty by the evaporation of the water is filled with a nonreactive gas such as nitrogen.

Separating monomers from the polymer

3 Next, the kettle is heated to a temperature of approximately 305 degrees Fahrenheit (150 degrees Celsius). Heating the mixture causes thermal cracking of the polymer, creating reactive monomers (chemically, ethyl cyanoacrylate esters; with a slightly different process, methyl cyanoacrylate esters are possible) that will, when the finished glue is applied, recombine to form a bond.

4 Because the monomers are lighter than the polymer, they volatize upward and are piped out of the kettle into a second collector. The process is not unlike distilling, although the goal is a glue rather than an alcoholic beverage. In going from one vessel to the other, the monomers move through a series of cooling coils that allow them to

become liquid. A second distilling might be performed for a high-quality product, and some manufacturers might even distill the monomers a third time.

Preventing curing

5 The contents of the second collecting container (the one holding the liquid monomers) are effectively the C.A. glue, although they still need to be protected against curing. Various chemicals called free radical inhibitors and base scavengers are added to precipitate out impurities that would otherwise harden the mixture. Because the quantities of impurities and precipitates are small (measurable in nothing larger than parts per million), there is no need to remove them from the C.A. mixture. If particles of precipitate were visible, even under several hundred magnifications, it would be a sign of severe contamination, and the batch would be destroyed.

Additives and packaging

6 The C.A. glue can, at this point, receive any additives that the manufacturer wishes. These additives can control the viscosity of the C.A. (in fact, at least three different thicknesses are sold), or they can allow the glue to work on material types that

earlier C.A.s could not. A thicker viscosity is desired when bonding is to be done on surfaces that don't meet very well; the thicker viscosity allows the glue to fill the empty spaces before it sets. Without other additives, C.A.s might need to be restricted to nonporous surfaces. With additives in the C.A. or with some surface preparation, the C.A. will work very well. C.A. technology is sufficiently mature that a manufacturer can meet a request from a customer for a C.A. that will bond almost any given pair of surfaces.

7 The C.A. can now be added to tubes using conventional, albeit humidity-free, techniques. Once a tube is filled, a top is fitted and crimped on, and the bottom of the tube is crimped closed. Because most metal tubes would react with the C.A., packaging tubes are usually made of a plastic material such as polyethylene, although aluminum tubes are possible. Once the C.A. is exposed to moisture or an alkaline, either in the air or on the surfaces being glued, the monomers will repolymerize and harden, forming a tremendously strong bond between the two substances. The reaction is total; the entire amount of C.A. that has been placed on the substances will polymerize.

Quality Control

Careful quality control must be exercised if the product is to work as it is supposed to. Because the polymerization of monomers is a universal reaction (it spreads throughout the amount of glue put on a surface, so that by the time the reaction has ended there is no glue left unpolymerized), any flaw in any step of the manufacturing process can affect thousands of gallons of material.

Tremendous emphasis is placed on the quality of chemicals and supplies coming into the plant. Ideally, all suppliers have approved quality control procedures to assure delivery of quality product to the plant.

Although the manufacturing process is automatic, it is carefully monitored in the plant at all stages of operation. The duration of the mixing, the amount of mixture at each stage, and the temperature all need to be watched by operators ready to adjust the machines if necessary.

The finished product also is tested before shipping. Most important is shear resistance, a measure of the force necessary to break the holding power of the glue. Measures of shear strength commonly reach several thousands of pounds of force per square inch.

Where To Learn More

Books

Lee, Lieng-Huang. *Adhesive Bonding.* Plenum Press, 1991.

Packham, D. E., ed. *Handbook of Adhesion.* Longman Publishing Group, 1993.

Skeist, Irving. *Handbook of Adhesives.* Van Nostrand Reinhold, 1977.

Swezey, Kenneth M., updated by Robert Scharff. *Workshop Formulas, Tips & Data.* Sterling Publishing Co., 1989, pp. 194-212.

Periodicals

"Which Glue for Which Job?" *Consumer Reports.* January, 1988, pp. 46-51.

Hand, A. J. "What to Know About Super Glues," *Consumers' Research.* November, 1990, pp. 32, 40.

Hand, A. J. "Secrets of the Superglues," *Popular Science.* February, 1989, pp. 82-84+.

Sterling, Bruce. "Superglue." *The Magazine of Fantasy and Science Fiction.* June, 1993, p. 107.

—Lawrence H. Berlow

Thermometer

The thermoscope, developed by Galileo around 1592, was the first instrument used to measure temperature qualitatively. It comprised a large bulb flask with a long, open neck and used wine to indicate the reading, making it extremely sensitive to barometric pressure.

Background

A thermometer is a device used to measure temperature. The thermoscope, developed by Galileo around 1592, was the first instrument used to measure temperature qualitatively. It was not until 1611 that Sanctorius Sanctorius, a colleague of Galileo, devised and added a scale to the thermoscope, thus facilitating quantitative measurement of temperature change. By this time the instrument was called the thermometer, from the Greek words *therme* ("heat") and *metron* ("measure"). About 1644 it became obvious, however, that this instrument—comprising a large bulb flask with a long, open neck, using **wine** to indicate the reading—was extremely sensitive to barometric pressure. To alleviate the problem, Grand Duke Ferdinand II of Tuscany developed a process to hermetically seal the thermometer, thereby eliminating outside barometric influence. The basic form has varied little since.

There are many types of thermometers in use today: the recording thermometer uses a pen on a rotating drum to continuously record temperature readings; the digital readout thermometers often coupled with other weather measuring devices; and the typical household types hung on a wall, post, or those used for medical purposes.

With a thermometer, temperature can be measured using any of three primary units: Fahrenheit, Celsius, or Kelvin. At one point during the eighteenth century, nearly 35 scales of measure had been developed and were in use.

In 1714 Gabriel Daniel Fahrenheit, a Dutch instrument maker known for his fine crafts-manship, developed a thermometer using 32 (the melting point of ice) and 96 (the standard temperature of the human body) as his fixed points. It has since been determined that 32 and 212 (the boiling point of water) are the scale's fixed points, with 98.6 being accepted as the healthy, normal body temperature.

Swedish scientist Anders Celsius, in 1742, assigned 0 degrees as the point at which water boiled and 100 degrees as the point at which ice melted. These two figures were eventually switched—creating the scale we know today—with 0 degrees as the freezing point of water and 100 degrees as the boiling point. Use of this scale quickly spread through Sweden and to France, and for two centuries it was known as the centigrade scale. The name was changed in 1948 to Celsius to honor its inventor.

In 1848 another scientist, Lord Kelvin (William Thomson), proposed another scale based on the same principles as the Celsius thermometer, with the fixed point of absolute zero set at the equivalent of -273.15 degrees Celsius (the units used on this scale are called Kelvin [K]). The freezing and boiling points of water are registered at 273 K and 373 K respectively. The Kelvin scale is most often used in scientific research studies.

Design

The operating principle of a thermometer is quite simple. A known measure of liquid (mercury, alcohol, or a hydrocarbon-based fluid) is vacuum-sealed in a glass tube. The liquid expands or contracts when air is heated or cooled. As the liquid level changes, a corresponding temperature scale can be read to indicate the current temperature.

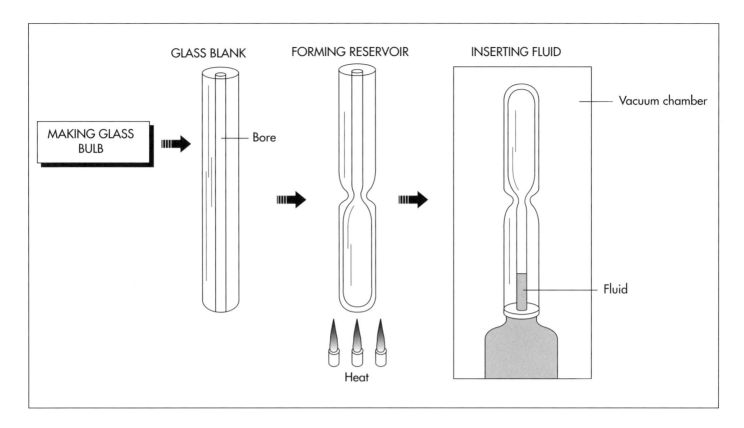

GLASS BLANK   FORMING RESERVOIR   INSERTING FLUID

MAKING GLASS BULB

Bore

Heat

Vacuum chamber

Fluid

Thermometers are designed according to pre-defined standards identified by the National Institute of Standards and Technology (NIST, formerly the National Bureau of Standards) and standard manufacturing practices. Within the regulatory guidelines there are provisions for the custom manufacture of thermometers. Custom thermometers can be as varied as those who use them. Different sizes exist for the amount, weight, and length of glass used, the type of liquid filled into the glass, the frequency of gradations laid onto the glass tube or enclosure, and even the color of the gradation scale marks.

A design engineer will look at the travel limits for the liquid to be used in the thermometer. Once precise limits are established, the dimensions of the glass tube and size of the glass bulb can be determined.

Use of electronic components in thermometers has grown. Many of today's broadly used thermometers contain digital readouts and sample program cycles to feed back the current temperature to a **light-emitting diode (LED)** or **liquid crystal display (LCD)** panel. For all the electronic wizardry available, a thermometer must still contain a heat-cold sensitizing element in order to respond to environmental changes.

Raw Materials

Thermometers consist of three basic elements: spirit-filled liquid, which responds to changes in heat and cold; a glass tube to house the temperature-measuring liquid; and black ink to color in the engraved scale marks with legible numbers. In addition, other elements are necessary for the manufacture of thermometers, including a wax solution used to engrave the scale marks on the glass tube; an engraving engine that makes permanent gradations on the glass tube; and a hydrofluoric acid solution into which the glass tube is dipped to seal the engraving marks.

The glass material forming the body of the thermometer is usually received from an outside manufacturer. Some thermometer products are made with an enclosure, which can be made of plastic or composites and may contain scale gradations as opposed to having these on the glass tube itself. The enclosure also serves to protect and mount the thermometer on a wall, post, or in a weather shelter box.

The Manufacturing Process

Although there are numerous types of thermometers, the production process for the

Thermometer manufacturers start with glass blanks with bores down the middle; these are usually received from glass manufacturers. The bulb reservoir is formed by heating one end of the glass tube and pinching it closed. The bulb is sealed at its bottom, leaving an open tube at the top.

Next, with the open end down in a vacuum chamber, air is evacuated from the glass tube, and the hydrocarbon fluid is introduced into the vacuum until it penetrates the tube about 1 inch. Due to environmental concerns, contemporary thermometers are manufactured less with mercury and more with a spirit-filled hydrocarbon liquid.

most common of these—the classic household variety—is described below.

The glass bulb

1 First, the raw glass material is received from an outside manufacturer. The tube is made with a fine passage, or bore, throughout its length. The bored tubes are checked for quality; any rejected parts are sent back to the manufacturer for replacement.

2 The bulb reservoir is formed by heating one end of the glass tube, pinching it closed, and using glassblowing and the application of an air-driven torch to complete it. Alternately, the bulb can be made by blowing a separate piece of lab material that is then joined with one end of the glass tube. The bulb is sealed at its bottom, leaving an open tube at the top.

Adding the fluid

3 With the open end down in a vacuum chamber, air is then evacuated from the glass tube, and the hydrocarbon fluid is introduced into the vacuum until it penetrates the tube about 1 inch (2.54 centimeters). Due to environmental concerns, contemporary thermometers are manufactured less with mercury and more with a spirit-filled hydrocarbon liquid. Such a practice is mandated (with tolerance for a limited use of mercury) by the Environmental Protection Agency (EPA).

The vacuum is then gradually reduced, forcing the fluid down near the top of the tube. The process is the same when mercury is used, except heat is also applied in the vacuum chamber.

4 Once full, the tube is placed upon its bulb end. A heating-out process is then conducted by placing the thermometer into a warm bath and raising the temperature to 400 degrees Fahrenheit (204 degrees Celsius). Next, the temperature is reduced to room temperature to bring the residual liquid back to a known level. The open end of the thermometer is then sealed by placing it over a flame.

Applying the scale

5 After the tube is sealed, a scale is applied based on the level at which the fluid rests when inserted into a water bath of 212 degrees Fahrenheit (100 degrees Celsius) versus one at 32 degrees Fahrenheit (0 degrees Celsius). These reference points for the desired scale are marked on the glass tube before engraving or silkscreening is done to fill gradations.

6 The range lengths vary according to the design used. A scale is picked that best corresponds to even marks between the reference points. For accuracy purposes, engraving is the preferred method of marking. The marks are made by an engraving engine after the thermometer is placed in wax. The numbers are scratched onto the glass and, once complete, the thermometer is dipped in hydrofluoric acid to seal the engraved markings. Ink is then rubbed into the marks to highlight the scale values. When enclosures are used on the scales, a silkscreening process is used to apply the marks.

7 Finally, the thermometers are packaged accordingly and shipped to customers.

Quality Control

The manufacturing process is controlled by widely adopted industry standards and specific in-house measures. Manufacturing design considerations include quality control checks throughout the production process. The equipment used to perform fabrication tasks must also be carefully maintained, especially with updated design protocol.

Waste materials accrued during manufacturing are disposed of according to environmental regulatory standards. During the manufacturing cycle, equipment used to heat, evacuate, and engrave the thermometer must be checked and calibrated regularly. Tolerance tests are also performed, using a known standard, to determine the accuracy of the temperature readings. All thermometers have a tolerance for accuracy. For the common household, this tolerance is usually plus or minus 2 degrees Fahrenheit (16 degrees Celsius). For laboratory work, plus or minus 1 degree is generally acceptable.

The Future

Although the longstanding simple glass thermometer is unlikely to change, other ther-

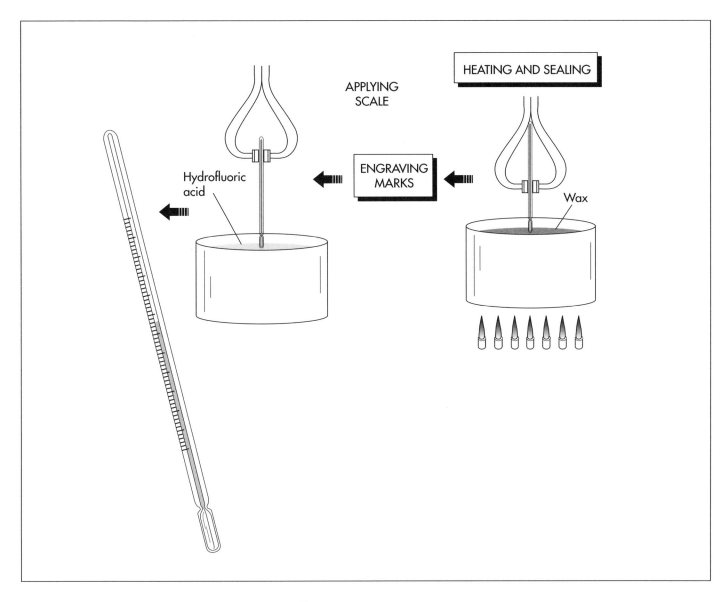

APPLYING
SCALE

HEATING AND SEALING

ENGRAVING
MARKS

Hydrofluoric
acid

Wax

mometer forms continue to evolve. With technological advances and the more widespread use of lighter and stronger materials, manufacturers of electronically integrated temperature instruments can provide more accurate measurements of temperature with minimal equipment bulk and at an affordable price. Analog box thermometers, for example, were once used with a long wire and probe tip for in-ground temperature measurements, among other uses. Today, the probe tips are made of lighter materials, and the boxes, loaded with digital electronics, are not as bulky and square. Looking ahead, further work with the microchip may provide the impetus to fully digitize the temperature measuring process. Also, it may eventually be possible to direct an infrared beam into soil and extract a temperature reading from a target depth without even touching the soil.

Where To Learn More

Books

Gardner, Robert. *Temperature and Heat.* Simon & Schuster, 1993.

McGee, Thomas D. *Principles and Methods of Temperature Measurement.* John Wiley & Sons, 1988.

Pavese, F., ed. *Modern Gas-Based Temperature and Pressure Measurements.* Plenum Publishing, 1992.

Periodicals

Alderman, Lesley. "Stick It In An Ear," *Money.* January, 1993, p. 19.

"Fever Thermometers," *Consumer Reports.* December, 1988, p. 214.

After the bulb reservoir is formed and the liquid inserted, the unit is heated and sealed. Next, the scale markings are added. This is done using engraving, in which the bulb is dipped in wax, the marks engraved, and the bulb dipped in hydrofluoric acid to seal the marks on the glass.

DiChristina, Mariette. "Thermometer You Swallow," *Popular Science*. March, 1990, p. 113.

"Taking the Heat from Inside," *Discover*. June, 1988, p. 12.

Joyce, Mary E. "Thermometer Assists in Cancer Therapy," *Design News*. September 21, 1992, p. 46.

—*Matthew Fogel*

Tire

Background

A tire is a strong, flexible rubber casing attached to the rim of a wheel. Tires provide a gripping surface for traction and serve as a cushion for the wheels of a moving vehicle. Tires are found on **automobile**s, trucks, buses, aircraft landing gear, tractors and other farm equipment, industrial vehicles such as forklifts, and common conveyances such as baby carriages, shopping carts, wheel chairs, bicycles, and motorcycles.

Tires for most vehicles are pneumatic; air is held under pressure inside the tire. Until recently, pneumatic tires had an inner tube to hold the air pressure, but now pneumatic tires are designed to form a pressure seal with the rim of the wheel.

Scottish inventor Robert Thomson developed the pneumatic tire with inner tube in 1845, but his design was ahead of its time and attracted little interest. The pneumatic tire was reinvented in the 1880s by another Scotsman, John Boyd Dunlop, and became immediately popular with bicyclists.

Natural rubber is the main raw material used in manufacturing tires, although synthetic rubber is also used. In order to develop the proper characteristics of strength, resiliency, and wear-resistance, however, the rubber must be treated with a variety of chemicals and then heated. American inventor Charles Goodyear discovered the process of strengthening rubber, known as *vulcanization* or *curing*, by accident in 1839. He had been experimenting with rubber since 1830 but had been unable to develop a suitable curing process. During an experiment with a mixture of india rubber and sulfur, Goodyear dropped the mixture on a hot stove. A chemical reaction took place and, instead of melting, the rubber-sulfur mixture formed a hard lump. He continued his experiments until he could treat continuous sheets of rubber.

Today, large, efficient factories staffed with skilled workers produce more than 250 million new tires a year. Although automation guides many of the steps in the manufacturing process, skilled workers are still required to assemble the components of a tire.

Raw Materials

Rubber is the main raw material used in manufacturing tires, and both natural and synthetic rubber are used. Natural rubber is found as a milky liquid in the bark of the rubber tree, *Hevea Brasiliensis*. To produce the raw rubber used in tire manufacturing, the liquid latex is mixed with acids that cause the rubber to solidify. Presses squeeze out excess water and form the rubber into sheets, and then the sheets are dried in tall smokehouses, pressed into enormous bales, and shipped to tire factories around the world. Synthetic rubber is produced from the polymers found in crude oil.

The other primary ingredient in tire rubber is carbon black. Carbon black is a fine, soft powder created when crude oil or natural gas is burned with a limited amount of oxygen, causing incomplete combustion and creating a large amount of fine soot. So much carbon black is required for manufacturing tires that rail cars transport it and huge silos store the carbon black at the tire factory until it is needed.

Sulfur and other chemicals are also used in tires. Specific chemicals, when mixed with

The tire-building machine invented by W. C. State of Goodyear Tire Company in 1909 dramatically increased workers' productivity.

The history of tires provides an excellent example of how innovations in one industry can cause massive changes in another. Simply put, the "take-off" of the automobile industry transformed the rubber industry in the United States during the early years of the twentieth century. The late-nineteenth century rubber industry concentrated on producing footwear and bicycle and carriage tires. By World War I, rubber and automobile tires were virtually synonymous in the public mind. Seven thousand new car sales in 1901 were accompanied by sales of 28,000 tires as original equipment (OE) and an additional 68,000 replacement tires. By 1918, with tires forming about fifty percent of rubber sales, OE tire sales exceeded four million for the one million new cars produced and total tire production reached 24.5 million.

This vast increase in production was accompanied by the emergence of now well-known firms like Goodyear, Goodrich, and Firestone, and the formation of the industry's center in Akron, Ohio. And while employment soared, production increases were possible only with the aid of technology. The fundamental innovation was the mechanization of core building. Before 1910, tires were built up by workers stretching, cementing, and stitching each ply and the beads around an iron core. In 1909, W. C. State of the Goodyear company patented a machine that carried the plys, beads, and tread on rollers carried on a central turret. The worker pulled the appropriate material over the core while the machine's electric motor held the proper tension so the worker could finish cementing and stitching. Skill and dexterity remained important, but the core-building machine simplified and sped-up production from six to eight tires per day per worker to twenty to forty a day, depending upon the type.

William S. Pretzer

rubber and then heated, produce specific tire characteristics such as high friction (but low mileage) for a racing tire or high mileage (but lower friction) for a passenger car tire. Some chemicals keep the rubber flexible while it is being shaped into a tire while other chemicals protect the rubber from the ultraviolet radiation in sunshine.

Design

The main features of a passenger car tire are the tread, the body with sidewalls, and the beads. The tread is the raised pattern in contact with the road. The body supports the tread and gives the tire its specific shape. The beads are rubber-covered, metal-wire bundles that hold the tire on the wheel.

Computer systems now play a major role in tire design. Complex analysis software acting on years of test data allows tire engineers to simulate the performance of tread design and other design parameters. The software creates a three-dimensional color image of a possible tire design and calculates the effects of different stresses on the proposed tire design. Computer simulations save money for tire manufacturers because many design limitations can be discovered before a prototype tire is actually assembled and tested.

In addition to tests of tread design and tire body construction, computers can simulate the effects of different types of rubber compounds. In a modern passenger car tire, as many as twenty different types of rubber may be used in different parts of the tire. One rubber compound may be used in the tread for good traction in cold weather; another compound is used to give increased rigidity in the tire sidewalls.

After tire engineers are satisfied with computer studies of a new tire, manufacturing engineers and skilled tire assemblers work with the designers to produce tire prototypes for testing. When design and manufacturing engineers are satisfied with a new tire design, tire factories begin mass production of the new tire.

The Manufacturing Process

A passenger car tire is manufactured by wrapping multiple layers of specially formulated rubber around a metal drum in a tire-forming machine. The different components of the tire are carried to the forming machine, where a skilled assembler cuts and positions the strips to form the different parts of the

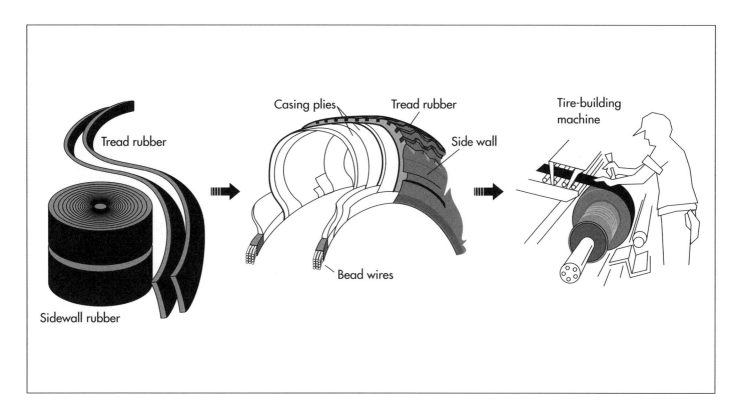

Tread rubber

Sidewall rubber

Casing plies

Tread rubber

Side wall

Bead wires

Tire-building machine

tire, called a "green tire" at this point. When a green tire is finished, the metal drum collapses, allowing the tire assembler to remove the tire. The green tire is then taken to a mold for curing.

1 The first step in the tire manufacturing process is the mixing of raw materials to form the rubber compound. Railcars deliver large quantities of natural and synthetic rubber, carbon black, sulfur, and other chemicals and oils, all of which are stored until needed. Computer control systems contain various recipes and can automatically measure out specific batches of rubber and chemicals for mixing. Gigantic mixers, hanging like vertical cement mixers, stir the rubber and chemicals together in batches weighing up to 1,100 pounds.

2 Each mix is then remilled with additional heating to soften the batch and mix the chemicals. In a third step, the batch goes through a mixer again, where additional chemicals are added to form what is known as the final mix. During all three steps of mixing, heat and friction are applied to the batch to soften the rubber and evenly distribute the chemicals. The chemical composition of each batch depends on the tire part—certain rubber formulations are used for the body, other formulas for the beads, and others for the tread.

Body, beads, and tread

3 Once a batch of rubber has been mixed, it goes through powerful rolling mills that squeeze the batch into thick sheets. These sheets are then used to make the specific parts of the tire. The tire body, for instance, consists of strips of cloth-like fabric that are covered with rubber. Each strip of rubberized fabric is used to form a layer called a *ply* in the tire body. A passenger car tire may have as many as four plies in the body.

4 For the beads of a tire, wire bundles are formed on a wire wrapping machine. The bundles are then formed into rings, and the rings are covered with rubber.

5 The rubber for the tire tread and sidewalls travels from the batch mixer to another type of processing machine called an *extruder*. In the extruder, the batch is further mixed and heated and is then forced out through a die—a shaped orifice—to form a layer of rubber. Sidewall rubber is covered with a protective plastic sheet and rolled. Tread rubber is sliced into strips and loaded into large, flat metal cases called *books*.

Tire-building machine

6 The rolls of sidewall rubber, the books containing tread rubber, and the racks of

The first step in the tire manufacturing process is the mixing of raw materials—rubber, carbon black, sulfur, and other materials—to form the rubber compound. After the rubber is prepared, it is sent to a tire-building machine, where a worker builds up the rubber layers to form the tire. At this point, the tire is called a "green tire."

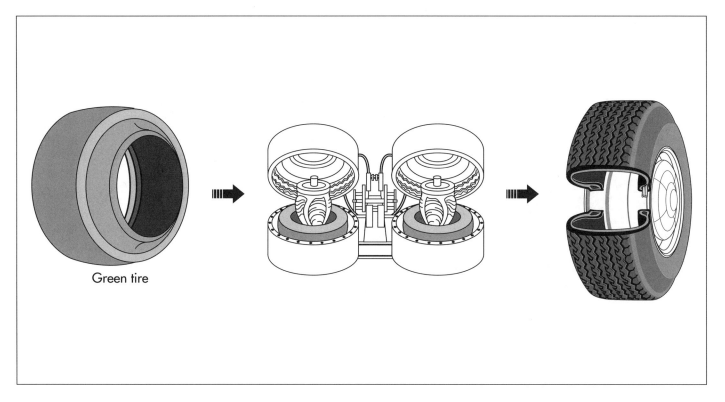

Green tire

After the green tire is made, it is put in a mold for curing. Shaped like a clam, the mold contains a large, flexible balloon. The tire is placed over the balloon (bladder), and the mold closes. Next, steam is pumped into the balloon, expanding it to shape the tire against the sides of the mold. After cooling, the tire is inflated and tested.

beads are all delivered to a skilled assembler at a tire-building machine. At the center of the machine is a collapsible rotating drum that holds the tire parts. The tire assembler starts building a tire by wrapping the rubber-covered fabric plies of the body around the machine drum. After the ends of these plies are joined with glue, the beads are added and locked into place with additional tire body plies laid over the beads. Next, the assembler uses special power tools to shape the edges of the tire plies. Finally, the extruded rubber layers for the sidewalls and tread are glued into place, and the assembled tire—the green tire—is removed from the tire-building machine.

Curing

7 A green tire is placed inside a large mold for the curing process. A tire mold is shaped like a monstrous metal clam which opens to reveal a large, flexible balloon called a *bladder*. The green tire is placed over the bladder and, as the clamshell mold closes, the bladder fills with steam and expands to shape the tire and force the blank tread rubber against the raised interior of the mold. During this curing process, the steam heats the green tire up to 280 degrees. Time in the mold depends on the characteristics desired in the tire.

8 After curing is complete, the tire is removed from the mold for cooling and then testing. Each tire is thoroughly inspected for flaws such as bubbles or voids in the rubber of the tread, sidewall, and interior of the tire. Then, the tire is placed on a test wheel, inflated, and spun. Sensors in the test wheel measure the balance of the tire and determine if the tire runs in a straight line. Because of the design and assembly of a modern tire, rarely is one rejected. Once the tire has been inspected and run on the test wheel, it is moved to a warehouse for distribution.

Quality Control

Quality control begins with the suppliers of the raw materials. Today, a tire manufacturer seeks suppliers who test the raw materials before they are delivered to the tire plant. A manufacturer will often enter into special purchasing agreements with a few suppliers who provide detailed certification of the properties and composition of the raw materials. To insure the certification of suppliers, tire company chemists make random tests of the raw materials as they are delivered.

Throughout the batch mixing process, samples of the rubber are drawn and tested to confirm different properties such as tensile strength and density. Each tire assembler is responsible for the tire components used. Code numbers and a comprehensive computer record-keeping system allow plant managers to trace batches of rubber and specific tire components.

When a new tire design is being manufactured for the first time, hundreds of tires are taken from the end of the assembly line for destructive testing. Some of the tires, for example, are sliced open to check for air pockets between body plies, while others are pressed down on metal studs to determine puncture resistance. Still other tires are spun rapidly and forced down onto metal drums to test mileage and other performance characteristics.

A variety of nondestructive evaluation techniques are also used in tire quality control. X-ray videography provides a quick and revealing view through a tire. In an X-ray tire test, a tire is selected at random and taken to a radiation booth where it is bombarded with X-rays. A test technician views the X-ray image on a video screen, where tire defects are easily spotted. If a defect shows up, manufacturing engineers review the specific steps of tire component assembly to determine how the flaw was formed.

In addition to internal testing, feedback from consumers and tire dealers is also correlated with the manufacturing process to identify process improvements.

The Future

Constant improvements in rubber chemistry and tire design are creating exciting new tires that offer greater mileage and improved performance in extreme weather conditions. Manufacturers now offer tires estimated to last up to 80,000 miles. Treads, designed and tested by computer, now feature unique asymmetrical bands for improved traction and safety on wet or snowy roads.

Tire design engineers are also experimenting with non-pneumatic tires that can never go flat because they don't contain air under pressure. One such non-pneumatic tire is simply one slab of thick plastic attached to the wheel rim. The plastic curves out from the rim to a point where a rubber tread is secured to the plastic for contact with the road. Such a tire offers lower rolling resistance for greater fuel economy and superior handling because of a greater area of contact between tread and road.

Where To Learn More

Books

Kovac, F. J. *Tire Technology.* Goodyear Tire and Rubber Co., 1978.

Mechanics of Pneumatic Tires. U. S. Dept. of Transportation, 1981.

Periodicals

"Winners: The Best Product Designs of the Year," *Business Week.* June 8, 1992, pp. 56-57.

"Computer Simulation Saves Money, Enhances Tire Design Before Prototypes Are Built," *Elastomerics.* July 1992, pp. 14-15.

"PZero: Pushing the Performance Envelope with Pirelli's Newest Offering," *European Car.* July, 1992, pp. 62-63.

"Tires: A Century of Progress," *Popular Mechanics.* June 4, 1985, pp. 60-64.

—*Robert C. Miller*

Tortilla Chip

One of the most important advancements in tortilla chip manufacture has been the production of dry masa flour, a shelf-stable product. This dry flour has become popular because it reduces requirements for energy, labor, floor space, processing time, and equipment, and is convenient and easy to use.

Background

The Spaniards first brought the word *tortilla* (from *torta*, "cake") to Mexico; the Mexicans, in turn, used it to describe their flat corn and flour cakes. The bread staple of the Mexican diet, all tortillas were originally made from the pulp of ground corn, the native grain of the New World. When the Spanish brought wheat to the New World, white flour tortillas became prevalent. Corn tortillas, now mostly machine-made, still hold the highest nutritional value. Cut into wedges and deep fried, these flat cakes became tortilla chips. After tortilla products were first introduced in the United States by Latin Americans living in the southwestern states, the popularity of new food item spread rapidly. Tortilla chips can come in many different sizes and shapes, such as triangles, rounds, and rectangular strips. The seasonings of tortilla chips can vary greatly, and they can be eaten with a variety of **salsa**s and toppings.

The basic method of tortilla and tortilla chip production has changed little since ancient times. Traditional tortilla preparation involves cooking the corn in pots over a fire, steeping (soaking) for 8 to 16 hours, pouring off the cooking liquor or nejayote, and washing the nixtamal (the end product of the cooking, steeping, and washing/draining process). The nixtamal is then ground into masa (dried and ground corn flour) with hand-operated grinders or metates (grinding stones). The masa is either hand-molded or molded using a tortilla press to form thin disks, which are then baked on a hot griddle called a *comal*.

One of the most important industrial advancements has been the production of dry masa flour, a shelf-stable product. This dry flour has become popular because it meets standards for certain applications, reduces requirements for energy, labor, floor space, processing time, and equipment, and is convenient and easy to use. When compared with fresh masa flour, however, foods made from dry masa flour tend to be less flavorful and the cost per unit is higher. Smaller manufacturers that supply local restaurants with tortilla chips usually use dry masa flour, while larger manufacturers use fresh masa flour that is produced on-site.

Raw Materials

Tortilla chips are made using yellow corn, white corn, flour, whole wheat, or blue cornmeal. Coarse masa is used in making corn tortilla chips. Masa consists of corn that has been soaked in a food-grade lime and water solution to break down the hulls; the kernels are then ground into flour. Frying oil, salt, and various seasonings complete the list of main ingredients. Other ingredients, such as preservatives, emulsifiers, gums, and acidulants, are used mainly in the United States to improve shelf life and to maintain certain properties of the product. The characteristics of the raw material determine the tortilla chips' quality, cooking parameters, and color.

The Manufacturing Process

Preparing the masa (dough)

1 The first major process in tortilla chip manufacturing is the production of coarse masa or dough. In a typical mixture, 2.5 to 3.0 liters of water, 1 kilogram of 12 percent moist corn, and 0.01 kilogram of food-grade lime (usually quicklime or hydrated lime) are

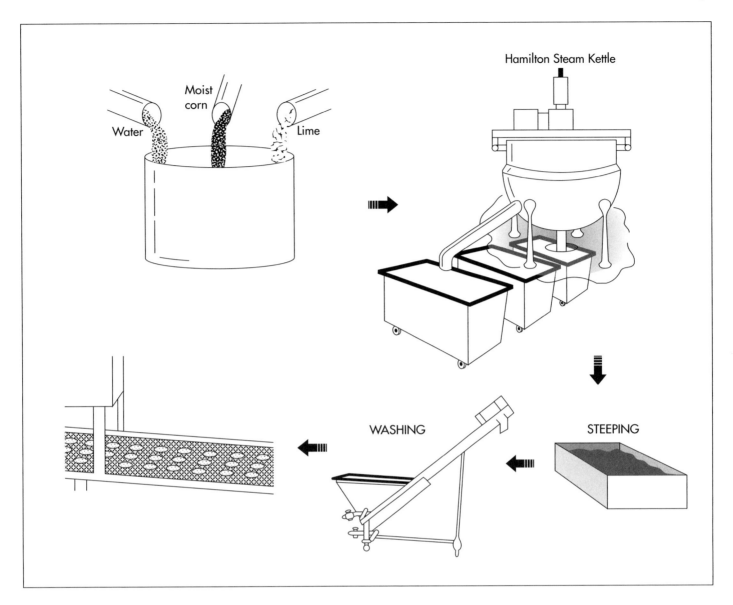

Water　Moist corn　Lime

Hamilton Steam Kettle

WASHING　STEEPING

added together in a large industrial cooker. The lime is used primarily as an aid in removing the pericarp (hull or skin) during cooking and steeping. The lime also helps to increase the product shelf life by controlling microbial activity, and it affects the flavor, aroma, color, and nutritional value of the chips.

2 This mixture is then batch-cooked in either a Hamilton steam kettle or a vertical closed cooker. The Hamilton kettle is indirectly heated by steam, and the grain contents are mechanically agitated. It is designed for cooking at or near the boiling point of the lime-water-corn solution. An elaborate agitation system ensures the uniform transfer of heat by condensing steam through the kettle wall and into the lime-water-corn solution. The capacity of these steam-jacketed kettles ranges from 300 to

595 pounds (136 to 270 kilograms). The vertical closed cooker uses direct steam injection to heat and agitate the lime-water-corn solution in a large tank, which serves for both cooking and steeping. Additional agitation is accomplished with compressed air. Because this system is designed for cooking at temperatures well below the solution boiling point (185 degrees Fahrenheit or 85 degrees Celsius), the cooking time is longer than in the Hamilton steam kettles. The capacity of the vertical cookers ranges from 3,000 to 6,000 pounds (1,360 to 2,730 kilograms). Cooking time can vary greatly from a few minutes to a half hour, depending upon which system is used. In general, temperatures above 155 degrees Fahrenheit (68 degrees Celsius) are considered to be the optimum cooking temperatures. Cooking depends on the characteristics of the corn and

To make tortilla chips, manufacturers first mix the raw ingredients—water, moist corn, and lime—to form the masa or dough. Next, the mixture is heated in a large kettle such as a Hamilton kettle, which is heated indirectly by steam. After steeping, which allows water to be absorbed, the solution is washed and pumped onto a conveyor belt for transport to the grinder.

the interaction of time, temperature, lime concentration, cooking vessel size, and agitation. Nixtamal used for fried products is generally cooked less than nixtamal used for table tortillas.

3 Immediately after cooking, the solution is quenched (rapidly cooled) to about 154 to 162 degrees Fahrenheit (68-72 degrees Celsius). This lower temperature decreases water absorption during the steeping process and the cooking time of the nixtamal. The result is a more consistent masa, which absorbs less oil during frying.

4 The grain is then steeped for 8 to 16 hours in the cooking vat (if a vertical cooker was used) or transferred to a holding vat (if a Hamilton steam kettle was used). The steeping process allows water to be absorbed, which helps to disintegrate the hull and soften the kernel. During the steeping process, the temperature is dropped to 104 degrees Fahrenheit (40 degrees Celsius).

5 After steeping, the solution is pumped into the washers. The cooking liquor is drained off, and the resulting nixtamal is washed with pressurized water or spraying systems. Most of the pericarp and excess lime is removed during this step. Washing in commercial processes is done in two types of equipment: the drum washer and the "lowboy" system. A drum washer consists of a conveyor that transports the nixtamal into a rotating perforated cylinder with internal flights and water sprayers located within the drum. After spraying, the nixtamal passes into a drain conveyor, where the excess water is removed. The lowboy system consists of a receptacle equipped with internal screens and sprayers. The washed nixtamal is continuously removed from the bottom of the receptacle by an inclined belt conveyor. In both systems, a conveyor transports the washed, drained nixtamal into a hopper, which then feeds the stone grinder. The end result, using the typical corn and lime mixture, will be 54 ounces (1.53 kilograms) of 47 percent moist nixtamal.

Grinding

6 The washed nixtamal is then ground using two matched carved stones, one stationary and the other rotating at about 500 to 700 rpm. The stones are usually composed of

lava or volcanic materials, although they can also consist of synthetic materials made of aluminum oxide (Al_2O_3). For optimum efficiency, the lava stones must be frequently recarved; the synthetic stones last longer and require less recarving. A typical stone is 10 centimeters thick and 40 centimeters in diameter and has radial grooves. The grooves become more shallow as they approach the perimeter of the stone. The number, design, and depth of the grooves in the stones vary with the intended product: stones carved for the production of table tortillas have more shallow grooves to produce a finer masa, whereas coarser masa for tortilla chips comes from deeper-grooved stones.

The grinding or milling starts when a screw conveyor at the base of the hopper forces the nixtamal through a center opening and into the gap between the stones, where shearing occurs. The material travels outward from the center to the perimeter of the stones. Water added during milling cools the stones, prevents excessive wear, and reduces the masa temperature. For a grinder with a capacity of 600 kg/hr, about 0.6 to 1.2 liters of water per minute (0.16-0.32 gpm) is added. This amount of water increases the masa moisture content to the optimum for sheeting. Like the grinding stones, the moisture content depends upon the resulting product. The masa particle size is the result of several interacting factors: degree of nixtamal cooking; size and depth of the grooves in the grinding stones; gap or pressure between the grinding stones; amount of water used during milling; and the type of corn used. The grinding breaks up the kernel structure and promotes "plastic" and cohesive properties in the masa. Once the masa is produced, it is important to use it immediately or to protect it against moisture loss. After grinding, the resulting mixture will be 1.65 kilograms of 51 percent moist coarse masa.

Forming chips

7 Next, actual chips are produced using the coarse masa, which is kneaded and mixed into plastic masa by mixers and extruders and then fed to sheeter rolls. The plastic masa is sheeted into a thin layer, which is then cut or forced into a specific configuration; the thickness of the sheet determines the final product weight. The sheeting starts when the masa is fed onto a pair of smooth rollers, usually

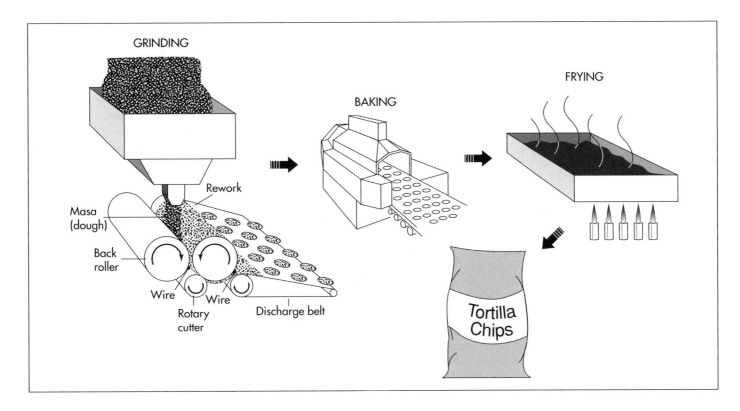

GRINDING

Rework

Masa
(dough)

Back
roller

Wire   Wire

Rotary
cutter   Discharge belt

BAKING

FRYING

Tortilla
Chips

coated with Teflon, one rotating counterclockwise and the other clockwise. The gap between the rollers is adjustable, so that products of different thicknesses can be produced. The masa is forced between the rolls and separated by wires located on the front and back rolls. The back wire cleans the sheeted masa from the back roll and allows it to adhere to the front roll, and the front wire or wires strip the masa pieces from the roll. The cutter rotates underneath the front roll. Different cutter configurations (triangular, circular, rectangular, etc.) are used for various products. Copper or plastic bands surround the end of the first roll and help to recycle excess masa. The masa pieces leave the front roller on a discharge belt, which feeds directly into the oven.

Baking and cooling

8 A three-tiered gas-fired oven is used to bake the formed masa. Generally, the chips are baked at temperatures ranging from 500 to 554 degrees Fahrenheit (260-290 degrees Celsius), with the baking time varying from 35 to 50 seconds. Baking enhances the alkaline flavor and reduces moisture and oil absorption during frying.

9 The tortilla chips are then cooled by moving through a series of open tiers or cooling racks. The chips are sometimes cooled for up to 20 minutes before frying to produce a more uniform consistency and to reduce blistering during frying. During this cooling process, the chips lose additional moisture (up to 3 percent), and the moisture within each chip becomes more evenly distributed.

Frying and seasoning

10 The next step involves frying the chips using oil temperatures ranging from 338 to 374 degrees Fahrenheit (170-190 degrees Celsius) for 50 to 80 seconds. The frying temperature and time depend on the type of product. Tortilla chips made from yellow corn require a lower frying temperature and a longer time than chips made from white or blended white and yellow corn. For example, corn chips made from yellow corn are fried at 320 degrees Fahrenheit (160 degrees Celsius), while those made from blended white and yellow corn are fried at temperatures up to 410 degrees Fahrenheit (210 degrees Celsius) for 60 to 90 seconds. Most of the commercial fryers used are the continuous type with direct or indirect heating elements. Indirect-fired fryers are more expensive but more efficient, with lower operational costs. Modern fryers are designed to filter out fines (very small pieces) continu-

The washed solution is ground using two matched carved stones, one stationary and the other rotating. From there, the resulting coarse masa is cut into actual chips. The masa is fed onto a pair of smooth rollers, usually coated with Teflon, one rotating counterclockwise and the other clockwise. The masa is forced between the rolls, cut, and discharged into the oven for baking. After frying and seasoning, the chips are packaged accordingly.

ously and be easy to clean. These commercial fryers are available in sizes that can process from 160 to 1,360 kg/hr (353-3,000 lbs/hr). The process yield, using the typical corn/lime mixture, will be 0.96 kilograms (2.1 pounds) of tortilla chips, with 22 to 24 percent oil and less than 2 percent moisture.

11 The salt and seasonings are applied immediately after frying while the chips are still hot. The hot chips are conveyed into an inclined rotating cylinder, where a liquid seasoning mix is sprayed on them. Generally, the liquid mix consists of hot oil, salt, seasonings, and flavoring and coloring agents. Upon cooling, the oil crystallizes, forming the seasoning coat. Salt can also be deposited on the chips as a liquid spray or by a granulated salt dispenser positioned over the conveying belts after the tumbling operation. The amount of salt usually added to tortilla chips is about 1 to 1.5 percent by weight.

Cooling and packaging

12 The tortilla chips are then cooled to ambient temperature and immediately packaged in moistureproof bags. Because fried products are very hygroscopic (they readily absorb and retain moisture), delayed packaging can cause a loss of crispness. The cooled tortilla chips, with about 1.5 percent moisture, are conveyed into a bagging machine. This machine automatically weighs and deposits them in a bag, which is then sealed.

Quality Control

The quality control aspect of tortilla chip production is essential so that the chips can reach the customer at their freshest. The major parameters controlled during tortilla chip production are: temperature and relative humidity of corn silos and storage rooms for ingredients and products; the cooking, quenching, steeping, baking, and frying times and temperatures; types of grinding stones and their adjustment during milling; moisture content of the corn, nixtamal, masa, and, finally, the tortilla chips; operating condition of the equipment (such as the cooker, sheeter, oven, fryer, cooling rack, packaging equipment, etc.); frying oil and product deterioration; and the sanitation of equipment and personnel.

The Future

The future trends for the corn and tortilla chip market are toward thinner, lighter, and smaller chips. Recently, tortilla chips made from white corn, whole wheat flour, and the blue cornmeal of the Southwest have become available and increasingly popular. Combinations of masa flour with wheat, legumes, and other flours will lead to interesting new products. New products fried with oils containing more unsaturated fatty acids or made from nutritionally improved corn will enhance the image of tortilla chips. Modified frying and new baking techniques that produce foods with a texture like that of fried foods will be used to make lower calorie snacks. The industry will move toward higher-speed production lines, more automation, better quality control, and higher labor and equipment efficiency.

It is estimated that the consumption of tortilla chips will continue to increase in the United States. Corn and tortilla chips are becoming popular in other areas of the world as well. Corn chip plants have been started in Australia, the People's Republic of China, India, Korea, and other countries. Experiencing a 50 percent increase in wholesale sales during the past five years, corn and tortilla snacks are rapidly moving into mainstream popularity. Future growth, however, depends on the industry's ability to keep pace with changing consumer demands.

Where To Learn More

Books

Booth, R. Gordon. *Snack Food.* Van Nostrand Reinhold, 1990.

Gleason, Carolyn J. *Handbook of Mexican American Foods: Recipes, Nutritional Analysis, Diabetic Exchanges & Common Practices.* Intercultural Development Research Association, 1982.

Matz, Samuel A. *Snack Food Technology.* Pan-Tech International, 1993.

Sparks, Pat and Barbara Swanson. *Tortillas!* St. Martin's Press, Inc., 1993.

Wise, Victoria and Susanna Hoffman. *The Well-Filled Tortilla Cookbook.* Workman Publishing, 1990, pp. 32-33.

Periodicals

de Lisser, Eleena. "Tortilla Chips Tempt Snackers With Changes," *Wall Street Journal.* May 6, 1993, p.B1.

"Thin Tortilla Chips," *Fortune.* October 19, 1992, p. 109.

Mack, Toni. "Tortilla Wizard," *Forbes.* July 20, 1992.

Serna-Saldivar, S. O., M. H. Gomez, and L. W. Rooney. "Technology, Chemistry, and Nutritional Value of Alkaline-Cooked Corn Products," *Advances in Cereal Science & Technology.* 1990, pp. 243-307.

—*Glenn G. Whiteside*

Trumpet

Assyrians, Israelites, Greeks, Etruscans, Romans, Celts, and Teutonic tribes all had some form of horn, and many were decorated. These instruments, which produced low, powerful notes, were mainly used in battle or during ceremonies. They were not usually considered to be musical instruments.

Background

A trumpet is a brass wind instrument noted for its powerful tone sounded by lip vibration against its cup-shaped mouthpiece. A trumpet consists of a cylindrical tube, shaped in a primary oblong loop that flares into a bell. Modern trumpets also have three piston valves as well as small, secondary tubing that act as tuning slides to adjust the tone. Almost all trumpets played today are B-flat. This is the tone naturally played when the trumpet is blown. They have a range between the F-sharp below middle C to two and a half octaves above (ending at B), and are comparatively easier to play than other brass instruments.

The first trumpets were probably sticks that had been hollowed out by insects. Numerous early cultures, such as those in Africa and Australia, developed hollow, straight tubes for use as megaphones in religious rites. These early "trumpets" were made from the horns or tusks of animals, or cane. By 1400 B.C. the Egyptians had developed trumpets made from bronze and silver, with a wide bell. People in India, China, and Tibet also created trumpets, which were usually long and telescoped. Some, like Alpine horns, rested their bells on the ground. Assyrians, Israelites, Greeks, Etruscans, Romans, Celts, and Teutonic tribes all had some form of horn, and many were decorated. These instruments, which produced low, powerful notes, were mainly used in battle or during ceremonies. They were not usually considered to be musical instruments. To make these trumpets, the lost-wax method was used. In this process, wax was placed in a cavity that was in the shape of a trumpet. This mold was then heated so that the wax melted away, and in its place molten bronze was poured, producing a thick-walled instrument.

The Crusades of the late Middle Ages (A.D. 1095-1270) caused most of Europe to come into contact with Arabic cultures, and it is believed that these introduced *trumpas* made from hammered sheets of metal. To make the tube of the trumpet, a sheet of metal was wrapped around a pole and soldered. To make the bell, a curved piece of metal shaped somewhat like an arc of a phonograph record was dovetailed. One side was cut to form teeth. These teeth were then splayed alternately, and the other side of the piece of metal was brought around and stuck between the teeth. Hammering the seam smoothed it down. Around A.D. 1400 the long, straight trumpets were bent, thus providing the same sound in a smaller, more convenient instrument. Molten lead was poured into the tube and allowed to solidify. This was then beaten to form a nearly perfect curve. The tube was next heated and the lead was poured out. The first bent trumpets were S-shaped, but rapidly the shape evolved to become a more convenient oblong loop.

A variety of trumpets were developed during the last half of the eighteenth century, as both musicians and trumpet makers searched for ways to make the trumpet more versatile. One limitation of the contemporary trumpet was that it could not be played chromatically; that is, it could not play the half-step range called the chromatic scale. In 1750 Anton Joseph Hampel of Dresden suggested placing the hand in the bell to solve the problem, and Michael Woggel and Johann Andreas Stein around 1777 bent the trumpet to make it easier for the player's hand to reach the bell. The consensus was that this created

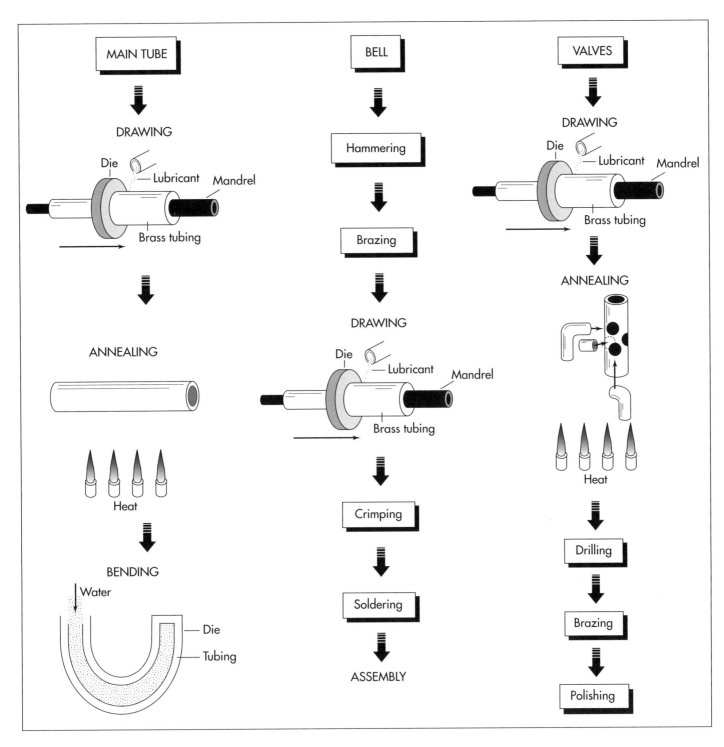

more problems than it solved. The keyed trumpet followed, but it never caught on, and was replaced rapidly by valve trumpets. The English created a slide trumpet, yet many thought the effort to control the slide wasn't worth it.

The first attempt to invent a valve mechanism was tried by Charles Clagget, who took out a patent in 1788. The first practical one, however, was the box tubular valve invented by Heinrich Stoelzel and Friedrich Bluhmel in 1818. Joseph Riedlin in 1832 invented the rotary valve, a form now only popular in Eastern Europe. It was Francois Perinet in 1839 who improved upon the tubular valve to invent the piston valved trumpet, the most preferred trumpet of today. The valves ensured a trumpet that was fully chromatic because they effectively changed the tube length. An open valve lets the air go through the tube fully. A closed valve diverts the air

The various parts of a trumpet are manufactured in drawing, hammering, and bending operations. In drawing, brass tubing is put over a tapered steel rod (mandrel), and a die is drawn down its length. At various times, the brass parts must be annealed (heat-treated) to improve their workability.

through its short, subsidiary tubing before returning it to the main tube, lengthening its path. A combination of three valves provides all the variation a chromatic trumpet needs.

The first trumpet factory was founded in 1842 by Adolphe Sax in Paris, and it was quickly followed by large-scale manufacturers in England and the United States. Standardized parts, developed by Gustave Auguste Besson, became available in 1856. In 1875 C. G. Conn founded a factory in Elkhart, Indiana, and to this day most brass instruments from the United States are manufactured in this city.

Today some orchestras are not satisfied with only using B-flat trumpets. There has been a revival of natural trumpets, rotary trumpets, and trumpets that sound higher than the standard B-flat. Overall, however, modern trumpets produce high, brilliant, chromatic musical tones in contrast with the low, powerful, inaccurate trumpets of the past.

Raw Materials

Brass instruments are almost universally made from brass, but a solid **gold** or silver trumpet might be created for special occasions. The most common type of brass used is yellow brass, which is 70 percent copper and 30 percent zinc. Other types include gold brass (80 percent copper and 20 percent zinc), and silver brass (made from copper, zinc, and nickel). The relatively small amount of zinc present in the alloy is necessary to make brass that is workable when cold. Some small manufacturers will use such special brasses as Ambronze (85 percent copper, 2 percent tin, and 13 percent zinc) for making certain parts of the trumpet (such as the bell) because such alloys produce a sonorous, ringing sound when struck. Some manufacturers will silver- or goldplate the basic brass instrument.

Very little of the trumpet is not made of brass. Any screws are usually steel; the water key is usually lined with cork; the rubbing surfaces in the valves and slides might be electroplated with chromium or a stainless nickel alloy such as monel; the valves may be lined with felt; and the valve keys may be decorated with mother-of-pearl.

Design

Most trumpets are intended for beginning students and are mass produced to provide fairly high quality instruments for a reasonable price. The procedure commonly used is to produce replicas of excellent trumpets that are as exact as possible. Professional trumpeters, on the other hand, demand a higher priced, superior instrument, while trumpets for special events are almost universally decorated, engraved with ornate designs. To meet the demand for custom-made trumpets, the manufacturer first asks the musician such questions as: What style of music will be played? What type of orchestra or ensemble will the trumpet be played in? How loud or rich should the trumpet be? The manufacturer can then provide a unique bell, specific shapes of the tuning slides, or different alloys or plating. Once the trumpet is created, the musician plays it and requests any minor adjustments that might need to be made. The trumpet's main pipe can then be tapered slightly. The professional trumpet player will usually have a favorite mouthpiece that the ordered trumpet must be designed to accommodate.

The Manufacturing Process

The main tube

1 The main tube of the trumpet is manufactured from standard machinable brass that is first put on a pole-shaped, tapered mandrel and lubricated. A die that looks like a doughnut is then drawn down its entire length, thus tapering and shaping it properly. Next, the shaped tube is annealed—heated (to around 1,000 degrees Fahrenheit or 538 degrees Celsius) to make it workable. This causes an oxide to form on the surface of the brass. To remove the oxidized residue, the tube must be bathed in diluted sulfuric acid before being bent.

2 The main tube may be bent using one of three different methods. Some large manufacturers use hydraulic systems to push high pressure water (at approximately 27,580 kilopascals) through slightly bent tubing that has been placed in a die. The water presses the sides of the tubing to fit the mold exactly. Other large manufacturers send **ball bearing**s of exact size through the tubing. Smaller manufacturers pour pitch into the

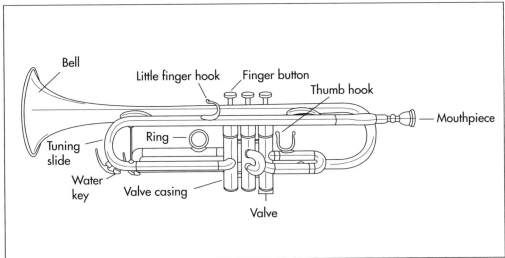

Trumpets are almost universally made from brass, but a solid gold or silver trumpet might be created for special occasions. The most common type of brass used is yellow brass, which is 70 percent copper and 30 percent zinc. Other types include gold brass (80 percent copper and 20 percent zinc), and silver brass (made from copper, zinc, and nickel). The relatively small amount of zinc present in the alloy is necessary to make brass that is workable when cold.

tube, let it cool, then use a lever to bend the tube in a standard curve before hammering it into shape.

The bell

3 The bell is cut from sheet brass using an exact pattern. The flat dress-shaped sheet is then hammered around a pole. Where the tube is cylindrical, the ends are brought together into a butt joint. Where the tube begins to flare, the ends are overlapped to form a lap joint. The entire joint is then brazed with a propane oxygen flame at 1,500 to 1,600 degrees Fahrenheit (816 to 871 degrees Celsius) to seal it. To make a rough bell shape, one end is hammered around the horn of a blacksmith anvil. The entire tube is then drawn on a mandrel exactly like the main tube, while the bell is spun on the mandrel. A thin wire is placed around the bell's rim, and metal is crimped around it to give the edge its crisp appearance. The bell is then soldered to the main tube.

The valves

4 The knuckles and accessory tubing are first drawn on a mandrel as were the tube and bell. The knuckles are bent into 30-, 45-, 60-, and 90-degree angles, and the smaller tubes are bent (using either the hydraulic or ball bearing methods used to bend the main tubing), annealed, and washed in acid to remove oxides and flux from soldering. The valve cases are cut to length from heavy tubing and threaded at the ends. They then need to have holes cut into them that match those of the pistons. Even small manufacturers now have available computer programs that precisely measure where the holes should be drawn. The valve cases can be cut with drills whose heads are either pinpoint or rotary saws that cut the holes, after which pins prick out the scrap disk of metal. The knuckles, tubes and valve cases are then placed in jigs that hold them precisely, and their joints are painted with a solder and flux mixture using a blow torch. After an acid bath, the assembly is polished on a buffing machine, using wax of varying grittiness and muslin discs of varying roughness that rotate at high speeds (2,500 rpm is typical).

Assembly

5 The entire trumpet can now be assembled. The side tubes for the valve slides are joined to the knuckles and the main tubing is united end to end by overlapping their ferrules and soldering. Next, the pistons are then inserted, and the entire valve assembly is screwed onto the main tubing. The mouthpiece is then inserted.

6 The trumpet is cleaned, polished, and lacquered, or it is sent to be electroplated. The finishing touch is to engrave the name of the company on a prominent piece of tubing. The lettering is transferred to the metal with carbon paper, and a skilled engraver then carves the metal to match the etching.

7 Trumpets are shipped either separately for special orders or in mass quantities for high school bands. They are wrapped carefully in thick plastic bubble packaging or other insulating material, placed in heavy

boxes full of insulation (such as packaging peanuts) then mailed or sent as freight to the customer.

Quality Control

The most important feature of a trumpet is sound quality. Besides meeting exacting tolerances of approximately 1×10^{-5} meters, every trumpet that is manufactured is tested by professional musicians who check the tone and pitch of the instrument while listening to see if it is in tune within its desired dynamic range. The musicians test-play in different acoustical set-ups, ranging from small studios to large concert halls, depending on the eventual use of the trumpet. Large trumpet manufacturers hire professional musicians as full-time testers, while small manufacturers rely on themselves or the customer to test their product.

At least half the work involved in creating and maintaining a clear-sounding trumpet is done by the customer. The delicate instruments require special handling, and, because of their inherent asymmetry, they are prone to imbalance. Therefore, great care must be taken so as not to carelessly damage the instrument. To prevent dents, trumpets are kept in cases, where they are held in place by trumpet-shaped cavities that are lined with velvet. The trumpet needs to be lubricated once a day or whenever it is played. The lubricant is usually a petroleum derivative similar to kerosene for inside the valves, mineral oil for the key mechanism, and axle grease for the slides. The grime in the mouthpiece and main pipe should be cleaned every month, and every three months the entire trumpet should soak in soapy water for 15 minutes. It should then be scrubbed throughout with special small brushes, rinsed, and dried.

To maintain the life of the trumpet, it must occasionally undergo repairs. Large dents can be removed by locally annealing and hammering, small dents can be hammered out and balls passed through to test the final size, fissures can be patched, and worn pistons can be replated and ground back to their former size.

Where To Learn More

Books

Barclay, Robert. *The Art of the Trumpet-Maker.* Oxford University Press, Inc., 1992.

Bate, Philip. *The Trumpet and Trombone.* Ernest Benn, 1978.

Dundas, Richard J. *Twentieth Century Brass Musical Instruments in the United States.* Richard J. Dundas Publications, 1989.

Mueller, Kenneth A. *Complete Guide to the Maintenance and Repair of Band Instruments.* Parker Publishing, 1982.

Tarr, Edward. *The Trumpet.* Amadeus Press, 1988.

Tetzlaff, Daniel B. *Shining Brass.* Lerner Publications, 1963.

Tuckwell, Barry. *Horn.* Schirmer Books, 1983.

Whitener, Scott. *A Complete Guide to Brass.* Schirmer Books, 1990.

Periodicals

Benade, Arthur H. "How to Test a Good Trumpet." *The Instrumentalist.* April, 1977, pp. 57-58.

"Yamaha Allows Players to Design Custom Trumpets," *Down Beat.* December, 1991, p. 12.

Fasman, Mark J. "Brass Bibliography: Sources on the History, Literature, Pedagogy, Performance, and Acoustics of Brass Instruments," rev. by Doug Rippey in *RQ,* Summer, 1991, p. 555.

Smithers, Don, Klaus Wogram, and John Bowsher. "Playing the Baroque Trumpet." *Scientific American.* April, 1986, pp. 108-115.

Weaver, James C. "The Trumpet Museum." *Antiques and Collecting Hobbies.* January, 1990, p. 30.

—Rose Secrest

Umbrella

Background

The umbrella as we know it today is primarily a device to keep people dry in rain or snow. Its original purpose was to shade a person from the sun (*umbra* is Latin for "shade"), a function that is still reflected in the word "parasol," (derived from the French *parare*, "to shield" and *sol*, "sun") a smaller-sized umbrella used primarily by women. There is an abundance of references to the usage of parasols and umbrellas in art and literature from ancient Africa, Asia, and Europe. For example, the Egyptian goddess Nut shielded the earth like a giant umbrella—only her toes and fingertips touched the ground—thus protecting humanity from the unsafe elements of the heavens. Although the Egyptians, like the Mesopotamians, used palm fronds and feathers in their umbrellas, they also introduced stretched papyrus as a material for the canopy, thereby creating a device that is recognizably an umbrella by modern standards.

About 2,000 years ago, the sun-umbrella was a common accessory for wealthy Greek and Roman women. It had become so identified as a "woman's object" that men who used it were subjected to ridicule. In the first century A.D., Roman women took to oiling their paper sunshades, intentionally creating umbrellas for use in the rain. There is even a recorded lawsuit dating from the first century over whether women should be allowed to open umbrellas during events held in amphitheaters. Although umbrellas blocked the vision of those behind them, the women won their case.

It was not until 1750 that the Englishman Jonas Hanway set out to popularize the umbrella. Enduring laughter and scorn, Hanway carried an umbrella wherever he went; not only was the umbrella unusual, it was a threat to the coachmen of England, who derived a good portion of their income from gentlemen who took cabs in order to keep dry on rainy days. (In the late 1700s and early 1800s, another name for an umbrella was a "Hanway.") Braving similar ridicule in 1778, John MacDonald, a well-known English gentlemen, carried an umbrella wherever he went.

Due to the efforts of Hanway, MacDonald, and other enterprising individuals, the umbrella became a common accessory. In nineteenth-century England, specially designed handles that concealed flasks for liquors, daggers and knives, small pads and **pencil**s, or other items were in high demand by wealthy gentlemen. The umbrella became so popular that by the mid-twentieth century, if not earlier, etiquette demanded that the uniform of the English gentleman include hat, gloves, and umbrella.

Among the qualities one might look for in an umbrella is the comfort of the handle, the ease with which the umbrella is opened and closed, and the closeness with which the canopy segments are connected to the ribs.

Raw Materials

Materials used to manufacture umbrellas have, of course, improved through the years. One of the most important innovations came in the early 1850s, when Samuel Fox conceived the idea of using "U" shaped steel rods for the ribs and stretchers to make a lighter, stronger frame. Previously, English umbrellas had been made from either cane or whalebone; whalebone umbrellas especially

In the first century A.D., Roman women took to oiling their paper sunshades, intentionally creating umbrellas for use in the rain. There is even a recorded lawsuit dating from the first century over whether women should be allowed to open umbrellas during events held in amphitheaters. Although umbrellas blocked the vision of those behind them, the women won their case.

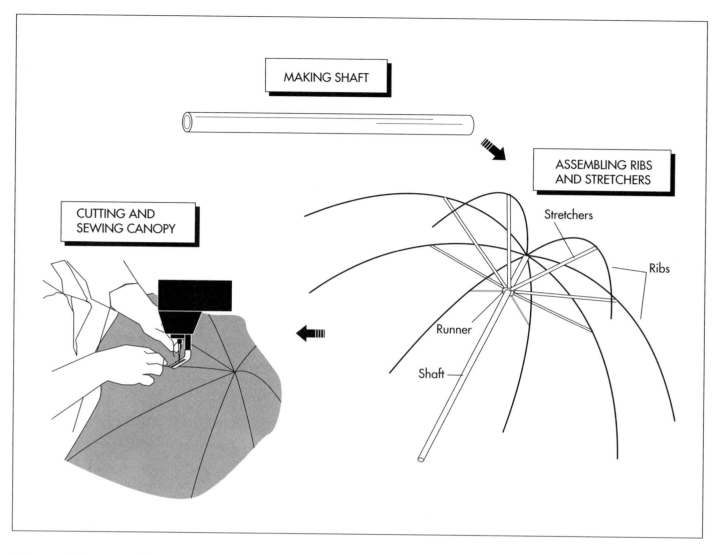

MAKING SHAFT

ASSEMBLING RIBS AND STRETCHERS

Stretchers

Ribs

Runner

Shaft

CUTTING AND SEWING CANOPY

Modern umbrellas are made by a hand-assembly process that, except for a few critical areas, can be done by semi-skilled workers. First, the shaft—whether wood, metal, or fiberglass—is made, and then the ribs and stretchers are assembled. Next, the nylon canopy is hand-sewn in sections (a typical umbrella has 8 sections).

were bulky and awkward. Rounded ribs and stretchers are frequently seen today only on parasols and patio umbrellas. Advancements in metal-producing technology have made rounded metal ribs and stretchers more feasible, however, and some manufacturers produce umbrellas with these components. Modern rain umbrellas are made with fabrics (nylon, most commonly) that can withstand a drenching rain, dry quickly, fold easily, and are available in a variety of colors and designs.

The Manufacturing Process

Modern umbrellas are made by a hand-assembly process that, except for a few critical areas, can be done by semi-skilled workers. Choices of materials and quality control occur throughout the manufacturing process. Although a well-made umbrella need not be expensive, almost every purchasing

decision impacts directly upon the quality of the final product.

Collapsible rain umbrellas that telescope into a length of about a foot are the most recent innovations in umbrellas. Though mechanically more complicated than stick umbrellas, they share the same basic technology. Among the differences between a stick umbrella and a collapsible umbrella is that the collapsible uses a two piece shaft that telescopes into itself, and an extra set of runners along the top of the umbrella. This section will focus on the manufacture of a stick umbrella.

The shaft

1 The stick umbrella will usually begin its life as a shaft of either wood, steel, or aluminum, approximately 3/8 inch (.95 centimeter) thick. Fiberglass and other plastics are occasionally used, and in fact they are common in the larger golf umbrella. Wood

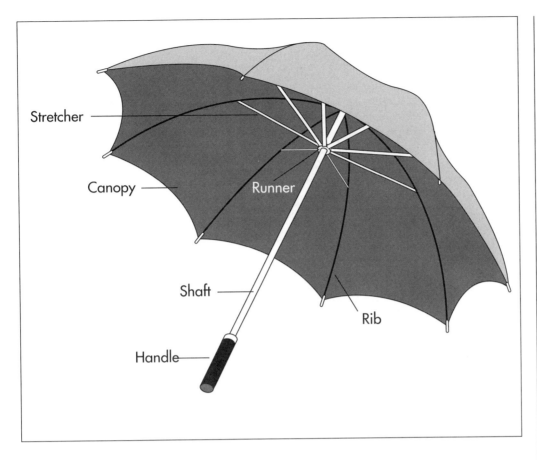

Stretcher

Canopy

Runner

Shaft

Rib

Handle

The fabric for the canopy is usually a nylon taffeta with an acrylic coating on the underside and a scotchguard type finish on the top. The coating and finish are usually applied by the fabric supplier. Other fabrics besides nylon might be used according to need or taste; a patio umbrella attached to an outdoor table does not have to be lightweight and waterproof as much as a customer might want it to be large, durable, and attractive.

from various types of ash trees, including Rowan wood from Asia, is among the popular choices for a sturdy wood shaft. While wood shafts are made using standard wood-shaping machines such as turning machines and lathes, metal and plastic shafts can be drawn or extruded to the proper shape.

Ribs and stretchers

2 The ribs and stretchers are assembled first, usually from "U" shaped or channeled steel or other metal. Ribs run underneath the top or canopy of the umbrella; stretchers connect the ribs with the shaft of the umbrella. The ribs are attached to the shaft of the umbrella by fitting into a top notch—a thin, round nylon or plastic piece with teeth around the edges, and then held with thin wire. The stretchers are connected to the shaft of the umbrella with a plastic or metal runner, the piece that moves along the shaft of the umbrella when it is opened or closed.

3 Next, the ribs and stretchers are connected to each other with a joiner, which is usually a small jointed metal hinge; as the umbrella is opened or closed, the joiner opens or closes through an angle of more than 90 degrees.

4 There are two catch springs in the shaft of each umbrella; these are small pieces of metal that need to be pressed when the umbrella is slid up the shaft to open, and again when the umbrella is slid down the shaft for closing. Metal shafts are usually hollow, and the catch spring can be inserted, while a wood shaft requires that a space for the catch spring be hollowed out. A pin or other blocking device is usually placed into the shaft a few inches above the upper catch spring to prevent the canopy from sliding past the top of umbrella, when the runner goes beyond the upper catch spring.

Canopy

5 The cover or canopy of the umbrella is hand sewn in individual panels to the ribs. Because each panel has to be shaped to the curve of the canopy, the cover cannot be cut in one piece. Panels are sewn at the outer edges of the ribs, and there are also connections between the ribs and the panels about one-third of the way down from the outer edge of the canopy. Each panel is cut sepa-

rately from piles of materials called *gores*; machine cutting of several layers at once is possible, although hand-cutting is more typical. The typical rain umbrella has eight panels, although some umbrellas with six panels (children's umbrellas and parasols usually have six panels) and as many as twelve can occasionally be found. At one point, the number of panels in an umbrella may have been an indication of quality (or at least of the amount of attention the umbrella maker paid to his product). Today, because of the quality of the material available to the umbrella maker, the number of panels is usually a matter of style and taste rather than quality.

The fabric used in a good-quality umbrella canopy is usually a nylon taffeta rated at 190T (190 threads per inch), with an acrylic coating on the underside and a scotch-guard type finish on the top. The coating and finish are usually applied by the fabric supplier. Fabric patterns and designs can be chosen by the manufacturer, or the manufacturer might add his own patterns and designs using a rotary or silk screening process, especially for a special order of a limited number of umbrellas. Similarly, other fabrics besides nylon might be used according to need or taste; a patio umbrella attached to an outdoor table does not have to be lightweight and waterproof as much as a customer might want it to be large, durable, and attractive.

6 The tip of the umbrella that passes through the canopy can be covered with metal (a ferrule) that has been forced over and perhaps glued to the tip, or left bare, depending on the desire of the manufacturer. The handle is connected to the shaft at the end of the process, and can be wood, plastic, metal, or any combination of desired ingredients. Though handles can be screwed on, bet-

ter-quality umbrellas use glue to secure the handle more tightly.

7 The end tips of the umbrella, where the ribs reach past the canopy, can be left bare or covered with small plastic or wood end caps that are either pushed or screwed on, or glued, and then sewn to the ends of the ribs through small holes in the end caps.

8 Finally, the umbrella is packaged accordingly and sent to customers.

Where To Learn More

Books

Crawford, T. S. *A History Of The Umbrella.* Taplinger Publishing, 1970.

Stacey, Brenda. *The Ups and Downs of Umbrellas.* Alan Sutton Publishing, 1991.

Periodicals

"How to Choose a Good Umbrella," *Consumer Reports.* September, 1991, pp. 619-23.

"Nylon Ribs Toughen Umbrella Frame," *Design News.* June 16, 1986, p. 49.

Jones, Arthur. "Personal Affairs—Sticks of Distinction," *Forbes.* February 24, 1986, pp. 116-18.

Sedgwick, John. "Let It Pour: Getting a Handle on the Best Umbrella," *Gentlemen's Quarterly.* March, 1992, p. 51.

Shenker, Israel. "Yoicks! Yoicks! And Brolly Ho! Rah for the Parapluie!" *Smithsonian.* November, 1989, p. 130.

—*Lawrence H. Berlow*

Washing Machine

Background

Mechanical washing machines appeared in the early 1800s, although they were all hand-powered. Early models cleaned clothes by rubbing them, while later models cleaned clothes by moving them through water. Steam-powered commercial washers appeared in the 1850s, but home washing machines remained entirely hand-powered until the early 1900s, when several companies started making electric machines. The Automatic Electric Washer Company and Hurley Machine Corporation both began selling electric washers in 1907, while Maytag offered an electric wringer washer in 1911. In 1947, Bendix offered the first fully automatic washing machine, and by 1953 spin-dry machines overtook the wringer types in popularity.

The last wringer washer manufactured in the United States was made in June of 1990 at Speed Queen's plant in Ripon, Wisconsin. The major U.S. manufacturers today are General Electric, Maytag (Montgomery Ward), Speed Queen (Amana and Montgomery Ward), Whirlpool (Kenmore), and White Consolidated (Frigidaire and Westinghouse).

Many models with many varying features are now available; however, with a few exceptions, only the controls are different. The only difference between the washer in your home and the top-load washers in the laundromat is the ruggedness of construction.

The washing machine operates by a motor, which is connected to the agitator through a unit called a transmission. The motor and transmission are near the bottom of the machine, while the agitator extends up through the middle of the machine. The transmission is similar to the transmission in your **automobile** in that it changes the speed and direction of the agitator. In one direction (agitate), the transmission changes the rotation of the agitator and spin tub—the inside tub with small holes in it—into a back-and-forth motion. When the motor is reversed by the controls (spin), the transmission locks up and the agitator, transmission, and spin tub all rotate as a unit. Without the transmission changing the speed or direction, the unit uses centrifugal force to remove as much water from the clothes as possible. The motor is also connected to a pump. When the motor is moving in the spin direction, the pump removes the water from the tub and discards it through the drain pipe.

Models designed for use in other countries offer different features. One component required on all models sold in England (and possibly soon in the rest of Europe) is called the lid lock. Normally when the lid is raised the washer must stop for safety reasons. However, in England, when the washer is operating the lid must be locked closed.

Raw Materials

Many parts of a washing machine are manufactured from sheet steel, usually coated with zinc to improve rust resistance. The steel manufacturer supplies the metal in a coil, which allows the material to be cut to size with minimum waste or automatically fed into the forming process. On some models made by Speed Queen, the spin tub is made of **stainless steel**. All other models use a steel (called enameling iron) designed for a **porcelain** coating. For the wash tub, which

Early washing machines cleaned clothes by rubbing them, while later models cleaned clothes by moving them through water. Steam-powered commercial washers appeared in the 1850s, but home washing machines remained entirely hand-powered until the early 1900s, when several companies started making electric machines.

Most sheet metal parts, including the body, are formed by a machine that presses a piece of sheet metal between two halves of a mold (die). Because metal in parts shaped by only one die tends to wrinkle, crack, or tear, multiple dies are generally used to form each component.

The tub sub-assembly is manufactured automatically. After being rolled into a drum shape, the side is welded. The weld is then smoothed out and the drum is placed on an expander, which stretches the tub into its final shape. A bottom is then welded onto the drum, and this weld is also smoothed.

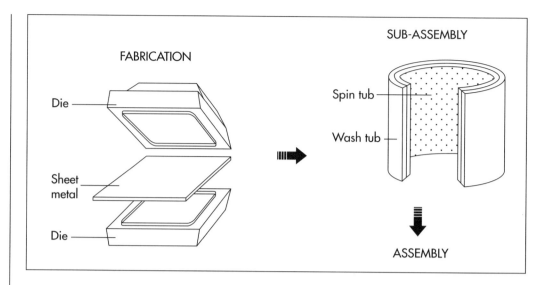

isn't visible unless you open the machine cabinet, enameling iron with a porcelain coating is generally used. Whirlpool is the exception, using plastic instead of enameling iron for the outer wash tub.

Many other parts are plastic as well. Manufacturers receive raw plastic from which they fabricate parts in pieces about the size of a small ant, using them for machine components that do not bear weight and/or require extremely good rust resistance. Such parts include the pump, the tub guards (which prevent your clothes from being thrown out of the spin tub into the wash tub or the cabinet area), and the agitator.

The transmission is generally made from cast aluminum, which arrives from the manufacturer in ingots—20 pound slabs of aluminum. Scrap parts are usually remelted and reused. Hoses, controls (timers, switches, etc.), and motors are purchased in prefabricated form from other manufacturers.

The Manufacturing Process

The manufacturing process is split into fabrication (making parts), sub-assembly (putting parts together to make components), and assembly (putting the components together to form the final product). The fabrication process comprises several different procedures, each specific to a particular type of raw material—sheet metal, plastic, or aluminum. Once the constituent parts have been made, they are assembled; major sub-assemblies, or components, include the transmis-

sion, the pump, the spin and wash tubs, the balance ring, and the painted parts. Finally, the sub-assemblies are put together inside the shell of the washer, which is then complete.

Fabrication

1 Most sheet metal parts are formed by a machine called a press. This name is quite descriptive, as the machine actually presses (or squeezes) a piece of sheet metal between two halves of a mold called a die. The metal will take the form of the space between the halves of the die. Because metal in parts shaped by only one die tends to wrinkle, crack, or tear, multiple dies are generally used to form each component. Where possible, the metal is fed directly from a coil into the press. When this is not possible, the metal is cut to length and manually (or, with larger parts like the cabinet, automatically) placed into the die.

2 Plastic parts are formed in an injection molding machine, a metal mold with one or more cavities in the shape of the desired part. After being heated to its melting point, the plastic is forced into the mold under high pressure. Next, water is passed through the mold to cool and solidify the part. The mold is then opened and the part pushed out by ejector pins. When you look at a plastic part, you often can see small circles created by these pins.

3 Aluminum transmission parts are formed into a rough shape in a die cast machine, which works much like an injection mold except that it does not use pressure. The

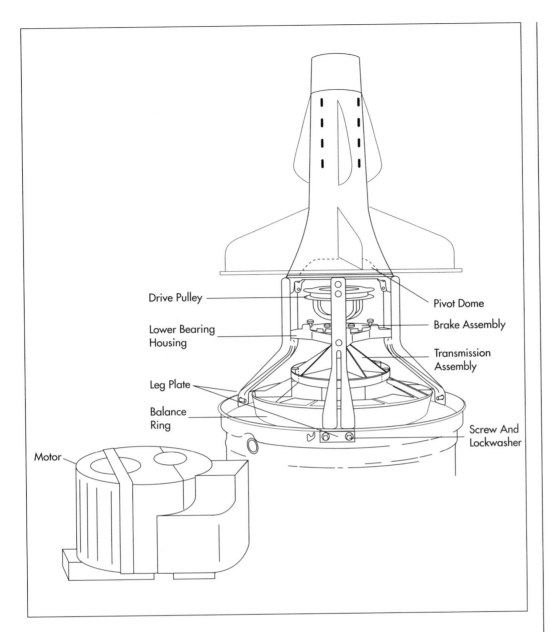

Drive Pulley

Lower Bearing Housing

Leg Plate

Balance Ring

Motor

Pivot Dome

Brake Assembly

Transmission Assembly

Screw And Lockwasher

Most of the key components—transmission, motor, brake assembly—are housed below the agitator. The balance ring is a weighted ring that keeps the washer from moving around during operation.

molten metal is mechanically ladled into the mold and cooled. The ensuing rough casting is then given its final shape by various machines which drill holes, shave excess metal off critical surfaces, or cut metal away from the part.

Sub-assemblies

4 The transmission is assembled manually by workers who bolt, snap, or press (tight fit) several shafts and gears together. Workers then add a metered amount of oil and bolt the unit together.

5 The pump is assembled automatically. Robots place the impeller and seals in the cover and body, and seal the pump. Some

manufacturers use heat and others vibration (which generates heat) as a sealant.

6 The tub parts are made in presses, and the sub-assembly is manufactured automatically. After being rolled into a drum shape, the side is welded. The weld is then smoothed out and the drum is placed on a unit called an *expander,* which stretches the tub into its final shape. A bottom is then welded onto the drum, and this weld is also smoothed. If the tub is stainless steel it is polished so it won't snag the clothes. Otherwise the tub is dipped in a solution called a *ground coat* and heated to about 1600 degrees until this coating hardens. If the tub will not be visible (the wash tub), the unit is done. If the tub will be visible (the spin tub), a finish coat

is applied following the same procedure used with the ground coat; this final coat gives the tub either a white or blue color.

7 The balance ring is a large weight that stabilizes the washer. Its outside structure is plastic, with a ring of metal melted into the plastic for strength. Cement is added and balanced precisely. This ring, which weighs more than twenty pounds, keeps the machine from "walking," or moving about, when it is in use.

8 Washing machine manufacturers use any one of several painting processes. One manufacturer uses steel that has been pre-painted by the steel manufacturer. Although cheaper, this type of steel does not offer the best rust protection because the cut edges are not painted. Other companies treat their parts with various chemicals to clean and ready them before applying **paint**. In some cases, the paint comes in a powder with a flour-like consistency. Mixed with air and given an electrical charge, the powder is sprayed on the part, which is hung from an overhead conveyor and given an opposite charge so that it and the powder will attract one another. After spraying, the conveyor moves the part into an oven that melts the paint; when the part cools, the paint process is completed.

Assembly

9 This process begins with mounting the transmission on the balance ring. The transmission is set on a bearing that is bolted on the wash tub; the wash tub is sitting on a conveyor. Another bearing (the lower bearing), the brake assembly, and the drive pulley are put on the end of the transmission. Next, a pivoting mechanism called the *pivot dome* and legs are bolted on the assembly to hold all the pieces together.

10 Using a hydraulically operated mechanism, workers then lift this assembly, called the *module,* onto the washer base. Springs are added to hold module and base together. A seal is added, the spin tub is bolted to the transmission inside of the wash tub, and its plastic covers are snapped into place. A plastic hub, which attaches the agitator to the transmission, is bolted onto the output end of the transmission shaft. Then the agitator is snapped onto the hub.

11 The pump and a mounting bracket are now bolted onto the motor, which is then fitted with a shield to protect against potential leaks. This assembly is bolted to the base of the washing machine and connected to the transmission module with a belt and hoses.

12 Next, the lid hinges are attached to the lid and the top. The top of the washer is bolted to the cabinet with a hinge for easy maintenance. A mixing valve to control the mixture of hot and cold is bolted to the back of the cabinet. The graphics panel, which provides words and pictures to explain the controls, is mounted on the control panel; the controls themselves are attached from the back. The wiring, connected as one unit, is called a *harness.* The harness is clipped to the control connectors at one end, and the other end is passed through a hole in the top to be mounted to the motor. Because of its large size and weight, the cabinet assembly is then placed in the washer by a robot.

13 The cabinet is bolted to the base, and the controls are snapped together with the mating connectors on the module and motor. The drain hose is pulled through the cabinet and a part called the *gooseneck* is added. This part is what gives the hose its hook shape so that it will fasten into the drain. After being tested, the front panel is bolted on, and a packet of information and accessories is added.

14 The finished unit is crated automatically. A machine opens the cardboard box, which was flat for shipment, and drops it over the washer. The top and bottom flaps are simultaneously folded over and glued. Then the machine applies pressure on the top and bottom of the crate to make sure the glue sets properly. After the glue has set, the machine puts a banding strap around the top of the crate to add strength for lift truck transportation (the units are carried from the top to reduce the risk of damage).

Quality Control

All parts purchased from outside manufacturers are spot checked before use, and most sub-assemblies are checked as well. For instance, all transmissions are automatically tested for operation, noise, and vibration. All pumps are leak-tested using air, automatically if their assembly was automated and manually if it was manual. All painted parts are visually inspected for defects. Daily samples are put in detergent, bleach, and steam baths for corrosion testing. Once it has been completely assembled, the machine is filled with water and tested for noise, vibration, and visual defects, as well as properly functional controls and mechanisms. After packaging, some units are put through severe tests to simulate the transportation conditions to test the cartoning process.

Byproducts/Waste

Leftover scraps of sheet metal are sold to metal recycling centers, and leftover aluminum is remelted for use. The leftover plastic is ground into small chunks and reused on non-visible parts because the color cannot be kept consistent. The unused paint (in powder form) is reclaimed and reused automatically. The chemicals from processes such as paint are reacted into forms of harmless waste and disposed of safely.

The Future

As motors become less expensive and more durable, it will become economical to offer washing machines driven directly by motors instead of by belts, making the washers more versatile and less noisy. Another likely trend will be the gradual displacement of top-load washers by front-load washers, which, because they require less water, satisfy government restrictions on water use. In Japan, a washer is being tested that cleans with bubbles rather than with an agitator. Using a computer, this machine "senses" how soiled each load of clothing is and then generates the bubble activity necessary to remove that amount of dirt. This is called "fuzzy logic" because it imitates human logic more closely than normal computers. If successful, these machines will become available elsewhere. Further in the future people may use washers that clean using ultrasonics—sound waves that, vibrating at frequencies of more than

20,000 cycles per second, cannot be distinguished by the human ear.

Where To Learn More

Books

Woolridge, Woody. *Repair Master for Frigidaire Automatic Washers: Unimatic & Pulsamatic Design.* Longhurst, Rey, 1990.

—. *Repair Master for Maytag Automatic Washers: All Models.* Longhurst, Rey, 1990.

Periodicals

"To Be Fuzzy, or Not To Be Fuzzy." *Appliance Manufacturer.* February, 1993, pp. 31-32.

"Whirlpool Goes Off on a World Tour." *Business Week.* June 3, 1991, pp. 98-100.

"The Future Looks 'Fuzzy.'" *Newsweek,* May 28, 1990, pp. 46-47.

Stafanides, E. J. "Frictional Damping Smooths Automatic Washer Spin Cycles," *Design News.* February 15, 1988.

—*Barry M. Marton*

Although at present most home washing machines in the United States are top-loading, these will likely be gradually displaced by front-load washers. Because they require less water, front-load washers satisfy government restrictions on water use. Also, in Japan a washer is being tested that cleans with bubbles rather than with an agitator. Using a computer, this machine "senses" how soiled each load of clothing is and then generates the bubble activity necessary to remove that amount of dirt.

Watch

Quartz watches make use of piezoelectricity, which is the current that flows from or through a piece of quartz when the quartz is put under electrical and/or mechanical pressure. A quartz watch uses the electricity from a piece of quartz subjected to the electricity from a battery to send a regular, countable series of signals to one or more microchips.

Background

The oldest means of determining time is by observing the location of the sun in the sky. When the sun is directly overhead, the time is roughly 12:00 noon. A slightly later development, and one less subject to an individual's judgment, is the use of a sundial. During the daylight hours, sunlight falls on a vertical pole placed at the center of a calibrated dial, thus casting a shadow on the dial and providing the reader with a relatively accurate time reading.

The invention of the mechanical clock in the fourteenth century was a major advancement—it provided a more concise and consistent method of measuring time. The mechanical clock includes a complicated series of wheels, gears, and levers powered by a falling weights and with a pendulum (or later a wound-up spring). These pieces together moved the hand or hands on a dial to show the time. The addition of chimes or gongs on the hour, half hour, and quarter hour followed soon afterward. By the eighteenth century, smaller clocks for the home were available, and, unlike their predecessors, were closed and sealed in a case.

The more exacting the workmanship of the moving parts, the more accurate the clock was. From invention through to the middle of the twentieth century, developments in clock-making focused on making the moving parts work as accurately as possible. Developments in metal technology and in miniaturization, the lubrication of small parts, and the use of first, natural sapphires (and then artificial sapphires) at the spots that received the most stress (the jeweled movement) all became integral components of horological science.

Small pocket watches, perhaps two to three inches (five to seven centimeters) in diameter, were available by the end of the nineteenth century. Mechanical wristwatches were an everyday item in the United States by the 1960s. And yet, the central problem faced by watch and clockmakers remained the same: mechanical parts wear down, become inaccurate, and break.

In the years immediately following World War II, interest in atomic physics led to the development of the atomic clock. Radioactive materials emit particles (decayed) at a known, steady rate. The parts of a mechanical clock that ratcheted to keep the time could be replaced by a device that stimulated the watch movement each time a particle was emitted by the radioactive element. Atomic clocks, incidentally, are still made and sold, and they are found to be consistently accurate.

With the development of the microchip in the 1970s and 1980s, a new type of watch was invented. Wristwatches that mixed microchip technology with quartz crystals became the standard; there are few non-quartz wristwatches made today. The microchip is utilized to send signals to the dial of the watch on a continual basis. Because it is not a mechanical device with moving parts, it does not wear out.

The use of quartz in watches makes use of a long-known type of electricity known as *piezoelectricity*. Piezoelectricity is the current which flows from or through a piece of quartz when the quartz is put under electrical and/or mechanical pressure (*piezo* is from the Greek verb meaning "to press"). A quartz watch uses the electricity from a piece of quartz subjected to the electricity from a **battery** to send

478

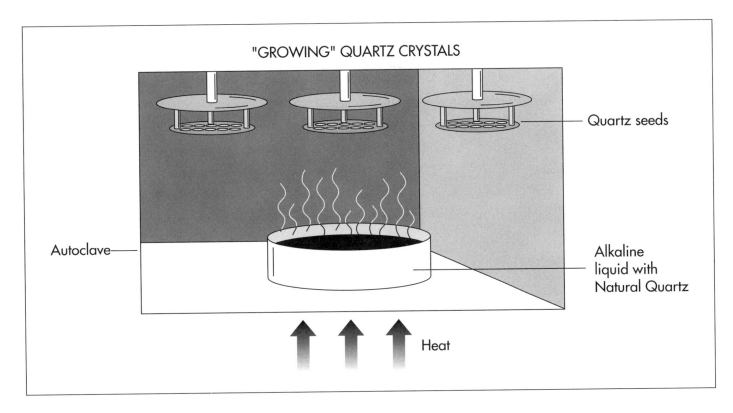

"GROWING" QUARTZ CRYSTALS

Quartz seeds

Autoclave

Alkaline
liquid with
Natural Quartz

Heat

a regular, countable series of signals (oscillations) to one or more microchips. (Electrical wall clocks, in contrast, use the regularity of wall current to keep track of time.)

The most accurate quartz watches are those in which the time appears in an electronically controlled digital display, produced via a **light-emitting diode (LED)** or a **liquid crystal display (LCD)**. It is possible, of course, to have the microprocessor send its signals to mechanical devices that make hands move on the watch face, creating an analog display. But because the hands are mechanically operated through a portion of the watch known as a gear train, analogue watches usually are not as accurate as digitals and are subject to wear. Both types of watches achieve tremendous accuracy, with digital watches commonly being accurate to within three seconds per month.

Raw Materials

Electronic watches make use of many of the most modern materials available, including plastics and alloy metals. Cases can be made of either plastic or metal; watches with metal cases often include a **stainless steel** backing. Microchips are typically made of silicon, while LEDs are usually made of gallium arsenide, gallium phosphide, or gallium

arsenide phosphide. LCDs consist of liquid crystals sandwiched between glass pieces. Electrical contacts between parts are usually made of a small amount of **gold** (or are gold-plated); gold is an almost ideal electrical conductor and can be used successfully in very small amounts.

The Manufacturing Process

This section will focus on quartz digital watches with LED displays. Although the assembly of such watches must be performed carefully and methodically, the most essential aspects of the manufacturing process are in the manufacture of the components.

Quartz

1 The heart of a quartz watch is a tiny sliver of quartz. The synthetically produced quartz is cut by the manufacturer with a diamond saw and shipped to the watchmaker to use. The production of "grown" quartz is a critical step in the process.

Quartz, in a natural form, is first loaded into a giant kettle or autoclave (the same device used by doctors and dentists to sterilize instruments). Hanging from the top of the autoclave are seeds or tiny particles of quartz

The heart of a quartz watch is a tiny sliver of quartz. In a natural form, quartz is first loaded into a giant kettle or autoclave. Hanging from the top of the autoclave are seeds or tiny particles of quartz with the desired crystalline structure. An alkaline material is pumped into the bottom of the autoclave, and the autoclave is heated to a high temperature, dissolving the quartz in the hot alkaline liquid, evaporating it, and depositing it on the seeds. After about 75 days, the chamber can be opened, and the newly grown quartz crystals can be removed and cut into the correct proportions.

In watch assembly, the entire set of crystal and microchips is set onto a circuit board. A battery is also installed that generates electricity for the quartz crystal and supplies the power for the LED display.

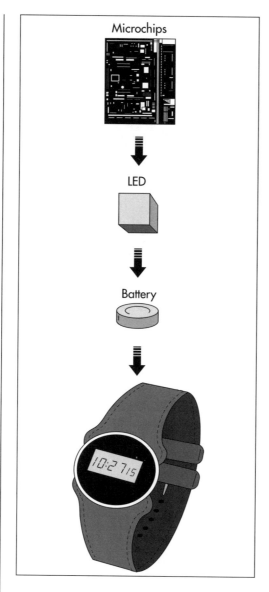

Microchips

LED

Battery

with the desired crystalline structure. An alkaline material is pumped into the bottom of the autoclave, and the autoclave is heated to a temperature of roughly 750 degrees Fahrenheit (400 degrees Celsius). The natural quartz dissolves in the hot alkaline liquid, evaporates, and deposits itself on the seeds. As it deposits itself, it follows the pattern of the crystalline structure of the seeds. After about 75 days, the chamber can be opened, and the newly grown quartz crystals can be removed and cut into the correct proportions. Different angles and thicknesses in the cutting lead to predictable rates of oscillation. The desired rate of oscillation for quartz used in wristwatches is 100,000 megaHertz or 100,000 oscillations per second.

2 To work most effectively, the piece of quartz needs to be sealed in a vacuum chamber of one sort or another. Most commonly, the quartz is placed into a sort of capsule, with wires attached to both ends so that the capsule can be soldered or otherwise connected to a circuit board.

The microchip

3 The electronic leads generated by a battery through the quartz (producing oscillations) will go to a microchip that serves as a "frequency dividing circuit." Microchip manufacture, like the quartz, is also carried out by the supplier to the watch manufacturer. An extensive and complex process, making microchips involves chemical and/or x-ray etching of a microscopic electronic circuit onto a tiny piece of silicon dioxide.

4 The oscillation rate of perhaps 100,000 vibrations/second is reduced to 1 or 60 or some other more manageable number of oscillations. The new pattern of oscillation is then sent to another microchip that functions as a "counter-decoder-driver." This chip will actually count the oscillations that it receives. If there are sixty oscillations per second, the chip will change the reading on an LED every second. After 3,600 oscillations (60 x 60), the counter will instruct the LED to change the reading for minutes. And, after 60 x 60 x 60 oscillations (216,000), the counter will change the hour reading.

Assembly

5 The entire set of crystal and microchips is set onto a circuit board. The board incorporates a space to hold the battery that supplies electricity to the quartz crystal and supplies the power for the LED display. Generally, the space for the battery is on the outside of the surface facing the back of the case. The battery can be replaced by removing the back of the watch, shaking out the old one, and dropping in the new battery.

6 The mechanism used for setting the watch is then connected. This mechanism involves two pins that extend beyond the case of the watch. One pin lets the counter circuit know which reading to reset—seconds, minutes, or hours. The second pin is pushed a number of times to bring the display to the desired reading.

7 The entire circuit board, along with a battery, is then closed into a case, and a wrist strap is attached.

Additional Watch Features

Because the microchips in a quartz watch are capable of holding large quantities of information, it is possible, from an engineering standpoint, to add other functions to a watch without much difficulty. An additional push button on the case connected to the counter circuit can provide alarms, tide information, and more. The microchip can just as easily be programmed to set the watch forward or back a defined amount at the push of a button, so that an owner can determine the time in another time zone, or perhaps have two, three, or more time zone times displayed successively.

Quality Control

All components of electronic watches are manufactured under a strict system of quality control. Quartz crystals, for example, have their frequencies tested before being used in a watch. Microchips must be made in a "clean room" environment with specially filtered air, since even the tiniest dust particles can render a chip useless. Microchips are examined carefully and are also bench tested for accuracy before use.

After a watch is manufactured, it is again tested before being shipped to market. In addition to its time-keeping accuracy, it is also subjected to a drop-test in which it must continue to operate properly after being dropped and otherwise abused; a temperature test; and a water test. While a watchmaker may, with proper testing and proof, claim that a watch is "water resistant" at certain, known specifications, it is inaccurate to say a watch is "waterproof" because without particular specification that designation is meaningless.

Large watch companies make all of their own components, ensuring that product quality standards are in place at the earliest point in the manufacturing process.

The Future

Because today's electronic watches are by design so accurate, accuracy is not the only goal for which a watch manufacturer aims. Future changes in product will take advantage of other technologies from other fields such as the addition of a calculator function to a watch, or even the addition of a radio-transmitter that can send out a traceable signal if the wearer is lost or in trouble.

Where To Learn More

Books

Billings, Charlene W. *Microchip: Small Wonder*. Dodd, Mead & Company, 1984.

Carpenter, Alice B. *Questions and Answers in Quartz Watch Repairing*. American Watchmakers Institute, 1989.

Ford, Roger, and Oliver Strimpel. *Computers: An Introduction*. Facts On File, 1985.

Periodicals

Becker, Dan. "Crystal Oscillators," *Electronics Now*. January, 1993, pp. 45-54.

Beller, Miles. "Consumer Corner: The Ultra-watches," *Los Angeles*. September, 1986, p. 14.

"A Good Watch Is More Than Just a Pretty Face," *Changing Times*. March, 1981, pp. 72-74.

Hathaway, Bruce. "Circuitry Wizards and New Agers Alike Can Get Good Vibes from Quartz," *Smithsonian*. November, 1988, p. 83.

"Kit Report: Clock Module," *Radio-Electronics*. November, 1987, pp. 122-123.

Schmidt, Leon W. "Build The Hyper Clock," *Radio-Electronics*. February, 1992, pp. 33-41.

Wassef, Ayyam. "Quartz Time," *The Unesco Courier*. April, 1991, pp. 33-36.

—*Lawrence H. Berlow*

Wind Turbine

The first large-scale wind turbine built in the United States was completed by Palmer Cosslett Putnam in 1941. The machine was huge. The tower was 36.6 yards high, and its two stainless steel blades had diameters of 58 yards. Putnam's wind turbine could produce 1,250 kilowatts of electricity, or enough to meet the needs of a small town.

Background

A wind turbine is a machine that converts the wind's kinetic energy into rotary mechanical energy, which is then used to do work. In more advanced models, the rotational energy is converted into electricity, the most versatile form of energy, by using a generator.

For thousands of years people have used windmills to pump water or grind grain. Even into the twentieth century tall, slender, multi-vaned wind turbines made entirely of metal were used in American homes and ranches to pump water into the house's plumbing system or into the cattle's watering trough. After World War I, work was begun to develop wind turbines that could produce electricity. Marcellus Jacobs invented a prototype in 1927 that could provide power for a radio and a few lamps but little else. When demand for electricity increased later, Jacobs's small, inadequate wind turbines fell out of use.

The first large-scale wind turbine built in the United States was conceived by Palmer Cosslett Putnam in 1934; he completed it in 1941. The machine was huge. The tower was 36.6 yards (33.5 meters) high, and its two **stainless steel** blades had diameters of 58 yards (53 meters). Putnam's wind turbine could produce 1,250 kilowatts of electricity, or enough to meet the needs of a small town. It was, however, abandoned in 1945 because of mechanical failure.

With the 1970s oil embargo, the United States began once more to consider the feasibility of producing cheap electricity from wind turbines. In 1975 the prototype Mod-0 was in operation. This was a 100 kilowatt turbine with two 21-yard (19-meter) blades. More prototypes followed (Mod-0A, Mod-1, Mod-2, etc.), each larger and more powerful than the one before. Currently, the United States Department of Energy is aiming to go beyond 3,200 kilowatts per machine.

Many different models of wind turbines exist, the most striking being the vertical-axis Darrieus, which is shaped like an egg beater. The model most supported by commercial manufacturers, however, is a horizontal-axis turbine, with a capacity of around 100 kilowatts and three blades not more than 33 yards (30 meters) in length. Wind turbines with three blades spin more smoothly and are easier to balance than those with two blades. Also, while larger wind turbines produce more energy, the smaller models are less likely to undergo major mechanical failure, and thus are more economical to maintain.

Wind farms have sprung up all over the United States, most notably in California. Wind farms are huge arrays of wind turbines set in areas of favorable wind production. The great number of interconnected wind turbines is necessary in order to produce enough electricity to meet the needs of a sizable population. Currently, 17,000 wind turbines on wind farms owned by several wind energy companies produce 3.7 billion kilowatt-hours of electricity annually, enough to meet the energy needs of 500,000 homes.

Raw Materials

A wind turbine consists of three basic parts: the tower, the nacelle, and the rotor blades. The tower is either a steel lattice tower similar to electrical towers or a steel tubular tower with an inside ladder to the nacelle.

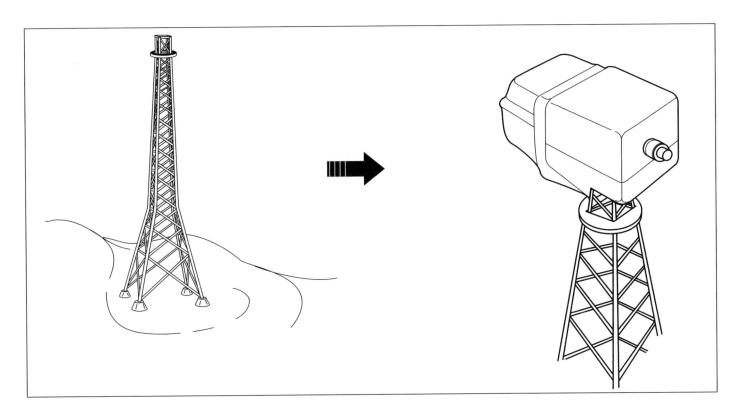

Most towers do not have guys, which are cables used for support, and most are made of steel that has been coated with a zinc alloy for protection, though some are painted instead. The tower of a typical American-made turbine is approximately 80 feet tall and weighs about 19,000 pounds.

The nacelle is a strong, hollow shell that contains the inner workings of the wind turbine. Usually made of fiberglass, the nacelle contains the main drive shaft and the gearbox. It also contains the blade pitch control, a hydraulic system that controls the angle of the blades, and the yaw drive, which controls the position of the turbine relative to the wind. The generator and electronic controls are standard equipment whose main components are steel and copper. A typical nacelle for a current turbine weighs approximately 22,000 pounds.

The most diverse use of materials and the most experimentation with new materials occur with the blades. Although the most dominant material used for the blades in commercial wind turbines is fiberglass with a hollow core, other materials in use include lightweight woods and aluminum. Wooden blades are solid, but most blades consist of a skin surrounding a core that is either hollow or filled with a lightweight substance such as

plastic foam or honeycomb, or balsa wood. A typical fiberglass blade is about 15 meters in length and weighs approximately 2,500 pounds.

Wind turbines also include a utility box, which converts the wind energy into electricity and which is located at the base of the tower. Various cables connect the utility box to the nacelle, while others connect the whole turbine to nearby turbines and to a transformer.

The Manufacturing Process

Before consideration can be given to the construction of individual wind turbines, manufacturers must determine a proper area for the siting of wind farms. Winds must be consistent, and their speed must be regularly over 15.5 miles per hour (25 kilometers per hour). If the winds are stronger during certain seasons, it is preferred that they be greatest during periods of maximum electricity use. In California's Altamont Pass, for instance, site of the world's largest wind farm, wind speed peaks in the summer when demand is high. In some areas of New England where wind farms are being considered, winds are strongest in the winter, when the need for

The first step in constructing a wind turbine is erecting the tower. Although the tower's steel parts are manufactured off site in a factory, they are usually assembled on site. The parts are bolted together before erection, and the tower is kept horizontal until placement. A crane lifts the tower into position, all bolts are tightened, and stability is tested upon completion.

Next, the fiberglass nacelle is installed. Its inner workings—main drive shaft, gearbox, and blade pitch and yaw controls—are assembled and mounted onto a base frame at a factory. The nacelle is then bolted around the equipment. At the site, the nacelle is lifted onto the completed tower and bolted into place.

The nacelle is a strong, hollow shell that contains the inner workings of the wind turbine, such as the main drive shaft and the gearbox. It also contains the blade pitch control, a hydraulic system that controls the angle of the blades, and the yaw drive, which controls the position of the turbine relative to the wind. A typical nacelle for a current turbine weighs approximately 22,000 pounds.

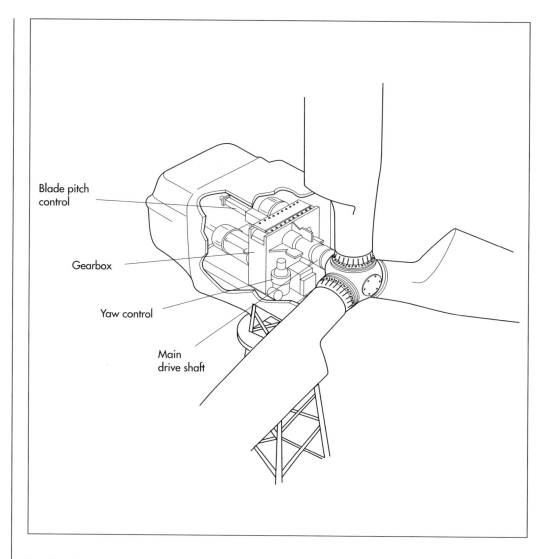

Blade pitch control

Gearbox

Yaw control

Main drive shaft

heating increases the consumption of electrical power. Wind farms work best in open areas of slightly rolling land surrounded by mountains. These areas are preferred because the wind turbines can be placed on ridges and remain unobstructed by trees and buildings, and the mountains concentrate the air flow, creating a natural wind tunnel of stronger, faster winds. Wind farms must also be placed near utility lines to facilitate the transfer of the electricity to the local power plant.

Preparing the site

1 Wherever a wind farm is to be built, the roads are cut to make way for transporting parts. At each wind turbine location, the land is graded and the pad area is leveled. A **concrete** foundation is then laid into the ground, followed by the installation of the underground cables. These cables connect the wind turbines to each other in series, and also connect all of them to the remote control cen-

ter, where the wind farm is monitored and the electricity is sent to the power company.

Erecting the tower

2 Although the tower's steel parts are manufactured off site in a factory, they are usually assembled on site. The parts are bolted together before erection, and the tower is kept horizontal until placement. A crane lifts the tower into position, all bolts are tightened, and stability is tested upon completion.

Nacelle

3 The fiberglass nacelle, like the tower, is manufactured off site in a factory. Unlike the tower, however, it is also put together in the factory. Its inner workings—main drive shaft, gearbox, and blade pitch and yaw controls—are assembled and then mounted onto a base frame. The nacelle is then bolted

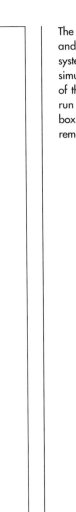

The utility box for each wind turbine and the electrical communication system for the wind farm is installed simultaneously with the placement of the nacelle and blades. Cables run from the nacelle to the utility box and from the utility box to the remote control center.

Pendent cables

Cross braces

Midtower junction box

Utility box

around the equipment. At the site, the nacelle is lifted onto the completed tower and bolted into place.

Rotary blades

4 Aluminum blades are created by bolting sheets of aluminum together, while wooden blades are carved to form an aerodynamic propeller similar in cross-section to an airplane wing.

5 By far the greatest number of blades, however, are formed from fiberglass. The manufacture of fiberglass is a painstaking operation. First, a mold that is in two halves like a clam shell, yet shaped like a blade, is prepared. Next, a fiberglass-resin composite mixture is applied to the inner surfaces of the mold, which is then closed. The fiberglass mixture must then dry for several hours; while it does, an air-filled bladder within the mold helps the blade keep its shape. After the fiberglass is dry, the mold is then opened and the bladder is removed. Final preparation of the blade involves cleaning, sanding, sealing the two halves, and painting.

6 The blades are usually bolted onto the nacelle after it has been placed onto the tower. Because assembly is easier to accomplish on the ground, occasionally a three-pronged blade has two blades bolted onto the nacelle before it is lifted, and the third blade is bolted on after the nacelle is in place.

Installation of control systems

7 The utility box for each wind turbine and the electrical communication system for the wind farm is installed simultaneously with the placement of the nacelle and blades. Cables run from the nacelle to the utility box and from the utility box to the remote control center.

Quality Control

Unlike most manufacturing processes, production of wind turbines involves very little concern with quality control. Because mass production of wind turbines is fairly new, no standards have been set. Efforts are now being made in this area on the part of both the government and manufacturers.

While wind turbines on duty are counted on to work 90 percent of the time, many structural flaws are still encountered, particularly with the blades. Cracks sometimes appear soon after manufacture. Mechanical failure because of alignment and assembly errors is common. Electrical sensors frequently fail because of power surges. Non-hydraulic brakes tend to be reliable, but hydraulic braking systems often cause problems. Plans are being developed to use existing technology to solve these difficulties.

Wind turbines do have regular maintenance schedules in order to minimize failure. Every three months they undergo inspection, and every six months a major maintenance checkup is scheduled. This usually involves lubricating the moving parts and checking the oil level in the gearbox. It is also possible for a worker to test the electrical system on site and note any problems with the generator or hookups.

Environmental Benefits and Drawbacks

A wind turbine that produces electricity from inexhaustible winds creates no pollution. By comparison, coal, oil, and natural gas produce one to two pounds of carbon dioxide (an emission that contributes to the greenhouse effect and global warming) per kilowatt-hour produced. When wind energy is used for electrical needs, dependence on fossil fuels for this purpose is reduced. The current annual production of electricity by wind turbines (3.7 billion kilowatt-hours) is equivalent to four million barrels of oil or one million tons of coal.

Wind turbines are not completely free of environmental drawbacks. Many people consider them to be unaesthetic, especially when huge wind farms are built near pristine wilderness areas. Bird kills have been documented, and the whirring blades do produce quite a bit of noise. Efforts to reduce these effects include selecting sites that do not coincide with wilderness areas or bird migration routes and researching ways to reduce noise.

The Future

The future can only get better for wind turbines. The potential for wind energy is largely untapped. The United States Department of Energy estimates that ten times the amount of electricity currently being produced can be achieved by 1995. By 2005, seventy times current production is possible. If this is accomplished, wind turbines would account for 10 percent of the United States' electricity production.

Research is now being done to increase the knowledge of wind resources. This involves the testing of more and more areas for the possibility of placing wind farms where the wind is reliable and strong. Plans are in effect to increase the life span of the machine from five years to 20 to 30 years, improve the efficiency of the blades, provide better controls, develop drive trains that last longer, and allow for better surge protection and grounding. The United States Department of Energy has recently set up a schedule to implement the latest research in order to build wind turbines with a higher efficiency rating than is now possible. (The efficiency of an ideal wind turbine is 59.3 percent. That is, 59.3 percent of the wind's energy can be captured. Turbines in actual use are about 30 percent efficient.) The United States Department of Energy has also contracted with three corporations to research ways to reduce mechanical failure. This project began in the spring of 1992 and will extend to the end of the century.

Wind turbines will become more prevalent in upcoming years. The largest manufacturer of wind turbines in the world, U.S. Windpower, plans to expand from 420 megawatt capacity (4,200 machines) to 800 megawatts (8,000 machines) by 1995. They plan to have 2,000 megawatts (20,000 machines) by the year 2000. Other wind turbine manufacturers also plan to increase the numbers produced. International committees composed of several industrialized nations have formed to discuss the potential of wind turbines. Efforts are also being made to provide developing countries with small wind turbines similar to those Marcellus Jacobs built in the 1920s. Denmark, which already produces 70 percent to 80 percent of Europe's wind power, is developing plans to expand manufacture of wind turbines. The turn of the century should see wind turbines that are properly placed, efficient, durable, and numerous.

Where To Learn More

Books

Assessment of Research Needs for Wind Turbine Rotor Materials Technology. National Academy Press, 1991.

Eggleston, David M. *Wind Turbine Engineering Design.* Van Nostrand Reinhold, 1987.

Hunt, Daniel V. *Windpower: A Handbook on Wind Energy Conversion Systems.* Van Nostrand Reinhold, 1981.

Kovarik, Tom, Charles Pupher, and John Hurst. *Wind Energy.* Domus Books, 1979.

Park, Jack. *The Wind Power Book.* Cheshire Books, 1981.

Putnam, Palmer Cosslett. *Power from the Wind.* Van Nostrand Company, 1948.

Periodicals

Frank, Deborah. "Blowing in the Wind," *Popular Mechanics,* August, 1991, pp. 40-43+.

Mohs, Mayo. "Blowin' in the Wind," *Discover.* June, 1986, pp. 68-74.

Moretti, Peter M. and Louis V. Divone. "Modern Windmills," *Scientific American.* June, 1986, pp. 110-118.

Price, Marshall. "Basement-Built Wind Generator," *Mother Earth News.* July-August, 1986, p. 103.

Stefanides, E. J. "Hydraulic Yaw Control Upgrades Wind Turbine," *Design News.* March 3, 1986, p. 240.

Vogel, Shawna. "Wind Power," *Discover.* May, 1989, pp. 46-49.

—Rose Secrest

Wine

The name of a wine almost invariably is derived from one of three sources: the name of the principal grape from which it was made, the geographical area from which it comes, or—in the case of the traditionally finest wines—from a particular vineyard or parcel of soil.

Background

Wine is an alcoholic beverage produced through the partial or total fermentation of grapes. Other fruits and plants, such as berries, apples, cherries, dandelions, elder-berries, palm, and rice can also be fermented.

Grapes belong to the botanical family *vitaceae*, of which there are many species. The species that are most widely used in wine production are *Vitis labrusca* and, especially, *Vitis vinifera*, which has long been the most widely used wine grape throughout the world.

The theory that wine was discovered by accident is most likely correct because wine grapes contain all the necessary ingredients for wine, including pulp, juice, and seeds that possess all the acids, **sugar**s, tannins, minerals, and vitamins that are found in wine. As a natural process, the frosty-looking skin of the grape, called "bloom," catches the airborne yeast and enzymes that ferment the juice of the grape into wine.

The cultivation of wine grapes for the production of wine is called "viticulture." Harvested during the fall, wine grapes may range in color from pale yellow to hearty green to ruby red.

Wine can be made in the home and in small-, medium- or large-sized wineries by using similar methods. Wine is made in a variety of flavors, with varying degrees of sweetness or dryness as well as alcoholic strength and quality. Generally, the strength, color, and flavor of the wine are controlled during the fermentation process.

Wine is characterized by color: white, pink or rosé, and red, and it can range in alcohol content from 10 percent to 14 percent. Wine types can be divided into four broad categories: table wines, sparkling wines, fortified wines, and aromatic wines. Table wines include a range of red, white, and rosé wines; sparkling wines include champagne and other "bubbly" wines; aromatic wines contain fruits, plants, and flowers; and fortified wines are table wines with brandy or other alcohol added.

The name of a wine almost invariably is derived from one of three sources: the name of the principal grape from which it was made, the geographical area from which it comes, or—in the case of the traditionally finest wines—from a particular vineyard or parcel of soil. The year in which a wine is made is only printed on bottles that have aged for two or more years; those aged less are not considered worthy of a date. Wine years are known as "vintages" or "vintage years." While certain wines are considered good or bad depending on the year they were produced, this can vary by locality.

In general, red wines are supposed to age from seven to ten years before being sold. Because white and rosé wines are not enhanced by additional ageing, they are usually aged from only one to four years before being sold. And, since the quality of wine can depend on proper ageing, older wines are generally more expensive than younger ones. Other factors, however, can affect the quality of wine, and proper ageing does not always ensure quality. Other factors affecting quality include the grapes themselves, when the grapes are picked, proper care of the grapes, the fermentation process, as well as other aspects of wine production.

Most wineries bottle wine in different size bottles and have different product and

graphic designs on their labels. The most common bottle sizes are the half bottle, the imperial pint, the standard bottle, and the gallon bottle or jug. Most red and rosé wine bottles are colored to keep light from ageing the wine further after they are on the market.

While viticulture has remained much the same for centuries, new technology has helped increase the output and variety of wine.

History

Well documented in numerous Biblical references, evidence of wine can be traced back to Egypt as far as 5,000 B.C. Tomb wall paintings showing the use of wine as well as actual wine jars found in Egyptian tombs provide evidence of this fact. Because more northern climates and soil produce better wine, the growth of the wine industry can be traced from its emergence along the Nile River in Egypt and Persia northward into Europe and, eventually, to North America.

Though the wines of old were coarse and hard and had to be mixed with water, ancient Greek wine proved to be somewhat better than Egyptian wine. For this reason, Egyptians began importing it. Then Roman wines (from what would emerge to be Italy,

Spain, and France) became notably superior. Eventually, French and German wines grew to be the most desirable, thereby shifting the center of wine production from the Mediterranean to central Europe. Some of the best wine in the world is still produced in southern France, particularly in the Bordeaux region, where wine has been made for more than 2,000 years.

The colonists brought wine production to the east coast of the New World by the mid-1600s. The earliest account of wine used in the New World may be when the Pilgrims fermented grapes to celebrate their first Thanksgiving in 1623. Settlers tried to grow imported grape cuttings they brought from Europe, but unfortunately the European cuttings had not developed immunities to the North American plant diseases that eventually killed them. By the middle of the nineteenth century (using the fruits of the abundant native Vitis labrusca grape plants) wineries were established in Pennsylvania, Virginia, Ohio, Indiana, Alabama, Mississippi, and North Carolina.

In 1697, European cuttings of *Vitis vinifera* grapes were successfully introduced to California by Franciscan priests at the Mission San Francisco Xavier. They soon became the dominant grape species in

Vineyardists inspect sample clusters of wine grapes with a refractometer to determine if the grapes are ready to be picked. The refractometer is a small, hand-held device that allows the vineyardist to accurately check the amount of sugar in the grapes. If the grapes are ready for picking, a mechanical harvester gathers and funnels the grapes into a field hopper, or mobile storage container.

Some mechanical harvesters have grape crushers mounted on the machinery, allowing vineyard workers to gather grapes and press them at the same time. The result is that vineyards can deliver newly crushed grapes, called *must*, to wineries, eliminating the need for crushing at the winery.

California wine making. A great boost to California wine making came from Colonel Agoston Haraszthy, a Hungarian nobleman, who introduced more high-quality European cuttings during the 1850s. His knowledge made him the founder of California's modern wine industry.

Today, California and New York state are by far the largest American producers of wine, and California is one of the largest wine producers in the world. Though many of its table wines are known for their quality, the enormous wineries of central and southern California produce gigantic quantities of neutral, bulk wines that they ship elsewhere to make specific wines, such as dessert wines, or to blend with other wines. They also make grape concentrates to fortify weaker wines and brandies that use large quantities of grapes.

Raw Materials

As mentioned above, the wine grape itself contains all the necessary ingredients for wine: pulp, juice, sugars, acids, tannins, and minerals. However, some manufacturers add yeast to increase strength and cane or beet sugar to increase alcoholic content. During fermentation, winemakers also usually add sulfur dioxide to control the growth of wild yeasts.

The Manufacturing Process

The process of wine production has remained much the same throughout the ages, but new sophisticated machinery and technology have helped streamline and increase the output of wine. Whether such advances have enhanced the quality of wine is, however, a subject of debate. These advances include a variety of mechanical harvesters, grape crushers, temperature-controlled tanks, and centrifuges.

The procedures involved in creating wine are often times dictated by the grape and the amount and type of wine being produced. Recipes for certain types of wine require the winemaker (the vintner) to monitor and regulate the amount of yeast, the fermentation process, and other steps of the process. While the manufacturing process is highly auto-

mated in medium- to large-sized wineries, small wineries still use hand operated presses and store wine in musty wine cellars.

A universal factor in the production of fine wine is timing. This includes picking grapes at the right time, removing the must at the right time, monitoring and regulating fermentation, and storing the wine long enough.

The wine-making process can be divided into four distinct steps: harvesting and crushing grapes; fermenting must; ageing the wine; and packaging.

Harvesting and crushing grapes

1 Vineyardists inspect sample clusters of wine grapes with a refractometer to determine if the grapes are ready to be picked. The refractometer is a small, hand-held device (the size of a miniature telescope) that allows the vineyardist to accurately check the amount of sugar in the grapes.

2 If the grapes are ready for picking, a mechanical harvester (usually a suction picker) gathers and funnels the grapes into a field hopper, or mobile storage container. Some mechanical harvesters have grape crushers mounted on the machinery, allowing vineyard workers to gather grapes and press them at the same time. The result is that vineyards can deliver newly crushed grapes, called *must*, to wineries, eliminating the need for crushing at the winery. This also prevents oxidization of the juice through tears or splits in the grapes' skins.

Mechanical harvesters, or, in some cases, robots, are now used in most medium to large vineyards, thereby eliminating the need for hand-picking. First used in California vineyards in 1968, mechanical harvesters have significantly decreased the time it takes to gather grapes. The harvesters have also allowed grapes to be gathered at night when they are cool, fresh, and ripe.

3 The field hoppers are transported to the winery where they are unloaded into a crusher-stemmer machine. Some crusher-stemmer machines are hydraulic while others are driven by air pressure.

The grapes are crushed and the stems are removed, leaving liquid must that flows

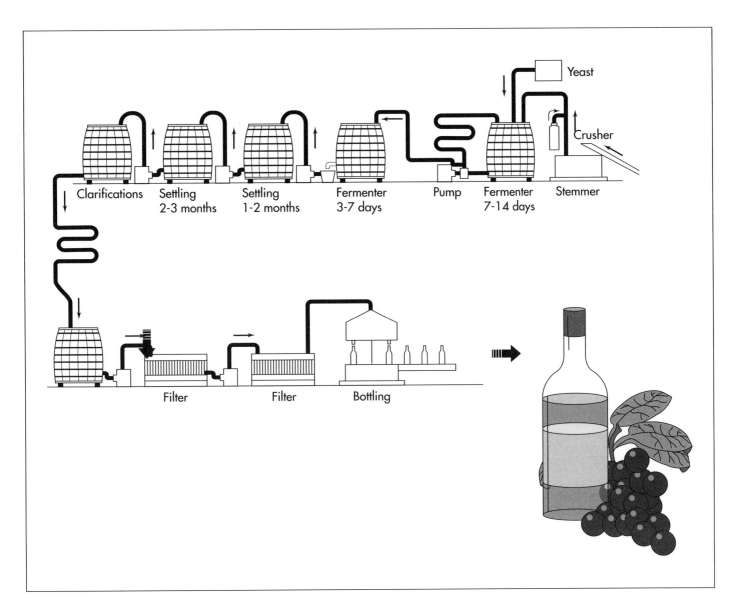

Yeast

Crusher

Clarifications Settling 2-3 months Settling 1-2 months Fermenter 3-7 days Pump Fermenter 7-14 days Stemmer

Filter Filter Bottling

either into a **stainless steel** fermentation tank or a wooden vat (for fine wines).

Fermenting the must

4 For white wine, all the grape skins are separated from the "must" by filters or centrifuges before the must undergoes fermentation. For red wine, the whole crushed grape, including the skin, goes into the fermentation tank or vat. (The pigment in the grape skins give red wine its color. The amount of time the skins are left in the tank or vat determines how dark or light the color will be. For rosé, the skins only stay in the tank or vat for a short time before they are filtered out.)

5 During the fermentation process, wild yeast are fed into the tank or vat to turn

the sugar in the must into alcohol. To add strength, varying degrees of yeast may be added. In addition, cane or beet sugar may be added to increase the alcoholic content. Adding sugar is call *chaptalization*. Usually chaptalization is done because the grapes have not received enough sun prior to harvesting. The winemaker will use a handheld hydrometer to measure the sugar content in the tank or vat. The wine must ferments in the tank or vat for approximately seven to fourteen days, depending on the type of wine being produced.

Ageing the wine

6 After crushing and fermentation, wine needs to be stored, filtered, and properly aged. In some instances, the wine must also be blended with other alcohol. Many wineries

Once at the winery, the grapes are crushed if necessary, and the must is fermented, settled, clarified, and filtered. After filtering, the wine is aged in stainless steel tanks or wooden vats. White and rosé wines may age for a year to four years, or far less than a year. Red wines may age for seven to ten years. Most large wineries age their wine in large temperature-controlled stainless steel tanks that are above ground, while smaller wineries may still store their wine in wooden barrels in damp wine cellars.

still store wine in damp, subterranean wine cellars to keep the wine cool, but larger wineries now store wine above ground in epoxy-lined and stainless steel tanks. The tanks are temperature-controlled by water that circulates inside the lining of the tank shell. Other similar tanks are used instead of the old redwood and concrete vats when wine is temporarily stored during the settling process.

After fermentation, certain wines (mainly red wine) will be crushed again and pumped into another fermentation tank where the wine will ferment again for approximately three to seven days. This is done not only to extend the wine's shelf life but also to ensure clarity and color stability.

The wine is then pumped into settling ("racking") tanks or vats. The wine will remain in the tank for one to two months. Typically, racking is done at 50 to 60 degrees Fahrenheit (10 to 16 degrees Celsius) for red wine, and 32 degrees Fahrenheit (0 degrees Celsius) for white wine.

7 After the initial settling (racking) process, certain wines are pumped into another settling tank or vat where the wine remains for another two to three months. During settling the weighty unwanted debris (remaining stem pieces, etc.) settle to the bottom of the tank and are eliminated when the wine is pumped into another tank. The settling process creates smoother wine. Additional settling may be necessary for certain wines.

8 After the settling process, the wine passes through a number of filters or centrifuges where the wine is stored at low temperatures or where clarifying substances trickle through the wine.

9 After various filtering processes, the wine is aged in stainless steel tanks or wooden vats. White and rosé wines may age for a year to four years, or far less than a year. Red wines may age for seven to ten years. Most large wineries age their wine in large temperature-controlled stainless steel tanks that are above ground, while smaller wineries may still store their wine in wooden barrels in damp wine cellars.

10 The wine is then filtered one last time to remove unwanted sediment.

The wine is now ready to be bottled, corked, sealed, crated, labeled, and shipped to distributors.

Packaging

11 Most medium- to large-sized wineries now use automated bottling machines, and most moderately priced and expensive wine bottles have corks made of a special oak. The corks are covered with a peel-off **aluminum foil** or plastic seal. Cheaper wines have an aluminum screw-off cap or plastic stopper. The corks and screw caps keep the air from spoiling the wine. Wine is usually shipped in wooden crates, though cheaper wines may be packaged in cardboard.

Quality Control

All facets of wine production must be carefully controlled to create a quality wine. Such variables as the speed with which harvested grapes are crushed; the temperature and timing during both fermentation and ageing; the percent of sugar and acid in the harvested grapes; and the amount of sulfur dioxide added during fermentation all have a tremendous impact on the quality of the finished wine.

Where To Learn More

Books

Adams, Leon. *The Wines of America.* McGraw Hill, 1978.

Anderson, Stanley F. *Winemaking.* Harcourt Brace & Company, 1989.

Churchill, Creighton. *The World of Wines.* Collier Books, 1980.

Farkas, J. *The Technology & Biochemistry of Wine.* Gordon & Breach Science Publishers, Inc., 1988.

Hazelton, Nika. *American Wines.* Grosset Good Life Books, 1976.

Johnson, Hugh. *The Vintner's Art: How Great Wines are Made.* Simon & Schuster Trade, 1992.

McGee, Harold. *On Food and Cooking.* Collier Books, 1984.

Ough, Cornelius S. *Winemaking Basics.* Haworth Press, Inc., 1992.

Rainbird, George. *An Illustrated Guide to Wine.* Harmony Books, 1983.

Zaneilli, Leo. *Beer and Wine Making Illustrated Dictionary.* A. S. Barnes & Company, 1978.

Periodicals

Asimov, Isaac. "The Legacy of Wine," *The Magazine of Fantasy and Science Fiction.* July, 1991, p. 81.

Merline, John W. "What's in Wine? (Calling All Consumers)," *Consumers' Research Magazine.* November 1986, p. 38.

Oliver, Laure. "Fermenting Wine the Natural Way," *The Wine Spectator.* October 31, 1992, p. 9.

Robinson, Jancis. "Spreading the Gospel of Oak," *The Wine Spectator.* August 31, 1991, p. 20.

Roby, Norm. "Getting Back to Nature," *The Wine Spectator.* October 15, 1990, p. 22.

—*Greg Ling*

Wool

As Britain began to prosper, it sought to enhance its position by enacting laws and embargoes that would stimulate its domestic production of wool. Some laws, for example, required that judges, professors, and students wear robes made of English wool. Another law required that the dead be buried in native wool.

Background

As with many discoveries of early man, anthropologists believe the use of wool came out of the challenge to survive. In seeking means of protection and warmth, humans in the Neolithic Age wore animal pelts as clothing. Finding the pelts not only warm and comfortable but also durable, they soon began to develop the basic processes and primitive tools for making wool. By 4000 B.C., Babylonians were wearing clothing of crudely woven fabric.

People soon began to develop and maintain herds of wool-bearing animals. The wool of sheep was soon recognized as one of the most practical to use. During the eleventh and twelfth centuries, wool trade prospered. The English had become proficient in the raising of sheep, while the Flemish had developed the skills for processing. As a result, the British began to sell their wool to the Flemish, who processed the raw material and then sold it back to the English.

The ambitious British soon realized the advantages of both producing and processing their own wool. As Britain began to prosper, it sought to enhance its position by enacting laws and embargoes that would stimulate its domestic production. Some laws, for example, required that judges, professors, and students wear robes made of English wool. Another law required that the dead be buried in native wool. When the American colonies began to compete with the motherland, the English passed a series of laws in an attempt to protect their "golden fleece." One law even threatened the amputation of the hand of any colonist caught trying to improve the blood line of American sheep.

Today, wool is a global industry, with Australia, Argentina, the United States, and New Zealand serving as the major suppliers of raw wool. While the United States is the largest consumer of wool fabric, Australia is the leading supplier. Australian wool accounts for approximately one-fourth of the world's production.

What for centuries was a small home-based craft has grown into a major industry. The annual global output is now estimated at 5.5 billion pounds. Though cotton is the number one plant used for fabrics and the number one fiber overall, the number one source for animal fiber is still wool.

Raw Materials

While most people picture only sheep when they think of wool, other animals also produce fine protein fiber. Various camels, goats, and rabbits produce hair that is also classified as wool.

In scientific terms, wool is considered to be a protein called *keratin*. Its length usually ranges from 1.5 to 15 inches (3.8 to 38 centimeters) depending on the breed of sheep. Each piece is made up of three essential components: the cuticle, the cortex, and the medulla.

The cuticle is the outer layer. It is a protective layer of scales arranged like shingles or fish scales. When two fibers come in contact with each other, these scales tend to cling and stick to each other. It's this physical clinging and sticking that allows wool fibers to be spun into thread so easily.

The cortex is the inner structure made up of millions of cigar-shaped cortical cells. In natural-colored wool, these cells contain melanin. The arrangement of these cells is also responsible for the natural crimp unique to wool fiber.

Rarely found in fine wools, the medulla comprises a series of cells (similar to honeycombs) that provide air spaces, giving wool its thermal insulation value. Wool, like residential insulation, is effective in reducing heat transfer.

Wool fiber is hydrophilic—it has a strong affinity for water—and therefore is easily dyed. While it is a good insulator, it scorches and discolors under high temperatures. Each fiber is elastic to an extent, allowing it to be stretched 25 to 30 percent before breaking. Wool does, however, have a tendency to shrink when wet.

Design

While some of the characteristics of wool can be altered through genetic engineering of sheep, most of the modifications of design are implemented during the manufacturing of the fabric. Wool can be blended with any number of natural or synthetic fibers, and various finishes and treatments can also be applied.

Different types of fleece are used in producing wool. Lambs' wool is fleece that is taken from young sheep before the age of eight months. Because the fiber has not been cut, it has a natural, tapered end that gives it a softer feel. Pulled wool is taken from animals originally slaughtered for meat and is pulled from the pelt using various chemicals. The fibers of pulled wool are of low quality and produce a low-grade cloth. Virgin wool is wool that has never been processed in any manner before it goes into the manufacturing phase. This term is often misunderstood to mean higher quality, which is not necessarily the case.

These wools and others can be used in the production of two categories of woolen fabrics: woolens and worsteds. Woolens are made up of short, curly fibers that tend to be uneven and weak. They are loosely woven in plain or indistinct patterns. Usually woolens have a low thread count and are not as durable as worsteds. They do, however, make soft, fuzzy, and thick fabrics that are generally warmer than their counterparts.

The deep wrinkles on imported A-type Merino ewes (left) and rams (right) contributed to increased wool yields per sheep for American wool producers.

The mechanization of the woolen cloth industry provides a heady example of the extent of nineteenth-century industrial change. Every step of the process, except shearing the sheep and sorting the wool into different grades, was mechanized between 1790 and 1890. Only the organic aspects of shearing live animals and the value judgments required of human sorters resisted mechanical replication until the twentieth century.

Growth of the American woolen trade was based on more than mechanical change, however. In the seventeenth and eighteenth centuries, American sheep provided wool that was quite satisfactory for "homespun," the rough, durable cloth woven by hand on looms owned by professional weavers who set up shop or moved from town to town with their looms. But domestic cloth was overshadowed in quality by imported material.

Several varieties of sheep bred in England and Europe produced wool vastly superior in quality to American-produced wool. The importation of breeds such as the English Southdowns and Spanish Merinos improved domestic quality and allowed the American woolen industry to compete with the best imports.

The Merino sheep, in particular, with their deeply wrinkled folds producing large quantities of wool, caused a stir among American farmers in the early part of the century. A few "gentlemen farmers" avoided Spanish export restrictions and imported some Merinos. As wool prices rose during the embargo of 1807, a "Merino craze" occurred that pushed the price of fine wool and purebred animals to record levels. Then, in 1810, an American diplomat arranged the importation of 20,000 purebred Merinos, and the woolen industry from Vermont to Pennsylvania to Ohio was changed forever.

William S. Pretzer

Worsted fabrics are made of long, straight fibers with considerable tensile strength. They are usually woven in twill patterns and have a high thread count. The finish tends to be hard, rough, and flat. Also, the insulation

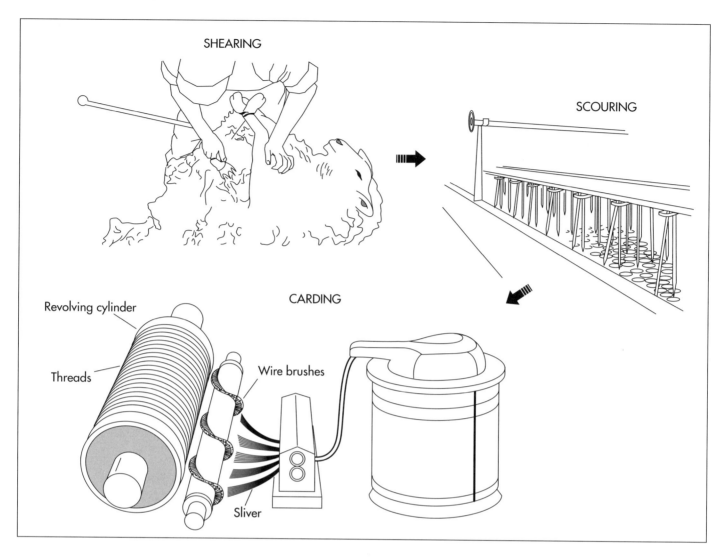

SHEARING

SCOURING

CARDING

Revolving cylinder

Threads

Wire brushes

Sliver

Wool manufacture begins with shearing the sheep. After grading and sorting, the fleece is scoured in a series of alkaline baths containing water, soap, and soda ash or a similar alkali. This process removes sand, dirt, grease, and dried sweat from the fleece.

Next, the fleece is carded—passed through a series of metal teeth that straighten and blend the threads into slivers. Carding also removes residual dirt and other matter left in the fibers.

value is normally not as high as woolens. Worsted fabrics also tend to be more expensive than woolens.

The Manufacturing Process

The major steps necessary to process wool from the sheep to the fabric are: shearing, cleaning and scouring, grading and sorting, carding, spinning, weaving, and finishing.

Shearing

1 Sheep are sheared once a year—usually in the springtime. A veteran shearer can shear up to two hundred sheep per day. The fleece recovered from a sheep can weigh between 6 and 18 pounds (2.7 and 8.1 kilograms); as much as possible, the fleece is kept in one piece. While most sheep are still sheared by hand, new technologies have been

developed that use computers and sensitive, robot-controlled arms to do the clipping.

Grading and sorting

2 Grading is the breaking up of the fleece based on overall quality. In sorting, the wool is broken up into sections of different quality fibers, from different parts of the body. The best quality of wool comes from the shoulders and sides of the sheep and is used for clothing; the lesser quality comes from the lower legs and is used to make rugs. In wool grading, high quality does not always mean high durability.

Cleaning and scouring

3 Wool taken directly from the sheep is called "raw" or "grease wool." It contains sand, dirt, grease, and dried sweat (called *suint*); the weight of contaminants accounts for about 30 to 70 percent of the

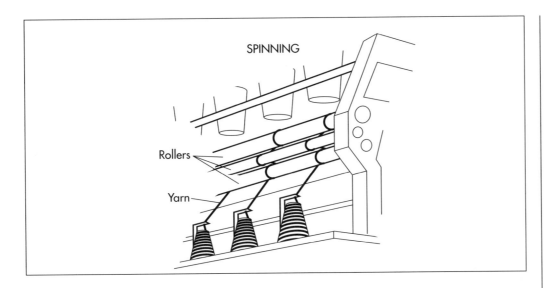

SPINNING

Rollers

Yarn

After being carded, the wool fibers are spun into yarn. Spinning for woolen yarns is typically done on a mule spinning machine, while worsted yarns can be spun on any number of spinning machines. After the yarn is spun, it is wrapped around bobbins, cones, or commercial drums.

fleece's total weight. To remove these contaminants, the wool is scoured in a series of alkaline baths containing water, soap, and soda ash or a similar alkali. The byproducts from this process (such as lanolin) are saved and used in a variety of household products. Rollers in the scouring machines squeeze excess water from the fleece, but the fleece is not allowed to dry completely. Following this process, the wool is often treated with oil to give it increased manageability.

Carding

4 Next, the fibers are passed through a series of metal teeth that straighten and blend them into slivers. Carding also removes residual dirt and other matter left in the fibers. Carded wool intended for worsted yarn is put through gilling and combing, two procedures that remove short fibers and place the longer fibers parallel to each other. From there, the sleeker slivers are compacted and thinned through a process called *drawing*. Carded wool to be used for woolen yarn is sent directly for spinning.

Spinning

5 Thread is formed by spinning the fibers together to form one strand of yarn; the strand is spun with two, three, or four other strands. Since the fibers cling and stick to one another, it is fairly easy to join, extend, and spin wool into yarn. Spinning for woolen yarns is typically done on a mule spinning machine, while worsted yarns can be spun on any number of spinning machines. After the yarn is spun, it is wrapped around bobbins, cones, or commercial drums.

Weaving

6 Next, the wool yarn is woven into fabric. Wool manufacturers use two basic weaves: the plain weave and the twill. Woolen yarns are made into fabric using a plain weave (rarely a twill), which produces a fabric of a somewhat looser weave and a soft surface (due to napping) with little or no luster. The napping often conceals flaws in construction.

Worsted yarns can create fine fabrics with exquisite patterns using a twill weave. The result is a more tightly woven, smooth fabric. Better constructed, worsteds are more durable than woolens and therefore more costly.

Finishing

7 After weaving, both worsteds and woolens undergo a series of finishing procedures including: fulling (immersing the fabric in water to make the fibers interlock); crabbing (permanently setting the interlock); decating (shrink-proofing); and, occasionally, dyeing. Although wool fibers can be dyed before the carding process, dyeing can also be done after the wool has been woven into fabric.

Byproducts

The use of waste is very important to the wool industry. Attention to this aspect of the business has a direct impact on profits. These wastes are grouped into four classes:

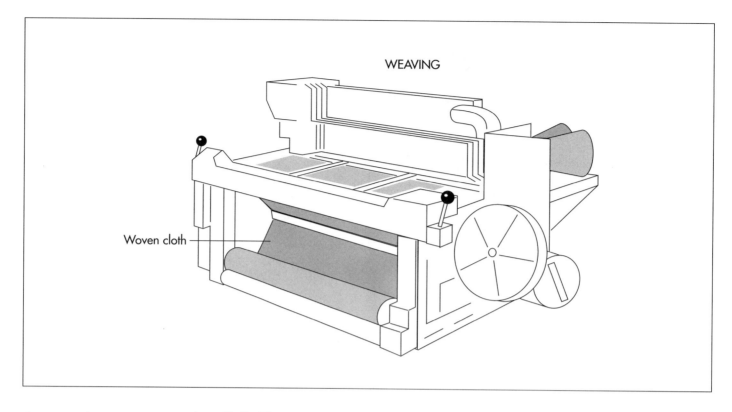

WEAVING

Woven cloth

The spun wool yarn is woven into fabric using two basic weaves: the plain weave and the twill weave. Woolen yarns are made into fabric using a plain weave (rarely a twill), which produces a fabric of a somewhat looser weave and a soft surface (due to napping) with little or no luster. The napping often conceals flaws in construction.

Worsted yarns can create fine fabrics with exquisite patterns using a twill weave. The result is a more tightly woven, smooth fabric. Better constructed, worsteds are more durable than woolens and therefore more costly.

- *Noils.* These are the short fibers that are separated from the long wool in the combing process. Because of their excellent condition, they are equal in quality to virgin wool. They constitute one of the major sources of waste in the industry and are reused in high-quality products.

- *Soft waste.* This is also high-quality material that falls out during the spinning and carding stages of production. This material is usually reintroduced into the process from which it came.

- *Hard waste.* These wastes are generated by spinning, twisting, winding, and warping. This material requires much re-processing and is therefore considered to be of lesser value.

- *Finishing waste.* This category includes a wide variety of clippings, short ends, sample runs, and defects. Since this material is so varied, it requires a great deal of sorting and cleaning to retrieve that which is usable. Consequently, this material is the lowest grade of waste.

Quality Control

Most of the quality control in the production of wool fabrics is done by sight, feel, and measurement. Loose threads are removed with tweezer-like instruments called *burling irons*; knots are pushed to the back of the cloth; and other specks and minor flaws are taken care of before fabrics go through any of the finishing procedures.

In 1941, the United States Congress passed the Wool Products Labeling Act. The purpose of this act was to protect producers and consumers from the unrevealed presence of substitutes and mixtures in wool products. This law required that all products containing wool (with the exception of upholstery and floor coverings) must carry a label stating the content and percentages of the materials in the fabric.

This act also legally defined many terms that would standardized their use within the industry. Some of the key terms identified in the Act are:

- *Wool.* Refers to new wool. Can also include new fiber reclaimed from scraps and broken threads.

- *Repossessed Wool.* Material that is obtained from scraps and clips of new woven or felted fabrics made of previously unused wool.

- *Reused Wool.* Wool obtained from old clothing and rags that have been used or worn.

The Future

The current widespread use and demand for wool is so great that there is little doubt that wool will continue to maintain its position of importance in the fabric industry. Only a major innovation that encompasses the many attributes of wool—including it warmth, durability, and value—could threaten the prominence of this natural fiber.

Where To Learn More

Books

Botkin, M. P. *Sheep and Wool: Science, Production, and Management.* Prentice Hall, 1988.

Corbman, Bernard P. *Textiles: Fiber to Fabric,* 6th ed. McGraw-Hill, 1983.

Ensiminger, Eugene. *Sheep and Wool Science.* Interstate Printers, 1970.

Periodicals

Hyde, Nina. "Fabric of History: Wool," *National Geographic.* May, 1988, p. 552.

Ryder, Michael L. "The Evolution of the Fleece," *Scientific American.* January, 1987, p. 112.

—Dan Pepper

Zipper

Zippers for the general public were not produced until the 1920s, when B. F. Goodrich requested some for use in its company galoshes. It was Goodrich's president, Bertram G. Work, who came up with the word zipper, but he wanted it to refer to the boots themselves, and not the device that fastened them, which he felt was more properly called a slide fastener.

Background

Fasteners have come a long way since the early bone or horn pins and bone splinters. Many devices were designed later that were more efficient; such fasteners included buckles, laces, safety pins, and buttons. Buttons with buttonholes, while still an important practical method of closure even today, had their difficulties. Zippers were first conceived to replace the irritating nineteenth century practice of having to button up to forty tiny buttons on each shoe of the time.

In 1851, Elias Howe, the inventor of the sewing machine, developed what he called an *automatic continuous clothing closure*. It consisted of a series of clasps united by a connecting cord running or sliding upon ribs. Despite the potential of this ingenious breakthrough, the invention was never marketed.

Another inventor, Whitcomb L. Judson, came up with the idea of a slide fastener, which he patented in 1893. Judson's mechanism was an arrangement of hooks and eyes with a slide clasp that would connect them. After Judson displayed the new clasp lockers at the 1893 World's Columbian Exposition in Chicago, he obtained financial backing from Lewis Walker, and together they founded the Universal Fastener Company in 1894.

The first zippers were not much of an improvement over simpler buttons, and innovations came slowly over the next decade. Judson invented a zipper that would part completely (like the zippers found on today's jackets), and he discovered it was better to clamp the teeth directly onto a cloth tape that could be sewn into a garment, rather than have the teeth themselves sewn into the garment.

Zippers were still subject to popping open and sticking as late as 1906, when Otto Frederick Gideon Sundback joined Judson's company, then called the Automatic Hook and Eye Company. His patent for Plako in 1913 is considered to be the beginning of the modern zipper. His "Hookless Number One," a device in which jaws clamped down on beads, was quickly replaced by "Hookless Number Two", which was very similar to modern zippers. Nested, cup-shaped teeth formed the best zipper to date, and a machine that could stamp out the metal in one process made marketing the new fastener feasible.

The first zippers were introduced for use in World War I as fasteners for soldiers' money belts, flying suits, and life-vests. Because of war shortages, Sundback developed a new machine that used only about 40 percent of the metal required by older machines.

Zippers for the general public were not produced until the 1920s, when B. F. Goodrich requested some for use in its company galoshes. It was Goodrich's president, Bertram G. Work, who came up with the word *zipper*, but he wanted it to refer to the boots themselves, and not the device that fastened them, which he felt was more properly called a slide fastener.

The next change zippers underwent was also precipitated by a war—World War II. Zipper factories in Germany had been destroyed, and metal was scarce. A West German company, Opti-Werk GmbH, began research into new plastics, and this research resulted in numerous patents. J. R. Ruhrman and his associates were granted a German patent for developing a plastic ladder chain. Alden W. Hanson, in 1940, devised a method

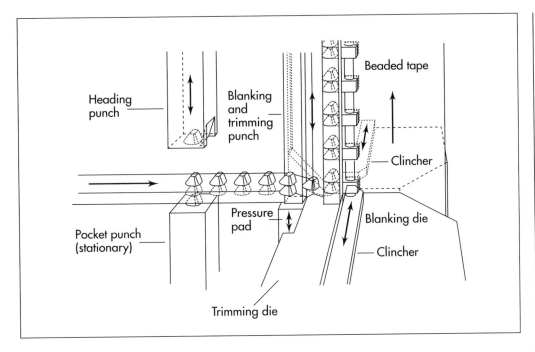

Heading punch

Blanking and trimming punch

Beaded tape

Clincher

Pocket punch (stationary)

Pressure pad

Blanking die

Clincher

Trimming die

A stringer consists of the tape (or cloth) and teeth that make up one side of the zipper. One method of making the stringer entails passing a flattened strip of wire between a heading punch and a pocket punch to form scoops. A blanking punch cuts around the scoops to form a Y shape. The legs of the Y are then clamped around the cloth tape.

that allowed a plastic coil to be sewn into the zipper's cloth. This was followed by a notched plastic wire, developed independently by A. Gerbach and the firm William Prym-Wencie, that could actually be woven into the cloth.

After a slow start, it was not long before zipper sales soared. In 1917, 24,000 zippers were sold; in 1934, the number had risen to 60 million. Today zippers are easily produced and sold in the billions, for everything from **blue jeans** to sleeping bags.

Raw Materials

The basic elements of a zipper are: the stringer (the tape and teeth assembly that makes up one side of a zipper); the slider (opens and closes the zipper); a tab (pulled to move the slider); and stops (prevent the slider from leaving the chain). A separating zipper, instead of a bottom stop that connects the stringers, has two devices—a box and a pin—that function as stops when put together.

Metal zipper hardware can be made of **stainless steel**, aluminum, brass, zinc, or a nickel-silver alloy. Sometimes a steel zipper will be coated with brass or zinc, or it might be painted to match the color of the cloth tape or garment. Zippers with plastic hardware are made from polyester or nylon, while the slider and pull tab are usually made from

steel or zinc. The cloth tapes are either made from cotton, polyester, or a blend of both. For zippers that open on both ends, the ends are not usually sewn into a garment, so that they are hidden as they are when a zipper is made to open at only one end. These zippers are strengthened using a strong cotton tape (that has been reinforced with nylon) applied to the ends to prevent fraying.

The Manufacturing Process

Today's zippers comprise key components of either metal or plastic. Beyond this one very important difference, the steps involved in producing the finished product are essentially the same.

Making stringers—metal zippers

1 A stringer consists of the tape (or cloth) and teeth that make up one side of the zipper. The oldest process for making the stringers for a metal zipper is that process invented by Otto Sundback in 1923. A round wire is sent through a rolling mill, shaping it into a Y-shape. This wire is then sliced to form a tooth whose width is appropriate for the type of zipper desired. The tooth is then put into a slot on a rotating turntable to be punched into the shape of a scoop by a die. The turntable is rotated 90 degrees, and another tooth is fed into the slot. After another 90 degrees turn, the first tooth is

To make the stringer for a spiral plastic zipper, a round plastic wire is notched and then fed between two heated screws. These screws, one rotating clockwise, the other counterclockwise, pull the plastic wire out to form loops. A head maker at the front of each loop then forms it into a round knob. This method requires that a left spiral and right spiral be made simultaneously on two separate machines so that the chains will match up on a finished zipper.

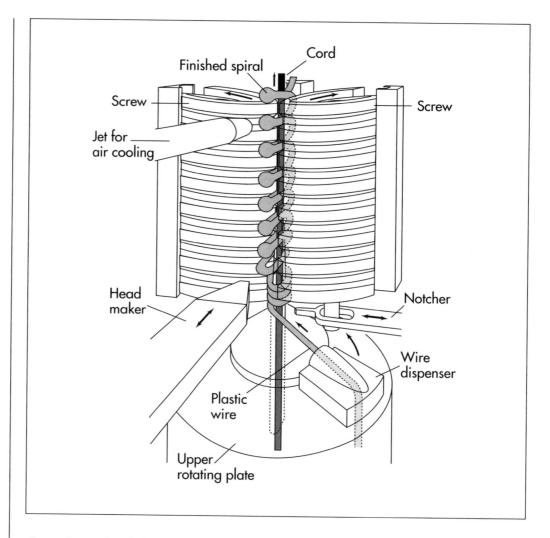

clamped onto the cloth tape. The tape must be raised slightly over twice the thickness of the scoop—the cupped tooth—after clamping to allow room for the opposite tooth on the completed zipper. A slow and tedious process, its popularity has waned.

Another similar method originated in the 1940s. This entails a flattened strip of wire passing between a heading punch and a pocket punch to form scoops. A blanking punch cuts around the scoops to form a Y shape. The legs of the Y are then clamped around the cloth tape. This method proved to be faster and more effective than Sundback's original.

2 Yet another method, developed in the 1930s, uses molten metal to form teeth. A mold, shaped like a chain of teeth, is clamped around the cloth tape. Molten zinc under pressure is then injected into the mold. Water cools the mold, which then releases the shaped teeth. Any residue is trimmed.

Making stringers—plastic zippers

3 Plastic zippers can be spiral, toothed, ladder, or woven directly into the fabric. Two methods are used to make the stringers for a spiral plastic zipper. The first involves notching a round plastic wire before feeding it between two heated screws. These screws, one rotating clockwise, the other counterclockwise, pull the plastic wire out to form loops. A head maker at the front of each loop then forms it into a round knob. Next, the plastic spiral is cooled with air. This method requires that a left spiral and right spiral be made simultaneously on two separate machines so that the chains will match up on a finished zipper.

The second method for spiral plastic zippers makes both the left and right spiral simultaneously on one machine. A piece of wire is looped twice between notches on a rotating forming wheel. A pusher and head maker simultaneously press the plastic wires firmly into the notches and form the heads. This process makes two chains that are already linked together to be sewn onto two cloth tapes.

4 To make the stringers for a toothed plastic zipper, a molding process is used that is similar to the metal process described in step #2 above. A rotating wheel has on its edge several small molds that are shaped like flattened teeth. Two cords run through the molds to connect the finished teeth together. Semi-molten plastic is fed into the mold, where it is held until it solidifies. A folding machine bends the teeth into a U-shape that can be sewn onto a cloth tape.

5 The stringers for a ladder plastic zipper are made by winding a plastic wire onto alternating spools that protrude from the edge of a rotating forming wheel. Strippers on each side lift the loops off the spools while a heading and notching wheel simultaneously presses the loops into a U shape and forms heads on the teeth, which are then sewn onto the cloth tape.

6 Superior garment zippers can be made by weaving the plastic wire directly into the cloth, using the same method as is used in cloth weaving. This method is not common in the United States, but such zippers are frequently imported.

Completing the manufacturing process

7 Once the individual stringers have been made, they are first joined together with a temporary device similar to a slider. They are then pressed, and, in the case of metal zippers, wire brushes scrub down sharp edges. The tapes are then starched, wrung out, and dried. Metal zippers are then waxed for smooth operation, and both types are rolled onto huge spools to be formed later into complete zippers.

8 The slider and pull tab are assembled separately after being stamped or die-cast from metal. The continuous zipper tape is then unrolled from its spool and its teeth are removed at intervals, leaving spaces that surround smaller chains. For zippers that only open on one end, the bottom stop is first clamped on, and then the slider is threaded

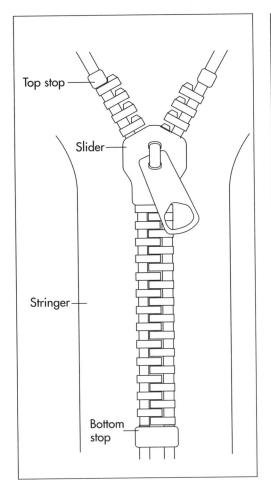

The basic elements of a zipper are the stringer (the tape and teeth assembly that makes up one side of a zipper); the slider (opens and closes the zipper); a tab (pulled to move the slider); and stops (prevent the slider from leaving the chain).

onto the chain. Next, the top stops are clamped on, and the gaps between lengths of teeth are cut at midpoint. For zippers that separate, the midpoint of each gap is coated with reinforcing tape, and the top stops are clamped on. The tape is then sliced to separate the strips of chain again. The slider and the box are then slipped onto one chain, and the pin is slipped onto the other.

9 Finished zippers are stacked, placed in boxes, and trucked to clothing manufacturers, luggage manufacturers, or any of the other manufacturers that rely on zippers. Some are also shipped to department stores or fabric shops for direct purchase by the consumer.

Quality Control

Zippers, despite their numbers and practically worry-free use, are complicated devices that rely on a smooth, almost perfect linkage of tiny cupped teeth. Because they are usually designed to be fasteners for garments, they must also undergo a series of tests similar to those for clothing that undergo frequent laundering and wear.

A smoothly functioning zipper every time is the goal of zipper manufacturers, and such reliability is necessarily dependent on tolerances. Every dimension of a zipper—its width, length, tape end lengths, teeth dimensions, length of chain, slide dimensions, and stop lengths, to name a few—is subject to scrutiny that ascertains that values fall within an acceptable range. Samplers use statistical analysis to check the range of a batch of zippers. Generally, the dimensions of the zipper must be within 90 percent of the desired length, though in most cases it is closer to 99 percent.

A zipper is tested for flatness and straightness. Flatness is measured by passing a gauge set at a certain height over it; if the gauge touches the zipper several times, the zipper is defective. To measure straightness, the zipper is laid across a straight edge and scrutinized for any curving.

Zipper strength is important. This means that the teeth should not come off easily, nor should the zipper be easy to break. To test for strength, a tensile testing machine is attached by a hook to a tooth. The machine is then pulled, and a gauge measures at what force the tooth separates from the cloth. These same tensile testing machines are used to test the strength of the entire zipper. A machine is attached to each cloth tape, then pulled. The force required to pull the zipper completely apart into two separate pieces is measured. Acceptable strength values are determined according to what type of zipper is being made: a heavy-duty zipper will require higher values than a lightweight one. Zippers are also compressed to see when they break.

To measure a zipper for ease of zipping, a tensile testing machine measures the force needed to zip it up and down. For garments, this value should be quite low, so that the average person can zip with ease and so that the garment material does not tear. For other purposes, such as **mattress** covers, the force can be higher.

A finished sample zipper must meet textile quality controls. It is tested for laundering durability by being washed in a small amount of hot water, a significant amount of bleach, and abrasives to simulate many washings. Zippers are also agitated with small steel balls to test the zipper coating for abrasion.

The cloth of the zipper tapes must be colorfast for the care instructions of the garment. For example, if the garment is to be dry cleaned only, its zipper must be colorfast during dry cleaning.

Shrinkage is also tested. Two marks are made on the cloth tape. After the zipper is heated or washed, the change in length between the two marks is measured. Heavyweight zippers should have no shrinkage. A lightweight zipper should have a one to four percent shrinkage rate.

Where To Learn More

Books

Petroski, Henry. *The Evolution of Useful Things.* Knopf, 1992.

Zipper! An Exploration in Novelty. W. W. Norton & Co., Inc., 1994.

Periodicals

Berendt, John. "The Zipper," *Esquire.* May, 1989, p. 42.

Getchell, Dave. "Zip It Up: How to Care For and Repair Zippers," *Backpacker.* May, 1993, p. 94.

Kraar, Louis. "Japanese Pick Up U.S. Ideas," *Fortune,* Spring-Summer, 1991, p. 66.

"Zip," *The New Yorker.* December 17, 1979, pp. 33-34.

Weiner, Lewis. "The Slide Fastener," *Scientific American.* June, 1983, pp. 132-144.

—*Rose Secrest*

Zirconium

Background

Zirconium, symbol Zr on the Periodic Table, is a metal most often found in and extracted from the silicate mineral zirconium silicate and the oxide mineral baddeleyite. In its various compound forms, the grayish-white zirconium is the nineteenth most plentiful element in the earth's crust, where it is far more abundant than copper and lead. It belongs to the titanium family of metals, a group that also includes titanium and hafnium and that is favored in industry for its members' good electrical conductivity as well as their tendency to form metallic salts. Because it is stable in many electron configurations and physical states, zirconium can be made into many products. However, since the 1940s, its most significant applications have been in various structural components of nuclear reactors.

Zirconium was discovered by German chemist Martin Heinrich Klaproth, who first isolated an oxide of the mineral zircon in 1789. The first metallic powder was produced in 1824 by a Swedish Chemist, Jons J. Berzelius. The forms of the metal that could be isolated during the nineteenth century, however, were impure and thus very brittle. The earliest method of purifying useable quantities of the metal was developed in 1925 by Dutch chemists Anton E. van Arkel and J. H. de Boer, who invented a thermal iodide process by which they thermally decomposed zirconium tetraiodide. The drawback with van Arkel and de Boer's method was its cost, but twenty years later William Justin Kroll of Luxembourg invented a cheaper process, using magnesium to break down zirconium tetrachloride. Relatively inexpensive, this process produced zirconium in quantities large and pure enough for industrial use.

Since Kroll's breakthrough, zirconium has become an important element in several industries: steel, iron, and nuclear power. It is used in the steel industry to remove nitrogen and sulfur from iron, thereby enhancing the metallurgical quality of the steel. When added to iron to create an alloy, zirconium improves iron's machinability, toughness, and ductility. Other common industrial applications of zirconium include the manufacture of photoflash bulbs and surgical equipment, and the tanning of leather.

Despite its ability to be used for many different industrial applications, most of the zirconium produced today is used in water-cooled nuclear reactors. Zirconium has strong corrosion-resistance properties as well as the ability to confine fission fragments and neutrons so that thermal or slow neutrons are not absorbed and wasted, thus improving the efficiency of the nuclear reactor. In fact, about 90 percent of the zirconium produced in 1989 was used in nuclear reactors, either in fuel containers or nuclear product casings.

Raw Materials

Of the two mineral forms in which zirconium occurs, zircon is by far the more important source. Found mainly in igneous rock, zircon also appears in the gravel and sand produced as igneous rock erodes. In this form, it is often mixed with silica, ilmenite, and rutile. The vast majority of the zircon used in industry today originates in these sand and gravel deposits, from which the purest zircon is extracted and refined to be used as zirconium metals. Less pure deposits are used in the form of stabilized zirconia for refractories and ceramic products. The world's largest zircon mines are in Australia, South Africa,

Most of the zirconium produced today is used in water-cooled nuclear reactors. Zirconium has strong corrosion-resistance properties and can improve the efficiency of a nuclear reactor. In fact, about 90 percent of the zirconium produced in 1989 was used in nuclear reactors, either in fuel containers or nuclear product casings.

The sand and gravel that contain zircon are typically collected from coastal waters by a floating dredge, a large steam shovel fitted on a floating barge. After the shovel has scooped up the gravel and sand, they are purified by means of spiral concentrators, and then unwanted material is removed by magnetic and electrostatic separators.

End-product manufacturers of zircon further refine the nearly pure zircon into zirconium by using chlorine to purify the metal and then sintering (heating) it until it becomes sufficiently workable for industrial use. Less-pure zircon is made into zirconia, an oxide of zirconium, by fusing the zircon with coke, iron borings, and lime until the silica is reduced to silicon that alloys with the iron.

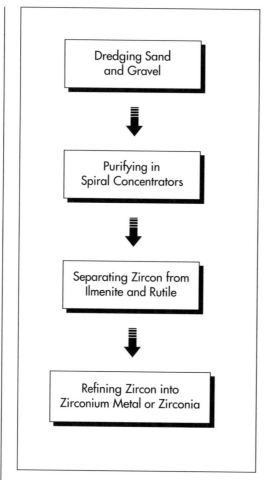

Dredging Sand and Gravel

↓

Purifying in Spiral Concentrators

↓

Separating Zircon from Ilmenite and Rutile

↓

Refining Zircon into Zirconium Metal or Zirconia

and the United States, but rich beds also exist in Brazil, China, India, Russia, Italy, Norway, Thailand, Madagascar, and Canada. Like zircon, baddeleyite is extracted from sand and gravel deposits. Unlike zircon, commercially viable baddeleyite deposits contain relatively high concentrations of zirconium oxide, and baddeleyite can thus be used without refining. The mineral is, however, much more scarce than zircon, with significant amounts occurring only in Brazil and Florida.

Extraction and Refining

Extracting zircon

1 The sand and gravel that contain zircon mixed with silicate, ilmenite, and rutile are typically collected from coastal waters by a floating dredge, a large steam shovel fitted on a floating barge. After the shovel has scooped up the gravel and sand, they are purified by means of spiral concentrators, which separate on the basis of density. The ilmenite and rutile are then removed by magnetic and electrostatic separators. The purest

concentrates of zircon are shipped to end-product manufacturers to be used in metal production, while less pure concentrations are used for refractories.

Refining zircon

2 End-product manufacturers of zircon further refine the nearly pure zircon into zirconium by using a reducing agent (usually chlorine) to purify the metal and then sintering (heating) it until it becomes sufficiently ductile—workable—for industrial use. For small-scale laboratory use, zirconium metal may be produced by means of a chemical reaction in which chloride is used to reduce the zircon.

3 The less-pure zircon is made into zirconia, an oxide of zirconium, by fusing the zircon with coke, iron borings, and lime until the silica is reduced to silicon that alloys with the iron. The zirconia is then stabilized by heating it to about 3,095 degrees Fahrenheit (1,700 degrees Celsius), with additions of lime and magnesia totalling about five percent.

Refining baddeleyite

4 As mentioned above, baddeleyite contains relatively high, pure concentrations of zirconium oxide that can be used without filtering or cleansing. The only refining process used on baddeleyite involves grinding the gravel or sand to a powder and sizing the powder with different sized sieves. All zirconium oxide that comes from baddeleyite is used for refractories and, increasingly, advanced ceramics.

Quality Control

The quality control methods implemented in the production of zirconium metal are typical Statistical Process Control (SPC) methods used in most metal production. These involve tracking and controlling specific variables determined by the end product requirements. Stringent government quality control is applied to all zirconium metal produced for nuclear applications. These controls assure that the zirconium produced for use in a nuclear plant has been processed correctly and also allow for accountability: processing is tracked so that it can be traced back to each individual step and location.

Quality control methods for zirconium used in refractory applications also focus on SPC. However, in the refractory industries, it is also necessary to ascertain the beach (and even what part of the beach) from which the zirconium mineral was extracted. Manufacturers need to know exactly where the zirconium came from because each source contains slightly different trace elements, and different trace elements can affect the end product.

Byproducts/Waste

Silicate, ilmenite, and rutile—all byproducts of the zircon refining process—are typically dumped back in the water at the extraction site. These elements compose typical beach sand and are in no way detrimental to the environment. Magnesium chloride, the only other notable byproduct of zirconium manufacturing, results from the reduction of the zircon with chlorine in the refining process and is typically sold to magnesium refineries. No byproducts or waste result from baddeleyite refining.

The Future

Many believe that the future of zirconium lies in its use as an advanced ceramic. Advanced ceramics—also called "fine," "new," "high-tech," or "high-performance" ceramics—are generally used as components in processing equipment, devices, or machines because they can perform many functions better than competing metals or polymers. Zirconium is fairly hard, doesn't conduct heat well, and is relatively inert (i.e., it doesn't react readily with other elements), all excellent qualities for advanced ceramics. Zirconium oxide, manufactured as a ceramic, can be used to make crucibles for melting metals, gas turbines, liners for jet and rocket motor tubes, resistance furnaces, ultra-high frequency furnaces, and refractories such as the facing of a high-temperature furnace wall.

Where To Learn More

Books

Heuer, A. H., ed. *Science and Technology of Zirconia*. American Ceramic Society, 1981.

Specifications for Zirconium and Zirconium Alloy Welding Electrodes and Rods. American Welding Society, 1990.

Zirconium and Hafnium. Gordon Press Publishers, 1993.

Periodicals

Burke, Marshall A. "Ceramics Enter the Foundry," *Design News*. June 16, 1986, p. 56.

"Fuel Cell's Future Gets a Boost," *Design News*. August 18, 1986, p. 38.

"Zirconium," *Machine Design*. April 14, 1988, pp. 234-35.

"Zirconium Holds Down Costs of Making Zirconium," *Metal Progress*. November, 1983, pp. 11-12.

"Adding Strength to Glassy Ceramics," *Science News*. September 13, 1986, p. 170.

—*Alicia Haley and Blaine Danley*

Index

Bold-faced items and page numbers refer to main entries.